PRAGUE
MEDIEVAL
STUDIES ❡ 3

Centre for the Study of
THE MIDDLE AGES

Peasantry in the Cheb City-State in the Late Middle Ages

Socioeconomic Mobility and Migration

Tomáš Klír

Charles University
Karolinum Press 2024

KAROLINUM PRESS
Karolinum Press is a publishing department of Charles University
Ovocný trh 560/5, 116 36 Prague 1, Czech Republic
www.karolinum.cz
© Tomáš Klír, 2024
Coverphoto © ÖNB/Wien Handschriftensammlung, Cod. 3085, fol. 2r.
Layout by Jan Šerých
Set and printed in the Czech Republic by Karolinum Press
First English edition

This work was supported by the European Regional Development Fund project
"Creativity and Adaptability as Conditions of the Success of Europe in an Interrelated World"
(reg. no.: CZ.02.1.01/0.0/0.0/16_019/0000734).

EUROPEAN UNION
European Structural and Investment Funds
Operational Programme Research,
Development and Education

MINISTRY OF EDUCATION,
YOUTH AND SPORTS

A catalogue record for this book is available from the National Library of the Czech Republic.

ISBN 978-80-246-5706-6
ISBN 978-80-246-5775-2 (pdf)

https://doi.org/10.14712/9788024657752

The original manuscript was reviewed by Prof. Piotr Guzowski (University of Białystok)
and Dr. Jonas Lindström (Uppsala University).

For Danka, Tomášek, František, and my parents

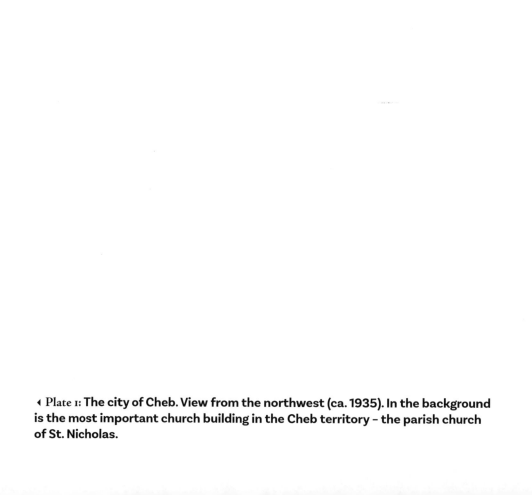

◄ Plate I: **The city of Cheb. View from the northwest (ca. 1935). In the background is the most important church building in the Cheb territory – the parish church of St. Nicholas.**

Contents

Supplementary materials available at www.karolinum.cz

Acknowledgments

The completion of this manuscript demanded a long time, and at this point I would like to express my gratitude to all those who made it possible and shaped its form in various ways. My first thanks go to my patient family and friends. For discussions and research recommendations I am particularly indebted to Prof. Sheilagh Ogilvie (Oxford), Prof. Emmanuel Huertas (Toulouse), as well as Prof. Mateusz Goliński (Wrocław), Prof. Matthias Hardt (Leipzig), Prof. Haio Zimmermann (Bockhorn), Prof. Karlheinz Hengst (Chemnitz), Prof. Thomas Ertl (Berlin), Prof. Thomas Frank (Pavia), Prof. Nikolai A. Makarov (Moscow), Prof. Eduard Maur, Prof. Hana Pátková, Prof. Jan Klápště, Prof. Josef Žemlička, Assoc. Prof. Martin Musílek, Assoc. Prof. Martin Nodl and Dr. Martin Janovský (all Prague). For substantial comments, I am very grateful to both reviewers of the English version of the monograph, Dr. Jonas Lindström (Uppsala) and Prof. Piotr Guzowski (Białystok), as well as to the reviewers of the partial studies adopted here, especially Assoc. Prof. Shami Ghosh (Toronto) and Dr. Lluís To Figueras (Girona). The manuscript would not have been written without the collegial support of the scholars in the field of Medieval Studies within the Faculty of Arts of Charles University, as well as the helpful approach of the staff of the State District Archives in Cheb. I would also like to thank Karolinum Press and the editors Dr. Adéla Petruželková and Karolína Klibániová. For the revision of the English text I owe thanks to Sean M. Miller, Karin Stark, and Scott Alexander Jones in particular.

The first stage of the research was supported by the Grant Agency of the Czech Republic (GPP405/12/P715). The chapters on the land transfer activity of Cheb's burghers and the relationship between the town and its hinterland were written within the framework of the following project supported by the Grant Agency of the Czech Republic (16-20763S). The final version of the work was written within the framework of the project Creativity and Adaptability as a Prerequisite for European Success in an Interconnected World (reg. no.: CZ.02.1.01/0.0/0.0/16_019/0000734, financed by the European Regional Development Fund). The book is internally affiliated with the Cooperatio program of Charles University, in the field of Medieval Studies.

Note on the English Translation/Edition

The presented monograph is a modified translation of the Czech-language monograph *Rolnictvo na pozdně středověkém Chebsku v pozdním středověku: sociální mobilita, migrace a procesy pustnutí*, published in 2020 by Karolinum Press.[1] The English version has been updated and complemented with references to the latest literature. The section on field patterns in the city-state of Cheb (*chap. 27–28*) and on the processes of abandonment in the Late Middle Ages (*chap. 29*) were omitted, as they were only loosely related to the main topic. Moreover, processes of late medieval abandonment in the region of Cheb had recently been developed into a comprehensive monograph.[2] Furthermore, the chapters on demographic structures (*chap. 16*) and on the changing monetary values of landholdings (*chap. 21*) were left out, as both were not absolutely necessary to resolve the main aim. Some chapters were reduced and/or merged with others; for this reason, the numbering changed in relation to the Czech version. Some data of regional/local historical significance has been retained in the text for potential German readers.

Extensive supplemental materials accompany the English version in the same way they accompanied the original Czech version. We refer to these attachments as appendices. They are available for download on the publisher's website.

---

1   Tomáš Klír, *Rolnictvo na pozdně středověkém Chebsku v pozdním středověku: sociální mobilita, migrace a procesy pustnutí* [Peasantry in the city-state of Cheb in the Late Middle Ages: Social mobility, migration, and abandonment of settlements] (Prague: Karolinum, 2020). According to Tomáš Klír. "Sociální mobilita rolnictva a procesy pustnutí v pozdním středověku. Díl 2. Sociální a geografická mobilita rolnictva v pozdním středověku: Chebsko 1392–1469" [Social mobility of the peasantry and the processes of abandonment in the Late Medieval Period. Volume 2. Social and geographical mobility of the peasantry in the Late Medieval Period: The Cheb Region 1392–1469] (PhD diss., Charles University, 2018).

2   Tomáš Klír, *Zánik a pustnutí venkovských sídlišť v pozdním středověku. Chebsko a Slavkovský les* [The abandonment of rural settlements in the Late Middle Ages. The region of Cheb and the Slavkov Forest] (Prague: Karolinum, 2023).

The Czech edition of the monograph was preceded by several Czech[3] and English studies.[4] Additionally, a study on the land market was also published in the volume *Busy Tenants: Peasant Land Markets in Central Europe (15th to 16th Century)*, which we take into account in this English translation.[5] We therefore thank the publishing houses Franz Steiner Verlag and Taylor & Francis Group for kindly granting us the licensing rights. Further independent studies have proposed a new conceptualization of the migration of the Cheb peasantry in the Late Middle Ages. The Cheb findings were also placed in the context of the existing knowledge of local peasant migration in the pre-modern period. We do not expound on these research findings, except for a short summary (*chap. 23.9*), and we thus invite the reader to consult the relevant paper published in the *Journal of Migration History*.[6]

3   Tomáš Klír, et al., *Knihy chebské zemské berně z let 1438 a 1456* [Die Egerer Landsteuerbücher von 1438 und 1456], Libri Civitatis X. (Prague: Filozofická fakulta Univerzity Karlovy, 2016); Tomáš Klír, "Procesy pustnutí, válečné škody a tzv. sociální úhory. Chebsko v pozdním středověku" [The processes of village abandonment, war damage, and social fallows. The Cheb region in the late Middle Ages], *Archaeologia historica* 42 (2017): 547–577; Tomáš Klír, "Sociálně-ekonomická mobilita rolnictva v pozdním středověku. Chebsko v letech 1438–1456" [The socio-economic mobility of peasants in the late Middle Ages: The city-state of Cheb in 1438–1456], in *Wieś miniona, lecz obecna. Ślady dawnych wsi i ich badania*, ed. Przemysław Nocuń, Agnieszka Przybyła-Dumin, and Krzysztof Fokt. Monografie i materiały MGPE 13 (Chorzów: Muzeum Górnośląski Park Etnograficzny w Chorzowie," 2018), 159–231. Partial or complete parallels to Klír, *Rolnictvo*, chaps. 3.1–3.3, 6, 7, 14, 18, 20.4, and 22.3.
4   Tomáš Klír, "Socioeconomic mobility and property transmission among peasants. The Cheb region (Czech Republic) in the late Middle Ages," in *Settlement change across Medieval Europe: Old paradigms and new vistas*, ed. Niall Brady and Claudia Theune, Ruralia 12 (Leiden: Seidestone, 2019), 341–355 (this study is an excerpt from the extensive Czech study Klír, "Sociálně-ekonomická mobilita"); Tomáš Klír, "Rural credit and monetarisation of the peasantry in the late Middle Ages. The Eger city-state c. 1450," in *A history of the credit market in Central Europe. The Middle Ages and Early Modern Period*, ed. Pavla Slavíčková (London, New York: Routledge, 2020), 113–130. Partial or complete parallels to Klír, *Rolnictvo*, chaps. 14–15, app. 19.4, and app. 20.3.
5   Tomáš Klír, "Land transfer in a late medieval city-state. Cheb Region 1438–1456," in *Busy tenants. Peasant land markets in Central Europe (15th to 16th century)*, ed. Thomas Ertl, Thomas Frank, and Samuel Nussbaum, Vierteljahrschrift für Sozial- und Wirtschaftsgeschichte, Beiheft 253 (Stuttgart: Franz Steiner Verlag, 2021), 151–192. Partial or complete parallels to this monograph chaps. 5, 7–8; 15; app. 16, app. 19.4, *and* app. 20.3.
6   Tomáš Klír, "Local migration of peasants in the late Middle Ages: A quantitative analysis of the city-state of Cheb 1442–1456," *Journal of Migration history* 8 (2022): 191–219.

There are many Czech titles in the bibliography. To simplify the orientation of the reader, we have included the title of the foreign-language summary, if one is provided (usually in German or English). We do not otherwise translate the Czech titles into English.

The terminology used regarding socioeconomic mobility and the economic reproduction of the peasantry in the pre-modern world is based largely on Jonas Lindström's monograph *Distribution and Differences: Stratification and the System of Reproduction in a Swedish Peasant Community 1620–1820*. The selection of English equivalents for the typical Czech or German terms has been particularly informed by the studies of Markus Cerman and Sheilagh Ogilvie.

User's Note

In terms of data, this monograph is based largely on the edition of the *1438 Cheb Land Tax Register* and the *1456 Taxation Book*, as well as on a tabular extract from the land tax registers for 1424 and 1469, all of which is part of an unpublished manuscript of a habilitation work submitted to the Faculty of Arts of Charles University.[7] Additionally, the data contained in the tax registers from 1442–1456 is summarized in tabular form in an appendix to the habilitation work.

The text is interspersed with tables and figures that are numbered according to their location within the respective chapters. The appendices are attached separately and numbered in relation to the chapters that they relate to. They are not included in the printed monograph but are available for download from the web portal of Karolinum Press.

For settlements now located within the Czech Republic, we cite their names in their current official form (Czech settlement names), followed by their historical German equivalents in brackets or after a slash. In the appendices and on maps, we use the German settlement names. The correlation between Czech and German settlement names can be found in a separate appendix. For German settlement names located outside of the Czech Republic, we have chosen to use the customary English version, if in existence and common usage (e.g., Nuremberg instead of Nürnberg). We also cite the customary English versions of medieval Czech and German baptismal names, where applicable (e.g., Nicholas instead of Mikuláš or Niclas, Wenceslaus instead of Václav or Wenzel).

Certain passages contain transliterations of various medieval and/or modern written documents. Unless specified otherwise, these were transliterated in the same manner as in the two edited tax books.

The cover depicts the illumination of the month of March, accompanying the calendar parts of the so-called *Book of Medical Astrology*, which is part of a lengthier codex, housed today in the Austrian National Library.[8] The manuscript is dated to 1475 and its place of origin is considered to most likely be the

7   Klír, et al., *Knihy*.
8   Österreichische Nationalbibliothek Wien, Handschriftensammlung, *Cod.* 3085, fol. 2r, 7r.

Passau, Regensburg, Salzburg, or Brixen diocese.[9] The depicted life and institutions correspond to the idea we have of the late medieval city-state of Cheb.

On the dividing pages, the reader is introduced to the Cheb countryside via a selection of photographs taken by local amateur photographers from 1890–1940. As with the medieval texts, these pictures evoke a forgotten peasant world, arousing a yearning for further exploration.[10]

9   Astrid Böhm, "Das Iatromathematische Hausbuch des Codex ÖNB, 3085 (fol. 1r–39v). Stoffgeschichtliche Einordnung, dynamisch-mehrstufige Edition und Glossar" (master's thesis, Karl-Franzens-Universität Graz, 2014), esp. 21–22.
10 Zbyněk Černý, Příznivé světlo: chebské fotografické ateliéry (1849–1945) – Gutes Licht: Egerer Fotoateliers (1849–1945) (Cheb: Muzeum Cheb, 2016), 129.

Abbreviations

Ar Cheb	State Regional Archive Plzeň – State District Archive Cheb, fonds Město Cheb
dt.	dedit (he paid)
FPS	family property society
GFPS	genetically connected family property society
gr.	groschen (if not stated otherwise, Prague groschen)
GRIMM	Grimm, *Das Deutsche Wörterbuch* (cf. bibliography)
ME	Gradl, ed., *Monumenta Egrana* (cf. bibliography)
Mg	Morgen (arable plot); cf. measurement
ss	threescore (usually threescore of Prague groschen)
Tgw	Tagwerk (meadow plot), cf. measurement
[…]	elaboration of the scribe's abridgements
⟨…⟩	abridged text
»…«	full transliteration of the passage of a medieval document

Measurements

korec (*Strich*) | a Bohemian measurement of dry grain, figuratively also a seed and area measurement;
ca. 93.6 liters
ca. 0.28 ha

kar (*Khar, Khor, Kar*) | a Cheb measurement of dry grain, figuratively also a seed and area measurement
1 kar of rye = ca. 297 liters
1 kar of oats = ca. 308 liters
ca. 0.95 ha
(10 Bohemian *korec* = 3 Cheb *kar*)

morgen (*Morgen*) | measured arable plot;
ca. 0.57 ha

tagwerk (*Tagwerk*) | measured meadow plot;
ca. 0.57 ha

(Slavík, "O popisu Čech," 79–80; Pekař, *České katastry*, 217; Sedláček, *Míry*, 43, 100–101; Steiner, "Alte Masse"; Langhammer, *Waldsassen*, 155; Schreiber, *Der Elbogener Kreis*, 235; Maťa and Dragoun, *Lán*, 104–107; Klír, et al., *Knihy*, 155–156)

The agricultural land of the late medieval city-state of Cheb was counted by the amount of land that could be worked daily, i.e., how much of a field could be ploughed by a pair of horses (*morgen*) or the amount of meadowland from which hay could be harvested (*tagwerk*) in a single day. The distinction between a *morgen* and *tagwerk* was gradually lost, and by the end of the 15th century, the fields were already counted predominantly in *tagwerk* (Singer, ed., *Das Landbuch*, 115). Everything indicates that a *morgen* and a *tagwerk* were more or less the same in size (Singer, ed., *Das Landbuch*, 115). In the city-state of Cheb in the 18th century, the arable land was already counted by sown area, hence in *kar* (Pekař, *České katastry*, 217; Sedláček, *Míry*, 100–101).

The areas or sizes of a *morgen* and *tagwerk* is not known and probably varied. In West Bohemia in the 14th century, the so-called German *morgen* was known and corresponded to two Bohemian *korec* (ca. 0.57 ha; Sedláček, *Míry*, 43; Maťa and Dragoun, *Lán*, 104–107). In Upper Franconia (the area of Bayreuth and Wunsiedel) in the 17th through the 19th centuries, old and new measures of *tagwerk* were distinguished. The old *tagwerk* was larger than the new *tagwerk* (Singer, ed., *Das Landbuch*, 115). The areal size of the more undefined *tagwerk* in Upper Franconia from the 16th to the beginning of the 19th centuries fluctuated between 0.39 and 0.53 ha. In 1811, a standardized Bavarian *tagwerk* (0.34 ha) was introduced, also called the new *tagwerk* (Singer, ed., *Das Landbuch*, 115). In the Bohemian Loket district in the 17th century, a *tagwerk* was introduced as a measurement of fields and meadows. When converted, 0.7–3.5 Bohemian *korec* were sown for each *tagwerk*, in 80% of the cases 0.8–2.2 *korec*. Historians therefore worked with an average of 1.5 Bohemian *korec* (Slavík, "O popisu Čech," 79–80; Schreiber, *Der Elbogener Kreis*, 235). In this monograph, we tend to accept that the Cheb *morgen* corresponded to two Bohemian *korec* (thus 0.57 ha) and that a *morgen* and a *tagwerk* were equivalent in size.

Vocabulary

This study contains a large number of specialized terms, which we define the first time they appear or where it is suitable. Below, the reader will find the definitions of those terms that are not common in the literature and are used in this study with a specific meaning in mind.

landholding	an integral economic unit usually made up of dwellings, economic buildings, gardens, fields, and meadows, or other properties (farm, holding; Czech: *usedlost*; German: *Hof, bäuerliche Anwesen*)
Herberge	a landholding/cottage of a smallholder or landless person; in modern terminology, it corresponds to a cottager's dwelling, a smallholding, or the dwelling of a rural craftsman (Czech: *chalupa, chalupnická usedlost*)
Hof	a full-fledged peasant landholding; a "peasant" landholding with enough land for subsistence (Czech: *selská usedlost*)
Höfel	a full-fledged peasant landholding with limited land
non-landholding plot	freely disposable land, not an integral part of any landholding
"free" landholding	in this monograph it means a wide range of non-"subject" landholdings (free and hereditary fief landholdings; hereditary fief landholdings)
tenant	usually "subject" tenant; a head of a peasant household on a "subject" landholding; a tenant of a "subject" landholding ("subject" peasant, peasant farmer)
holder	a holder of a "free" landholding

farmstead   a plot with a dwelling house, economic buildings, and
                             a garden; a part of a landholding

rent   surplus claimed by a landlord (land rent/feudal rent),
                             the church (ecclesiastical tithes), and the state (land
                             tax)

Cf. Klein and Ogilvie, "Occupational structure"; Cerman, "Social structure";
Cerman, *Villagers*.

Figure 1. Administrative division of the city-state of Cheb according to the parishes in 1395.

Source: Ar Cheb, book Nr. 974, *Musterungsbuch der Bauernschaft.*
Note: Parish districts were identical to the districts of the Land Peasant Militia. The basis of the visualization is the modern cadastral territories (1841). In cases where a modern cadastral area included more settlements, the area is divided according to the relevant farmlands.

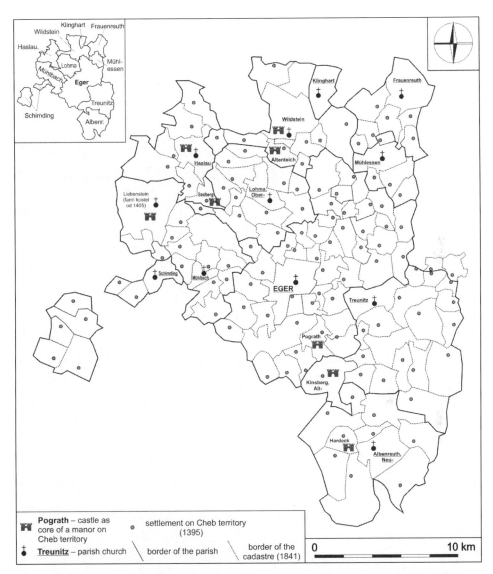

Figure 2. Administrative division and parishes of the city-state of Cheb in 1395. Complemented by the modern cadastral territories (1841) and locations of castles.

Source: Ar Cheb, book Nr. 974, *Musterungsbuch der Bauernschaft.*
Note: If the cadastral area included more settlements, it is divided in the map according to the perimeter of the respective field patterns.

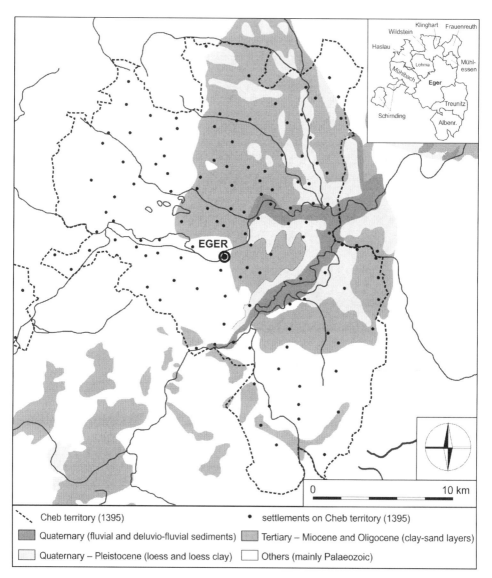

Figure 3. The city-state of Cheb in 1395 and the area of the Cheb Basin.

Source: Cf. *fig. 1*. Geological characteristics according to the Geologische Karte von Bayern.
Scale 1:500 000; H. Arndt et al., ed., *Bayerisches Geologisches Landesamt* (Munich, 1954). Modified.

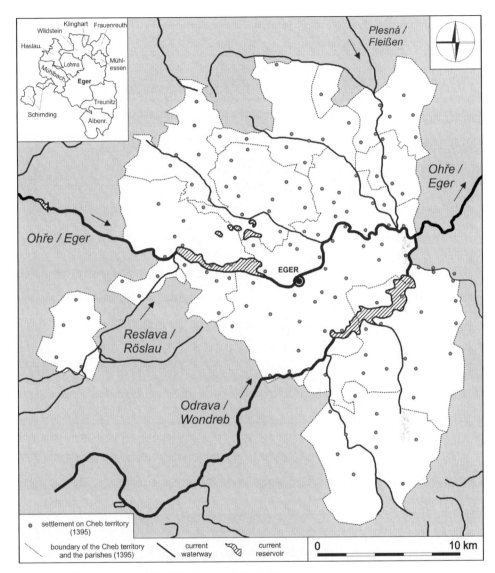

Figure 4. Water network in the city-state of Cheb.

Source: Cf. *fig. 1.*

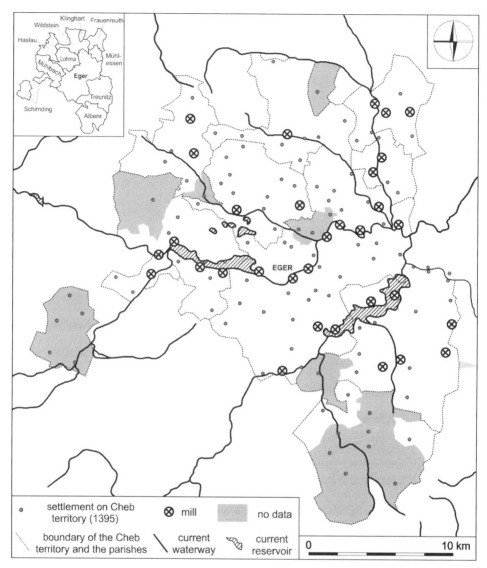

Figure 5. **Mills in the city-state of Cheb during the first half of the 15ᵗʰ century.**

Source: Ar Cheb, book Nr. 1060, *Klosteuerbuch 1424*; book Nr. 1067, *Klosteuerbuch 1438*; book Nr. 1084, *Klosteuerbuch (Schätzungsbuch) 1456.*

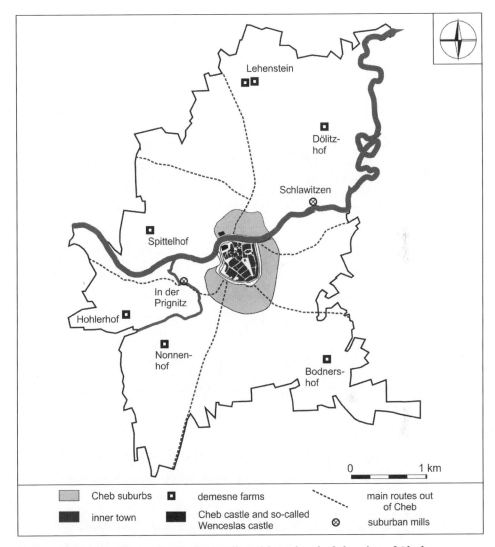

Figure 6. Demesne farms in the immediate hinterland of the city of Cheb in the Late Middle Ages and Early Modern Period.

Source: H. RIMPEL, *Eger*, Plan 14.

Note: The border of the hinterland according to the cadastral border of the city of Cheb in a stable cadastre (1841). Lehenstein (Malý and Velký Chlumeček), originally a settlement under the land tax, consisted of demesne farms in the 15th century under the city tax; Dölitzhof (Dolnice) was originally a settlement in the 15th century under the land tax, later a demesne farm; Bodnershof (Bodnerův Dvůr) was formerly known as Leubner's demesne farm in the 15th century under the land tax; Nonnenhof was a demesne farm of the Cheb Poor Clares, not subject to land or city tax; Hohlerhof was a demesne farm in the 15th century under the land tax; Spittelhof was a demesne farm of the Knights of the Cross with the Red Star, not subject to land or city tax.

◄ Plate 2: **Okrouhlá (Scheibenreuth). A shepherd boy near Březová Mýť (1893).**
A landscape of rolling hills on the right bank of the Odrava River in the Cheb Basin.

I.
General Points

1.
Introduction

1.1 Research objectives

The present study deals with a peasant society living in one of the many territories of the Holy Roman Empire, amidst a long and inexorable cycle of late medieval population stagnation. As most of the questions we ask have not been comprehensively addressed for this period and this part of Europe, we are offering a new perspective. Historians dealing with late medieval social and economic history in areas north of the Alps and east of the Rhine focus primarily on the socioeconomic structures and institutions of peasant communities, namely socioeconomic stratification, the legal framework for land tenure, and transfer or inheritance rights. Much has also been written about the position of the peasantry within the manorial system, as well as surplus exploitation and peasant revolts. Our goal, however, is to penetrate deeper below the surface and illuminate the processes underlying these structures. Therefore, we examine socioeconomic mobility within the life cycle, intergenerational property transfer, migration, the level of monetization and involvement of the peasantry in the credit market, the specific impacts of land rent and land taxes on the peasant economy, and complementary links between the city and the countryside.

It should be added that these themes are rarely accessible to medievalists, while they are systematically addressed by historians of the Early Modern Period, since they have adequate written sources. However, the very existence of such documents is also a sign of a profound difference between the late medieval and early modern situations. Regional studies across Central Europe show that in the 16th century, the lives of peasant communities changed profoundly, as members began to be controlled much more intensely than ever before by peasant elites, landlords, and the state. Internal control, regulation, and monetization also permeated internal family relationships. These changes were accompanied by the onset of adequate means of control, such as collective and detailed written records of assets and property transfers. While the medievalist must reconcile themself with a series of testimonies from a limited range of predominantly normative sources, the historian of the Early Modern Period is faced with a real flood of manorial landlord and state records continually maintained and variable in type in the form of village land-transfer registers, court records, tax records, and church registers. Knowledge of the Early Modern Period cannot simply be projected deeper into the past, as the secular economic cycle beginning around 1500 was of a different nature, characterized by rapid and long-term population growth, declining free agricultural land, rising agricultural product prices, and wage cuts. Social processes should, therefore, develop principally differently and with different consequences for the early modern and late medieval peasantry. In writing this study, we often felt like a cartographer mapping an exotic and almost unknown landscape.

But how is it possible that in the middle of Europe, there is a region like the city-state of Cheb with written sources that—quite unexpectedly—make it possible to break the boundaries of knowledge of the late medieval peasantry? How could it have happened that sources with testimony comparable to village land-transfer registers and modern land tax registers were created and preserved, and why have they gone hitherto unnoticed in the archive?

First, the presence of detailed and continually kept written records of the peasantry in the medieval city-state of Cheb was due to the fact that the Cheb city council obtained territorial rights from the king (1400), and the city office's agenda also included the annual collection of the land tax. The fiscal records for the countryside thus acquired a similar character and informational depth to that of the city itself. Second, while the fiscal documents of many imperial territories were deliberately destroyed in later stages of political integration, as they testified to prior autonomy and the prior level of taxes, the opposite was the case in the city-state of Cheb. Although the Habsburgs attached Cheb to Bohemia in the 18th century, the city-state sought to prove its original geographical scope in territorial disputes with the imperial princes, and it sent the best Bohemian archivist to the Cheb Archive to find and preserve fiscal documents. The Cheb Archive retained its wealth also because the importance of the city decreased significantly in the modern era, and the city office and its registry did not undergo reorganization for a long time. In addition, the city itself has generally avoided catastrophic fires and war-related looting. Third, the Cheb region is situated in the middle of the mountains on the border of several states, in a distressed landscape far from regional centers, and it has had its autonomous status for a long period of time. As such, it has never been fully integrated into Bohemian, Bavarian, Franconian, or Saxon historiography. Cheb's written sources were used mainly by local historians, with little interest in current issues of social and economic history. Although the situation changed in the 1930s, the promising, burgeoning research then was ended by war.

The late medieval Cheb countryside, controlled by the city, had a size of approximately 400 km²; it was comprised of 11 parishes and included significantly different ecological zones.[11] In the fiscal records, we can follow in detail about 100 settlements with 800–900 peasant households, in a fragmented manner since 1392, continuously from 1442–1757. The late medieval and early modern fiscal records are not separated by a sharp divide. Initially, therefore, we faced the dilemma of how to limit our research spatially and temporally. It was possible to narrow our attention to a smaller sample of settlements and to investigate a longer period or to analyze the whole city-state of Cheb in a shorter time interval. We chose the second option, although this meant abstaining from capturing developmental tendencies and telling the story of the long-term transformation of the peasant society. Instead, we focused on the beginnings of the detailed written records and analyzed the time interval of 1438/1442–1456, with overlaps from 1424 to 1469.

Several reasons led us to limit the analyzed period to such a short time span. The first is the densification of the richest sources of information in the period up to the mid-15th century, and the desire to critically evaluate them in their entirety. We believe that this step, which includes understanding the details and the local context, is essential for any further research into the continuity and change of Cheb's peasant society between the Late Middle Ages and the Early Modern Period. The second reason was the effort to identify, in their tremendous diversity, the essential phenomena and generally valid social and

---

11   We leave aside the market village of Marktredwitz, which belonged directly to the city of Cheb and along with the adjacent villages represented an administratively special enclave. Cf. Heribert Sturm, *Districtus Egranus. Eine ursprünglich bayerische Region*, Historischer Atlas von Bayern – Altbayern II/2 (Munich: Kommission for Bayerische Landesgeschrifte, 1981), 125–131.

economic patterns. In this respect, we build on a research strategy based on the knowledge that local socioeconomic structures were shaped largely by the possibilities for agricultural production and market sales of products. The comprehensive understanding of early modern Czech peasant communities, therefore, relies on detailed and comparatively oriented research of micro-regions with different ecological, and thus socioeconomic, conditions. A similar epistemic effect is achieved in the city-state of Cheb by considering it in the research as a whole, while also separating the individual ecological zones, including both the agronomically favorable belt inhabited in prehistory and in the Early Middle Ages and the climatically harsh foothill terrain settled in the High Middle Ages. As a result, we capture internal variation and diversity, while at the same time, we learn about the general processes experienced by all peasant communities. The third reason we did not reduce the sample analyzed was to obtain quantified and statistically sufficiently substantiated answers to our questions. We applied a qualitative analysis to the historical context and institutional framework.

Although we deal with the late medieval population, we were inspired by economic-anthropological studies of the Early Modern Period. These comprehensive and comparative studies not only provided us with appropriate methods but also led us to ask new questions. The ongoing confrontation of partial results has always shown how different the nature and results of social processes were, depending on whether they occurred in the late medieval cycle of population stagnation or the long-term Early Modern Period of growth.

Our study is not comprehensive; because of the many processes we could follow based on the available sources, we have emphasized socioeconomic mobility and migration. This selection was catalyzed by a dramatic and highly sophisticated debate initiated by Russian prerevolutionary sociologists on the principles of the socioeconomic stratification of the peasantry, as well as the belief that this is an issue of extraordinary importance, the resolution of which impacts not only a deeper understanding of the past but also present populations dominated by the peasant mode of production. For this reason, we discuss the theory, models, and analytical tools for recognizing socioeconomic mobility in our study, while approaching other social processes and structures as a necessary backdrop.

I.2 **Synopsis of the book**

We divide the book into five main parts.

+ In the first part, we present the issue of socioeconomic stratification and the mobility of peasant communities, thereby outlining the scope of our research and the text that follows. In accordance with agrarian history and peasantology, we then identify the differentiating and leveling forces that determined the specific nature of socioeconomic stratification and the trajectory of the socioeconomic mobility of the peasantry (*chap. 3*). We also address the current state of research concerning the historical knowledge of socioeconomic stratification (*chap. 4*).

+ In the second part, we turn our attention to the wider historical context of the city-state of Cheb, as well as the crucial environmental, demographic, and socioeconomic processes that characterized the period in question (*chap. 5*). The readers are then introduced to the main written sources we use and their importance in the Central European context (*chap. 6*).

+ The third part deals with the institutions and other factors that played an important role in the formation of peasant society. This includes the practice of property and inheritance rights, the distribution and power of landlords' rights, and the nature and weight of the feudal burden of peasant production in the form of land rent and land tax (*chap. 8–13*).

+ In the fourth part, we turn our attention to the socioeconomic stratification of the Cheb peasantry, the level of property inequality, and the demographic structure, as well as the differences between different settlements and ecological zones (*chap. 14–16*).

+ The core of the study is presented in the fifth part, which directly concerns the socioeconomic mobility and migration of the peasants of the city-state of Cheb. We examine and interpret changes in the property position of families during an individual's life cycle, as well as intergenerational differences; the proportion of landholding transfers between relatives; the proportion of transfers due to tenant migration; the socioeconomic position of migrating tenants on their original and on the target landholding; the number of landholding transfers undergone by individual landholdings; and fluctuations between tax amounts prescribed for tenants of individual landholdings (*chap. 17–22*). However, we are not interested in absolute monetary values but rather in relative differences between rich and poor, fullholding peasants and "sub-peasant" groups, "subject" and "free" landholding tenants. We also touch on the social aspects of the migration of peasants to the city of Cheb (*chap. 23*).

+ In one specific chapter, we investigate the links between social mobility, migration, and processes of the abandonment of settlements in the Late Middle Ages. We test the hypothesis that abandonment and long-term vacant landholdings were the reverse side of certain forms of social mobility and migration (*chap. 24*).

Our focus of interest was primarily the transalpine region of Europe (*fig. 1.1*); for methodological and theoretical inspiration, no time-related, geographical, or discipline restrictions were imposed.

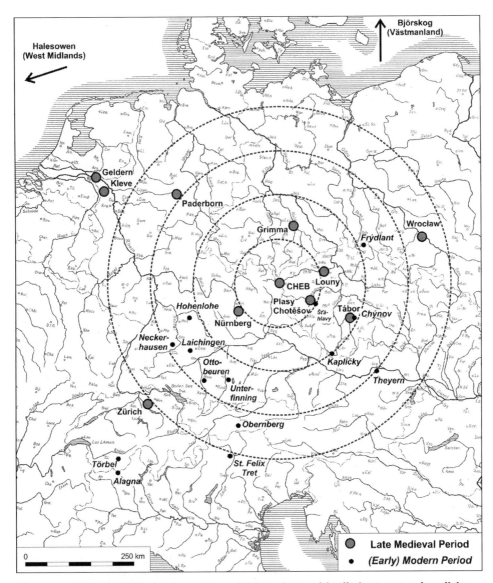

Figure 1.1. Focus territory. An overview of historiographically important localities and regions mentioned in the text.

Source: Prepared by the author.

Note: Circular perimeters of 100 km. Most of the reference sites were located in the area of so-called impartible inheritance of land, i.e., indivisible peasant landholdings handed over to only one of the descendants.

2.
Terminology

2.1 Social mobility and migration

People differ in their living standards all the time and everywhere—in their lot in life and in their expectations of the future. Such differences stem from the uneven distribution of scarce commodities, such as economic resources, power, and prestige. Every society is *stratified*, i.e., made up of many various hierarchical positions (*statuses*) and related expected behaviors (*roles*), which correspond to a certain quantity of scarce commodities. The aggregate of the stable relations and rules of behavior that govern social interaction, which are independent of concrete individuals and are meant to satisfy a certain social need, are identified as *institutions*. Social institutions are also the main reproduction tool of the social stratification system. Social stratification (i.e., statuses, roles, and the relationships between them) is generated through the process of social *differentiation*, which can create various types of economic and non-economic inequalities.[12]

For a long time, *social mobility* was not studied as a separate topic in sociology but was instead viewed as an automatic component of studies of social stratification and differentiation.[13] The first comprehensive theory of social mobil-

---

[12]   In Czech cf. Jadwiga Šanderová, *Sociální stratifikace. Problém, vybrané teorie, výzkum* (Prague: Karolinum, 2004), 13, 15, 21–22, 25–26. For more about the starting points of the approach, cf. esp. Gerhard Emmanuel Lenski, *Power and privilege: A theory of social stratification*, McGraw-Hill Series in Sociology (New York: McGraw-Hill, 1966); James Littlejohn, *Social stratification: An introduction*, Studies in Sociology 7 (New York: Routledge, 2021). In Czech also cf. relevant topic headings in Miloslav Petrusek, Hana Maříková, and Alena Vodáková, et al., *Velký sociologický slovník*, Vols. 1 and 2 (Prague: Karolinum, 1996).

[13]   In medieval studies see also Sandro Carocci and Isabella Lazzarini, "Introduction," in *Social mobility in medieval Italy (1100–1500)*, ed. Sandro Carocci and Isabella Lazzarini, Viella

ity was presented by Pitirim Aleksandrovič Sorokin (1889–1968), a Russian sociologist who spent most of his life—after a short intermezzo in Czechoslovakia[14]—in exile in North America.[15] In his classic 1927 monograph, he defined *social mobility* as the transition of people, social objects, and values from one status to another. Transitions between statuses on the same level (i.e., in the same stratum) can be identified as *horizontal* mobility, and transitions between strata as *vertical* mobility. Social mobility can be either upward or downward. According to Sorokin, despite that individuals in a social space are organized hierarchically, stratification has several dimensions; several stratification principles exist, and the individual may hold several different statuses at once, depending on the concrete situation. Research on mobility can then be directed at identifying various categories of social mobility, such as class/rank, economic, professional, and political mobility. Sorokin also introduced an essential term—the "channel" of vertical social mobility, which identifies the most typical manner of social transition.[16] In general terms, social mobility also includes geographical mobility.[17]

Historical Research 8 (Rome, 2018), 9–20, on 10–11; recently see also contributions published in Giampiero Nigro, ed., *Disuguaglianza economica nelle società preindustriali: cause ed effetti / Economic inequality in pre-industrial societies: causes and effect* (Firenze: Firenze University Press, 2020); esp. Guido Alfani, "Economic inequality in preindustrial Europe, 1300-1800: methods and results from the EINITE project", 21–36.

14   Alexander Nikulin and Irina Trotsuk, "Pitirim Sorokin's contribution to rural sociology: Russian, European, and American milestones of a scientific career," *Journal of Peasant Studies* 45 (2018): 1203–1220, on 1212–1213.

15   In addition, e.g., Miloslav Petrusek, "Od víry ve společnost bez trestů ke společnosti altruistické a nezištné lásky (Na okraj Sorokinovy Krise našeho věku)" [From faith in a society without punishments to a society of altruistic love (on the margins of Sorokin's Crisis of our Age)], in *Aktéři, systémy, rizika*, ed. Jiří Šubrt, Acta Universitatis Carolinae, Philosophica et Historica 1/2006, Studia Sociologica 15 (Prague, 2009), 9–25, on pp. 10–11. More recently, cf. Pitirim Sorokin and Edward A. Tiryakin, eds., *Sociological theory, values, and sociocultural change: Essays in honor of Pitirim A. Sorokin* (New York: Free Press of Glencoe, 2017); V. V. Sapov, ed., *Pitirim Aleksandrovich Sorokin*, Nauchnoe izdanie, Filosofiia Rossii pervoĭ poloviny dvadtsatogo veka (Moskow: ROSSPĖN, 2013).

16   Pitirim Sorokin, *Social Mobility* (New York: Harper & Brothers, 1927). A brief Czech summary appears in Pitirim Sorokin, *Sociologické nauky přítomnosti*, Laichterova filosofická knihovna 13, trans. Blažena Jirsová (Prague: Jan Laichter, 1936), 610–614.

17   On the same topic, see, Josef Grulich, *Migrace městského a vesnického obyvatelstva: Farnost České Budějovice 1750–1824*, Monographia historica 13 (České Budějovice: Jihočeská univerzita v Českých Budějovicích, 2013), esp. 59–60.

In contemporary sociological research, mobility is operationalized and ideologized in many ways, and there is no single shared concept.[18] Since the 1960s–1970s, the dominant trend stemming from social anthropology (P. Bourdieu) has emphasized the constant reproduction and transformation of the social space taking place against a backdrop of numerous, changing social interactions. Social stratification, then, is not a static set of statuses between which an individual crosses and which can be sharply defined, but rather a process during which the scale for evaluating economic resources, power, prestige, and the relevant constellation of statuses and roles are changed, constructed, and reproduced through everyday activities. It is not only individuals, groups, and social objects that can be mobile, but also values, statuses, and their hierarchies. As such, factors and tools with which people actively create and represent social statuses have become a focus of interest, and attention is also paid to the changing nature of social mobility channels. In analytic and model terms, social mobility is operationalized as a result of the active efforts (*agency*) of the individual and their economic, cultural, and subjectively most significant symbolic capital, which always go hand in hand together.[19]

Currently, social anthropological and sociological concepts are also being applied to medieval studies to clarify how written sources and material culture shed light on contemporaneous social values, recognition, statuses, formative and manipulative representation, and constantly mutating social mobility channels over a long time period. Despite the lack of quantitative data, each evaluation of social stratification and mobility—due to their dynamics, relativity, and multidimensional nature—is always just approximate.[20]

Sociology defines geographical (i.e., spatial) mobility as the movement of people in a physical space. The term refers not only to the spatial relocation of a person, but also to related processes. The range of types of geographical mobility can be differentiated; among them, *migration* holds a special position,

18   Cf. Wiemer Salverda, Brian Nolan, and Timothy M. Smeeding, eds., *The Oxford Handbook of Economic Inequality* (Oxford: Oxford University Press,[2] 2011).

19   Summarized from a medievalist viewpoint in Sandro Carocci, "Social Mobility and the Middle Ages," *Continuity and Change* 26 (2011): 367–404, on pp. 369–371, 382–385; Carocci, and Lazzarini, "Introduction," 10–12. From the point of view of early modern Bohemian agrarian history, see, e.g., Grulich, *Migrace*, 22–25.

20   Carocci, "Social Mobility," esp. 370–371; Carocci and Lazzarini, "Introduction," esp. 14.

which indicates a one-off removal and change of residence.[21] In this study, we use the term *moving* as an equivalent for *migration*.[22]

2.2 The peasantry

We conceived of this study as a component of the broader study of European society in the preindustrial period, the primary characteristics of which were the peasantry and the peasant mode of production.[23] Although it is possible to find various broad definitions of the *peasantry*, here we are inclined to use those that take into account both the typical production unit (a peasant family household) and the milieu in which such units operated.[24] European *peasantry*

21   Petrusek, Maříková, and Vodáková, *Velký sociologický slovník*. Cf. Carocci, *Social mobility*, 369; Grulich, *Migrace*, 39–41; Hans-Jörg Gilomen, "Neue Forschungen zur Migration im Spätmittelalter und in der Frühen Neuzeit. Einleitung," in *Migration in die Städte. Ausschluss – Assimilierung – Integration – Multikulturalität – Migrations vers les villes. Exclusion – assimilation – intégration – multiculturalité*, ed. Hans-Jörg Gilomen, Schweizerische Gesellschaft für Wirtschafts- und Sozialgeschichte 16 (Zürich: Chronos, 2000), 1–16, on pp. 14–15.

22   Also cf. František Graus, *Dějiny venkovského lidu v Čechách v době předhusitské II. Od poloviny 13. stol. do roku 1419*, Studie a prameny 13 (Prague: Státní nakladatelství politické literatury, 1957), 256–257.

23   Jane C. Whittle, *The development of agrarian capitalism: Land and labour in Norfolk, 1440–1580*, Oxford Historical Monographs (Oxford: Oxford University Press, 2000), 11–16. For the Czech terminology cf. Václav Husa, "K methodice studia dějin lidových hnutí v období pozdního feudalismu," in Václav Husa and Josef Petráň, *Příspěvky k dějinám třídních bojů v Čechách I. Nevolnické povstání r. 1775*, Acta Universitatis Carolinae, Historica VI (Prague: Karlova University, 1955), 5–34; Graus, *Dějiny*, 194–207; Alois Míka, *Poddaný lid v Čechách v první polovině 16. století* [Die untertänige Bevölkerung in Böhmen in der ersten Hälfte des 16. Jahrhunderts], Studie a prameny 19 (Prague: Nakladatelství Československé akademie věd, 1960), 8, 134–177; Josef Petráň, *Poddaný lid v Čechách na prahu třicetileté války* [Serfs in Bohemia on the verge of the Thirty Year' War] (Prague: Nakladatelství Československé akademie věd, 1964), 13–14; František Matějek, *Cesta poddaného lidu na Moravě ke znevolnění*, Knižnice Matice moravské 5 (Brno: Matice moravská, 2000); František Matějek, *Feudální velkostatek a poddaný na Moravě. S přihlédnutím k přilehlému území Slezska a Polska: Studie o přeměnách na feudálním velkostatku v druhé polovině 15. a v první polovině 16. století*, Studie a prameny 18 (Prague: Nakladatelství Československé akademie věd, 1959), 15; Jaroslav Čechura, "Sedlák," in *Člověk českého středověku*, ed. František Šmahel and Martin Nodl (Prague: Argo, 2002), 436–459.

24   Whittle, *Development*, 11.

is defined as a group composed primarily of agricultural producers with the following characteristics:[25]

1. They are consumers of their own products; the primary aim of their agricultural production is to cover their own subsistence needs, not to be sold in the market.

2. They primarily use their own family labor; wage labor is sought mainly for seasonal peaks, not because of commercial or profit-maximizing production.

3. They cultivate land in various legal forms of tenure; to achieve acquisition and tenure, they conclude contracts with the sovereign landowners.

4. They exist within larger political units (states), and they are in a dependent relationship with other social groups that extract the peasant surplus through various means (peasants are the subject of non-economic exploitation).[26] Peasants prosper or suffer not only based on how much they produce

---

25 For the classical anthropologizing conception see: Eric R. Wolf, *Peasants* (Englewood Cliffs, NJ: Prentice-Hall Englewood, 1966); the sociologizing conception: Theodor Shanin, "Peasantry: Delineation of a sociological concept and a field of study," *European Journal of Sociology* 12 (1971): 289–300; Theodor Shanin, "Introduction: Peasantry as a concept," in *Peasants and peasant societies: selected readings*, ed. Theodor Shanin (Oxford: Blackwell,² 1990), 1–11; the economic conception: Frank Ellis, *Peasant economics: Farm households and agrarian development*, Wye Studies in Agricultural and Rural Development (Cambridge: Cambridge University Press,² 2003), 4–16; Haroon A. Akram-Lodhi and Kay Cristóbal, eds., *Peasants and globalization: Political economy, rural transformation and the agrarian question* (London, New York: Routledge, 2009), 3. From the view of late medieval and early modern history, see, e.g., Gérard Béaur and Jürgen Schlumbohm, "Einleitung: Probleme einer deutsch-französischen Geschichte ländlicher Gesellschaften," in *Ländliche Gesellschaften in Deutschland und Frankreich, 18.–19. Jahrhundert*, ed. Reiner Prass, Jürgen Schlumbohm, Gérard G. Béaur, and Christophe Duhamelle, Veröffentlichungen des Max-Planck-Instituts für Geschichte 187 (Göttingen: Vandenhoeck & Ruprecht, 2003), 11–29, on 22–27; Whittle, *Development*, 11–12; Paul Warde, "Subsistence and sales: The peasant economy of Württemberg in the early seventeenth century," *The Economic History Review* 56 (2006): 289–319, on 289–293. Modern sociological concepts of the peasantry were introduced into the Czech agrarian history of the late Middle Ages by Jaroslav Čechura, "Rolnictvo v Čechách v pozdním středověku. Perspektivy dalšího studia," *Český časopis historický* 88 (1990): 465–498, on 465, 483–484; in the German version: Jaroslav Čechura, "Die Bauernschaft in Böhmen während des Spätmittelalters: Perspektiven neuer Orientierungen," *Bohemia* 31 (1990): 283–311, on 283, 290–291.

26 e.g., Philip R. Schofield, *Peasant and community in late medieval England, 1200–1500*, Medieval Culture and Society (Basingstoke: Springer, 2003), 6; Whittle, *Development*, 11–12.

through their work, but also based on how much surplus the socially dominant groups leave them.[27]

5. They operate in an incomplete and imperfect market; they are partially integrated into the market but are not existentially dependent on the market. The peasant economy is dual in nature, i.e., subsistence and market oriented.[28]

6. They are dependent on towns, which consume their products and at the same time supply them with specific tools and services.[29] In order to sell their surplus agricultural production, obtain cash, and purchase items that they themselves do not produce, they negotiate with merchants.

7. Peasants try to make use of their land, their capital, and their own labor force in an optimal way; they also adapt to local ecological conditions and actively shape them. If the labor capacity of peasants remains unused or can be applied for profit, they may even attempt to enter the labor market.[30]

Traditional scholarship has characterized the peasantry as dual, operating within both subsistence and market systems simultaneously. Today, we go further and define *peasantry* as a group that normally acts within a three-part system: subsistence (points 1–2), market (points 5–7), and exploitation (points 3–4).

We see the peasantry as an exemplary and ideal type due to its knowledge and its analytical and comparative potential. The concept of the peasantry, therefore, is not intended to express the uniformity or homogeneity of a particular social group, but it rather presupposes the existence of internal differences that help to identify it even in temporally or spatially distant societies.

Given that Europe between the High Middle Ages and the capitalist period was characterized by the peasant mode of production, the non-economic extraction of the surplus, imperfect markets, and the position of cities as the centers of non-agrarian market production, some historians have suggested that *peasant society* should replace the controversial and vague term *feudal society*. In other words, the model of feudal production would be replaced by the more flexible and politically less burdened model of peasant society and

27   Shanin, "Introduction," 3–5; Akram-Lodhi and Cristóbal, *Peasants*, 3.
28   Ellis, *Peasant Economics*, 3.
29   E.g., Schofield, *Peasant*, 6; Whittle, *Development*, 11–12.
30   Akram-Lodhi and Cristóbal, *Peasants*, 3.

the peasant economy (ca. 13th–18th centuries).[31] In this study, we use the term *feudal*, in spite of the reservations and in keeping with tradition, while acknowledging that it does not necessarily involve the peasantry's personal dependence.

A peasant may be part of several *personal networks* and *communities*, the most important one being the community with which they shared a settlement and economic resources. Members of such a community are linked by common interests in the sphere of production activities, the maintenance of safety and security, the provision of services, and the use of common resources. The community is the key domain for social, economic, and demographic interaction. The members of the community, who may be treated as neighbors, are born into or come to live in the same external conditions, gain similar experiences in life, meet more or less daily during a wide range of activities, lack any space for anonymity, and have a strong sense of common interdependence and proximity. Peasant communities, therefore, behave according to a special cultural model stemming from the relatively small numbers of members.[32]

One social category that indicated membership in certain communities was the neighborhood, which formally erased other social differences, ensured the functioning, cohesion, and stability of communities, determined the use of local economic resources, created collective memory—thereby ensuring certain rights—and also constituted an economic safety net for its members.[33]

In recent decades, historical research has been addressing the concepts of peasant communities, neighborhoods, social domains, and personal networks. Thanks to such research, new insights have developed not only in self-regulation, mutual support, control, and the resilience of peasant households—and in their shared memories and prejudices—but also in the ingrained inner tensions and differences and the factors causing them.[34]

31   Whittle, *Development*, 10–11.

32   Shanin, "Peasantry"; Shanin, *"Introduction"*; Christopher Dyer, "The English mediaeval village community and its decline," *Journal of British Studies* 33 (1994): 407–429, on 408–411; Peter Blickle, *Kommunalismus: Skizzen einer gesellschaftlichen Organisationsform, Band 1: Oberdeutschland; Band 2: Europa* (Munich: R. Oldenbourg Verlag, 2000); Crow Graham and Allan Graham, *Community life: An introduction to local social relations* (New York – London: Harvester Wheatsheaf, 1994).

33   Susan McDonough, "Being a neighbor: Ideas and ideals of neighborliness in the medieval west," *History Compass* 15/9 (September 2017): 1–11.

34   Schofield, *Peasant*, 5–6; for a recent overview, see also McDonough, "Being."

Medieval peasant communities were not homogeneous but rather were fragmented into numerous different social groups and contextually defined statuses and roles relating to such statuses.[35] A fascinating view of the constituent
elements of the peasant world was offered by Govind P. Sreenivasan's anthro-
pologically focused study on the early modern peasantry of the Ottobeuren
Abbey in Swabia, southwest of Augsburg.[36] The view of the social world here
had a dual nature in principle until the first half of the 16th century, and it
divided the community along various axes of "us and them"—those with full
rights and those without them, the strong and the weak, the powerful and
the vulnerable, protectors and the protected. Depending on the concrete situation and type of social interaction, various groups stood against each other:
(1) rich and poor, (2) fullholding peasant and "sub-peasant" groups, (3) kinship
and non-kinship, (4) insiders and outsiders, (5) men and women, (6) friends
and enemies, (7) families and strangers. These social distinctions dictated the
degree of respect for authority, family and group loyalty, inequality in access to
property, regulation of marriages, economic vulnerability, violence, and hospi-
tality.[37]

A mere list of social categories that categorized the course of peasant life
would be misleading and two-dimensional. Social statuses were not mutually
equal; some were primary and stable, others flexible and manipulative. It was
the rich who, to a great extent, controlled peasant communities and for various
reasons determined who would end up in which social category and where the
boundary between kinship and non-kinship or between friends and enemies
lay. As Sreenivasan and other researchers have shown, it was the peasant elites
who, in cooperation with the landlords, shaped and stabilized social statuses in
early modern peasant communities.[38] It is no coincidence that in our research
we concentrate primarily on social stratification as expressing differences in
control over precious, scarce commodities, as this was the most important axis

---

35   E.g., Rainer Beck, *Unterfinning. Ländliche Welt vor Anbruch der Moderne* (Munich: Beck,
      2004), 217–253.

36   Govind P. Sreenivasan, *The Peasants of Ottobeuren, 1487–1726. A rural society in Early
      Modern Europe*, Past and Present Publications (Cambridge: Cambridge University Press,
      2004).

37   Sreenivasan, *Peasants*, 51–71.

38   Sreenivasan, *Peasants*, 107–279; Thomas Robisheaux, *Rural society and the search for order
      in Early Modern Germany* (Cambridge: Cambridge University Press, 1989), 95–146.

of social distinction according to which a large portion of other distinctions were governed.

Due to the specific nature and structure of the written sources, the fundamental analytic units in social history and historical demography are most often settlements, parishes, or manors, which are considered to be independent social and economic units. The fruits of this approach, especially in English medieval studies of the 1970s and 1980s, were myriad studies from the so-called Toronto School and Zvi Razi's study of the parish of Halesowen. Examples from other countries where a sufficiently detailed range of sources exist are also available to medievalists. However, this approach has been criticized for being too determined by the structure of the sources.[39] Anne Reiber DeWindt, a key player in the Toronto School, emphasized that peasants shared diverse circumstances and destinies, performed diverse activities, and only rarely spent their lives in just one settlement, parish, or manor. Thus, a complex network of relationships spread like a spider web over the socially and geographically mobile peasant population. When studying social and geographical mobility, the focus on individual settlements, parishes, or manors must be put aside, and the paths of peasants and their families in various communities must be followed.[40] This is the approach that we have chosen for this study, where individual families, landholdings, ecological zones, and the city-state of Cheb as a whole are given prominence, not specific settlements or parishes.

[39]   Anne Reiber DeWindt, "Redefining the peasant community in medieval England: The regional perspective," *Journal of British Studies* 26 (1987): 163–207.

[40]   DeWindt, "Redefining," 163–166. On the same subject see Christopher Dyer, "Villages in crisis: Social dislocation and desertion, 1370–1520," in *Deserted Villages Revisited*, ed. Christopher Dyer and Richard Jones, Explorations in Local and Regional History 3 (Hatfield: University of Hertfordshire Press, 2010), 28–45, esp. 30.

3.
Theoretical framework

3.1 The Differentiation model versus the life-cycle model of socioeconomic stratification and mobility

Marxist–Leninist political economics was one of the first prominent models to attempt to explain, at least partially, the changes in the distribution of the basic means of production. According to this materialistic concept, economic development was accompanied by the social division of labor, the creation and reinforcement of market relations, the accumulation of capital, and vertical social differentiation. The full development of these forces and the investment of capital in further production were meant to take place after the weakening and disintegration of feudal relations.[41] The polarization processes first hit the towns and craft production, and subsequently the peasants and agrarian production as well. This caused a fairly uniform class of self-sufficient peasant households to approach inevitable disintegration, since a minority of them had accumulated ever more advantages, agriculture tools and equipment, land, and livestock, while the majority went into economic decline and had to fight just to survive while their offspring became nothing more than a reserve of agrarian wage laborers (*fig. 3.1. A*). Huge social tensions resulted from this disparity,

---

41   Peter C. M. Hoppenbrouwers and Jan Luiten van Zanden, eds., *Peasants into farmers? The transformation of rural economy and society in the low countries (Middle Ages – 19th century) in light of the Brenner debate*, CORN Publication Series 4 (Turnhout: Brepols, 2001); Whittle, *Development*, 17–27; Trevor H. Aston and Charles H. E. Philpin, eds., *The Brenner debate: Agrarian class structure and economic development in pre-industrial Europe*, Past and Present Publications (Cambridge: Cambridge University Press, 1985).

erupting into anti-feudal—and later anti-capitalist—revolution characterized by the struggle of the rural poor against the wealthy and prosperous peasants: the Kulaks.[42] To begin with, this Marxist concept, first formulated in its entirety by V. I. Lenin in the 1890s against a backdrop of development in Russia after the abolition of serfdom in 1861 and modified after experience with revolutions at the beginning of the 20th century, was more or less copied by Marxist-oriented agrarian history across Europe.[43]

The idea that the peasantry would inevitably transform and disintegrate due to market forces was based on experience with Western European development in the industrial era and therefore was long considered final and unquestionable. However, since the end of the 19th century, Russian and then Soviet (hereafter simply Russian) agrarian research formulated a fundamentally different theoretical concept that was not based on mechanical deduction, but rather attempted to explain an extraordinary quantity of unusually high-quality data that did not make sense in either traditional neoclassical economics or Marxist political economy. The relevant data were collected between the

---

42   For more on the Marxist–Leninist concept and its modification given the development of the Russian peasantry, see, e.g., Theodor Shanin, *The awkward class: Political sociology of peasantry in a developing society: Russia 1910–1925* (Oxford: Clarendon Press, 1972); Theodor Shanin, *Late Marx and the Russian road: Marx and the "peripheries of capitalism"* (New York: Monthly Review Press, 1983); Theodor Shanin, "Defining peasants: Conceptualizations and deconceptualizations," in *Defining peasants: Essays concerning rural societies, expolary economies, and learning from them in the contemporary world*, ed. Theodor Shanin (Oxford: Blackwell, 1990), 49–74, on 56–61; Theodor Shanin, "Socio-Economic Mobility and the Rural History of Russia 1905–30," in *Defining peasants: Essays concerning rural societies, expolary economies, and learning from them in the contemporary world*, ed. Theodor Shanin (Oxford: Blackwell, 1990), 209–227, on 210–215; William Roseberry, "Rent, differentiation, and the development of capitalism among peasants," *American Anthropologist* 78 (1977): 45–58; Natalia Rozinskaya, Alexander Sorokin, and Dmitry Artamonov, "Peasants' inequality and stratification: Evidence from pre-revolutionary Russia," *Scandinavian Economic History Review* 69 (2021): 253–277, on 255.

43   An overview of Marxist–Leninist documents, essential for agrarian history is summarized in, e.g., Boris Timofeevich Rubtsov, *Evoljucija feodal'noj renty v Čechii (XIV – načalo XV v.)* (Moscow: s.n., 1958), 170; in more general terms also by John Hatcher and Mark Bailey, *Modelling the Middle Ages* (Oxford: Oxford University Press, 2001), 66–120; Antón María Isabel Alfonso, ed., *The rural history of medieval European societies: Trends and perspectives*, The Medieval Countryside 1 (Turnhout: Brepols, 2007). For more on heated Marxist-oriented historiographic debate cf. the recent Terry J. Byres, "Differentiation of the peasantry under feudalism and the transition to capitalism: In defence of Rodney Hilton," *Journal of Agrarian Change* 6 (2006): 17–68.

1870s and 1928, when research practically ceased due to new agrarian policy. Thus came into being a fascinating collection of information, methodological procedures, and theoretical concepts without comparison today, which afford countless unique views into the behavior and development of the traditional peasantry.[44] In opposition to neoclassical economics and also to the original Marxist–Leninist concept, this research created an image of (1) a specific peasant economy that requires a special theory to describe it, and (2) peasants as a peculiar social group that is only partially integrated into the market and monetary relationships and resists their influence because it is capable of existing outside of the market and for a range of reasons does not strive to maximize yields. This view also emphasized the stability of the peasantry as a class that, despite being stratified for a range of reasons, also resists further polarization, has exceptional resilience as a whole, and follows a different development trajectory than the craftsmen in towns, since they pose no threat to each other in existential terms. Relevant theoretical concepts identified simply as *neopopulationist* were perfected and popularized for the foreign audience by

---

44   Rozinskaya, Sorokin, and Artamonov, "Peasants' inequality," 255; Alexander M. Nikulin, "An Omitted Intellectual Tradition: The Chaianov School on Collective Farming," *Jahrbücher für Geschichte Osteuropas* 65 (2017): 423–444; Shanin, *Awkward Class*, 1–4, 74–82, 122–131, 145–166; Shanin, "Socio-Economic Mobility," 210–211; Theodor Shanin, "Measuring peasant capitalism," in *Defining peasants: Essays concerning rural societies, expolary economies, and learning from them in the contemporary world*, ed. Theodor Shanin (Oxford: Blackwell, 1990), 229–247, on 234–242; Mark Harrison, "Resource allocation and agrarian class formation: The problem of social mobility among Russian peasant households, 1880–1930," *Journal of Peasant Studies* 4 (1977): 127–161; Robert E. Johnson, "Family life-cycles and economic stratification: A case-study in rural Russia," *Journal of Social History* 30 (1997): 705–731, on 706–708. Cf. Aleksandr Vasil'evich Chaianov, *Bjudzhetnye issledovanija: istorija i metody* (Leningrad, 1929); Aleksandr Vasil'evich Chaianov, *Ocherki po Ekonomike Trudovogo Selskogo Khazyaistva* (Moscow: Narodnyi komissariat zemledeliya, 1924); Aleksandr Vasil'evich Chaianov and Gennadij Aleksander Studenskii, *Istoriya byudzhetnykh issledovanii* (Moscow: Izd. Tsentral'nogo statisticheskogo upravleniya, 1922); Aleksander Tchayanov, "The organization and development of agricultural economics in Russia," *Journal of Farm Economics* 12 (1930): 270–277.

Alexander Vasilievich Chayanov.[45] However, his work is just the proverbial tip of the iceberg.[46] Therefore, the Chayanov school is often referred to.[47]

Prerevolutionary and postrevolutionary analyses of the Russian peasantry all showed fairly extreme stratification into relatively rich and poor peasants, and therefore it seemed that nothing contradicted the Leninist interpretation and neoclassical models. However, more sophisticated research that not only compared the degree of stratification at a particular time but also traced the social development of concrete families over time showed that the main form of mobility was not polarization and continuing enrichment of one at the expense of another, but multidirectional or even cyclic movement (*fig. 3.1. D–E*). Or rather, the higher the socioeconomic position of the peasant family household, the higher the likelihood that in subsequent years its situation would deteriorate; conversely, the poor stood a good chance of improvement in the future. Polarization tendencies were constantly counterbalanced by opposing forces

45   Daniel Thorner et al., eds., *A. V. Chayanov on the theory of peasant economy* (Manchester: Manchester University Press, 1986); Aleksandr Vasil'evich Chaianov, *Organizatsiia krestianskogo khoziaistva* (Moscow: Kooperativnoe Izdatel'stvo, 1925). Further, see particularly Aleksandr Vasil'evich Chaianov, *Ocherki po Ekonomike Trudovogo Selskogo Khazyaistva* (Moscow: Narodnyi komissariat zemledeliya, 1924); Aleksandr Vasil'evich Chaianov, *Krest'janskoe khozijaistvo: izbrannye trudy*, ed. A. A. Nikonov (Moscow: Ekonomika, 1989); Aleksandr Vasil'evich Chaianov, *Izbrannye proizvedenija*, ed. Evgenija Viktorovna Serova (Moscow: Moskovskii rabochii, 1989). Along with Chayanov, cf. Shanin, *Awkward Class*, 45–80; Theodor Shanin, "Chayanov's message," in *A. V. Chayanov on the theory of peasant economy*, ed. Daniel Thorner (Manchester: Manchester University Press, 1986), 15–18; Vladimir Nikolaevich Baliazin, *Professor Aleksandr Chaianov, 1888–1937* (Moscow: Agropromizdat, 1990); Aleksandr Vasil'evich Chaianov, *A.V. Chaianov: Chelovek—uchenyi—grazhdanin* (Moscow: Izdatel'stvo mSChA, 1998); Alexander Alexandrowitsch Nikonow and Eberhard Schulze, *Drei Jahrhunderte Agrarwissenschaft in Russland. Von 1700 bis zur Gegenwart*, Studies on the Agricultural and Food Sector in Central and Eastern Europe (Halle: IAMO, 2004), 42–76; Eberhard Schulze, ed., *Alexander Wasiljewitsch Tschajanow. Die Tragödie eines grossen Agrarökonomen*, Studies on the Agricultural and Food Sector in Central and Eastern Europe 12 (Kiel: IAMO, 2001).
46   One of the extremely extensive book collections of Russian agrarian sociology and economy is kept at the Slavonic Library in Prague, thanks to Russian emigrés and the activities of the Ukrainian Academy of Economics. Cf. Nikulin and Trotsuk, "Pitirim Sorokin's contribution," 1212–1213.
47   A recent overview in English is provided in Nikulin, "An Omitted Intellectual Tradition"; Joachim Zweynert et al., "The Enigma of A.V. Chayanov," in *Economics in Russia: Studies in intellectual history*, ed. Joachim Zweynert and Vincent Barnett (Aldershot: Ashgate, 2008), 91–105.

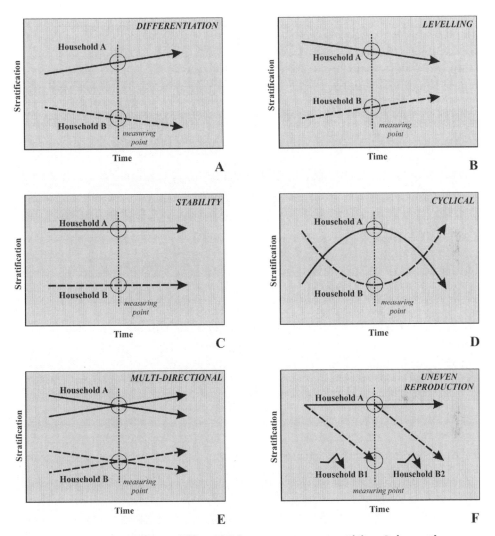

Figure 3.1. **Socioeconomic mobility within peasant communities. Schematic illustration of the main model variations. The graphics demonstrate how diverse processes may be hidden behind the same socioeconomic stratification. The position of households A and B are always the same at the measuring point, while their past and future are always different.**

Source: Lindström, *Distribution*, figs. 1.3–1.5, 4.8, 7.1. Supplemented by a leveling and multidirectional model according to Shanin, "Measuring Peasants," 218, fig. 14.1; cf. Tschajanow, *Die Lehre*, 100–101.

dictated in the first place by life cycles and endeavors to achieve the optimum economic operation of a household. The socioeconomic status and quantity of resources of a peasant household therefore changed on a cyclic basis, depending on the moment in the life cycle, while large family landholdings were often divided into smaller units; conversely, landholdings that were too small merged with others. The concept of *social differentiation* was thus supplemented by the idea of *demographic differentiation* and the theory of the *cyclic redistribution* of economic resources.[48]

The method, which follows the fates of peasant households not statically but dynamically, in the way that demographers or sociologists follow the fates of separate population cohorts, proved that in certain social categories during various time segments, different kinds of households emerged. In other words, different concrete households were always hiding behind a façade of seemingly similar social structures. The greatest movement was visible on both extreme poles; therefore, the largest—or conversely, the poorest—households were the least stable. Russian agrarian economists found the same phenomena in various time periods and geographic areas, using all thinkable indicators from traditionally analyzed items, from areas of arable land or numbers of horses to the accumulation of capital or the employment of wage labor.[49] Also, later revisions provided by several scholars from the end of the 20th century who concentrated on a contextual analysis of the data confirmed the original neo-populationistic observation and interpretation.[50] Nevertheless, the latest analysis, published by Russian researchers in 2021, showed that the level of socioeconomic inequality within the Russian peasantry only deepened over time, thus challenging Chaynov's hypothesis of a positive correlation between the size of the family and the amount of ploughed land.[51]

48   Shanin, *Awkward Class*, 28–32, 76–88, 101–109, 119, 151–155; Shanin, "Socio-Economic Mobility," 216–220; Harrison, "Resource allocation," chap. 2; Johnson, "Family Life-Cycles," 705–707; Heinz-Dietrich Löwe, "Differentiation in Russian peasant society: Causes and trends, 1880–1905," in *Land commune and peasant community in Russia: Communal forms in imperial and early Soviet society*, ed. Robert Bartlett (London: Springer, 1990), 165–195.
49   Shanin, *Awkward Class*; Shanin, "Socio-Economic Mobility"; Shanin, "Measuring Peasant"; Harrison, "Resource allocation"; Johnson, "Family Life-Cycles."
50   Johnson, "Family Life-Cycles." Other studies summarized in Rozinskaya, Sorokin, and Artamonov, "Peasants' inequality," 255.
51   Rozinskaya, Sorokin, and Artamonov, "Peasants' inequality."

Russian agrarian economists also offered an interpretation of this socio-economic pattern whose main characteristics were cogently summarized many decades later by peasantologist Teodor Shanin. Differentiating forces really did act on the peasant community, as predicted by neoclassical economics and Marxist–Leninist models; nevertheless, their influence was attenuated by a range of leveling tendencies—so-called organic changes, such as (a) the preferred division of large landholdings among several sons, (b) the merging of weak landholdings by means of a strategic marriage, and (c) the demise of the weakest landholdings and emigration to towns, which cleansed the peasant community of the socially weakest. A range of processes initiated by external forces were by nature multidirectional and unpredictable. Natural factors, market fluctuations, state intervention, coincidences, or luck played a considerable role. Russian research managed to quantify these random factors, as demonstrated by their records of farms impoverished by bad luck, alcoholism, illness, or other unlucky circumstances.[52]

In the first quarter of the 20th century, Russian agrarian statistics challenged Lenin's mechanical deduction on the development of the Russian peasantry and simultaneously explained why the agrarian reforms at the time met with failure and why the well-intended interventions by the state had unexpected consequences.[53] Nevertheless, knowledge of Russian theoretical concepts and research methods is limited to a small circle of agrarian economists outside Russia, unlike Lenin's extensively translated but antiquated texts.[54] It was not until the 1960s, when investments and economic reforms in third world countries had failed catastrophically and the development of the peasantry again followed a seemingly shocking and unpredictable course, that Russian neopop-

---

52   Shanin, *Awkward Class*; Shanin, "Socio-Economic Mobility," 220–222. For more about the explanation models, which, however, concern the Swedish peasantry, see the recent Jonas Lindström, *Distribution and differences: Stratification and the system of reproduction in a Swedish peasant community 1620–1820*, Studia Historica Upsalensia 235 (Uppsala: Uppsala Universitet, 2009), 203–218.

53   Shanin, "Socio-Economic Mobility," 212–216; David Moon, *The Russian peasantry 1600–1930. The world the peasants made* (London, New York: Longman, 1999), 316–324, 343–365; Judith Palloth, *Land reform in Russia. Peasant responses to Stolypin's project of rural transformation* (Oxford: Clarendon Press, 1999). Cf. also articles in the compendium Ben Eklof and Stephen Frank, eds., *The world of the Russian peasant: Post-emancipation culture and society* (Boston: Unwin Hyman, 1990), esp. 81–100 (R. E. Johnson), 193–218 (M. Perrie).

54   More recently, the debate was summarized by Henry Bernstein, "V. I. Lenin and A. V. Chayanov: Looking back, looking forward," *Journal of Peasant Studies* 36 (2009): 55–81.

ulationists were rediscovered, and their theories were significant for the formation of peasant studies and development economics while they were both still
in their infancy.[55] Paradoxically, a similar failure of investment into agriculture and mistakenly estimated developments occur even in today's European
Union, so here too we are experiencing a renaissance of interest in the peasant
method of production.[56]

Agrarian history has long ignored Russian neopopulationist concepts,
as they were developed for an institutionally different environment. While
in modern Russia the basic economic unit was the *peasant family household,*
which was fairly flexible in determining the degree of exploitation of the
means of production (mainly land), in Central Europe of the Early Modern
Period, these were usually *"subject" landholdings* with relatively fixed economic
resources and demands on labor that remained stable, and their continuity
was assured by appropriate inheritance rights. In other words, in Russia and in
a range of other developing countries, it was the demographic characteristics
of families, their immediate labor capacity, and consumption demands that
determined the nature of the household and the amount of cultivated land,
while in feudal Central or Northern Europe it was the quantity of the means of
production (i.e., the amount of permanently allocated land) that regulated the
demographic behavior of the family household and the degree of integration
of extra labor forces—servants and inmate-lodgers[57] (*fig. 3.2*). For this reason,
German terminology distinguishes between *Familienwirtschaft* and *Hofwirtschaft.*[58] Such differing behavior of peasants is most frequently explained

---

55   E.g., Tomáš Klír, *Osídlení zemědělsky marginálních půd v mladším středověku a raném novověku* [Besiedlung und landwirtschaftliche Nutzung marginaler Böden im späten Mittelalter
      und der frühen Neuzeit − The settlements and agriculture of the margins in the later
      Middle Age and Early Modern Period], Dissertationes archaeologicae Brunenses/Pragensesque 5 (Prague: Univerzita Karlova v Praze, 2008), 186−195.

56   Jan van der Ploeg, *Peasants and the art of farming: A Chayanovian manifesto,* Agrarian
      Change and Peasant Studies Series (Winnipeg: Fernwood, 2013).

57   Czech: podsedek/podruh, German: Hausleute/Hausgenoßen.

58   This principal difference is emphasized, for instance, in Josef Ehmer and Michael Mitterauer, "Zur Einführung: Familienstruktur und Arbeitsorganisation in ländlichen Gesellschaften," in *Familienstruktur und Arbeitsorganisation in ländlichen Gesellschaften,* ed. Josef
      Ehmer and Michael Mitterauer (Vienna: Böhlau, 1986), 7−30; Gert Spittler, "Tschajanow
      und die Theorie der Familienwirtschaft," in *Die Lehre von der bäuerlichen Wirtschaft. Versuch
      einer Theorie der Familienwirtschaft im Landbau,* ed. Aleksander Tschajanow (Frankfurt,
      New York: Campus-Verlag, 1987), vii−xxxvii. Cf. also Otto Brunner, "Das ‚ganze Haus‘ und

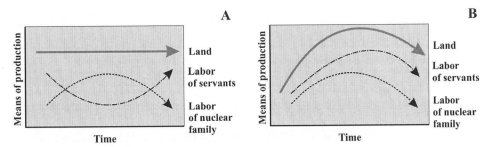

Figure 3.2. **Use of labor force and means of production (land) in diverse institutional systems. A: Land as the main means of production of peasant households is controlled by the landlord and so the household maintains constant labor capacity by the integration of servants, inmate-lodgers, or wage labor (limited land market). B: The peasant family household has land freely available to it and the extent of the use of such land corresponds to the demographic cycle (limited labor market).**

Source: Lindström, *Distribution*, fig. 4.2 (based on Dribe, *Leaving Home*).

by the fact that land resources were usually controlled by the landlord and therefore peasant households could not adapt freely to their immediate demographic situation. The land market, therefore, was limited, and fluctuations in family numbers were balanced by the labor market.[59] This theory has been confirmed by Swedish research, which proved that there was greater stability in the size of land resources held by tenants on "nobility land" and, conversely, indications of cyclic redistribution in the case of "freeholders."[60] However, the situation could also have been the opposite, and the redistribution of land as occurred in Tsarist Russia could be interpreted as a reaction to the limited labor market.[61]

Given the prevalence of subject landholdings with a relatively constant size of held land resources, the neopopulationist theories unsurprisingly began to be applied intensively in early modern agrarian history not as a result of research

die alteuropäische ‚Ökonomik,'" in *Neue Wege der Verfassungs- und Sozialgeschichte*, Otto Bruner (Göttingen: Vandenhoeck & Rupprecht, 1980), 103–127, on 105–113.

59 Lindström, *Distribution*, 100.
60 Martin Dribe, *Leaving home in a peasant society: Economic fluctuations, household dynamics and youth migration in Southern Sweden, 1829–1866*, Lund Studies in Economic History 13 (Lund: Lund University, 2000), 59–79.
61 Lindström, *Distribution*, 100.

into full-fledged peasant strata, bound by feudal relationships, but rather as a result of research into proto-industrialization and "sub-peasant" groups that combined livelihoods both in agrarian and non-agrarian production.[62]

3.2 Cultural-anthropological research

Similar phenomena as seen in Tsarist and Soviet Russia (i.e., demographic differentiation and the cyclic redistribution of economic resources) were regularly recorded during research into other peasant communities existing in a period of transition towards capitalism or socialism, especially in developing countries such as China, India, and Iran, and all European countries where traditional forms of peasantry survive.[63] The most important aspect of cultural anthropology for our purposes is that it regularly discovers and discusses phenomena that usually are not recorded in written sources of an official nature.[64] At the same time, it was demonstrated that the polarization tendencies and class differentiation in peasant communities were commonly weakened not just by

---

62   For a classic viewpoint, e.g., see David Warren Sabean, *Property, production, and family in Neckarhausen, 1700–1870* (Cambridge: Cambridge University Press, 1990); Hans Medick, *Weben und Überleben in Laichingen. 1650–1900. Lokalgeschichte als Allgemeine Geschichte*, Veröffentlichungen des Max-Planck-Instituts für Geschichte 126 (Göttingen: Vandenhoeck & Ruprecht, 1997); Sheilagh Ogilvie, *State Corporatism and Proto-Industry: The Württemberg Black Forest, 1580–1797* (Cambridge: Cambridge University Press, 1997).

63   A summary of the issue from a peasantological point of view is Robert McC. Netting, *Smallholders, householders: Farm families and the ecology of intensive, sustainable agriculture* (Stanford: Stanford University Press, 1993), 189–231. From the viewpoint of agrarian history of the Early Modern Period see Lindström, *Distribution*, 15–21, 101–102. Further, for example: James C. Scott, *The moral economy of the peasant: Rebellion and subsistence in southeast Asia* (New Haven: Yale University Press, 1976), 78–80. The following are analytically inspiring: Donald W. Attwood, "Why some of the poor get richer: Economic change and mobility in rural western India [and Comments]," *Current Anthropology* 20 (1979): 495–516 (for India); Shanin, "Socio-Economic Mobility," 225–227; Shanin, "Measuring Peasant" (for Russia and India). Additionally, see, e.g., Bogusław Gałęski, *Basic concepts of rural sociology* (Manchester: Manchester University Press, 1972), esp. 100–133 (for Poland); Göran Hoppe and John Langton, *Peasantry to capitalism: Western Östergötland in the nineteenth century*, Cambridge Studies in Historical Geography 22 (Cambridge: Cambridge University Press, 1994) (for Sweden).

64   Wolf, *Peasants*, 78–80.

demographic cycles and the division of large landholdings among several heirs, but also by other leveling mechanisms that reduced the wealth of the rich and ensured a subsistence minimum for the poor. The accumulation of property could result in various social and often even institutionalized sanctions.[65] The basis of such sanctions were systemic cultural patterns, for example, the "image of limited good" or the notion that rich families should support the poor. Furthermore, manipulative tales were told in peasant communities that justified the existing inequalities—e.g., tales maintaining that the wealth of certain families was earned somewhere externally, and not at the expense of other members of the community.[66]

Modern anthropological research has also been extremely valuable for cultivating methods and interpreting masses of data, the danger of which is that they can erase differences between families and differing lifestyles. The prevalent quantitative tendencies may ignore less frequent cases that do not follow the general trend, which is crucial for interpretation purposes. In this respect, striking results came from diachronic analyses of peasant communities conducted between the 1950s and 1980s in various parts of the Alps: an analysis of St. Felix and Tret by John W. Cole and Eric R. Wolf, of Törbel by Robert McC. Netting, of Alagna by Pier Paolo Viazzo, and the empirically most extensive analysis of Obernberg in Tirol by Leopold Pospíšil.[67]

For example, research on tax data for Törbel in the Alps for the period 1851–1915 proved that (1) social mobility generally followed a multidirectional trajectory, (2) the wealth of parents did not determine the wealth of their children, (3) there was no connection between wealth and demographic behavior, (4) more children of richer families survived until adulthood, which could

---

65   Randall McGuire and Robert McC. Netting, "Leveling peasants? The maintenance of equality in a Swiss Alpine community," *American Ethnologist* 9 (1982): 269–290, on 270–271, 283–286.

66   E.g., Wolf, *Peasants*, 4–10; Lindström, *Distribution*, 173–202.

67   John W. Cole and Eric R. Wolf, *The hidden frontier: Ecology and ethnicity in an Alpine valley* (New York: Academic Press, 1974); Robert McC. Netting, *Balancing on an Alp: Ecological change and continuity in a Swiss mountain community* (Cambridge: Cambridge University Press, 1981); McGuire and McC. Netting, "Leveling peasants?"; Pier Paolo Viazzo, *Upland communities: Environment, population, and social structure in the Alps since the sixteenth century*, Cambridge Studies in Population, Economy, and Society in Past Time 8 (Cambridge: Cambridge University Press, 1989); Leopold Pospisil, *Obernberg: A quantitative analysis of a Tirolean peasant economy*, Memoirs of The Connecticut Academy of Arts and Sciences 24 (New Haven: Connecticut Academy of Arts and Sciences, 1995).

then result in the increased fragmentation of property. On the other hand, it was the richest families who diverged from the general trend, and thanks to a combination of conscious decisions—such as deliberate marriage strategies, a life of celibacy for certain family members, and the integration of hereditary transfers—they managed to retain supreme social status and enormous property for several consecutive generations. At the other end of the social spectrum, some of the poorest families also diverged from the general trend. Fewer members of such families got married; they had fewer children and more often left their village.[68] An important discovery was that members of the peasant community had a realistic awareness of the social inequalities, and as late as the 1960s, old consultants were able to rank the families they remembered from their youth more or less correspondingly to relevant tax documents dating to the first third of the 20th century. Members of the small face-to-face peasant community in Törbel knew each other intimately and were able to very accurately estimate their own wealth and that of others.[69] The findings from Törbel may be applied to historical situations in which agricultural production maintained its subsistence nature, investment in land or cattle turned out to not be very worthwhile, and the accumulation of the means of production from a certain point in quantity of economic resources meant an increase of work burden for family members rather than an increase in the standard of living.[70]

Another inspiring benefit of the anthropological research was the finding that, in reality, identical practices may lie behind differing cultural and legal norms. In this respect, we refer to the neighboring South Tyrolian villages of St. Felix and Tret. In the German-speaking St. Felix impartible inheritance (primogeniture) applied, while in the Italian-speaking Tret landholdings were divided up equally. Despite this fundamental difference in inheritance rights, both communities demonstrated similar demographic and property-related behavior, whereby landholdings did not tend to be divided up.[71] These findings from the Alps cannot be generalized, since the marginal ecological conditions dramatically limited the options of peasant communities in mountainous

---

68   McGuire and McC. Netting, "Leveling peasants?," 277–283.
69   McGuire, and McC. Netting, "Leveling peasants?," 284–285.
70   McGuire and McC. Netting, "Leveling peasants?," 282–283.
71   Cole and Wolf, *Hidden Frontier*, 175–205. Cf. Hermann Zeitlhofer, *Besitzwechsel und sozialer Wandel: Lebensläufe und sozioökonomische Entwicklungen im südlichen Böhmerwald, 1640–1840*, Sozial- und wirtschaftshistorische Studien 36 (Vienna, Cologne: Böhlau, 2014), 17.

areas to adapt and also constrained free choice. The declared division of land-holdings between offspring was therefore practically impossible to enact, due to limited economic resources.[72]

3.3 A model of uneven reproduction

Historical evidence

New ideas on the nature of socioeconomic stratification and mobility among the peasantry in the medieval period have arisen in English historical demography, thanks to analyses of a unique collection of sources: the *Manorial Court Rolls*. Tel Aviv medievalist Zvi Razi, for example, conducted a pioneering study of the manor and parish of Halesowen near Birmingham, reacting to, among other things, contemporary discussion between Marxist and demographic interpretations of the uneven distribution of the means of production.[73] According to Marxist historians such as J. A. Kosminsky, economic inequalities led to reinforcing the position of the rich at the expense of the poor and to differences in living standards. Conversely, M. M. Postan attempted implicitly to confirm Chayanov's notion that economic inequalities were caused by family life cycles and that the quantity of the means of production in reality copied the size of family labor capacity. In his view, the balancing mechanism was the land market—wealthy families with few members sold their land to the smallholders with a surplus labor force.[74]

Although Zvi Razi in principle confirmed Marxist theory, he described the distribution mechanisms differently and explained why the stratification of peasant communities remained unchanged in the long-term. In populous Halesowen during the pre-plague period (1270–1348), the lack of land and

---

72   Cf. Viazzo, *Upland Communities*, 2–3, 263–264, 269.

73   Zvi Razi, *Life, marriage and death in a medieval parish: Economy, society and demography in Halesowen 1270–1400*, Past and Present Publications (Cambridge: Cambridge University Press, 1980), esp. 86–97.

74   Razi, *Life*, 86–89. Cf. Eugenij Aleksevic Kosminskij, *Studies in the agrarian history of England in the thirteenth century* (Oxford: Basil Blackwell, 1956), 197–255; Michael M. Postan, "The charters of the villeins," in *Essays on medieval agriculture and general problems of the medieval economy*, ed. Michael M. Postan (Cambridge: Cambridge University Press, 1973), 107–149.

the low wages gave an advantage to the propertied groups in the peasant community at the expense of others. The propertied profited from their wealth and from the low wages paid to their laborers; they also operatively exploited high market prices and failed harvests by lending poorer peasants grain and cash, subsequently buying up their land. The data also demonstrated a strong connection between the property situation of a family and the number of descendants who survived until adulthood. The poor had markedly fewer such descendants than the rich, since they got married later, and higher mortality could also have had an influence due to chronic undernutrition and an overall lower quality of life. Land reserves were exhausted, and for those born into a landless or smallholder's family, there was no easy way of acquiring any. The only solution was to have a small family. Conversely, the sons of the rich entered into marriage at a fairly early age, had large families, and received large inheritances; further, their wives brought large dowries and their parents supported them and bought extra land if necessary. In Halesowen, where inheritance practice was that of primogeniture, these economic differences led to diverse demographic characteristics within the peasant community, but not vice versa. The rich also expanded their property—though they were unable to divide the acquired landholding—by acquiring for their sons the land of the poor and the economically weak who had left their landholding and often the parish itself.[75] This rigid and harsh social system, with its predominantly reverse socioeconomic mobility, came to an end only as a result of the plague mortality crisis.

Razi's interpretation, labeled neo-Malthusian, significantly influenced notions about the social mobility of the peasantry, even though it has been subjected to criticism from many sides since the end of the 1980s. The main objection was that on the one hand, it ignored the possibility of upward social mobility due to engagement with non-agrarian production and commercial activities available to second-born peasant sons, and on the other hand, it ignored the possibility of shifts in social stratification and the scale of social values. In other words, the focus of Razi's interest neglected an analysis of the social mobility channels of the time and an evaluation of scarce goods.[76]

---

75   Razi, *Life*, 86–97.
76   Carocci, "Social Mobility," 378–379, 381. See also Schofield, *Peasant*, 84–89, 97–98, 120–121, 145–146; Christopher Dyer, "Social mobility in medieval England," in *Social mobility*

Reproduction models

Razi's findings were formalized by Jonas Lindström in his *model of uneven reproduction* in a study of a peasant community in the Swedish parish of Björ-skog from the 16th to 19th centuries. Based on socioeconomic and demographic data, he tested a differentiation, leveling, cycle, and stability model (the stability model states that the economic resources of peasant households remained fixed and were handed down from generation to generation; *fig. 3.1.* C).[77] He first ruled out both the differentiation and the leveling models, since both analyses showed that, although the peasant community was markedly stratified, in most cases the inequalities did not deepen fundamentally and remained more or less structurally stable over time. In this respect, Björskog fully corresponded to the characteristics of most peasant communities in the feudal period.[78] There is also discussion concerning what is known as "stratification without differentiation," which might correspond to the cycle or stability model. Ultimately, these two models were rejected and replaced by the *model of uneven reproduction.*[79]

The classic materialist theory, which posits that stratification and its development trajectory reflect the constant reproduction of economic resources and that inequality is the result of the uneven distribution of surplus, stands at the core of the model of uneven reproduction.[80] Integral to the ideal reproduction of a peasant household are the annually renewed means of production and labor force, which results in the consumption of a household (subsistence) and

in medieval Italy (1100–1500), ed. Sandro Carocci and Isabella Lazzarini, Viella Historical Research 8 (Rome, 2018), 23–43, on 31–34.

77   Lindström, *Distribution*, 11–21, 73, 94–135, 203–207; here is a reference to a further similar study.

78   The exceptions were of course communities exposed to dramatic changes in exterior conditions, from a strong influence of commercialization in the hinterland of the towns or mining regions to closer integration into a landlord's demesne farming. The peculiar status of the Swedish peasantry should be noted at this point, since in the Early Modern Period its nucleus comprised free peasants.

79   Lindström, *Distribution*, 203–205.

80   Lucidly explained in Ellis, *Peasant Economics*, 45–60; Lindström, *Distribution*, 95–96; Jacques Chevalier, "There is nothing simple about simple commodity production," *Studies in Political Economy* 7 (1982): 89–124; Jacques Chevalier, "There is nothing simple about simple commodity production," *Journal of Peasant Studies* 10 (1983): 153–186.

at the same time the produced surplus exploited by rent (*fig. 3.3*).[81] *Simple repro-duction* means that the resources invested in renewal are always the same, the subsistence level does not change, and the level of overall production remains constant. In *extended reproduction*, part of the surplus is returned into produc-tion, leading to an increase in both the subsistence level and overall production. In *imperfect reproduction*, less and less is returned into subsistence every year and the overall level of production therefore falls. Several main situations may arise that correspond to models that explain processes in the social stratifica-tion of peasant communities:

1) The *differentiation (polarization) model* states that rich households had extended reproduction, while the poor had imperfect reproduction. Rich households expanded at the expense of poor households, which acquired economic resources in exchange for part of their surplus. Therefore, the stratification of peasant communities deepened over time: the tenants of rich landholdings accumulated more and more resources, while the tenants of poor landholdings became landless (*fig. 3.1. A*).

2) The *leveling model* is the opposite of the differentiation model (*fig. 3.1. B*).

3) The *cycle model* assumes the simple reproduction of all households, i.e., a subsistence economy and almost total exploitation of surplus; peasant households did not retain any significant disposable surplus. Subsistence needs, labor capacity, and the amount of the means of production changed depending on the demographic cycle of the households. A characteristic feature of the cycle model is the assumption that the trajectory of socio-economic mobility was the same in all households, but in shifted phases (*fig. 3.1. D*).

4) The *stability model* assumes stable subsistence needs, surplus, and level of overall production of all households; peasant households did not retain a disposable surplus (*fig. 3.1. C*).

5) The *model of uneven reproduction* assumes extended reproduction and a dis-posable surplus for rich peasant households on the one hand, and imperfect reproduction for poor peasant households on the other hand. Rich peasants were expected to expand at the expense of the poor. In these respects, this coincides with the differentiation model. Nevertheless, the excess surplus

---

81   Rent = surplus claimed by a landlord, the Church, and the state (land rent + ecclesiastical tithes + land tax).

that rich peasant households retained after paying rent was accumulated in the form of capital, not to increase production and maximize profit but rather to improve the life and well-being of themselves and their descendants.[82] In this respect, this model coincides with the cycle model. In practice this meant that the core of a rich peasant's property was passed down to the primary heir, but, with the help of their parents and siblings, the other descendants were able to buy up poorer landholdings left by the original and indebted tenants. In extreme cases, a rich landholding and its resources might be subdivided. The model of uneven reproduction requires a difference in the conditions of reproduction not only between rich and poor peasants, but also between the descendants of the rich. There was a high probability in rich peasant households that their offspring would remain on their original parents' landholding or acquire a different one nearby, albeit smaller and poorer. Some of the descendants of rich peasant households maintained their social position (the primary heir), while others found their status falling in comparison with their parents. A poor peasant could therefore have a rich ancestor but could scarcely have rich offspring. The degree of stratification of "settled" (i.e., landholding) peasants did not change, and the stratification of landholdings remained the same ("stratification without differentiation"). Rich landholdings were more often passed down to one of the offspring; his siblings expanded to poorer landholdings and further social decline awaited their offspring.[83] A characteristic feature of the model of uneven reproduction is the combination of research in social and geographical mobility (fig. 3.1. F).

6) In the case of the *multidirectional model*, a situation may also occur in which the analyzed sample is too heterogenic, and individual peasant landholdings or communities are exposed to external forces and operate under various conditions, so their stratification changes along different trajectories (fig. 3.1. E).[84]

---

82   See Shami Ghosh, "Rural Economies and Transitions to Capitalism: Germany and England Compared (c. 1200–c. 1800)," *Journal of Agrarian Change* 16 (2016): 255–290, on 260, 268; Dyer, "Social mobility," 32.

83   Lindström, *Distribution*, 203–205.

84   Cf. Jan van der Ploeg, "The genesis and further unfolding of farming styles research," *Historische Anthropologie* 20 (2013): 427–439.

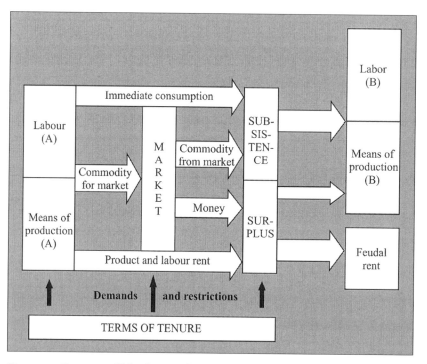

Figure 3.3. System of ideal reproduction of peasant households in a milieu of feudal relations.

Source: Lindström, *Distribution*, fig. 4.1.

Note:

Simple reproduction: (labor force A + means of production A) = (labor force B + means of production B)

Extended reproduction: (labor force A + means of production A) < (labor force B + means of production B)

Imperfect reproduction: (labor force A + means of production A) > (labor force B + means of production B)

3.4 Operationalization of research

Distribution factors

In socioeconomic mobility and reproduction models, the size of a disposable surplus and the method of its exploitation are of key significance. Hence, the following questions arise: (1) How large an amount of the means of production did the family have at its disposal? (2) How great were their production level and subsistence needs? And (3) what proportion of the surplus was extracted by rent? This cannot be separated from the issue of the (4) legal framework, i.e., local agrarian institutions and relations between "subject" tenants and landlords, and (5) market mechanisms. The relationships between these factors are described by a range of economic models for peasant households operating under feudal conditions.[85] Jonas Lindström named them directly as *explanatory elements* that should be examined in all research into social stratification and mobility (*tab. 3.1*). In this study, we will speak about *direct distributional factors*. Of course, the distribution of resources and the exploitation of the surplus were influenced by *indirect distributional factors*, which acted in a mediated way, including, for instance, ecological factors influencing the level of production, further demographic factors, and gender issues that affected the labor force and the institutional framework.[86]

Principles

Jonas Lindström also identified the main forces or principles that determined the direction and result of reproduction processes in peasant households. These principles are (1) the equilibrium between labor capacity and means of production; (2) the imperfect exploitation of the surplus; and (3) property fission.[87] We may also add (4) the principle of the accumulation of the surplus and means of production, whose objectives can be many and various (*tab. 3.2*). All of these principles were integral to the Marxist and neopopulationist interpretation, the difference being the degree of significance awarded to them (*tab. 3.3*). In reality, all four forces were omnipresent; the degree of their application depended on the concrete historical situation; therefore, some strengthened each other, while some acted against each other (*fig. 3.4*).

For instance, the principle of the accumulation of the means of production could be best applied where the labor market functioned. If agricultural production was supported only by family labor, then the accumulation of land

---

85   See esp. Walter Achilles, *Landwirtschaft in der frühen Neuzeit*, Enzyklopädie deutscher Geschichte 10 (Munich: Oldenbourg, 1991), 76–85; Walter Achilles, "Überlegungen zum Einkommen der Bauern im späten Mittelalter," *Zeitschrift für Agrargeschichte und Agrarsoziologie* 31 (1983): 5–26. For the High Middle Ages, see Harry Kitsikopoulos, "Standards of living and capital formation in pre-plague England: A peasant budget model," *The Economic History Review* 53 (2000): 237–261. For grain production in the environment of the early modern subdivision of landholdings, see Warde, "Subsistence."

86   Lindström, *Distribution*, 23–25, 33–67, 207–211.

87   Lindström, *Distribution*, 96–135, 207–211.

resources above a certain level no longer brought benefit but instead represented an unnecessary burden. In this case, the opposing principle of the
equilibrium of labor and means of production prevailed over the principle of

Table 3.1. **Direct distribution factors in the peasant household reproduction model.**

	Distribution factor	Characteristics
a	Means of production	- circulating and fixed (land, livestock, seed, and tools); - the degree of stratification is usually measured according to the amount of the means of production; - the means of production form an interconnected system, with the quantity of one usually proportionate to the quantity of another.
b	Labor force	- the basis is the labor capacity of a peasant family; - essential is the nature of the labor market and the degree of perfection, i.e., the extent to which labor has the nature of free commodity.
c	Subsistence	- the degree of subsistence and the size of the surplus are interconnected; - subsistence needs are determined by the extent of the means of production and by the size of the labor force; - the size of the surplus is determined by the level of production on the one hand and by subsistence needs on the other;
d	Surplus	- the level of production reflects the amount of the means of production and the size of the labor force; - the management of the surplus is essential; it may be accumulated and invested, consumed, used to support offspring, or redistributed within the community.
e	Market mechanisms (reallocation by the market)	- the means of production, labor force, means of subsistence, and surplus are distributed by the market; - the degree of distribution depends on the size and nature of the market; - the market may deepen inequalities among peasants, since it favors the rich over the poor; - the market may also level the differences if the poor are allowed access to credit.
f	Terms of tenure – institutional framework	- particularly the security of land tenure and inheritance rights and customs; - the institutional framework influenced the land and labor market and also the degree of exploitation of surplus.

Source: Lindström, *Distribution*, 23–25, 33–67, 207–211.
Note: Supplemented and modified.

accumulation, as Russian neopopulationists showed. Even under these conditions, the principle of property fission encouraged the endeavor to accumulate
the means of production even over and above the optimal point of equilib-

Table 3.2. **Principles in the peasant household reproduction model.**

	Principle	Characteristics
1.	Accumulation of means of production	- emphasized by the Marxist model; - a large amount of the means of production could: (a) mean higher, more secure, and more effective (re)production; (b) allow for the optimum organization of a landholding; (c) transfer the labor burden onto several persons and give the head of the household time for other activities, including commerce; (d) provide material supports for offspring (did not lead to polarization); (e) create reserves and transform surplus into capital (led to polarization).
2.	Equilibrium of labor and the means of production	- lies at the heart of the demographic model; - labor capacity, subsistence, and amount of the means of production should be in equilibrium; - a large amount of the means of production does not necessarily equate to an advantage, as it could also be a burden; - the amount of the means of production correlates with the size, subsistence needs, and labor capacity of the peasant family, and so the amount of the means of production falls; - the peasant family chooses a compromise between maximum yields and the labor effort required to achieve them.
3.	Imperfect exploitation of surplus	- emphasized by the Marxist model; - every peasant landholding is burdened by rent paid to the landlord (land/feudal rent), territorial power (land tax), and to the Church (tithe); - fixed rent tended to deepen differences; - progressive rent tended to even out differences; - the level of disposable surplus determines the degree of the development of stratification.
4.	Property fission	- lies at the center of the demographic model; - surplus and property were accumulated during a single generation to provide for all offspring; - the production unit was not permanently reinforced, and the accumulated surplus was used to create new or reinforce weak units; - property position depended on the demographic characteristics of the family, primarily the number of adult offspring.

Source: Lindström, *Distribution*, 96–135, 207–211. *Note:* Supplemented and modified.

rium, since properties were accumulated with the aim of future division. The property expansion of peasant households sought not only to increase living standards but also to ensure security for their offspring. Another force that acted against the accumulation of wealth was surplus exploitation (rent). We can therefore model and test a large quantity of diverse situations on historical material.

We see Lindström's model of uneven reproduction as an integral analytic tool that connects the theoretical and empirical aspects of our knowledge. In addition, it facilitates a Europe-wide comparison and the effective transfer of the acquired knowledge. We believe that the nature of the stratification and socioeconomic mobility of the peasantry was influenced throughout the feudal period by identical principles and depended on the concrete situation, i.e., the character of other factors (elements) that outweighed the principles. For this reason, the reproduction models that we use to simplify and analyze a single

Table 3.3. Explanation of "stratification without differentiation".

	Model	Characteristics
1.	Marxist polarization model	- households differed from each other in the size of their respective surpluses, all of which, however, were exploited to pay rent; - accumulation of property meant accumulation of dues and obligations to a landlord; - the disruption of feudal relations and the onset of capitalism was a turning point that meant fast polarization and the disintegration of the peasantry as a uniform social class.
2.	Neopopulationist cycle model	- large amounts of the means of production meant a larger labor force and a larger family; - any surplus was minimal, since higher production was consumed at a higher rate by members of the family and the permanently integrated labor force; - although peasant landholdings had different amounts of means of production, the quantity per head remained the same.
3.	Model of uneven reproduction	- although a surplus was accumulated, it was used to acquire property for offspring.
4.	Stability model	- although landholdings were unequal, they reproduced at the same rate and did not create a surplus.

Source: Lindström, *Distribution*, 96–135.

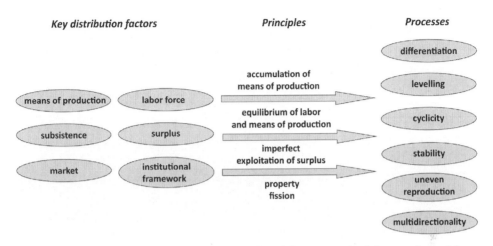

Figure 3.4. **Relationships between distributional factors, principles, and resulting processes in the peasant household reproduction model.**

Source: **Prepared by the author.**

fact cannot be carried across from one historical context to another; they could be theoretically applicable in all contexts. In other words, models are general, while past experience is always unique.

3.5 Summary

The concept of the social mobility of the peasantry is closely connected with the phenomena of social stratification and the uneven distribution of scarce goods. Since the late 19th century, against a backdrop of social reform experiments, some generally applicable principles and forces that applied to the reproduction of peasant households and maintained or changed stratification within peasant communities began to be discovered. These were opposing differentiating (polarizing) forces on the one hand and leveling forces on the other. Which of the two forces would dominate depended on the specific historical conditions. Differentiating forces arose due to the impact of the market exchange and fixed rents. Leveling forces came about due to the need for equilibrium between the size of the labor force and the amount of the means of production, progressive land tax, demographic factors leading to the fission of property, and non-economic institutions redistributing the surplus within peasant communities. The accumulation of production resources in itself did not deepen social stratification automatically, since the results depended on whether their purpose was to react to the life cycle, i.e., to prepare family property for fission and provide support for their offspring, or to increase the surplus and transform it into capital.

For the preindustrial period, with its imperfect market, the more or less stable social stratification of the peasantry (known as "stratification without differentiation") is documented throughout Europe, which concealed a high rate of internal social mobility that could take various forms. The social mobility of the Russian peasantry after the abolition of serfdom was described well by the *cycle model*, which assumes that the means of production were constantly transferred between households in connection with their family life cycle. The social mobility of the peasantry in the feudal conditions of Europe during the High Middle Ages and Early Modern Period was described by the *model of uneven reproduction*. According to this model, rich peasants held temporary control over the accumulation of the means of production and surplus. They did not strive to maximize profits but rather to ensure the well-being, prestige, and property of their offspring. Social mobility in this case was more complex in nature—the offspring of the rich either maintained the same position as their parents (primary heir) or suffered a decline in their position (the others); the offspring of the poor usually suffered decline, because they tended to be pushed out by the offspring of the rich. Behind the façade of stable social stratification, a person's lot in life was determined by relentless polarizing forces. This particular form of the model of uneven reproduction need not be generally applicable, since it applies to peasant communities operating under conditions of demographic pressure and a lack of available land.

4.
State of the research

4.1 Late Middle Ages

Central and East-Central Europe

Contemporary overviews of research on the social structures, institutions, and processes that the late medieval peasantry experienced have been published several times.[88] This research is often motivated by the image of the Late Middle Ages as a turbulent period of "creative destruction" and the search for the prerequisites for the economic growth of some European regions in the Early Modern Period.[89] Many researchers have pointed to the need to cross traditional boundaries between periods and to analyze the development of the

---

[88] Carocci, "Social Mobility"; Alfonso, *Rural history*; Harry Kitsikopoulos, ed., *Agrarian change and crisis in Europe, 1200–1500*, Routledge Research in Medieval Studies 1 (New York: Routledge, 2011); Harry Kitsikopoulos, "Social and economic theory in medieval studies," in *Handbook of medieval studies: Terms, methods, trends*, ed. Albrecht Classen (Berlin, New York: De Gruyter 2010), 1270–1292. Cf. also for England Miriam Müller, "A divided class? Peasants and peasant communities in Later Medieval England," in *Rodney Hilton's Middle Ages: An exploration of historical themes*, ed. Christopher Dyer, Past and Present Supplements 195, 2007, Suppl. 2 (Oxford: Oxford Journals, 2007), 115–131; Schofield, *Peasant*. For Western Europe and the Pyrenees, cf. Frederic Romero Aparisi and Vicent Royo Pérez, eds., *Beyond lords and peasants: Rural elites and economic differentiation in pre-modern Europe* (Valencia: Publicacions de la Universitat de València, 2014). For research on social inequality and mobility across social groups in European historiography, cf. articles in *Continuity and Change* 24/3, 2009.

[89] Sreenivasan, *Peasants*, 4.

Late Middle Ages and the Early Modern Period together.[90] On a methodological level, research centers attempting to research the economically progressive regions on the shores of the North Sea have proven to be the most innovative.[91] Central European research is also moving in a new direction thanks to the absorption of anthropological and demographic approaches and the new institutional economics.[92] For a comprehensive summary of the state of knowledge

90	E.g., Markus Cerman, *Villagers and lords in Eastern Europe, 1300–1800*, Studies in European History (Basingstoke, 2012); Whittle, *Development*. For theoretical approaches see: Michael Kopsidis, *Agrarentwicklung: Historische Agrarrevolutionen und Entwicklungsökonomie*, Grundzüge der modernen Wirtschaftsgeschichte 6 (Stuttgart: Steiner, 2006).
91	Cf. the Comparative Rural History of the North Sea Area publication series. E.g., Bas J. P. van Bavel and Peter C. M. Hoppenbrouwers, eds., *Landholding and land transfer in the North Sea area (late Middle Ages – 19th century)*, CORN Publication Series 5 (Turnhout: Brepols, 2004); Hoppenbrouwers and van Zanden, *Peasants into farmers?*; Eric Vanhaute, Isabelle Devos, and Lambrecht Thijs, eds., *Making a living: Family, income and labour*, Rural Economy and Society in North-Western Europe, 500–2000 (Turnhout: Brepols, 2011); Bas J. P. van Bavel, ed., *Social relations: Property and power*, Rural Economy and Society in North-Western Europe, 500–2000, 1 (Turnhout: Brepols, 2010); Guido Alfani, and Erik Thoen, eds., *Inequality in rural Europe (Late Middle Ages-18th century)* (CORN Publication Series 18. Brepols: Turnhout, 2020); Thijs Lambrecht, and Wouter Ryckbosch, "Economic inequality in the rural Southern Low Countries during the fifteenth century: sources, data and reflections." In *Disuguaglianza economica nelle società preindustriali: cause ed effetti / Economic inequality in pre-industrial societies: causes and effect*, ed. Giampiero Nigro, Datini Studies in Economic History (Firenze: Firenze University Press, 2020), 205–229; Bas van Bavel, "Looking for the islands of equality in a sea of inequality: Why did some societies in pre-industrial Europe have relatively low levels of wealth inequality?" In *Disuguaglianza economica nelle società preindustriali: cause ed effetti / Economic inequality in pre-industrial societies: causes and effect*, ed. Giampiero Nigro, Datini Studies in Economic History (Firenze: Firenze University Press, 2020), 431–456.
92	Julien Demade, "The Medieval countryside in German-language historiography since the 1930s," in *The rural history of medieval European societies: trends and perspectives*, ed. Antón María Isabel Alfonso, The Medieval Countryside 1 (Turnhout: Brepols, 2007), 173–252; Piotr Górecki, "Medieval peasants and their world in Polish historiography," in *The rural history of medieval European societies: Trends and perspectives*, ed. Antón María Isabel Alfonso, The Medieval Countryside 1 (Turnhout: Brepols, 2007), 253–296; Grzegorz Myśliwski, "Central Europe," in *Agrarian change and crisis in Europe, 1200–1500*, ed. Harry Kitsikopoulos, Routledge Research in Medieval Studies 1 (New York: Routledge, 2011), 250–291; Markus Cerman, "Social structure and land markets in Late Mediaeval Central and East-central Europe," *Continuity and Change* 23 (2008): 55–100, on 55–76. From an anthropological perspective see: Mary K. Shenk et al., "Intergenerational wealth transmission among agriculturalists: Foundations of agrarian inequality," *Current Anthropology* 51 (2010): 65–83; Monique Borgerhoff Mulder et al., "Intergenerational wealth transmission and the dynamics of inequality in small-scale societies," *Science* 326.5953 (2009): 682–688;

in the Czech and Austrian lands, we can rely on the ongoing studies by Markus Cerman and Shami Ghosh (*fig. 4.1*).[93] In relation to the bordering geographical position of the city-state of Cheb, it is necessary to emphasize Cerman's thesis that in the Late Middle Ages—unlike the early modern development—a principal difference between the western and eastern parts of Central Europe has not been demonstrated. The differences at the level of individual—often even neighboring—regions and microregions were much more significant.[94]

Recent scholarship has focused on the socioeconomic structure and institutions of the late medieval peasantry and the mechanisms of its change.[95] In East-Central Europe, certain prevailing tendencies are supposed, but a high degree of regional variability and deviation from the prevailing development trajectory are also documented (*fig. 4.2*).[96]

The 14th century saw a disintegration of the original forms of the manor, a retreat from demesne farming, and a fragmentation of demesne farms in large parts of East-Central Europe. This meant a real improvement in the status of "subject" tenants, a reinforcement of their rights to land, a stronger interaction with the market, and commercialization.[97] The relationship between the landlord and his "subject" tenants acquired a purely material nature where their "subject" status stemmed from land tenure, without personal dependency. Despite its various origins and the normative framework, the legal status of "subject" tenants throughout East-Central European regions had standardized to a great extent, with the hereditary tenure of "subject" landholdings giving tenants a secure and fairly wide range of disposal and inheritance rights. Upon

Samuel Bowles et al., "The emergence and persistence of inequality in premodern societies: Introduction to the special section," *Current Anthropology* 51 (2010): 7–17.

93 Cerman, "Social structure"; Markus Cerman, "Open fields, tenurial rights and the development of land markets in medieval East-central Europe," in *Property rights, land in market and economic growth*, ed. Gérard Béaur, Rural History in Europe 1 (Turnhout: Brepols, 2013), 405–424. See also a recent overview in Ghosh, "Rural Economies," 256–267.

94 Cerman, "Open fields," 406, 409, 414, 419–420.

95 Cf. also Rosemary L. Hopcroft, *Regions, institutions, and agrarian change in European history*, Economics, Cognition, and Society (Ann Arbor: University of Michigan Press, 1999), 15–45, 157–195.

96 Cerman, "Social structure", 55–56.

97 Concerning the peasant land market see the recent Thomas Ertl, Thomas Frank, and Samuel Nussbaum, eds., *Busy tenants: Peasant land markets in Central Europe (15th to 16th century)*, Vierteljahrschrift für Sozial- und Wirtschaftsgeschichte, Beiheft 253 (Stuttgart: Franz Steiner Verlag, 2021).

Figure 4.1. Central and East-Central Europe.

Source: From Cerman, "*Social Structure*," fig. 1; Cerman, "*Open fields*," fig. 20.1.

Note: Focus of long-term interest of Markus Cerman (marked with a thick line).

fulfiling certain conditions, a tenant could pass his "subject" landholding to his offspring, sell it, or abandon it. The influence of the landlord on everyday activities was minimal if the "subject" tenant met his dues and obligations, which were firmly set and theoretically unchanging. A lower level of jurisdictional rights that handled inheritance procedures and land transfers was mainly in the hands of the peasant elites.[98]

A crucial issue for the peasants was the potential for the flexible disposition of land—that is, the subdivision of landholdings and the separation of certain land plots that could circulate freely among peasants based on market relations. In this respect, the significance of so-called "non-landholding plots," which were under the weaker institutional control of peasant communities and

---

98   Cerman, "Social structure," 57–67; Cerman, "Open fields," 409, 415–416; Ghosh, "Rural Economies," 258–259, 263–265.

the landlord, should be emphasized. The source of disposable land was sometimes a subdivision of demesne farms, and other times common land, deserted settlements, or newly cleared arable land, depending on local conditions. In practice, such lands could be alienated from the land attached to "subject" landholdings, even though this was inadmissible under the law.[99]

Despite the one-sided testimony of manorial records, which tended to be normative and not reflective of the real situation, the legal or illegal subdivision of large landholdings and the separation of individual land plots are documented. The landlord accepted this fact, sometimes even encouraging it himself.[100]

The circulation of land was increased by any disintegration of an institutional framework, either the disruption of family or community ties or the disintegration of the originally integrated manor and subdivision of demesne farms. A significant role was played by cities, which affected the countryside in several fundamental ways: (1) they changed the economic structure of their hinterland with specific market demands; (2) the acquisition of property by burghers disrupted the rights of landlords, which were originally compact; (3) the accumulation of land resources and the creation of residential demesne farms led to new social statuses that could be adopted by peasant elites too; (4) more flexible town laws concerning property and disposal rights began to apply to various extents in the hinterland; (5) market-oriented activities, speculation, loans, and rents infiltrated the countryside; (6) diversified livelihoods allowed for the development of a labor market and the existence of a reserve of seasonal wage labor.[101]

An important indicator of a dynamic social structure and a flexible land market was the establishment and expansion of the "sub-peasant" groups— smallholders and cottagers. Their presence was fundamental, as they represented a reservoir of labor force, making the existence of extremely large landholdings possible. The "sub-peasant" groups could obtain their livelihoods through the division of larger landholdings or the acquisition of additional land resources and land outside of the traditional core of peasant farmland.[102]

---

99   Cerman, "Social structure," 69–76; Cerman, "Open fields," 410–414.
100   Cerman, "Social structure," 63–64; Cerman, "Open fields," 409–413.
101   Cerman, "Social structure," 68–69; Ghosh, "Rural Economies," 263.
102   Cerman, "Social structure," 64–65, 71–73; Cerman, "Open fields," 414–418; Ghosh, "Rural Economies," 257–261.

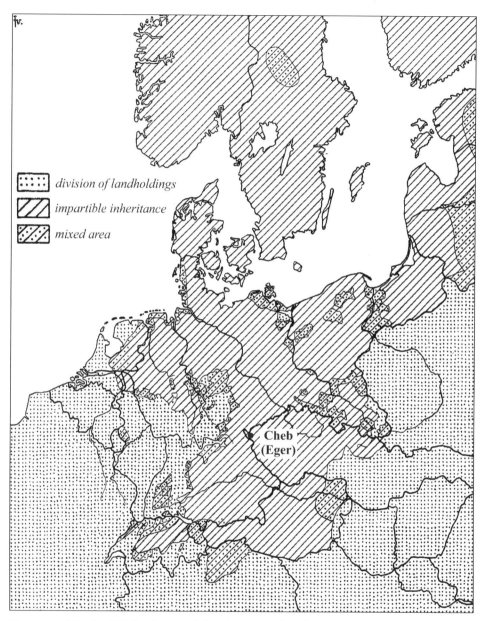

Figure 4.2. "Subject" inheritance rights in Central and Northern Europe.

Source: From Huppertz, *Räume*, Karte IV.

Bohemia

Prewar Bohemian agrarian history focused on the legal status of the peasantry and agrarian structures and edited the main written sources, which included emphyteutic deeds, estate registers, and tax registers. The quiet consensus preferred a *stability model*,[103] although radical change at that time was heralded by studies written by Václav Husa.[104] In the postwar years, extensive empirical materials collected by earlier historiography were put to use by František Graus in his monograph *History of the Peasantry in Pre-Hussite Bohemia* (*Dějiny venkovského lidu v Čechách v době předhusitské*), in which he arranged the historical data so that it would correspond to the classic Marxist–Leninist view of the so-called agrarian question, regardless of the institutional difference between feudal and capitalist periods.[105]

According to František Graus, in the late 13th and early 14th centuries, as economic development began in pre-Hussite Bohemia, advances in agrarian technologies arose, production increased, the legal status of "subject" tenants improved, and towns, market relations, and monetary forms of land rent developed.[106] In the subsequent period, due to the intensive effect of market relations, the social differentiation of the peasantry became more profound, even though written sources that would support Graus's claim do not exist, since the estate registers and tax registers inform us only of stratification at a particular time, not of its dynamics over time. As of the 1360s–1370s, the deteriorated

103 The earlier literature is summarized by Boris Timofeevich Rubtsov, *Evoljucija feodal'noj renty v Čechii (XIV – načalo XV v.)* (Moscow: s.n., 1958), 3–32; Boris Timofeevich Rubtsov, *Issledovaniia po agrarnoi istorii Chekhii, XIV-nachalo XV v.* (Moscow: Izd-vo Akademii nauk SSSR, 1963), 3–24; Graus, *Dějiny*, 7–29, 317–338; Čechura, "Rolnictvo," 469 (in German see Čechura, "Die Bauernschaft," 287–288); Jaroslav Čechura, *Die Struktur der Grundherrschaften im mittelalterlichen Böhmen unter besonderer Berücksichtigung der Klosterherrschaften*, Quellen und Forschungen zur Agrargeschichte 39 (Stuttgart: Steiner 1994), 11–15, 26. For the subsequent period see Míka, *Poddaný lid*, 338–346.

104 See esp. Václav Husa, "Třídní boje – tabu československého dějepisectví" [Les luttes de classe – un tabou de l'historiographie tchécoslovaque], *Dějiny a přítomnost* 1 (1937): 39–47.

105 Graus, *Dějiny*, esp. 307–316; cf. Čechura, *Die Struktur*, 16–17, 27–28; Čechura, "Rolnictvo," 470–474 (in German see Čechura, "Die Bauernschaft," 289–292). Cf. also Jaroslav Čechura, "František Graus jako vítěz. (Dějiny venkovského lidu v Čechách v době předhusitské II.)," in *František Graus: Člověk a historik, Sborník z pracovního semináře Výzkumného centra pro dějiny vědy konaného 10. prosince 2002* (Prague: Výzkumné centrum pro dějiny vědy, 2004), 69–88.

106 Graus, *Dějiny*, esp. 49–158.

economic situation resulted in a drop in the buying power of "subject" tenants, the impairment of their legal status, a more thorough exploitation of "subject" tenants by landlords, and ruthless land rent.[107] Internal polarization of the peasantry, intensifying class struggle, growing feudal repression, and economic crisis, along with rising tensions in society as a whole, resulted in the Hussite Revolution, thanks to which social antagonisms lessened and the status of the peasantry temporarily improved.[108] Graus's theory ignored not just the influence of demographic development and changes in the natural environment, but also to a large extent changes in institutional framework, since these supposedly only passively reflected economic development.[109] On the other hand, it should be said that in later years Graus departed from his original vision of social development in pre-Hussite Bohemia.[110] Furthermore, at about the same time, Graus's materialistic view, assuming fast polarization of the peasantry due to market relations, was also applied to the close of the Middle Ages and the beginning of the Early Modern Period by Dušan Třeštík.[111]

---

107   Graus, *Dějiny*, esp. 159–267.

108   Graus, *Dějiny*, esp. 268–316; Míka, *Poddaný lid*. On Graus's theory as a whole, cf. Čechura, "Rolnictvo," 466–471 (in German see Čechura, "Die Bauernschaft," 284–292); Čechura, *Die Struktur*, 27–31; Čechura, "František Graus."

109   Graus, *Dějiny*, esp. 233–267. Also, for instance, cf. Jiří Kejř and Vladimír Procházka, "Právně historické glosy k dějinám venkovského lidu v Čechách v době předhusitské," *Právněhistorické studie* 5 (1959): 291–321; Vladimír Procházka, *Česká poddanská nemovitost v pozemkových knihách 16. a 17. století* [Die tschechische Untertanenliegenschaft in den Grundbüchern des 16. und 17. Jhdts.], Právněhistorická knižnice 6 (Prague: Nakladatelství Československé akademie věd, 1963), 367.

110   E.g., Graus, *Dějiny*; František Graus, "Krize středověku a husitství" [Die Krise des Mittelalters und das Hussitentum], *Československý časopis historický* 17 (1969): 507–526; František Graus, "From resistance to revolt: The late medieval peasant wars in the context of social crisis," *Journal of Peasant Studies* 3 (1975): 1–9; František Graus, *Pest – Geissler – Judenmorde. Das 14. Jahrhundert als Krisenzeit*, Veröffentlichungen des Max-Planck-Instituts für Geschichte 86 (Göttingen: Vandenhoeck & Ruprecht, ²1994). On the thought development of František Graus see, e.g., Čechura, "František Graus"; Martin Nodl, "František Graus – Proměny pojetí krize pozdního středověku," in *František Graus: Člověk a historik, Sborník z pracovního semináře Výzkumného centra pro dějiny vědy konaného 10. prosince 2002* (Prague: Výzkumné centrum pro dějiny vědy, 2004), 99–118; Naďa Morávková, *František Graus a československá poválečná historiografie* (Prague: Academia, 2013).

111   Dušan Třeštík, "Příspěvky k sociální diferenciaci venkovského lidu v šestnáctém století" [Contributions au problème de la différenciation sociale des paysans au XVIe siècle], *Sborník historický* 4 (1956): 189–225. In addition, critically, Antonín Kostlán, "'Cenová revoluce' a její odraz v hospodářském vývoji Čech" ["Die Preisrevolution" und ihr Widerhall in

Boris Timofeevich Rubtsov, a young member of the Soviet agrarian history school, independently made a similar interpretation of pre-Hussite development as seen through the prism of Hussitism as a peasant revolt.[112] Areas where he diverged from Graus included (1) on a heuristic level (that is, his dependence on source editions); (2) on a methodological level (his sophisticated, then pioneering, statistical approach); and (3) his interpretational emphasis on the geographically specific socioeconomic diversity of Bohemia.[113]

In discussions about B. T. Rubtsov and F. Graus's results, Rostislav Nový in particular, and later Jaroslav Čechura, launched a new stage in Bohemian research, turning their attention away from the aggregate processing of very diverse data to the integral analysis of the economic functioning and development of specific manors (estates), each understood as a unique "micro-cosmos."[114] Thanks to this approach, the social stratification of peasant communities began to be interpreted contextually, i.e., in relation to the function that a concrete settlement had in the framework of the manor in question.[115] Several studies with this exciting perspective gradually changed the image of the developing trajectories and forms of the manor in pre-Hussite Bohemia and, at the same time, of the socioeconomic position of peasants and

der wirtschaftlichen Entwicklung Böhmens], *Folia Historica Bohemica* 11 (1987): 161–212, on 190; Petráň, *Poddaný lid*, 60–62.

112 Rubtsov, *Evoljucija*.

113 František Graus, "Vývoj feudální renty v Čechách v 14. a 15. století," *Československý časopis historický* 7 (1959): 301–303; Boris Timofeevich Rubtsov, "K otázce některých zvláštností vývoje feudální renty v Čechách ve 14. a na počátku 15. století," *Československý časopis historický* 8 (1960): 856–863.

114 On the discussion itself see: Boris Timofeevich Rubtsov, "Dopis redakci (doplnění a opravy k článku B.T. Rubcov, K otázce . . .)," *Československý časopis historický* 9 (1961): 927–928; Rostislav Nový, Review of *Issledovanija po agrarnoj istorii Čechii 14 – načalo 15 vv*, Moscow 1963, by Boris Timofeevich Rubtsov, *Československý časopis historický* 12 (1964): 541–544; Boris Timofeevich Rubtsov, "Ještě o některých sporných otázkách agrárního vývoje v předhusitských Čechách," *Československý časopis historický* 18 (1970): 601–608; Zdeněk Šimeček, "O poddanských poměrech v nejjižnější oblasti Čech v období předhusitském," *Československý časopis historický* 19 (1971): 568–574. Their discussion was also summarized in František Šmahel, *Husitská revoluce I. Doba vymknutá z kloubů* (Prague: Karolinum, 1995), 423–426.

115 For example, Rostislav Nový, "Studie o předhusitských urbářích I" [Studien über die vorhussitischen Urbarien I], *Sborník historický* 13 (1965): 5–64; Čechura, *Die Struktur*, (here see also the historical summary on 11–31).

their relationship to the landlord.[116] Čechura formulated a new research perspective on the peasantry in late medieval Bohemia based on his own empirical findings, a comparison with the latest European findings, and also theoretical-methodological concepts.[117] On a regional and institutional level, he used as a basis his own analysis of the status of "subject" tenants on the western Bohemian manors of Plasy and, to a certain extent, Chotěšov,[118] as well as F. Šmahel's investigations of the Rosenbergs' "subject" tenants in the Tábor region (esp. 1379–1423/1433).[119] The main theses are:

+ The period between the mid-14th and early 16th centuries (1350–1500) may be viewed as uniform and closed in terms of development. After the mid-14th century, the social, economic, and legal position of "subject" tenants generally stabilized and/or improved.

116   Čechura, *Die Struktur*, 109–134; Čechura, "Rolnictvo," 476–487 (part of this source can also be found partially in German, see Čechura, "Die Bauernschaft," 293–301); Jaroslav Čechura, *Adelige Grundherrn als Unternehmer: Zur Struktur südböhmischer Dominien vor 1620*, Sozial- und wirtschaftshistorische Studien 25 (Munich: Oldenbourg Verlag, 2000).

117   Čechura, "Rolnictvo," 476–487, 490–497 (in German see Čechura, "Die Bauernschaft," 293–311); Čechura, *Die Struktur*, esp. 121–125; Čechura, "Sedlák." For another overview, see Jaroslav Čechura, *Sedláci si dělají, co chtějí: sborník vybraných prací profesora Jaroslava Čechury*, ed. Veronika Boháčová and Veronika Kucrová (Prague: NLN, Nakladatelství Lidové noviny, 2012). Cf. Šmahel, *Husitská revoluce*, 425–432.

118   Jaroslav Čechura, "Dvě studie k sociálně ekonomickému vývoji klášterního velkostatku v předhusitských Čechách" [Zwei Studien zur sozialökonomischen Entwicklung des Klostergrossgrundbesitzes im vorhussitischen Böhmen], *Sborník Národního Muzea v Praze*, řada A – Historie 42 (1988): 1–72, on 46–69; Jaroslav Čechura, "Chotěšov v 15. století" [Chotěšov im 15. Jahrhundert], *Minulostí Západočeského kraje* 27 (1991): 51–78; Jaroslav Čechura, "Liber antiquus kláštera v Plasech z let 1339–1441" [Der ,Liber antiquus' des Klosters Plass aus den Jahren 1339–1441], *Časopis Národního muzea v Praze*, Řada A – Historie 153 (1984): 166–179. Cf. also Eduard Maur, "Nejstarší chotěšovské pozemkové knihy (1497–1566) – významný pramen pro poznání populačního vývoje Čech v 16. století" [The oldest Chotěšov land registry books (1497–1566) – an important source for the research of the population development of Bohemia in the 16th century], *Historická demografie* 41 (2017): 131–149; Dana Koutná-Karg, "Das Register des Klosters Chotieschau," *Verhandlungen des Historischen Vereins für Oberpfalz und Regensburg* 131 (1991): 305–312; Václav Bok, "Hospodářský vývoj kláštera chotěšovského do roku 1421" (PhD diss., Univerzita Karlova, 1961).

119   František Šmahel, "Dvanáct pramenných sond k sociálním poměrům na Táborsku od poloviny 14. do konce 15. století" [Zwölf Quellensonden zu den sozialen Verhältnissen im Taborer Gebiet von der Mitte des 14. bis Ende des 15. Jahrhunderts], *Husitský Tábor* 9 (1987): 277–322. Cf. Ute Henningsen, *Besitz und Einkünfte der Herren von Rosenberg in Böhmen nach dem Urbar von 1379–1384*, Historische und landeskundliche Ostmitteleuropa-Studien 5 (Marburg a. Lahn: J.-G.-Herder-Institut, 1989).

+ Agricultural production relied on "subject" landholdings held by peasant households that functioned basically similarly in the Early Modern Period; therefore, the models of early modern agrarian history and peasant studies may be applied.
+ The social structure of peasant communities was stabilized thanks to the indivisibility of "subject" holdings. Those sons who did not obtain the land-holding were partially absorbed by the towns.[120]
+ The reduction of demesne farming corresponded with developments in "subject" tenant farming. A reduction of labor duties allowed peasants to concentrate on their own production and more intensive interaction with the market.
+ The relationships between "subject" tenants and the landlord were not of a personal nature. The level of land rent was nominally fixed and was not unilaterally increased on the part of the landlord.
+ A certain quantity of land was available. "Subject" tenants also leased separated non-landholding plots from the landlord. A document that provides a helpful, if not completely clear, illustration is the land rent register for two districts on the Zlatá Koruna Monastery manor for 1415–1420, which documents small but annual and intensive changes in areas of land among "subject" tenants.[121]
+ Hereditary land tenure to which "subject" tenants had extensive disposal rights was secured legally and factually. No attempts of the landlord to restrict this practice were documented. Once they had met their dues and obligations to the landlord, tenants could sell or transfer and then leave the "subject'" landholding.

---

120   Rostislav Nový, "Hospodářský region Prahy na přelomu 14. a 15. století" [Die Wirtschafts-region Prags an der Wende des 14. und 15. Jahrhunderts], *Československý časopis historický* 19 (1971): 397–418, on 414.

121   Graus, *Dějiny*, 196–197, 352–353; Jaroslav Kadlec, *Dějiny kláštera Svaté Koruny* (České Budějovice: Knihkupectví ČAT «U zlatého klasu," 1949), 73–91; about the source, cf. Josef Šusta, "Úroční rejstřík kláštera zlatokorunského z počátku 15. věku," *Český časopis historický* 13 (1907): 312–322; regarding the context, cf. Jaroslav Čechura, "K některým otázkám hos-podářského a správního systému cisterciáckých klášterů (Zlatá koruna v předhusitském období)" [Zu einigen Fragen des Wirtschafts- und Verwaltungssystems des Zisterzienserk-lostern (Kloster Goldenkron in der vorhussitischen Zeit)], *Československý časopis historický* 29 (1981): 228–257.

+ Crisis theories of Western European agrarian history cannot be applied to the peasantry of Bohemia.[122]
+ The internal functioning of peasant communities, commercialization, and monetization, as well as the material aspects of the peasantry's life, profoundly changed as a result of the so-called price revolution in the first half of the 16th century.[123]

Opinions on social stratification concurred that it was more or less stable and did not deepen over time (Tábor region, Chotěšov manor). One can find peasants here who accumulated large properties and bought their way out of "subject" status, with unstable "sub-peasant" strata at the other end of the scale.[124] At the same time, the intensive social mobility and migration of the peasantry is assumed. The activities of the richest peasants who managed to buy their way out of their "subject" obligations and become creditors to the landlord are well documented in sources (Plasy manor, Chotěšov manor). Nevertheless, genuinely large accumulations of money were possible from non-agricultural, rather than agricultural, production. Relevant documents pertain to holders of special businesses (taverns) and manorial officials (Plasy manor).

In this respect, the expectations of neoclassical economics and Marxist models are confirmed. On the other hand, polarization between peasant households growing richer and those growing poorer was counterbalanced by a range of other factors, from biologically determined demographic tendencies to the individual characteristics of concrete peasants.[125] Hypothetically,

---

122   Jaroslav Čechura, "Krize pozdního středověku – mýtus 20. století?," in *Středověký kaleidoskop pro muže s hůlkou: věnováno Františku Šmahelovi k životnímu jubileu* (Prague: NLN, Nakladatelství Lidové noviny, 2016), 34–45; Čechura, *Die Struktur*, 130–134; Jaroslav Čechura, "Teorie agrární krize pozdního středověku: teoretický základ koncepce hospodářského a sociálního vývoje předhusitských Čech: metodologická studie" [Die Theorie von der Agrarkrise des späten Mittelalters: theoretische Grundlagen eines Entwurfs der wirtschaftlichen und sozialen Entwicklung im vorhussitischen Böhmen], *Archaeologia historica* 12 (1987): 129–141, in summary form see Čechura, *Sedláci*, 17–61. Similarly, see Šmahel, *Husitská revoluce*, 414–456.
123   On this see Kostlán, "Cenová revoluce."
124   On the expansion of sub-peasant strata, cf. Markus Cerman, "Mittelalterliche Ursprünge der unterbäuerlichen Schichten," in *Untertanen, Herrschaft und Staat in Böhmen und im "Alten Reich." Sozialgeschichtliche Strukturen*, ed. Markus Cerman and Robert Luft, Veröffentlichungen des Collegium Carolinum 99 (Munich: Oldenbourg, 2005), 323–350.
125   Šmahel, *Husitská revoluce*, 426.

movements took place in both directions. However, such statements by Czech historians are the result of logical deduction; the necessary verification for this is missing in the sources.[126] Property data mostly concerns just one particular time period; the chance of following changes over an extended time period is limited to very few cases.[127] Following the development trajectories of concrete households seems to be impossible.[128]

4.2 Early Modern Period

While medieval studies only rarely conceptualize the social mobility and migration of the peasantry, it is a frequent topic for early modern social and economic history.[129] In recent years, the international research project *Social Structures in Early Modern Bohemia 1650–1750* played an important role, following up on the Czech historiographical knowledge of the time.[130] The

---

126 The possibilities of the source base for Bohemia are summarized by Čechura, *Die Struktur*, 109–125; for Central and Eastern Europe, see Cerman, "Social structure," 56–76.

127 See particularly Šmahel, "Dvanáct pramenných sond," 314–316; Čechura, *Die Struktur*, 114–116. For the more recent period cf. also František Šmahel, "Táborské vesnice na Podblanicku v letech 1420–1547," *Sborník vlastivědných prací z Podblanicka* 22 (1981): 171–201.

128 An exception is the Tábor region's sources from the transition between the Middles Ages and the Modern Period: Šmahel, "Táborské vesnice." Cf. also Zdeněk Boháč, "Vesnice v sídelní struktuře předhusitských Čech" [Das Dorf in der Siedlungsstruktur des vorhussitischen Böhmens], *Historická geografie* 21 (1983): 37–116.

129 E.g., Carocci, "Social Mobility," 371. Cf. also articles in Carocci and Lazzarini, eds. *Social mobility*.

130 See esp. Josef Pekař, *České katastry* (Prague: Historický klub, 1932); Kamil Krofta, *Dějiny selského stavu: Přehled dějin selského stavu v Čechách a na Moravě*, ed. Emil Janoušek Laichterův výbor nejlepších spisů poučných 80, Dílo Kamila Krofty 3 (Prague: Jan Laichter, ²1949); Míka, *Poddaný lid*; Petráň, *Poddaný lid*; Procházka, *Česká poddanská nemovitost*; Eduard Maur, *Český komorní velkostatek v 17. století: Příspěvek k otázce „druhého nevolnictví" v českých zemích*, Acta Universitatis Carolinae. Philosophica et historica. Monographia 59 (Prague: Univerzita Karlova, 1976); Aleš Chalupa, "Venkovské obyvatelstvo v Čechách v tereziánských katastrech (1700–1750)" [La population tchéque de la campagne dans les cadastres thérésiens (1700–1750)], *Sborník Národního muzea v Praze, řada A – Historie* 23 (1969): 197–378; Eduard Maur, *Gutsherrschaft und „zweite Leibeigenschaft" in Böhmen: Studien zur Wirtschafts-, Sozial- und Bevölkerungsgeschichte (14.–18. Jahrhundert)*, Sozial- und wirtschaftshistorische Studien 26 (Vienna: Verlag für Geschichte und Politik; Munich: Oldenbourg, 2001); Josef Petráň, ed., *Problémy cen, mezd a materiálních podmínek života od*

empirical part of the project was conducted in the 1990s by Czech and Austrian researchers, as well as individual researchers from other countries. In addition to numerous separate studies[131] under this project, several syntheses,[132] influential volumes,[133] and dissertations were composed (1999–2008), conceived as case studies, and gradually published over the previous decade (2008–2015).[134] The main goal of the project was to more deeply understand

16. *do poloviny 19. století*, Acta Universitatis Carolinae. Philosophica et Historica 1 (Prague: Univerzita Karlova, 1971); Josef Petráň, ed., *Problémy cen, mezd a materiálních podmínek života lidu v Čechách v 17.–19. století II*, Acta Universitatis Carolinae. Philosophica et Historica 3 (Prague: Univerzita Karlova, 1977); in addition see also Jan Horský, "Pojmy, objekty, vztahy a systémy. Poznámky o místě historické demografie ve vývoji dějepisectví" [Concepts, objects, relations and systems. Notes on local historical demographics in the development of history], *Lidé města* 14 (2012): 421–455; Jiří Mikulec, "Dějiny venkovského poddaného lidu v 17. a 18. století a česká historiografie posledních dvaceti let," *Český časopis historický* 88 (1990): 119–130.

131   A list of publications from 1996–2004 is contained in Markus Cerman and Robert Luft, eds., *Untertanen, Herrschaft und Staat in Böhmen und im "Alten Reich": sozialgeschichtliche Studien zur Frühen Neuzeit*, Veröffentlichungen des Collegium Carolinum 99 (Munich: Oldenbourg, 2005), 353–367.

132   Markus Cerman and Eduard Maur, "Proměny vesnických sociálních struktur v Čechách 1650–1750" [Der Wandel der ländischen Sozialstrukturen in Böhmen, 1650–1750], *Český časopis historický* 98 (2000): 737–774; Markus Cerman and Eduard Maur, "Die wirtschaftliche und soziale Entwicklung im frühneuzeitlichen Böhmen aus mikro- und makrohistorischer Sicht," in *Soziale Strukturen in Böhmen. Ein regionaler Vergleich von Wirtschaft und Gesellschaft in Gutsherrschaften, 16.–19. Jahrhundert*, ed. Markus Cerman and Hermann Zeitlhofer, Sozial- und Wirtschaftshistorische Studien 28 (Vienna – Munich, 2002), 101–110; Markus Cerman and Hermann Zeitlhofer, eds., *Soziale Strukturen in Böhmen. Ein regionaler Vergleich von Wirtschaft und Gesellschaft in Gutsherrschaften, 16.–19. Jahrhundert*, Sozial- und Wirtschaftshistorische Studien 28 (Vienna – Munich, 2002).

133   Articles in the *Historická demografie* magazine nr. 20 (1996); Cerman and Zeitlhofer, *Soziale Strukturen*; Cerman and Luft, *Untertanen*.

134   Josef Grulich, *Populační vývoj a životní cyklus venkovského obyvatelstva na jihu Čech v 16. až 18. století* [Die demographische Entwicklung und der Lebenszyklus der Dorfbewohner (Südbohmen, 16.–18. Jahrhundert)], Monographia historica 10 (České Budějovice: Jihočeská univerzita v Českých Budějovicích, 2008); Dana Štefanová, *Erbschaftspraxis, Besitztransfer und Handlungsspielräume von Untertanen in der Gutsherrschaft. Die Herrschaft Frýdlant in Nordböhmen, 1558–1750*, Sozial- und wirtschaftshistorische Studien 34 (Vienna: Verlag für Geschichte und Politik, 2009); Alice Velková, *Krutá vrchnost, ubozí poddaní? Proměny venkovské rodiny a společnosti v 18. a první polovině 19. století na příkladu západočeského panství Šťáhlavy* [Cruel landlords, poor subjects? Transformations of the rural family and society in the 18th and the first half of the 19th centuries], Opera Instituti historici Pragae, Řada A, Monographia 27 (Prague: Historický ústav, 2009); Hermann Zeitlhofer, *Besitzwechsel und sozialer Wandel: Lebensläufe und sozioökonomische Entwicklungen im südlichen Böhmerwald, 1640–1840*, Sozial- und wirtschaftshistorische Studien 36 (Vienna, Cologne:

the long-term development tendencies of the social and economic setting of the rural population in post–White Mountain Bohemia (1620) based on (1) a comparison of a carefully selected and representative sample of estates and (2) macro-analyses of nationwide data and their combination with the micro-historical view of selected peasant communities. Over the course of the project, individual researchers specialized and shifted their research focus to population development and the life cycle (Josef Grulich, Alice Velková, Markéta Pražáková Seligová) and/or to an analysis of landholding transfer, inheritance practices, the roles of village communities, the institutional framework in the context of the estates (demesne farming), and the status of women (Sheilagh Ogilvie, Dana Štefanová, Hermann Zeitlhofer).[135] The macroanalytic approaches of Sheilagh Ogilvie and Alexander Klein continued in the original ideals of the research project.[136] It must be mentioned at this point that in addition to the research and publications by scholars involved with the *Social Structures* project in the past, complementary, lively research activities have been focused on other prominent researchers in Bohemia[137] and Mora-

Böhlau, 2014); Markéta Pražáková Seligová, *Život poddaných v 18. století: osud, nebo volba?: K demografickým, hospodářským, sociálním a rodinným aspektům života venkovských poddaných na panství Horní Police* [The lives of serfs in the 18th century: Destiny or choice? Towards demographic, economic, social, and family aspects of the lives of rural serfs living in the estate of Horní Police] (Prague: Togga, 2015).

135   Cf. also Eduard Maur, Review of *Besitzwechsel und sozialer Wandel: Lebensläufe und sozioökonomische Entwicklungen im südlichen Böhmerwald, 1640–1840*, by Hermann Zeitlhofer, *Historie – otázky – problémy* 9 (2017): 301–303, on 301; Eduard Maur, "Dějiny rodiny v české historiografii" [Die historische Familienforschung in der tschechischen Historiographie], in *Rodina a domácnost v 16.–20. Století*, Acta Universitatis Carolinae. Philosophica et historica 2/2006, Studia historica 60 (Prague: Karolinum, 2010), 9–22, esp. 15–16. Further, see, e.g., Sheilagh Ogilvie, "Vesnická obec a tzv. „druhé nevolnictví" v raně novověkých Čechách" [Communities and the "Second Serfdom" in early modern Bohemia], *Český časopis historický* 107 (2009): 46–94; Sheilagh Ogilvie and Jeremy Edwards, "Frauen und „zweite Leibeigenschaft" in Böhmen," *Bohemia* 44 (2003): 101–145.

136   Alexander Klein and Sheilagh Ogilvie, "Occupational structure in the Czech lands under the second serfdom," *The Economic History Review* 69 (2015): 493–521.

137   Summarized in Eduard Maur, "Venkov v raném novověku," in *Základní problémy studia raného novověku*, ed. Marie Šedivá Koldinská, Ivo Cerman, et al., České dějiny 6 (Prague: NLN, Nakladatelství Lidové noviny, 2013), 307–334; Jaroslav Čechura, "Mikrohistorie a raněnovověká studia: možnosti a meze jednoho historiografického konceptu" [Mikrogeschichte und Frühneuzeitstudien. Möglichkeiten und Grenzen eines hisoriographischen Konzepts], *Časopis Matice moravské* 135 (2016): 361–393; Jan Horský and Markéta Seligová, *Rodina našich předků*, Knižnice Dějin a současnosti 2 (Prague: NLN, Nakladatelství Lidové

via.[138] Overall, therefore, it can be said that thanks to this extraordinary, diverse research and intensive networking with international research groups across Europe,[139] early modern Czech historical research has maintained a progressive and inspiring spirit that has brought to light essential comparative materials useful also for the study of late medieval situations.

The findings of Czech early modern agrarian history are significant, as the norms and inheritance practices both in Bohemia and the city-state of Cheb were of an impartible inheritance nature, maintaining the integrity of the peasant landholding. Nevertheless, despite this partial institutional similarity, there were also principal differences. Bohemian early modern peasant communities operated in the context of various forms of labor-rent demesne farming, relatively strong landlord regulations, higher levels of commercialization, and the monetization of family property relations. However, we consider the following conclusions derived by the researchers of early modern agrarian history to be methodologically and conceptually inspiring for an analysis of the city-state of Cheb:

+ Emphasis was placed on the formal classification of property transactions (sales), particularly on the difference between landholding transfer and inheritance practices.[140]

noviny, 1997); Jiří Koumar, "‚Má doplaceno, žádnému nic nedluží . . .': Finanční aspekty majetkového transferu poddanské nemovitosti na mělnickém panství v 17. století" [„Er hat alles beglichen, er schuldet niemandem etwas . . ." Finanzielle Aspekte des Vermögenstransfers einer Untertanenliegenschaft im Dominium Mělník im 17. Jahrhundert], *Ústecký sborník historický* 1 (2011): 7–43; Pavel Himl, *Die ‚armben Leüte' und die Macht. Die Untertanen der südböhmischen Herrschaft Český Krumlov / Krumau im Spannungsfeld zwischen Gemeinde, Obrigkeit und Kirche (1680–1781)*, Quellen und Forschungen zur Agrargeschichte 48 (Stuttgart: Steiner, 2003); Pavel Himl, "Marginální vrstvy raně novověké společnosti," in *Základní problémy studia raného novověku*, ed. Marie Šedivá Koldinská, Ivo Cerman, et al., České dějiny 6 (Prague: NLN, Nakladatelství Lidové noviny, 2013), 370–409.

138   E.g., Bronislav Chocholáč, *Selské peníze: Sonda do finančního hospodaření poddaných na západní Moravě koncem 16. a v 17. století* [Das Bauerngeld. Finanzwirtschaft der Bauern in Westmähren am Ende des 16. und im 17. Jahrhundert], Knižnice Matice moravské 4 (Brno: Matice moravská, 1999).

139   University research units in Vienna and Bielefeld, as well as the *Annales* platform, working group *Cambridge Group for the History of Population and Social Structure, Max-Planck-Institut für Geschichte v Göttingen*, and others.

140   Štefanová, *Erbschaftspraxis*, 68–70; Zeitlhofer, *Besitzwechsel*, 22–23. Concisely (Just the word "concisely" is a little vague; it would be helpful to add a few more words for clarity, possibly something like: *Procházka, Česká poddanská nemovitost*.

- An anthropological and also a systemic interpretation of tenancy and material goods (the material subsystem) around which dependencies, relationships, conflicts, social prestige, and emotions formed (social subsystem).[141]
- There was regional and local diversity in the terms of land tenure and inheritance rights and flexibility of both norms and practices.[142]

Concerning changes in social mobility and migration, in terms of concrete information, the following findings are of comparative significance for the city-state of Cheb:

- The proportion of land transfers (sales) between relatives and non-relatives differed significantly according to the circumstances. The proportion of *intrafamilial* transfers was considerably lower in *inter vivos* transfers, while *causa morti* transfers were conducted for the most part within the family. The high proportion of *intrafamilial* transfers would indicate that a majority of peasants held the "subject" landholdings until their death, while a small proportion indicated market transfers and migration of peasants between landholdings.[143]
- Like elsewhere across Europe, a positive relationship is documented between social status and (1) the frequency of land transfers and (2) the proportion of transfers between relatives. According to the type of sources available, we are able to establish differences between full-fledged peasant and "sub-peasant" groups or among individual tenants of different valuable "subject" landholdings. With the falling socioeconomic status and monetary value of the landholding, the proportion of *intrafamilial* transfers and the frequency of "subject" tenants replacing each other increased.[144]
- Different destinies were identified not just among the offspring of rich and poor peasants, but also among the individual children of the rich. Thanks to the relaxed practice regarding "subject" landholding tenure, up until the mid-18th century, upward social mobility was possible, while later a rigid system of downward mobility prevailed, where usually only the primary heir main-

141 Štefanová, *Erbschaftspraxis*, 49.
142 Procházka, *Česká poddanská nemovitost.*
143 Grulich, *Populační vývoj*, 302–309; Velková, *Krutá vrchnost*, 124–246; Štefanová, *Erbschaftspraxis*, 74–85; Zeitlhofer, *Besitzwechsel*, 206–212.
144 Chocholáč, *Selské peníze*, 117–124; Grulich, *Populační vývoj*, 294–312, 326–330; Velková, *Krutá vrchnost*, 129–134, 136–139, 144–149; Štefanová, *Erbschaftspraxis*, 74–80; Zeitlhofer, *Besitzwechsel*, 197–212, 227–237.

tained his parent's position. His siblings awaited a drop in status unless they managed to enter an advantageous marriage.[145]

+ Also evident are the differences over time that may be only partially explained by the demographic and economic situations. Intensive alternation of "subject" tenants was characteristic not only during the massive drop in population that occurred after the Thirty Years' War, but records exist indicating this pattern also in the second half of the 16th century. The situation stabilized in the 18th century, when "subject" landholdings could be acquired, except from parents, and so those without peasant origin were almost unable to get hold of a "subject" landholding.[146]

4.3 Geographical mobility and migration

The options for identifying the concrete features of geographical mobility and the migration horizon of the medieval population are limited and usually can only be done in a town's hinterland.[147] Sources do allow us to follow rural-urban migration.[148]

Of the exceptionally rich sources that have been used quantitatively for the study of peasant mobility in Europe so far, we should mention the English *Manorial Court Rolls* for the 13th–14th centuries. Back in the 1980s, Anne Reiber DeWindt used extensive databases containing information from several parishes and manors in the Midlands of England to trace the movements of the

---

145 Summarized in Alice Velková, "Proměny venkovské společnosti v letech 1700–1850" [Transformations of rural society between 1700–1850], *Český časopis historický* 105 (2007): 809–857, on 824–834; Velková, *Krutá vrchnost*, 304–334.

146 Chocholáč, *Selské peníze*, 117–124; Grulich, *Populační vývoj*, 302–318, 326–330; Štefanová, *Erbschaftspraxis*, 78–80; Zeitlhofer, *Besitzwechsel*, 197–199, 206–207; in summary form, see Velková, "Proměny," 826–838.

147 For more on the study of the migration of the peasantry in the Early Modern Period, cf. Grulich, *Migrace*.

148 Rainer Christoph Schwinges, ed., *Neubürger im späten Mittelalter. Migration und Austausch in der Städtelandschaft des Alten Reiches (1250–1550)*, Zeitschrift für historische Forschung. Beiheft 30 (Berlin: Duncker & Humblot, 2002); David Postles, "Migration and mobility in a less mature economy: English internal migration, c. 1200–1350," *Social History* 25 (2000): 285–299, on 285–287.

same peasant in various communities.[149] Using the manorial rolls, she encountered several problems, from identifying the same person in various sources to
the fact that the manorial rolls did not record all peasant groups with equal
representation. Despite this, the results convincingly showed an unusually
wide active radius for peasant families, the individuality of the motives for
the geographical mobility, and the differences between members of various
property-owning and social groups within the peasantry. Other English
studies have arrived at similar conclusions and therefore generalization is possible.[150] Peasants regularly crossed the boundaries of their village, even if membership in a concrete community remained essential for managing common
local economic resources and the right to use them. The main reasons for the
geographical mobility of peasants are unsurprising and included (1) changing
landholdings during their lifetime, (2) seeking a spouse, (3) being attracted
to market and administrative centers where peasants had to perform several
duties but could also choose between a range of livelihoods even outside of
the non-agricultural sphere, and (4) attempting to leave their past behind and
start a new life. Although the concrete active radius of social and economic
activities of peasants, their family ties, and intensive relations were very individual, in principle it depended on the social status of the peasant and their
family. It was this status that presented the concrete options and needs to use
certain sources of livelihood and to become a part of certain personal networks
across a wide region. As for the absolute spatial values that characterized the
extent of peasant activities, these depended on the particular network of settlements and the concrete distribution of places with a higher degree of centrality.
In central England, the active radius of rich peasants extended for 20–30 km,
while that of the poor was 7–11 km. Smallholders and the landless often lacked
access to common economic resources and so their sources of income, whether
agricultural or non-agricultural, were fairly sparse and lacking a firm foundation in one particular village. Although these poorest peasants were very
mobile, their activities were limited to just a few neighboring villages. Rich

---

149   DeWindt, "Redefining." A classic study by the Toronto School, introducing the topic of
       social and geographical mobility appears in James Ambrose Raftis, *Tenure and mobility.
       Studies in the social history of the mediaeval English village* (Toronto: Pontifical Institute of
       Mediaeval Studies, 1964).
150   Schofield, *Peasant*, 94–127; Bethany Jane Hamblen, "Communities of the hinterland: Social
       networks and geographical mobility beyond the walls of late medieval York" (PhD diss.,
       University of York, 2008).

peasants had a firm family foundation in the form of a large landholding and were thus able to enter geographically more extensive personal networks.[151]

English sources make it possible to follow, more or less, all types of geographical mobility of the medieval peasantry and also to reconstruct the networks that peasants joined throughout their lives. However, the sources available for the transalpine part of Europe generally make only partial knowledge possible or they apply only to the Early Modern Period.[152] A manifestation of the exceptionally strong family bonds at the time was the maintenance of contact even over relatively long distances extending beyond the borders of the region and even the country.[153] Certain aspects of geographical mobility may be learned by studying the geographical horizon of the peasantry, i.e., their mental spatial map.[154]

4.4 Summary

To date, East-Central European medieval studies have emphasized research into the social stratification of the late medieval peasantry, but due to a lack of data, a deeper analysis of social mobility has remained neglected. The same may be said of continental medieval studies as a whole. There is no doubt that the social rise or fall of individuals and entire groups was omnipresent.[155]

The materialist concept of social differentiation used to be applied in a pure, crystalline form in Bohemian historiography (B. T. Rubtsov, F. Graus, A. Míka, R. Nový), but this was later replaced by the concept of the commercialization of the peasantry (J. Čechura, F. Šmahel). Neo-Malthusian theories empha-

---

151   DeWindt, "Redefining," esp. 163–166, 188–189, 191–195; Postles, "Migration and mobility."
152   Grulich, *Migrace*; Petráň, *Poddaný lid*, 241–251.
153   E.g., Sreenivasan, *Peasants*, 52–53.
154   For Bohemia, cf. Zdena Wiendlová, "Geografický horizont středočeských vesničanů na konci 14. století" [Der geographische Horizont der Landbewohner in Mittelböhmen am Ende des 14. Jahrhunderts], *Český časopis historický* 93 (1995): 65–85; Barbora Mlynaříková, *Geografický horizont prostého člověka v Čechách v letech 1740–1830*, sv. 1–2, Národopisná knižnice 39 (Prague: Etnologický ústav Akademie věd České republiky, 2001).
155   Carocci, "Social mobility," esp. 368–369, 371–375.

sizing demographic growth and mortality crises have been applied only marginally.[156]

Research on the social stratification and mobility of the peasantry has been considerably influenced by the agrarian history of the Early Modern Period, which crossed the lower time boundary if sources allowed (J. Petráň, E. Maur). In this regard, the project *Social Structures in Early Modern Bohemia 1650–1750* is frequently mentioned. Previously, research on Bohemia in the Early Modern Period had suggested that the trajectory of social mobility might be described well by the model of uneven reproduction, the nature of which depended on concrete demographic and economic conditions.

---

156   Petr Čornej, *Dějiny zemí Koruny české. I., Od příchodu Slovanů do roku 1740* (Prague: Paseka, 1997), 133–140. Cf. Čechura, "Mor," esp. 287–288.

◄ Plate 3: **Starý Hrozňatov (Kinsberg, Alt-). View from the southeast (1899). In the background is the former "ministerial" castle, the core of a small estate in the 15th century held by the Cheb patrician Frankengrüner family. The castle was then open to the town.**

II.
Region and Sources

In this part of the study, we introduce readers to the late medieval Cheb countryside and characterize the long-term economic cycle. In doing so, we also describe those factors determining the social stratification and mobility of the peasantry, which we refer to as *indirect* in Chapter 3. Moreover, we describe the main collection of our written sources.

5.
The city-state of Cheb

5.1 Historical overview

The historical Cheb region (Czech: *Chebsko*; German: *Egerland*) was formed during the 12th century as an imperial territory ruled by the Hohenstaufen dynasty through the ministerial system.[157] The administrative center of the land was the *Kaiserpfalz* (imperial palace) in Cheb (German: *Eger*) on the Ohře River (German: *Eger*), under which the settlement agglomeration spread, which already at the beginning of the 13th century proved to be a city. At the time that is the subject of our analysis, the Cheb region had the status of an imperial lien to the Bohemian king (1322; *fig. 5.1*), later the Crown of Bohemia (1348), and its territory was more or less geographically stabilized by 1413. The city council of Cheb exercised territorial power, which was materialized by the annual collection of the land tax and the organization of the land peasant militia.[158] We can therefore speak of a Cheb city-state from the turn of the 15th century. In this regard, the city-state of Cheb had many characteristics that connected it with other city-states, especially with members of the Swabian-Frankish group, such as Nuremberg, Rothenburg ob der Tauber,

---

157 That is, a system of lower nobiliar vassals. František Kubů, *Die staufische Ministerialität im Egerland. Ein Beitrag zur Siedlungs- und Verwaltungsgeschichte*, Otnant-Gesellschaft für Geschichte und Kultur in der Euregio Egrensis. Quellen und Erörterungen 1 (Pressath: Bodner, 1995); in Czech see František Kubů, *Štaufská ministerialita na Chebsku* (Cheb: Chebské muzeum, 1997).

158 Extensive literature concerning historical development and the city-state governance aspects of the Cheb Region are summarized by Klír et al., *Knihy*, 31–59, 194; Klír, "Procesy pustnutí," 548–550.

and Ulm.[159] Nevertheless, the city-state of Cheb has a fundamentally different beginning.[160] Within the Church, the Cheb region belonged to the Regensburg diocese.[161]

The strategic significance of the Cheb region stemmed from its location at the crossroads of the highways that connected Bohemia to Franconia and from Bavaria to Saxony (fig. 5.2). Concretely it was an ideal halfway point between (1) Prague and Nuremberg, the latter of which was one of the three most populated imperial cities of the 14th–16th centuries, and (2) Regensburg and Leipzig (fig. 5.3). In the Late Middle Ages, Cheb, with its approximately 630 houses and estimated population of between 5,000–8,000 inhabitants, was one of the most populous cities of the Lands of the Bohemian Crown[162]; compared with others across the Empire, it could be categorized as a medium-large city.[163] Since the High Middle Ages, the agroclimatically favorable Cheb Basin and the town of Cheb played an increasingly important role as an economic and organizational base for exploiting the mineral wealth of the neighbouring mountain areas.

The period under detailed consideration spans from the Hussite Wars to the Poděbrad period. The Hussite Wars created tighter bonds between Cheb and the Holy Roman Emperor, Sigismund (1410–1437), while maintaining factual autonomy that it had been granted during the reign of Wenceslaus IV (1378–1419). The war years of 1420–1434 affected the economic functioning of the city and the land, leading to the mobilization of economic resources and to the concentration of their administration into the hands of a few prominent patricians. Cheb actively participated in the political and military activities of

---

159   Klír et al., *Knihy*, 31–59; František Kubů, *Chebský městský stát: Počátky a vrcholné období do počátku 16. Století* (Cheb: Veduta, 2006). Cf. Tom Scott, "The city-state in the German-speaking lands," in *Politics and reformations: Essays in honor of Thomas A. Brady, Jr.*, ed. Christopher Ocker et al., Studies in Medieval and Reformation Traditions 128 (Leiden, 2007), 3–66; Tom Scott, *The city-state in Europe, 1000–1600: Hinterland, territory, region* (Oxford: Oxford University Press, ²2012).

160   Klír et al., *Knihy*, 50–59.

161   Klír et al., *Knihy*, 10–11, 22–23.

162   Klír et al., *Knihy*, 46–50.

163   Hektor Ammannm, "Wie gross war die mittelalterliche Stadt? (1956)," in *Die Stadt des Mittelalters 1*, ed. Carl Hasse, Wege der Forschung 243 (Darmstadt: Wissenschaftliche Buchgesellschaft, 1977), 408–415; Eberhard Isenmann, *Die deutsche Stadt im Mittelalter 1150–1550: Stadtgestalt, Recht, Verfassung, Stadtregiment, Kirche, Gesellschaft, Wirtschaft* (Cologne, Weimar, Vienna: Böhlau,² 2014), 58–63.

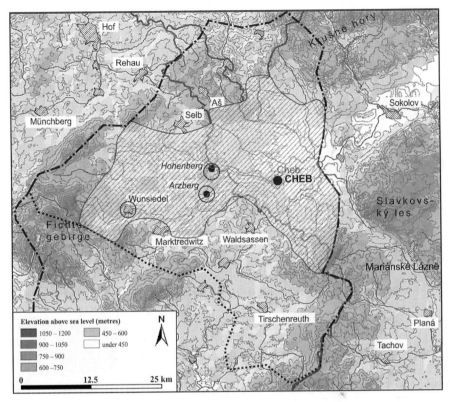

Figure 5.1. Historic Cheb region and the extent of the imperial lien in 1322.

Source: From Klír et al., *Knihy*, fig. 1.

Note: The boundary of the northern part of the Diocese of Regensburg (chain-dotted) in the Late Middle Ages, the Deaconry of Wunsiedel and Cheb in 1438 (dotted—corresponds to the historical Cheb region), and the Cheb imperial lien granted by Ludwig I of Bavaria to Jan of Luxembourg in October 1322 (dashed).

the anti-Hussite alliance, performing the function of a support and supply point during operations against Hussite Bohemia led from the west, while in 1429–1430 it faced actual invasion by Hussite armies.[164]

After the end of the Hussite Wars and the death of Sigismund of Luxembourg (1437), Cheb's position in the arising power vacuum became more complicated. The new lienholder and Sigismund's successor, Albrecht II (1437–1439),

---

164   Klír et al., *Knihy*, 19–20; on the raid of the Hussite armies, see Klír, "Procesy pustnutí," 726–727. Cf. also Jiří Jánský, *Kronika česko-bavorské hranice 2 – Chronik der böhmisch-bayerischen Grenze 2 (1427–1437)* (Domažlice: Nakladatelství Český les, 2003).

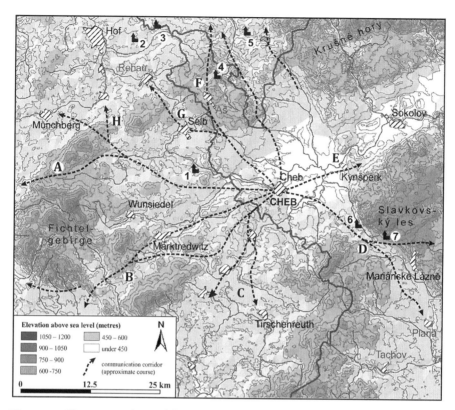

Figure 5.2. The strategic position of the Cheb region. Transport corridors leading from Cheb in the High and Late Middle Ages.

Source: From Klír et al., *Knihy*, fig. 2.

Note: Mountain passes and gullies: A – saddle separating the sources of the Main River and the Ohře River; B – Röslau-Naab Gulley; C – Naab-Wondreb Gulley; D – Žandov Pass; E – ravine between the Cheb Basin and Sokolov Basin; F – headwaters of the White Elster, Saale, and Ohře Rivers; G – saddle between Selbe and Rehau; H – Lamitz river valley.

could not provide the city actual protection, and so the city of Cheb arranged for protection themselves in 1438/1440–1452/1454 by repeatedly entering into protection treaties with their most powerful neighbors. The financial costs connected with the protection treaties were paid from the land tax collections.[165]

165   Klír et al., *Knihy*, 20. Cf. also Jiří Jánský, *Kronika česko-bavorské hranice 3 – Chronik der böhmisch-bayerischen Grenze 3 (1437–1457)* (Domažlice: Nakladatelství Český les, 2003), 22–26, 214–216.

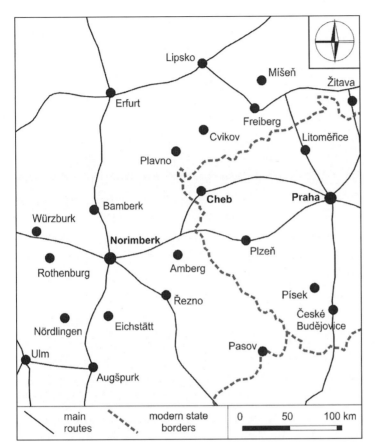

Figure 5.3. The position of Cheb in the network of important late medieval cities. What is striking is the central position of Cheb between Prague and Nuremberg.

Source: Petráň, "Doprava a cestování," 817, fig. 735. Cf. Musílek, *Patroni*, 158–159, fig. 23. Modified.

In the 1440s, Cheb lacked a generally recognized lienholder and in practice the city was brought into the immediate influence of the Empire. An intensive renewal of relations with Bohemia came about during the period of stabilization under the governance of George of Poděbrady (1452–1458), to whom Cheb provided diplomatic support in an expensive yet successful clash with Henry II of Plauen, Burgrave of Meissen (1452–1453). In 1453, Cheb rendered homage to the Bohemian King Ladislaus (1453–1457), receiving the traditional confirmation of all privileges in return. In January 1454, King Ladislaus declared his protection over Cheb and ordered that annual payments to their previous protectors be halted. The provisional practice of private protection therefore ended and was replaced by protection by the lienholder. Five years later, Cheb's privileges were affirmed by King George of Poděbrady (1458–1471) as the new lienholder. Cheb played an important contact role in his imperial policy, and important meetings took place there, including two imperial diets (1459, 1461) and the weddings of George's children to the children of Saxon dukes. Cheb remained loyal to George even during the period of conflicts in the second half of the 1460s and only concentrated pressure from the anti-Poděbrady camp, bolstered by the declaration of an interdict, led the city to change its stance in 1470. The Jagiellonian era, beginning upon the delayed recognition of King Vladislaus II of Hungary (1471–1516) as the lienholder in 1477, caused a turnaround in the balance of power and a weakening of the city's independent status.[166]

5.2 Central settlements and the administrative division of the territory

One of the characteristics of the city-state of Cheb was the separation of fief and landlord rights. The overlords loaned a large part of their holdings as fiefs with varying related obligations. Fiefs were distributed among vassals of varying rank, some nearing the status of lower regional nobility and others being more like free peasants. A range of fiefs were also transferred back and forth between burghers and ecclesiastical institutions. From today's point of view, property relations in the city-state of Cheb were unwieldy and complex, landlord rights were not compact but dispersed. The countryside had an abundance of (1) "subject" landholdings, (2) landholdings where lower vassals themselves farmed and lived and that could have a separate residential dwelling resembling a stronghold, and (3) strategically important and prestigious castles with their own demesne farms and whose holders steadily concentrated more

---

166   Klír et al., *Knihy*, 20–21; on the military conflicts of 1453–1454, 1459–1463 and 1468–1470 see Klír, "Procesy pustnutí," 727–731. Cf. also Jánský, *Kronika česko-bavorské hranice 3*; Jiří Jánský, *Kronika česko-bavorské hranice 4 – Chronik der böhmisch-bayerischen Grenze 4 (1458–1478)* (Domažlice: Nakladatelství Český les, 2004).

and more landlord rights in their hands.[167] Historiography of the city-state of Cheb attempts to address its stratified and dynamic past through the concept of small manors that sprang up around prestigious castles in the Late Middle Ages and Early Modern Period.[168] Alongside strategic castles, we may also include demesne farms, which tended to be held by Cheb's burghers.[169]

Settlements in the city-state of Cheb differed not only in the number of land-holdings, but also in the degree of centrality. Some settlements had a parish church[170] or a castle as the center of a small manor;[171] other settlements were located at crossroads, and in many a mill operated (fig. 5).[172] Therefore, in models, we differentiate a range of settlements, from those with a greater degree of centrality (i.e., centers consisting of small manors with a castle, a parish church, and a mill) to settlements with a lesser degree of centrality where some of the central functions were lacking, and finally to settlements with no central functions. The degree of centrality naturally had a fundamental influence on the socioeconomic structure of the settlement. Central settlements facilitated non-agrarian modes of subsistence and thus the expansion of the non-peasant strata. For this reason, during analysis it is essential to strictly differentiate settlements with a large degree of centrality from others.[173]

Insight into the internal administrative structures of the late medieval city-state of Cheb is afforded by an exceptional written document—the 1395 *Land Militia Register*—which recorded armed peasants and their weapons in settlements directly controlled by the lienholder and the city of Cheb.[174] Unlike contemporaneous land tax collection registers for 1392 and 1395, this list also included peasants from the settlements of Cheb Castle and in the castle village of Ostrov/Seeberg. The list recorded a total of 1,237 armed peasants in

167   An overview of material relicts is offered by Jiří Úlovec, *Hrady, zámky a tvrze na Chebsku* (Cheb: Chebské muzeum, 1998). For the more significant localities, cf. Tomáš Karel and Vilém Knoll, "Hrady na Chebsku jako reprezentanti moci" [Die Burgen des Egerlandes als Machtrepräsentanten], *Castellologica bohemica* 16 (2016): 153–178.
168   Sturm, *Districtus Egranus*, 190–237.
169   Klír et al., *Knihy*, 136–138; Ar Cheb, book 1424, *Losungsbuch 1446*.
170   Cf. Ar Cheb, book 974, *Musterungsbuch der Bauernschaft*.
171   Cf. Sturm, *Districtus Egranus*, 190–237.
172   *App. 5.1*.
173   *App. 5.1*.
174   Ar Cheb, book 974, *Musterungsbuch der Bauernschaft*. Additionally see Jan Durdík, "Vojenská hotovost chebského venkova v roce 1395," *Historie a vojenství* (1966): 561–583; František Kubů, "Ozbrojené síly chebského městského státu," *Sborník Chebského muzea* (2001): 9–23.

133 settlements (see *chap. 10.4*).[175] Individual settlements were categorized in the register according to parish and fanning out in a circular fashion, i.e., they started with the parish village, followed by other settlements ordered more or less clockwise.[176] The parish of Cheb was the largest, and unlike the others, it was internally divided into 5 districts (*app. 5.3*). The administrative division of the city-state of Cheb according to parish districts, as described in 1395, functioned into the 15th century.[177]

The testimony offered by the register of the land militia is extraordinary. With its help, we have been able, for the first time, to group together settlements according to parish church, thereby determining the degree of cohesion between peasant communities, with the city of Cheb and with other central settlements.[178] Compared to the picture painted on the basis of tax registers, the extent of Cheb's territorial power is more clearly defined geographically.

5.3 Geographical zonality of the Cheb territory

The imperial territory enfeoffed to the Bohemian Crown and controlled by the city of Cheb in the 15th century comprised the entire Cheb Basin (elev. 400–500 m), including areas extending into the mountainous areas surrounding it (elev. 500–650/700 m). Small enclaves of Cheb's territorial power lay in the Röslau Valley, which lies in the Upper Franconian Fichtel Mountains. Individual settlements lay in significantly different geomorphological, geolog-

---

175   The picture of the Cheb countryside provided by registers of the Land Militia was confronted by Wilhelm Heisiner, "Die Egerer Klosteuerbücher als Quellen für die Bevölkerungs- und Wirtschaftsgeschichte des Egerlandes im späten Mittelalter" (Phd diss., Deutsche Universität, 1938), 105–124.

176   *App. 5.2.*

177   *App. 5.3.* Cf. Klír et al., *Knihy*, 417, note 572.

178   In contemporaneous documents from the Diocese of Regensburg only settlements with deaconries or parishes can be traced. Cf. Heribert Sturm, "Egerländer Pfarreien in der Diözese Regensburg," *Jahrbuch der Egerländer* 6 (1956): 38–44; Johann Baptist Lehner, "Ein Pfarreienverzeichnis des Bistums Regensburg aus dem Jahre 1326," *Jahresbericht des Vereins zur Erforschung der Regensburger Diözesangeschichte* 2 (1927): 24–36; Johann Baptist Lehner, "Beiträge zur Kirchengeschichte des Egerlandes," *Jahresbericht des Vereins zur Erforschung der Regensburger Diözesangeschichte* 12 (1939): 79–211, on 94–111.

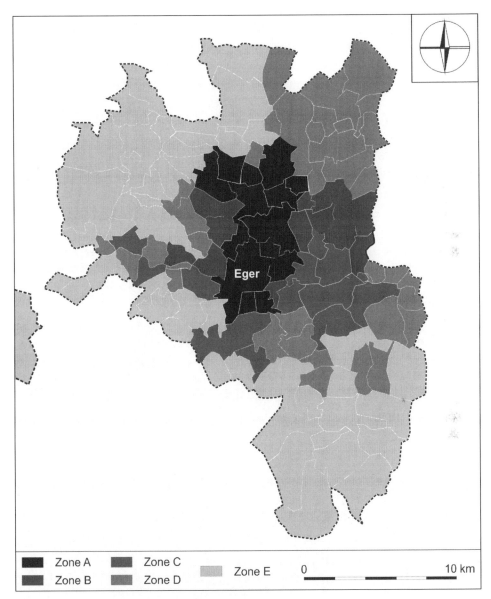

Figure 5.4. **Main ecological zones in the city-state of Cheb. The area of the reach of the Cheb land tax according to the 1438 register.**

Source: Cf. *app. 5.4.* Prepared by the author.

ical, pedological, and agroclimatic zones (from the agriculturally optimal zone A to the least favorable zone E; *figs. 3–4; 5.4*).[179]

The most favorable conditions for settlements in the focus area are in the fairly expansive Cheb Basin (271 km²). It is usually described as a continental climate, which characteristically has fairly hot summer months and very cold winters. The internal zonality of the Cheb Basin is greatly determined by the heterogenic geological subsoil, on which the soil quality is dependent. Overall, the Cheb Basin is made up of tertiary and quaternary sediments, the nature of which is dictated by the geological composition of the mountain range from which they were carried.[180] Ethnographic reports from the first third of the 19th century differentiated between peasants farming in clay-based (approximately zone A), sandy (B), and mixed (A) soils, as well as marshland. They also differentiated peasants farming in harsh, submountainous conditions (corresponding to zones D and E).[181]

Favorable agroclimatic conditions are offered by a belt of land from Cheb following the Ohře downriver with elevations of around 390–450 m (zones A and B). Agriculturally high-quality soils lay in the heart of this belt (zone A). The remaining parts of the Cheb Basin at higher elevations have a harsh and cooler climate with higher precipitation (zones C and D; elev. 450–550 m). An enclave running along the banks of the Ohře River westerly from Cheb, leading all the way to the Fichtel Mountains, had variable conditions. Considerably worse agricultural opportunities were offered by hilly

179 *App. 5.4.* Margita Kurpelová, Lubomír Coufal, and Jaroslav Čulík, *Agroklimatické podmienky ČSSR* (Bratislava: Príroda, 1975), esp. 252–253, map nr. 14; Jaromír Demek and Petr Mackovičin, eds., *Zeměpisný lexikon ČR. Hory a nížiny* (Brno: AOPK ČR,³ 2006); Emil Meynen and Josef Schmitüsen, *Handbuch der naturräumlichen Gliederung Deutschlands* (Remagen: Bundesanstalt für Landeskunde; Bad Godesberg: Bundesanstalt für Landeskunde und Raumforschung, 1953–1962).

180 Rudolf Käubler, *Die ländlichen Siedelungen des Egerlandes* (Leipzig: Verlag der Werksgemeinschaft, 1935). Also cf. Gretl Fischer, *Die Flurnamen des Gerichtsbezirkes Eger*, Sudetendeutsches Flurnamen-Buch 4 (Reichenberg: Kraus/Deutsche Gesellschaft der Wissenschaften und Künste für die Tschechoslowakis, 1941); Ernst Ettel, *Beiträge zur Siedlungsgeschichte des Egerer Kreises unter besonderer Berücksichtigung der Orts- und Flurformen*, Quellen und Erörterungen 4 (Pressath: Bodner / Otnant-Gesellschaft für Geschichte und Kultur in der Euregio Egrensis, 2004).

181 Sebastian Grüner and Alois John, *Über die ältesten Sitten und Gebräuche der Egerländer: 1825 für J. W. von Goethe niedergeschrieben*, Beiträge zur deutsch-böhmischen Volkskunde 4/1 (Prague: J. G. Calve, 1901), 62–63.

areas forming part of the Fichtel Mountains and the Upper Palatinate / Bohemian Forest (zone E; 550–650 m).

5.4 The market and consumption area of Cheb[182]

The question is: to what extent did the territory of the city-state of Cheb overlap with the area of the local city market? This is defined as the territory (1) from which the city was regularly supplied with food and raw materials, (2) which was an outlet for urban craft products, and (3) in which the rural population was intensively involved in services for the city (transport, mining). This market area formed one functional organism with the city, and their social, economic, and demographic characteristics were closely linked.[183] Within the zonality model of the economic hinterland of medieval towns, the area, on the one hand, was bounded by the immediate hinterland of the city, which was used directly by burghers living both *intra* and *extra muros*, and on the other hand, it extended into a wider market area, from which the town was irregularly supplied with selected raw materials and specific craft products from other cities.[184] In cities with larger consumer demands, the market and

---

182 Subchapter 5.4 is a substantially broadened version of Klír, "Rural credit," 119–121. © Routledge 2020. Reproduced by permission of Taylor & Francis Group.

183 Nový, "Hospodářský region," 397–399, 402–404; Franz Irsigler and Herbert Eiden, "Environs and hinterland: Cologne and Nuremberg in the Later Middle Ages," in *Trade, urban hinterlands and market integration c. 1300–1600*, ed. James A. Galloway, Centre for Metropolitan History. Working Papers Series 3 (London: Centre for Metropolitan History, Institute of Historical Research, 2000), 43–57, on 57; Piet J. Cruyningen and Erik Thoen, "Food supply, demand, and trade. Aspects of the economic relationship between town and countryside (Middle Ages – nineteenth century). Book introduction," in *Food supply, demand and trade. Aspects of the economic relationship between town and countryside (Middle Ages – nineteenth Century)*, ed. Piet J. van Cruyningen and Erik Thoen, 1–6. CORN 14 (Turnhout: Brepols, 2012).

184 E.g., Michel Pauly and Martin Uhrmacher, "Das Versorgungsgebiet der Stadt Luxemburg im späten Mittelalter," in *Städtische Wirtschaft im Mittelalter: Festschrift für Franz Irsigler zum 70. Geburtstag*, ed. Rudolf Holbach (Cologne: Böhlau, 2011), 211–254, on 212–213, 247–252; Thomas Hill, *Die Stadt und ihr Markt. Bremens Umlands- und Außenbeziehungen im Mittelalter (12.–15. Jahrhundert)*, Vierteljahrschrift für Sozial- und Wirtschaftsgeschichte. Beihefte 172 (Stuttgart: Steiner, 2004), 16–26; Irsigler and Eiden, "Environs and hinterland," 43–44; Christopher Dyer, "Trade, urban hinterlands and market integration,

consumption area was structured more complexly, with an accessible part that directly interacted with the city, and another part where contact was mediated by a network of market villages and smaller towns. In the former case, more or less all the direct agrarian producers came to the city market; in the latter, agrarian production was largely directed first to the transit market center and from there to the city market.[185]

Ideally, the complex of the local city market area was intended to embody and protect the "mile law" principle, but the geographical reality varied for each medieval city.[186] Historians therefore must define the spatial extent of the local market of a given city, recognize its structure, and trace its transformations over time.[187] Here, we endeavor only to produce a static reconstruction of the Cheb local market in the time period we are studying (1442–1456). We will rely on the data contained in the *City Court Records*, which recorded creditors' claims against debtors and, to a lesser extent, debtors' declarations of specific commitments, repayments, and guarantees (*Schuldprotokolle*; *Schuldenbücher / books of obligations*).[188]

Outside of important religious holidays, the Cheb city court convened relatively regularly on Mondays and Fridays and exceptionally on Wednesdays. A wide range of persons could turn to the court if they had claims against Cheb burghers—not only Cheb burghers themselves, burghers from other towns, or

1300–1600: A summing up," in *Trade, urban hinterlands and market integration c. 1300–1600*, ed. James A. Galloway, Centre for Metropolitan History. Working Papers Series 3 (London: Centre for Metropolitan History, Institute of Historical Research, 2000), 103–109, on 103.

185   E.g., Nový, "Hospodářský region," 406–407; Dyer, "Trade," 103.

186   Nový, "Hospodářský region," 402.

187   For the latest model reconstructions cf., e.g., Kate Giles and Christopher Dyer, eds., *Town and country in the Middle Ages: Contrasts, contacts, and interconnections, 1100–1500*, Monograph series. The Society for Medieval Archaeology 22 (Leeds: Taylor & Francis Group, 2005); Stephan R. Epstein, ed., *Town and country in Europe 1300–1800*, Themes in International Urban History 5 (Cambridge: Cambridge University Press, 2001); Thomas Holger Gräf and Katrin Keller, eds., *Städtelandschaft = Réseau urbain = Urban network: Städte im regionalen Kontext in Spätmittelalter und früher Neuzeit*, Städteforschung A 62 (Cologne: Böhlau, 2004); James A. Galloway, ed., *Trade, urban hinterlands and market integration c. 1300–1600*, Centre for Metropolitan History. Working Papers Series 3 (London: Centre for Metropolitan History, Institute of Historical Research, 2000); John S. Lee, *Cambridge and its economic region, 1450–1560* (Hertfordshire: University of Hertfordshire Press, 2001).

188   From the medieval period, several large books have been preserved from 1387–1496, with continual records beginning in 1405. Ar Cheb, books 894–900, *Schuldprotokolle 1387–1496*. Cf. Sturm, *Das Archiv*, 55–56.

Jews, but also servants of burghers or "subject" tenants from the countryside. The creditor first lodged the initial action, and if the claim was not paid, it was followed by the second and finally the third action, after which the pledge was forfeited or another remedial action was taken.[189] Notably, in the period under review, even relatively small debts (less than 10 Prague groschen) were dealt with in court.[190] The record was associated with a relatively low fee (4 hellers), which was ultimately to be paid by the defendant.[191]

When reconstructing the geographical scope of the local market in Cheb, we proceeded from the assumption that both the direct producers and suppliers of the city market and intermediaries from transit market settlements will appear in the court protocols. Of course, we only see part of the claims in the protocols, because only the unpaid were brought to court. However, the sample should be sufficiently representative. Among the 12,276 complaints from 1442–1456, we have identified a total of 257 (2.1%) in which the plaintiff came from a rural settlement, market village, or township, whether from Cheb territory or outside of it.[192] Of these, 165 were the primary complaint; the rest were repeated complaints. Among the plaintiffs it was possible to identify 133 unique persons, most of whom were demonstrably peasants (*tab. 5.1*). In the registers of the Cheb land tax, it was possible to find directly in the year of the complaint 61 plaintiffs who were peasants. Among the other plaintiffs, rural millers had a significant share (9% plaintiffs; 17% of complaints), and even parish priests were represented (2 people; 3 claims).

The specific cause of the creation of the debt can be found only exceptionally in the protocols—three times unpaid wages appeared (*lidtlohn*), twice an unspecified commercial transaction, twice loaned money, once likely an unpaid hereditary share, twice the debt arose from the sale of grains (oats, barley) and once dill. Nevertheless, a total of 47 primary claims (29.7%) were brought

189 The time periods were set by a resolution of the council from 1455. Ar Cheb, book 898, *Schuldprotokolle 1452–1470*, p. 129 (record 2 May 1455).

190 Ar Cheb, book 894, *Schuldprotokolle 1387–1416*, p. 1–3.

191 Ar Cheb, book 894, *Schuldprotokolle 1387–1416*, p. 3.

192 We have left aside the claims from cities like Prague, Würzburg, Pilsen, Loket, Tirschenreuth, Kemnitz, and others, because they belonged to the wider market circle of Cheb. Claims from outside of Cheb by place of origin were recorded in the books systematically in the first claim; in repeated claims that was no longer the rule. In the analysis, we carefully assured that the new burghers from the countryside were not counted among the collection of claimants from outside of Cheb (cf. *Chap.* 24).

Table 5.1. **Receivables of the complaints outside of Cheb discussed before the Cheb city court in 1442–1456.**

		Primary complaints					
		Number	%	Persons	%	Localities	%
Cheb territory	village or hamlets	111	67.3	86	64.7	55	66.3
	transit market centers	15	9.1	13	9.8	4	4.8
Outside of the territory	village or hamlets	22	13.3	20	15.0	16	19.3
	transit market centers	17	10.3	14	10.5	8	9.6
Total		165	100.0	133	100.0	83	100.0

Source: Ar Cheb, books 897 and 898, *Schuldprotokolle 1439–1452* and *Schuldprotokolle 1452–1470.*

against burghers, who, according to their name, performed the butcher's trade or, according to the *1446 City Tax Register,* owned a butcher's bench (*tab. 5.2*).[193] Six actions were related to Cheb millers.

The monetary amount of the debt, most often in Prague groschen, was listed in 158 primary complaints (*tab. 5.1*). A total of 61% of the debts can be considered to be small, not exceeding one threescore of Prague groschen. Another 20% of the debts was between one or two threescore groschen. Receivables from the Cheb butchers had the highest representation in the category from one-half to two threescore groschen. Since the monetary value of a cow around the middle of the 15th century in the city-state of Cheb was between 50 and 55 Prague groschen, a calf about 10 groschen, a sheep roughly 7–8 groschen, and one Cheb "kar" of oats (ca 3 hl) was purchased for approximately 10 groschen,[194] a large proportion of the receivables may be regarded as a reflection of usual local trade in agricultural, especially livestock products. The amount of defendant claims also tells us how much cash the peasants had received at one time.

Among the places of origin of the complaints from outside of Cheb, we identified 71 rural settlements, of which 55 were directly in Cheb territory, and

193   Ar Cheb, book 1424, *Losungsbuch 1446.*
194   Cf. *Chap. 11.4; 13.2; 14.6.*

Table 5.2. Amount of the debt with the claims of those accused by plaintiffs from outside of Cheb before the Cheb city court in 1442–1456.

Amount of debt (Prague groschen)	Primary complaints			
	Number	%	Cheb "butchers"	%*
7–30	50	31.6	12	25.5
31–60	47	29.7	17	36.2
61–120	31	19.6	12	25.5
121–300	23	14.6	6	12.8
300–3,600	7	4.4	0	0.0
Total	158	100.0	47	100.0

Source: From Klír, "Rural credit," 119, Tab. 9.3. © Routledge 2020. Reproduced by permission of Taylor & Francis Group. Data according to Ar Cheb, books 897 and 898, *Schuldprotokolle 1439–1452* and *Schuldprotokolle 1452–1470.*
Notes: * – share within the monetary category mentioned.

12 localities, which can be considered small market centers (4 in Cheb territory).[195] The mapping of all these places shows the extent and internal zonality of the Cheb local market area (*fig. 5.5*). It is quite clear that Cheb was supplied with agricultural products directly from an area extending 12–18 km from the town. At this distance, at the same time, a belt of transit market centers began to form around them, creating their own catchment area. Most of the city-state of Cheb territory was directly connected to the Cheb market; only the northern part at the foot of the Elster Mountains and the southern part at the Upper Palatinate / Bohemian Forest were connected via transit centers. Overall, we can say that the area of the local Cheb market was asymmetrical, directly or indirectly encompassing the entire territory of the city-state of Cheb and extending along the Ohře River, especially into the Loket region in Bohemia.

195　We included in the category of transit places those that formally acquired the status of market village or township not only in the Late Middle Ages but also in the Early Modern Period.

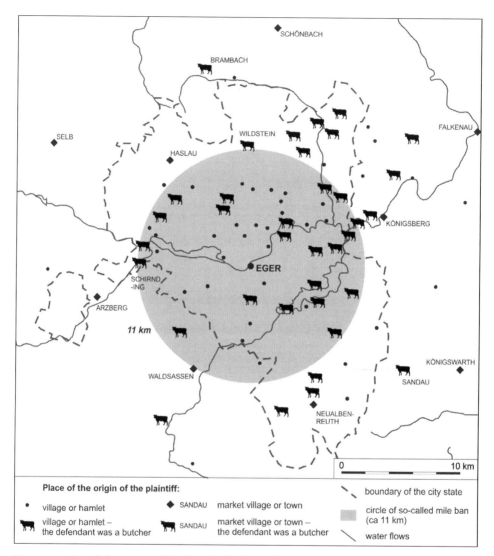

Figure 5.5. Spatial extent of the local Cheb market according to the place of origin of the creditors outside of Cheb, who sued Cheb burghers in 1442–1456.

Source: From Klír, "Rural credit," 126, fig. 9.8. © Routledge 2020. Reproduced by permission of Taylor & Francis Group. Data according to Ar Cheb, books 897 and 898, *Schuldprotokolle 1439–1452* and *Schuldprotokolle 1452–1470*.

Notes: Cf. *tab. 5.1.*

5.5 The size of rural settlements

The stability or changes in the number of landholdings in settlements was essential to the dynamics of socioeconomic stratification. The numbers of Cheb landholdings based on tax registers from the 15th century was reconstructed by W. Heisinger at five-year intervals for 101 settlements. We may accept its results after discarding certain insufficiently documented settlements (*figs. 5.6–5.7*).[196]

Settlements in the city-state of Cheb proved to be remarkably stable in the 15th century. None of them were abandoned, and the number of landholdings in most settlements remained approximately the same for the entire period. In terms of general tendencies, between 1392/1395 and 1438, the number of landholdings gradually fell by 10%, while later it stagnated or rose slightly (*fig. 5.6*).[197] This trend is fully in line with the development usually documented in regions between the Alps and northern Germany, where the number of peasant landholdings fell in the last quarter of the 14th century, subsequently stagnating and then rising as of the last quarter of the 15th century.[198]

Another important indicator is the size of the settlement itself, which informs us of the nature of peasant communities, their fragmentation, the mutual cohesion of their members, and also the chances of migration between settlements. From the point of view of the number of landholdings in the city-state of Cheb, small settlements predominated (*fig. 5.7*).[199] Small settlements with no more than ten landholdings accounted for approximately 70% of all

---

196   *App. 5.6a–b.* Heisiner, "Die Egerer Klosteuerbücher," 125–165; Tabelle 8; Klír et al., *Knihy*, 124–135.

197   *App. 5.6a; App. 5.5.* Cf. Klír, "Procesy pustnutí." The abandonment process in the last quarter of the 14th century only affected the mountainous areas.

198   For the Zurich region, see Konrad Wanner, *Siedlungen, Kontinuität und Wüstungen im nördlichen Kanton Zürich (9.-15. Jahrhundert)*, Geist und Werk der Zeiten. Arbeiten aus dem Historischen Seminar der Universität Zürich 64 (Bern: P. Lang, 1984), 204–226, 232–234, 238–246, 265–267; Walter Bauernfeind, *Materielle Grundstrukturen im Spätmittelalter und der Frühen Neuzeit. Preisentwicklung und Agrarkonjunktur am Nürnberger Getreidemarkt von 1399 bis 1670*, Nürnberger Werkstücke zur Stadt- und Landesgeschichte 50 (Neustadt a. d. Aisch: Korn und Berg, 1993), 138–159; for the surroundings of Leipzig see Uwe Schirmer, *Das Amt Grimma 1485–1548. Demographische, wirtschaftliche und soziale Verhältnisse in einem kursächsischen Amt am Ende des Mittelalters und zu Beginn der Neuzeit*, Schriften der Rudolf-Kötzschke-Gesellschaft 2 (Beucha: Sax Verlag, 1996), 27–32.

199   *App. 5.6a.* On Bohemia at that time, cf. Boháč, "Vesnice."

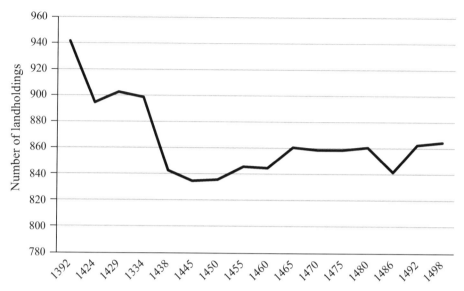

Figure 5.6. Total number of landholdings in 101 researched settlements in the city-state of Cheb from the end of the 14ᵗʰ century to the end of the 15ᵗʰ century.

Source: Data according to Heisinger, "Die Egerer Klosteuerbücher," Tabelle 8.
Note: For certain settlements for which a complete description has not survived, the number of landholdings has been interpolated according to the tax register nearest in time.

Cheb settlements throughout the 15ᵗʰ century. Medium large and large villages with more than 15 landholdings accounted for just 6–10% of the total number. However, the small number of landholdings was often compensated by their farmland size, so even seemingly small settlements had relatively large economic resources available to them. We receive a bit of a different image from the perspective of peasant families. Overall, 60–70% of landholdings lay in settlements of 6–15 landholdings in size and just 10–15% in small settlements of up to 5 landholdings, and the same amount also applied to settlements comprising 16 or more landholdings (*fig. 5.8*).[200]

200   *App. 5.6b.*

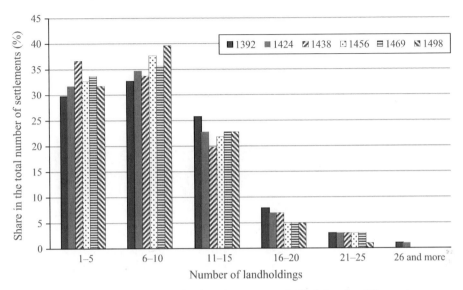

Figure 5.7. Size of settlements in the city-state of Cheb in the 15th century. Relative overview.

Source: Data according to Heisinger, "Die Egerer Klosteuerbücher," Tabelle 8.

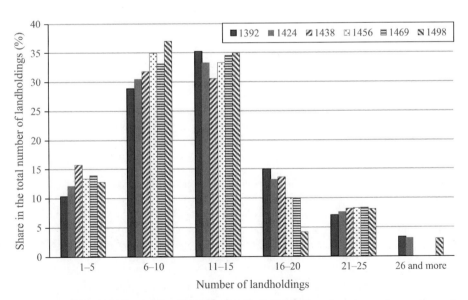

Figure 5.8. Distribution of landholdings in settlements of various size categories in the city-state of Cheb in the 15th century. Relative overview.

Source: Data according to Heisinger, "Die Egerer Klosteuerbücher," Tabelle 8.

5.6 Agricultural system and agrarian cycle

A three-field fallow system was used in the late medieval and modern period in the city-state of Cheb.[201] This effective system, based on the spatial rotation of the agricultural use of land and the synchronization of work activities, gave the soil time to regenerate and divided the workload and harvest risk evenly, at the same time leaving a considerable part of the farmland fallow for cattle grazing. The natural conditions in the city-state of Cheb did not allow all of the land resources to be used as arable land, and so large areas were left as meadows or permanent common pasture.[202]

The concrete agricultural strategies used in the city-state of Cheb were captured by members of a commission preparing materials for the *Theresian Cadastre* in the mid-18th century and economic reports from the first half of the 19th century.[203] The fundamental features of the regional agriculture practices of Cheb in the period of serfdom were described also by Cheb magistrate and criminal chief inspector, Joseph Sebastian Grüner, in an ethnographic manu-script for J. W. Goethe.[204] A special method of ploughing exceptionally narrow strips composed of just four furrows, 110–130 cm wide, was typical. In this respect, the city-state of Cheb was similar to Franconian and Bavarian regions, where such narrow cultivated strips were standard.[205] Vernacular researcher,

201   Alois John, *Oberlohma: Geschichte und Volkskunde eines egerländer Dorfes*, Beiträge zur deutsch-böhmischen Volkskunde IV/2 (Prague: J.G. Calve'sche k.u.k. Hof- u. Universi-täts- Buchhandlung (Josef Koch), 1903), 116–120; Alois John, "Saat und Ernte im Egerlande (1896)," in *Egerländer Heimatbuch. Gesammelte Aufsätze*, ed. Alois John (Eger: Selbstverlag, 1907), 207–217; Alois John, *Sitte, Brauch und Volksglaube im deutschen Westböhmen*, Bei-träge zur deutsch-böhmischen Volkskunde 6 (Reichenberg: Kraus, ²1924), 183–223. Cf. also Singer, *Das Landbuch*, 85.

202   Václav Černý, *Hospodářské instrukce. Přehled zemědělských dějin v době patrimonijního vel-kostatku v XV. – XVI. století* [Wirtschaftsinstruktionen – Übersicht einer Geschichte der Landwirtschaft zur Zeit der Patrimonialherrschaft im XV.–XIX. Jahrh. Les instructions économiques – Esquisse d'une histoire de l'agriculture pendant le régime seigneurial aux XVe–XIXe siècles], Prameny a základy vydávané Československou akademií zemědělskou A 2 (Prague: Československá akademie zemědělská, 1930), esp. 31–39; Beck, *Unterfinning*, 56–60, 96–139.

203   Pekař, *České katastry*, 204–205, 217; Černý, *Hospodářské instrukce*, 131.

204   Grüner and John, *Über die ältesten Sitten*, 62–74. Cf. also Hermann Braun, "Sitte und Brauchtum im Jahreskreis," in *Eger und das Egerland: Volkskunst und Brauchtum*, ed. Lorenz Schreiner (Munich: Lang Müller, 1988), 371–395.

205   E.g., Beck, *Unterfinning*, 125–126.

Alois John, informed us of further details of the distribution of agricultural labor in the last third of the 19th century, enabling us to reconstruct the traditional agrarian cycle.[206] The appearing dates should be considered merely for orientation, since the reality of each year was naturally different.[207] What is clear, though, is that unlike agroclimatically optimum areas of Bohemia, springtime work in the fields was delayed by about a month and the beginning of the harvest time by fourteen days, while conversely autumnal work began and ended earlier.[208]

Our reconstruction of the agrarian cycle was not just an end in itself, because all important moments of life both in the countryside and in the city correlated with it (see *chap. 9–13*). In the Late Middle Ages, city council accounting closed with the beginning of the harvest and the sale of new grain, and the new economic year began (St. James' Day). After September's ploughing had ended and winter crops were sown, land rents in grain were made to the landlord (Michaelmas). At the very end of the agricultural year, with the end of grazing on the commons, the slaughter of cattle, the departure of shepherds, and changes in servants, the land tax was raised (St. Martin's Day). These dates in the city-state of Cheb aligned with those in the Loket region, but they differed from inland Bohemia, where the agrarian cycle was three weeks longer.[209]

5.7 Mining

The Cheb Basin is surrounded on all sides by ore-rich mountains of importance in Europe—the Ore Mountains, Slavkov Forest, the Upper Palatinate

206 *App. 5.7.* John, *Oberlohma*, 116–122; John, *Sitte*, esp. 183–198; John, "Saat"; Alois John, "Das egerländer Volkstum und die Ursachen seines Verfalls (1896)," in *Egerländer Heimatsbuch, Gesammelte Aufsätze*, ed. Alois John (Eger: Selbstverlag, 1907), 234–242.

207 Rudolf Brázdil et al., "Climate variability and changes in the agricultural cycle in the Czech Lands from the sixteenth century to the present," *Theoretical and Applied Climatology* (2018): 1–21.

208 Cf. Klír, *Osídlení*, 62–79.

209 E.g., Rudolf Schreiber, *Das Elbogener Urbar der Grafen Schlick von 1525*, Sudetendeutsches historisches Archiv 1 (Prague: Deutsche Gesellschaft der Wissenschaften und Künste für die Tschechoslowakische Republik, 1934), 17.

/ Bohemian Forest, and the Fichtel Mountains.[210] In the Middle Ages, there were primary and secondary deposits of tin, silver, copper, and iron ores and also deposits of gold. This raises the question of the extent to which mining might have influenced the late medieval city-state of Cheb and whether it distorted its socioeconomic structure.

In the course of territorialization at the turn of the 15th century, the lienholder and the city of Cheb were unable to maintain power over any of the mining districts in the territory of the so-called historical Cheb region.[211] Rich fields of tin ore in the Fichtel Mountains around Wunsiedel and Thiersheim and iron ores between Arzberg and Röthenbach were controlled by the Burgraves of Nuremberg;[212] the monastery in Waldsassen controlled the iron ore fields around and between Neualbenreuth and Altmugel, where gold mining also took place to some extent. Nevertheless, Cheb held a key position in the distribution of certain products, thanks to extensive privileges and also to direct links to the commercial centers of Nuremberg and Leipzig.[213] The commer-

---

210   Cf. Franz Michael Ress, "Geschichte und wirtschaftliche Bedeutung der oberpfälzischen Eisenindustrie von den Anfängen bis zur Zeit des 30jährigen Krieges," *Verhandlungen des Historischen Vereins für Oberpfalz und Regensburg* 91 (1950): 5–186; Mathias Hensch, "Montanarchäologie in der Oberpfalz – von der Forschung vergessen?," *Bericht der bayerischen Bodendenkmalpflege* 43/44 (2002/2003): 273–287; Norbert Hirschmann, "Zum bergbaulichen Verbrauchszentrum Oberpfalz im 16. Jahrhundert: Möglichkeiten und Grenzen einer Analyse anhand von Zoll- und Mautakten sowie verwandtem Quellenmaterial," in *Bergbaureviere als Verbrauchszentren*, ed. Ekkehard Westermann, Vierteljahrschrift für Sozial- und Wirtschaftsgeschichte, Beihefte 130 (Stuttgart: Steiner, 1997), 59–84; Helmut Wolf, *Eisenerzbergbau und Eisenverhüttung in der Oberpfalz von den Anfängen bis zur Gegenwart*, Hefte zur bayerischen Geschichte und Kultur 3 (Munich: Haus der Bayerischen Geschichte, 1986); Reinhard Höllerich, "Der historische Bergbau im Rehauer Gebiet: Zur Rekonstruktion einer Bergbaulandschaft," *Archiv für die Geschichte von Oberfranken* 96 (2016): 71–97; Jiří Majer, *Těžba cínu ve Slavkovském lese v 16. století* [Die Zinnförderung im Kaiserwald im 16. Jahrhundert] (Prague: Národní technické muzeum, 1970); Herbert Heinritz, "Bergbau in Oberfranken," published May 11, 2009, in *Historisches Lexikon Bayerns*, www.historisches-lexikon-bayerns.de/Lexikon/Bergbau_in_Oberfranken; Wolfgang Schwabenicky, *Der mittelalterliche Bergbau im Erzgebirgsvorland und im westlichen Erzgebirge* (Chemnitz: Klaus Gumnior, 2009); Hauke Kenzler, *Die hoch- und spätmittelalterliche Besiedlung des Erzgebirges: Strategien zur Kolonisation eines landwirtschaftlichen Ungunstraumes*, Bamberger Schriften zur Archäologie des Mittelalters und der Neuzeit 4 (Bonn: Habelt, 2012), 162–164.

211   Cf. Klír et al., *Knihy*, 24–25, 40–41.
212   Cf. Singer, *Das Landbuch*, 93–96.
213   Cf. Majer, *Těžba*, 10–11.

cial significance of Cheb is illustrated by merchant and benefactor Sigmund Wann from Wunsiedel (c. 1395–1469), who accumulated considerable wealth in his hometown by producing tinplate but moved to Cheb in 1446 to further develop his commercial activities.[214]

In the 15th century, bordering on territory where the Cheb land tax was collected, there were mining districts on the banks of the Röslau near Arzberg (iron ore), in a district near Neualbenreuth (gold and iron ore), and further afield, in districts on the southwest edge of the Slavkov Forest near Kynžvart (tin and silver ore). Although mining is documented in all of these districts in the 15th century, it is not particularly intensive and is overshadowed by the later mining boom towards the end of the Late Middle Ages and the beginning of the Early Modern Period.[215] The boom hit the Fichtel Mountains and the Ore Mountains first in the 1460s–1470s and then the Slavkov Forest in the first half of the 16th century.[216]

Mining regions provided peasants a chance to supplement their income in various areas of non-agrarian production, which permitted the growth of "sub-peasant" groups. In the same manner as a well-documented situation in the Early Modern Period, peasants from settlements in the parish of Schirnding near Arzberg, in the parish of Neualbenreuth, and then from settlements scattered between Arzberg and Marktredwitz were able to take advantage of this opportunity.[217] Given the intermingling of Cheb power and the power of the Nuremberg burgraves and the monastery in Waldsassen, only some peas-

---

214 Sabina Zehentmeier, "Sigmund Wann (um 1400–1469). Unternehmer, Handelsherr, Bankier und Stifter," in *Religion Kultur Geschichte: Beiträge zur historischen Kulturforschung vom Mittelalter bis zur Gegenwart; Festschrift für Klaus Guth zum 80. Geburtstag*, ed. Heidrun Alzheimer, Michael Imhof, and Ulrich Wirz (Petersberg: Michael Imhof, 2015), 63–74.

215 On mining in the late Middle Ages, cf. Reinhard H. Seitz and Helmut Wolf, "Zum Erzbergbau im Stiftsland Waldsassen," *Acta Albertina Ratisbonensia* 31 (1971): 15–56, on 24–29; Ernst Schmidtill, *Zur Geschichte des Eisenerzbergbaus im südlichen Fichtelgebirge*, Die Plassenburg 18 (Bayreuth: Freunde der Plassenburg EV, 1963).

216 Jiří Majer, "Konjunkturen und Krisen im böhmischen Silberbergbau des Spätmittelalters und der Frühen Neuzeit: Zu ihren Ursachen und Folgen," in *Konjunkturen im europäischen Bergbau in vorindustrieller Zeit. Festschrift für Ekkehard Westermann zum 60. Geburtstag*, ed. Christoph Bartels, Vierteljahrschrift für Sozial- und Wirtschaftsgeschichte. Beihefte 155 (Stuttgart: Steiner 2000), 73–83, on 78–79; Majer, *Těžba*, 7–16; Schwabenicky, *Der mittelalterliche Bergbau*; Klír, *Zánik a pustnutí*, exkurz V.

217 For a discussion on the settlements in the parish of Neualbenreuth, cf. Käubler, *Die ländlichen Siedelungen*, 40–43; Heisinger, "Die Egerer Klosteuerbücher," 118–119.

ants in these settlements paid land tax, and in addition, the landholdings there were not described in detail in the 1438 register or the 1456 *Taxation Book*.[218] For this reason, we are not using these settlements for analysis of socio-economic mobility.

In summary, in the case of the settlements and peasant communities that we study in the city-state of Cheb, the influence of mining activities on the socioeconomic structure in the Late Middle Ages may be ignored. Overall, it can be said that Cheb's urban territory had a purely agrarian character, and the economic relationship between town and country had a traditional form.

5.8 Early forerunner of the Little Ice Age

When characterizing the wider historical context, consideration of climatic variability cannot be avoided, since this influenced the level of agricultural production and thereby also of demographic and economic development. A detailed and still applicable description of climatic characteristics during the analyzed period for the Bohemian Crown Lands, including the Cheb region, was presented by Rudolf Brázdil and Oldřich Kotyza.[219] They based their reconstruction on the interpretation of the temperature and precipitation extremes for each season according to narrative written sources (1000–1500). Locally limited data for Bohemia and Moravia was compared critically with

---

218   Namely, Schirnding, Dietersgrün, Oschwitz, Seußen, Neualbenreuth. Klír et al., *Knihy*, 225–232, appendix II.

219   For a complete overview and with a list of interpreted narrative reports, see Rudolf Brázdil and Oldřich Kotyza, *History of Weather and Climate in the Czech Lands 1: Period 1000–1500*, Zürcher Geographische Schriften 62 (Zürich: ETH, 1995), esp. 120–151, 161–165, 169–175; in summary form see Rudolf Brázdil and Oldřich Kotyza, "Kolísání klimatu v českých zemích v první polovině našeho tisíciletí" [Climate fluctuation in the Czech lands during the first part of the last millennium], *Archeologické rozhledy* 49 (1997): 663–699, esp. 669–676, 686–690. Cf. also Rudolf Brázdil and Oldřich Kotyza, "Současná historická klimatologie a možnosti jejího využití v historickém výzkumu" [Contemporary historical climatology and possibilities of its utilization in the historical research], in *Historie a interdisciplinární výzkum*, Časopis Matice moravské, Supplementum 1 (Brno: Matice moravská, 2002), 17–59.

reports from adjacent areas in Europe and against a backdrop of data from farther afield in Europe.[220]

An analysis of narrative sources has concurrently demonstrated that 1400–1419 tended to be cool and wet, with 1420 considered to be a warm anomaly at the start of the hot and dry decade of the 1420s. The following five decades around the mid-15th century (1430–1479) were extremely cool and wet and so are spoken of as one of the first and actually palpable blows of the so-called Little Ice Age.[221] The 1430s in particular came as a shock to contemporaneous observers; later the temperature considered "normal" probably shifted slightly, but even so, the chronicles' accounts of cold winters remained dramatic. According to climatic reconstructions, the cool fluctuation culminated during the decade of the 1450s (fig. 5.9).[222]

In overall comparison with other decades during the period of 1000–1500, the following can be concluded:[223]

+ Between 1430 and 1460, cold winter months predominated, most occurring in the decade of the 1450s. Winters identified as harsh followed one after another between 1439 and 1444, and 1454 and 1460.
+ The summer months conversely were characteristically cool, especially during the decade of the 1450s. Wet summers were extremely abundant in the decade of the 1450s.
+ An unusual number of cool springs accumulated in the decade of the 1440s.
+ The decade of the 1450s had an exceptional number of cool autumns.

---

220   Cf. the recently published Rüdiger Glaser and Dirk Riemann, "A thousand-year record of temperature variations for Germany and Central Europe based on documentary data," *Journal of Quaternary Science* 24 (2009): 437–449; Rüdiger Glaser and Dirk Riemann, "Klimageschichte im späten Mittelalter und in der frühen Neuzeit in Südwestdeutschland im Kontext der mitteleuropäischen Klimaentwicklung," in *Landnutzung und Landschaftsentwicklung im deutschen Südwesten: zur Umweltgeschichte im späten Mittelalter und in der frühen Neuzeit*, ed. Lorenz Sönke and Peter Rückert, Veröffentlichungen der Kommission für geschichtliche Landeskunde in Baden-Württemberg, Reihe B 173 (Stuttgart: W. Kohlhammer, 2009), 219–232.

221   Cf. also Kelly Morgan, "Debating the Little Ice Age," *Journal of Interdisciplinary History* 45 (2014): 57–68; Ulf Büntgen and Lena Hellman, "The little ice age in scientific perspective: Cold spells and caveats," *Journal of Interdisciplinary History* 44 (2014): 353–368; Jean M. Grove, *The Little Ice Age* (London: Routledge, 1988).

222   Brázdil and Kotyza, *History*, esp. 161–165; Brázdil and Kotyza, "Kolísání klimatu," 671–676.

223   Brázdil and Kotyza, *History*, esp. 161–165; Brázdil and Kotyza, "Kolísání klimatu," 671–676.

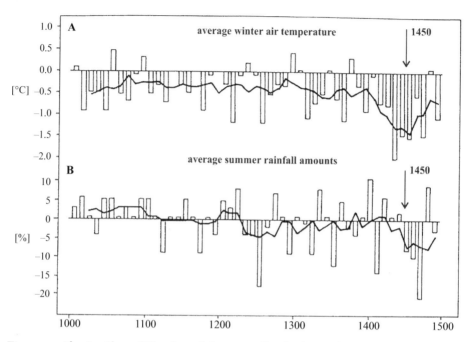

Figure 5.9. Fluctuation of the decade's anomalies (columns) of winter air temperatures (A) and summer precipitation sums (B) in 1000–1499. Model made from measurements recorded at Prague-Klementinum observatory.

Source: From Brázdil and Kotyza, "Kolísání klimatu," 677, fig. 6. The core of our reference period is indicated with an arrow.

Note: Smoothed by running averages of five decades each (dashed line). Reference period 1851–1950.

The cool spate around the middle of the 15th century in Central Europe began with a series of very long and harsh winters in the 1430s. For Bohemia, four harsh winters are confirmed in 1431–1432, 1432–1433, 1434–1435, and 1436–1437. More recent Cheb chronicles recorded recollections of the exceptionally long, snowy, and icy winters of 1429–1430 and 1450–1451.[224]

The cooling around the mid-15th century could have had fatal consequences for settlements protruding into agroclimatic border zones, whereas elsewhere the period was quite easily overcome, which was also the case in the Cheb region.[225]

---

224 Brázdil and Kotyza, *History*, 125, 132.
225 For instance, in the mid-15th century a large village of Spindelbach on the ridges of the Ore Mountains (elev. 800–880 m), disappeared. Tomáš Klír, "Zaniklé středověké vsi ve výz-

5.9 Mortality crisis

The mobility of the late medieval peasantry was largely influenced by demographic factors, especially long-term population stagnation. Generally speaking, by the 15th century the outbreaks of plague were losing their vigor as the population was becoming immune, although a high death rate probably continued in children. It is important to address how outbreaks of plague were distributed in our period of interest and how severe they were. Overviews produced for Nuremberg may be applied, supplemented by information available concerning Bohemia.[226] In the future, it will certainly be possible to provide a chronological and quantitatively detailed report on Cheb itself, whose demographic development should be captured in the city tax registers that have been kept continuously since 1390.[227]

The main waves of plague usually hit both the Nuremberg region and Bohemia alike, but often with a year's delay. It is essential for our study that the mortality crisis that struck all of transalpine Europe in 1437–1439 barely touched the city-state of Cheb. The following fifteen-year period, which represents the core of our interest, was fairly calm in demographic terms, with probably just one weak wave of plague washing over the region in 1450 and 1462.

kumném záměru Ústavu pro archeologii Univerzity Karlovy v Praze. Zaniklý Spindelbach (Krušné hory), Kří a Hol (střední Čechy)" [Research of Deserted Medieval Villages Conducted by the Institute of Archaeology at Charles University in Prague], in *Wieś zaginiona. Stan i perspektywy badań*, ed. Przemysław Nocuń, Agnieszka Przybyła-Dumin, and Krzysztof Fokt, Monografie i materiały MGPE 5 (Chorzów: Muzeum "Górnośląski Park Etnograficzny w Chorzowie," 2016), 17–59, on 36.

226   *App. 5.8.* Bauernfeind, *Materielle Grundstrukturen*; Eduard Maur, "Příspěvek k demografické problematice předhusitských Čech (1346–1419)" [Ein Beitrag zur demographischen Problematik Böhmens in vorhussitischer Zeit (1346–1419)], in *Acta Universitatis Carolinae – Phil. et Hist., Studia historica* 34 (Prague: Univerzita Karlova, 1989), 7–71; Eduard Maur, "Obyvatelstvo českých zemí ve středověku," in *Dějiny obyvatelstva českých zemí*, ed. Ludmila Fialová et al. (Prague: Mladá ronta, 1996), 35–73, on 60–64; Petr Čornej, "Epidemie a kalamity v letech 1419–1471 očima českých kronikářů," *Documenta Pragensia* 7 (1987): 193–224; Josef Macek, *Jagellonský věk v českých zemích (1471–1526) 1. Hospodářská základna a moc* (Prague: Academia, 1992), 50–62; David Ch. Mengel, "A Plague on Bohemia? Mapping the Black Death," *Past and Present* 211 (2011): 3–34.

227   Cf. Klír, "Procesy pustnutí," 723.

5.10 Agricultural production and prices

From the viewpoint of agrarian history, changing grain prices are the ideal periodization criteria for following economic development, since they reflect the level of agricultural production (i.e., supply) on the one hand, and the contemporary demographic situation on the other hand. The approaches of Wilhelm Abel formulated between the 1930s and the 1950s, while having been criticized in many respects, have been adopted for transalpine Europe; Abel identified important periods or secular cycles over a long timescale, which can be classified as (1) agrarian growth with a higher number of inhabitants, higher demand, and relatively higher prices for agricultural products and (2) agrarian depressions (crises) caused primarily by a lower demographic level and relatively high wages and prices of non-agricultural products.[228]

The history of transalpine Europe as a whole is divided up according to convention, into the growth periods of the High Middle Ages, the depression of the Late Middle Ages, and renewed growth at the very end of the Late Middle Ages, peaking at the price revolution of the second third of the 16th century.[229] While there is not much doubt concerning the main development tendencies, there seem to be extreme differences in the precise course of events both in shorter time segments and also in various regions. For instance, while in upper and central Germany, the number of inhabitants, agricultural production, and grain prices fell dramatically around 1380, the same did not occur in Silesia

---

228 Wilhelm Abel, *Agrarkrisen und Agrarkonjunktur. Eine Geschichte der Land- und Ernährungswirtschaft Mitteleuropas seit dem hohen Mittelalter* (Hamburg, Berlin: Parey, ³1978), 13–26; Wilhelm Abel, *Strukturen und Krisen der spätmittelalterlichen Wirtschaft*, Quellen und Forschungen zur Agrargeschichte 32 (Stuttgart: Fischer, 1980). Discussion summarized, for instance, by Achilles, *Landwirtschaft*, 2–4, 63–75. More recently, e.g., see Harry Kitsikopoulos, "Introduction," in *Agrarian change and crisis in Europe, 1200–1500*, ed. Harry Kitsikopoulos, Routledge Research in Medieval Studies 1 (New York: Routledge 2011), 1–22.

229 Cf. articles in Michael North, ed., *Geldumlauf, Währungssysteme und Zahlungsverkehr in Nordwesteuropa 1300–1800*, Beiträge zur Geldgeschichte der späten Hansezeit, Quellen und Darstellungen zur hansischen Geschichte 35 (Cologne, Vienna: Böhlau, 1989). Also, see esp. Rainer Metz, *Geld, Währung und Preisentwicklung. Der Niederrheinraum im europäischen Vergleich 1350–1800*, Schriftenreihe des Instituts für Bankhistorische Forschungen 14 (Frankfurt a. M.: Knapp, 1990).

until 1425, due to external factors.[230] In both areas, the depression passed in the closing decades of the 15th century.

Of course, the contraction of the agrarian sector did not immediately mean a deterioration in the economic position of the peasantry, since due to various compensation factors, their income could even rise. Models of the peasant economy showed that in the period of the so-called agrarian crisis, the efficiency of agricultural production and peasant monetary income were able to improve. It depended on the direction of transformation of agricultural production. A decisive role was played by institutional factors such as local agrarian institutions and the severity of landlord restrictions. If the transformation was successful, it presented the potential for increasing the part of rent that was levied in cash, as well as according to the level of income, not according to the area of cultivated land or grain yields.[231] We have good reason to mention this issue, as the imposition of the Cheb land tax around the year 1400 fits only too well into this scheme and also indicates a profound transformation of the Cheb countryside in the Late Middle Ages.

Although Cheb's written sources containing data on prices are rich, they have not yet been analyzed.[232] Therefore, we lack a precise picture of the development of agricultural production, the significance of non-agrarian activities, and population development tendencies, nor do we have lists of the prices of key commodities. Knowledge from neighboring regions must be applied here too for basic orientation.

230   Richard Charles Hoffmann, *Land, liberties, and lordship in a late medieval countryside: Agrarian structures and change in a Duchy of Wroclaw*, The Middle Ages Series (Philadelphia, PA: University of Pennsylvania Press, 1989), 273–369.

231   Frank Konersmann, "Von Betriebsgrössen zu Wirtschaftspraktiken: Die Betriebsgrössenfrage in der deutschen Agrar- und Sozialgeschichte," in *Ländliche Gesellschaften in Deutschland und Frankreich, 18.–19. Jahrhundert*, ed. Reiner Prass, Jürgen Schlumbohm, Gérard G. Béaur, and Christophe Duhamelle, Veröffentlichungen des Max-Planck-Instituts für Geschichte 187 (Göttingen: Vandenhoeck & Ruprecht, 2003), 125–143; Achilles, "Überlegungen"; Achilles, *Landwirtschaft*, 78–82; Hubert Freiburg, "Agrarkonjunktur und Agrarstruktur in vorindustrieller Zeit. Die Aussagekraft der säkularen Wellen der Preise und Löhne im Hinblick auf die Entwicklung der bäuerlichen Einkommen," *Vierteljahrschrift für Sozial- und Wirtschaftsgeschichte* 64 (1977): 289–327. For the Bohemian environment, cf. Čechura, "Teorie"; Jaroslav Čechura, "Mor, krize a husitská revoluce" [Die Pest, die Krise und die hussitische Revolution], *Český časopis historický* 92 (1994): 286–303, in synoptic form, see Čechura, *Sedláci*, 17–61.

232   Klír et al., *Knihy*, 40–50, 60–65.

Thanks to Walter Bauernfeind's dissertation on Bayreuth, a quantity of unusually high-quality information on central Franconia is at our disposal.[233] Unfortunately, data regarding Bohemian regions in the second half of the 14th century and the 15th century are mainly just a fragment, allowing at most a comparison of some isolated points.[234] A certain substitute exists in the form of Richard C. Hoffmann's comprehensive study of the Duchy of Wrocław.[235]

Central Franconia is relevant for the city-state of Cheb. Written sources for these areas were critically analyzed using sophisticated statistical methods to compensate for the weaknesses of Wilhelm Abel's mechanical approaches.[236] In his dissertation, Bauernfeind was not satisfied with the simple assembly of a series of grain prices for Nuremberg and other places in its market radius between 1339 and 1670, but for comparison, he analyzed the price series for the Rhine-Main area with Frankfurt and Cologne; for comparison, he also used schedules of changing price series for Würzburg on the Main River and for Augsburg in Swabia.[237] This made it possible for him to differentiate general tendencies from regional and local variations. He also monitored changes in price for other commodities. For a historical interpretation of price series, it is essential to know the supply-and-demand situation. As an indicator of the fluctuating level of supply, Bauernfeind used grain tithe registers, which fairly reliably inform us of the relative results of the harvests, crop failures, and record yields. The indicator of demand for Bauernfeind were reports in chronicles on mortality crises, especially outbreaks of plague. As a result, he could convincingly determine what lay behind movements in grain prices—either a failed harvest, a surplus, or changes in numbers of inhabitants. On a methodological level, Bauernfeind founded his work on (1) smoothed annual averages, (2) the conversion of prices to the gold standard (*Goldpreisen*), and (3) the transformation of long-term price series according to the buying power of gold

---

233   Bauernfeind, *Materielle Grundstrukturen*.
234   E.g., Čechura, *Die Struktur*, 130–134.
235   Hoffmann, *Land*.
236   Bauernfeind, *Materielle Grundstrukturen*, 1–6.
237   Earlier literature concerning series of early modern grain prices and the principles for their evaluation in the medieval and modern periods are summarized esp. in Hans-Jürgen Schmitz, *Faktoren der Preisbildung für Getreide und Wein in der Zeit von 800 bis 1350*, Quellen und Forschungen zur Agrargeschichte 20 (Stuttgart: Fischer, 1968); Wilhelm Abel, *Massenarmut und Hungerkrisen im vorindustriellen Europa. Versuch einer* Synopsis (Hamburg – Berlin: Parey, 1974).

(the conversion of *Goldpreisen to Realpreisen*). The conversion of grain prices to the gold standard proved to be appropriate only for year-to-year comparison, or perhaps for comparison in a medium long-term horizon of 10–30 years, but insufficient for comparison on a level of more long-term (secular) trends. Bauernfeind therefore took into account the well-founded criticism raised against mechanical price conversion into precious metal.[238] In this phase of the analysis, he drew methodological inspiration from Rainer Metz's dissertation on Trier, which provoked heated discussion at the time.[239]

In the grain prices series for 1339–1670, Bauernfeind identified eight long waves, which were further divided internally into three or four cycles that express medium-term fluctuation (*fig. 5.10*). For our study, it is the third wave (1420–1465) that is relevant, since it matches the period that we are analyzing in the city-state of Cheb (*fig. 5.11*). In detail, this wave may be further divided into three separate cycles. In the first cycle (1420–1440), grain prices initially stagnated at a very low level but then, due to a series of poor harvests and a catastrophic failed harvest in 1437, a wave of high prices followed, not just in Nuremberg but everywhere in Central, Western, and Northern Europe. Not even the fall in demand in the Nuremberg region as a result of a severe outbreak of plague could prevent the enormous prices of 1437. Then in 1438 and 1439, there was a sharp drop in grain prices to the level of the 1420s. The next cycle (1440–1449) was an unusually calm period in terms of prices, with a slight upward tendency after 1443, not just in the Nuremberg region but across Central Europe. A gentle price fall continued in the third cycle as well (1450–1465), by the end of which grain prices had reached rock bottom. The First Margrave War had only a small influence on Nuremberg grain prices, which devastated the countryside and led to a significant fall in agricultural production in 1449–1455.[240]

The price series calculated by the conversion of nominal prices to the gold standard (*Goldpreisen*) illustrated the development of grain prices over the course of fairly short- to medium-length time segments. Not even the value

238 Bauernfeind, *Materielle Grundstrukturen*, 7–10, 13–14, 61–73, 84–98, 307–354. For more on Czech reactions to the discussion concerning the conversion of prices into precious metal, cf. in particular Josef Petráň et al., "Současný stav bádání o dějinách cen a mezd" [Der gegenwärtige Stand in der Forschung der Preis- Lohngeschichte (Übersicht für den Zeitraum 1962–1971)], *Československý časopis historický* 21 (1973): 45–72, on 54.

239 Metz, *Geld*, 307–353.

240 Bauernfeind, *Materielle Grundstrukturen*, 178–201.

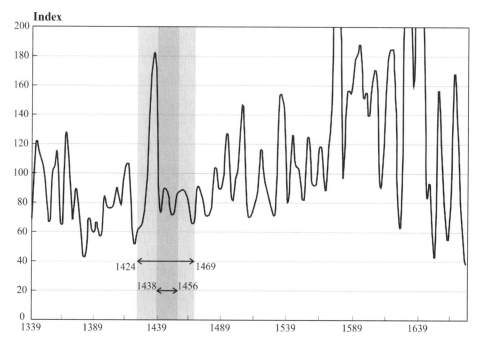

Figure 5.10. **Prices of rye in the Nuremberg region in 1339–1670. The graph shows that "real" grain prices were not the lowest in the period investigated, because they were still above the level of the last quarter of the 14ᵗʰ century.**

Source: Bauernfeind, *Materielle Grundstrukturen*, Abb. 102. Graphically adapted.
Note: Smoothed annual averages, the nominal prices converted to the gold standard and adjusted for purchasing power of gold (*Realpreisen*). The main period monitored in the city-state of Cheb is marked (1424–1469, 1438–1456).

of gold itself was stable in the long-term. Identifying the development trend of the buying power of gold is not easy and is always just an approximation. The development of prices for certain commodities with a lower degree of year-to-year fluctuation (e.g., butter) may facilitate some adjustment.[241] On this foundation, Bauernfeind assembled a long-term series of grain prices that should at least partially remove the influence of monetary factors (*Realpreisen*).[242] But this had no effect on the interpretation of the separate cycles;

241   Bauernfeind, *Materielle Grundstrukturen*, 307–353.
242   Bauernfeind, *Materielle Grundstrukturen*, 354–363.

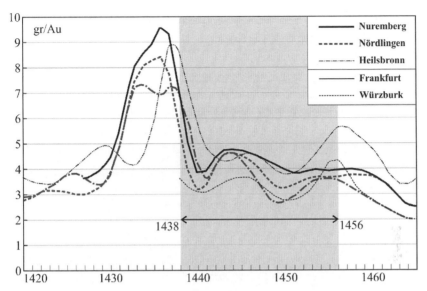

Figure 5.11. Rye prices in the Nuremberg region and other localities for 1420–1465 (third price wave).

Source: According to Bauernfeind, *Materielle Grundstrukturen*, Abb. 38. Graphically adapted.
Note: Main reference period for the city-state of Cheb (1438–1456) indicated with an arrow. Smoothed annual averages, nominal prices converted to the gold standard (*Goldpreisen*).

changes in grain prices in separate long waves appear in a slightly different light (*fig. 5.12*).

Given the fairly good source base, Bauernfeind could choose annual price data concerning salt, butter, and herring for comparison with grain prices. He converted nominal prices into the gold standard and this into index points, where 100 index points meant the average price of goods during the fifty-year period of 1500–1550. This approach enabled the relative comparison of the price developments of all commodities, regardless of the different units of measurement.[243] The interpretation of grain price series gained a new dimension thanks to this (*fig. 5.13*).

During the third wave (1420–1465), the prices of salt, butter, and herring had a long-term downward tendency without any significant fluctuations. The price of salt fell most dramatically, by 45 index points, while butter and herring

---

243   Bauernfeind, *Materielle Grundstrukturen*, 77–83, 124.

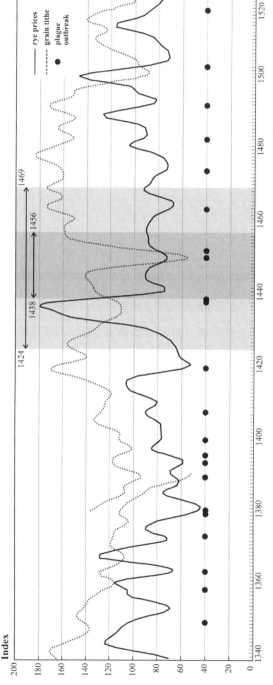

Figure 5.12. Rye price changes and relative tithe yields for the Nuremberg region 1339–1526. The years indicated are those with reports of outbreaks of plague in the Nuremberg region. The correlation between grain prices and mortality crises or size of harvest is clearly evident.

Source: According to Bauernfeind, *Materielle Grundstrukturen*, Abb. 103–104, 94. Graphically adapted.

Note: Smoothed annual averages, nominal prices converted to the gold standard and adjusted according to the buying power of gold (*Realpreisen*). Early series of relative grain tithe yields for Heilsbronn Abbey (1338–1391). More recent series specifically for the estates of the Bamberg Provostry, Bamberg Chapter, and the Holy Spirit Hospital in Nuremberg (from 1386 and 1387). Reference period for the city-state of Cheb (1424–1469, 1438–1456) indicated with arrows.

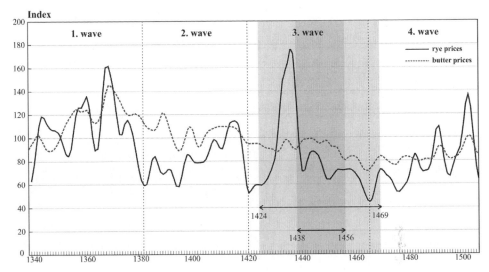

Figure 5.13. **Price series for rye and butter in the Nuremberg region between 1339 and 1506. Nominal prices converted to the gold standard (Goldpreisen). The long-term relative drop in rye prices in 1370–1481 is evident.**

Source: According to Bauernfeind, *Materielle Grundstrukturen*, Abb. 22, 37, 46, 54. Graphically adapted.
Note: Index 100 = average commodity prices in the first half of the 16th century. Main price waves indicated with arrows. Reference period for the city-state of Cheb (1424–1469, 1438–1456) indicated with arrows.

fell less, by 30 index points. Nevertheless, the relative position of rye improved until 1465; although rye prices fell slightly compared to gold, they rose against salt, butter, and herring. After a period of extremely high grain prices in the 1430s, the situation turned around and, by 1437, rye prices were 80 index points above butter prices. In this respect, the period of high prices in the 1430s fundamentally differed from the high prices of the 1360s, when grain prices did not rise above prices for other commodities. The high prices of 1437 may therefore be described as the first real subsistence crisis in the Nuremberg region in the Late Middle Ages. By 1465, grain prices had reached their lowest value compared to precious metals, not to other commodities.[244]

244   Bauernfeind, *Materielle Grundstrukturen*, 198–201.

5.11 **Summary**

The late medieval city-state of Cheb had a unique genesis, since unlike other Franconian or Swabian cities, the Cheb city council received a share in territorial and jurisdictional rights from the Czech king as lienholder, in other words, from above and not by means of gradual acquisitions from below. The territorialization of power and geographical stabilization of the city-state of Cheb occurred during the turn of the 15th century and manifested itself in the annual collection of land tax.

On a population scale, Cheb was one of the most populous medium-large imperial cities. The territory controlled by the city was over 400 km², which ranks it as one of the three largest city-states in the German-speaking parts of the Holy Roman Empire.

The period of our main analytic interest (1438–1456) was relatively calm, defined on one hand by the Hussite Wars, and on the other by the Bohemian–Hungarian War. A partial devastation of the countryside occurred only in 1452. This was also a period of a power vacuum, which the Cheb city council tackled with protection agreements and related financial payments to powerful neighbors that were paid out from the land tax. This practice ended after 1452, with a swing towards the strong Bohemian king as the recognized lienholder.

A feudal system developed in the Cheb region, with strict differentiation between landlord rights and fief rights. Although small manors had already sprung up around strategically situated castles, the overall character of the region was determined by dispersed landlord rights in the hands of Cheb ecclesiastical institutions and dozens of patrician families, which was reflected in the territorial scope of the city-state of Cheb. In places where patrician and Church holdings had not yet penetrated, the city was unable to impose its territorial power.

In administrative terms, the city-state of Cheb was divided into land militia districts that mirrored parish borders. The most expansive parish in Cheb was divided internally into five smaller districts. In terms of Church organization, the Cheb region was part of the Diocese of Regensburg.

According to the natural conditions for agricultural production, the city-state of Cheb may be divided into five ecological zones whose poles were at one end the agroclimatically optimal parts of the Cheb Basin along the banks of the Ohře River (A) and, at the other, the agriculturally unfavorable submountainous regions with a harsh climate (B). A heterogeneous social, economic, and demographic structure and varying degrees of agricultural commercialization should be assumed to apply in the city-state of Cheb. Although the surrounding mountainous areas were rich in ore, they had no direct influence on the socioeconomic structure of the Cheb countryside.

The market and consumption area of Cheb encompassed the entire territory of the city-state and extended beyond, especially to the Loket region in Bohemia. From a distance of up to 12 km, Cheb was largely supplied directly by agrarian producers (peasants), while from a greater distance it was supplied indirectly through market villages and smaller towns.

Except for a few settlements that had a certain degree of centrality, the city-state of Cheb was covered by a network of hamlets and small villages, often not exceeding 10 or 15 landholdings in size. Between 1392 and 1424, the total number of landholdings fell by 10%, while for the rest of the 15th century the number remained surprisingly stable.

Typical of agricultural production in the city-state of Cheb was the three-field fallow system, as well as commercially oriented cattle farming in the Cheb Basin in particular. The agrarian cycle affected not just the countryside but also the city. The beginning of harvest time coincided with the beginning of the accounting year of the city chancellory, the grain surplus being levied as fixed land rent at Michaelmas and cattle surplus in monetary form as land tax raised on St. Martin's Day. Surplus exploitation was timed so that the seasonal agricultural surplus was levied from peasants at a relatively optimal moment.

The years 1438–1456 fall into an extraordinarily cold period, when the characteristics of a continental climate dominated with long, hard, and snowy winters. In the overall comparison, these were some of the coldest decades medieval society had ever experienced. The onset of cold and wet years was exceptionally dramatic, which was manifested in poor harvest yields and a catastrophic grain failure in 1437, after which a subsistence and mortality crisis followed in 1438 and 1439. The actual culmination of the cold climate fluctuation in the decades of 1440–1459 did not significantly shake society, as the grain yields maintained a slightly lower but stable level. Of course, peripheral areas in cool mountainous locations were at risk.

The series of subsistence and mortality crises in 1437–1439 is important for us, since it is in these years that our analysis of the peasants of the city-state of Cheb begins. However, the *1438 Land Tax Register* that we use describes the peasantry existing before the mortality crisis and not after or during the crisis. It was compiled at the very beginning of the year, when a plague epidemic had hit the Main River region, though neighboring Swabia and Bohemia did not experience it until the summer of the following year.

According to the closer data from Nuremberg, we can determine that the period between 1440 and 1465 was as a whole abnormally calm in terms of fertility, demographics, and grain prices, which was also true for the city-state of Cheb. Production levels and the demographic situation were disrupted by local military conflicts and minor outbreaks of plague or other illnesses. The prices of all commodities fell very slowly over a long period of time, although grain products improved their price position compared to animal products and other products. It was still more or less applicable that grain production provided relatively lower cash income than in the period before the agrarian depression or in the first half of the 16th century.

6.
Tax documents

This study uses a specific group of sources abundantly—the Cheb land tax registers and a taxation book. In this chapter, we acquaint the reader with them in more detail. The question is to what extent similar sources may be found elsewhere in Central Europe of the Late Middle Ages and whether in other regions the peasantry may be analyzed in the same way as the city-state of Cheb.

It should be stressed in advance that the Cheb land tax registers are among the oldest preserved in German-speaking imperial territories. Moreover, they are the only ones that have been preserved continuously every year since the late medieval period. While registers from other imperial territories were only preserved for some years and therefore can generally only provide assessments of socioeconomic stratification at certain moments in time, the Cheb registers allow us to follow the life trajectories of concrete individuals, families, and landholdings over time.

6.1 Land tax documents[245]

For a long time, the historical Cheb region (and later the city-state) was not integrated into the Bohemian land tax collection system. Here, the lienholder collected a special land tax called the "hoof tax" (*Klauensteuer* or *Klosteuer*). Originally, this tax was raised only exceptionally, and the lienholder's officials

---

245   Summarized also in Klír, "Land transfer," 153–155.

cooperated with the Cheb city council in its collection. At the end of the 14th century, tax collection was completely in the hands of the city council, which, as of 1395, collected tax biannually and, as of 1403, annually. The city-state of Cheb therefore became one of the first territories in the Holy Roman Empire where the annual collection of land tax was imposed. The geographical scope of tax collection was reduced at the beginning of the 15th century, also stabilizing geographically. Independent land tax collection then remained one of the significant symbols of the original autonomy of Cheb, which it lost due to the Theresian reforms of the 18th century.[246]

The series of Cheb's land tax books begins, with gaps, in 1392 intermittently and starting in 1441 with continuity, and it ends more than three centuries later in 1757, when the former Cheb region was first included in nationwide taxation based on the *Theresian Cadastre*. According to the current archive inventory, 311 volumes of various tax books, mostly registers, survive in the Cheb Archive, not including other auxiliary written documents. The variety of types and the development tendencies of Cheb's land tax books correspond in many respects with the situation in territories of the Holy Roman Empire.[247]

In the earliest part of the Cheb land tax documents up until 1500, the following five categories may be identified: (1) hybrid tax registers, (2) clean copies thereof, (3) tax registers, (4) specially kept arrears registers, and (5) a special taxation book (taxable property valuation ledger) (*tab. 6.1*).[248]

The method for making entries in the tax registers in the first half of the 15th century was dynamic. Until 1441, registers were fairly variable in form and had hybrid content, since they comprised not only (1) a register of taxpayers, (2) both prescribed and actually made land tax payments, (3) income accounts, and (4) sometimes also valuation of taxable property, but also (5) lists of all expenditure from the tax collection and (6) relevant accountancy, all rounded off by (7) total balance of income and expenditure.[249]

Following the reform of the city accountancy and the entire city chancellory in Cheb in 1441, the tax registers changed in form, with expenditure entries

246   Klír et al., *Knihy*, 18, 22, 36–40.
247   Georg Vogeler, "Spätmittelalterliche Steuerbücher deutscher Territorien, Teil 1: Überlieferung und hilfswissenschaftliche Analyse," *Archiv für Diplomatik* 49 (2003): 165–295; Georg Vogeler, "Spätmittelalterliche Steuerbücher deutscher Territorien, Teil 2: Funktionale Analyse und Typologie," *Archiv für Diplomatik* 50 (2004): 57–204.
248   Klír et al., *Knihy*, 71–74.
249   Klír et al., *Knihy*, 74–81.

Table 6.1. The Cheb land tax books for 1392–1498 in the Cheb City Archive.

Type	Number*	Years
hybrid tax registers – these registers were used during tax collection, formed base material for clean copies, and could serve for several years consecutively	6	1397–1434**
clean copies of hybrid tax registers	11	1392–1438**
tax registers	57	1441–1498
special taxation book	1	1456
arrears registers in the form of bound fascicles	1 (fascicles and loose sheets – book fragments)	1469–1492

Source: Klír et al., *Knihy*, 72.

Note: * – including fragments, copies
** – survives but with considerable gaps; it is hard to decide reliably whether or not the register for 1438 is a clean copy

being transferred to newly established city accounts books. The tax registers now contained simply a list of taxpayers, prescribed and paid payments, and a list of arrears; therefore, they contained only land tax income accounts.[250]

Cheb land tax system

The genesis of the Cheb land tax has been addressed in detail in another study.[251] In the 15th century, land tax was levied on all "subject" and "free" immovable and movable property in the territory controlled by the Cheb city council, except for (1) directly held property of persons with citizenship, since these persons paid not land tax but city tax; (2) directly held property of the nobility (noble land); and (3) property belonging directly to the parish or Church (parish lands). Therefore, the land tax was paid by the "subject" tenants of the burghers of Cheb but not by burghers' demesne farms. Exempt from the land tax were also "subject" tenants of (4) Cheb Castle, (5) Cheb city hospital, and (6) Waldsassen Abbey in the enclave later known as Frais.[252]

---

250 Klír et al., *Knihy*, 81–84.
251 Klír et al., *Knihy*, 36–40, 71–85, 124–133.
252 Klír et al., *Knihy*, 135–144.

Table 6.2. **Cheb territory after 1424.**

Geographical scope	ca. 400 km²
Settlements with landholdings subject to the territorial power of the lienholder	138
Settlements where land tax was levied	130
Settlements with landholdings exempt from land tax	8
Settlements where land tax was levied from all "subject" and "free" landholdings	113

Source: Klír et al., *Knihy,* 135, 214–220, Appendix 9.

Note: * – three settlements of Cheb Castle; one settlement at Ostroh Castle (Seeberg); four settlements in the enclave of the Cheb hospital, the so-called "Vierdörfer"

After the territorialization and geographical stabilization of the city-state of Cheb in the first quarter of the 15th century, land tax was collected from about 130 settlements in a territory of almost 400 km² (*tab. 6.2*). However, in 17 settlements not all landholdings paid the land tax,[253] since some settlements were under the territorial power of the Burgraves of Nuremberg or Margraves of Meissen.[254]

The vernacular name of the Cheb land tax—*Clostewr* ("hoof" tax)—suggests that the amount of the tax was initially measured according to the number of horses and cattle. Nevertheless, at the latest from the first quarter of the 15th century, the amount of the tax was determined according to the monetary value of (1) the tenure right to the landholding as a whole, whether "subject" tenure or "free"; (2) horses, cattle, and sheep; (3) non-landholding plots, thus plots that were not directly attached to a particular landholding and that the holder could dispose of relatively freely; and (4) further rights and properties, e.g., the right to a fishery, large beehives, fishponds, parts of forests, etc. Other taxed items were rarely listed. Most taxpayers paid taxes only for their landholding and livestock, and a fair number also declared their non-landholding plots. A small number of taxpayers had no landholding, only a non-landholding plot or a herd of sheep or cattle.[255]

253   *App. 6.1.*
254   Klír et al., *Knihy,* 124–135.
255   Klír et al., *Knihy,* 144–157.

Cheb land tax had a progressive character. The tax rate fluctuated during the 15th century and in some cases could even been individual; however, between 1438 and 1456, this represented about one-sixtieth or one-fortieth of the estimated monetary value of property (1.5–2.5%; see *chap. 12*).[256]

The Cheb tax system was diametrically different from the contemporary system in neighboring Bohemia because an extraordinary, general, and direct land tax from the "subject" land was collected there. The tax rate then either had a flat rate (1453, 1479) or reflected the amount of the land rent (1459, 1462, 1487).[257] A direct property tax was first implemented in Bohemia in 1517 and annual collection began, in fact, around the middle of the 16th century.[258]

Tax books with exceptional information

Among the preserved late medieval registers of the Cheb land tax, the annually kept registers dominate, the core of which comprises an alphabetical list of the settlements. Within each settlement, the names of the taxpayers, the set amount of the tax, and a note on its payment are listed. The registers from 1424 and 1438 were different because they contained a detailed description of the taxed items. The 1469 register was also exceptional, presenting additionally the perpetual, fixed land rent of the "subject" tenants given to their landlords. A detailed description of the taxed property items is also provided by the special 1456 *Taxation Book*. These documents constitute our main sources.

The 1438 register and the 1456 *Taxation Book* have already been described in detail and published in edition form.[259] Registers from 1424 and 1469 are currently undergoing preparation for publication. So here we shall limit ourselves to the basic characteristics.

256 Klír et al., *Knihy*, 175–177.
257 Kamil Krofta, "Začátky české berně," *Český časopis historický* 36 (1930): 1–26, 237–257, 437–490, on 483–486.
258 Otto Placht, *České daně 1517–1652* (Prague: Jednota československých matematiků a fysiků, 1924), 7–35, 85–91; Antonín Gindely, *Geschichte der böhmischen Finanzen von 1526 bis 1618* (Vienna: Kaiserl.-Königl. Hof- u. Staatsdruckere, 1868).
259 Klír et al., *Knihy*.

1424 Register

The 1424 *Tax Register* documented, for the first time, some of the taxed items—both the landholding and the non-landholding plots. The PEASANT FULLHOLDING (*Hof*) was the most common type, and the "SUB-PEASANT" HOLDING (*Herberge*; smallholders and cottagers; the dwellings of craftsmen as well) also appeared relatively often. Even a small PEASANT FULLHOLDING (*Höfel*) was represented.[260] A landholding could be formally whole, half, one-third, or one-quarter, or even one-and-a-half or two landholdings together. Some taxpayers held even more landholdings.

Usually one line concerned one taxpayer, divided into six columns containing the taxpayer's personal name, type of landholding, the amount of tax prescribed, and a note confirming payment. For instance, in the village of Sebenbach/Chvoječná (fol. 46v) a standard taxpayer entry was as follows:

> *Steffan   I hof XX g[roschen] d[edi]t*

An entry for propertied taxpayers was frequently amended, most often with information concerning further taxable items, the special legal status of property, and the localization of non-landholding plots. For instance, in the village of Sebenbach/Chvoječná a typical expanded entry stated (fol. 46v):

> *Hirsler I hof XVIII morg[en] in Schöner raynu[n]ge*
> *I[1/2] morg[en] bey der Stat III tagb[er]g IIII kar erb czins III[1/2]*
> *s[chokken] d[edi]t*

Taxpayers had tenure of a landholding usually on the basis of "purchase" right (*emphyteusis*), which therefore was not even mentioned. Only exceptional legal statuses such as a "free" inheritable fief or inheritable fief (a further "free" landholding) were recorded.[261]

---

260   Ar Cheb, book 1060, *Klosteuerbuch 1424*; Klír et al., *Knihy*, 77–78.
261   Unfortunately, the binding of the register has fallen apart, and therefore several double-pages are missing; in total, loose sheets containing an originally detailed description of about 12 settlements are missing.

1438 Register

The *1438 Tax Register* has not been preserved in its original form, but two reliable copies from 1769 have been maintained. The base of the register is an alphabetized list of the settlements. Under the name of the settlement, a list of the individual taxpayers usually follows; each taxpayer is identified by their personal name followed by a basic characteristic, an assessment of the landholding (*Hof*, *Höfel*, and *Herberge* are distinguished), its legal status, and the value of their taxed livestock are listed. Additionally, in many cases, other, separately taxed properties, such as non-landholding fields, meadows, parts of forests, or other various incomes are listed before the livestock. Following this is the determination of the monetary fiscal value of the landholding with all these details, the amount of the prescribed annual tax, and a note on payment (*tab. 6.3*).[262] The entry for each taxpayer is a single paragraph separated by a blank line.

Table 6.3. **An example of the entry of one of the taxpayers in the village of Háje (Gehaag) in the *1438 Tax Register*.**

Entry			Explanation
Hans Gotzel			– personal name of the taxpayer
ein Hof das Kaufr[echt]		XX ss	– landholding and legal status
drey Morgen		VIIII ss	– non-landholding plots
Kie und Kelber		VI ss	– cattle
Pferd		VII ss	– draft animals (horses)
und Schaf		II ss	– sheep
	facit	XLIIII ss	– total fiscal monetary value of the taxed property
		XLVIII gr. dt.	– prescribed tax

Source: Ar Cheb, book 1067, *Klosteuerbuch 1438*; cf. Klír et al., *Knihy*, 90.
Note: Format adjusted.

1456 Taxation Book

The *1456 Taxation Book* begins with an introductory declaration describing its purpose and the taxable items. Settlements are recorded in alphabetical order, as in the *1438 Tax Register*. The settlement name is usually followed by the tax-

---

262   Klír et al., *Knihy*, 85–103.

payers, while the structure of the entry is largely identical to the *1438 Tax Register*. The fundamental difference is that the total value of all individual items is not specified; instead, the prescribed level of annual tax typically immediately follows the description. Landholdings are no longer differentiated into *Hof*, *Herberge*, or *Höfel*; only their legal status is specified ("subject" or "free"). Another difference is that several times the number of horses, cattle, and sheep is also recorded.[263]

1469 Register

The *1469 Tax Register* differs from the others mainly in that the standard list of taxpayers, and prescribed tax amounts were subsequently added to (1) the type and amount of the land rent and (2) the name of the landlord.[264] Due to inflation, in 1469 twice the normal tax amount was collected from each taxpayer, and it was noted in the register whether they had actually delivered the required amount. Therefore, an entry for a standard registered settlement was divided into a total of 7 columns (*tab. 6.4*).

Table 6.4. **Taxpayer registration in the village of Salajna (Konradsgrün) in the 1469 Tax Register.**

	Taxpayer's name and tax	Main annual payment and the landlord	Note concerning payment
Record in the register	*Hanns Per XXVIII g[roschen]*	*1 k[ar] Cumpth[errn]*	*d[edi]t 2fach*
Notes	Hanns Per 28 Prague groschen	1 "kar" of grain (½ rye, ½ oats) of annual payment to the commandery of the Teutonic Order in Cheb	payment twice the normal tax amount (56 Prague groschen)

Source: Ar Cheb, book 1096, *Klosteuerbuch 1469*, fol. 3v.
Note: Modified format.

---

263   Klír et al., *Knihy*, 104–118.
264   Ar Cheb, book 1096, *Klosteuerbuch 1469*; Klír et al., *Knihy*, 83, 159–161.

6.2 **Cheb land tax registers in Central European comparison**

A database of land tax registers (books) for the territory of today's Germany, Austria, and parts of the Netherlands is contained in a dissertation completed by Georg Vogeler.[265] He excluded registers concerning land tax collection from city-states, since in his opinion cities only rarely developed the administration of a certain territory.[266] Such a characteristic certainly applies to taxes collected from gradually emerging imperial city territories such as Nuremberg, Ulm, Rothenburg ob der Tauber, and Zurich, but not to Cheb. As for the Cheb land tax, this was the lienholder's territorial tax that the city controlled and transformed.[267] Cheb tax registers would fit into Volgeler's dataset. At this point, we are interested in the extent to which Cheb tax registers resemble or differ from other important collections of tax registers of the lands of the Holy Roman Empire and what their informational capabilities are.

Rarely have land tax registers from German-speaking imperial territories prior to the mid-14th century survived. After 1380, however, they became more frequent, and it was not until the mid-15th century that any significant quantitative growth occurred (*fig. 6.1*). This number of surviving land tax registers corresponds very well with the formation of territorial states in the Late Middle Ages, where a regular, annually collected land tax was not generally imposed until the first half of the 16th century, which was also the case for neighboring Bohemia. The Cheb series of land tax registers are among the oldest in existence, and they correspond, for instance, with the origin of surviving land tax registers for individual Bavarian duchies (1390).

According to Georg Vogeler, there are 677 physically surviving originals and a further 99 complete copies, extracts, or other documents testifying to their existence, dating back to the end of the Middle Ages (1506/35) or earlier. Therefore, 775 registers for 47 different imperial territories are documented. If Bohemia[268] and the city-state of Cheb were to be included, this number would

265 Vogeler, "Spätmittelalterliche Steuerbücher, Teil 1," 211–235.
266 Vogeler, "Spätmittelalterliche Steuerbücher, Teil 1," 168.
267 Klír et al., *Knihy*, 178–179.
268 Georg Vogeler, "Die böhmischen Berna-Register als „Steuerbücher deutscher Territorien"?," in *Böhmen und das Deutsche Reich: Ideen- und Kulturtransfer im Vergleich (13.–16. Jahrhundert)*, ed. Eva Schlotheuber and Hubertus Seibert, Veröffentlichungen des Collegium Carolinum 116 (Munich: R. Oldenbourg, 2009), 203–222.

Figure 6.1. Number of surviving land tax registers from the German-speaking imperial territories.

Source: According to Vogeler, "Spätmittelalterliche Steuerbücher I," 212, Abb. 1. Adapted.
Note: Total indicated for the preceding 15 years in all cases. Without the city-state of Cheb.

rise to 892 registers. This quantity is not distributed evenly; four territories with the greatest number of registers contain almost 60% of the entire stock (*fig. 6.2*). The most registers survive for the Duchy of Geldern with the county of Zutphen (hereafter referred to as Geldern; 163 registers; 18%). The Duchy of Bavaria-Landshutis in second place (134 registers; 15%), the city-state of Cheb is in third place (112 registers; 13%), and the Bavarian Duchy of Munich is in fourth place (103 registers; 12%). This simple and purely quantitative comparison must be described in more detail.

Land tax in the Duchy of Geldern, stipulated as a progressive tax on all movable and immovable property, was collected irregularly and originally with long gaps between collections of around 5 to 10 years. Tax collection did not increase in intensity until halfway through the 15th century, and tax was collected every year starting in the first half of the 16th century. The large quantity of tax registers in Geldern is due to the fact that this was a geographically large area, divided into four subregions that themselves were divided further into smaller administrative districts for which separate registers were kept. The oldest such surviving registers are for 1369, 1382, and 1387. Land tax was

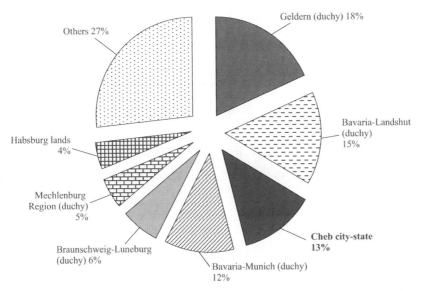

Figure 6.2. Proportion of Cheb land tax registers compared to the entire stock for the German-speaking imperial territories in the Late Middle Ages.

Source: Cf. Klír et al., *Knihy*, 181–183, graphics 2, table 27–28.
Note: Germany, Bohemia, Austria, Low Countries.

paid by propertied inhabitants both in towns and in the countryside, including the nobility and the clergy. The registers did not record all inhabitants, just heads of households. The total population of the duchy around the year 1500 is therefore estimated at between 130,000 and 140,000.[269] Although as a whole the Geldern registers are numerous and exceptional in scope, in qualitative terms they are typical fiscal documents that provide insight into the population at a particular time. In this respect, tax registers were also analyzed in a dissertation by Remi van Schaïk, who concentrated on analyzing the principles and organization of the Geldern tax system, demographic development, and the socioeconomic structure of the duchy. The Geldern registers are currently the best socially and demographically sourced collection of tax registers for the German-speaking territory of the late medieval Holy Roman Empire,

---

269 Remigius Wenceslaus Maria van Schaïk, *Belasting, bevolking en bezit in Gelre en Zutphen 1350–1550*, Middeleeuwse Studies en Bronnen 6 (Hilversum: Verloren, 1987), esp. 270–287, 312–313.

and they are of fundamental significance for understanding the relationship between public finances and economic development.[270]

Similar possibilities as those offered by the Geldern tax registers are offered by less plentiful tax registers surviving for the Duchy of Cleeves, which Norbert Becker partially evaluated in his dissertation.[271] It is believed that land tax in this region might have been collected every year, but only a fragment of registers kept for each separate administrative district has survived (20 registers for 1384 and 1385). In this case too, only very static information is available concerning the population and its socioeconomic structure for a specific time segment.

The enormous number of tax registers that have survived for Bavarian duchies is due to the quantity of administrative districts, not due to annual tax collection. The Bavarian registers have not yet been evaluated as a whole from a socioeconomic or demographic perspective, but they have been analyzed from a diplomatic point of view.[272]

The Zurich tax registers as of the 1440s also included the city-controlled countryside. Tax determined by the monetary value of property was not collected annually in the countryside and in some years was increased by a fixed head tax imposed on the entire adult population, men and women alike.[273] Particularly detailed registers have survived for 1450, 1467, and 1470. The Zurich

---

270   Cf. also Remigius Wenceslaus Maria van Schaïk, "Taxation, public finances and the state-making process in the late Middle Ages. The case of the duchy of Guelders," *Journal of Medieval History* 19 (1993): 251–271; Remigius Wenceslaus Maria van Schaïk, ed., *Economies, public finances, and the impact of institutional changes in interregional perspective. The Low countries and neighbouring German territories (14th–17th centuries)*, Studies in European Urban History 36 (Turnhout: Brepols, 2015).

271   Norbert Becker, *Das Land am unteren Niederrhein. Untersuchungen zur Verfassungs-, Wirtschafts- und Sozialgeschichte des ländlichen Raumes vom Hohen Mittelalter bis zur Frühen Neuzeit (1100–1600)*, Rheinisches Archiv 128 (Cologne: Böhlau, 1992), esp. 330–339.

272   Vogeler, "Spätmittelalterliche Steuerbücher, Teil 1"; Vogeler, "Spätmittelalterliche Steuerbücher, Teil 2."

273   A basic description may be found in the introductions to editions of Zurich tax documentation, esp.: Hans Nabholz and Friedrich Hegi, eds. *Die Steuerbücher von Stadt und Landschaft Zürich des XIV. und XV. Jahrhunderts, 1: Die Steuerrödel des XIV. Jahrhunderts, 1357–1379* (Zürich: Beer, 1918), IX–XXVI; Hans Nabholz and Edwin Hauser, eds. *Die Steuerbücher von Stadt und Landschaft Zürich des XIV. und XV. Jahrhunderts, 2/1: Steuergesetzgebung von 1401–1470, Steuerrödel von 1401–1450* (Zürich: Beer, 1939), XIII–XVII. For more on Zurich see: Elisabeth Raiser, *Städtische Territorialpolitik im Mittelalter. Eine vergleichende Untersuchung ihrer verschiedenen Formen am Beispiel Lübecks und Zürichs*, Historische Studien 406

registers also provide knowledge of the rural population only for a certain time segment, but they are unique in that they record all adults. In this regard, they are unparalleled in transalpine Europe.[274]

The Cheb land tax registers are exceptional in that their great number is due not to the large spatial scope of the territory, as it is elsewhere, but to the annual collection of tax. Nevertheless, in overall comparison, the oldest group of Cheb tax registers for 1392–1435 has proven to be fairly standard in terms of information, as it provides unrelated data for various years at fairly long intervals, which allows only basic findings to be made as to the size of the population and socioeconomic stratification. The potential for finding comprehensive data in the registers changes dramatically starting in 1441, after which the registers survive in continuity for every year. In combination with the information-rich registers for 1424, 1438, and 1469 and the 1456 *Taxation Book*, they allow a very detailed and dynamic insight into a rural population that is unique across Europe.

Among the unique advantages of the Cheb collection are records with descriptions and valuations of peasant property from 1438 and 1456. If we were to seek close parallels, we would not find them until the onset of the Early Modern Period, in what was known as the Turk tax, which played a significant role in imperial territories with the establishment of stable forms of land tax. For instance, in his extensive dissertation in which Uwe Schirmer examined the GRIMMA region, registers of land tax collected in the Margrave of Meissen and later in Saxony from 1421 and 1495 have survived that recorded only the amount of tax to be paid by each taxpayer.[275] The Turk tax registers for 1531 also recorded the total value of property as sworn under oath by the "subject" tenant.[276] It was not until the registers relating to the 1542 Turk tax that they achieved an informational level comparable to the Cheb land tax registers, since they contained concrete information about "subject" landholdings, the quantity of livestock, and amount of land.[277]

(Lübeck, Hamburg: Matthiesen, 1969), esp. 97–98, 104–110, 131–135; Scott, *City-State in Europe*, 168–173. From a settlement history perspective, cf. Wanner, *Siedlungen*, esp. 19–53.

274   Randolph C. Head, "Haushalt und Familie in Landschaft und Stadt Zürich, nach Steuerbüchern des 15. Jahrhunderts," *Zeitschrift für Agrargeschichte und Agrarsoziologie* 40 (1992): 113–132, on 113–115.

275   Schirmer, *Das Amt Grimma*, 43–49.

276   Schirmer, *Das Amt Grimma*, 49–52.

277   Schirmer, *Das Amt Grimma*, 52–56.

6.3 City tax registers[278]

In this study, we also use the Cheb city tax registers (*Losungsbücher* in German). Cheb city tax (*Losung*), the rate of which was decided by the city council, was paid by all members of the city community (burghers). The clergy (parish, monasteries, city hospital), inhabitants of the castle, and squires were not subject to this tax; however, Jews paid a fixed amount. Even burghers' immediate properties in the countryside were subject to city tax. A more or less complete series of these registers running from 1390 to 1758 survives in Cheb's archive (359 registers).[279]

We are quite well informed about the tax rate and principles of taxation.[280] According to the oldest surviving city tax register, from 1390, 1 pound of hellers was payable on property worth 100 pounds of hellers; therefore, the tax rate was 1%. Already in 1395, 6 pounds were payable on 100 pounds (6% tax), plus an additional hearth tax of 6 pounds, i.e., the equivalent of 18 Prague groschen. The introductory text in the 1396 register specifies a change that involved a differentiation between movable ("Parschaft," 4% tax) and immovable property ("Erbe," 2% tax). Hearth tax was set at 3 pounds of hellers, i.e., 9 Prague groschen. The different taxation of movable and immovable property endured in the city tax system at least until 1441/42, with the current rate regularly announced in the introductory text of the tax registers. An overview for individual years may be found in Schönstetter's *Chronicle* (mid-16th century), including the hearth tax.[281] However, Schönstetter's data does not always correspond to fact, or rather are chronologically displaced.[282] According to the introductions of the city tax registers, between 1438 and 1456, movable property was most often taxed at a ratio of 1:50 (2%), immovable 1:60 (1.7%); and hearth tax was 7 ½ Prague groschen.

---

278   For a summary see also Klír, "Land transfer," 155.

279   Karl Siegl, "Das älteste Egerer Stadtsteuerbuch vom Jahre 1390," *Kalender für das Egerland* 21 (1931): 83–106; 22 (1932): 55–78.

280   Klír et al., *Knihy*, 175–177; Ar Cheb, book 984, *Chronik des Hans Schönstetter 1390–1576*.

281   For more on the chronicle, cf. Heribert Sturm, "Der Egerer Losungsschreiber Hans Schönstetter und seine Chronik," in *Heimat und Volk: Forschungsbeiträge zur sudetendeutschen Geschichte: Festschrift für Universitätsprofessor Dr. Wilhelm Wostry zum 60. Geburtstage*, ed. Anton Ernstberger (Brünn: Rudolf M. Rohrer, 1937), 247–285.

282   Klír et al., *Knihy*, 175–176.

Table 6.5. **An example of the entry of a wealthy Cheb burgher in the city tax register 1446.**

Entry	Explanation
Vlrich Weiss Czu ersten sein herstat	- hearth tax
Sein hawsung dorinn er siczt fur I[1/2]^c X ß	- house
V morgen velds in d[er] Frawngaß fur XXV ß	
IIII morge[n] auf den Gensßpẅhel fur XXVI ß	
II morge[n] czu dem Gal[gen]p[er]g fur XX ß	
It[em] II morge[n] kenseyt dez Gerichts fur XVI ß	- plots in the Cheb agricultural
It[em] III morge[n] an dez Hallers velde fur XXII[1/2] ß	area (farmland)
It[em] V morge[n] kenseyt Lestein fur XXV ß	
It' IIII[1/2] Tagwerck Wiesmat vnt[er] Lestein fur L ß	- non-landholding plots in the
It[em] VIII tagw[er]ck Wiesmat pey Tursnicz fur XLVI ß	countryside
It[em] III tagwerck neb[e]n Kotschwicz fur XXII[1/2] ß	
It[em] die Rame fur X ß	- clothmaker's frame
It[em] czu Ob[er]ndorff reichsleh[e]n	
It[em] ab[er] czu Ob[er]ndorff VI k fur XXXVI ß	- land rent from "subject"
It[em] czu Markhaẅsen VI[1/2] k reichs leh[e]n fur XXXII[1/2] ß	tenants in the countryside
It[em] d[ie] czinß fur IIII[1/2] ß	- unspecified rent
It[em] den hof czu Meczelspach I^{c}XL ß	- demesne farm in the countryside
It[em] eine[n] halb[e]n stadel fur IIII ß	- barn in Cheb
Schuld war vnd parschafft fur LXXXX ß	- loans, goods, cash
It[em] dora[n] hat er schuld <vnd par> abczogen II[1/2]^{c}XXIIII ß	- debts (subtracted from the property)
VIIII[1/2] sex[agenas] IIII g[roschen]	- overall amount of the annual city tax

Source: Ar Cheb, book 1424, *Losungsbuch 1446*, fol. 42r.

Note: Format adjusted.

* – A significant part of his property were the plots in Cheb, non-landholding plots in some rural settlements, and land rent collected from "subject" tenants.

In analyzing land transfers and the circulation of land between burghers and peasants in the Late Middle Ages, the 1446 register has the greatest significance, because it contains additional data on the nature of property declarations (*tab. 6.5*).[283] We are informed about the owners and the monetary values of the individual taxed items—houses, places of work (clothmakers' frames, shops, butchers' benches, mills, hammer forges, malthouses, breweries,

283   Ar Cheb, book 1424, *Losungbuch 1446.*

brickyards, etc.), plots in the city and in rural areas (gardens, fields, meadows, forests, fishponds), rents, land rents collected from "subject" tenants in the countryside, etc.

Notably, the registers of the city and land taxes were kept by the city office. The two series of registers were formally similar, making it possible to understand several phenomena that appear in one set of registers by studying the second set.

6.4 Summary

In the 15th century, the land tax was direct, property-based, and collected annually. The Cheb city council had control over the tax, which included setting the tax rates and ensuring the collection and availability of the collected amount.

The land tax was a progressive tax and was determined according to the monetary value of all of the taxpayer's immovable and movable property (1.5–3.0%), which the taxpayers declared under oath. Whether they had tenure of "subject" or "free" landholdings or simply non-landholding plots, all propertied peasant households paid tax, with some precisely specified exceptions. Tax was collected from up to 130 settlements over a territory of about 400 km^2.

Prior to 1441, tax registers were of a hybrid nature, since they also contained expenditure entries and survived in a very fragmented form. After the reform of the city chancellory in 1441, only a list of taxpayers and prescribed and collected amounts could be found in them, but they survived almost without interruption until 1757, when the Cheb region was incorporated into the Bohemian land tax system.

The value of the tax registers in terms of findings is magnified by the exceptionally information-rich registers of 1424 and 1438 and a special *1456 Taxation Book*, which contain detailed inventories and descriptions of taxable items. The *1469 Tax Register* even contains data about the landlords and land rents paid by "subject" tenants.

The late medieval collection of Cheb land tax books is exceptional in many respects. Its quantity of surviving land tax registers ranks the city-state of Cheb in third place among the German-speaking parts of the Empire, representing 13% of all known books. It is significant that in the Late Middle Ages, land tax was not collected annually in any other Holy Roman Empire territory, or if so, no continuous series of tax registers has survived. The large number of written sources surviving for other territories is due to their division into separate administrative districts and not due to annually kept registers. Therefore, it seems that for now, annual and nominally recorded tax data are available only for the Cheb peasantry, supplemented in certain years by tax declaration.

A combination of factors lies behind these favorable source records: firstly, annual tax collection; secondly, the overlapping of city and territorial administration and the systematic keeping of tax registers at the city "chamber"; and thirdly, the existence of information-rich tax books.

The testimony of the Cheb land tax registers is supplemented by the city tax registers. Thanks to the 1446 register, which contains burghers' tax declarations, we are able to follow movable and immovable property both in the city and in the countryside. This makes our survey of the city and the region uniquely complete, as we are informed on the land resources of almost the entire city-state.

◂ Plate 4: **Horní Lomany (Lohma, Ober-). Two women with their knives in the vicinity of Antonínovy Výšiny (March 19, 1905). A remarkable image from the period, when amateur interest in Cheb ethnography and its comprehensive documentation was at its peak.**

III.
Social Institutions and Surplus Extraction

In the following chapters, we shift the reader's attention to the factors that influenced the distribution of the peasant surplus and the possibility of accumulating wealth and thus the extent to which socially differentiating forces were applied (*direct distribution factors*). We will focus on the practice of property and inheritance rights, the power of peasant communities, the intensity of landlords' control, and the degree of peasant surplus exploitation by all the components of rent.

7.
Institutional framework[284]

7.1 Introduction

A significant share of the shaping of peasant communities was determined by the norms and practices of the institutional controls over land tenure, use, and transfer. The question is to what extent these means of control were in the hands of the peasant community vs. the landlord.

The study of social and economic institutions over the past decades has been invigorated by new institutional economics (NIE), which conceptualized the partial factors influencing transaction costs as:[285]

+ The legal framework of land transfer: the security of tenure, disposal, and inheritance rights
+ Tools for monitoring and control, records, and registration of land transfers
+ Methods of measuring land plots
+ The physical shape of land plots, field pattern, the agricultural system, and communal rights

---

284 Summarized in Klír, "Land transfer," 159–167.

285 Rosemary L. Hopcroft, *Regions, institutions, and agrarian change in European history*, Economics, Cognition, and Society (Ann Arbor, MI: University of Michigan Press, 1999), 1–9, 15–57; Bas J. P. van Bavel and Peter C. P. Hoppenbrouwers, "Landholding and land transfer in the North Sea area (late Middle Ages – 19ᵗʰ century)," in *Landholding and land transfer in the North Sea area (late Middle Ages – 19ᵗʰ century)*, ed. Bas J. P. Van Bavel and Peter C. M. Hoppenbrouwers, CORN Publication Series 5 (Turnhout: Brepols, 2004), 13–43, on 25–27; Schofield, *Peasants*, 3. Cf. Sheilagh Ogilvie and André W. Carus, "Institutions and economic growth in historical perspective," in *Handbook of Economic Growth 2A*, ed. Steven N. Durlauf and Philippe Aghion (Amsterdam: Elsevier, 2014), 405–514.

From these factors, we will deal with the legal framework in detail.

We have only limited normative data on the late medieval legal framework concerning land tenure and transfer in the city-state of Cheb; however, entries in the tax registers show much about the practice. This is because the basis of the land tax was the monetary value of both immovable and movable properties held by the taxpayer, and tax officials annually noted the property changes and the circumstances surrounding them. In principle we can reconstruct both the concrete disposal rights to the immovable property of various legal statuses and the practices of family property and inheritance rights.

In order to reveal the legal institutions and practices of the Cheb countryside we comprehensively extracted the data contained in the land tax registers from 1424, 1438, and 1441–1456, and also from the *1456 Taxation Book*.[286] The resulting catalogue of relevant entries is very long, since it was necessary to link up entries concerning the same landholding or a single taxpayer scattered on the pages of several tax registers.[287] The catalogue is enclosed in the appendix, divided into a section comprising evidence of the exercise of *property and inheritance rights*[288] and also into a section systematically recording all entries demonstrating *kinship*.[289] We have made use of other available written sources.[290]

In the late medieval city-state of Cheb, the disposal rights to land were governed by two overlapping legal customs: the institutions of *fief right* (*Lehensrecht*) and "*purchase*" *right* (*emphyteutic right*; *Kaufrecht*). On the strength of findings in the neighboring area, we assume that the application of both rights was adapted and applied as needed to a broad spectrum of specific situations that in turn transformed these customs.

---

286   Ar Cheb, books 1068–1083, *Klosteuerbücher 1441–1456*.
287   Klír et al., *Knihy*, 198–199, Appendix 3.
288   *App. 7.1.*
289   *App. 7.2.*
290   Friedrich Wilhelm Singer, ed., *Das Nothaftische Lehensbuch von 1360. Besitz und Verwaltung der Reichsministerialen Nothaft im Historischen Egerland, Faksimile und Übertragung des Originals im Bayerischen Hauptstaatsarchiv München* (Arzberg, Hohenberg: G. Arzberger, 1996); Ar Cheb, book 1003, *Urbar der Clarissinnen ab 1464*; Heinrich Gradl, *Die Chroniken der Stadt Eger* (Prague: Verlag des Vereines für Geschichte der Deutschen in Böhmen, 1884); Ar Cheb, book 1424, *Losungsbuch 1446*. For the western area of the so-called the historical Cheb region, so-called Sechsämterland, see: Singer, *Das Landbuch*.

7.2 **Fief right**

General characteristics

The situation in the city-state of Cheb in the Late Middle Ages is easier to understand thanks to the results of analyses in the territory of Bavaria[291] and the Franconian regions.[292]

The essence of the fief system here was the transfer of landlord rights in return for which the vassal would perform certain obligations (usually services) for the overlord, typically knight services. He was not obligated to any cash or in-kind payments, apart from a symbolic fee upon the ritual handover of fiefs.[293] The vassal generally conferred the land to peasants, most by "purchase" right, i.e., by hereditary tenure and subject to a fixed annual payment

---

291   Fiefs of a lower order in the territory of Bavaria are addressed in detail by: Ludwig Holzfurtner, "Die Grundleihepraxis oberbayerischer Grundherren im späten Mittelalter," *Zeitschrift für Bayerische Landesgeschichte* 48 (1985): 647–676; Herbert Klein, "Ritterlehen und Beutellehen in Salzburg," *Mitteilungen der Gesellschaft für Salzburger Landeskunde* 80 (1940): 87–128; Ernst Klebel, "Freies Eigen und Beutellehen in Ober- und Niederbayern," *Zeitschrift für Bayerische Landesgeschichte* 11 (1938): 45–85; Hans Constantin Faussner, "Vom salmannischen Eigen zum Beutellehen. Zum bäuerlichen Grundeigentum im bayerisch-österreichischen Rechtsgebiet," *Forschungen zur Rechtsarchäologie und rechtlichen Volkskunde* 12 (1990): 11–37. For a bibliographic overview, see: Matthias Bader, "Lehenswesen in Altbayern," published on Sept. 16, 2013, in *Historisches Lexikon Bayerns*, www.historisches-lexikon-bayerns.de/Lexikon/Lehenswesen_in_Altbayern.

292   Rolf Sprandel, "Der Würzburger Lehenhof 1345–1372," *Zeitschrift für Bayerische Landesgeschichte* 47 (1984): 791–794; Hermann Hoffmann, ed., *Das älteste Lehenbuch des Hochstifts Würzburg 1303–1345*, Vol. 1–2, Quellen und Forschungen zur Geschichte des Bistums und Hochstifts Würzburg 25 (Würzburg: Schöningh, 1973); Joachim Wild, "Schriftlichkeit und Verwaltung am Beispiel der Lehenbücher in Bayern," in *Schriftlichkeit und Lebenspraxis im Mittelalter. Erfassen, Bewahren, Verändern*, ed. Hagen Keller, Christel Meier, and Thomas Scharff, Münstersche Mittelalterschriften 76 (Munich: Fink, 1999), 69–77. For a bibliographic overview, see: Hans-Peter Baum, "Lehenswesen in Franken," published on Feb. 13, 2014, in *Historisches Lexikon Bayerns*, www.historisches-lexikon-bayerns.de/Lexikon/Lehenswesen_in_Franken.

293   Stefan Patzold, *Das Lehnswesen* (Munich: Beck, 2012), esp. 94–119; Karl-Heinz Spiess and Thomas Willich, eds., *Das Lehnswesen in Deutschland im hohen und späten Mittelalter* (Stuttgart: Steiner, ³2011); Jürgen Derndorfer and Roman Deutinger, eds., *Das Lehnswesen im Hochmittelalter. Forschungskonstrukte – Quellenbefunde – Deutungsrelevanz*, Mittelalter-Forschungen 34 (Ostfildern: Thorbecke, 2010). Cf. Susan Reynolds, *Fiefs and vassals. The medieval evidence reinterpreted* (Oxford: Oxford University Press, 1994). For the field of Saxon rights, see esp. Jan Zelenka, *Beneficium et feudum: podoba a proměny lenního insti-*

(*see below*). Ideally, we would record "subject" tenants who paid land rent to a landlord who was the vassal of a more powerful overlord.

The system was more complex in reality, since certain properties were assigned under fief right including annual payment in cash and/or kind. These were individual landholdings and all parts thereof, as well as various types of plots, such as meadows, fields, vineyards, pastureland, and segments of forest that did not belong to any specific landholding (so-called non-landholding plots). The tenants of these small land plots were usually burghers or peasants.

To make the variability of feudal ties easier to deal with, in the second half of the 15th century, dual division was introduced in the Bavarian regions, which divided fiefs into *higher-order fiefs*, reserved for nobility with military capability (so-called knight's fiefs), and *lower-order fiefs*, which were acquired abundantly by burghers and peasants for an annual payment.[294] The characteristics of higher-order fief tenure in the Late Middle Ages were:

1) heritability;
2) possibility of further disposal, either sale of the fief with the consent of the overlord or conveyance of the property to a third party for an annual payment;
3) divisibility of a fief, especially during the inheritance procedure.[295]

These characteristics did not apply fully to lower-order fiefs, especially non-landholding plots. In those cases, both heritability and, for practical reasons, divisibility were limited, because such lands were elemental plots of land, firmly physically bordered in the terrain and practically indivisible.

In practice, fief right found an unusually wide range of applications, since it generally afforded wider disposal rights than "purchase" right or a time-limited rental lease. In this way, practices rising from fief right expanded considerably in the Late Middle Ages to include non-landholding plots especially. Their formal status as lower-order fiefs ensured that they were not subject to strict landlord control and therefore nothing stopped them from being put on the market, transferred between peasant landholdings or burghers' households, worked by the buyer, or rented out. Moreover, this allowed the overlord to

---

tutu, Práce Historického ústavu AV ČR, řada A, Monographia = Opera Instituti Historici Pragae, Series A, Monographia 66 (Prague: Historický ústav, 2016).

294 Klebel, "Freies Eigen," 67–68; Klein, "Ritterlehen," 91–92; Faussner, "Vom salmannischen Eigen"; Sprandel, "Der Würzburger Lehenhof," 792–793.

295 Holzfurtner, "Die Grundleihepraxis," 655–662.

make some money from a property without having to sell it and completely lose control over it.

Fief right in the city-state of Cheb

The division into higher and lower-order fiefs may be applied to the late medieval city-state of Cheb. The higher-order fief system was studied in considerable detail in connection with the fate of the Cheb ministeriales.[296] The matter of small fiefs in the form of individually registered and taxed meadows and fields, which littered the Cheb countryside, has not yet become a topic of research.

The important overlords of the late medieval city-state of Cheb were:[297]

1) The King of Bohemia as the lienholder of the Cheb territory, controlling through his representatives both imperial fiefs and the immediate fiefs of Cheb Castle;[298]

2) Nobility with origins in the ministeriales of the Hohenstaufen era—mainly the Nothaft, Paulsdorfer, and Sparneck families;[299]

---

296   That is, the lower nobility—vassals of the Cheb Castle. Cf. Kubů, *Die staufische Ministerialität*.

297   In summary form on the genesis of fiefs see, e.g., Sturm, *Districtus Egranus*, 50–60. For the western part of the historical Cheb region (Sechsämterland), cf. Singer, *Das Landbuch*, 41–47.

298   No detailed medieval register has survived for the imperial fiefs of Cheb, so our records of them are very fragmentary and incomplete. The following castles in the vicinity of the city of Cheb were imperial "knight's fees": Hazlov (Haslau), Starý Hroznatov (Kinsberg), Libá (Liebenstein), Podhrad (Pograt), and Skalná (Wildstein); Ostroh (Seeberg) Castle was an independent fief of Cheb Castle. See Sturm, *Districtus Egranus*, 173–179, 189–235; Karl Siegl, "Geschichte der Egerer Burgpflege," *Mittheilungen des Vereines für Geschichte der Deutschen in Böhmen* 50 (1912): 546–594, on 550–552. References to small imperial fiefs are scattered in a range of documents, or in a more concentrated form in the Cheb Poor Clares' cartulary of 1476. See Siegl, "Das Salbuch," 26, nr. 7; 57–58, nr. 95; 69–70, nr. 136; 90, nr. 204; 94, nrs. 217, 219; 100, nr. 236; 101–102, nr. 241; 103–104, nr. 248; 116–117, nr. 289; 119, nr. 301; 128–129, nr. 326.

299   Cf. Peter Braun, "Die Herren von Sparneck. Stammbaum, Verbreitung, Kurzinventar," *Archiv für die Geschichte von Oberfranken* 82 (2002): 71–106; Michael Döberl, *Die Landgrafschaft der Leuchtenberger. Eine verfassungsgeschichtliche Studie mit anhängenden Regesten und Urkunden* (Munich: Killinger 1893); Harald Stark and Herbert Maurer, *Die Familie Notthaft – auf Spurensuche im Egerland, in Bayern und Schwaben* (Weissenstadt: Heinz Späthling, 2006); Harald Stark et al., *Po stopách šlechtického rodu Notthafftů – Notthaffti v Čechách a v Bavorsku / Auf den Spuren eines Adelsgeschlechts – die Notthaffte in Böhmen und Bayern* (Cheb: HB Print, 2007); Harald Stark, "Die Stammlehen der Familie Nothaft im Eger-

3) The Landgraves of Leuchtenberg, who had inherited extensive fief rights after a ministerial family died out without a successor;[300]

4) The monastery in Waldsassen.[301]

Several findings on practices relating to fiefs in the late medieval city-state of Cheb may be found in the oldest Nothaft fief register (ca. 1360–1405). In this fief register: (1) it is easy to differentiate between high- and low-order fiefs; (2) small fiefs were fairly well specified, including the payments required from them annually; and (3) one can also easily trace factual and formal heritability of fiefs in the male and female lines.[302]

The Poor Clares nuns of Cheb's cartulary informs us comprehensively about further aspects of fief tenure and transfer.[303] Various copies in the cartulary document the various ways the Poor Clares nuns gained landlords' rights from the original vassals, which they endeavored to complement with fief rights as

land," *Archiv für die Geschichte von Oberfranken* 75 (1995): 39–69. Earlier literature on the lower noble families is summarized by Kubů, *Die staufische Ministerialität*, 76–79. A complete list has survived for Paulsdorfer fiefs in a charter from a period around the year 1299 (ME, 186–187, nr. 512). The oldest Nothaft German-language fief register dates to the last third of the 14th century (Singer, *Das Nothaftische Lehensbuch*; Stark, "Die Stammlehen"; Josef Hemmerle, "Kolonisation und Lehenbesitz der Herren von Nothaft im westlichen Böhmen," *Stifter-Jahrbuch* 4 (1955): 57–78, information on the tenure of imperial, Nothaft, Paulsdorfer, Sparneck, and other fiefs held by burghers of Cheb is contained in the 1446 City Tax Register (*App. 7.3*; Ar Cheb, book 1424, *Losungsbuch 1446*).

300   Illuminatus Wagnr, *Geschichte der Landgrafen von Leuchtenberg I* (Kallmünz: Laßleben, 1940). The oldest fief register from Leuchtenberg, also written in the German language, dates to the end of the 14th century (Georg Völkl, ed., "Das älteste Leuchtenberger Lehenbuch," *Verhandlungen des Historischen Vereins für Oberpfalz und Regensburg* 96 (1955): 277–404; Tomáš Velička, "Lantkrabata z Leuchtenberka v politice lucemburských králů a jejich lenní knihy s ohledem na majetky na Chebsku a Loketsku" [Landgrafen von Leuchtenberg in der Politik der luxemburgischen Könige und ihre Lehensbücher in Hinsicht auf die Besitztümer im Eger- und Elbogenland], *Sborník muzea Karlovarského kraje* 22 (2014): 169–212, on 192–202).

301   The oldest fief book, written in Latin, for the Waldsassen Abbey fiefs was begun in the first half of the 14th century. Cf. Hans Muggenthaler, *Kolonisatorische und wirtschaftliche Tätigkeit eines deutschen Zisterzienserklosters im 12. und 13. Jahrhundert*, Deutsche Geschichtsbücherei 2 (Munich: Hugo Schmidt, 1924) 172–173; Rudolf Langhammer, *Waldsassen. Kloster und Stadt 1. Aus der Geschichte der ehedem reichsunmittelbaren und gefürsteten Zisterzienserabtei bis zur Reformation* (Waldsassen: Albert Angerer, 1936), 137–138; Heribert Sturm, *Tirschenreuth*, Historischer Atlas von Bayern – Altbayern 21 (Munich: Kommission for Bayerische Landesgeschrifte, 1970).

302   *App. 7.5.*

303   *App. 7.3.*

well. In certain cases, the Poor Clares received annual payments directly from overlords who simultaneously surrendered their fief rights as a whole.[304] An example of this is seen in the fate of a meadow near Plesná (Fleissen) on the boundary between the regions of Cheb and Loket, which was a Nothaft fief from which an annual payment of seven hens was levied on its users. Firstly, the overlord, Albrecht Nothaft of Weißenstein, loaned this levy to the Franciscans of Cheb in 1443, and then in 1458 he donated it, at the same time also transferring his rights to the fief to them. At that time, the meadow was used by the peasants Ulrich Klarner, Maier, and Matel Peczel, who paid the Franciscans to use it.[305] Fiefs that were bought back were identified in various ways, usually in the sense of a "free" heritable fief or "free" holding (*freies Erbe*; *freies Erbe und Eigen*).

In the same way as other sovereign overlords in the city-state of Cheb, the Poor Clares could loan their own holding, freed from their original feudal obligations, as if it were their own fief. The former vassals therefore became overlords.[306] Other tenants, too, released their properties from fief status, including the burghers of Cheb. Consequently, non-landholding plots with fief status came into circulation. These land plots naturally intermingled with "free" properties, where it was sometimes especially emphasized that they were not fiefs. This was the case in 1355, when a burgher of Cheb, Gotfreid Becherer, gifted to the Poor Clares substantial grain levies from three landholdings in various villages to mark the occasion of his two daughters entering the convent.[307]

The fief nature of land tenure in the late medieval city-state of Cheb and the varying rigidity, origin, and hierarchy of feudal relations naturally did nothing to improve the clarity of written records. Nevertheless, for this study we need not decode the complex feudal relations of the city-state of Cheb; rather we identify the concrete disposal rights and obligations of peasants as the actual users of landholdings and non-landholding plots.

---

304   Siegl, "Das Salbuch," 30, nrs. 15–16.
305   Siegl, "Das Salbuch," 106, nr. 257; 117, nr. 291.
306   Siegl, "Das Salbuch," 40, nr. 44; Ar Cheb, book 1003, *Urbar der Clarissinnen ab 1464*, 5 (fields in Dřenice/Treunitz), 6 (fishing rights on the Wondreb River), 19 (meadows in Nový Drahov/Rohr).
307   Siegl, "Das Salbuch," 58, nr. 97.

7.3 "Purchase" right

The legal norms, customs, and practice of "purchase" right (*emphyteusis*) in the late medieval Cheb countryside have not yet been analyzed. The situation in early modern Bohemia (16th–17th centuries), reconstructed by Vladimír Procházka and newly also by the participants of the project *Social Structures in Early Modern Bohemia 1650–1750*, seems to be a suitable starting point and comparative framework, based on the village land-transfer registers and knowledge of the broader Central European context.[308] On a regional level, we may use the relevant detailed information from the neighboring late medieval and early modern Loket region[309] and also some adjacent German regions.[310] The medieval roots of the legal customs and practical procedures recorded in early modern Czech written sources are indisputable; isolated elements of this may also be found in emphyteutic deeds dating to the 14th and 15th centuries.[311]

Tenurial right

The majority of Cheb landholdings had "subject" (German: *untertänig*) status and were purchased (German: *Kaufrecht*).[312] The peasant had a relatively broad tenure right to such a landholding, including extensive disposition, family

---

308   Procházka, *Česká poddanská nemovitost*. See also newly summarized by Eduard Maur, "Das bäuerliche Erbrecht und die Erbschaftspraxis in Böhmen im 16.–18. Jahrhundert," *Historická demografie* 20 (1996): 93–118; Maur, "Dějiny," 17; Cerman, "Social Structure"; Velková, *Krutá vrchnost*, 86–303; Štefanová, *Erbschaftspraxis*, esp. 49–72; Zeitlhofer, *Besitzwechsel*, esp. 11–28.
309   Rudolf Schreiber, *Der Elbogener Kreis und seine Enklaven nach dem dreissigjährigen Kriege*, Sudetendeutsches historisches Archiv 2 (Prague: Deutsche Gesellschaft der Wissenschaften und Künste für die Tschechoslowakische Republik, 1935). Demographic analyses for the Loket and Sokolov regions in the Early Modern Period have only marginal application, since they concern mountainous regions with a wide range of livelihood options in non-agrarian production. Cf. Jan Horský, Iva Sedláčková, and Markéta Seligová, "Ein einheitliches ,altes demographisches Regime' oder die Bindung eines demographischen Verhaltens zu ,Ökotypen,'" *Historická demografie* 20 (1996): 57–91. Cf. Antonín Haas, ed., *Sbírka pramenů práva městského království českého IV/1, Privilegia nekrálovských měst českých z let 1232–1452* (Prague: Nakladatelství Československé akademie věd, 1954), 419–420, no. 294.
310   Werner Rösener, *Bauern im Mittelalter* (Munich: Beck, ³1987), 228–240, 267–276.
311   Graus, *Dějiny*, 233–267; Maur, "Das bäuerliche Erbrecht," 93–94. Cf. also Míka, *Poddaný lid*, 187–226.
312   For terminology cf. Cerman, "Social Structure," 59–60.

property, and inheritance rights. The peasant could sell, exchange, or sublease the landholding or pass it on to his children and relatives; in the case of death, the landholding went to his heir by inheritance procedure. In the city-state of Cheb, the existence of fees required by the landlord for the transfer of land cannot be proven.[313] The "subject" landholding was understood to be an integral economic unit made up of dwellings, economic buildings, gardens, fields, and meadows or other properties to which certain rights and obligations to the landlord, state, and church were bound, usually in the form of payments in cash and/or in kind. The possibility of alienating the component parts that comprised the "subject" landholding was limited normatively and practically. Firstly, the landholding formed a balanced and time-tested—over many generations—economic unit whose balance and prosperity could be jeopardized by any land separation or fragmentation. Secondly, the potential transfer of individual plots could take place only between landholdings subject to the same landlord, who had to give his consent. Both the "subject" tenants and the landlord were keen to maintain the integrity of landholdings. On the other hand, in many situations and for various reasons it was advisable to adapt the size of landholdings to suit both parties, e.g., to divide off or exchange distant or unfavorably situated plots.[314]

In the Cheb land tax registers, mainly only more significant changes can be identified, which occurred with the consent or acceptance of the landlord, such as the subdivision or merging of landholdings, or significant changes in the size of land property held. In practice, it is possible to encounter the subdivision/merging of landholdings and their obligations and the temporary or permanent subdivision/integration of retirement dwellings and cottages. The

---

313   For a similar situation in the neighboring part of Smrčiny, cf. Singer, *Das Landbuch*, 60.

314   For more on the situation in early modern Bohemia, cf. Procházka, *Česká poddanská nemovitost*, 65–105. For the Central European context see Cerman, "Social Structure," 58–64, which also contains an overview of the Czech literature. Cf. also Stefan Sonderegger, "Active Manorial Lords and Peasant Farmers in the Economic Life of the Late Middle Ages: Results from New Swiss and German Research." In *Peasants, Lords, and State: Comparing Peasant Conditions in Scandinavia and the Eastern Alpine Region, 1000–1750*, ed. Tore Iversen, John Ragnar Myking, and Stefan Sonderegger, The Northern World 89 (Leiden and Boston: Brill, 2020), 292–318; Birgit Heinzle, "Transactions Intertwined. Land Transfer Among Tenants in the Aflenz and Veitsch Estate." In *Busy tenants. Peasant land markets in Central Europe (15th to 16th century)*, ed. Thomas Ertl, Thomas Frank, and Samuel Nussbaum, Vierteljahrschrift für Sozial- und Wirtschaftsgeschichte, Beiheft 253 (Stuttgart: Franz Steiner Verlag 2021), 75–108.

small extent of such organic changes in the long-term is indicated by the fact that the number of landholdings in settlements remained stable for the entire Late Middle Ages in the city-state of Cheb.

The degree of the "subject" tenants' personal dependence on the landlords was minimal; their relationship was economic and was expressed by payment of the fixed land rent. The peasant could leave the landholding at any time, provided they had a successor in place.[315] Several times in the tax registers a situation when several "subject" tenants moved in one year or two tenants exchanged their "subject" landholdings can be noted (chap. 23). Escheat was limited to the lowest possible degree. According to the tax registers, the Cheb "subject" landholdings were inherited by male and female heirs in descending, ascending, and secondary lines—that is, sons and daughters, spouses, more rarely siblings and the children of siblings, uncles from the brother's children, and others.[316] Nothing indicates that the late medieval Cheb situation differed in this way from early modern Bohemia.[317]

Family property right

As in Bohemia, we also encounter in the city-state of Cheb FAMILY PROPERTY SOCIETIES (hereinafter FPSs), which were formed based on family relations and usually were created by spouses and their children. At the head of such an FPS was the tenant, commonly the father of the family (95%), more rarely the mother—a widow (3–5%). Only in extraordinary cases did other types of societies emerge, such as those with stepparents with children from a previous marriage, the husband of the child, or relatives in the branch line.[318] Such FPSs were usually concluded due to the premature death of the father-tenant and often were only temporary.[319]

---

315 On the situation in high and late medieval Bohemia and Moravia, cf. Graus, Dějiny, 244–246, 256–257; Míka, Poddaný lid, 189–203.

316 App. 7.2, passim.

317 Grulich, Populační vývoj, 302–309; Velková, Krutá vrchnost, 155–173; Štefanová, Erbschafts-praxis, 73–86, 94–124; Zeitlhofer, Besitzwechsel, 200–227.

318 App. 7.2, nrs. 1; 4; 6; 10; 23; 32; 37; 43; 62–63.

319 Cf. Procházka, Česká poddanská nemovitost, 365–373. For more on the head of the household, see Grulich, Populační vývoj, 265–268; Velková, Krutá vrchnost, 149–273. For more on the provisional nature of marginal types of FPS (in this case families) from an early modern demographic perspective, see, e.g., Markéta Seligová, "Die Entwicklung der Familie auf der

A widow might become the head of the FPS, unless she was forced to enter a new marriage to secure a male labor force for the landholding.[320] This was possible only when the children were almost adults and one of them was about to take tenure of the landholding and establish a new FPS. In such a situation, a widow was the head of an FPS only for a limited period, usually a year or two. Occasionally one can trace the progression in land tax registers: father → widow → widow and son → son. Landholdings and FPSs where male labor was not urgently lacking, even after the death of the father, were in an exceptional situation and the widow could then remain head of the FPS for many years until her death. Widows at the head of a landholding in the long-term indicate two socially and economically opposing poles. The male labor force was superfluous on the richest landholdings, where the tenant himself did not have to work because he used the labor of other men—servants, inmate-lodgers, wage laborers, or subtenants. The widow then assumed just the role of manager. The opposite applied to landholdings with a minimum of its own economic resources, where the male labor force found no application, and during his lifetime, the man had worked elsewhere. Landholdings with long-term farming widows indicate contrasting socioeconomic stratification.

Family continuity on a landholding where an adult son was lacking could be ensured by someone else other than the widow. The Cheb land tax registers recorded two cases where the daughter of the original tenant paid land tax for a landholding for a year or more before her brother took over the property.[321] It is unclear, however, whether or not the daughter was married.

Another option was a society with the children from the previous marriage where a widower tenant took a new wife or a widow took a new husband. This meant that the original FPS endured on the landholding but with the addition of new members.[322] However, we were unable to identify such situations in the tax registers.

Herrschaft Děčín in der Mitte des 17 Jh. unter Berücksichtigung seines wirtschaftlichen Charakters," *Historická demografie* 20 (1996): 119–175, on 164, 175.

320 Cf. Procházka, *Česká poddanská nemovitost*, 373–376. For more on the status of widows, see esp. Ogilvie and Edwards, "Women"; Grulich, *Populační vývoj*, 268–278; Velková, *Krutá vrchnost*, 247–259; Štefanová, *Erbschaftspraxis*, 153–160; Zeitlhofer, *Besitzwechsel*, 219–227; Maur, *Dějiny*, 18–19.

321 *App.* 7.2, nrs. 1; 4; 27; 37; 43; 62–63.

322 On this topic in general, see Procházka, *Česká poddanská nemovitost*, 376–380.

In tax registers we sometimes find property societies of siblings, comprising children in general or specifically brothers or a brother and a sister.[323] This typically served as a short-term arrangement following the death of both parents, until the siblings had started their own families, and one of them had acquired the landholding and paid the others off. Long-term cohabitation of siblings would otherwise have resembled one of the variations of the complex family, the so-called "joint" family.[324]

More frequent were societies consisting of a father tenant or widow with their son-in-law.[325] The question is why such a situation occurred during the lifetime of the tenant. The endeavor to ensure the transfer of the landholding or to prioritize one of the heirs might have played a role in this. We might also imagine behind this a situation where, although an adult daughter had started her own family, her husband did not have the opportunity to have his own landholding, or his labor was needed by the parents. A society of a farmer with his son-in-law indicated the absence of an adult son who could inherit the landholding.[326]

One may also come across societies formed with relatives from a different family line, mainly uncles and nephews or nieces.[327] This is evidenced by the fact that in all cases the entry contained a formulation like "*und sein Bruder Kinder*," which indicates that the uncle was acting in the role of guardian of his brother's children. In some exceptional cases, an entry documented an FPS comprising an uncle, his brother's children, and his mother (grandmother) and an FPS composed of a tenant and other unspecified relatives.[328]

We know little of the form of the **spousal property right** based on the Cheb tax registers, but in some settlements and with wealthier families we could expect the influence of town law and modifications of the property relations by the nuptial contract.[329] This would correspond to several recorded cases showing the separability of the property of both spouses, when the widow

323   *App. 7.2*, nrs. 32; 47.
324   On this in general terms, see Procházka, *Česká poddanská nemovitost*, 380–382.
325   *App. 7.2*, passim.
326   On this topic in general, see Procházka, *Česká poddanská nemovitost*, 382–384.
327   On this generally, see Procházka, *Česká poddanská nemovitost*, 385–386.
328   *App. 7.2*, nrs. 1; 32; 47.
329   On this topic in general, see Procházka, *Česká poddanská nemovitost*, 389–404. See also, e.g., also Velková, *Krutá vrchnost*, 149–246; Štefanová, *Erbschaftspraxis*, 131–135; Zeitlhofer, *Besitzwechsel*, 23–24.

received priority over the children or possessed her own property. Its origin may have lain in a sizeable dowry that the widow brought to the landholding and thanks to which, as a widow, she had a right to a retired tenant's dwelling and preferential inheritance. For example, we may mention the widow of a certain blacksmith (*Smid*) from Pomezná (Markhausen) who kept fields worth 6 threescore of Prague groschen, while her son took over the landholding,[330] or the mother of a miller (*Mülner*) from Krásná Lípa (Schönlind), who as a widow living with her brother-in-law in the city of Cheb had an unspecified inheritance at her disposal, even though she had an adult son.[331]

We cannot know the specifics of the **property rights of children** without more information.[332] In principle, also in the city-state of Cheb everything indicates that children, at birth, automatically joined an FPS and had a right to a certain share of the property. This claim was ideally fulfilled in two ways: first, as the equipment for a separate household, and second, as a hereditary claim in the dissolution of the original FPS. Both fulfilments could be fulfilled at the same time in the form of a one-off payment. The Cheb land tax registers do not inform us about the equipment; sometimes only the inherited share can be reconstructed.

The position of **orphans** again did not differ in their basic features from the Bohemian situation known from the 16th century.[333] Until they reached adulthood, farming on their father's landholding was performed by (1) the mother (widow); (2) the widow's next husband, who was not accepted with full rights into the FPS and passed on the landholding to the orphans once they reached adulthood; or (3) the uncle. It could happen that until they reached adulthood, the landholding could be (4) leased out. The indicator for options (2) and (4) is a series of direct taxpayers according to the model A → B → A (such as Worss → Winckler → Worss).[334]

---

330 *App. 7.2, nr. 40.*

331 *App. 7.2, nr. 68.*

332 On this generally, see Procházka, *Česká poddanská nemovitost*, 404–417. See also, e.g., Štefanová, *Erbschaftspraxis*, 130–140; Velková, *Krutá vrchnost*, 149–246.

333 On this generally, see Procházka, *Česká poddanská nemovitost*, 417–435.

334 *App. 7.2, nrs. 1; 6; 17; 37.*

The entries in the Cheb tax registers contain data on the material security of **overaged family members.**[335] It was mentioned, for instance, in the village of Klest (Reißig) in 1448 that one of the landholdings was transferred to new hands and the original tenant had moved his retired dwelling (*Herberge*) to his son's property. This case proves the existence of a separate small house and perhaps even an independent subsistence holding of a retired peasant. It was unnecessary to list the most common situation, a society made up of a retired peasant and the family of the new tenant, in the tax registers.

Family inheritance right

In the event of the real dissolution of a family property society and its division, the individual members were not equal in property, because the share of the sons was greater than the shares of the daughters and perhaps even the widows. The determination of the exact proportions of the individual ideal shares is known only fragmentarily, but in principle they would correspond to the early modern West Bohemian system of preferring the male offspring. At the core of this asymmetric system could be land militia duty, which was bound to the landholding.[336] Nevertheless, the separation of property based on a testament is also documented.

If the heirs were only the sons, the original property was passed on to them under the system of equal ideal shares.[337] The specific shares that went to daughters in the city-state of Cheb are unknown to us, with one exception.[338] If the survivors were mother and daughter, the property was divided evenly between them.[339] If there were no sons and the surviving family member was a married daughter, her husband would become the new tenant.

Upon the dissolution of the original family property society, the "subject" landholding was usually transferred to a single heir (the so-called primary heir). The remaining members of the society would instead receive an ideal

335   On this topic in general, see Procházka, *Česká poddanská nemovitost*, 435–452. See also, e.g., Grulich, *Populační vývoj*, 339–356; Velková, *Krutá vrchnost*, 274–303; Štefanová, *Erbschafts-praxis*, 167–218; Zeitlhofer, *Besitzwechsel*, 272–302.
336   Durdík, "Vojenská hotovost"; Kubů, "Ozbrojené síly."
337   *App. 7.2, nrs. 3; 24.*
338   *App. 7.2, nr. 27.*
339   *App. 7.2, nr. 69.*

share of its value.[340] If the landholding was extremely large, or the property of the FPS included more landholdings, it was divided, and each of the sons acquired his own landholding.

Upon the demise of an FPS, the total monetary value of all significant property items in the inheritance was calculated, and according to certain principles, each of the heirs' ideal share was specified. This could occur based on a will or inheritance agreements. The value was most frequently set by estimation, although certain items might have previously gone through the market, and their value was therefore known. Representatives of the peasant community, the village bailiff, aldermen, and other leading neighbors participated in the estimation.[341] In the city-state of Cheb, the subject of the hereditary share most often included (1) the landholding as a whole, more precisely the "purchase" right to the "subject" landholding; (2) the flexible accessories of the landholding, especially horses and cattle; (3) non-landholding plots and other special property items such as ponds; and (4) cash or receivables.[342] The primary heir took the landholding into his new FPS, the other members either flexible items and/or monetary receivables from the primary heir.

The specific value of the inheritance of persons who did not inherit the landholding in the city-state of Cheb is known only in a few cases, because these people, whether sons or daughters, brought their share to the landholding that they married into or bought. We are unable to reliably distinguish between these genetically different parts in the frame of an FPS. However, we can see them if their tenant had not been incorporated into any landholding taxed by the land tax, or if his part was taxed and listed separately for another reason. We can thus determine the form of the inheritance shares in the case of persons who (1) lived in Cheb but taxed properties in the countryside in the framework of land tax, (2) resided at a landholding that was not subject to land tax, or (3) lived at the landholding of a relative, and other persons such as (4) orphans living on the landholding of an uncle or (5) widows.

340   Procházka, *Česká poddanská nemovitost*, 83–95, 365–371, 453. See also, e.g., Velková, *Krutá vrchnost*, 174–190; Štefanová, *Erbschaftspraxis*, 73, 130–140; Zeitlhofer, *Besitzwechsel*, 174–180, 193–195.

341   Procházka, *Česká poddanská nemovitost*, 466–468; Josef Hanzal, "Poznámky ke studiu ceny poddanské nemovitosti v 16.–17. století," in *Příspěvky k dějinám cen nemovitostí v 16.–18. století* (Prague: Univerzita Karlova, 1963), 39–48; Petráň, *Poddaný lid*, 25–26; Choholáč, *Selské peníze*, 72–75.

342   *App. 7.2*, passim.

Specific examples of property division

Of the many documents of concrete inheritance, we may mention:
+ The landholding of the peasant Clugel in Okrouhlá (Scheibenreuth). In 1438, the FPS was comprised of the "subject" landholding with a value of 7 threescore of Prague groschen, seven tagwerk of non-landholding meadows with a value of 20 threescore, and livestock for 17 threescore. In 1447, the father was dead, and the FPS was temporarily comprised of three sons: Hans, Fritz, and Nicolas. A year later, the landholding was already held only by Hans; the other two brothers had left for the city of Cheb. For 1456, Hans's property was comprised of a landholding with a value of 6 threescore, 2.5 tagwerk of non-landholding meadows for 7.5 threescore, and livestock with a value of 8 threescore. Hans Clugel thus inherited the landholding and one-third of the non-landholding meadows; Fritz and Nicolas got one-third of the meadows each, and Hans had to pay them money and/or livestock as well.[343]
+ The property of the peasant Michael Mÿssler in Okrouhlá (Scheibenreuth), where one of the sons inherited the landholding and half of the non-landholding meadows, while the other was paid off and in addition received the other half of the non-landholding meadows.[344]
+ Distribution of the inheritance of Peter Vogelsanck of Poustka (Oedt). In 1446, Petr's tax obligations were assumed by his son, Hans, paying 30 Prague groschen on the landholding and another 30 groschen on his brother's children's share of the inheritance ("Erb/e"), indicating that they were orphans.[345]
+ A vivid description of the method of disbursement of their inheritance share is contained in a crossed-out note in the 1454 register for Hans Fischer in Dolní Dvory (Kunreuth, Unter-), as follows: "hat dez H[ans] Mayers tocht[er] vn[d] sein Brud[er] hab[e]n in geb[e]n XIIII[1/2] ss II kvh[e] vnd ein tagwerk Wismat fur X ss."[346] The entry says that Hans Fischer was to settle with Hans Mayer's daughter and her brother. Specifically, he was to give them 14.5 threescore, 2 cows, and a meadow.

343   *App. 7.2, nr. 62.*
344   *App. 7.2, nr. 63.*
345   *App. 7.2, nr. 47.*
346   *App. 7.2, nr. 27.*

In the examples of the peasants Clugel, Mÿssler, and Vogelsanck, we see evidence of the distribution of paternal inheritance in equal shares between brothers. The fourth example documents a combined disbursement involving a cash sum, non-landholding plots, and cattle.

7.4 Items of land transfer

Like in other Central European regions, land transfer in the late medieval city-state of Cheb took place in two principally different forms. The first was land comprising an integral part of the landholding (A); the second, individual and freely disposable plots that were not part of the inalienable equipment of the landholding, so-called non-landholding plots (B).[347] At the same time, it is not possible to prove that the spatial pattern would have differed between the two types of plots, i.e., that the non-landholding plots would have been located outside of the actual core of the open-fields farmland.[348] The possible difference in the placement of the plots rather arose from their agricultural use, because meadows especially were often situated outside of the open-field farmland.

A. Landholdings

In the Cheb countryside during the 15th century, two legally different types of landholdings are documented, both of which were subject to land tax (*tab. 7.1*):[349]
1) "Subject" landholdings under "purchase" right, from which perpetual and fixed annual payments (land rent) were made by tenants to the landlord; this landlord could be the vassal of an overlord. The "purchase" right was so general that it was not even explicitly stated in the land tax registers from 1424 and 1469. The entries in the 1438 register and in the 1456 *Taxation Book* listed "purchase" right for ca. 95% of all landholdings.[350]

---

347   Cerman, "Open fields," 410; Van Bavel and Hoppenbrouwers, "Landholding," 17.
348   Cerman, "Open fields," 410–411.
349   *App. 7.9.*
350   Klír, *Knihy*, 148–150, 159–161, 597–598.

2) Various privileged landholdings, usually with the status of hereditary/
heritable or free hereditary/heritable fiefs (*Erbhof*), whose holder was
(i) a vassal, usually obligated to their overlord for military service with
a horse; or (ii) free, without obligations to landlords and overlords, usually
with payments to the parish church only (*freier Hof*; *eigener Hof*). The
denomination of these landholdings fluctuated in the tax registers throughout the 15th century.[351] Throughout this analysis, we are simplifying terminology and the complex reality, and we use the term "*free*" *landholding* for all
privileged landholdings, because in practice they were disposed similarly. In
the *1469 Tax Register*, free and heritable fiefs were not differentiated from
hereditary fiefs, since in both cases these were landholdings without payments due to a landlord.

The land tax registers and taxation book inform us of property transactions
involving "free" landholdings. Free division, separation, and sale of subdivisions
are all documented.[352] Determining the quantity and distribution of "free"
landholdings across the city-state of Cheb is difficult, since legal status was
not always strictly and precisely specified in tax documentation and could also
fluctuate. The numbers of "free" landholdings specified in the table should be
considered to represent a minimum, especially for 1438 and 1456 (*tab. 7.2*).[353]

The genesis and original difference in the legal position of the "subject"
and "free" (privileged) landholdings in the city-state of Cheb and the situation before the 15th century are unclear. All of the landholdings, except for the
economically weakest, were obligated to maintain a prescribed and variously
expensive armament (depending on economic possibilities) and if needed,
to provide one armiger for the land militia. "Free" landholdings provided an
equestrian warrior, sometimes also with a page. This was related to the hereditary nature of the male line (*Mannlehen*).[354] The label of "free" landholdings
as hereditary can be connected with their being different in this respect from
common "subject" holdings, which were not originally hereditary.[355]

---

351   *App. 7.7.*
352   App. 7.2, nrs. 65; 85; 147.
353   *App. 7.8.*
354   Durdík, "Vojenská hotovost"; Singer, *Das Landbuch*, 42, 60.
355   Singer, *Das Landbuch*, 42.

Table 7.1. **Overview of disposition rights with landholdings of different legal statuses.**

Legal status of the landholding		Land tax	Land rent	Inheritability	Possibility of sale	Possibility to sublease to a third person under payment	Divisibility
"Purchase" right	"Subject" landholdings	yes	yes	yes	need to ensure successor	no	with consent
Heritable fief	"Free" landholdings	yes	yes	yes	with consent	yes	yes
Freely heritable fief; "free" landholding		yes	**no**	yes	free sale	yes	yes

Table 7.2. **Frequency of the "subject" and "free" landholdings in the city-state of Cheb in the 15th century.**

	Absolute terms				%			
	1424	1438	1456	1469	1424	1438	1456	1469
Number of evaluated settlements	99	113	93	99	x	x	x	x
Landholdings in total	935	935	728	817	100.0	100.0	100.0	100.0
"Subject" landholdings	879	905	714	766	94.0	96.8	98.1	93.8
"Free" landholdings (Freely heritable fief)	51	21	11	51	5.5	2.2	1.5	6.2
"Free" landholdings (Heritable fief)	5	9	3		0.5	1.0	0.4	

Source: From Klír, "Land transfer," 167, tab. 4. Data according to Ar Cheb, book 1060, *Klosteuerbuch 1424*; book 1067, *Klosteuerbuch 1438*; book 1084, *Klosteuerbuch (Schätzungsbuch) 1456*; book 1096, *Klosteuerbuch 1469*.

Note: * – only a fragment of the register has been preserved

B. Non-landholding plots

General characteristics

In the city and land tax registers in the late medieval city-state of Cheb, independent and separately taxed plots without firm ties to a specific landholding, which the tenant could dispose of relatively freely, appear in abundance. In modern Austrian terminology, the corresponding designation would be non-landholding properties or land plots (*unbehauste Gründer*),[356] in German legal studies *"walzende Stücke,"*[357] in Upper German regional studies also *"einzechtige, einschichtige, einfältige, absonderliche, fliegende . . . Güter,"*[358] and one also comes across the term *"walzende Gründe."*[359] Within this study, we speak of NON-LANDHOLDING PLOTS. They were most often meadows, fields, pastureland, or fallow lands, which were not usually integral components of the open-field system and enforced crop rotations, allowing flexible property disposition and individual agricultural cultivation.[360] It is necessary to stress the particular importance of this type of land as a relatively flexible resource that could be used to adjust landholdings to demographic changes.

According to the tax registers from 1424 and 1438 and the *1456 Taxation Book*, about one-quarter of all taxpayers in the city-state of Cheb had at least one non-landholding plot at their disposal (*tab. 7.3*). Taxpayers with non-landholding plots were found to various degrees in most of Cheb's rural settlements. In some, however, they were rather an exception, thus, one taxpayer with a single non-landholding plot represented an entire settlement; elsewhere, on the contrary, they appeared in mass. At least one appeared in 94 of 113 villages.

Detailed analysis demonstrated that non-landholding plots circulated amongst peasant households and as a result, some taxpayers held non-

356   Procházka, *Česká poddanská nemovitost*, 85.
357   E.g., Carl August Gründler, *Polemik des germanischen Rechts Land- und Lehnrecht (jus controversum germanicum privatum et feudale)*, Bd. 4 (Leipzig: Reimann, 1838), 74. Cf. also Holzfurtner, "Die Grundleihepraxis," 658.
358   Hans Jänichen, *Beiträge zur Wirtschaftsgeschichte des schwäbischen Dorfes*, Veröffentlichungen der Kommission für geschichtliche Landeskunde in Baden-Württemberg. Reihe B 60 (Stuttgart: Kohlhammer, 1970), 130, 133, 139–140.
359   Cerman, "Social Structure," 69–70.
360   Cerman, "Social Structure," 70; Cerman, "Open fields," 411–413. For the Upper Palatinate cf. esp. Georg Leingärtner, *Die Wüstungsbewegungen im Landgericht Amberg vom ausgehenden Mittelalter bis zur Neuorganisation des Landgerichts im Jahre 1803*, Münchener Historische Studien, Abt. Bayerische Geschichte 3 (Kallmünz: M. Lassleben, 1956), 6.

landholding plots outside of the settlement where their own landholding stood (*fig. 7.2*). Short-term rental of more distant land plots may be assumed.

Late medieval written sources relating to the city-state of Cheb show that non-landholding plots could have one or more of a wide range of uses and legal statuses. Specifically documented as being in peasant tenure are the following:[361]

+ Rented non-landholding plots
+ "Purchased" ("subject") non-landholding plots
+ "Free" non-landholding plots (non-heritable fiefs, heritable fief, and free heritable fiefs)

It was not the legal status but the monetary value of non-landholding plots that was decisive for the collection of land tax. The precise legal status of a large part of the non-landholding plots therefore did not have to be recorded; the quantitative distinction between the individual types is thus impossible.

A favorable framework for the tenure of non-landholding plots was presented under *fief right* where tenure could be lifelong or heritable.[362] For instance, the Cheb Poor Clares' estate register informs us how common non-heritable fief tenure was in the city-state of Cheb.[363] *"Purchase" right* could compete with fief right, since it could be modified, and factual differences between both types of right could become blurred.[364] Detailed research on the situation in the city-state of Cheb based on tax sources is unfortunately complicated by the variety of terms and, in all probability, careless entries too. In summary, a large quantity of non-landholding plots of diverse legal status were in circulation

361   Rented, purchased, and non-heritable non-landholding plots are specified in the Cheb Cla-
       rissines' estate register: Ar Cheb, book 1003, *Urbar der Clarissinnen ab 1464*, 5, 6, 19, 60–61.
362   On this in general, see Holzfurtner, "Die Grundleihepraxis," 660–661; Jänichen, *Beiträge*,
       131.
363   Ar Cheb, book 1003, *Urbar der Clarissinnen ab 1464*, 6: "*das wasser und die fischwaid ynnen
       hat der sol das lehen von dem Closter nemen und der wirt erblos als ander guter in dem land zu
       Eger.*"
364   The fairly wide, adaptive spectrum of "purchase" right for disposal with non-landhold-
       ing plots in late medieval Bohemia is demonstrated, for instance, by Jaroslav Čechura,
       "Zákup na statcích vyšehradské kapituly ve 14. a 15. století" [Der Ankauf an den Gütern des
       Wyschehrader Domkapitels im 14. und 15. Jahrhundert], *Právněhistorické studie* 34 (1997):
       39–62.

in the city-state of Cheb, but in many cases we are unable to determine their status.[365]

Table 7.3. **Number and main types of non-landholding plots, without the forest parts and less common types of property.**

	1424	1438	1456
Number of evaluated settlements	99	113	93
Settlements with non-landholding plots	65 (65.7%)	81 (71.7%)	70 (75.3%)
Number of evaluated taxpayers	968	950	783
Taxpayers with non-landholding plots	243 (25.1%)	261 (27.5%)	212 (27.1%)
Meadows (Tgw = "tagwerk" of meadow)	543.5	367.5	351.3
Fields (Mg = field "morgens")	785.3	440.3	353.0
Meadows without measured areas (number of items)	2	31	41
Fields without measured areas (number of items)	4	56	57
Unspecified hereditary fiefs (number of items)	1	62	11
Gardens (number of items)	5	4	2

Source: From Klír, "Land transfer," 167, tab. 5. Data according to Ar Cheb, book 1060, *Klosteuerbuch 1424*; book 1067, *Klosteuerbuch 1438*; book 1084, *Klosteuerbuch (Schätzungsbuch) 1456*.

Transfer and disposal

A sufficient amount of data has survived concerning the immediate genesis and transfer of non-landholding plots of various legal statuses. Peasants acquired non-landholding plots through market transactions among themselves, as well as through inheritance,[366] purchase from a burgher,[367] or purchase from a landlord.[368] The selling off of the component parts of a "free" landholding is

365   Klír, *Rolnictvo*, app. 7.10.
366   *App. 7.2*, passim.
367   *App. 7.2*, nrs. 1, 24, 26, 36, 38, 86.
368   *App. 7.2*, nrs. 50, 60, 67, 87.

proved several times.[369] As a rule, the tax officials entered in the registers the monetary value of the non-landholding plots of land that were the subject of a property transfer.

Several examples show that at least some of the non-landholding plots were fiefs of a lower order, namely of the Nothaft family.[370] Among the holders of Nothaft fiefs in the last third of the 14th century, we can identify Cheb burghers and peasants, of which some later also purchased fief right from the Nothaft family, and therefore could already entirely freely dispose of the properties. Cheb burghers played a large role in the emergence and transfer of non-landholding and flexibly transferred plots.[371]

Another question that arises is: what was the primary source of the non-landholding plots, whatever their legal status, function, or agricultural use? The potential sources considered are: (i) newly cleared land, (ii) divided commons, (iii) separated parts of "free" or "subject" landholdings, (iv) parts of subdivided demesne farms, or (v) the land resources of abandoned landholdings and entire deserted settlements.[372] Direct evidence exists of non-landholding plots originally consisting of abandoned land—either individual landholdings or the farmland of deserted villages.[373] A large role was indisputably also played by the burghers of Cheb in the creation and transfer of fragmented and flexibly transferrable land plots.[374]

The defining characteristic was that the tenant of non-landholding plots in the 15th century could dispose of them fairly freely—he could sell them, lease them to third parties, pay off his siblings with them, or endow his children. Specifically, we have identified the following examples:

+ On several occasions a peasant exchanged or sold a "subject" landholding, but kept his non-landholding plots and transferred them from the original landholding to another (figs. 7.1–7.2).[375]

---

369 App. 7.2, nrs. 65, 85, 147.
370 Klír, Rolnictvo, 140–141.
371 App. 7.2, nr. 34.
372 On this in general, see Cerman, "Social Structure," 70.
373 Cf. Klír et al., Knihy, 128–129, 152–155; Klír, "Procesy pustnutí."
374 For an overview the influence of cities on the dynamics of land transfer in the late Middle Ages, see Cerman, "Social Structure," 66–69.
375 App. 7.2, nrs. 32–33, 48, 54, 73, 76, 80, 85, 91, 99, 105, 109–111, 123, 126, 132, 135, 147.

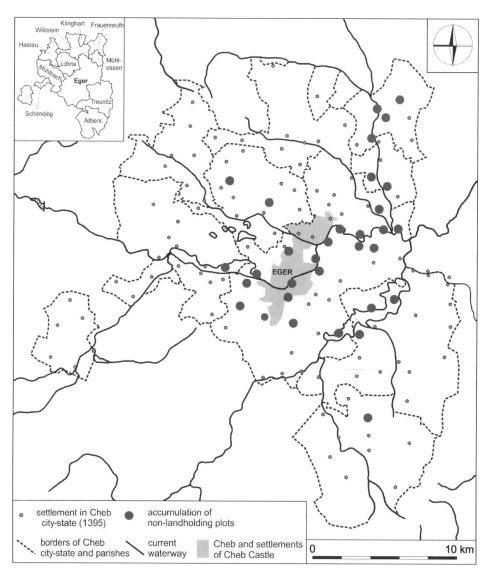

Figure 7.1. **Settlements with the relatively highest representation of non-landholding plots in the farmland of 1456. What is striking is the concentration of these settlements in proximity to the city, along the Ohře River and Plesná Brook, where a large number of non-landholding meadows were found.**

Source: Ar Cheb, book 1084, *Klosteuerbuch (Schätzungsbuch) 1456.*
Note: Measured according to the number of non-landholding plots falling on average to one FPS in the settlement. Settlements belonging to the first quartile are depicted with a circle.

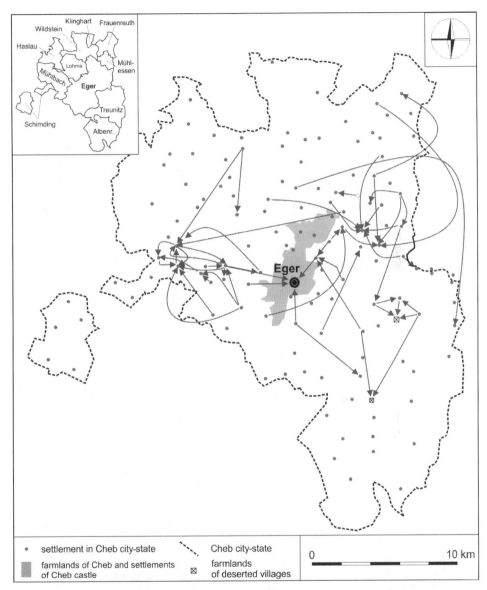

Figure 7.2. **Externally located non-landholding plots according to the 1456 Taxation Book—i.e., the situation when the taxpayer (FPS) held non-landholding plots outside his home settlements. The dispersion pattern is proof of the intensive migration and mutual connection of the peasantry in the city-state of Cheb in the Late Middle Ages.**

Source: Ar Cheb, book 1084, *Klosteuerbuch (Schätzungsbuch)* 1456.
Note: The base of the arrow marks a landholding taxpayer (FPS), the tip of the arrow the location of the non-landholding plots.

+ A peasant's property was divided among his sons, where one acquired the "subject" landholding, the second the non-landholding plots.[376]
+ A peasant sold a "subject" landholding and left for the city, where he acquired citizenship but continued to keep the non-landholding plots and paid city tax from them.[377]
+ A peasant left a "subject" landholding and sold the non-landholding plots.[378]
+ Purchased non-landholding plots could become components of subject landholdings.[379]

The non-landholding plots therefore appear in the tax registers both with the taxpayers holding entire landholdings and, in some cases, also independently, because their tenant did not own a landholding or had a landholding not subject to land tax (e.g., in the settlements of Cheb Castle).[380]

Overall share of the non-landholding plots in the land resources

Both the 1456 *Taxation Book* and the register of the city tax from 1446 especially make the reconstruction of the scope and spatial distribution of the non-landholding plots in the countryside possible.[381] According to them, there were then in the city-state of Cheb at least 466.8 "tagwerks" of meadow, 72.5 unmeasured meadows, 442.0 arable "morgens," 49 unmeasured fields, and 13 other unspecified plots. Converted, there were then 280.1 ha of measured non-landholding meadows and 265.2 ha of measured non-landholding fields.

Unfortunately, we do not know the size of the land belonging to the integral equipment of "subject" and "free" landholdings. For orientation, though, we can use the data in the early modern *Teresian Cadastre* (1757).[382] According to it, a total of 14,353.8 ha of arable lands, 1,175.1 ha of fallow lands, pastures corresponding to 651.5 wagons of harvested hay and rowen, and meadows corresponding to 8,418.5 wagons of harvested hay and rowen belonged to the landholdings in the settlements, which were listed also in the 1456 *Taxation*

---

376   *App. 7.2, nr. 37.*
377   *App. 7.2, nrs. 53, 147.*
378   *App. 7.2, nr. 6.*
379   *App. 7.2, nr. 50*; Ar Cheb, book 1003, *Urbar der Clarissinnen ab 1464*, 19.
380   *App. 7.2, nrs. 1, 13, 43, 104, 123, 135.*
381   Ar Cheb, book 1424, *Losungsbuch 1446*.
382   Aleš Chalupa, Marie Lišková, Josef Nuhlíček, and František Rajtoral, eds., *Tereziánský katastr český, sv. 1, Rustikál, kraje A–CH* (Prague: Archivní správa ministerstva vnitra ČR, 1964), 282–293.

Book. According to the early modern data, one "tagwerk" of meadow (0.57 ha) should provide a harvest on average of 5 wagons of hay and rowen (1–9 wagons).[383] The harvest of hay and rowen, listed in the *Teresian Cadastre*, would then correspond to 1,684 "tagwerks" of meadow (1,010 ha) in the city-state of Cheb.

According to available data, we can best estimate the extent of non-landholding arable land, which was approximately 2% of all of Cheb's land resources. In the agro-climatically favorable zone, however, it was more, about 5%, while in the submontane areas the share was almost zero. These differences indicate significant social and economic disparities between these ecological zones (see also *chap. 15*). The relative share of non-landholding meadows in the total number of meadows was significantly higher; in the city-state of Cheb as a whole it was more than 25%, in the agroclimatic zone it could have been even more. To summarize, non-landholding meadows had a fundamental significance on the land market, whereas the significance of non-landholding fields was marginal.

7.5 Summary

Family inheritance rights in the city-state of Cheb can be characterized as impartible inheritance (of land); the tenant of the landholding handed it over as a whole to only one of the offspring, who themselves took on the obligation to provide materially for their parents and settle affairs with their siblings.

If we leave aside the normative aspect of property right and concentrate on practices employed, rural land property in the late medieval city-state of Cheb circulated in two different economic and also legal systems.[384] The greater part of the land stock was compact, indivisible, and assigned as integral components to "subject" landholdings held under ***"purchase" right***. This land, tied to a landholding, was subject to the institutional control of the landlord, as well as the peasant communities. A considerably smaller, and also quantitatively more extensive, section of the land stock was outside of traditional institutional

---

383   Pekař, *České katastry*, 299. Cf. Beck, *Unterfinning*, 578; Černý, *Hospodářské instrukce*, 185–186; August Sedláček, *Paměti a doklady o staročeských mírách a váhách*, Rozpravy České akademie věd a umění I/66 (Prague: Nákladem České akademie věd a umění, 1923), 122–123.

384   For the Early Modern Period, cf. Zeitlhofer, *Besitzwechsel*, 19.

control, divisible to a certain extent, disposable, and traded on the market, and was subject to the fairly flexible *fief right* that we are familiar with in the neighboring Bavarian regions. This mostly concerned non-landholding plots and to a lesser extent entire landholdings. Fundamentally, non-landholding plots, normatively subject to fief right, were disposed of similarly to land plots in the Cheb farmland, which was subject to town law. Some non-landholding plots were traded on the market even when subject to the system of the "purchase" right, and peasants acquired them on heritable rental leases and paid regular annual payments to the landlord.

At the European level, the late medieval city-state of Cheb ranks among areas with lower landlord restrictions on land transfer where market mechanisms permitted the accumulation of land wealth, the flexible manipulation of economic resources, credit, and rentals. So, in practice, market and inheritance transfers created an effective and interwoven system maintaining the stability of the landholding despite demographic and economic fluctuations.[385]

---

385 For examples from the Early Modern Period, see Stefan Brakensiek, "Grund und Boden
     – eine Ware? ein Markt zwischen familialen Strategien und herrschaftlichen Kontrollen,"
     in *Ländliche Gesellschaften in Deutschland und Frankreich, 18.–19. Jahrhundert*, ed. Reiner
     Prass, Jürgen Schlumbohm, Gérard G. Béaur, and Christophe Duhamelle, Veröffentlichun-
     gen des Max-Planck-Instituts für Geschichte 187 (Göttingen: Vandenhoeck & Ruprecht,
     2003), 269–290; Thomas Robisheaux, *Rural society and the search for order in Early Modern
     Germany* (Cambridge: Cambridge University Press, 1989), 79–83.

8.
Classification
of landholdings

8.1 Introduction

The tax registers from 1424 and 1438 systematically specified the legal status and socioeconomic category of landholdings. Both registers differentiated between peasant fullholdings (hereafter *Hof* landholdings), "sub-peasant" holdings (smallholdings; smallholders' and cottagers' holdings; hereafter *Herberge* landholdings), peasant small fullholdings (hereafter *Höfel* landholdings), and also mills, fisherman dwellings, and taverns (*tab. 8.1*). A similar categorization of landholdings may be found in great quantities of written documents recording fief and landlord rights in areas neighboring the city-state of Cheb, i.e., contemporary Upper Palatinate, Franconia, and western Bohemia.[386] Nevertheless, traditional classification had no direct significance for the Cheb land tax in the 15th century, since it was the monetary value of a landholding that was important, and so the 1456 *Taxation Book* no longer differentiated between types of landholding.[387]

---

386 The geographically closest include the oldest Nothaft and Leuchtenberg fief registers (last third of the 14th century), the Waldsassen Abbey estate register (c. 1360), and the Loket estate register (1525). See Singer, *Das Nothaftische Lehenbuch*; Völkl, "Das älteste Leuchtenberger Lehenbuch"; Langhammer, *Waldsassen*; Schreiber, *Das Elbogener Urbar*. The Herberge in the Leutenberg fief registers were mistakenly considered to mean inns by Velička, "Lantkrabata," 201.

387 Klír et al., *Knihy*, 146–150. See also Klír, "Land transfer," 157.

A "subject" *Hof* landholding and a *Herberge* landholding could differ on three main levels:[388]

1) In the scope of the relevant land resources held, the type of farming operation, and potentially the form of buildings.
2) Differing status within the peasant community—*Herberge* landholdings did not have full rights, such as the right to use the commons, and their lands were separate from the core of the farmland; their land tenure therefore was more flexible and under reduced institutional control.[389]
3) Rights and obligations towards the landlord.

Draft animals

Records of draft animals in the late medieval city-state of Cheb refer almost exclusively to horses. As far as it was possible to trace, in 1438, 85% of *Hof* landholdings and 79% of *Höfel* landholdings were equipped with at least one horse. The situation was the opposite with *Herberge* landholdings—only 14% of them owned a horse. Only a quarter of millers owned a horse (*tab. 8.2*).

8.2 Individual categories

Hof landholdings

Ideally, peasant landholdings were self-sufficient, had adequate land resources and a paired draught team, and were capable of providing for the family, as well as creating a sufficient agricultural surplus. Peasant land plots lay in the heart of the farmland and their tenants had a share in the use of the commons.

Hof landholdings in the late medieval city-state of Cheb comprised a wide range of economic units from relatively small to large and commercialized landholdings. According to the land tax registers from 1424 and 1438 and the 1456 *Taxation Book*, *Hof* landholdings were the dominant type—over 75% of all landholdings (*tab. 8.1*).

---

388   E.g., Petráň, *Poddaný lid*, 15–16; Cerman and Maur, "Proměny," 745–760; Velková, "Proměny," 813–818.
389   Cerman, "Social Structure," 69–70.

Table 8.1. **The main landholding categories in the city-state of Cheb according to the tax registers from 1424 and 1438.**

Settle-ments	Total	Hof landholdings		Höfel landholdings		Herberge landholdings		Mills		Taverns	
		N	%	N	%	N	%	N	%	N	%
1424	97	935	693	74.1	22	2.4	189	20.2	27	2.5	4	0.2
1438	117	949	714	75.2	48	5.1	166	17.5	21	2.2	0	0.0

Note: N – Number
Source: Ar Cheb, book 1060, *Klosteuerbuch 1424*; book 1067, *Klosteuerbuch 1438*.

Table 8.2. **Landholdings with or without a horse in various economic categories in the city-state of Cheb, 1438.**

Assessed land-holdings	Hof land-holdings	Höfel land-holdings	Herberge land-holdings	Mills	Fisherman dwellings	Total
Total	497	24	84	19	7	628
Horses	420	19	12	5	0	456
%	85.0	79.2	14.3	26.3	0.0	72.6

Source: Ar Cheb, book 1067, *Klosteuerbuch 1438*.

Höfel landholdings

A landholding with the status of a peasant fullholding but for various reasons had only a very modest amount of land resources was called a *Höfel*. Certain *Höfel* landholdings whose classification did not change may be positively identified in both land tax registers. Forty-eight *Höfel* landholdings were registered in the *1438 Land Tax Register*, eight of which were part of other, larger peasant landholdings. In these cases, it seems that a *Höfel* was a relict of a *Hof* landholding that was integrated into another larger landholding. Approximately one-third of *Höfel* landholdings in the tax register were also designated as half, which most likely represented fragmentation of a larger peasant fullholding (1 Hof → ½ Höfel + ½ Höfel).[390] Therefore, a landholding designated as

390   Klír et al., *Knihy,* 149.

a *Höfel* was likely the fiction of a peasant fullholding that no longer existed from an economic standpoint, but only from a legal one.

"Sub-peasant" holdings (Herberge)

It is evident from the entries that the term *Herberge* was used to cover a wide range of small "sub-peasant" holdings and dwellings with limited or no land resources.[391] According to Bohemian early modern estate register and land tax register classification, Cheb's *Herberge* could be smallholder, gardener, or cottager holdings, as well as craftsmen, inmate-lodger, or retirement dwellings. Therefore, sometimes the designation *Herberge* really meant a simple dwelling without land.

Smallholders and cottagers were often forced to find a livelihood away from their own holding and exploit all types of labor opportunities in the city and in the countryside, on more sizeable landholdings and demesne farms, in transportation, forest crafts, mining, etc. The fact that a considerable portion of the smallholdings were actually inhabited by rural craftsmen is shown in the number of occupational surnames that is particularly apparent in large villages grouped around castles. Also, almost all fishermen held only cottages, not *Hof* landholdings.

Some inmate-lodgers and their dwellings could be permanently categorized as part of the essential labor force for larger, market-oriented peasant landholdings and demesne farms. Situations in which smallholdings were taxed together with large *Hof* landholding indicate such links.[392] Contemporaneous evidence of the functional symbiosis of cottages (*Herberge*) and a large landholding or demesne farm appears in an entry in the 1409 *Land Tax Register*: *"Des Elbel Symons hof czu Wagaw mit der herberge . . ."*[393]

---

391   On the definition of the "sub-peasantry," see for medieval Bohemia esp. Graus, *Dějiny*, 216–219; Míka, *Poddaný lid*, 146–150; Šmahel, *Husitská revoluce*, 425–432; Cerman, "Mittelalterliche Ursprünge"; Cerman, "Social structure," 63, 69. On this topic in general, see Ghosh, "Rural Economies," 257. See also Klír, "Land transfer," 157.

392   Cetnov (Zettendorf), Háje (Gehaag), Chocovice (Kötschwitz), Hněvín (Knöba), Horní Lomany (Lohma, Ober-), Skalka (Rommersreuth), Všeboř (Schöba), Krásná Lípa (Schönlind).

393   Ar Cheb, book 1059, *Klosteuerbuch 1409*, fol. 50r.

Certain smallholdings could temporarily serve as retirement dwellings, indicated by the existence of tenants with the denomination "*alt.*"[394] An explicit
case of this may be found in the 1448 *Land Tax Register*, where a note for the
taxpayer "*Alt Hamer*" in the village of Klest (Reissig) stated: "*v[n]d den hof hat
Walhan vnd ist pey sein sun in herb[er]g.*"[395]

Mills and taverns

Twenty-seven mills may be counted in the 1438 register, which more or less
corresponds with the situation of 1424 (*fig. 5*). Taverns were specified only in
1424 in villages with a certain degree of centrality and lying on main transport
routes—in the castle villages of Hazlov (Haslau) and in the parish village of
Schirnding.

8.3 "Partial" landholdings

In addition to entire landholdings, in 1424 and 1438, half, third, and quarter
Hof and *Herberge* landholdings appeared in entries (*fig. 8.1*). Such classification
can also be encountered in other contemporaneous and subsequent written
documents for the Loket region, the Upper Palatinate, and Franconia.[396] A systematic overview of "partial" landholdings appears in the 1424 *Land Tax Register*, while the 1438 *Land Tax Register* recorded them only in exceptional cases;
otherwise, "partial" landholdings were designated as entire. This assumption is
supported by the overall proportions—in the 1424 register, "partial" landholdings represented more than one-third of all landholdings (34%), while in the
1438 register, the number is negligible (3%). Such a significant difference may
be explained only by a change in the method of entry-making.[397]

---

394   A similar situation is indicated by the 1424 *Land Tax Register* (Ar Cheb, book 1060). Cf.
      Heisinger, "Die Egerer Klosteuerbücher," 143 (Nebanice/Nebanitz, Nový Drahov/Rohr).
395   KB 1448. This case was highlighted by Heisinger, "Die Egerer Klosteuerbücher," 182.
396   E.g., in the oldest Nothaft fief register: Singer, *Das Nothaftische Lehensbuch*, passim; Singer,
      Das Landbuch, 85–87; in the Loket 1525 *Estate Register*: Schreiber, *Das Elbogener Urbar*
      (cf. Schreiber, *Der Elbogener Kreis*, 146–147; Slavík, "O popisu Čech," 78).
397   Klír et al., *Knihy*, 148.

The existence of "partial" landholdings shows the antagonism between the ideal and impartible "subject" landholding with set obligations towards the landlord on the one hand, and the practice of splitting up certain landholdings on the other hand. Fragmentation of landholdings could be:

1) Real and permanent, where the landholding was physically divided up.
2) Formal and temporary, where, although the landholdings' tenants had separate households and shared in the rights and obligations, they farmed together and the dwelling itself and its economic buildings and economic operations were not physically separated.

According to available sources, none of the above options can be documented as a general rule.

The separate parts of the landholding could express the ratio of the division of rights and duties to the landlord, but not the setting of the land tax, which in 1424 was not demonstrably determined by the different parts of the landholdings. For instance, in the village of Dietersgrün, taxpayers from half *Hof* landholdings paid significantly diverse amounts—3, 9, 12, and 15 gr.

Table 8.3. **The hamlet of Mechová (Mies)—taxpayers, prescribed annual tax amount (1392, 1424, 1438), and landholding value (1438).**

1392		1424			1438			
Taxpayer	Tax	Taxpayer	Land-holding	Tax	Taxpayer	Land-holding	Tax	Land-holding value
Gaffel	36 gr.	**Hans Gaffel**	1 Hof	100 gr.	Michel	1 Hof	36 gr.	4.5 ss
Hufnagel	14 gr.	Michel	½ Hof	36 gr.	**Hans Gaffel**	⅓ Hof	45 gr.	30 ss
Crawse	11 gr.	Feyrer	½ Hof	20 gr.	**Jung Gaffel**	⅓ Hof	45 gr.	30 ss
					Aber Gafel*	⅓ Hof	30 gr.	30 ss
					Stroer	1 Hof	20 gr.	5 ss

Source: Ar Cheb, book Nr. 1009, *Klosteuerbuch 1392*, fol. 31v; book Nr. 1060, *Klosteuerbuch 1424*, fol. 20r–21v; book Nr. 1067, *Klosteuerbuch 1438*, 40b.

Note: * – probably Hans Gaffel; the landholding did not comprise cattle.
Landholding value = the monetary value of the "purchase" right to the landholding.

The land tax registers present a variety of evidence for the subdivision of entire landholdings into smaller units and, conversely, the merging of "partial" landholdings into one. The first case is in the hamlet of Mechová (Mies), where, instead of Gafell's landholding from 1424, we find three one-third landholdings in 1438 (*tab. 8.3*). The opposite situation is illustrated by the hamlet of Stodola (Stadel), which in 1392 contained four landholdings, then in 1424 four half landholdings held by just two taxpayers, and in 1438 just two remaining landholdings (*tab. 8.4*).

Table 8.4. **The hamlet of Stodola (Stadel) taxpayers, prescribed annual tax amount (1392, 1424, 1438), and landholding value (1438).**

1392		1424			1438			
Taxpayer	Tax	Taxpayer	Land-holding	Tax	Taxpayer	Land-holding	Tax	Land-holding value
Hans Nvnner	45 gr.	Hans Voyt	2× ½ Hof	50 gr.	Snur	1 Hof	45 gr.	10 ss
Possecker	36 gr.	Grym[m]e	2× ½ Hof	70 gr.	Langheintz	1 Hof	35 gr.	10 ss
Peczel	24 gr.							
Stadelman	60 gr.							

Source: Ar Cheb, book 1009, *Klosteuerbuch 1392*, fol. 55v; book 1060, *Klosteuerbuch 1424*, fol. 48v; book 1067, *Klosteuerbuch 1438*, 72a.
Note: ss – threescore of Prague groschen
Landholding value = the monetary value of the "purchase" right to the landholding.

8.4 Summary

We know the socioeconomic categories of landholdings for 1424 and 1438. In the city-state of Cheb as a whole, approximately 77–80% were *Hof* landholdings, 18–20% were *Herberge* landholdings, and the remainder were mills and taverns. Diametrical differences existed among settlements, with *Herberge* landholdings being the greatest in number in settlements with a certain degree of centrality. In early modern classification, these *Herberge* landholdings in the

city-state of Cheb would have comprised smallholders, cottagers, and gardeners. Draft horses were a characteristic for *Hof* landholdings, while their absence is characteristic for *Herberge* landholdings.

Figure 8.1. "Partial" landholdings in individual settlements in the city-state of Cheb, 1424.

Source: Ar Cheb, book 1060, *Klosteuerbuch 1424.*

Note: Settlements without "partial" landholdings (0% of "partial" landholdings): Altenteich, Au, Berg, Döba, Dölitz, Dürr, Fonsau, Förba, Gehaag, Haid, Harlas, Hatzenreuth, Höflas (Lohma), Höflas (Konersreuth), Honnersdorf, Konradsgrün, Kornau, Kreuzenstein, Lapitzfeld, Liebeneck, Ober-Lindau, Ober-Losau, Unter-Losau, Matzelbach, Nonnengrün, Ottengrün (Albenreuth), Ottengrün (Haslau), Palitz, Schüttüber, Schönlind (Schloppenhof), Sorgen, Taubrat, Thiemreuth, Thurn, Trebendorf, Triesenhof, Ulrichsgrün, Hinter-Voitersreuth, Wogau.

9.
Landlords' rights

9.1 Introduction

The degree of institutional control over land transfers and also the intensity of the commercial activities of the peasantry was dependent on (1) the compactness and strength of landlords' rights and (2) the share that burghers had in them. We assume that fragmented tenure, wherein "subject" tenants in the same settlement paid rent to various landlords, weakened the strength of landlord control on the one hand, and strengthened the landlord's interest in maintaining the integrity of "subject" landholdings on the other. The transfer of land resources between landholdings in settlements with fragmented landlords' rights brought great administrative and also economic complications. Burgher tenure of landlords' rights is generally attributed to the potential for innovation in the sphere of progressive market institutions, agrarian production structures, and the expansion of rental and credit.[398]

9.2 Overall characteristics

Unfortunately, the testimony of the 1469 *Tax Register* is incomplete; data for certain settlements are missing. In total, the landlord can be traced for land-

---

398 Cerman, "Social Structure," 67–69; in more general terms see, e.g., the following selected studies: Scott, *Town*; Jean-Marie Duvosquel and Erik Thoen, eds., *Peasants and townsmen in medieval Europe: Studia in honorem Adriaan Verhulst* (Gent: Snoeck-Ducaju), esp. 603–774.

holdings in 99 settlements[399] where we know the landlord of 670 taxpayers; a further 55 taxpayers held "free" landholdings.[400] A detailed view shows that (*fig. 9.1*):[401]

+ Both secular and ecclesiastic landlords were approximately equally represented in documented settlements (337.5 : 311.5 "subject" tenants).
+ The property of ecclesiastical institutions was largely held by the Cheb Poor Clares, the Teutonic Order, and the Knights of the Cross with the Red Star (city hospital), which together controlled 255.6 "subject" tenants (39.5%). No significant spatial concentrations are observed in the distribution of the landlords' rights (*figs. 9.2–9.3*).
+ A considerable proportion of the annual payments to churches was exceptionally fragmented and intended for serving requiem Mass in rural parish churches—in Cheb in the Church of St. Nicholas, in Cheb Castle's Chapel of St. Erhart and St. Ursula, and in Cheb's monasteries, including the Dominican and Franciscan monasteries (49.8% of "subject" tenants; 7.5% of the whole).
+ Burghers were predominant among secular landlords (204 subjects; 32%).[402]
+ Sixty-four "subject" tenants (9.6%) were distributed among just four burghers whose holdings included castles in the countryside, and the local nobility had a further 51.5 "subject" tenants (7.7%).

9.3 Compactness of landlords' rights

Most of the researched settlements were fragmented in terms of landlords' rights, with only 14 of 99 settlements being compact.[403] The tenure of Cheb's burghers was significantly dispersed. A total of 80 burghers, including owners of castles, participated in landlords' rights over 269 "subject" tenants (*fig. 9.3*).[404] Of the 99 researchable settlements, at least one "subject" tenant

---

399   Cf. also Heisinger, "Die Egerer Klosteuerbücher," 158–195, Tab. 5. Cf. Klír et al., *Knihy*, 159–161, appendix 14.
400   *App. 9.1.*
401   *App. 9.2.*
402   *App. 9.5.*
403   *App. 9.1.*
404   *App. 9.1, 9.3.–9.5.*

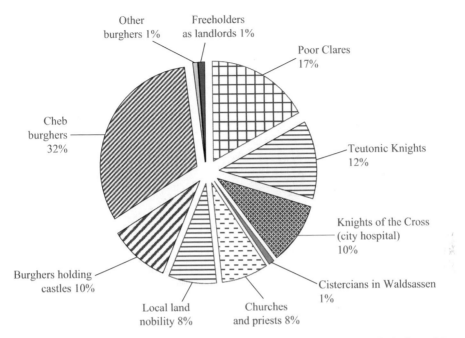

Figure 9.1. The distribution of landlords' rights in the city-state of Cheb, 1469.

Source: Ar Cheb, book 1096, *Klosteuerbuch 1469*.
Note: Without the "free" landholdings.

in 72 such settlements paid land rent to burghers (73%). Cheb burghers had a majority share in 26 settlements; in the other settlements their share was not more than half of the subjects (46 settlements). Burghers' landlords' rights were not geographically concentrated; they controlled around 30–40% of the "subject" tenants across all ecological zones.

9.4 Summary[405]

Compact landlords' tenure was lacking in the Cheb countryside. Landlords' rights were dispersed mostly between Cheb's ecclesiastical institutions and bur-

---

405   See also Klír, "Land transfer," 155–156.

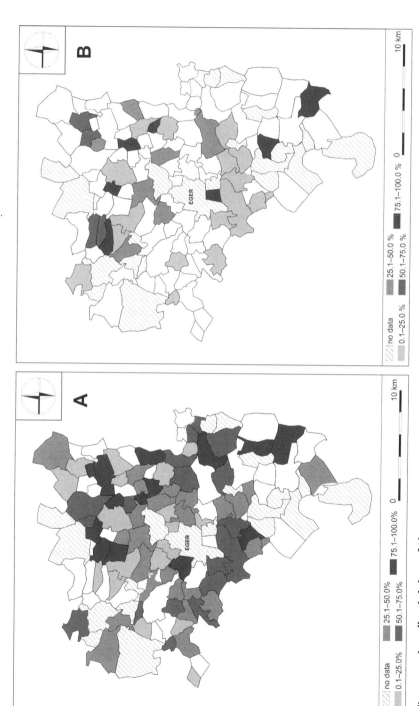

Figure 9.2. **Landlord rights of the most prominent entities. Percentage share of landlord rights in the city-state of Cheb, 1469. A – Cheb burghers; B – Cheb Poor Clares.**

Source: Ar Cheb, book 1096, *Klosteuerbuch 1469*.

Note: In certain settlements, the data may be misleading because only some subjects were subject to land tax. Cf. *app. 9.1*.

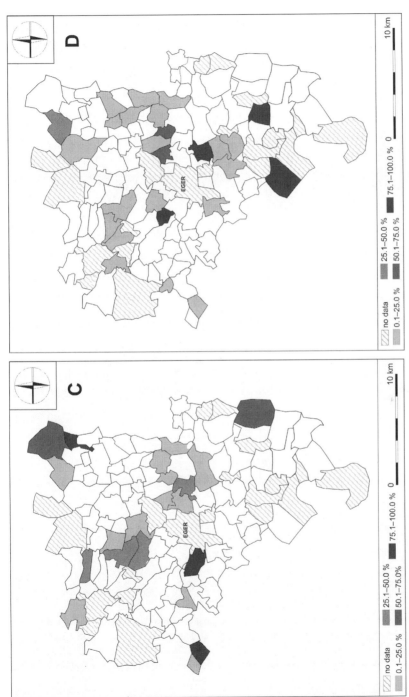

Figure 9.3. **Landlord rights of the most prominent entities. Percentage share of landlord rights in the city-state of Cheb, 1469. C – Teutonic Order; D – Knights of the Cross with the Red Star (city hospital).**

Source: Ar Cheb, book 1096, *Klosteuerbuch 1469.*

Note: In certain settlements, the data may be misleading because only some subjects were subject to land tax. Cf. *app. 9.1.*

ghers. Just 14% of settlements that were described in detail in the exceptional *1469 Land Tax Register* were homogenous in terms of landlords' rights. Eighty burghers of Cheb held landlords' rights, and frequent landholding transfers presumably took place between them. Burgher tenure was not concentrated in any one ecological zone but permeated the entire city-state of Cheb more or less equally. Therefore, hypothetically, we can assume that (1) the peasant communities were not exposed to concentrated pressure on the part of the landlord and their institutional control, (2) the landlord was interested in the stability and land integrity of the landholding, and (3) no serious obstacles were placed on the commercial activities of the peasantry.[406]

---

406 In general terms, e.g., Bavel van and Hoppenbrouwers, "Landholding," 33–36; Chris Wickham, "Conclusions," in *Le marché de la terre au Moyen Âge*, ed. Laurent Feller and Chris Wickham, Collection de l'École Française de Rome 350 (Rome: École Française de Rome, 2005), 625–642, on 634–635; Markus Cerman, "Bodenmärkte und ländliche Wirtschaft in vergleichender Sicht: England und das östliche Mitteleuropa im Spätmittelalter," *Jahrbuch für Wirtschaftsgeschichte* 2 (2004): 125–150; Cerman, "Social Structure," 67–69; Cerman, "Open fields," 409–413.

10.
Exploitation
of the peasantry

10.1 Problem-posing

Feudal relations and their attendant burdens, such as the imposition of various forms of rent, are considered to be a significant factor in preventing the commercial activities of the peasantry.[407] The method of rent distribution and the degree of the non-market extraction of the surplus are therefore key indicators of the economic potential of peasant communities and the nature of their socioeconomic stratification.[408] Unlike Bohemia, the overall degree of the exploitation of the peasantry in the late medieval city-state of Cheb has yet to be systematically studied.[409]

407 E.g., Witold Kula, *An economic theory of feudal system: Towards a model of the Polish economy 1500–1800* (London: NLB and Humanities Press, 1976), 62–75. See also the recent Ghosh, "Rural Economies," 260–261. Further literature is summarized in, e.g., Lindström, *Distribution*, 118–125.

408 Lindström, *Distribution*, 118.

409 For the pre-Hussite period in Bohemia, cf. *chap. 4.3*. For the second half of the 15th century, cf. Míka, *Poddaný lid*, 227–280; Kostlán, "Cenová revoluce," 173–197; Antonín Kostlán, "K rozsahu poddanských povinností od 15. do první poloviny 17. století ve světle odhadů a cen feudální držby" [Zum Umfang der Untertanenpflichten vom 15. Jahrhundert bis zur 1. Hälfte des 17. Jahrhunderts im Lichte der Schätzungen und Preise des Feudalbesitzes], *Folia Historica Bohemica* 10 (1986): 205–248, on 215–221. We do not draw on the unpublished manuscript Antonín Kostlán, "Feudální zatížení českého venkova po husitské revoluci. K hospodářským a sociálním dějinám jagellonského období českých dějin (1471–1526)" (CSc diss., Historický ústav ČSAV, 1988).

If—purely hypothetically—rent were to extract all of a peasant's surplus, the stratification of peasant communities would not exist; a larger property would not denote greater wealth, but rather a greater burden, and so there would be no desire to accumulate "subject" land superfluously. In reality, however, for a range of reasons, the surplus was not extracted entirely; some landholdings were favored by rent (surplus exploitation), while others were overburdened. The final result of this was that rent could either deepen property-related stratification of the peasantry or level it out.

Due to changing yields and prices of agricultural products, the volume of peasant production and cash income fluctuated year-to-year. The level at which rent was set was decisive for an overall balanced economy of households. In principle, rent should have corresponded to minimum yield values, meaning that the complete extraction of the surplus would occur only in bad years (*fig. 10.1. A*). If the level of rent was any higher, in some years the reproduction of peasant households might be jeopardized and various compensatory mechanisms, such as a temporary exemption, postponement of payments, or credit (*fig. 10.1. B*) would need to be activated.[410] Setting rent at the lower yield level meant that in good years peasants could keep the resulting part of the surplus. Therefore, the year-to-year fluctuation of agricultural yields was beneficial for peasants in the long-term perspective, although situations could arise where long-term average yields fell, bringing the rent level uncomfortably high.

The main questions that arise are:

1. To what extent did rent extract the peasant surplus?

The solution is to follow its annual collection—if peasants were unable to pay in certain years, the level of rent exceeded their production capabilities. The level of rent would therefore lie above the lower margin level. If gaps in rent payments occurred only exceptionally, we may assume a low rent and in good years a fairly large surplus that remained in the hands of the peasants. To answer this question, it is not necessary to investigate the collection of the entire sum of rent; it is enough just to analyze one part, in our case the Cheb land tax collection (*chap. 12.4*). In this, we assume that a gap in land tax also meant a gap in land rent payments.

---

410   In a similar vein already in Bohemian historiography, see, e.g., Rostislav Nový, "Struktura feudální renty v předhusitských Čechách," *Československý časopis historický* 9 (1961): 60–74, on 61; and for more, see, e.g., *Poddaný lid*, 27.

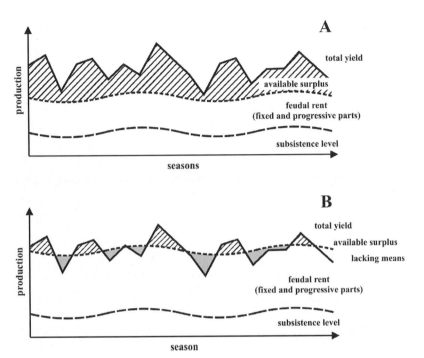

Figure 10.1. **Size of disposable surplus that the peasants retained—a model.**

Source: Prepared by the author.
Note: A – the level of rent (land rent, land tax, ecclesiastical tithes) is set low; surplus is extracted imperfectly, and the peasant households retain a high disposable surplus.
B – the level of rent is set high; in some years, the surplus is extracted completely, and sometimes rent cannot even be paid because the peasant households would have to limit their own subsistence (in gray).

2. Did rent deepen socioeconomic inequalities between landholdings—and if so, to what extent? Or did rent, on the contrary, reduce them (*chap. 13.3–13.4*)? Did a high land rent mean a high land tax too, or did both elements of rent balance out in the city-state of Cheb? For instance, if a landholding was overburdened with a fixed land rent that did not correspond with its actual economic capabilities, was its land tax reduced?

3. How large was the total exploitation of rent and how large was the landholding's disposable surplus? Was accumulation of wealth possible (*chap. 13.5*)? Before answering these questions, we will look at some general characteristics of rent in the city-state of Cheb (*chap. 10.2–10.3*) and the form of land rent (*chap. 11*).

10.2 The complementarity of land rents and land tax[411]

In the city-state of Cheb, "subject" tenants who held their landholding by "purchase" right paid regular land rent, regularly collected land tax, and also ecclesiastical tithes; tenants of "free" landholdings were obligated to pay land tax and ecclesiastical tithes only. Land rent applied to "subject" landholdings and was a fixed sum, while land tax applied to the entire property of the FPS and was progressive.

Agricultural production was seasonal, as was the extraction of the peasant surplus.[412] Consequently, land rent and land tax were complementary. Land rent first extracted the grain surplus, either through grain payments or indirectly in cash. Payments in cash could be favorable for "subject" tenants with a low grain surplus who acquired cash for payment of rent in other ways. Land tax extracted livestock surplus in cash payments. The distribution of collection dates in the city-state of Cheb was planned accordingly—land rents in grain were generally collected at Michaelmas, thus after the harvest (see *chap. 11.2*), and, during the first half of the 15th century, land tax collection commenced on St. Martin's Day, thus after the end of common grazing, when the cattle were slaughtered. The actual collection usually took place at the end of the autumn and subsequently during the winter.[413] Seasonal distribution of peasant income from livestock production in the city-state of Cheb can be followed continually from 1442 onward in city income from butchers' shops that were recorded in accounts books at weekly intervals (*fig. 10.2*). Other seasonal products were extracted in the form of extraordinary and symbolic payments such as eggs and cheese at Easter, poultry in the autumn, and suckling pigs at Christmas (*fig. 10.5*; see *chap. 11.2*).

The options for analyzing the relationship between land tax and land rent are generally very limited. Serious discussion of the parallel application of forms of surplus exploitation in the Zurich Region has been conducted, although the

---

411   See also Klír, "Land transfer," 156–157.
412   In general terms, e.g., see Julien Demade, "Grundrente, Jahreszyklus und monetarische Zirkulation: Zur Funktionsweise des spätmittelalterlichen Feudalismus," *Historische Anthropologie* 17 (2009): 222–244.
413   Klír et al., *Knihy*, 167–168. The Brandenburg margrave in the western part of the historical Cheb region (Sechsämterland) collected the land tax at Candlemas (Singer, *Das Landbuch*, 54).

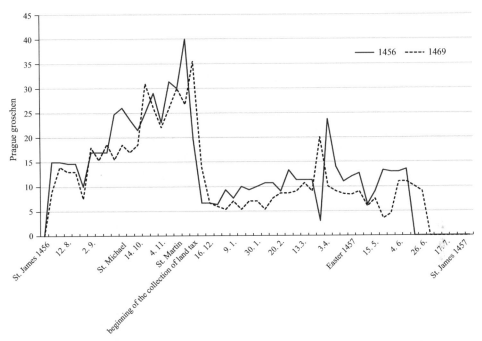

Figure 10.2. Distribution of city income from butchers' shops for 1456 and 1469.

Source: According to Ar Cheb, books 2157; 2169; *Allgemeine Umgeldbücher 1456* (fol. 27r), 1469 (fol. 22r).
Note: The sampled income collected from the Cheb meat shops in 1456 and 1469 reflects the annual dynamics of the payment capacity of the peasants, which was generated by the sale of cattle. The peak during the autumn slaughter of cattle was typical, coinciding with the start of the collection of tax on St. Martin's Day.

burdensome taxation of the countryside by land tax was instituted only in the mid-15th century.[414]

10.3 The fight over rent

Land rent in the city-state of Cheb predominantly took the form of fixed grain payments (*chap. 11.3*). If grain prices fell or stagnated due to an agrarian depression and low demand, the first to suffer from this was the landlord. From the

414   Wanner, *Siedlungen,* 212–213.

late 14th century to the early 15th century onward, the cash income of peasant landholdings rose, which may be explained by structural changes, from the move towards market-oriented livestock production to increasing productivity and reorganization of the distribution of agricultural land. We can see an improvement in the economic results of peasant landholdings according to the fairly high land tax, the annual collection of which was instituted in the city-state of Cheb in 1403.

It was in the landlord's interest for their "subject" tenants not to pay land tax. Landlords strove to ensure this, not to protect their "subject" tenants economically, but to appropriate the relevant sum. This is documented in the situation of the "subject" tenants of Cheb Castle who, despite not paying land tax directly, paid the burgrave a fixed equivalent. The land rent paid by Cheb Castle "subject" tenants was paid in kind, while they paid the equivalent of the land tax in cash (*chap. 11.2*).

The annual collection of the land tax in the city-state of Cheb was instituted fairly easily because at the beginning of the 15th century the prominent burgher families and the city council controlled the castles in the countryside, including the landlord rights. The remaining landlord rights were more or less taken up by Cheb's ecclesiastical institutions, in practice also controlled or influenced by burgher families. The regular income flowing into the land tax coffers was largely at the disposal of the same people whose "subject" tenants paid the land tax.[415] In the second quarter of the 15th century, the situation began to change when the descendants of the first generation of burghers who had acquired castles and accumulated landlord rights underwent a transformation into the landed nobility, losing their burghers' rights and access to the city council. This trend increased in the second half of the 15th century and the beginning of the 16th century.[416]

In the first half of the 15th century, evidence of any serious disputes over payment of land tax is lacking. The only known dispute was with the noble Paulsdorfer family and was decided by Emperor Sigismund in 1430 in favor of the city council. A serious feud between the local landed nobility and the city council raged from the 1470s to the 1480s.[417] At that time, a large portion of

---

415   Klír et al., *Knihy*, 412–423.

416   Cf. Gradl, *Die Chroniken*; Sturm, *Districtus Egranus*, 169–237; Heribert Sturm, *Eger. Geschichte einer Reichsstadt* (Augsburg: Kraft,' 1951), 385–400.

417   Klír et al., *Knihy*, 162–163; Heisinger, "Die Egerer Klosteuerbücher," 93–94. Cf. also Jánský, *Kronika česko-bavorské hranice 2.*

"subject" tenants stopped paying land tax, although we are unable to determine to what extent this was due to local military conflicts or to the resistance of landlords.[418] The feud over payment of land tax, settled in 1481, enabled King Vladislaus to intervene on behalf of the city and, at the same time, burden it with a new, indirect tax.[419]

10.4 Land Militia

The "subject" and "free" landholdings in the late medieval city-state of Cheb were burdened in another, specific way, namely the obligation to maintain pre-scribed armament and if needed provide one armiger on foot or a mounted one for the land militia.[420] Only the poorest landholdings were freed of this obliga-tion and perhaps also peasants who paid an annual fee to the parish churches for requiem Masses.[421] The local historical research indicates that the land militia was created, or at least reorganized, at the beginning of the 1390s due to the establishment of land peace agreements (*Landfrieden*).[422] Notably, the land militia was controlled by the city council from this period at the latest. The 1395 *Land Militia Register*, which registered 1,237 armigers in 133 settlements, allows us to look into the structure of the land militia.[423] Unless specified otherwise, two peasants living in the parish village were charged with the function of mayor (*Hauptmann*) of the relevant district of the militia. The parish of Cheb was the largest and, unlike others, was internally divided into 5 districts, each headed by a pair of peasant mayors.[424]

The specific armament associated with the individual landholdings recorded in 1395 reveals a well-organized system (*fig. 10.3*). The rural militia was com-

---

418   Klír, "Procesy pustnutí," 730–731; Heisinger, "Die Egerer Klosteuerbücher," 95–101, 315–318. Cf. also Jiří Jánský, *Kronika česko-bavorské hranice 4 – Chronik der böhmisch-bayerischen Grenze 4 (1458–1478)* (Domažlice: Nakladatelství Český les, 2004).
419   Heisinger, "Die Egerer Klosteuerbücher," 95.
420   Ar Cheb, book 974, *Musterungsbuch der Bauernschaft*. Cf. Heisinger, "Die Egerer Klosteuer-bücher," 116–124; Durdík, "Vojenská hotovost"; Kubů, "Ozbrojené síly."
421   Heisinger, "Die Egerer Klosteuerbücher," 116–124.
422   Durdík, "Vojenská hotovost," 563, 570; Ar Cheb, book 1009, *Klosteuerbuch 1392*, fol. 76r.
423   The analysis provided by Durdík, "Vojenská hotovost."
424   *App. 5.3.*

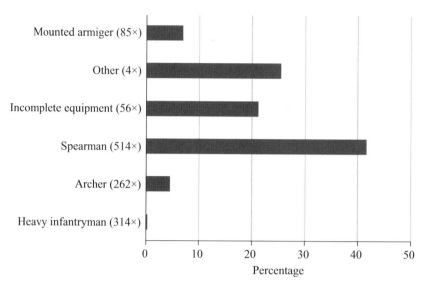

Figure 10.3. **The Cheb land rural militia by type of armament, 1395.**

After: Durdík, "Vojenská hotovost," 565, table I. Simplified.

prised of mounted soldiers (7%) and dismounted troops (93%). The foot soldiers can be divided into well-armored heavy infantrymen equipped perhaps
with gisarmes (25%), less protected archers with crossbows (21%), and the
most numerous spearmen (42%), whose defensive armor was relatively differentiated.[425]

The specific equipment prescribed for each landholding must have corresponded to its economic capabilities, as the analysis of the best-documented
parishes showed an extremely strong positive correlation between the type of
armament and the tax amounts recorded in the 1392 register (*fig. 10.4*). The
wealthiest group of taxpayers were the mounted warriors, sometimes also with
a page, then the heavy infantry. Larger, medium-sized landholdings armed
the archers, while the poorer ones only equipped the spearmen, though in
extremely varied quality.[426]

The imposition of military service on the Cheb peasantry can be seen as
a specific, one-off burden. The acquisition of individual pieces of armor was

425   Durdík, "Vojenská hotovost," 566–570.
426   Durdík, "Vojenská hotovost," 573–577.

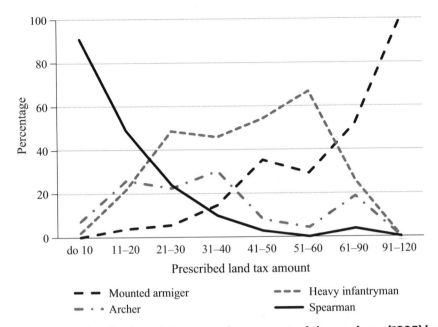

Figure 10.4. **Distribution of the type of armament of the armigers (1395) by the amount of tax prescribed (1392). Parishes of Cheb and Dřenice. Percentage.**

After: Durdík, "Vojenská hotovost," 575, table V. Simplified.

certainly financially demanding, as evidenced by the fact that in the accounts of war-related damage to farmsteads, in addition to the number of horses and cattle, there were also damages to mandatory armament.[427] On the other hand, there was no need to repeat these expenditures for a prolonged period. Furthermore, the degree of encumbrance corresponded to the property status and the amount of land tax prescribed. Therefore, we do not address military duties any further in this monograph.

10.5 Summary

Rent in the city-state of Cheb was composed of three annually collected amounts: land rent, land tax, and ecclesiastical tithes. The main question

427 Klír, "Procesy pustnutí," 736.

is whether rent extracted the entire surplus or whether part of the surplus remained in the hands of the peasants. The influence of the separate components of rent on Cheb's peasantry would be varied, as some were fixed and others progressive. We will therefore test the hypothesis that the land rent and ecclesiastical tithes deepened socioeconomic differences, while the progressive land tax evened them out.

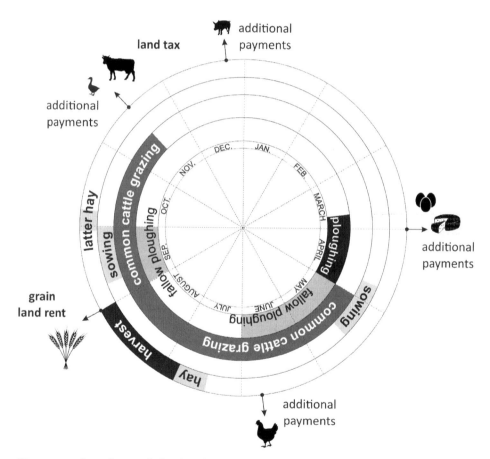

Figure 10.5. Agrarian cycle in the city-state of Cheb and collection of rent throughout the year (ca. 1450).

After: Cf. *chap. 5.6.; app. 5.7.; tab. 11.1.*
Note: For monetary land rent, cf. *chap. 11.2.* Surcharges (i.e., extraordinary payments) are depicted for the "subject" tenants of the Cheb Castle (*chap. 11.2*).

The two main forms of rent were complementary, with land rent aiming at the direct and in-kind extraction of the grain surplus after the harvest, and with land tax aiming at the indirect extraction of the livestock surplus before the coming of winter. A combined rent, which, in addition to land rent and ecclesiastical tithes, comprised the annual land tax, was introduced in the city-state of Cheb in a specific historical context at the turn of the 15th century, when landlord rights in Cheb were controlled directly or indirectly by burgher families who also governed the city council. The disintegration of this originally homogeneous ruling group in terms of interests and the transition of the original patricians into Cheb's landed nobility led to an unsuccessful attempt to increase land rents to the detriment of land tax.

11.
Land rent

11.1 Introduction

In this chapter we provide basic information about land rent in the late medieval city-state of Cheb. We investigate: (1) the nature of land rents, (2) the amount of rent and the ratio of cash and in-kind payments, (3) the degree of nominal stability of land rents from the first half of the 14th century until the second half of the 15th century, (4) the distribution of land rents and inequalities between individual ecological zones and also between individual "subject" landholdings, and (5) the material aspects of land rents—model labor costs as well as the subsistence capacity of landholdings.

For an insight into land rents in the late medieval city-state of Cheb, several important sources may be used.[428] We use primarily the *1469 Land Tax Reg-*

---

428 The *1469 Cheb Land Tax Register* (cf. chap. 6.1; Ar Cheb, book 1096, *Klosteuerbuch 1469*; Klír et al., *Knihy*, 83, 159–161); the Cheb *1446 City Tax Register* (cf. chap. 6.3; Ar Cheb, book 1424, *Losungsbuch 1446*; the Cheb Poor Clares' *1464 Estate Register* (Ar Cheb, book 1003, *Urbar der Clarissinnen ab 1464*); the Cheb Poor Clares' cartulary of 1476 (*App. 7.6*; Siegl, "Das Salbuch"; Ar Cheb, book 975, *Salbuch der Klarissinen vom Jahre 1476*); the Cheb Castle estate register from ca. 1400 (*tab. 11.1*; a copy created in 1771 or shortly before survives amongst the documents of the Bohemian Governorate Border Committee, NA, fond HS, Lit. O, Num. 37, ad Subn. 35, Lit. M, 19, *Zinß und Rent zur der Pfleg zur Eger*; cf. Siegl, "Geschichte," 553); the estate register of Waldsassen Monastery dating to the second quarter of the 14th century (Langhammer, *Waldsassen*, 154–170). Of the later sources, the Starý Hrozňatov/Alt-Kinsberg 1516 register should also be mentioned (Jan Boukal, "Rytíř Kryštof z Týna. Válečník a diplomat pozdního středověku" [Knight Christoph of Týn. Warrior and diplomat of the Late Middle Ages] (B.A. thesis, Charles University, 2013), 39–43; Adam Wolf, ed., "Die Selbstbiographie Christophs von Thein. 1453–1516," *Archiv für österreichische Geschichte* 53

ister, firstly because it informs us about "subject" tenants across the entire city-state of Cheb, regardless of concrete landlord, and secondly because it makes it possible to establish the amount paid in both land tax and land rent for each taxpayer.[429] The disadvantage of this register is that it identifies only the main annual payments given by "subject" tenants and not the complete structure of land rents. Therefore, we supplement the data using the Cheb Poor Clares' estate register and the Cheb Castle estate register. The dynamic aspects of land rent may be established thanks to the Cheb Poor Clares' cartulary and estate register. The *1446 City Tax Register* is essential for completely establishing the land rents in the hands of Cheb burghers.

The question is, what was behind the creation of such an exceptional source as the tax register, expanded by data on the taxpayers' annual payments to their landlords? We assume that the purpose of such careful record-keeping was an endeavor by the Cheb city council to extract peasant surplus more systematically and more fully, and/or it was an attempt to set the tax amount according to land rents, as was the case in neighboring Bohemia.[430]

11.2 The form of land rent

For the use of land by right of purchase, "subject" tenants originally paid a tithe from their agricultural production, of which two-thirds belonged to the holders of landlord rights and one-third to the Church, represented by the parish church. In the 15th century, and probably in the previous century as well, ideal conditions were no longer a reality. The tithe from cereal produc-

(1875): 105–123). Some detailed data on the late medieval land rent are provided by the estate register of the parish church of St. Nicholas in Cheb, compiled in the 16th century, and includes copies of relevant documents securing a funeral Mass for donors (Ar Cheb, book 933, *Zins- und Copienbuch, 16. Jh.*). The estate register of the Brandenburg margraves is extremely important for comparison for the western part of the historical Cheb region (Sechsämterland) (Singer, *Das Landbuch*).

429   Cf. *App. 11.2.*
430   Míka, *Poddaný lid*, 268.

tion, therefore, also called the main tithe, played a key role, while the tithe from animal production was called the small tithe.[431]

Main tithes/payments

In the 14th century, the grain tithe paid to the landlord was a fixed amount for almost all "subject" tenants, and sometimes it was formally commuted to a cash or a mixture of cash and in-kind payment. Thus we speak of the main payment, not the tithe. Grain payment was collected at Michaelmas, but it depended on the type of grain. The subjects of the Waldsassen Monastery paid part of their grain payments also on St. James' Day, St. Martin's Day, Twelfth Night, and Walpurgis Eve (oats, wheat).[432] Cash payments were normally divided up to be paid at Michaelmas and then on Walpurgis Eve, although sometimes they were collected in full on Michaelmas alone, and in very exceptional cases on St. George's Day.[433]

It was specific to the city-state of Cheb that grain payments were most often composed of two equal halves, one of rye and one of oats.[434] It was usual that a certain volume of the grain payment automatically meant payment of both types of grain without this fact needing to be specified. So a reference to a payment of 10 "kar" of grain normally meant a payment of 5 "kar" of rye and 5 "kar" of oats.[435] The Cheb Poor Clares' cartulary and estate register contain entries of cases where the main grain payment was paid only in rye, oats, or partly included wheat, or else the ratio of rye to oats was not 1:1.[436] According

---

431   Singer, *Das Landbuch*, 47–52. Cf. documents in František Vacek, "Emfyteuse v Čechách ve XIII. a XIV. století II," *Agrární archiv* (1919): 130–144, on 137–138. In documents, depending on the context and custom, this payment was called tithe, grain tithe, great tithe, full tithe, rent, great rent, grain rent, or monetary rent (in German texts "Zehnte" and "Zins" in various variants). Cf. Jacob Grimm and Wilhelm Grimm, *Das Deutsche Wörterbuch von Jacob Grimm und Wilhelm Grimm*, http://dwb.uni-trier.de/de/das-woerterbuch/das-dwb/, Bd. 6, Sp. 4494; Bd. 31, Sp. 459, 1473–1505.

432   Langhammer, *Waldsassen*, 159.

433   Ar Cheb, book 1003, *Urbar der Clarissinnen ab 1464*. For dates in the neighboring Loket region, cf. Schreiber, *Der Elbogener Urbar*. For the Sechsämterland, cf. Singer, *Das Landbuch*, 47–49.

434   The estate register of the Brandenberg margraves mentioned ". . . egerischen Zehnt, halb korn und halb habern." Singer, *Das Landbuch*, 48.

435   This ratio is explicitly substantiated by cases cited in *app. 7.6.*, nrs. 8, 13, 17, 23, 25–26, 36.

436   *App. 11.3b*. For the cartulary, cf. *App. 7.6.*, nrs. 6–7, 11, 17.

to the *1464 Estate Register*, the customary composition of grain rent (1 part rye to 1 part oats) applied to two-thirds of the 130 assessed "subject" tenants, or else the proportion of rye accounted for half of the grain rent for 74% of "subject" tenants, while the second half was made up of grains other than oats.[437] For the "subject" tenants of Cheb Castle, oats were predominant in the grain rent (60%), which most likely had something to do with fodder requirements for the castle regiment's horses (*tab. 11.1*).

The data in the Cheb Poor Clares' cartulary, in which the authors of the copies also added the situation at the time of copying (1476), document a surprising stability of the main grain and cash payments. If we consider 21 comparable cases, the level of 17 grain payments remained the same (7x over a period of 100–146 years; 5x over 50–99 years; 5x over 16–49 years); in three cases the grain payments were reduced (16 → 14 "kar"; 4 → 3 "kar"; 8 → 6 "kar"); and in one case 6 "kar" of rye changed to 3 "kar" of rye and 3 "kar" of oats, which may have been merely due to the terminological inaccuracy of the scribe of the original or of the copy.[438] Grain payments converted into pounds or shillings of hellers into Prague groschen also remained stable.[439] Changes in the level of the main payment and the reasoning behind them may be found in places in the Cheb Poor Clares' *1464 Estate Register*.[440]

Main payments made by one "subject" landholding could be divided between several landlords—or more accurately, beneficiaries. We may mention the extreme case of a donation made by Cheb burgher Elizabeth Golderl, who at the end of the winter of 1343 divided her main payments totaling 8 "kar" of grain and also an unspecified additional payment on one landholding that she held in the village of Nový Drahov (Rohr) by paying two "kar" of grain each to the Cheb Poor Clares, Minorites, Dominicans, and the Teutonic Order. This meant that the salvation of this burgher was ensured several times over.[441]

---

437 *App. 11.3b.*

438 For concurrences, cf. *App. 7.6*, nrs. 3, 9–11, 13, 16–17, 21–23, 26, 28, 30–32, 34–35. For differences, cf. as above, nrs. 3, 4, 8.

439 Cf. *App. 7.6*, nrs. 5, 14. On the situation and coin changes, cf. Karel Castelin, "Chebské mincovnictví v době grošové (1305–1520)," *Numismatický sborník* 3 (1956): 73–113.

440 Hněvín (Knöba; farmer Per); Žírovice (Sirmitz; farmer Hanuš Karg); Potočiště (Dürrnbach; farmer Perner). Ar Cheb, book 1003, *Urbar der Clarissinnen ab 1464*, 23, 28.

441 *App. 7.6*, nr. 8.

Small tithes and additional payments

A further substantial burden on "subject" tenants were small tithes and additional payments, known also as extraordinary payments or recognition payments, identified in German documents as "*Weisat.*" As a rule, they were taken from animal products.[442] Here we will present a simplified overview of additional payments. These were collected on various dates and differed in scope and structure among individual "subject" tenants and landlords. Unlike main payments, they were not particularly firm, and property-related legal documents often did not even mention them. The complete normative data may be found in the Cheb Poor Clares' *1464 Estate Register*, according to which 80% of all listed tenants paid complete land rent, i.e., a main payment plus additional payments.[443] The rest paid either just the main payment or the church tithe, which cannot be considered a component to land rent, while additional payments may have been paid to somebody other than the Poor Clares. The Poor Clares' estate register also recorded development trends, specifically two cases of "reliution," wherein part of the additional payment (a wheel of cheese) was commuted to a cash payment and added to the main payment.

The beneficiaries of main and additional payments sometimes varied. Sale of the main payments took place quite frequently, while additional payments would be kept by the original overlord.[444] This may have had something to do with the fact that the form of some extraordinary (recognition) payments implied the fief status of a landholding.

The Poor Clares' "subject" tenants most often paid 2 hens (chickens), 30 eggs, 1 or 2 wheels of cheese, more rarely also a goose, a loaf of white bread (roll), and 2 sheaves of flax.[445] Some documents also cited lambs.[446] The quantity of additional payments was in no way burdensome for individual landholdings; when converted, they had a value of a few Prague groschen at the most, although when amassed this was a significant income for the Poor Clares. According to the final estate register balance sheet, this constituted a grand

---

442 Singer, *Das Landbuch*, 49–52. Cf. Grimm and Grimm, *Das Deutsche Wörterbuch*, Bd. 28, Sp. 1010–1011; *App. 7.6, nr. 37.*

443 *App. 11.3a.*

444 *App. 7.6, nrs. 28, 30.*

445 *App. 11.3c–d.*

446 *App. 7.6, nrs. 1–5, 8, 12, 14–17, 26, 28, 34, 36–37.*

total of 289 wheels of cheese, more than 268 hens, 3,328 eggs, and 6 geese received from their subjects.[447]

The collection of additional payments was spread out over the year in order to extract specific seasonal surplus. The Poor Clares' cartulary documents payments at Easter, Pentecost, and Christmas.[448] For illustration, we may cite an extract from the estate register for Cheb Castle, whose key subjects made additional payments on St. Martin's Day (geese), Christmas (suckling piglets), Easter (eggs and cheese), and St. John's Day (chickens) (*tab. 11.1*).[449] The subjects of the Waldsassen Monastery provided cheese at Pentecost, eggs before Ash Wednesday or Easter, and chickens in the autumn.[450]

Labor rent

Labor rents were almost unknown in the city-state of Cheb and if the landlord ran a demesne farm, he relied on wage labor. Demesne farms lay mainly in the close hinterland of the city of Cheb, although most of them were owned or rented by individual burghers, without further significant land tenure (*fig. 6*). Labor duties were vaguely referred to in documents copied into the Cheb Poor Clares's cartulary, even in cases where this was really just a formal expression. In the *1464 Estate Register*, specific labor duties were prescribed only for "subject" tenants of the village of Dřenice (Treunitz), specifically hay-making on meadows of an area of 8.5 "tagwerks" (ca. 4.8 hectares).[451] Concrete labor duties were also prescribed for Cheb Castle's "subject" tenants. Significantly, Cheb Castle' "subject" tenants did not perform labor on a demesne farm but provided for the castle's needs by transporting firewood from the forest to the castle (*tab. 11.1*). In summary, it may be claimed that for the late medieval city-state of Cheb, the rent economy activities of the landlord were crucial, while demesne farming was of marginal importance and was mainly carried out by wage labor.

The territory of the city-state of Cheb differed from the neighboring area of the so-called Sechsämterland of the Brandenburg margraviate, where manual

447 Ar Cheb, book 1003, *Urbar der Clarissinnen ab 1464*, 52 (including three villages lying outside of the Cheb Region).
448 *App. 7.6*, nrs. 4, 14.
449 NA, fond HS, fasc. O, Num. 37, Nr. 19. *Zinß und Rent zur der Pfleg zur Eger*.
450 Langhammer, *Waldsassen*, 159.
451 Ar Cheb, book 1003, *Urbar der Clarissinnen ab 1464*, 5.

and draught labor was relatively widespread, very diverse, and often performed over long distances and tied to large demesne farms near central settlements.[452]

Table 11.1. **Annual payments and duties of Cheb Castle "subject" tenants.**

Type of payment or duty	Date	Total payment amount	Average for one landholding
Main payments (main tithes)	Michaelmas	66 "kar" of rye	11 "kar" of rye
		108 "kar" of oats	18 "kar" of oats
		108 viertel (quarters) of peas	18 viertel of peas
Additional payments (small tithes)	St. Martin's Day	60 geese	10 geese
	Christmas	6 suckling pigs, each worth 10 groschen	1 suckling pig at 10 groschen
	Easter	9 threescore of eggs, 3 threescore and 20 cheeses	90 eggs and 30 cheeses (50 cheeses instead of 30 for one of the landholdings)
	St. John's Day	2 threescore of chicken	20 chickens
Labor duties	according to need	transport firewood from the forest	transport firewood from the forest
	haymaking	mowing 12 "tagwerks" of meadows and baling hay; during work received cheese, beer, and bread	mowing 2 "tagwerks" of meadows and baling hay
Land tax equivalent	when land tax is raised	6 threescore of groschen	1 threescore of groschen
	when double land tax is raised	12 threescore of groschen	2 threescore of groschen
Ecclesiastical tithes	(without mention)		

Source: NA, HS, fasc. O, Num. 37, Nr. 19, *Zins und Rent zur der Pfleg zur Eger* (ca. 1400; modern copy from the second half of the 18th century).
Note: A total of 6 landholdings in Doubek (Aag), Tršnice (Tirschnitz), and Dlouhé Mosty (Langenbruck).

452   Singer, *Das Landbuch,* 55–58.

11.3 Types of main payments

According to the 1469 *Land Tax Register*, we may determine the nature of the main land rent for 586 "subject" tenants in 94 settlements. We come across in-kind, cash, and mixed rents. Only the main annual payments were entered into the tax register. A comparison with the Cheb Poor Clares' estate register and cartulary demonstrated that the unspecified term "kar" indicated the customary grain payments, which corresponded to 1 part rye to 1 part oats.[453]

As for the nature of the main payments, most "subject" tenants paid only in kind (71%), fewer only in cash (23%), and the smallest number paid in both manners (6%) (*chap 11.4a*).[454] The ecological zones of the city-state of Cheb differed fundamentally from each other (*fig. 11.1*). Pure in-kind payments were most frequent in the agriculturally favorable zones in the vicinity of Cheb (86%), while pure cash payments applied to marginal, submountainous areas (33%). If we assess the methods of payment in separate settlements, almost half of them contained "subject" tenants paying only in kind, while in others the subjects also made at least partial cash payments.[455] The nature of land rent varied from landlord to landlord.[456]

Various reasons may explain the larger proportion of cash payments in the agriculturally less favorable areas, from historical, settlement-related, and genetic areas to economic areas. In the first case, we should emphasize the differing historical conditions and agreements between the landlords and "subject" tenants at the time of the establishment of the settlements; in the second case, we should emphasize ecological and economic differences. We assume that in the agriculturally less favorable areas, with a high risk of harvest failure, it was easier for peasants to acquire cash from a combination of various agricultural and non-agricultural activities than to deliver a specific, firmly set amount of grain.

453   Ar Cheb, book 1003, *Urbar der Clarissinnen ab 1464. App. 7.6,* nrs. 8, 13, 17, 23, 25–26, 36.
454   *App. 11.1.*
455   1–3 "subject" tenants with this data. *App. 11.1; App. 11.4b.*
456   *App. 11.5.*

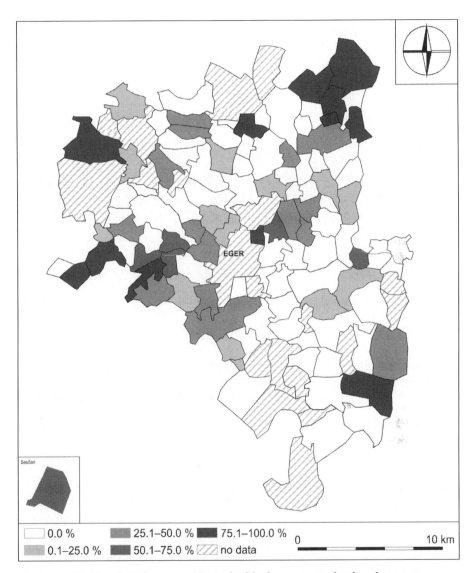

Figure 11.1. **Ratio of cash payments to in-kind payments in the city-state of Cheb, 1469. The predominantly peripheral locations of settlements with predominant cash payments are striking.**

Units: Number of persons who could be supported from the area's yield. (Arranged according to the extent of the area necessary to ensure the production of the rye part of the natural land rent.)
Source: Ar Cheb, book 1096, *Klosteuerbuch 1469.*
Note: In certain cases, the data may be misleading because only some "subject" tenants paid the land tax. Cf. *app. 11.1.*

11.4 The level of main payments and inequalities in its distribution

A total of 170 "subject" tenants paid **cash rent**, some in combination with in-kind payments, adding up to over 73 threescore of Prague groschen in total.[457] One hundred thirty-two "subject" tenants paid cash rent only, totaling 65 threescore of groschen. Large differences existed between the annual payments of separate subjects, the lowest rent being just 1 Meissen groschen (ca. 0.33 of a Prague groschen) and the most being 4 threescore Meissen groschen (240 Prague groschen). In the agriculturally optimal zone, annual payments were generally higher, ranging from 12 to 240 groschen, with an average of almost 91 groschen; in the submountainous zone the average was just 17 groschen, with payments ranging from 2 to 60 groschen (*figs. 11.2; 11.4*).[458]

In-kind rent was paid by 454 "subject" tenants and amounted to a grand total of 2,733.2 "kar" of grain (half rye, half oats), 104.8 "kar" of oats, and 17.8 "kar" of rye.[459] Every year, a total of 2,708.5 "kar" of grain was meant to be collected from 399 "subject" tenants who paid just rent in kind in grain. Therefore, this was ideally divided into 1,354.3 "kar" of rye and 1,354.3 "kar" of oats. The lowest grain payment was just a quarter of a "kar," the highest was 24 "kar." In agriculturally favorable zones, an average of 9–10 "kar" was due from each taxpayer, the minimum being 1 "kar," the maximum being 24 "kar"; in the submountainous zone, the average was 3.62 "kar," with payments ranging from a quarter up to 12 "kar" (*figs. 11.3; 11.5*).[460]

A detailed view of the level of cash and in-kind rent for individual landholdings according to ecological zone is presented in *figures 11.2–11.3*. The curves demonstrate that cash rent reflected geographic differences more clearly than in-kind rent. The average level of cash rent noticeably and continually fell with worsening natural conditions, and we can see a glaring difference between landholdings in the favorable zones A+B on the one hand and the unfavorable zones C+D+E on the other.

457   *App. 11.4c.*
458   *App. 11.4c.*
459   *App. 11.4e.*
460   *App. 11.4e.*

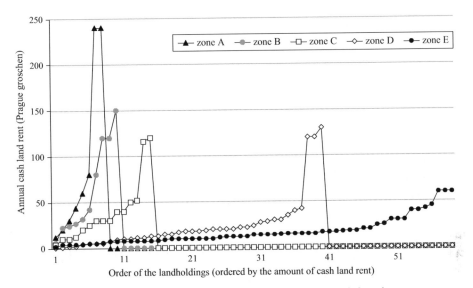

Figure 11.2. The level of cash land rent in ecological zones of the city-state of Cheb, 1469.

Source: Ar Cheb, book Nr. 1096, *Klosteuerbuch 1469.*
Note: Each dot represents one "subject" landholding. Landholdings paying just cash rent.

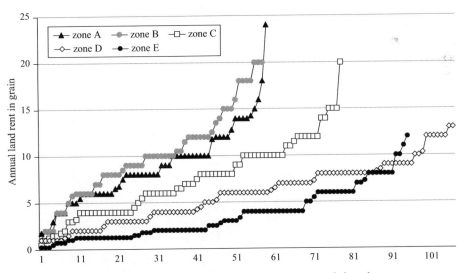

Figure 11.3. Level of land rent in grain in ecological zones of the city-state of Cheb (rye and oats), 1469.

Source: Ar Cheb, book Nr. 1096, *Klosteuerbuch 1469.*
Note: Each dot represents one landholding. Landholdings paying just grain rent.

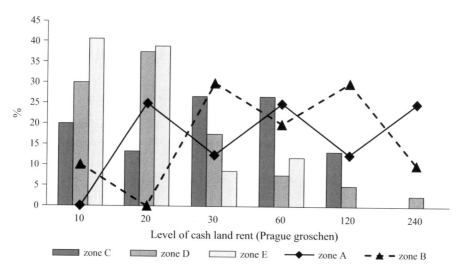

Figure 11.4. The level of cash land rent in ecological zones of the city-state of Cheb, 1469. To highlight the contrast, the agriculturally optimal zones are represented by a line, the average and unfavorable zones by a column.

Source: Ar Cheb, book Nr. 1096, *Klosteuerbuch 1469*.
Note: Landholdings paying just cash rent.

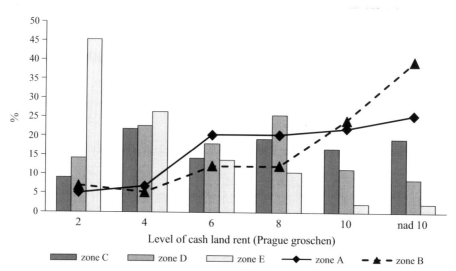

Figure 11.5. Level of land rent in grain in individual ecological zones of the city-state of Cheb, 1469. To highlight the contrast, the agriculturally optimal zones are represented by a line, the average and unfavorable zones by a column.

Source: Ar Cheb, book Nr. 1096, *Klosteuerbuch 1469*.
Note: Landholdings paying just grain rent.

Rate of inequality of land rent

The rate of inequality in the distribution of cash and in-kind payments between landholdings in the different ecological zones may best be illustrated using the *Lorenz curve* (*fig. 11.6*) and with the *Gini coefficient* (*tab. 13.1*). The results are as follows. Firstly, in zones A–D cash rent led to deeper inequalities between landholdings than in-kind rent, while the opposite applied in zone E. Secondly, in-kind rent most differentiated landholdings in the agriculturally least favorable zone E (Gini 0.49), while cash rent most differentiated landholdings in the agriculturally optimal zone A (Gini 0.54). Conversely, we find the smallest differentiation between landholdings in terms of cash rent in the agricul-

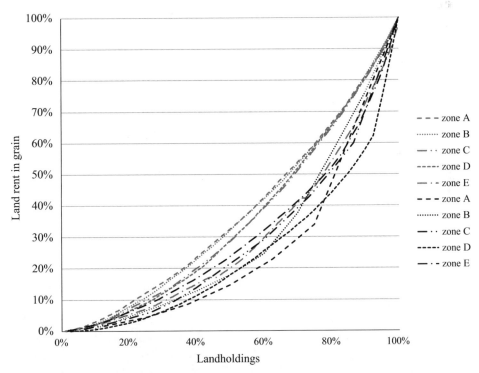

Figure 11.6. **Rate of inequality in the distribution of cash (in gray) and in-kind land rents (in black) in ecological zones of the city-state of Cheb, 1469.**

Source: Ar Cheb, book Nr. 1096, *Klosteuerbuch* 1469.
Note: Cash rent differentiated "subject" landholdings more than in-kind rent, except for submountainous and agriculturally unfavorable zone E. The most striking contrast may be seen in ecological zone A. Cf. *tab. 13.1*.

turally least favorable zone E (Gini 0.37), and in in-kind rent in the optimal zones A and B (Gini 0.43–0.44). These findings have significant consequences for interpretation and also demand explanation.

The varying degrees of differentiation of landholdings due to cash and in-kind rent is unsurprising. In-kind rent prescribed in "kar" of grain was rounded up or down more than cash rent stipulated in groschen. Also, the absolute span of in-kind rent (0.25–24 "kar") was lower than that for cash rent (0.33–240 groschen). However, the surprising aspect is the more or less opposite effect on landholdings in the different ecological zones. This fact may be explained against a backdrop of land tax collection that functioned in tandem with land rent.

11.5 Labor demands and subsistence capacity of land rents

Figure 11.3 shows striking inequalities in the level of land rents between individual ecological zones. On average, a higher grain rent applied to peasant landholdings in agriculturally favorable zones than to those in less favorable zones. The amount of rent received was essential primarily for the landlord, not for their "subject" tenants, for whom the amount of labor they had to endure was more important. Although agriculturally favorable zones paid more on average, less labor was required to achieve a certain grain yield. We can calculate this inequality at least approximately with the help of the relatively varied yield/seed ratios estimated for the separate zones of the city-state of Cheb by the *Theresian Cadastre* of the Early Modern Period.

Our simplified calculation assumes that all "subject" landholdings operated in the same agricultural system (the traditional three-field fallow system) and that the grain land rent was paid half in rye and half in oats.[461] In fact, the situation of each individual landholding (*fig. 11.7*) differed from year to year depending on the course of the concrete agrarian cycle and the size of the harvest. In order to capture this variability, we model data also for years where the average yield/seed ratio fell or rose in all locations by half a seed.[462] It is

461   *App. 11.6.*
462   *App. 11.6.*

Table 11.2. **Arable land area necessary for covering the grain land rents of "subject" landholdings, 1469.**

Zone	Number of landholdings	Min.–Max. (ha)	Average (ha)
A	59	0.74–10.20	3.78
B	58	0.51–10.20	5.14
C	78	0.32–12.80	4.74
D	106	0.85–11.05	5.04
E	95	0.21–15.30	4.64

Source: Ar Cheb, book 1096, *Klosteuerbuch 1469.* Cf. Chalupa, Lišková, Nuhlíček, and Rajtoral, *Tereziánský katastr český, Vol. 1, Rustikál, kraje A–CH,* 282–293.
Note: Calculated according to the *Theresian Cadastre* yield/seed ratio model.

apparent that fluctuation had a markedly different impact in different ecological zones—in an agriculturally favorable zone with, on average, a higher yield/seed ratio, the difference was considerably lower than in unfavorable submountainous areas. Alternatively, the labor demand connected with a yield of one "kar" of grain remained more or less the same in the optimal zone for most of the year, while in submountainous areas, this fluctuated considerably from year to year.

If we convert the level of grain land rent to the arable land area, then the differences between ecological zones to a great extent evened out—averages relating to one "subject" landholding were fairly comparable in all zones (3.8–5.1 hectares; *tab. 11.2.*). Absolute area values in all zones were in a similar and real range, with most of them ranging between 10 and 15 hectares. Landholdings paying a high in-kind rent usually achieved the necessary yield more effectively—although the rent was high, the labor required per unit was less than for a landholding with a lower rent.

In-kind land rent may be approximately converted for an ideal number of persons who could survive from it during one year (*tab. 11.3*).[463] In our model, two Cheb "kar" of rye are necessary per adult, which equals four "kar" of grain land rent, where rye made up half of the payment.[464] The relevant limit values

---

463   *App. 11.7a–b.*
464   Summarized by Tomáš Klír, "Agrarsysteme des vorindustriellen Dorfes. Zur Interpretation mittelalterlicher Ortswüstungen im Niederungs- und Mittelgebirgsmilieu," in *Stadt – Land – Burg. Festschrift für Sabine Felgenhauer-Schmiedt zum 70. Geburtstag,* ed. Claudia Theune et al., Internationale Archäologie, Studia honoraria 34 (Rahden/West.: Leidorf, 2013), 139–157;

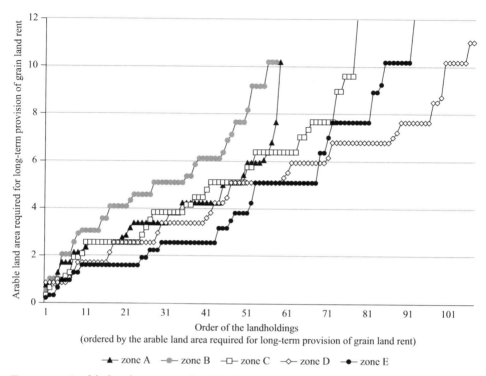

Figure 11.7. **Arable land area required for long-term provision of grain land rents for landholdings in ecological zones of the city-state of Cheb, 1469.**

Source: Entry data according to Ar Cheb, book 1096, *Klosteuerbuch 1469*.
Note: Modeled according to *Theresian Cadastre* yield/seed ratio. Each dot represents one "subject" land-holding. Arable land area required for producing 1 "kar" of rye and oats comprises 1 part winter crops, 1 part spring crops, and 1 part fallow field. Units of area correspond to the number of persons that can live off its yields.

are expressed by a horizontal line in *figure 11.7*, where the highest in-kind payments evidently corresponded to the quantity of rye needed to support 5–6 adults for a whole year. The subsistence value of in-kind payments was important from the landlord's standpoint, since they would cover their own subsistence needs and could put any surplus on the market.

Tomáš Klír and Dana Vodáková, "Economy and population of an Early Modern village: Milčice – home of the most famous Bohemian peasant F. J. Vavák," *Historie – otázky – problémy* 9 (2017): 106–151, on 111–113.

Table 11.3. **Subsistence value of grain land rent in individual ecological zones of the city-state of Cheb, 1469.**

Zone	Subject	Subsistence capacity (number of adults)	
		Min.–Max.	Average for one "subject" tenant
A	59	0.4–6.0	2.3
B	58	0.3–5.0	2.5
C	78	0.1–5.0	1.9
D	106	0.3–3.3	1.5
E	95	0.1–3.0	0.9

Source: Ar Cheb, book 1096, *Klosteuerbuch 1469.*
Note: Cf. *tab. 11.2.*

The in-kind payments recorded in the *1469 Land Tax Register* could ideally feed 687.5 adults for a year. In average years, the Cheb Poor Clares and the Teutonic Order certainly had a market surplus, while the Knights of the Cross with the Red Star probably used any potential surplus to operate the city hospital.

11.6 Summary

In the late medieval city-state of Cheb, the majority of land rent was typically paid in kind, while a smaller proportion of "subject" landholdings paid a cash payment and only a minimum of landholdings were burdened with mixed rent. Labor obligations are minimally documented. Where it proved possible to find earlier documents, land rent remained stable in the long-term.

On average, land rent for landholdings in agriculturally favorable zones was higher than for those in less favorable zones. Due to the more fertile land, the former landholdings required less arable land to achieve the necessary yields, and so the labor demands required for paying land rent were similar in all zones. Because of land rent, landholdings in the city-state of Cheb operating a three-field fallow system, leaving one field fallow, on average had to cultivate 4–5 hectares of land.

12.
Land tax

12.1 Formulation of the issue

The following chapter aims to assess the nature and degree of exploitation of Cheb's peasantry. The main question is to what extent rent extracted the peasant surplus. Was it extracted more or less completely? Or did a large part remain in the hands of peasant households? We also ask (1) what the land tax rate was, (2) whether the land tax rate was applied mechanically or adapted elastically on an individual basis, (3) whether the tax rate varied for rich and poor, (4) to what extent land tax reflected the impaired quality of coins and inflation, (5) whether the real tax burden increased or decreased, (6) what consequences an increasing tax had and whether those consequences different for the poor and the rich.

During the focus period, land tax was paid on the total monetary value of movable and immovable property. Thanks to the *1438 Land Tax Register* and the *1456 Taxation Book*, we can reconstruct the relationship between the tax amount and the monetary value of the property. We work with the term *tax rate*, which expresses how many groschen were paid on property with a monetary value of one threescore. A tax rate of 1.0 means a payment of one groschen for one threescore, or else a ratio of 1:60, i.e., taxation at a rate of 1.67%.

12.2 Analysis of the tax rate

Rate in 1438

There were 827 cases in the tax register where both the total monetary value of the taxpayer's property and the amount of tax was clearly specified (*fig. 12.1*).[465] In both values we can see great differences. The property value of individual taxpayers ranged from 1 to 324 threescore of Prague groschen, and prescribed tax amounts ranged from 1 to 260 threescore of groschen. The tax rate ranged between 0.50–3.60, but in almost 92% of cases its range was limited to 0.90–1.99. Extreme and almost incomprehensible values may be due either to past reality or to inconsistencies and errors made by the scribe in 1438 or by the author of the facsimile of 1769.

The analysis proves slight differences in the tax rate between:
1) The tenants of "subject" and "free" landholdings[466]
2) The tenants of different socioeconomic categories of "subject" landholdings[467]
3) Various property categories[468]

The standard tax rate of 1438 was 1 groschen for each threescore of property (the tax rate of 1.0; 42% of cases). We find a lower tax rate for 17% of taxpayers and a higher rate for 41%. The rate was most often increased for medium-rich and rich taxpayers, with property of between 21 and 60 threescore of groschen (increased for 39–51%). Conversely, the tax index was most frequently reduced for the extremely rich taxpayers, with property worth 91 threescore or more (reduced for 56%). For poorer peasants, the standard tax rate was usually maintained. It is an important finding that the monetary value of the taxpayer's total property did not directly reflect hisorrelay to pay, and tax officials therefore adapted the tax rate elastically so that the taxpayer's burden would be optimal in their view. In principle, land tax would level out potential socioeconomic differentiation between taxpayers.

---

465   *App. 12.1a; 12.6a.*
466   *App. 12.6a; 12.7a, 7e.*
467   *App. 12.4; app. 12.6b; 12.7a.*
468   *App. 12.4; app. 12.7a–e.*

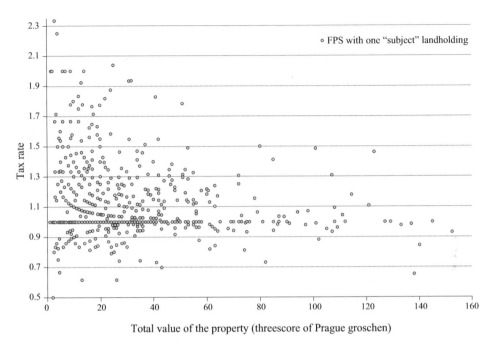

Figure 12.1. **Relation of the tax rate and the value of the taxed property, 1438.**

Source: Cf. app. 12.6a–e.

Rate in 1456

In the *1456 Taxation Book*, an entry for each taxpayer specified the tax and also the monetary value of the main items of property. Unlike in the 1438 register, however, their value was not added up by the scribe. Certain items were merely written in but not valued, so these taxpayers must be excluded from our analysis. Overall, we can work with 662 cases where we know the tax amount and can determine the total value of their property (*fig. 12.2*).[469] The monetary value of property ranged widely from 2 to 319 threescore of Prague groschen and the tax amount ranged between 3–420 groschen. The tax rate fluctuated from 0.25–3.44, but in almost 94% of cases its range was limited to 0.90–1.99. Therefore, in comparison with 1438, the tax rate had risen considerably. While

---

469   *App. 12.5; app. 12.1b; 12.8.a–b, 8f.*

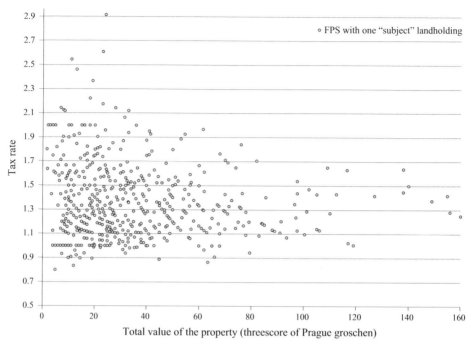

Figure 12.2. Relation of the tax rate and the value of the taxed property, 1456.

Source: Cf. app. 12.8a–f.

in 1438 on average 1.07 groschen were collected on one threescore of property, in 1456 the figure was 1.34 groschen, which is a rise of 125%.

Unlike the tax in 1438, no significantly predominant tax rate can be identified, with the vast majority of taxpayers having individually set land tax. We may consider a rate ranging from 1.10 to 1.39, which accounts for 46% of taxpayers. Eighteen percent of taxpayers paid a lower rate and 36% paid a higher rate. Due to the great variability of tax rates, we assume that in 1456, unlike in 1438, the total value of property was more for control and orientation purposes, while the practice of proceeding according to the tested potential of landholdings and taxpayers had greater significance.

Detailed analysis again showed that (1) taxpayers were treated on an individual basis and (2) various property categories varied in the application of low, standard (1.10–1.39) or high taxed rates.[470]

---

470   *App. 12.5; app. 12.8c–e.*

Unlike in 1438, relative differences in the taxation of the poorest, medium-rich, and rich taxpayers became less pronounced. While the low taxation of very rich taxpayers as a whole remained, a new group of the richest taxpayers emerged who also had the highest tax burden. Their status and ability to pay were therefore evaluated very differently than in 1438.

The pure fact of rising taxes is unsurprising given the impaired quality of the Prague groschen and its falling exchange rate against the Rhenish guilder.[471] However, the rising tax rate tells us that a real growth in burden came about. The tax burden rose between 1438 and 1456 considerably more than the monetary value of the taxed property, which may be seen in the summary in *appendix 12.1*. While in the case of tenants of "subject" landholdings, the average value of property belonging to one tenant rose by 118 %, the average tax amount rose by 147%. The difference in the case of tenants of "free" landholdings was even more pronounced: the average value of property rose by 139% and the tax amount by 181%. Meanwhile, the value of the Rhenish guilder against the Prague groschen rose by just 127%.

12.3 Tax changes from 1438–1456

In 1438, tax was prescribed fairly systematically according to the total value of each taxpayer's property. In subsequent years the tax amount changed, both universally and also individually in relation to the changing property situation of concrete taxpayers. To analyze the degree of taxpayer burden, it is essential to determine (1) the degree of increase, stability, or reduction of tax; (2) the consequences of increase; and (3) differences between variously wide tax ranges, i.e., between rich and poor taxpayers.

Given the large quantity of data, we do not analyze year-to-year changes in the tax amount, but the change at two- or four-year intervals. We limit ourselves to a four-year interval for the period 1438–1442 and 1451–1455, in the former case due to the absence of registers and in the latter case due to the devastation of the city-state of Cheb in 1452. We work with yearly intervals in

---

471 Wilhelm Heisinger even expressed the opinion that the increase in the Cheb land tax did not mean any real growth of burden. Heisiner, "Die Egerer Klosteuerbücher," 285–286.

1442–1443 and 1455–1456. The year 1443 has a special status because the relevant tax register lists two tax amounts for each taxpayer (identified as 1443a and 1443b). After tax had been announced and a new register started, tax was increased for all, and a second entry was made subsequently for each taxpayer with the actually demanded—and as a rule, paid—amount.[472]

The basis of our analysis are landholdings, not FPSs. We evaluated all changes in prescribed taxes when it was possible to identify the landholding in two "adjacent" registers, regardless of any change or continuity of the taxpayer. The number of evaluated cases in the separate interim periods fluctuated between 684 and 751; there were fewer just in the period 1438–1442 (565).

Changes and consequences of tax burden

During each of the focus interim periods, tax on individual landholdings changed to various degrees. A universal increase occurred in 1443 (changes in 97% of landholdings) and also in the interim period 1445–1447 (changes in 88% of landholdings; the increase occurred specifically in 1446).

+ During 1438–1442, tax remained stable for just below one-third of landholdings, was reduced for more than a quarter, and rose for 42% of landholdings. A universal increase did not occur, but the small quantity of stable tax amounts indicates a fairly unsettled period where we assume a greater degree of landholding transfers.
+ The universal increase that took place in 1443 and in the interim period of 1445–1447 (1446), led to tax revision for many landholdings over the subsequent year or two. Following the increase of 1443, tax had been reduced again by 1445 for 11% of landholdings, while a further increase affected just 4%. After the increase in the interim period of 1445–1447, it was reduced by 1449 for 23% of landholdings, while a continuing increase in tax affected just 5%.
+ In the subsequent 1449–1451 interim period, a change occurred for half of the landholdings both upward and downward (21% and 30%).
+ The changes in the period of 1451–1455 may have been due to the military devastation of 1452, although the tax burden remained the same for most landholdings.

472   Cf. Heisiner, "Die Egerer Klosteuerbücher," 22, 285.

• After assembling the taxation book in 1456, a tax revision occurred, meaning an increase for 50% of landholdings. However, the tax amount remained unchanged for 44% and was reduced for 7%.

Looking at the continuous increase or decrease in the prescribed amount of land tax, we ask whether these changes correlated with the exchange rate of the Prague groschen to the Rhenish guilder. A look at the comparative *figure 12.5* shows very little correlation.[473] It is therefore possible to interpret the blanket increases in 1443 and 1446 not as reactions to the decreasing quality of the groschen coins but rather as an effort by the Cheb city council to obtain more funds from the rural population. The real burden on the peasantry therefore increased. It was not until the 1450s that the rate of increase in land tax as a whole began to copy the inflationary trend.

The mass, although individually applied, reduction in tax that regularly followed each universal and mechanical increase provides an important testimony. For certain landholdings, the tax increase probably crossed the tolerance threshold and subsequently had to be reduced, whereas for other landholdings tax officials attempted to achieve this threshold. This again confirms that progressive and elastic Cheb land tax evened out the degree of burden and aimed towards socioeconomic leveling among FPSs. Simultaneously, it is evident that the Cheb city council sought to fully extract the peasant surplus product.

Crossing the tolerance threshold could have two effects. Firstly, it could mean crossing the **existential** threshold, when a landholding was burdened by tax to such an extent that its reproduction became imperfect and therefore tax reduction followed. Secondly, a tax increase could only cause glaring differences between landholdings, which were subsequently rectified. In the first case, the land tax was aimed at perfect exploitation, and thus, to a large extent, landholdings would lack a disposable surplus. In the second case, the burdens would be imperfect, and landholdings would retain the potential to create and accumulate surplus. We seek an answer to this question in *chapter 12.4.*

473   See *chap. 14.3.*

Differences between rich and poor landholdings

An increase or decrease in tax in the period 1438–1456 did not usually affect all landholdings in the city-state of Cheb universally, but some groups more, others less. At this point we ask to what extent landholdings differed if we order them according to the prescribed tax amount. Were poor taxpayers burdened in the same way as the rich? Or did differences exist between them? For this analysis, we use tax ranges of 10 Prague groschen, while we evaluate landholdings burdened with an amount of 90 groschen or more as one group. The overall distribution of landholdings into tax ranges in the focus period is illustrated in *figures 12.3* and *12.4*.

It is necessary to investigate the relative differences in the extent of the universal increases of 1443, 1446, and 1456.

+   When we evaluate the total monetary amount prescribed to all landholdings in a certain tax range, in 1443 there was the highest growth of landholdings in the lowest tax band up to 9 groschen (35% growth), and subsequently the growth rate fell (26–23% growth) and from 30 groschen growth more or less stabilized at 16–18%. Therefore, landholdings with lower tax were burdened more in relative terms in 1443 than landholdings with higher tax.
+   To a certain extent the tax increase of 1446 was similar, although more considerable, and the differences between landholdings with low and high taxes were no longer so contrasting. Tax on landholdings in the lowest tax band rose by 38%, while the increase for landholdings in subsequent bands fluctuated between 21–26%.
+   In 1456, the degree of burden also fell with the rising of the original land tax amount, in the lowest tax band up to 9 groschen the tax amount rose by 49%, while tax for landholdings in the highest group conversely fell by 4%.

12.4 Imperfect exploitation?

To determine the degree of exploitation of the peasantry, it is essential to examine the extent to which they actually accomplished their annual tax obligations. Two options present themselves. If exploitation was perfect or almost perfect, the taxpayer's ability to pay would copy year-to-year fluctuations in agricultural production and market prices, and so in bad years a considerable

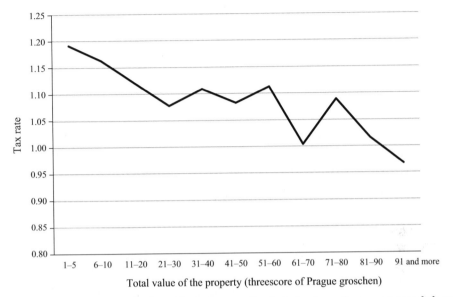

Figure 12.3. Relative relationship between the total value of property and the tax rate, 1438.

Source: Ar Cheb, book 1067, *Klosteuerbuch 1438.*
Note: Tax rate = tax amount*60/value of the property.

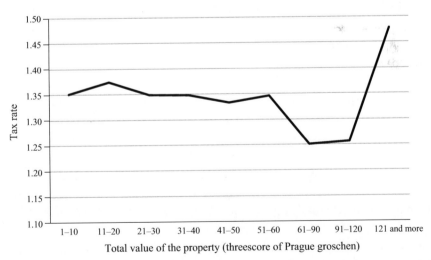

Figure 12.4. Relative relationship between the total value of property and the tax rate, 1456.

Source: Ar Cheb, book 1084, *Klosteuerbuch (Schätzungsbuch) 1456.*
Note: Tax rate = tax amount*60/value of the property.

proportion of taxpayers would have problems in paying the prescribed tax. If exploitation was imperfect, various volumes of disposable surplus would remain in the hands of the peasants, and we would expect an annual and balanced fulfillment of the prescribed obligations that would be disrupted only by a catastrophe. To find the answer, the period 1442–1456 is too short, and so we also included the land tax registers of 1457–1469 in this analysis (*figs. 12.5–12.6*).

In the land tax registers, we come across two possible reactions of the Cheb city council to a taxpayer's bad economic results in a certain year. Firstly, the tax could be reduced or completely exempted without being subsequently demanded in later years. In such cases, a note was entered concerning a taxpayer or an entire settlement explaining why tax had been exempted. The reason provided was most often damage caused by fire, looting, and occasionally extreme weather conditions; tax could be waived after the loss of a horse or cattle or upon the acquisition of an abandoned landholding. Secondly, the taxpayer or entire settlement paid taxes only partially or not at all, but they had to settle up the arrears the following year. It may be claimed that except for the warring years, exemption from or non-payment of tax was exceptional and limited to only a few individuals.

The tax registers kept after the reform of the Cheb city office in 1441 were uniform in structure. A regular component of the registers was the sum total of land tax collected, entered at the end. In many cases, amounts were added that were collected in arrears from the previous year, usually bearing a phrase such as: "*Mer nach der beslissung dt Grün II sex*" in the tax registers of 1446.[474] We understand this record as meaning that taxpayers from the settlement Úval (Grün) did not pay their flat rate of tax amount for 1446, which was meant to be collected from sometime between autumn 1446 and summer 1447 until sometime between autumn 1447 and summer 1448. Entries concerning paid arrears were not always recorded, but they do appear in the tax registers for 1443, 1446, 1448–1451, 1454, 1456, and 1462. Generally, the number and size of paid and recorded arrears was not large, 1–3 persons per year for the entire city-state, with the total sum ranging from a few dozen groschen to more than 4 threescore of Prague groschen. The exception is the 1448 register, which lists 14 persons from 10 settlements, which at that time paid arrears of 5 threescore and 40 groschen (approximately 1% of the total amount of tax collected).

---

474   Ar Cheb, book 1073, *Klosteuerbuch 1446*.

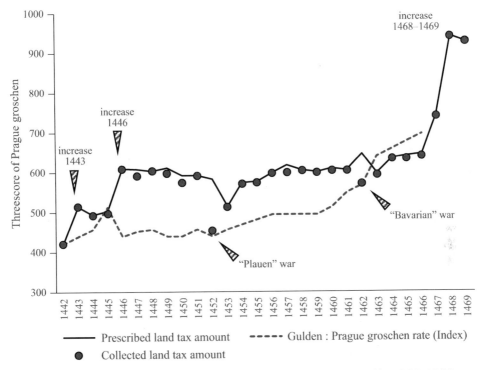

Figure 12.5. Nominal amount of land tax prescribed and collected in 1442–1469 and the currency ratios.

Source: According to total amounts noted in the *1442–1469 Land Tax Registers* (Ar Cheb, books 1069–1083, 1085–1096, *Klosteuerbücher 1442–1469*). Prague groschen : Rhenish guilder rate according to Ar Cheb, books 2144–2152, 2153–2169, *Umgeldbücher 1442–1450, 1452–1469*.
Note: Cf. Also Heisinger, "Die Egerer Klosteuerbücher," 278–281; Klír et al., *Knihy*, 45, graph 1. Cf. also *chap. 14.3.*

In the tax registers of 1455–1458, we come across another method in which arrears were recorded.[475] On the first page of each new tax register, the scribe wrote a list of those still in debt from the preceding year. In 1455, this list bore the caption "*Nota was pey den virn vor vns Closteẅr In den LIIII Jare hinterstellig plib[e]n ist [etc.].*" There followed a list of 21 taxpayers from 19 settlements and one entire settlement that had paid only partial or no tax at all in 1454. The owed amounts were not listed anywhere, and some taxpayers even owed tax for

---

475   Klír et al., *Knihy*, 83, appendix 5.

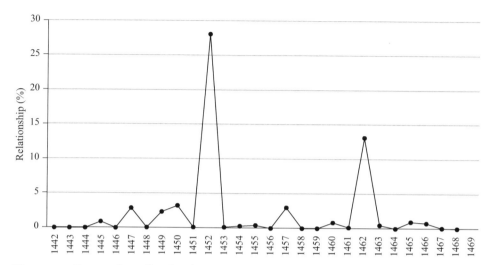

Figure 12.6. Proportion of waived tax amounts to the total amount collected in the city-state of Cheb, 1442–1469.

Source: According to the Ar Cheb, books 1069–1083, 1085–, *Klosteuerbücher* 1442–1469.

several years.[476] In 1456–1458, specific owed amounts appeared in lists, although they were not particularly large. Subsequent sources suggest that these arrears were paid in full or at least in large part. The low number of debtors and the limited level of arrears is almost shocking. After 1459, these systematic lists are absent from the registers, although at least until 1469 they were kept on separate sheets and later bound together into one book (1469–1492).[477]

Nonetheless, fairly systematic lists of waived tax were compiled, either on the last page of the register or on its back cover under the heading "*Abgangk.*"[478] The number of tax waivers fell year-to-year, since it depended on random circumstances. A more wide-ranging tax waiver is documented in the wake of the devastation caused by armies in 1452 and 1462, when the waived amount represented 28% or 13% of the total prescribed tax. In other years, tax was waived only for individuals, mainly as a result of a local catastrophe. Greater fluctua-

---

476 This concerned the tenants of non-landholding plots in Jindřichov (Honnersdorf) who were mechanically transcribed from one land tax register to another.

477 Book of arrears. Cf. Klír et al., *Knihy*, 83–84.

478 Klír et al., *Knihy*, 83, appendix 5. The absence of a list in the registers of 1456, 1459, and 1461 may have been because their covers have not survived.

tions were provoked when entire settlements were burned to the ground that had annually paid high levels of tax.[479]

Based on *appendices 12.2–12.3*, it may be said that taxpayers paid the prescribed tax amounts every year; year-to-year the agricultural fluctuations did not have a particularly significant influence and the tax did not threaten their reproduction even in bad years. Of course, we do not know whether or not the ability to pay was occasionally bolstered by a bridging loan, help of neighbors or relatives, or assistance from the landlord. If so, it seems that peasants soon came to terms with it, since no references to indebtedness exist.[480] Exploitation of the peasantry in the city-state of Cheb was therefore imperfect and peasants were able to retain a disposable surplus, which was particularly high in years of bountiful harvest. If a catastrophic event occurred, tax was temporarily waived.

12.5 Summary

The questions we posed at the beginning of this chapter have now been answered. The Cheb land tax rate was in the range of 1.7–3.0% of the monetary value of the property. The tax rate was not set completely mechanically, but where necessary could be modified to suit individual needs. In some years, wealthy FPSs were favored, while in others poor FPSs were. Overall, it may be claimed that there existed a dependency between the tax amount and property categories. Land tax was not only progressive but also elastic—property with the same monetary value could be taxed differently. "Free" landholdings, which did not pay the land rent, were the most burdened with the land tax. The progressive and elastic character of the land tax blurred the economic differences not only between the variously wealthy "subject" landholdings, but also between "subject" and "free" landholdings. Thus, the land tax acted as an important leveling factor on socioeconomic stratification, and it even seems that the rich landholdings became poorer, and the poor became richer.

The Cheb city council tried to exhaust the peasant surplus entirely, but at the same time it compensated for cases in which the tax rate set for the tax-

---

479   Such as the fire in the settlement of Třebně (Trebensdorf) in 1457, which meant a shortfall of 16 threescore and 25 groschen, which represented 2.7% of the land tax collected.

480   Perhaps only the list of arrears for 1455 stated: "*Oberndorff Mertil ist pfantt.*"

payer exceeded the acceptable limit. The Cheb countryside could handle the blanket increase of the tax in 1443, but after another increase in 1446 the tax for many taxpayers again had to be lowered.

Saltatory and universal increases in taxes occurred in 1443, 1446, and to a large extent also in 1456. These years of universal increase were then followed by a correction, which, however, did not exceed the landholdings' ability to pay, but rather the effort to balance out glaring differences within peasant communities.

We consider the finding that the blanket and, at the same time, a relatively significant increase in the prescribed land tax in the 1440s was not due to the deteriorating quality of the coin, as the ratio of Prague groschen to the Rhenish guilder remained relatively stable, but the efforts of the Cheb city council to draw more of the peasant surplus. The real weight of the land tax therefore increased.

The prescribed tax amounts, which were generally high, testify to the economic strength and commercialization of the Cheb peasantry as a whole. No written sources exist that would show what year the land tax exceeded the payment capacity of the taxpayers. Except for those whose landholding was burned to the ground in that particular year, or whose landholding had been plundered during local military conflicts, 99% of taxpayers regularly paid tax in full. However, this explanation for their good payment ability is not unequivocal. It points either to a high level of annual surplus, which was not extracted to the full even in bad years, or to an advanced system of bridging mechanisms such as loans, saved cash, and redistribution against a backdrop of solidarity within kinship networks.

Both the nominal and real tax burdens of the Cheb peasantry on average grew overall between 1438 and 1456. Two interdependent phenomena testify to an increase in the tax burden: (1) the tax rate rising and (2) the tax amount growing faster than the value of the taxed property. While an inflation trend and impairment of the quality of coins ranged between 10–25%, the tax amount rose by approximately 45%. Therefore, the growth in the tax burden was around 25%.

13.
The relationship between land tax and land rent

13.1 Introduction

In this chapter, we explore whether land tax and land rent grew in tandem, or conversely if they evened each other out. Land tax was not fixed, but unlike land rent it was progressive. Therefore, it could act against the differentiation of peasant households caused by land rent. This also raises the question as to the extent of the correlation between "fiscal" and "land" stratification.

13.2 Cheb land tax of 1469

In the *1469 Land Tax Register*, all taxpayers were prescribed a certain tax amount that in some cases remained nominally the same as the amount set during the last preceding valuation of 1456, while in other cases the amount varied to a greater or lesser extent. From 1463, tax officials collected a higher amount in the form of additional tax payments, which was due to the falling quality of groschen coins and rising prices. At first, the rise in tax affected only those taxpayers with a tax amount exceeding 30 Prague groschen, but by 1468 this affected everybody. From 1463–1467, for each threescore of prescribed payment, 6–7 Prague groschen extra were demanded, and in 1468 all taxpayers were required to pay one and a half times the prescribed amount, and in 1469

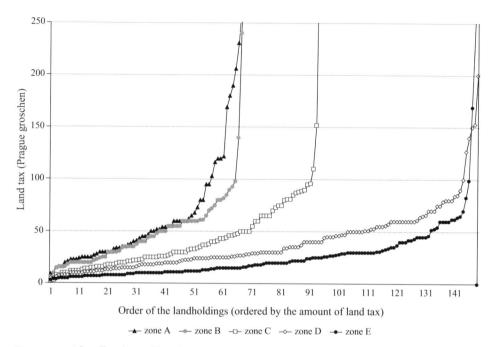

Figure 13.1. **Distribution of land tax set for "subject" landholdings in individual ecological zones in the city-state of Cheb, 1469.**

Source: Ar Cheb, book 1096, *Klosteuerbuch 1469.*
Note: Without extreme values (A: Triesenhof /540 gr./; B: Kornau /540 gr./).

double the amount.[481] However, the taxpayers' burden in 1469 did not grow in real terms, since the 100% increase in tax corresponded to the depreciation of coins and inflation.[482] Therefore, in our calculations, we may use the basic prescribed, pre-inflation tax amount.

Data on the nominal value of land tax, as well as land rents, is available for 586 taxpayers (*fig. 13.1*). If we leave aside relatively complicated cases where the taxpayer paid a combination of in-kind and cash rent or paid in-kind rent only

481   Heisinger, "Die Egerer Klosteuerbücher," 74–75.
482   For more on the depreciation of the groschen and the dramatic year 1469, cf. Jaroslav Vaniš, "Ceny v Lounech v druhé polovině 15. století" [The prices in Louny in the 2nd half of the 15th century], *Hospodářské dějiny* 8 (1981): 5–93; Jaroslav Vaniš, "Příspěvek k měnovým poměrům doby Jiřího z Poděbrad," *Numismatické listy* 16 (1961): 65–77. On the situation in the Cheb Region, see also Castelin, "Chebské mincovnictví," 95–102, 112.

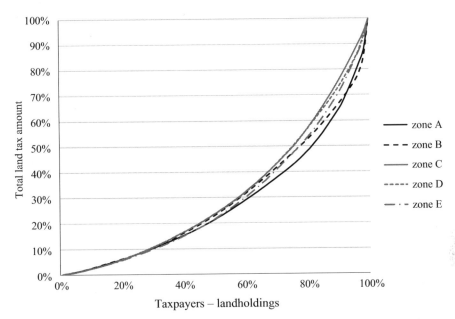

Figure 13.2. Rate of inequality in the distribution of land tax among "subject" landholdings in individual ecological zones in the city-state of Cheb, 1469.

Source: Ar Cheb, book 1096, *Klosteuerbuch 1469.*
Note: Demonstrated by the Lorenz curve. Cf. *tab. 13.1.*

in rye or oats, we may compare the data for 531 taxpayers,[483] which equates to 65% of the taxpayers listed in the *1469 Land Tax Register.*

The distribution of land tax among landholdings and their average level differed in the different ecological zones. In *figure 13.1* it is evident that in agriculturally favorable zones, landholdings were burdened by a significantly higher land tax than in submountainous zones. The average tax amount for one landholding in zone A was 66 Prague groschen, while in the least favorable zone E, this figure was three times less—22 groschen. Unlike land rents, the degree of inequality in the distribution of land tax among landholdings in different ecological zones was more or less identical (GINI 0.46–0.48; *tab. 13.1.; fig. 13.2*). Inequality between landholdings in the city-state of Cheb as a whole (Gini 0.49) was naturally higher than between landholdings within one ecological zone.

483   *App. 13.1.*

Table 13.1. **Rate of inequality in the distribution of land tax among "subject" landholdings in individual ecological zones in the city-state of Cheb, 1469.**

Zone	A	B	C	D	E	Range	A–E
	Number of units investigated						
Cash rent	8	10	15	44	61	8–61	138
In-kind rent	59	58	78	107	98	58–107	397
Land tax	67	68	93	149	147	67–149	524
Cash rent + land tax	8	10	15	44	61	8–61	138
	GINI						
Cash rent	0.54	0.50	0.49	0.52	0.37	0.37–0.54	0.52
In-kind rent	0.43	0.44	0.46	0.46	0.49	0.43–0.49	0.49
Land tax	0.47	0.46	0.48	0.48	0.48	0.46–0.48	0.49
Cash rent + land tax	0.41	0.47	0.48	0.48	0.44	0.41–0.48	0.49

Source: Ar Cheb, book 1096, *Klosteuerbuch 1469.*
Note: Expressed by the Gini coefficient. Cf. *figs. 11.6* and *13.2.*

13.3 The aggregate influence of land rent and land tax

Figures 11.2–11.6 and *13.1* may give the impression that the level of land rent and land tax differentiated "subject" landholdings in a similar way. In other words, the economically stronger a "subject" landholding was, the greater the burden of both land rent and land tax. However, the opposite may be true because land rent burdened "subject" landholdings relatively unevenly, i.e., "subject" landholdings in economically identical situations were often burdened differently. In other words, some "subject" landholdings were overburdened with land rent, while others were able to retain a large part of their surplus, which increased the monetary value of the landholding, thereby also increasing the land tax payable. In such a situation, land tax would level out the inequalities caused by land rent.

Two methods exist to answer the question as to whether land tax further deepened inequalities between landholdings or reduced them.
+ Firstly, we may calculate the **Gini coefficient** for the sum total of cash land rent and land tax. If this coefficient is lower than the relevant coefficient for cash rent, then land tax and land rent acted against each other. If it was the same or higher, the action of both forms of rent reinforced each other.

The results show that the total burden of "subject" landholdings created inequalities in a different way than just land rent or land tax and that land tax collection had a different effect in different ecological zones. The greatest rate of inequality in the overall burden of "subject" landholdings was found in zones B–D (Gini 0.47–0.48), while the lowest was in zone A (Gini 0.41); zone E fell somewhere between these two extremes (Gini 0.44). In zone A, land tax overall evened out the inequalities due to collected land rent (Gini 0.54→0.41), while conversely in zone E it deepened them (Gini 0.37→0.44), and in zones B–D it slightly reduced the rate of inequality (difference in Gini 0.02–0.04).

◆ Secondly, we may examine the ratio between *land tax and land rent*. If this ratio remained approximately the same, despite rising land rent, both forms of surplus exploitation acted against each other. If this ratio fell as land rent rose, they reinforced each other.

The resulting ratio between the level of land rent and land tax for individual landholdings and zones shows an extremely uneven situation and also warns of the overly simplifying and leveling effect of the Gini coefficient.[484] The ratio of land tax and cash land rent for individual landholdings ranged between 0.1–30.3 (i.e., the difference was as much as 303 times); the average was 1.33 (i.e., for every 1 groschen of land rent they paid 1.3 groschen of tax on average). The ratio of land tax in Prague groschen and in-kind land rent in "kar" of grain fluctuated between 0.8–120.0 (a difference of 150 times); the average was 6.08 (i.e., for each 1 "kar" of grain in-kind rent 6 Prague groschen was payable in land tax on average). Ecological zones differed to various extents; nevertheless, in principle it may be established, based on the correlation coefficients, that (1) the level of land rent and land tax were independent of each other and (2) a weak tendency emerges showing that with rising land rent the proportion of land tax on the total volume of surplus exploitation fell (*tab. 13.2*). The relationship between the tempo of the growth of land rents and land tax represented a medium-high negative correlation. However, occasionally the differences between landholdings were very marked (*fig. 13.3*). At this point we should be aware that our results are distorted by the fact that the land tax was set, amongst other factors, based on the monetary value of non-landholding

484   *App. 13.1.*

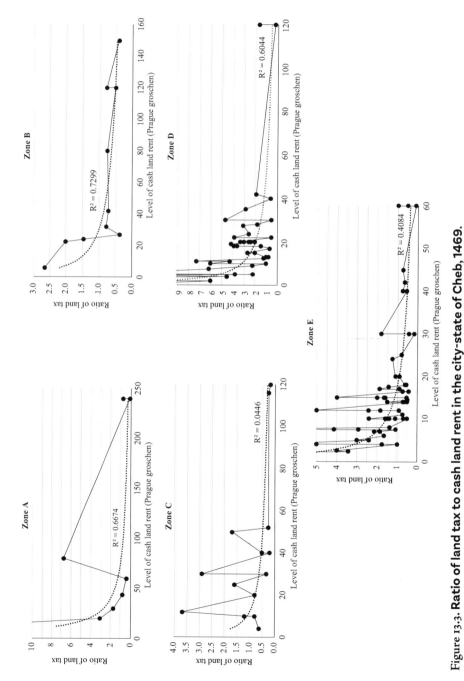

Figure 13.3. **Ratio of land tax to cash land rent in the city-state of Cheb, 1469.**

Source: Ar Cheb, book 1096, *Klosteuerbuch 1469. Note:* Without extreme values. Each dot represents one "subject" landholding.

Table 13.2. A – correlation between land rent and land tax; B – correlation between land rent and the ratio of land tax to land rent.

Correlation	Ecological zone				
	A	B	C	D	E
A1 – cash land rents and land tax	−0.01	0.81	0.12	0.34	0.27
A2 – in-kind land rents and land tax	0.32	0.06	0.30	0.26	0.42
B1 – cash land rents and ratio of land tax to land rent	−0.61	−0.61	−0.38	−0.31	−0.45
B2 – in-kind land rent and ratio of land tax to land rent	−0.34	−0.35	−0.48	−0.43	−0.37

Source: Ar Cheb, book 1096, *Klosteuerbuch 1469.*
Note: Cf. *fig. 13.3.*

plots that did not belong to the "subject" landholding but were in the tenure of a concrete taxpayer.

A comparison of land rent and land tax figures demonstrated the disproportionate burden that land rent imposed on "subject" landholdings. Many high-value landholdings with a large quantity of livestock and additional properties were burdened with a small land rent and vice-versa, while some low-value landholdings with a small quantity of livestock paid disproportionately high land rent. Three important conclusions stem from this:

1. Land rent in itself significantly deepened socioeconomic inequalities between "subject" landholdings, while land tax partially evened them out again. Landholdings with a high degree of surplus were taxed more than landholdings relatively overburdened by land rent.

2. Differences in the level of land rents, generally reflecting differences in the size of "subject" landholdings' land resources, are not in themselves a particularly reliable indicator of the socioeconomic differentiation of peasant communities.

3. Differences between the level of land rent and land tax can stem from the differing agrarian activities of landholdings. The level of land rent tended to reflect the size of grain production, while the nominal value of land tax reflected the scope of livestock production and the degree of commercialization.

13.4 Burden of aggregative land rent and land tax

We can know the total monetary burden for "subject" tenants who paid land rent purely in cash form, as its value can simply be added to the amount of the land tax (*fig. 13.4*).[485] Again, we find differences both between ecological zones and between landholdings in the individual ecological zones. Marked differences between zones are best illustrated by the average values of the monetary burden of landholdings, which was 231 Prague groschen in zone A, but just 37 in zone E. Internal differences within zones show ranges according to which the differences between "subject" landholdings were between 8 times (in zone A) and up to 31 times (in zone D). The most burdened landholding, paying annually a total of 620 Prague groschen (i.e., over 10 threescore) was located in zone A. The least burdened landholding, paying 6.5 groschen, lay in the rather unfavorable zone C.

We can determine the burden on "subject" landholdings that paid land rent in grain only indirectly and by estimation.[486] If we calculate that a Cheb grain "kar," comprising half rye and half oats, was equivalent to 15 Prague groschen, the monetary burden on "subject" landholdings in this group was approximately twice as high as that for the previous group of peasants who paid the land rent in cash, although the span was more or less the same. The price of grain year-to-year and in the course of one year would fluctuate, so the calculated values are only approximate.

An estimation closer to reality can be attained by converting the monetary sums into "kar" of grain and establishing how much grain "subject" tenants had to surrender and sell to meet their obligations for land tax and to fulfill their responsibility towards their landlord. Of course, "subject" tenants also acquired cash in ways other than by selling grain, so this calculation method is purely a model. The overall burden of "subject" landholdings paying grain rent ranged from half to 48 "kar" of grain, the average burden being 9.32 "kar." Certain landholdings therefore made payments capable of supporting up to three whole families, while the average would have supported two adults. For a better idea of the labor burden and the area of arable land necessary for ensuring payment of land rent and land tax, we may take into consideration the

485 *App. 13.2a.*
486 *App. 13.2b.*

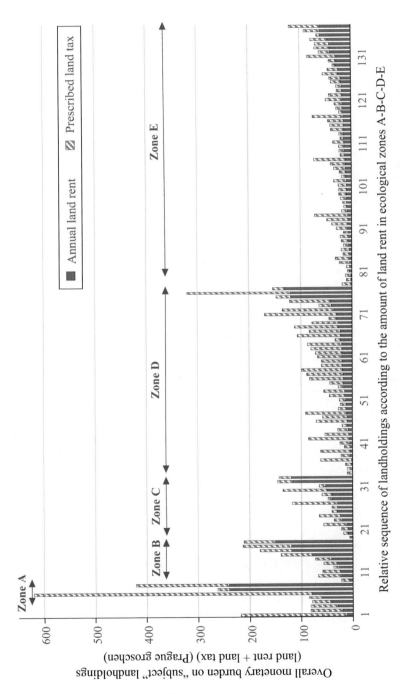

Figure 13.4. **Overall monetary burden on "subject" landholdings in the city-state of Cheb, 1469.**

Source: Ar Cheb, book 1096, Klosteuerbuch 1469

relative yield capabilities of separate ecological zones. In this case, differences between zones emerge in a rather different light. The burden on landholdings in the submountainous zone was on average one-third that of the agriculturally optimum zone. In other words, landholdings in the submountainous zone E were either considerably smaller than landholdings in the agriculturally optimal zone A or otherwise they were overburdened by land rent.

13.5 Tithes and overall rent burden

In the preceding chapters, we have focused on the main components of rent: land tax and land rent. Now we shall address a third component of rent: ecclesiastical tithes. In the city-state of Cheb, the ecclesiastical tithe was sometimes called a "small tithe."[487] We divide these into full tithes and fixed tithes.[488] The question is: what was its nature and to what extent did it increase the burden on the Cheb peasantry?

One of the main sources for knowledge about the structure and size of the ecclesiastical tithe in the city-state of Cheb is the Cheb Poor Clares' *1464 Estate Register*, which recorded in detail the ecclesiastical tithes coming in from landholdings in the villages of Dřenice (Treunitz), Všeboř (Schöba), and Polná (Hirschfeld). The final calculation also mentioned tithes coming from Horní Ves (Oberndorf), Vojtanov (Voitersreuth, Vorder-), Horní Pelhřimov (Pilmersreuth, Ober-), Střížov (Triesenhof), Lesná (Hart), and Lesinka (Harlas).[489] The Poor Clares also extracted a land rent from landholdings in Dřenice a Polná, while the land rent for Všeboř landed in the hands of the majority of the burghers of the city of Cheb.

In Dřenice, a full tithe of lambs, geese, and chickens was demanded, as well as a fixed tithe of rye and oats from most of the landholdings there. The size of the fixed tithe was substantial, with the grain payment for one landholding ranging between 1.25 and 2.5 Cheb "kar," which was between one-eighth

---

487 Ar Cheb, book 1003, *Urbar der Clarissinnen ab 1464*, 3. Cf. Singer, *Das Lehenbuch*, 47.

488 For more on the situation in Bohemia, cf. Graus, *Dějiny*, esp. 176–179; Míka, *Poddaný lid*, 261–267.

489 Ar Cheb, book 1003, *Urbar der Clarissinnen ab 1464*, 53–54.

and one-half of what "subject" tenants paid in grain payment as part of land rent.[490]

The ecclesiastical tithe in Všeboř collected from all "subject" landholdings took the form of a fixed grain payment, which was between 0.875 and 3.25 "kar." A full tithe of lambs and geese was extracted from two landholdings, and one landholding paid an extra fixed tithe of one chicken and two hens. In two cases, we were able to compare grain payments extracted as ecclesiastical tithes and land rent—in the first case, the ecclesiastical tithe was about one-fifth of land rent (1.5 : 7.0) and in the second case about one-third (3.1 : 9.0).[491]

In Polná, a full tithe of ten chickens and flax was commuted to a cash payment, with the "subject" tenants paying one Meissen groschen instead. It is possible that only part of the ecclesiastical tithe was payable to the Poor Clares.[492]

We were able to reconstruct the burden on "subject" tenants from all components of rent (i.e., land tax, land rent, and ecclesiastical tithe) in the case of two landholdings in Všeboř, six in Dřenice, and two in Polná (*tab. 13.3*).

In summary, the ecclesiastical tithe could take many different forms, and for some "subject" tenants it was a significant component of rent. Based on the Cheb Poor Clares's estate register, we can estimate that in comparison with land rent, the tithe was one-tenth to one-quarter in size (*tab. 13.3*).

13.6 Summary

Land rent was allocated among "subject" landholdings quite unevenly and did not correspond with their actual economic capabilities. Some landholdings were burdened relatively more than others. Despite this, all "subject" landholdings created a sufficiently large enough surplus to be able to pay land tax as well. However, this was apportioned in a different way than land rent. The general trend was that the share of land tax in the overall burden on "subject" landholdings fell as the level of land rent rose. Correlation coefficients showed a medium-high negative correlation. Land tax therefore differentiated land-

490   Ar Cheb, book 1003, *Urbar der Clarissinnen ab 1464*, 1–3.
491   Ar Cheb, book 1003, *Urbar der Clarissinnen ab 1464*, 24–27.
492   Ar Cheb, book 1003, *Urbar der Clarissinnen ab 1464*, 39.

Table. 13.3. **Overall burden of rent collected from peasants in the city-state of Cheb in the 1460s.**

	Name in the estate register (1464)	Land tax (1469) (Pr. Gr.)	Land rent (1464)			Ecclesiastical tithe** (1464)	
			grain payment (in "kar")	cash payment	additional payments	grain payment (in "kar")	other
Všeboř (Schöba)	Hanß Sebenpecker Richter	153	9*	–	–	3.1250	lambs, geese, and chickens
	Pertel Fischer	18	7	15	2 hens	1.5000	–
	Adlers	40	9	–	14 cheeses, 20 eggs, 2 hens	0	–
	Erhart Tvming	22	1.5	–	2 hens	0.3750	lambs, geese, and chickens
Dřenice (Treunitz)	Erhart Tᵥ̊mnyng	54	7	–	10 cheeses, 15 eggs, 1 hen	1.2500	lambs, geese, and chickens
	Jung Hagen	115	11	20	13 cheeses, 17 eggs, 2 hens	1.5625	lambs, geese, and chickens
	Leben	45	6	–	14 cheeses, 20 eggs, 2 hens	0	–
	Mwlner	44	3	–	2 hens	0.3750	lambs, geese, and chickens
Polná (Hirschfeld)	Seufrid	11	–	18	2 cheeses, 30 eggs	–	1 Meissen groschen
	Paulus Smyd	10	–	18	2 cheeses, 30 eggs	–	1 Meissen groschen

Source: Ar Cheb, book 1003, *Urbar der Clarissinnen ab 1464*, 1–3, 24–27, 39; book 1096, *Klosteuerbuch 1469*.
Note: * The land tax register specifies that 3 "kar" be given to the Cheb Poor Clares and 9 "kar" to a burgher of Cheb. The payment to the Poor Clares corresponds to the grain part of the tithe in the *1464 Estate Register*.
** Not necessarily complete.

holdings in the opposite way to land rent. This finding has important consequences for interpretation.

Firstly, the apportioning of tax amounts is not a particularly effective
approach for investigating socioeconomic stratification. "Subject" landholdings
with a relatively low land rent or with a higher share of livestock production
will be overrepresented amongst wealthy landholdings.

Secondly, land rent in the form of in-kind payments was extracted mainly
from the grain surplus, and therefore was suitable for the situation before the
last third or quarter of the 14th century. If this rent had remained fixed and not
supplemented by the exploitation of the peasantry by the land tax, differences
in the volume of disposable surplus between landholdings in the 15th century
would have been enormous. Against the backdrop of general findings and also
the situation in the neighboring Franconian and Bavarian regions, we assume
that as of the last quarter of the 14th century, the significance of livestock production grew, while the significance of grain production fell.[493] Land tax, commonly called "hoof tax," was collected in the 14th century only sporadically,
although after 1392 it rose significantly, and in 1403 it was transformed into an
annual payment. Unlike land rent, this was a progressive property tax, which
burdened primarily the market-oriented livestock production of landholdings. We may therefore see the fairly fast and effective introduction of land
tax as a reflection of the new power situation in the late medieval city-state of
Cheb,[494] as well as a reaction to the transformation of the peasant economy
that had been occurring since the last third of the 14th century. If land tax had
not been introduced, the peasantry of Cheb would have very quickly become
differentiated and some peasants would have been capable of accumulating
an exceptionally large surplus. The land tax thus could significantly stabilize
socioeconomic stratification and ameliorate the pressure within peasant communities.

The burden on peasants in the form of land tax occurred to the detriment
of the landlord, who lost the practical option of increasing annual payments;
on the other hand, the landlords were predominantly those burghers of Cheb
who controlled the tax "coffers."[495] The interconnection between the city, the

---

493   Achilles, "*Überlegungen*"; Achilles, *Landwirtschaft*, 78–82. Recently summarized in Ghosh,
      "Rural Economies," 262.
494   Cf. Klír et al., *Knihy*, 18, 25, 36–40.
495   Cf. Klír et al., *Knihy*, 41–46, 60–63, 168–170.

countryside, the landlords, and the city council partially explains why the annual collection of land tax in the late medieval city-state of Cheb was introduced so soon, so fast, and without visible resistance, unlike in any other imperial territory.[496]

The total burden on the Cheb peasantry was further increased with a tithe by a further 10–25% (a very rough estimate).

The sum total of land rent and land tax together was fairly high; a large number of "subject" landholdings paid so much that the sum would suffice to feed several adults all year long. This means that there was a high degree of surplus created by the peasantry, and also a reserve that they could source in bad years. It is very likely that in the event of a crisis or disaster, the landlord or the city council lowered their demands. This could explain the large regeneration potential and resiliency of Cheb's landholdings that were able to avoid social "fallows" and abandonment during the 15th century.

496   Cf. Klír et al., *Knihy*, 50–58.

◂ Plate 5: **Doubrava (Taubrath). A farmstead with a pigeon loft (1940). View of a dwelling house with a timbered and partly stone-built ground floor, on which a decorative half-timbered upper floor was built. This construction solution, considered to be a traditional form of Cheb folk architecture, as well as the four-sided enclosed courtyard, became common in the countryside relatively late, only in the second half of the 18th century. On Cheb folk architecture, cf. M. Tietz-Strödel, Ländlich-bäuerliche Architektur.**

IV.
Socioeconomic Stratification and Monetization

In the following part of the study, we examine the rate of the monetization of the Cheb peasantry and its engagement in market relations. We are interested in how large the monetary sums were that the peasantry needed to acquire to pay rent and meet the internal obligations arising from the property and inheritance family practices. How big and burdensome were these amounts? Did the need for money make the Cheb peasants raise their commercial agricultural production or even enter the credit market? Only after addressing these questions do we turn our attention to the depth of social, economic, and demographic inequalities within the Cheb peasantry. We also analyze the influence of the city and the complementarity of the socioeconomic structure of agrarian producers in the countryside and in the city.

14.
Monetary values, monetization, and the credit market

14.1 Initial assumptions

In this chapter, we will deal with three closely related problems. First, we deal with the interpretation of the monetary values of peasant property and try to learn about the mechanisms by which they were formed (*chap. 14.3–14.6*). We also ask what economic utility and benefit property of a certain value brought to its holder. The second question is about what the ratio between the main property items was, especially between the monetary value of the "purchase" right to a landholding and the value of livestock (*chap. 14.7*). The third question deals with the levels of the monetization of the Cheb peasantry and the extent of the credit market (*chap. 14.8–14.9*). We ask how much cash the peasant economy needed each year, in what form economic interactions with the outside world took place, and to what extent the family property situation and inheritance practices were penetrated by monetary relations. In this regard, was the late medieval peasantry like the early modern peasantry, or did they principally differ?

14.2 Monetary values in land-transfer registers

Written sources that recorded the monetary values of property in the hands of peasants began to appear across Central Europe in mass when peasant elites along with the landlords pushed through regulations and administrative control over the transfers of peasant land.[497] This occurred at the end of the Late Middle Ages and in the Early Modern Period, and the embodiment of this control became the village land-transfer registers.[498]

The significance of monetary values specified in connection with landholding transfers in village land-transfer registers in Bohemia was addressed by Josef Petráň at the beginning of the 1960s.[499] Despite the traditional objections that the monetary values mentioned here cannot be clearly interpreted in an economy that was only partially monetized and in which prices were distorted by feudal relations, the amount of the estimate should very reliably reflect the relative differences in the economic utility that landholdings of the same legal status and operating in similar conditions brought to their users. The reality of the monetary values of the landholdings was, moreover, assured by the long-term experience of the members of the peasant community and the personal interest of its members in the accuracy of the estimate. A similarly optimistic stance to that held by Josef Petráň was held by other historians associated with working groups in Prague and Brno, which were researching the history of prices and wages and analyzing the methods by which the prices of "subject"

---

497 Cf. Dana Štefanová, "Schöppenbücher," in *Quellenkunde der Habsburgermonarchie (16.–18. Jahrhundert). Ein exemplarisches Handbuch*, ed. Josef Pauser, Martin Scheutz, and Thomas Winkelbauer, Mitteilungen des Instituts für Österreichische Geschichtsforschung, Ergänzungsband 44 (Vienna, Munich: Oldenbourg, 2004), 511–515; Maur, "Nejstarší chotěšovské pozemkové knihy," 133–135.

498 Cf. Miloslav Volf, "Vývoj gruntovní knihy ve světle zákonů a hospodářských instrukcí," Zprávy českého zemského archivu 8 (1939): 43–108; Procházka, *Česká poddanská nemovitost*, esp. 310–313; Petráň, *Poddaný lid*, 25–26; Štefanová, *Erbschaftspraxis*, 14–15; Chocholáč, *Selské peníze*, 72–76; Bronislav Chocholáč, "O studiu pozemkových knih" [Über das Studium der Gründbücher], *Sborník prací Filozofické fakulty brněnské univerzity, řada historická (C)* 42/40 (1993): 51–61; Bronislav Chocholáč, "Grundbücher in Böhmen und Mähren," in *Quellenkunde der Habsburgermonarchie (16.–18. Jahrhundert). Ein exemplarisches Handbuch*, ed. Josef Pauser, Martin Scheutz, and Thomas Winkelbauer, Mitteilungen des Instituts für Österreichische Geschichtsforschung, Ergänzungsband 44 (Vienna, Munich: Oldenbourg, 2004), 530–539.

499 Petráň, *Poddaný lid*, 25–26.

properties were created.[500] However, other, skeptical voices still existed that pointed to the significance of other pricing factors such as landlord intervention and the insufficient awareness of peasants.[501] The significance of the monetary values of landholdings listed in the village land-transfer registers of the Early Modern Period were emphasized later by Bronislav Chocholáč. The estimated monetary values of landholdings in the Early Modern Period are thought to reflect (1) the tradition of earlier sales, (2) the situation of a landholding and its economic utility, and (3) the local supply-and-demand conditions.[502]

The question of how to understand the prices of "subject" landholdings was newly discussed by the project *Social Structures in Early Modern Bohemia 1650–1750*, against the backdrop of a wider European discussion.[503] The focus was on the non-economic aspects of the prices of "subject" holdings, which, in addition to common market factors, should also reflect the solidarity and relationships within peasant communities and individual families, the social statuses of the seller and buyer or the deceased and new tenant, emotions, and individuals' personal beliefs and perceptions. In the context of property transfers, we therefore speak of the social value of property, which was not the same as the market price or neutrally of the "purchase" price.[504] In principle, it

500 Hanzal, "Poznámky"; Procházka, *Česká poddanská nemovitost*, 310–314; Josef Válka, "K problému ceny poddanské usedlosti v 16.–17. století," in *Ceny, mzdy a měna 2* (Brno: Komise pro dějiny cen, mezd a měny, 1963), n. pag.; Josef Křivka, *Zadlužení poddanského zemědělství na roudnickém panství v 18. století*, Rozpravy ČSAV. Řada společenských věd 1986/2 (Prague: Academia, 1986), 83.

501 Eduard Maur, "K způsobu tvoření a splácení cen poddanských nemovitostí v 17. a počátkem 18. století," in *Příspěvky k dějinám cen nemovitostí v 16.–18. století* (Prague: Univerzita Karlova, 1963), 71–154; Eduard Maur, "Poddaní točnického panství v druhé polovině 17. století. Příspěvek k využití katastrů, soupisů obyvatelstva a pozemkových knih pro studium hospodářského a sociálního postavení venkovského lidu," *Sborník archivních prací* 14 (1964): 57–87; 15 (1965): 277–297. Cf. Štefanová, *Erbschaftspraxis*, 86–87.

502 Chocholáč, *Selské peníze*, 72–76, in the same vein see also Hanzal, "Poznámky. Also cf. Bronislav Chocholáč, "Güterpreise, Verschuldung und Ratensystem: Eine Fallstudie zu den finanziellen Transaktionen der Untertanen bei Besitzübertragungen in Westmähren im späten 16. und im 17. Jahrhundert," in *Untertanen, Herrschaft und Staat in Böhmen und im "Alten Reich." Sozialgeschichtliche Strukturen*, ed. Markus Cerman and Robert Luft, Veröffentlichungen des Collegium Carolinum 99 (Munich: Oldenbourg 2005), 89–125.

503 Primarily Štefanová, *Erbschaftspraxis*, 86–94. Cf. also Giovanni Levi, *Das immaterielle Erbe. Eine bäuerliche Welt an der Schwelle zur Moderne* (Berlin: Wagenbach, 1986), 85–88; Sabean, *Property*, 371–415; Medick, *Weben*, 330. Jiří Koumar's results have contributed significantly to this question as well (Koumar, "Má doplaceno").

504 Štefanová, *Erbschaftspraxis*, 88.

assumes that in a property transfer *inter vivos* the price of a property started from an agreement between the seller and buyer, whereas in a transfer by *causa morti* or in other specific situations a procedure of assessment was used, with the representatives of the village community playing a determining role. In the case of inheritance procedure, the price could also be set by the testament, and then the valuation procedure was unnecessary.[505]

Monetary values in the documents of the land tax

General knowledge on the creation of the prices contained in the Bohemian and Moravian village land-transfer registers from the 16th–17th centuries can be used also in the interpretations of the monetary values entered in the Cheb land tax registers from the 15th century. This should be done, naturally, with an awareness that they were created in an institutional context, in which there was no administrative landlord control of the transfers of peasant land.

The Cheb land tax had a progressive nature and was set as a share of the total monetary value of the family property society (FPS).[506] The values of the property items set for fiscal purposes corresponded to the values estimated within the inheritance procedures, the values stated in the testaments, or the values at which the property items of peasants were sold or pledged. The Cheb land tax officials used the assessment practice established inside the peasant communities, thanks to which all of the monetary values were effectively detectable and above all verifiable. This procedure was not exceptional in Central Europe; it was applied to the collection of land tax in other areas as well.[507]

Every "subject" tenant was aware of the arbitrary monetary value of property at the moment at which they inherited, bought, or pledged it. Similarly, the "subject" tenant was able to estimate the conventional value of their livestock. Using the land tax, the Cheb burghers thus had access to the money circulating *really* or *virtually* among the peasants without having to develop a complex bureaucratic apparatus. The relationship of the tax estimates to the practice of the landholding transfers taking place inside the peasant communities also explains why estimates are lacking for farmland plots, which were integral

505   Štefanová, *Erbschaftspraxis*, 88–93.
506   Klír et al., *Knihy*, 175–177.
507   Cf. Schirmer, *Das Amt Grimma*, 50, 52.

components of the "subject" landholdings, because these did not usually circulate among the peasants independently; they did not go through the market, nor were they subdivided in the inheritance partition of the property.

14.3 Coin quality and inflation

In interpreting fluctuations in the monetary values of the individual property items from 1438–1456, the value of the basic coins—Prague groschen, on which the estimates were based—is crucial. In the focus period, the quality of the Prague groschen decreased; the monetary values therefore grew due to inflation (127%). The Prague groschen's relation to the Rhenish guilder, as documented for Cheb, is presented in *figure 14.1* and summarized in *table 14.1*.[508] We ignore changes in the buying power of the Rhenish guilder and gold itself, since these changed only very little during the focus period.[509]

Proceeding mechanically, we could convert the values cited for 1438 and 1456 to a common denominator. However, the estimated values barely corresponded at all with the inflation trend. For instance, if a landholding did not go on the market or through inheritance procedures, its monetary value seems to have been estimated consistently at the same level. The same may apply also to non-landholding plots. We could expect that prices of horses and cattle increased in line with the inflation trend.

Table 14.1. **Monetary relations in the city-state of Cheb around the middle of the 15th century.**

Year	Gulden	Equivalent in groschen	Inflationary trend	
1435	1 Rhenish guilder	21 Prague groschen and 1 Meissen groschen	97.0 %	76.2 %
1438	1 Rhenish guilder	22 Prague groschen	100.0 %	78.6 %
1457	1 Rhenish guilder	28 Prague groschen	127.3 %	100.0 %

Source : Klír et al., Knihy, 98–101, 117.

---

508   Klír et al., *Knihy*, 98–101, 117. Cf. also Castelin, "Chebské mincovnictví," 88–94, 110–112 (the cited documents must be treated with discretion).
509   For more on this subject, see Bauernfeind, *Materielle Grundstrukturen*, 59–60, 339–353.

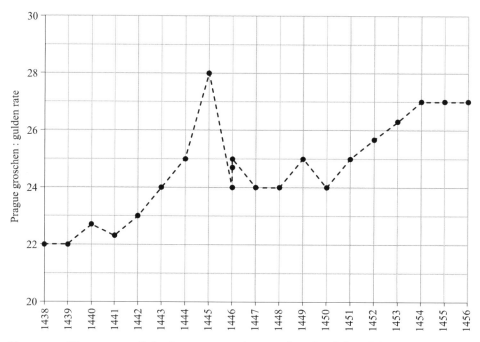

Figure 14.1. The course of the Prague groschen to the Rhenish guilder in 1442–1456.

Source: Ar Cheb, books 2144–2152, 2153–2169, Umgeldbücher 1442–1450, 1452–1469.
Note: Cf. also chap. 12.3; fig. 12.5.

14.4 Landholdings

In the tax documents, we encounter the monetary values of (1) the "purchase" right to landholdings (hereafter the monetary value of "subject" landholdings) and (2) the rights to "free" landholdings (hereafter the monetary value of "free" landholdings). We can see the monetary value of the landholdings as the utility that it brought to its tenant, thus, the overall economic balance and also the social prestige of the landholding. In the transformed form, the value of the "subject" or "free" landholding reflected the size and quality of the land resources, the character of the dwelling and economic buildings, or the number and quality of the inanimate inventory. Naturally, all of the values reflected the relevant institutional context, which was governed by the transactional costs and payment obligations that comprised components of the feudal quota. The prices of "subject" landholdings were distorted by non-market factors to a greater extent than "free" landholdings, which were not under the control of a landlord.

The *1438 Land Tax Register* makes a more accurate image of the value of the specific types of landholdings possible because it distinguishes between not only legal status but also the individual socioeconomic categories of landholdings. It is clear from the enclosed overview that (*tab. 14.2*):

+ Overall, the *Herberge* landholdings were appraised at, on average, approximately two to three times less than *Hof* landholdings.
+ The value of *Höfel* landholdings was approximately the same as *Herberge* landholdings.
+ The value of "free" *Hof* landholdings was on average 3–4 times higher than "subject" *Hof* landholdings.

It is not possible to distinguish between the categories of landholdings in the *1456 Taxation Book*. Nonetheless, it is evident that the average value of all the "subject" landholdings as a whole rose slightly compared to 1438 (*tab. 14.3*). While the average value of "subject" landholdings in 1438 was 10 threescore and 58 Prague groschen, in 1456 the average was already 13 threescore and 42 Prague groschen.[510] We may assume that this was a result of the inflation trend since the increase in prices from 1438–1456 is strikingly close to the increase in the value of the Prague groschen to the Rheinish guilder.

The greatest differences in the monetary values of the landholdings were due to their legal status—that is, the level of institutional control. If we eliminate the extreme values and concentrate on the interval in which 80% of landholdings are located, then striking contrasts appear in 1438. The values of the "subject" *Hof* landholdings lie in the interval of 3–25 threescore of Prague groschen, whereas those of "free" *Hof* landholdings lie in the interval of 25–60 threescore groschen. These relations had serious consequences. The high value of "free" landholdings meant that they brought both a high social and economic utility to their holders, but also the heavy burden of the land tax. Though the land rent was not paid from "free" landholdings, the surplus was all the more drained by the land tax. In this way, the exclusive economic advantage of the "free" landholdings was reduced, which as a final consequence contributed to socioeconomic leveling.

510   1438: based on 695 items at 7,621 threescore; 1456: 632 items.

Table 14.2. **Monetary values of "subject" and "free" landholdings in the city-state of Cheb, 1438.**

Legal status of landholding	Socioeconomic category of landholding	Number	Minimal – maximal value	Price in-terval ling 80% of the values	Average value
			(threescore grochen – ß)		
"Subject" ("purchase" right)	Hof	609	1–80	3–25	11 ß 45 gr.
	Herberge	86	1–16	2–9	5 ß 18 gr.
	Höfel	20	2–30	2–9	5 ß 56 gr.
"Free" (free fief right)	Hof	11	20–80	25–40	32 ß 55 gr.
	Herberge	6	5–30	–	15 ß 10 gr.
"Free" (free hereditary fief right)	Hof	9	10–84	25–60	43 ß 27 gr.
"Subject"	Cottage with the right to fishing (Herberge)	7	8–25	–	16 ß 26 gr.
	Mill	21	1–55	6–38	21 ß

Source: Ar Cheb, book 1067, *Klosteuerbuch 1438.* Cf. Klír et al., *Knihy,* 286–410.
Note: ß – threescore of Prague groschen (= 60 Prague groschen). gr. – Prague groschen

Table 14.3. **Approximate monetary values of "subject" and "free" landholdings in the city-state of Cheb, 1456.**

Type of landholding	Number	Min.–Max.	Price range (80% of values)	Average
		(threescore of grochen – ß)		
"Subject" landholdings	632	0.5–100.0 ß	3.1–30.0	13 ß 42 gr.
"Free" landholdings	11	10–110 ß	–	41 ß 26 gr.

Source: Ar Cheb, book 1084, *Klosteuerbuch (Schätzungsbuch) 1456.*
Note: ß – threescore of Prague groschen (= 60 Prague groschen). gr. – Prague groschen

14.5 Livestock

The monetary value of the horses, cattle, and sheep most faithfully reflected the real extent of the economic operations at the landholding. Behind the monetary value, and thus also the amount of draught power, we can see the size of the areas actually under cultivation and behind the value of the cattle, the minimal amount of human labor force that was permanently tied to the landholding.

The *1438 Tax Register* did not once list the specific number of horses, cattle, or sheep, the monetary value of which was merely estimated in summation. Detailed information from which it is also possible to determine the price of individual items is first available for some landholdings in the *1456 Taxation Book*.[511]

The monetary values of the horses, cattle, and sheep recorded in the tax documents cannot as of yet be compared with local market prices, since the contemporaneous medieval accounting books surviving in Cheb's archive have yet to be analyzed.[512] The closest relevant comparison to the city-state of Cheb are the data surviving for the city of Louny (1450–1472) published and evaluated by Jaroslav Vaniš.[513] A comparison shows that the average market prices recorded for Louny did not differ dramatically from the estimated prices for the Cheb countryside, which may be considered fairly reliable.[514]

The average value of a draft horse in the city-state of Cheb in 1456 ranged between 2 threescore to 2 threescore and 20 Prague groschen.[515] A price of 2 threescore may be a reasonable estimate for 1438. For 1438 and 1456, a cited value of 4–5 threescore for a horse may in reality have meant two quality horses or one paired team, a cited value of 8–10 threescore could have corresponded to four horses or two paired teams, etc.

The estimated value of cows, or cows with heifers, certainly fluctuated less than that of horses. Additionally, throughout the year a landholding usually kept a fairly wide range of beef cattle, which included animals at various stages of their reproductive cycle. Usually, therefore, alongside milk cattle, they kept heifers and bull calves. To simplify this otherwise very complicated situation, one threescore of groschen accounts for one cow and a calf. For example, the sum of 4–5 threescore could represent 4 cows or heifers plus 2–4 bull calves.

511   Klír et al., *Knihy*, 439–532.
512   Research on the income and expense books for 1441, 1442, 1456, and 1469 has yet to be done.
513   Vaniš, "Ceny," 75–77. Cf. Klír, *Rolnictvo*, app. 14.1.
514   For other Bohemian data, cf. Alois Míka, "Nástin vývoje cen zemědělského zboží v Čechách v letech 1424–1547," *Československý časopis historický* 7 (1959): 545–571, on 559–560, 566–569.
515   Cf. also Heisinger, "Die Egerer Klosteuerbücher," 247–248.

According to the Louny prices, the estimated value of the actual heifer was 8 groschen. The influence of inflation from 1438–1456 on this rough estimate was negligible. The estimated price of sheep in 1456 was most frequently around 7 groschen but ranged from 5 to 8 groschen in exceptional cases. We assume that for tax purposes, single animals were not valued or taxed; only herds of 12 head or more were taxed.

14.6 Non-landholding plots

The value of non-landholding plots expresses the real individual wealth of the FPS, because it was possible to freely dispose of these properties, pledge them, and increase their value further in terms of capital. These plots had a high collateral value. For the family, they also represented a reservoir of necessary resources and a valuable item to leave to their offspring. It is therefore unsurprising that they were highly valued. On the general level, ownership of non-landholding plots is one of the most important indicators of a peasant household's ability to accumulate wealth. A total of 257 of the 950 FPSs (27.05%) reported non-landholding plots in 1438, and a total of 211 of the 783 FPSs (26.95%) in 1456.[516]

Non-landholding fields were usually characterized by number of arable "morgens" (*Morgen*), meadows by "tagwerks" (*Tagwerk*). With some fields and meadows, however, the measurement was not listed. The summary *table 7.3* shows that individual FPSs usually had only a small number of non-landholding plots, so that especially non-landholding fields could have had a rather complementary role in the peasant household economy. However, their high monetary value contrasts with that.

The analysis showed a large gap between the values of one "morgen" of arable fields and one "tagwerk" of meadow. We assume that the price of a non-landholding plot reflected the legal status of tenure, the payments-related burden, and its yield capacity.

If an FPS in 1456 had non-landholding meadows, on average they were 3.25–3.50 "tagwerks," where the average value of one "tagwerk" of meadow was

516   *App. 14.1a–d.*

4.5 threescore of Prague groschen in 1438 and 5.0 threescore in 1456.[517] This difference partially corresponds also to the inflation of the coinage. In the case of the holdings of arable plots, one FPS owned 4.2–5.0 arable "morgens," with an average monetary value of 2.2 threescore for a "morgen" in 1438 and 2.8 three-score in 1456.[518] In this case, the increase in the average value corresponded to the inflationary trend. The large differences in the monetary value of one "morgen" can be explained by their different economic utility. The most valu-able were certainly "free" plots without any burden; the least valuable should be annually paid plots held by "purchase" right.

The overall size of non-landholding plots was in no way enormous. Based on data from the Early Modern Period, we assume that both one "morgen" and one "tagwerk" equaled about 0.6 of a hectare.[519] We also assume that an ideal hide contained an arable unit of 30 "morgen." In this case, the total size of taxed non-landholding arable "morgens" equaled 244.5 ha (13.6 hides) in 1438 and 187.5 ha (10.4 hides) in 1456; and 180.0 ha of meadow "tagwerks" in 1438 and 219.2 ha in 1456. It should be noted that in both of the above years, we assessed a different number of localities.

For the purpose of an overview, we list several other non-landholding plots that were recorded in the tax documents without specifying the area as meadows, and arable land without specifying the area as forest stands, fish-ponds, etc.[520]

14.7 Price relations

Individual FPSs usually had their taxable property divided into landholding and livestock, and sometimes non-landholding plots or other marginal items were also added. The share of the main property items in the total amount of the property can be expressed in many ways. On average, the value of the tenure right to a landholding had a share of approximately 45%, and livestock 35–38%,

---

517   *App. 14.1a.*
518   *App. 14.1b.*
519   More precisely 0.57 ha. Cf. also Beck, *Unterfinning*, 577; Sedláček, *Paměti*, 49.
520   *App. 14.1d.* A few isolated FPS reported tenure as well as items such as hollow trees or bee-hives and, in some cases, rents paid by other peasants.

of the monetary value of a peasant property in the city-state of Cheb.[521] Especially for "subject" *Hof* landholdings, it is then the case that the total value of
the "purchase" right equaled the value of the livestock. It was, therefore, from
a purely economic perspective, approximately as difficult to obtain a "subject"
landholding as it was to equip it with the necessary draft horses and cattle. Naturally, this statement is valid only as a generalization; the actual ratios of landholding value to livestock value for individual landholdings are shown in graphs
in the appendix.[522] The graphs in the appendix include only FPSs with tenure
of one landholding in the relevant year with a non-zero value of property items.

The correlation coefficients showed that the value of the tenure right to
the landholding and livestock together correlated noticeably positively with
the "free" landholdings (0.7), to a middling degree also with "subject" *Hof*
landholdings (0.5), and only a little or not at all with "subject" *Herberge* landholdings and mills (*tab. 14.4–15.5*). The difference in the level of the positive
correlation in the value of the tenure right to the landholding and livestock
between the "free" and "subject" landholdings indicates the different degree of
price distortion by non-market factors and the power of institutional control,
because the values of livestock can be considered to be relatively market-based,
and the items that correlated with them should thus also be distinctly formed
by the relationship between supply and demand. The higher correlation with
the "free" landholdings and lower correlation with the "subject" landholdings is
therefore unsurprising. The difference in the positive correlation of the value
of the tenure right to landholdings and livestock between the various socioeconomic categories of landholdings can again be explained by the fact that
Herberge landholdings contained a wide range of households, from retired
persons, inmate-lodgers, and craftsmen through relatively full-fledged agricultural management. The sizes of the cultivated areas and numbers of livestock
were extraordinarily variable with *Herberge* landholdings and did not directly
reflect their economic balance sheet and ability to pay.

The non-landholding plots represented an asset whose monetary value
should be largely determined by the market (*tab. 14.4–14.5*). This is unsurprising because, in their case, a strong positive correlation was also shown with the
value of the tenure right to a "free" landholding (0.7) and also with the value

---

521   *App. 14.2.*
522   *App. 14.3–14.4.*

Tables 14.4–14.5, **Relationship between the values of the main property items held by a single FPS in the city-state of Cheb, 1438 and 1456.**

Relationship between value of	Legal status	Socioeconomic category	1438 Number of FPS	1438 Correlation coefficient	1456 Number	1456 Correlation coefficient
Tenure right to the landholding : Livestock	"free" landholding	all types	26	0.74	23	0.73
	"subject" landholding	Hof	581	0.50	593	0.44
		Herberge	87	0.24		
		Höfel	30	-0.03		
		mill	20	0.27		
Tenure right to the landholding : Non-landholding plots	"free" landholding	all types	17	0.44	10	0.72
		Hof	161	0.25		
	"subject" landholding	Herberge	24	0.23	171	0.26
		Hof and Herberge	175	0.28	15	0.03
		tenants of more landholdings	28	0.49	186	0.42
		tenants of "subject" landholdings total	195	0.52		
Livestock : Non-landholding plots	"free" landholding	all types	17	0.67	10	0.65
		Hof	161	0.48		
	"subject" landholding	Herberge	24	0.27	171	0.49
		Hof and Herberge	175	0.48	15	0.05
		tenants of more landholdings	28	0.71	186	0.42
		tenants of "subject" landholdings total	195	0.52		

Source: Ar Cheb, book 1067, Klosteuerbuch 1438; book 1084, Klosteuerbuch (Schätzungsbuch) 1456.

of the livestock, both with the tenants of "subject" landholdings (0.5) and "free" landholdings (0.7). The correlation between the value of non-landholding plots and the "purchase" right to a *Hof* landholding was, by contrast, low, which also proves that even the tenants of less valuable landholdings could purchase—or through inheritance, accumulate—similar land capital to the tenants of highly valued landholdings. The relatively high correlation between the value of livestock and the value of non-landholding plots thus specifies that the greater the production of the landholding, the higher the chance for the accumulation of property.

What is noteworthy is the high monetary value of the non-landholding plots in the city-state of Cheb (*tab. 14.6–14.8*). The "morgens" and "tagwerks" had a total value of 2,223 threescore of Prague groschen in 1438, whereas the value of the 142 landholdings, held by their respective FPS, was 3,170 threescore. The areal size of the "morgens" and "tagwerks" altogether was only 424.5 ha. Similar relations can be proved also for 1456, when the "morgens" and "tagwerks" of a value of 2,680 threescore and a size of 406.7 ha were divided by 141 FPSs. If an FPS held a landholding, livestock, and non-landholding plots, their average ratio oscillated around 1:1:1. This ratio explains how the market profitability was distributed between individual types of property items and how the dissolution of an FPS and division of its property among the heirs could take place. Due to the relatively low value of the "purchase" right to a peasant landholding, the position of the primary heir was not extremely burdensome, because the obligations to the other heirs could be settled relatively easily and perhaps even immediately, or they could be left a share of the cattle or non-landholding plots.

Table 14.6. **Monetary value of the main property items in the city-state of Cheb, 1438 and 1456.**

	Year	Total	Tenure right to the land-holding	Live-stock	Non-land-holding plots	Fishing right (inde-pendently listed)	Other
Absolute (threescore of Pr. groschen)	1438	23,459	10,656	8,921	3,509	28	345
	1456	22,767	10,184	7,967	3,991	105	520
%	1438	100.0	45.4	38.0	15.0	0.1	1.5
	1456	100.0	44.7	35.0	17.5	0.5	2.3

Source: Ar Cheb, book 1067, Klosteuerbuch 1438; book Nr. 1084, Klosteuerbuch (Schätzungsbuch) 1456.

Table 14.7.–14.8. **Overall statistical synopsis of the monetary values of the main property items in the city-state of Cheb, 1438 and 1456.**

Year		Value of tenure right to the landholding	Live-stock	Non-landholding plots*	Fishing right (independently listed)	Other**
			(threescore of Prague groschen)			
1438	Number of tenants (FPS)	832	820	247	4	18
	Total value (threescore of Prague groschen)	10,656	8,921	3,509	28	345
	Average value falling to one FPS (threescore of Prague groschen)	12.81	10.88	14.21	7.00	19.19
	Min.-Max. (threescore of Prague groschen)	1-240	1-63	0.5-138.0	2-14	1-44
	Min.-Max. (80% of the values; threescore of Prague groschen)	2-30	2.5-36	2-33	–	4-40
1456	Number of tenants (FPS)	699	655	212	3	20
	Total value (threescore of Prague groschen)	10,184	7,967	3,991	105	520
	Average value for one FPS (threescore of Prague groschen)	14.57	12.16	18.82	35	25.97
	Range (threescore of Prague groschen)	0.5-100.0	0.83-70.00	1-101	15-50	1-148
	Range for 80% of the values	3.5-30.0	4-38	4-38	–	2.5-60

Source: Ar Cheb, book 1067, *Klosteuerbuch 1438*; book 1084, *Klosteuerbuch (Schätzungsbuch) 1456.*
Note: All of the monetary values are listed in threescore of Prague groschen.
* – Arable land, meadows, forest growth, fallow fields, fishponds, "Erbe."
** – Tithes, annual payments, military service.

14.8 Monetization[523]

Problem posing

The Cheb data encourages the thematicization of the key transformation that hit peasant communities across the whole of Central Europe at the beginning of the Early Modern Period, which is considered one of the prerequisites for the future development of agrarian capitalism in some regions.[524] It was a process of oligarchization, monetization, and commercialization of the peasant communities.[525] This structural transformation was enlighteningly explained by Govind Sreenivasan, using the example of villages in the Swabian abbey Ottobeuren and, to a certain extent, earlier by Thomas Robisheaux for the Lower Franconian Principality of Hohenlohe.[526] Both of these cases have a general validity, especially for regions where serfdom had not been implemented and where the peasantry was not burdened with significant labor rents,[527] thus, for regions like the city-state of Cheb.

During the transition from the Late Middle Ages to the Early Modern Period, peasant communities at Ottobeuren Abbey seemed to be socially fragmented and equipped with good properties, disposition, and inheritance rights (1480–1560). If necessary, the landholding could be divided among multiple descendants of the tenant. While peasants were connected to the external market economy, money was used relatively little, and internal property relations inside the family were not monetized; transactions took place predominantly in kind. On the other hand, the permanent growth of the popu-

---

523 The subchapter 14.8. is a substantially broadened version of Klír, "Rural credit," 115–118. © Routledge 2020. Reproduced by permission of Taylor & Francis Group.

524 Sreenivasan, *Peasants*, 7–8, 345–352.

525 E.g., Ghosh, "Rural Economies," 262–268; William W. Hagen, Review of *The Peasants of Ottobeuren, 1487–1726: A rural society in Early Modern Europe*, by Govind P. Sreenivasan, *Journal of Modern History* 78 (2006): 752–754, on 754. Recently, see also cf. Thomas Ertl, Thomas Frank, and Samuel Nussbaum, eds., *Busy tenants. Peasant land markets in Central Europe (15th to 16th century)*, Vierteljahrschrift für Sozial- und Wirtschaftsgeschichte, Beiheft 253 (Stuttgart: Franz Steiner Verlag, 2021); Piotr Guzowski, "Monetisation and economic inequality among peasants in medieval Poland," in *Monetisation and commercialisation in the Baltic Sea, 1050–1450*, ed. Dariusz Adamczyk and Beata Mozejko (London, New York: Routledge, 2021), 98–122.

526 Sreenivasan, *Peasants*; Robisheaux, *Rural society*.

527 Hagen, "Peasants," 753.

lation and lack of free arable land potentially threatened the community and its social order, because against the backdrop of the existing legal norms it could lead to a miniaturization of landholdings, the growth of poverty, and famines. The joint approach of the wealthiest peasants and the landlords therefore led to a profound transformation of the social institutions and thus also to the economic and demographic behavior of peasant families.[528] Property dispositions and transfer of peasant landholdings began to be regulated and strictly controlled. The social stabilization of peasant communities had no clear winner and came at a high price. Only one child was to acquire the landholding, namely in the form of a purchase, if possible while the parents were still alive (30–60% of the transfers). The new tenant himself took on the obligation to assure the livelihood of the original tenant (retirement) and pay off his siblings. Even though the retired tenant and other siblings did not usually demand the payment of the entire amount at one time, but were satisfied with bearable annual installments, the necessity for cash grew dramatically, which the tenant's family needed to acquire regularly because the prices of landholdings were relatively high. This led to the strengthening of the agrarian and non-agrarian commercial activities of the peasantry, engagement in the credit market, the monetization of family relationships, a relentless accounting mentality, marriage control, and the conclusion of detailed contracts concerning even smaller landholdings. Moreover, the eagerness of peasants to obtain cash even in rural non-agrarian production undermined the traditional economic ties between the city and the countryside and was also one of the prerequisites for proto-industrialization.[529]

It is well-known that similar situations to that of Ottobeuren during the 16th century were present in other parts of early modern Central Europe, including Bohemia and Moravia.[530] Scholars have discussed the permeation of

---

528 Sreenivasan, *Peasants*, 9–104. Cf. Robisheaux, *Rural society*, 10–11.

529 Sreenivasan, *Peasants*, 107–279; in summary, see also Randolph C. Head, Review of *The Peasants of Ottobeuren, 1487–1726: A rural society in Early Modern Europe* by Govind P. Sreenivasan. *The American Historical Review* 110 (2005): 1614–1615; Hagen, "Peasants." For Hohenlohe see Robisheaux, *Rural society*, 11–12.

530 Recently summarized by Ghosh, "Rural Economies," 264–267. From the latest Czech literature, cf. the outputs of the project *Soziale Strukturen in Böhmen*. For Moravia, e.g., see Chocholáč, *Selské peníze*; Bronislav Chocholáč, "Poddanský úvěr na Moravě v 16. a 17. století" [Kredit der Unteranenbevölkerung in Mähren im 16. und 17. Jahrhundert], *Český časopis historický* 99 (2001): 59–84. Cf. also Hermann Rebel, *Peasant classes: The bureaucratiza-*

commodity monetary relations into the peasant economy, changes in the practice of property disposition and inheritance rights, the high financial burdens of primary heirs, the credit and installment system, as well as of other striking shifts in the method of management, the consumption of the household, living standards, and material culture. At the same time, in Bohemia this all-inclusive transformation is connected with a price revolution.[531] Czech written sources, however, do not allow us to know on a larger and more detailed scale the previous, late medieval situation and the dynamics of change at the beginning of the Early Modern Period.[532] This information gap is at least partially filled by Cheb's written sources.

Cheb city-state

The legal framework for "subject" land tenure in Cheb was constituted during the High Middle Ages and in principle remained unchanged until the Modern Period. Inheritance rights were based on the impartibility of the landholding, the purchase of the landholding by the primary heir, and the property arrangement with other siblings. In principle, therefore, this was the same system whose onset in early modern Ottobeuren caused the radical transformation of peasant communities. The question is: what effect did this legal framework have on the late medieval city-state of Cheb? How great a need did peasant families have to obtain cash?

An economic historian would be surprised particularly by the price relations of the main peasant property items in the city-state of Cheb, specifically by the relatively low price of the "purchase" right for a landholding and the high price of non-landholding plots (*tab. 14.6–14.8; chap. 14.7*). For a subject landholding, the value of the "purchase" right for the landholding was around half the value of the entire property, while the other half was the value of the livestock. If the peasant FPS also owned non-landholding plots, then the value of the "purchase" right comprised on average one-third of the whole value, the second third went to the livestock, and the third to the non-landholding plots

tions of property and family relations under early Habsburg absolutism. 1511–1636 (Princeton: Princeton University Press, 1983).

531   Kostlán, "Cenová revoluce," esp. 190–195.
532   Cf. Čechura, "Rolnictvo" (in German see Čechura, "Die Bauerschaft"); Čechura, *Die Grundstrukturen*, 109–134; Chocholáč, "Poddaní," 300–303.

(1:1:1), or the average "subject" landholding itself could be acquired for the price of 10–12 cows, 3 draft horses, or 2–3 "tagwerks" of non-landholding meadows, and the "subject" smallholdings then for 5–6 cows or one "tagwerk" of non-landholding meadows.

The opportunities to compare—at least for orientation—the monetary relations found in the late medieval city-state of Cheb with the neighboring regions are scarce because mass data is available only starting in the 16th century. For the "subject" landholdings in the area of the town of Grimma near Leipzig, the data of the registers for the Turkish tax from 1542 were investigated, according to which the value of the livestock comprised approximately 10% of the total value of a peasant property.[533] Based on the data of the earliest village land-transfer registers, it is possible to estimate very roughly a similar relation also for Bohemia and Moravia at that time.[534] In the grain regions, horses and cattle accounted for less than one-tenth of the estimated price of wealthy peasant landholdings, and the ratio between the monetary value of livestock and the estimated price of buildings and "subject" land was around 1:8.[535] By way of comparison, an average peasant landholding at the Swabian abbey of Ottobeuren at the beginning of the 17th century could be obtained for the price of 50 or more cows.[536]

Although the norms of property and inheritance rights in the late medieval city-state of Cheb did not differ in principle from those of the Early Modern Period, their economic and social consequences for the functioning of peasant communities fundamentally differ regarding price relations and demographic regime. Due to the relatively low value of the "purchase" right to a "subject" landholding, the position of the primary heir was not in any way burdensome in the city-state of Cheb, because they were able to settle their liabilities to other heirs relatively easily and immediately in natural commodities, non-landholding plots, or with an accessible amount of cash. The model considerations show that loans or share repayments were rarely necessary. As a specific example, we can mention the family of the smallholder Clugel in Okrouhlá (Scheibenreuth; *chap. 7.3*).

---

533 Schirmer, *Das Amt Grimma*, 62.
534 Míka, *Poddaný lid,* 213–218, 352–405; Míka, "Nástin vývoje," 559–560, 566–568; Chocholáč, *Selské peníze,* 72–97.
535 Hanzal, "Poznámky," 42–44.
536 Cf. Sreenivasan, *Peasants,* 183, 197, 263, 265, Table 4.2.

The tenants of "free" landholdings in the city-state of Cheb ended up in a different situation, because their price was on average three times higher than "subject" landholdings (*tab. 14.9*). Nevertheless, in a significant majority of the cases, the tenants of these landholdings had non-landholding plots, or could divide the landholding. However, if the tenant had to pay off their siblings, and they wanted to preserve the inherited property, a substantially higher financial burden was placed on them, because livestock and landholding plots were barely enough to leave to the siblings.

The monetization of the Cheb peasantry due to internal family relations or property disposition and inheritance rights was thus not large at all. Another question is to what extent the individual components of rent led to monetization (*chap. 11–13*). The situations of individual families were enormously

Table 14.9. **Synopsis of the average monetary values of the property, financial, and barter demands put on a Cheb peasant landholding in 1438.**

		"Subject" landholding		"Free" landholding	
		Full-holding (*Hof*)	Smallhold-ing ("full-holding")	Smallholder landholding (*Hof*)	Cottager landholding (*Herberge*)
Average price	"purchase" right	11 ss 45 gr.	5 ss 18 gr.	32 ss 55 gr.	15 ss 10 gr.
	Horses and cattle	11 ss 38 gr.	3 ss 28 gr.	14 ss 22 gr.	4 ss
	1 arable Morgen (Mg)*	2 ss 12 gr.			
	1 meadow Morgen (Tgw)*	4 ss 30 gr.			
Average annual land tax		28 gr.	11.5 gr.	66.3 gr.	20.6 gr.
Average annual land rent only in cash (22.5% of landholdings)		29.5 gr.		0 gr.	
Average annual land rent only in grain (71% of landholdings)		6.8 grain kárs		0	
Church tithe		10–30% of the amount of the land rent		?	

Source: From Klír, "Rural credit," 117, Table 9.2. © Routledge 2020. Reproduced by permission of Taylor & Francis Group. Data according to Ar Cheb, book 1067, *Klosteuerbuch 1438*.
Note: Only the tenants of one landholding are included, without fishermen and millers. This is why some of the data are different from *chap. 12.2, 11.4, 13.5, 14.6*.
* – owned only by a minority of peasant families

diverse, so at this point we will simplify the reality to average values. In most cases, the *land rent* was of an in-kind nature, so it did not force the peasants to raise cash. Only one-fifth of landholdings had to pay cash rents, for which an average of 29.5 Prague groschen were required each year. The peasants could get this amount through the sale of four sheep. The *land tax* had an exclusively monetary form, representing an average annual burden of 28.5 Prague groschen for "subject" *Hof* landholdings and 11.5 Prague groschen for *Herberge* landholdings. If the land tax was combined with a monetary land rent for a peasant landholding, the average financial burden was 67.4 Prague groschen.[537] This corresponded to the price of one cow and one or two calves or sheep.

The average peasant family in the late medieval city-state of Cheb needed to raise at least 30–60 Prague groschen in cash every year. This is evidenced by the fact that these values correspond to the most frequent amounts of receivables that peasants requested from Cheb burghers, especially butchers (*tab. 5.2*), because the means by which peasants most often raised money was the seasonal sale of cattle.

Let us also add that all the previous analyses in the city-state of Cheb have shown immense differences between agriculturally favorable and foothill zones.[538] Unlike in the Early Modern Period, when all areas were monetized, in the late medieval city-state of Cheb, the agriculturally favorable zones A and B were monetized and commercialized. In zone E, the foothill area, the need for cash from peasants' landholdings for the collection of the land tax was 3–5 times lower than in zones A and B, corresponding to the price of 1–2 calves or sheep.

14.9 Credit market[539]

The issue of the relationship of late medieval peasantry and the credit market has attracted the attention of historians, especially in recent years, as shown by a series of monographs, anthologies, partial studies, and a special 2014 issue

---

537   *App. 13.2a.*

538   *App. 11.4.* Further esp. *chap. 15.*

539   The subchapter 14.9. is a substantially broadened version of Klír, "Rural credit," 122–128. © Routledge 2020. Reproduced by permission of Taylor & Francis Group.

of the journal *Continuity and Change*, edited by C. D. Briggs.[540] It discusses
inter alia the character and representativeness of the available sources, the
purpose of the loan, as well as its length, size, interest, and the amount of the
installments, the socioeconomic position of the different parties, the share of
the specialized and non-specialized creditors, the role of the cities and Jews,
institutional guarantees and security, the structure of the credit market and its
accessibility, the level of the informational awareness of the peasants, and the
positive and negative impacts of the market on the peasant economy. We focus
on these topics with the primary aim of deepening and verifying our current
knowledge of the monetization of the peasantry.

The main source for information about the peasant loan in the late medieval
city-state of Cheb are the protocols of the city court (*Schuldprotokolle*).[541] In
addition to the petitions that we analyzed in *chap. 5.1*, these also contain declarations from debtors accepting financial obligations to creditors. The records
present the date of the anticipated repayment or the installment schedule or
pledge. The amounts of the interests were never stated; many records were later
crossed out when the loan was paid off. From the records, an example from
January 10, 1446, concerning a peasant in the role of the debtor and a burgher
in the role of creditor can be presented:

---

540   Monographs: Chris Daniel Briggs, *Credit and village society in fourteenth-century England*
(Oxford: Oxford University Press, 2009). Volumes: Chris Daniel Briggs and C. Jaco Zuij-
derduijn, eds., *Land and credit: Mortgages in the Medieval and Early Modern European coun-
tryside*, Palgrave Studies in the History of Finance (London: Palgrave Macmillan, 2018);
Philip R. Schofield and Thijs Lambrecht, eds., *Credit and the rural economy in North-western
Europe, c. 1200–c. 1850*, CORN Publication Series 12 (Turnhout: Brepols, 2009); Philip
R. Schofield and Nicholas J. Mayhew, eds., *Credit and debt in medieval England, c.1180–c.1350*
(Oxford: Oxbow Books, 2002); Maurice Berthe, ed., *Endettement paysan et crédit rural dans
l'Europe médiévale et moderne: actes des XVIIes Journées Internationales d'Histoire de l'Ab-
baye de Flaran, Septembre 1995*, Flaran 17 (Toulouse: Presses universitaires du Midi, 1998).
Studies: Chris Daniel Briggs, "Money and rural credit in the Later Middle Ages revisited,"
in *Money, prices, and wages: Essays in honour of Professor Nicholas Mayhew*, ed. Marin R.
Allen and D'Maris Coffman, Palgrave Studies in the History of Finance (Basingstoke: Palgrave Macmillan, 2015), 129–142; Philip R. Schofield, "Dealing in crisis: External credit and
the early fourteenth-century English village," in *Medieval merchants and money: Essays in
honour of James L. Bolton*, ed. Matthew Davies and Martin Allen (London: University of
London Press, 2016), 253–270. For Bohemia and Moravia: Graus, *Dějiny*, esp. 213–214, 519–
523; Čechura, "Chotěšov," 76; for early modern parallels, see esp. Chocholáč, "Poddanský
úvěr."

541   Cf. *chap. 5.4*.

"Hans Cüncz vn[d] sein brud[er] vo[n] Hanersdorf sind bek[e]ntlich word[e]n dem
Lawber VI gute ss Czu beczal[e]n auf Weinacht[e]n do fur
seczt er Im ein czu pfant sein wiesen geleg[e]n czwisch[en]
dez Ditolz vn[d] Mewerlains wiß[e]n seins gelcz dar
auf czu bekan[en] wie er mage an alle sein sched[e]n"[542]

For the purposes of this study, the protocols from 1435–1456 were analyzed, comprising a total of 779 declarations of debtors accepting financial obligations. However, of this number, only 36 (4.6%) concerned Cheb peasants, who predominantly occupied the role of debtors, and occasionally of creditors.[543] The peasants were identified by their predicate and were subsequently sought in the registers of the Cheb land tax in order to exclude any possible new burghers of Cheb coming from the countryside.

A total of 31 debt declarations were made by 23 individual peasants or their societies. Most often, individual peasants are found (61%), while the representation of the "association" of two peasants and the "association" of a peasant and a burgher were approximately balanced (17% and 22% respectively). Cheb Jews were the primary creditors (61%); the rest were burghers. No declarations where a peasant was a creditor for another peasant were ever recorded. Peasants in the role of creditors of Cheb burghers were recognized in five cases; once the rural parish priest was the creditor.

Peasants in the role of debtors or creditors normally came from the core of the Cheb local market territory, predominantly from the Cheb and Loman parishes, from settlements within 10 km of Cheb, but there were also people from marginally located parts of the city-state of Cheb (*fig. 14.2*).

Some studies stress the important roles of millers in the rural credit market.[544] In court protocols, only the miller from Jindřichov (Honnersdorf; 2×) appeared among the debtors and in partnership with the Cheb burgher and miller from Krapice (Kropitz).[545] Considering the low number, these rural

---

542 Ar Cheb, book 897, *Schuldprotokolle 1439–1452*, 247.
543 Klír, *Rolnictvo*, app. 14.5a.
544 Most recently, see, e.g., Piotr Guzowski, "Village court records and peasant credit in fifteenth- and sixteenth-century Poland," *Continuity and change* 29 (2014): 115–142, on 134.
545 Ar Cheb, book 897, *Schuldprotokolle 1439–1452*, 08, 364 (entry crossed out).

millers were grouped together with the peasants. However, no rural millers appeared among the creditors.

It is necessary to say that in the analyzed sample, we see the interaction of the Cheb peasantry with the urban credit market. In particular, loans were recorded where the creditor wanted to assure his rights and the recoverability of the debt. It is thus unsurprising that the entries of Jewish creditors predominate. The creditors usually were satisfied with the declaration of the debtor himself before the city court, but in one case the presence of his landlord is also documented (28 July 1447):

> "*Erhart Struczel <ist> czu Nid[er] Pilgramsrait ist bek[e]ntlich
> word[e]n dem Kaczman Jud[e]n VII gute ss gr. vnd ain vnd
> czwaniczig guld[e]n do fur seczt er Im ein czu pfandt
> sein haws vn[d] alle sein habe samt vn[d] vnsamt
> wo er die hat czu beczal[en] an alle sein sched[en] d[er] clagt
> vnd d[er] fod[er]t sulche bek[e]ntniß ist gescheen vor seine[m]
> h[er]n Paul Ru[du]sch[e]n vn[d] Jud[e]n sched[en] vn[d] alle sein
> eck[er]n vn[d] wis[e]n geleg[e]n czu Pilgramsrait*"[546]

Peasants in the role of debtors

We are interested in the purpose of the loans to peasants. To gain an understanding, we need to know (1) the socioeconomic position of the peasant borrowers, (2) the absolute and relative value of the loans, (3) the duration and manner of repayment, (4) the seasons in which the peasants borrowed and when they repaid, and (5) the declared pledge.

Regarding the socioeconomic position of the peasants in the year of the debt declaration, we have relied on the testimony of the land tax registers (cf. *chap.* 22). For knowledge of the position of the Cheb burghers, we have excerpted only the registers of the city tax from 1446; we have not determined the economic position of the Jews (cf. *chap.* 23.4). The result of the analysis was unsurprising (*fig.* 14.3).[547] Only wealthy peasants borrowed money and at the same time the creditors were from the ranks of the wealthiest burghers.

---

546   Ar Cheb, book 897, *Schuldprotokolle 1439–1452*, 333 (entry crossed out).
547   Cf. Klír, *Rolnictvo*, app. 14.5b. The method is described in detail in *chap.* 17.5., 22.1. and 26.4.

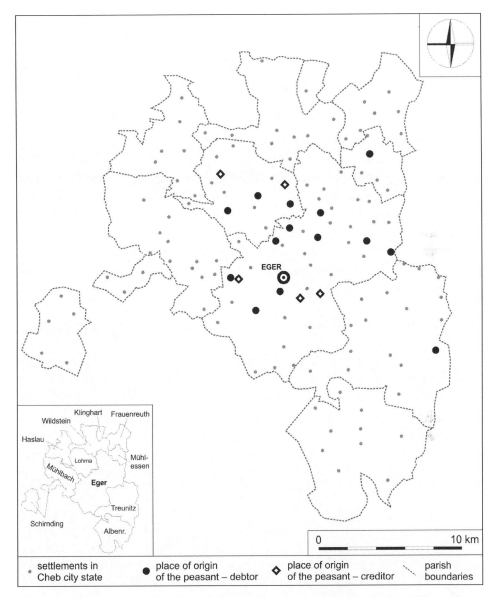

Figure 14.2. **Places of origin of the peasants connected to the Cheb credit market in 1435–1456.**

Source: From Klír, "Rural credit," 127, fig. 9.9. © Routledge 2020. Reproduced by permission of Taylor & Francis Group. Data according to Ar Cheb, book 897 and 898, *Schuldprotokolle 1439–1452* and *1452–1470.*

They were mainly tenants of "subject" landholdings, in one case of a "free" land-holding.

The amount of the loans—counted most often in Prague groschen, less often in Rheinish gulden or Meissen groschen—were not usually exceptionally high or low (*fig. 14.4*).[548] The minimum was 40 Prague groschen (2 threescore Meissen groschen), at most 26 threescore of Prague groschen. The peasants most often borrowed amounts from one to three threescore of Prague groschen and then from six to nine threescore of Prague groschen. The loans that were not over one threescore appeared only twice and the loans over 15 three-score thrice. The loans up to six threescore were, with exceptions, paid at one time. Higher amounts were already split into two to four installments in half of the cases.

Most of the loans had a short-term character. If the debt was covered in one payment, then the length of the loan never exceeded one year; it was usually paid back within half a year (*fig. 14.5*).[549] Most of the debts paid in the form of installments were also covered within one year.[550] At the same time, the first installment followed within a half-year of the provision of the loan. The longest loan was repaid in four installments over two years.[551]

The precise date of the entry of the debt depended on the schedule of the sessions of the city court during the year (*figs. 14.6–14.7*).[552] Almost two-thirds of the debtors' declarations fell in the winter months or the first annual quartal, namely in January (18%) and March (27%), never in February. One-quarter of the debts was recorded in the summer months, a tenth in the spring months, namely only in May, and we know of only one entry from the autumn months. In terms of repayment of debts or partial installments, their due dates were distributed relatively evenly across the winter, spring, and autumn months, with only a minimum falling in the summer months (*fig. 14.8*). The season of the repayment of debts and installments began on Michaelmas (29 Septem-ber) and ended at the time of the annual market, which in Cheb started two weeks after Pentecost.[553] The most popular date for the repayment of debts or

548   Cf. Klír, *Rolnictvo*, app. 14.5b.
549   Cf. Klír, *Rolnictvo*, app. 14.6a.
550   Cf. Klír, *Rolnictvo*, app. 14.6b.
551   Cf. Klír, *Rolnictvo*, app. 14.6c.
552   Cf. Klír, *Rolnictvo*, app. 14.7a–f.
553   E.g., Sturm, *Eger I*, 242.

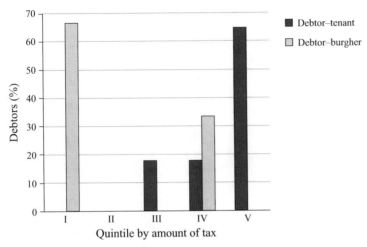

Figure 14.3. The socioeconomic position of the debtors and creditors in the city-state of Cheb 1435–1456.

Source: From Klír, "Rural credit," 123, fig. 9.3. © Routledge 2020. Reproduced by permission of Taylor & Francis Group. Cf. Klír, *Rolnictvo*, app. 14.5b.
Note: On the quintiles, cf. *chap.* 21.2 and 23.4; *app.* C. The socioeconomic position is determined only for a part of the debtors and creditors.

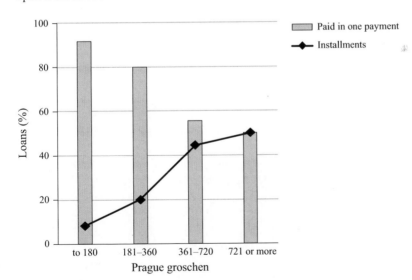

Figure 14.4. Nominal amount of the loans of the peasants in the city-state of Cheb, 1435–1456.

Source: From Klír, "Rural credit," 123, fig. 9.4. © Routledge 2020. Reproduced by permission of Taylor & Francis Group. Cf. Klír, *Rolnictvo*, app. 14.5b.

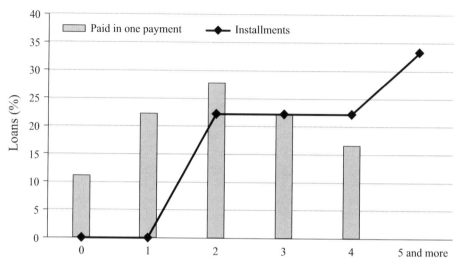

Figure 14.5. The length of the repayment of peasant loans.

Source: From Klír, "Rural credit," 124, fig. 9.5. © Routledge 2020. Reproduced by permission of Taylor & Francis Group. Cf. Klír, *Rolnictvo*, app. 14.6a–b.

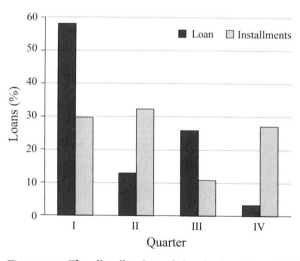

Figure 14.6. The distribution of the declaration of debt (date of the loan) and dates of the installments by a peasant before the Cheb city court, 1435–1456.

Source: Cf. Klír, *Rolnictvo*, app. 14.7a.

partial installments was Candlemas (2 February), which was also the only confirmed date in the first annual quartal. Two spring dates followed—St. Walpurgis (1 May) and Cheb's annual market. In the last quartal of the year, the most popular date was Christmas. The fluctuation of the peasant loan market thus corresponded to the normal agrarian cycle.

One-third of the entries also featured a pledge, which the debtor provided as a guarantee to the creditor (11×). The mention of a pledge was most often connected with nominally higher debts. The peasants or their "associations" most often used non-landholding plots (5×) or all their property (4×) as collateral. Of the other pledges, we can present the case of Niklas, the village bailiff in Salajna (Konradsgrün), who guaranteed a loan with his two landholdings, which he had in Šitboř (Schüttüber).[554] Erhart Strüczel from Dolní Pelhřimov (Pilmersreuth, Unter-) guaranteed a loan with all of his property; the non-landholding plots near Pelhřimov and an unidentified house were also mentioned specifically.[555] An "association" including Erhart Schepp and Niklas Pichler from Horní Lomany (Lohma, Ober-) guaranteed a loan with an unspecified house.[556] Noteworthy data on the relationship between the price of the pledge and the nominal amount of the loans is provided by the case of the peasant Strüczel, who held the landholding/demesne farm Hohlerhof in the immediate vicinity of Cheb and whose property was estimated at 106 threescore of Prague groschen. At the end of the winter of 1441, Strüczel borrowed 20 threescore of Prague groschen from the burgher Matel and his sister, which he promised to return on Candlemas the next year. The collateral was to be the meadow "In d[er] Prignicz."[557] The register of the Cheb land tax from 1438 actually did list 3.5 "tagwerks" of meadows of the value of 20 threescore precisely among the property of the peasant Strüczel.[558]

The purposes of loans were not mentioned in the court protocols. However, we can offer some suggestions in light of the price relations. The most frequent amount of 1–3 threescore of Prague groschen corresponded in price to one horse, several cows, or one "morgen" of non-landholding plots. The loans falling into the second most usual interval of 6–12 threescore corresponded in

554 Ar Cheb, book 896, *Schuldprotokolle 1429–1439*, 403.
555 Ar Cheb, book 897, *Schuldprotokolle 1439–1452*, 333.
556 Ar Cheb, book 897, *Schuldprotokolle 1439–1452*, 96.
557 Ar Cheb, book 897, *Schuldprotokolle 1439–1452*, 70.
558 Ar Cheb, book 1067, *Klosteuerbuch 1438*, 23b; Klír et al., *Knihy*, 320.

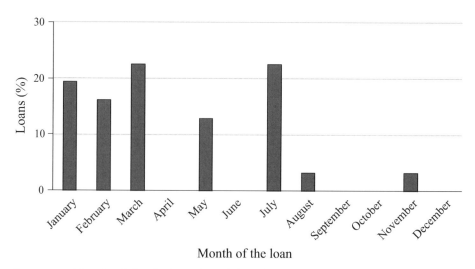

Figure 14.7. **Month of the declaration of debt (date of the loan) by a peasant before the Cheb city court, 1435–1456.**

Source: Cf. Klír, *Rolnictvo*, app. 14.7c–d.

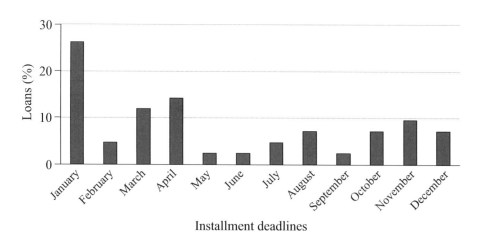

Figure 14.8. **Date of the repayment of a debt and its partial installments by a peasant in the city-state of Cheb, 1435–1456.**

Source: Cf. Klír, *Rolnictvo*, app. 14.7e–f.

price to the livestock equipment of the average fullholding, two "tagwerks" of non-landholding plots or four "morgens" of fields, or half the amount required to acquire the "purchase" right to an average "subject" smallholding.

An important testimony is provided by a comparison of the loaned amount to the total value of the debtor's property, or its relation to the land tax.[559] Based on the information from *chapter 12.2*, we have estimated the total value of a peasant's property in the year of the loan as 50× the amount of the land tax. If we stay with individual peasants, then the amount of the loan in 61% of the cases and with 46% of the unique people was up to four times the amount of the land tax paid each year (*fig. 14.9*). The loan surpassed ten times the annual land tax in 22% of cases and with 31% of unique people. It is naturally possible to find similar relations with the share of the total peasant property. In 72% of cases and with 62% of the unique persons, the loan was less than one-tenth of the total value of the property, and more than a quarter of the value of the property, with 17% of the cases and 23% of the people (*fig. 14.10*).

We can summarize that the short period of repayment, the relatively low loan amount, their relation to the land tax, and the total value of the property indicated that mainly seasonal bridging loans or investment loans for non-landholding plots were written into the court protocols. The peasant Adler from Střížov (Triesenhof) serves as a specific example of a bridging loan. At the end of the spring of 1454, he borrowed almost three threescore of Prague groschen from the Cheb Jew, Moshe. According to the 1456 *Taxation Book*, Adler's property had a value of 47 threescore of groschen, of which 15 threescore fell to the "purchase" right, twenty threescore to his horse and cattle, two threescore to his sheep, and ten threescore to non-landholding plots. Adler then paid one threescore and five Prague groschen annually in land tax.[560]

Peasants in the role of creditors

The court protocols from 1435–1456 contain only five records in which peasants from the city-state of Cheb loaned cash to Cheb burghers. The analysis of their socioeconomic position revealed a fact that is unsurprising—the creditors were rich peasants and the debtors, on the contrary, poor burghers. The

559   Cf. Klír, *Rolnictvo*, app. 14.8a–b.
560   Ar Cheb, book 1084, *Klosteuerbuch (Schätzungsbuch)* 1456, fol. 54r; Klír et al., *Knihy*, 521.

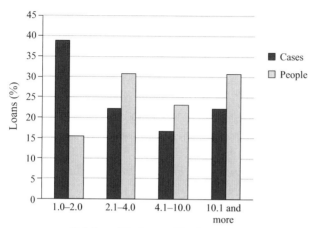

Figure 14.9. The relation of the nominal amount of the loan and the land tax in the city-state of Cheb, 1435–1456.

Source: From Klír, "Rural credit," 125, fig. 9.7. © Routledge 2020. Reproduced by permission of Taylor & Francis Group. Cf. Klír, *Rolnictvo,* app. 14.8a.

Note: For individual peasants, we could determine the amount of the land tax in the year of the loan for 18 declarations and 11 unique persons, for an "association" of peasants two declarations and four unique people, and for an "association" of a peasant and a burgher four declarations and three unique persons.

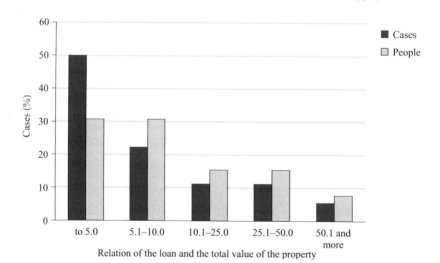

Figure 14.10. The relation of the nominal amount of the loan and the total value of the peasant property in the city-state of Cheb, 1435–1456.

Source: From Klír, "Rural credit," 125, fig. 9.7. © Routledge 2020. Reproduced by permission of Taylor & Francis Group. Cf. Klír, *Rolnictvo,* app. 14.8a.

amount of the loan was in the interval of cash that peasants could acquire in a lump sum (2–7 threescore of Prague groschen). The deadlines of the loans and installments followed the same model as with the peasants in the role of the debtors. That peasants were creditors proves the close interaction between the rural and urban economy. We assume that these peasant-creditors were among the rural elite because the basic characteristics of the urban elite were engagement in plural economic activities and diversity of income.[561]

Table 14.10. **The accessibility of cash for wealthy Cheb peasants.**

Sum	Accessibility	
Up to one threescore of Prague groschen.	An amount commonly available among peasants. A normal amount of the receivables of peasants in the city (chap. 5.4)	We suppose, if this amount was needed, peasants could obtain it through transactions among themselves; they did not have to turn to the city's credit market.
1–6 threescore of Prague groschen.	Amounts that were more difficult to obtain, and, in some cases, peasants were already turning to the city's credit market.	The peasants were able to obtain this amount all at once and repay it at one time; they could also offer it on the city's credit market.
More than 6 threescore of Prague groschen.		This amount was difficult for the peasants to obtain at once; it was typical to divide it into parts and repay the debt in installments.

14.10 Summary

In the first part of the chapter, we attempted to understand the significance of monetary values and determine what the ratio between the main property items was (chap. 14.2–14.7). We attempted to find what concrete objects and utility they represented. The price of a certain material asset was not formed based solely on its physical form and market profit, but also on the social and economic relationships that it entered into or could enter into, including its collateral value. The attractiveness and monetary value of individual property

561 E.g., Čechura, *Die Strukturen,* 115; Frederic Aparisi, "Village entrepreneurs: The economic foundations of Valencian rural elites in the fifteenth century," *Agricultural History* 89 (2015): 336–357, esp. 337–339, 352.

items in the eyes of peasants were based not on absolute yields but on the amount of such yields that remained in their possession after paying rent. This may explain the enormous monetary differences between materially similar assets. In principle, we can imagine two different systems where different economic and price rules applied. One was a subsistence economic system and expanded reproduction, and the second was a system of market economy and a freely disposable surplus. The prospects of the monetary appreciation of assets in the first system were little to none, while those in the second system were high. Non-market factors strongly influenced the price of the "purchase" right to "subject" landholdings. Market factors were of significant importance for the price of non-landholding plots. Peasants could accumulate money and non-landholding plots more or less regardless of the value of their "subject" landholding.

The prices of main property items may be explained based on market monetary yields. The majority of "subject" landholdings were oriented towards the fairly certain and predictable yet relatively low grain surplus that was extracted in land rent. Keeping cattle and horses was mainly of a subsistence nature and was always balanced against grain production. Non-landholding plots offered potential for expanding market-oriented cattle farming, so the degree of appreciation could rise dramatically. The second reason for the high price of non-landholding plots was the possibility of their free usage, including being the pledge for a loan; they had a collateral value. This explains why the average monetary value of one freely disposable non-landholding "tagwerk" of meadow compensated for the value of the "purchase" right to an average "subject" smallholding. The value of a non-landholding arable "morgen" was also high, since it was necessary for maintaining a balance between grain and livestock production. "Subject" landholdings in themselves covered subsistence and produced the surplus, which was, however, extracted by the landlord, so their monetary value was not generally high. However, if the threshold between simple reproduction and market surplus was exceeded, their value could rise sharply. This allows us to explain the exponential range of their monetary values.[562] In other words, the monetary values recorded in tax documents may be considered a true reflection of the market production capacity of a landholding and individual property items. Differences in monetary values expressed differences in

562 App. 14.3–14.4.

wealth and also different preconditions for the creation and accumulation of surplus. They are therefore ideal for investigating socioeconomic stratification.

In the third part, we dealt with the monetization of the Cheb peasantry and the extent of the credit market. On average, the rate of the commercialization and monetization of the late medieval Cheb peasantry was relatively low (*chap. 14.8*). In contrast to the situation in the Early Modern Period, only certain groups of the peasantry were significantly monetized, particularly those in the most agriculturally favorable zones near the city. Of the external factors, it was mainly the land tax that forced peasants to acquire cash, although to a bearable degree. The land rent and church tithe were paid mainly in kind and therefore did not push the peasantry towards monetization. Higher monetary sums were also not necessary for family property dispositions, because the prices of the landholdings were relatively low. While the landholding was impartible and only one of the offspring acquired it, the other heirs, thanks to the price relations, could choose to receive their share in kind, cattle, or non-landholding plots. It was the free transfer of non-landholding plots that significantly contributed to the stability of peasant economies in the institutional environment of the impartible inheritance of land and allowed for family property settlement, without the primary heir going into debt.

We verified the hypothesis that the average peasant household used cash only to a small extent by analyzing the credit market (*chap. 14.9*). The written sources give us a partial, but still sufficient, view of the interaction of the richest groups of the Cheb peasantry with the city credit market. Not even the richest peasants, who were the most monetized, sought funds in the city's credit market very often. The few loans we know of were short-term and used for operational or investment purposes, rather than to pay off siblings or even to purchase a landholding.

15.
Socioeconomic stratification[563]

15.1 Socioeconomic stratification and its measurement

Socioeconomic stratification may be assessed based on many criteria.[564] Earlier scholars focused only on the quantity of economic resources, an approach that is criticized today for various reasons, including the fact that in the feudal period, the accumulation of land resources automatically meant an increase in payment obligations.[565] Additionally, social prestige was not based directly on the extent of one's property but rather primarily on its symbolic value.

If we concentrate on economic resources, the decisive factor is what benefit they brought to the family, rather than the quantity or extent. To determine concrete economic utility, we would need to know not just the amount of means of production, but also the family's labor capacity, the volume of production, the level of rent (surplus exploitation), the volume of disposable surplus, and the legal term of tenure. We find some of these data in late medieval and early modern written sources, such as estate registers and tax documents.[566] In addition to economic utility, a social significance was linked to certain properties,

---

563 *App. 15.9–15. 11.*
564 For more on the operationalization process during the socio-economic analysis of the peasantry cf. Shanin, "Measuring."
565 Carocci, "Social Mobility," 381–382.
566 For an accurate account of Bohemian early modern written sources, see Petráň, *Poddaný lid,* 13–28.

including aspects connected to the socioeconomic status of the tenant, prestige, emotions, and family relationships and solidarity.[567]

The approaches of neoclassic and Marxist economics for analyzing Bohemian, primarily early modern peasantry were explicitly operationalized by Josef Petráň.[568] At the center of his ideas lay the economic model of a self-sufficient landholding that had the optimal quantity and ratio of means of production and labor force at its disposal to cover its own subsistence and to be capable of simple reproduction. The concrete amount of means of production and the form of this ideal landholding differed depending on historical, regional, and natural conditions. Real peasant landholdings approached or retreated from the comparative "model" to various degrees, and their position in the relative classification scale expressed the level of disposable surplus. In this way it was possible to differentiate between landholdings with a strong (1) entrepreneurial, (2) exploitational, (3) familial, and (4) non-agrarian and proletarian component, thereby solving the question of social polarization and primary accumulation of capital.[569] Naturally, Petráň's model classification was preceded by the land tax classification[570] and modified by other agrarian historians.[571] The important thing is that to this day, this classification, in different permutations, makes it possible to use the mass of data usually available in land tax and estate registers.[572] It describes primarily the economic—and to a lesser extent, the social—aspects of property ownership.

Josef Petráň also pointed out that the ideal source of information for assessing the socioeconomic stratification of peasant communities could be the monetary value of the landholdings specified in village land-transfer registers in the event of landholding transfers.[573] In the end, Petráň used these data to stratify "subject" landholdings only marginally, since the data available did not

---

567 For a classic view, see Levi, *Das immaterielle Erbe*, 104–105, 85–87. For further literature, cf. Medick, *Weben*, 330; Štefanová, *Erbschaftspraxis*, 87–88, 93–94.

568 Petráň, *Poddaný lid*, 13–28. For Bavarian sources, see Beck, *Unterfinning*, 217–253.

569 Petráň, *Poddaný lid*, 30–39, 53–163. Cf. Shanin, "Measuring," 237–239.

570 Cf. Pekař, *České katastry*, 13–17, 29–33, 40, 116–131, 206–207.

571 For the late Middle Ages in detail, see Kostlán, "Cenová revoluce," 176–195. Also cf. Graus, *Dějiny*, 188–190; Míka, *Poddaný lid*, 31–34; Šmahel, *Husitská revoluce*, 431; Rostislav Nový, "Hospodářství a sociální poměry doby Karla IV.," in *Karolus Quartus. Piae memoriae fundatoris sui Universitas Carolina D.D.D.* (Prague: Univerzita Karlova, 1984), 39–74, on 43.

572 Cerman and Maur, "Proměny."

573 Petráň, *Poddaný lid*, 25–26.

facilitate statistical processing for several reasons. The main problem was the uneven distribution of data over time and the fact that the monetary value of a landholding depends on the number of property transactions.

The starting point for understanding the late medieval city-state of Cheb is quite the opposite of the situation for early modern Bohemia, since we know a large quantity of commensurable monetary values of peasant properties as a whole, as well as their individual components, although clear information regarding the means of production at their disposal is lacking. The nature and criticism of our data are partially analogous to data contained in later village land-transfer registers.[574]

Cheb's land tax registers may be an ideal source for research on the socio-economic stratification of peasant communities. This chapter aims to identify and describe the basic and commonly monitored parameters of the socio-economic stratification of the Cheb peasantry, which is important for the context of its social mobility and migration. We are interested in (1) the pro-portion of *Hof* and *Herberge* landholdings, (2) the distribution of wealth amongst FPSs (i.e., fiscal stratification), (3) changes in the rate of inequality from 1438–1456, (4) the operational size of landholdings (i.e., stratification according to the amount of means of production), (5) the socioeconomic status of defined social groups (millers and fishermen), and (6) the structure of agrarian producers living in the city of Cheb itself.

15.2 *Hof* and *Herberge* landholdings

One of the main axes of the social distinction of peasant communities was that of the difference between the fullholding peasants and "sub-peasant" groups. Only fullholding peasants had complete rights and access to common eco-nomic resources. The city-state of Cheb was no exception, and we also encoun-ter here a division into *Hof* landholdings and *Herberge* landholdings.

In 1424, *Herberge* landholdings comprised 21% of all landholdings and in 1438 17% (*tab. 15.1*). The individual settlements differed from one another. In settle-

574 In contrast, detailed information on the extent of the land tenure of serf landholdings, including the share of fields and meadows, is available for the western part of the historical Cheb region (Sechsämterland). Cf. Singer, *Das Landbuch*.

Table 15.1. Share of Herberge landholdings at settlements with a varying degree of centrality in the city-state of Cheb, 1424 and 1438.

Year	Item	Settlements with a higher degree of centrality*	Other settlements total	Total
1424	Settlements	8	81	89
	Landholdings	161	730	891
	Of which *Herberge*	95	90	185
	Of which *Herberge*	59.0%	12.3%	20.8%
1438	Settlements	9	96	105
	Landholdings	149	783	932
	Of which *Herberge*	53	103	156
	Of which *Herberge*	35.6%	13.2%	16.7%

Source: Ar Cheb, book 1060, *Klosteuerbuch 1424*; book 1067, *Klosteuerbuch 1438*.
Note: * – settlements with a castle or parish church:
1424: (castle + parish church) – Skalná/Wildstein and Hazlov/Hazlau; (castle) – Starý Rybník/Altenteich; (parish church + mill) – Dřenice/Treunitz, Pomezí nad Ohří/Mühlbach, Mlýnek/Mühlessen and Schirnding; (parish church) – Kopanina/Frauenreuth.
1438: (castle + parish church) – Hazlov/Hazlau; (castle) – Starý Rybník/Altenteich; (parish church + mill) – Dřenice/Treunitz, Pomezí nad Ohří/Mühlbach, Mlýnek/Mühlessen and Schirnding; (parish church) – Kopanina/Frauenreuth, Horní Lomany/Lohma, Ober-.

ments with a higher degree of centrality, in which there was a parish church or castle, the *Herberge* landholdings comprised almost 60% of all the landholdings registered in 1424 and 36% in 1438, whereas at the other settlements, they had an average of only 12–13%. The differences between 1424 and 1438 are not due to development, but rather the different sets of settlements that we evaluated (the 1424 register is incomplete; some settlements are missing). It is true that the share of "sub-peasant" groups among the population of a certain settlement increased with the level of its centrality.[575]

575 We excluded the settlements that were not fully subject to the complete territorial control of Cheb from the analysis, and therefore we have only a partial insight into their structure. The *1424 Tax Register* includes (8 settlements): Albenreuth, Alt-/Mýtina; Grün (Thurn)/Úval; Hatzenreuth; Hirschfeld/Polná; Lapitzfeld/Lipoltov; Lindau/Lipina; Thurn/Tuřany; Tipessenreuth/Trpěš. The *1438 Tax Register* includes (12 settlements): Albenreuth, Alt-/Mýtina; Albenreuth, Neu-; Hatzenreuth; Hirschfeld/Polná; Lapitzfeld/Lipoltov; Lindau/Lipina; Querenbach; Thurn/Tuřany; Tipessenreuth/Trpěš; Tobiesenreuth/Dobrošov.

At the same time, we tested the influence of natural conditions, i.e., the distribution of *Herberge* landholdings in ecological zones A–E.[576] No correlation was found, so factors other than natural conditions influenced the proportion of *Herberge* landholdings.

15.3 Fiscal stratification

We included all the FPSs listed in the *1438 Land Tax Register* and the *1456 Taxation Book* in our analyzed set, without distinguishing the legal status of their tenure or if it comprised one or more landholdings. Our objective was to monitor the monetary value of the assets that the FPSs had at their disposal. Based on the knowledge we gained from *chapter 14.2*, we assume that the monetary value expressed the degree of economic utility of material assets, thus reflecting the degree of institutional control. We compiled the *tables in appendices 15.1–15.2* in the same manner, recording the number of landholdings with a specific monetary value of the tenure right to the landholding and livestock for each settlement. In analytic terms, we simplified and examined the distribution of wealth not within individual settlements, but in the city-state of Cheb as a whole and then in terms of the main ecological zones.[577]

We may consider the distribution of the **total monetary values** between FPSs to be *fiscal stratification*, as well as stratification based on the degree of access to sums of cash, and thus the degree of commercialization. We divided the FPSs according to the monetary value of all property into categories of 10 threescore of Prague groschen.[578] Comparatively, the largest number of FPSs had a total property value worth up to 10–20 threescore at their disposal (specifically

---

576 *App. 15.1a–b.*

577 We did not include all of the settlements in the analysis, only those that (1) were described in detail in the *1438 Land Tax Register* and the *1456 Taxation Book* and (2) were homogeneous from the point of view of territorial sovereignty, i.e., all landholdings were subject to the Cheb land tax. We limited the analysis in this way in an attempt to compare the situation in 1438 and 1456 and the need for familiarity with the complete social profile of the whole settlement not just in part, but as a whole. Settlements with a higher degree of centrality and a large number of smallholdings fundamentally cannot be a part of the set as they would distort the overall result (Hazlov/Haslau; Libá/Liebenstein; Schirnding).

578 *App. 15.2a.*

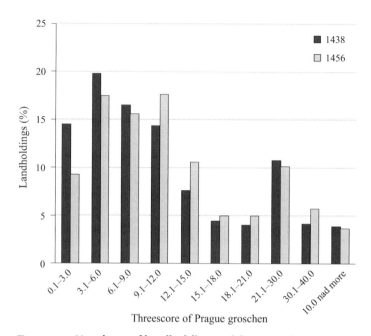

Figure 15.1. Numbers of landholdings with a certain monetary value of the tenure right in the city-state of Cheb as a whole, 1438 and 1456.

Source: Cf. app. 15.2b.

27% in 1438 and 1456). Differences exist between individual ecological zones (*figs. 15.3–15.4*).[579] It is clear that on average the wealth of the FPSs steadily declined as the conditions for commercial agricultural production worsened.

The differences in the **monetary values of landholdings** seem to be less contrasting than the differences in the total values of all property (*fig. 15.1*).[580] The value of landholdings was most often in a relatively low range of 3–6 threescore of Prague groschen (20% in 1438, 18% in 1456); approximately equally numerous were other ranges of up to 15 threescore, which 25% of FPSs exceeded. Notably, higher values were especially related to "free" landholdings. Values of landholdings were generally highest in agriculturally favorable zones and lowest in agriculturally unfavorable zones (*fig. 15.5–15.6*).[581]

---

579   *App. 15.2d; figs. 15.3–15.4.*
580   *App. 15.2d.*
581   *App. 15.2e.*

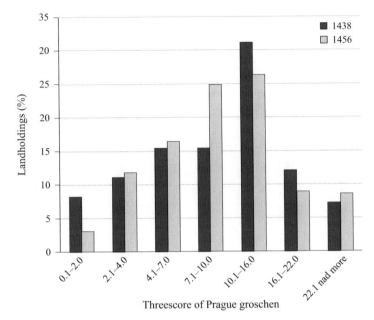

Figure 15.2. **Numbers of landholdings with a certain monetary value of livestock in the city-state of Cheb as a whole, 1438 and 1456.**

Source: Cf. *app. 15.2c.*
Note: Landholdings with zero monetary values of livestock not listed. Operationally medium-sized peasant landholdings with one or two paired horse teams (7.1–16.0 threescore of Prague groschen) predominated.

Concerning the **monetary value of livestock**, we excluded those FPSs from our analysis that did not list the value of livestock or that listed the combined value together with another item. We have decided to take this measure to eliminate the error that occurred due to unsystematic record-keeping in land tax-related documents. We divided up the monetary values of livestock into the categories of two, three, and six threescore of Prague groschen, to appropriately cover the uneven distribution of data (*fig. 15.2*).[582] The largest part of FPSs held livestock with a monetary value of 10–16 threescore (31% in 1438; 26% in 1456); a considerable quantity of FPSs also lay in the lower ranges of 4–7 threescore (16–17%) and 7–10 threescore (16–25%). If we consider the

582   *App. 15.2c.*

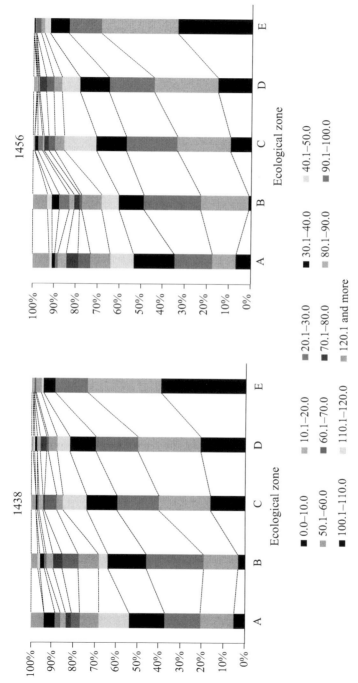

Figures 15.3–15.4. Monetary values of all property of individual FPSs in the main ecological zones of the city-state of Cheb.

Source: Cf. *app. 15.2d.*

Note: Values in threescore of Prague groschen.

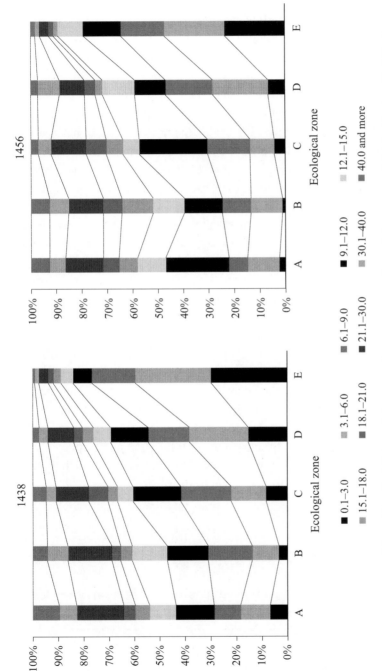

Figures 15.5–15.6. **Number of landholdings with a certain monetary value of the tenure right to the landholding in the main ecological zones in the city-state of Cheb, 1438 and 1456.**

Source: Cf. *app. 15.2e.*
Note: Values in threescore of Prague groschen.

uneven scope of ranges, then most FPSs were concentrated in the range of
7–10 threescore. Only a small number of FPSs held livestock worth only up
to 2 threescore (3–8%), while high values above 16 threescore were not a rarity
(18–19% of FPSs). The distribution of the monetary values of livestock had
the shape of an asymmetrical Gaussian curve, and therefore was in principle
different from the distribution of the values of landholdings. We can explain
the difference by saying that the value of livestock primarily reflected the operational size of landholdings held by FPSs, whereas the value of a landholding
reflected the extent of their market quota and commercialization.

The monetary values of all property and its main elements rose slightly
from 1438–1456 (cf. *chap. 14*), although the property distribution structure
remained more or less the same. The largest contrasts between zones lay in the
monetary values of all property, while the smallest lay in the values of livestock.
This leads us to assume that the subsistent core of the FPS was more or less
the same in all zones, although market-oriented livestock production developed to a greater extent solely at FPSs in the agriculturally favorable zones
A and B (*figs. 15.7–15.8*).

The extent of land resources available to individual FPSs is uncertain. The
differences in the range of the monetary values of all property across ecological
zones are too vast to be explained simply as a result of the different amounts
of land resources. The range of the monetary values of livestock is, after all, not
so different. We therefore see in the uneven distribution of monetary values
mainly the different ratios of subsistence to rent and market production quotas
for the analyzed FPSs. We can be sure that the agricultural production of the
FPSs in zones A and B was highly market-oriented, whereas in zone E high
subsistence agricultural production dominated. This characteristic is naturally
reflected in the monetary values of individual items of property.

15.4 Rate of inequality

In this chapter, we examine in detail how much the stratification of the Cheb
peasantry changed over the focus period. Did it remain stable, or did property inequalities deepen? What was the situation in the city-state of Cheb as
a whole and the situation in its individual ecological zones? What was the situation for the main items of property? The answers to these questions are

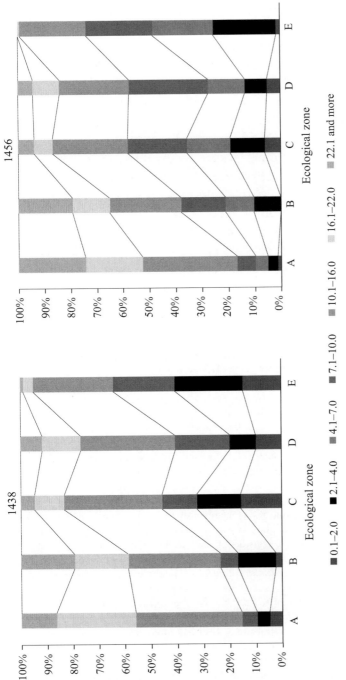

Figures 15.7–15.8. Number of landholdings with a certain monetary value of livestock in the main ecological zones in the city-state of Cheb, 1438 and 1456.

Source: Cf. *app. 15.2f.*

Note: Landholdings with zero monetary values of livestock not listed. General interpretation:
Up to 4 threescore of Prague groschen – cottagers, smallholders, and small peasant landholdings, without a paired team.
7–16 threescore of Prague groschen – medium-sized peasant landholdings, one or two paired teams.
16–22 threescore of Prague groschen – large peasant landholdings, two paired teams.
22 or more threescore of Prague groschen – extremely large landholdings, three or more paired teams.

an important prerequisite for an adequate interpretation of socioeconomic mobility and migration.

The rate of inequality in the distribution of material resources among the members of a specific population has been expressed and also simplified in several ways. A large number of them are derived from what is known as the Lorenz curve. The higher the rate of inequality in the distribution of resources among the population, the more the Lorenz curve curves, resulting in a larger area between the so-called equality diagonal and the arc of the actual Lorenz curve. The relative volume of this area, expressed by the Gini coefficient, may be used as an effective tool of comparison for several Lorenz curves. The Gini coefficient may have a value from "0" to "1"; the closer it is to "0," the more equal the distribution of resources within the population. Nevertheless, an equally large Gini coefficient does not mean an equal degree of relative distribution of resources, since it ignores the degree of asymmetry of the Lorenz curve, i.e., if inequality is caused by a large amount of poor or, conversely, wealthy tenants.[583]

---

583 Expression of socioeconomic inequality using the Lorenz curve began to appear in continental agrarian history in the 1970s and it celebrated the peak of its popularity in medieval studies during the 1980s and 90s. Cf. James P. Whittenburg and Randall G. Pemberton, "Measuring inequality: A Fortran program for the Gini index, Schutz coefficient, and Lorenz curve," *Historical Methods Newsletter* 10 (1977): 77–84; Randall H. McGuire, "Breaking down cultural complexity: Inequality and heterogeneity," *Advances in Archaeological Method and Theory* 6 (1983): 91–142. Data from 1460 showing the uneven distribution of land resources in Occitania's Saint-Thibéry is summarized in a table by E. Le Roy Ladurie and visualized by Randall H. McGuire (McGuire and McC. Netting, "Leveling Peasants?," 274, fig. 2). Changes in the fiscal stratification of the population of the Duchy of Geldern with the County of Zutphen between 1470, 1498, and 1541 were interpreted and compared using the Lorenz curve and the Gini coefficient by Remi van Schaïk (Schaïk, *Belasting*, 237–245). A similar interpretation of the inequalities and changes in the distribution of farmland among the peasantry of the Main River Valley applied by Dieter Rödel in the analysis of the late medieval estate registers of the Diocese of Würzburg (1468 and 1499) is relevant for the Cheb Region (Dietrich Rödel, *Das erste Salbuch des Hochstifts Würzburg. Agrargeschichtliche Analyse einer spätmittelalterlichen Quellen*, Studien zur bayerischen Verfassungs- und Sozialgeschichte 13 (Munich: Kommission für Bayerische Landesgeschichte, 1987); Dietrich Rödel, "Die spätmittelalterliche Dorfbevölkerung in Mainfranken," *Strukturen der Gesellschaft im Mittelalter, interdisziplinäre Mediävistik in Würzburg*, ed. Dietrich Rödel and Joachim Schneider (Wiesbaden: Reichert, 1996), 281–301, on 297–299). Cf. Demade, "The Medieval Countryside," 228. A similar analysis has been made of changes in uneven distribution of "subject" land tenure in the Duchy of Wrócław from the second half of the 15th century to the beginning of the 16th century, thanks to Richard C. Hofmann,

The significance of the Lorenz curve and the Gini coefficient lies in their comparative capabilities; when combined, they show how many people control how much wealth. The prerequisite for meaningful comparison and interpretation is a sufficient amount of principally corresponding data created by using identical methods of record-keeping. Therefore, in the analysis, we included precisely the same settlements and excluded ones where the number of taxed landholdings fluctuated in the analysis due to various circumstances.

We analyzed only those FPSs that held "subject" landholdings and not "free" landholdings. We also only included the FPSs that held landholdings that we were able to correlate in the 1438 *Land Tax Register* and the 1456 *Taxation Book* in the sample (*tab. 15.2*). We analyzed the inequality especially of (1) the total value of property, (2) the value of the "purchase" right to the landholding, (3) the total value of livestock, and (4) the value of non-landholding plots. We excluded the zero values due to incomplete tax records for the first three items. We depict the rate of inequality for individual years and items of property using Lorenz curves and express it using the Gini coefficient (*tab. 15.2; fig. 15.9*). The results are as follows:

+ The Gini coefficient reached medium-high values in all zones (0.43–0.50). One-fifth of the wealthiest landholdings thus held 34–54% of the value of the overall material wealth, while one-fifth of the poorest held 4–8%, depending on the concrete property item, year, and ecological zone.
+ We find the highest rate of inequality in the value of the "purchase" right to landholdings (maximum in zone A, 1438, one-fifth of the wealthiest here held 54%), and the lowest in the value of livestock (minimum in zone E, 1456, where one-fifth of the wealthiest held just 34%).
+ The degree of asymmetry of the Lorenz curve shows that inequality in the value of overall property was due to the large number of wealthy landholdings in the agriculturally optimal zone A, while this was due to the larger number of poorer landholdings in the unfavorable zone E.

Land, 247–251, 331–332, figs. 9.1, 11.1. Recently for property distribution among late medieval and early modern communities across Europe cf. Daniel R. Curtis, *Coping with crisis. The resilience and vulnerability of pre-industrial settlements*, Rural worlds: Economic, social, and cultural histories of agricultures and rural societies (London, New York: Routledge, 2016), 36–37. Recently see also chapters published in Alfani and Thoen, eds., *Inequality*; Nigro, ed., *Disuguaglianza*.

+ The distribution of non-landholding plots showed a different rate of inequality for which we do not display a Lorenz curve. Given that most FPSs did not hold non-landholding plots, the Gini coefficient reached extremely high values of 0.81–0.93.
+ The uneven distribution of non-landholding plots is also reflected in the Gini coefficient calculated using the total value of property of FPSs in 1438 and 1456, which is therefore higher than in the case of landholding or livestock values.

The answer to the opening question and the general development trend in 1438–1456 is the following: there was a moderate leveling in the distribution of the value of the "purchase" right, stability, or moderate leveling in livestock values, and both moderate leveling and differentiation occurred in the case of non-landholding plots. However, the differences were not overly dramatic in any of these cases, and in principle we may consider stratification during the focus period to be stable.

Table 15.2. **The rate of inequality in the distribution of material wealth in the city-state of Cheb, 1438 and 1456. Expressed by the Gini coefficient. Corresponding Lorenz curves, cf. fig. 15.9.**

Gini coeffi-cient	Total value (455)*		Landholding value (442)*		Livestock (424)*		Non-landholding plots (502)*	
	1438	1456	1438	1456	1438	1456	1438	1456
A	0.47	0.46	0.50	0.48	0.44	0.44	**0.81**	**0.83**
B	**0.44**	**0.47**	0.47	0.45	0.47	0.47	0.83	0.82
C	0.48	0.45	0.46	0.44	0.48	0.43	**0.82**	**0.83**
D	**0.46**	**0.47**	0.49	0.48	0.45	0.44	**0.87**	**0.88**
E	0.48	0.47	0.49	0.48	0.46	0.43	0.93	0.91

Source: Ar Cheb, book Nr. 1067, *Klosteuerbuch 1438*; book Nr. 1084, *Klosteuerbuch (Schätzungsbuch) 1456*.
Note: Corresponding Lorenz curves, cf. *fig. 15.9*.
* – number of FPSs in 1438 and 1456.
Red – leveling; **bold black** – differentiation; normal black – stability.

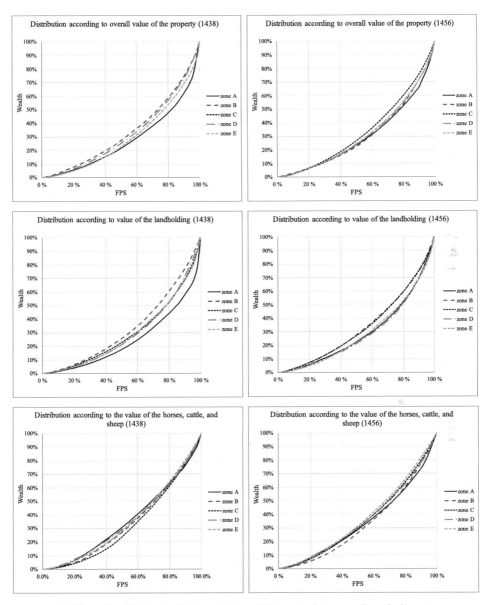

Figure 15.9. **The distribution of material wealth in the late medieval city-state of Cheb, 1438 and 1456.**

Source: Ar Cheb, book 1067, *Klosteuerbuch 1438*; book 1084, *Klosteuerbuch (Schätzungsbuch) 1456*.
Note: Expressed by the Lorenz curve. The main trend was stability to slight equalization. Corresponding Gini coefficients, cf. *tab. 15.2*.

15.5 Operational size of landholdings

The Cheb written documents do not inform us about how large the peasant landholdings actually were, i.e., what their operational size was. We consider this "detail" necessary for a general understanding of the peasantry. In this sub-chapter, therefore, we will attempt at least an indirect approximation.

Model

We may estimate the operational size of landholdings using the value of horses as draught power and cattle. In this respect, we follow the price summary from *chap. 14.4–14.5*.

The methods with which we may at least approximately estimate the economic category of a landholding based on the number of horses and cattle have been summarized in many studies.[584] The description of large peasant landholdings situated in the Cheb basin from the beginning of the 19th century by Sebastian Grüner is of great importance for the city-state of Cheb (*chap. 5.5*). Despite various methodological obstacles, it is possible to reconstruct the ideal monetary values of horses and cattle for the main economic categories of landholdings (*tab. 15.3–15.4*).[585] The estimation of the specific area of cultivated land according to the number of draft horses is naturally always burdened by substantial error; therefore, it should be applied mainly in a quantitative analysis of large sets of data, where we interpret general tendencies.

We have model data at our disposal regarding the relationship between the area of arable land and the number of draft animals for the Early Modern Period, although applying it to the Middle Ages is not without complications. One such complication is that this early modern data typically only concerns the work of servants and a strong paired team of horses on noble land.[586] The

---

584   Summarized for the Czech lands by Klír, "Agrarsysteme"; Klír and Vodáková, "Economy," 111–113.

585   Tomáš Klír and Michal Beránek, "A social-economic interpretation of the layouts of deserted villages: An example of a deserted village at the 'V Žáku' site in Klánovice Forest in Prague," in *Studies in Post-medieval Archaeology 4*, ed. Jaromír Žegklitz (Prague: Archaia, 2012), 289–364, on 306, Tab. 3 (model for early modern landholdings burdened by significant labor obligations); Míka, *Poddaný lid*, 141–146.

586   Černý, *Hospodářské instrukce*, 131; Pekař, *České katastry*, 8, 30, 119–121, 298; František Šach, "Potažní zvířata v českých zemích v průběhu šesti století" [Zugtiere in böhmischen Ländern

Table 15.3. **The size of adult labor forces in landholdings with various amounts of cattle, 1781, Alps.**

Number of head of cattle	1	2	3	4	5	6	7	8	9	10	11	12
Average number of adults	2.1	2.5	2.8	3.1	3.7	3.8	4.2	4.7	5.2	5.4	5.4	6.0
Most frequent number of adults	2		3		4					6		

Source: According to Mitterauer, "Formen," Tafel 2, simplified.
Note: People over 12 years of age, men, and women. Alpine valley Villgraten, Carinthia, predominantly cattle farming.

data for "subject" landholdings is burdened by the fact that their paired teams were usually oxen and that they were additionally burdened by labor duties. We can roughly limit the maximum capacity of a paired team of horses to one hide (usually 60 "korec"; ca. 16–18 ha), although ideally a team would work a landholding with an arable land area of 30–60 "korec" (ca. 8–18 ha). This of course depended on the landholding's specific agricultural system, as well as the climatic and soil conditions.

As a starting point, we may model for the late medieval city-state of Cheb an ideal medium peasant fullholding where the demographic structure of the members, the labor force, and economic resources are balanced. Such a landholding was farmed by one biological family with the labor force of the tenant, his wife, 1–2 adolescent children, a servant, and a maid—all in all, five adults. Their livestock inventory included 2–4 horses worth 5–10 threescore of Prague groschen and 4–6 cows, 1–2 heifers, and several calves worth in total 5–9 threescore—altogether, livestock with a total value of 10–19 threescore. The area of the arable land could have been between half a hide and one hide. Landholdings with livestock worth less than this could have extra labor capac-

im Laufe von sechs Jahrhunderten], *Vědecké práce Československého zemědělského muzea* 16 (1977): 5–28, on 7; Bořivoj Lůžek, "Špitální dvůr v Dobroměřicích v letech 1517–1542" [Spitalshof in Dobroměřice in Jahren 1517–1542], *Sborník Československé akademie zemědělských věd* 2 (1957): 175–201, on 179.

ity at their disposal, while landholdings with a larger amount could be forced to integrate an additional labor force such as servants or lodgers. Of course, we must analyze everything with appropriate care, bearing in mind the possibility of slight inaccuracy.[587]

Table 15.4. **Model of the correlation between the value of the livestock, their number, and the socioeconomic category of the landholding in the city-state of Cheb, 1438–1456.**

Socioeconomic category		*Herberge* landholdings		*Hof* landholdings		
		cottagers	small-holders	small	medium	large
Approximate size of the arable land*		0	(to 2–3 ha) (to ¼ hide)	to 9 ha (¼ – ½ hide)	to 18 ha (½ – 1 hide)	to 27 ha (more than 1 hide)
Livestock	draught power (number of horses)	0	1	2	2–4	5 or more
	cattle (number of cows)	1–3	2–4	3–5	4–6	6–12
Monetary value (threescore of Prague groschen)	horses**	0	2	4–5	5–10	10 or more
	cattle (number of cows)***	1–4	2–5	3–7	5–9	7 or more
	total livestock	4 and fewer	4–7	7–12	10–19	17 or more
Optimal number of adults / numbers of all persons including children****		2–3	3–5	3–5	5–8	11–18

Source: Ar Cheb, book 1067, *Klosteuerbuch 1438*; book 1084, *Klosteuerbuch (Schätzungsbuch) 1456*.
Note: * – calculated in a simplified way with a hide of ca. 16–18 ha in size.[588]
** – interval counted for the values of 2 threescore to 2 threescore 20 Prague groschen for one horse. Rounded to the whole threescore.
*** – interval counted for the values of 50 groschen to one threescore of 10 Prague groschen for one cow. Rounded to the whole threescore.
*** – for children, multiplied by the usual demographic coefficient 1.67 (cf. Head, "Haushalt," 119).

587   The relation between the level of land tax, the size of family, and the amount of livestock based on the so-called Turk tax of 1542 is analyzed by Schirmer, *Das Amt Grimma*, 52–56.

588   Sedláček, *Paměti*; Gustav Hofman, *Metrologická příručka pro Čechy, Moravu a Slezsko do zavedení metrické soustavy* (Plzeň: Státní oblastní archiv, 1984).

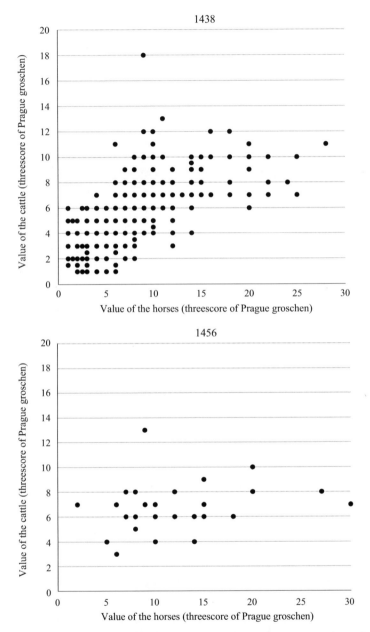

Figures 15.10–15.11. Ratio of monetary value of horses and cattle in the city-state of Cheb, 1438 and 1456.

Source: Ar Cheb, book 1067, *Klosteuerbuch 1438*; book 1084, *Klosteuerbuch (Schätzungsbuch) 1456*.

Note: Correlation coefficient 0.69 (1438) and 0.77 (1456).

Table 15.5. **Number of landholdings with or without a horse in various economic categories in the city-state of Cheb, 1438.**

Separately listed values	Absolute terms			%			
	Horses and cattle	Cattle only	Total	Horses and cattle*	Cattle only*	Total	Horses and cattle***
Herberge landholdings	12	72	84	2.6	41.9	13.4	14.3
Hof land-holdings***	420	74	494	92.1	43.0	78.7	85.0
Höfel land-holdings	19	5	24	4.2	2.9	3.8	79.2
Mills***	5	14	19	1.1	8.1	3.0	26.3
Fishermen	0	7	7	0.0	4.1	1.1	0.0
Total	456	172	628	72.6	27.4	100.0	100.0

Source: Ar Cheb, book 1067, *Klosteuerbuch 1438.*
Note:
* – proportion of the total number of landholdings with the given animals
** – proportion of the total number of landholdings in the given economic category
*** – the combination with a landholding of a different economic category included (e.g., *Hof* + *Herberge*)

For the above-mentioned model estimates to function, there must be a positive correlation between the value of horses and cattle. We were able to test this estimate on 469 landholdings in 1438 and 33 landholdings in 1456. In both cases, there was high positive dependency: in the first case the correlation coefficient reached 0.69 and in the second case 0.77 (*figs. 15.10–15.11*).

We can estimate the extent of a landholding's land resources with the highest degree of reliability if the monetary values of horses and cattle were listed separately.[589] We can deduce the number of horses from the independently listed value and determine the arable land equivalent from that value. A statistically sufficient amount of individual data exists only for the monetary value of horses in 1438 (628 values; *tab. 15.5; 15.7; fig. 15.12*).

The distribution of landholdings with various operational sizes in the city-state of Cheb paints the following image:

589   See also Klír, "Land transfer," 158.

Table 15.6. **Landholdings with no horses in the city-state of Cheb, 1438.**

Value of cows, heifers, and calves (three-score of Prague groschen*)	1	2	3	4	5	6	7	8	9	10–14	Total
Number	24	43	44	25	13	10	5	3	2	3	172
%	14.0	25.0	25.6	14.5	7.6	5.8	2.9	1.7	1.2	1.7	100.0

Source: Ar Cheb, book 1067, *Klosteuerbuch 1438.*
Note: Only the value of cattle listed.

Table 15.7. **Total value of horses held in individual FPSs in the city-state of Cheb, 1438.**

Hypothetical property category	Horses	Area of arable land	Value of horses (threescore of Prague groschen)	Number of cases	%
Landholdings with no horses	–	–	0	172	27.4
Smallholding	One or two (poor quality) horses (= without a full paired team).	around 15 "korec" (4.2 ha)	1–3	83	13.2
Medium fullholding	Two horses.	15–45 "korec" (4.2–12.6 ha)	4–5	77	12.3
	Two to three horses (= paired team).	30–60 "korec" (8.4–16.8 ha)	6–8	155	24.7
Large fullholding	Four to five horses (= two paired teams, four-in-hand paired team).	60–120 "korec" (16.8–33.6 ha)	9–12	94	15.0
Extremely large fullholding	More than 5 horses (= several paired teams)	90 or more (25.2 ha or more)	over 12	47	7.5
Total	–	–	–	–	–

Source: Ar Cheb, book 1067, *Klosteuerbuch 1438.* Cf. Klír et al., *Knihy,* 286–410.
Note: Only the cases where the value was listed separately, not in summary with other types of cattle.

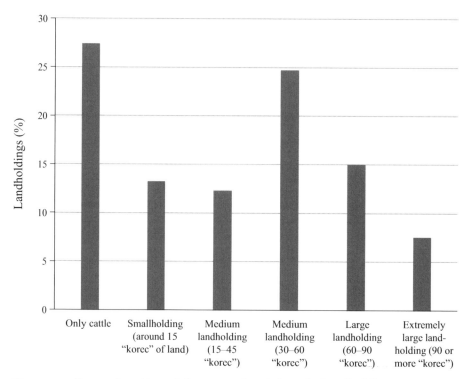

Figure 15.12. Reconstruction of the operational size of a landholding in the city-state of Cheb, 1438.

Source: Ar Cheb, book 1067, *Klosteuerbuch 1438*. See also Klír, "Land transfer," 158, fig. 1.
Note: 1 korec = ca. 0.29 ha.

+ The proportion of landholdings without horses (27%) or with an incomplete or partial paired team (13%) was substantial.
+ Medium-large landholdings with one paired team (37%) were the most common; large landholdings with two or more paired teams were also relatively frequent (23%).
+ For approximately half the landholdings without a paired team, this was a standard situation because they were designated as *Herberge* or they were held by millers and fishermen (54%). In the case of *Hof* landholdings, we may consider this a temporary absence of draft animals.

A prominent correlation can be seen between the absence/presence of horses and the socioeconomic category of the landholding (*tab. 15.6*). The basic characteristic of *Hof* landholdings was ownership of a horse and paired teams

(85% of them). The situation for *Herberge* landholdings was the exact opposite, most of which had no horses (85% of them). Additionally, millers (74%) and fishermen (100%) usually kept cattle, but not horses.

15.6 Millers

The most visible group of the late medieval rural population were those who accumulated extensive wealth and power from multiple sources. Their economic position was largely founded on the ownership and leasing of land or trading in agricultural products; however, they were distinguished from other villagers by a wide range of activities, financial business, and the provision of services. The core of this rural elite consisted of the richest peasants; it also included some millers, innkeepers, bailiffs, grangers, pastors, and some rural craftsmen.[590] These persons should be considered separately, because they may have deviated from the general trends of the peasant population.

In our sources, millers can be positively identified in the 1438 *Land Tax Register*, where mills were specially indicated. Even the right to fishing was listed in the land tax register and the 1456 *Taxation Book*, and people other than just fishermen may have had such a right too. Profession-related surnames appear profusely throughout the land tax register and the taxation book, but they cannot be relied upon. This leaves only the mill tenants for the analysis.

The millers formed a heterogenic group according to the structure of their property and the level of its monetary value.[591] Of the 23 millers whom we can analyze, three also held a further "subject" landholding. Millers ranked among the average or extremely wealthy taxpayers according to the total value of their property, and with only one exception they were not among the poorest of peasants. The value of the "purchase" right to a mill was equal to the values of medium to very expensive *Hof* landholdings. According to the amount and value of kept livestock, millers ranked among below-average taxpayers, although this was due to an absence of horses and not a small amount of

---

590 Aparisi, "Village Entrepreneurs," esp. 336–339, 352; for the best research on the Czech milieu, see Graus, *Dějiny*, 199–209; cf. also Čechura, *Die Strukturen*, 115; Šmahel, *Husitská revoluce*, 430–431.

591 *App.* 15.6.a–d.

cattle. As for the tenure of non-landholding plots, millers corresponded to the average, i.e., most of them did not own any.

15.7 Differences in the nature of settlements
(*figs. 15.15–15.21*)[592]

In this monograph, we analyze individual landholdings, FPSs, ecological zones, and the city-state of Cheb as a whole. We do not focus on individual settlements in our analysis, the main reason being their small and variable size, which limits the effectiveness of a comparison. Nevertheless, we sidestep this rule here and we shall attempt to describe some of the basic distinctions between individual settlements.

The socioeconomic stratification of each individual settlement was unique, and while describing it, we must make an ideal compromise between detail and simplification. The concrete distribution of various FPS property categories and landholdings in the settlements of Cheb is presented in tables in the appendix (*app. 15.9; 15.13–15.14*). Our attempt to characterize the uneven distribution of wealth within the settlements by using the Gini and LAC coefficients failed because it became evident that the Gini coefficient value correlates positively with the number of FPSs in the settlement (*tab. 15.8*). The settlements of the city-state of Cheb were too small to justify the use of the Gini coefficient. Therefore, we simplify reality in a different way, characterizing each settlement with a description of the average taxpayer. We are also interested in any change in a settlement's characteristics and their average taxpayers between 1438 and 1456.

Wilhelm Heisinger also worked with the characteristics of settlements according to a set of averages, and the respective results make up a large portion of his dissertation.[593] In the following segment, we will repeat his calculations, firstly concentrating on the differences between ecological zones and secondly excluding settlements that might distort the interpretation.[594]

---

592   *App. 15.8; 15.12–15.13.*
593   Heisinger, "Die Egerer Klosteuerbücher," 105–270.
594   Such settlements were under the territorial sovereignty of several different authorities; therefore, a part of them were not subject to the land tax. We also exclude those settlements

Table 15.8. **The degree of correlation between the number of FPSs in the settlement and the value of the Gini coefficient in the city-state of Cheb, 1438 and 1456.**

	Correlation coefficient	
	1438	1456
Value of landholding / Gini coefficient	0.78	0.81
Value of livestock / Gini coefficient	0.76	0.73

Source: Ar Cheb, book 1067, *Klosteuerbuch 1438*; book 1084, *Klosteuerbuch (Schätzungsbuch) 1456*.

Generally speaking, settlements with the richest FPSs on average were situated in the agriculturally optimal zone A in 1438 and 1456, while settlements with the poorest FPSs on average were always in the submountainous zone E (*tab. 15.9; figs. 15.13–15.14*).[595] This pattern held true in all cases if we analyze the average monetary value of (1) all property, (2) the tenure right to a landholding, and (3) non-landholding plots of all settlements (*figs. 15.15–15.16*).[596] Non-landholding plots in several zones consistently showed the lowest value of zero; in other words, none of the FPSs in the settlements owned that type of property, although the majority of zero value settlements lay in zone E. Average livestock values did not follow the common trend. In 1438, the settlements with the lowest average value of livestock lay in zone D, but in 1456 zone D contained settlements with the highest average value of livestock.

Also, in 1438 and 1456 settlements with a non-extreme average value of any item of property could exist in any ecological zone. Nevertheless, ecological zones differed in the quantitative representation of settlements with various average values. In this respect, zones A and B, representing the rich extreme of the city-state of Cheb, and zones D and E, representing the poor extreme of the city-state of Cheb, were similar in structure. Zone C fluctuated between both extremes, resembling zones A and B according to the average values of all property in settlements and landholdings and resembling zones D and E according to the average values of livestock. It was situated somewhere in between regarding the average values of non-landholding plots.

that were listed only in 1438 and not in 1456. We are therefore analyzing settlements identical to those in *chap. 14*, overall, 85 settlements in total in 1438 and 1456.

595 *App. 15.7–15.8.*
596 Cf. Klír, *Rolnictvo*, app. 15.15.

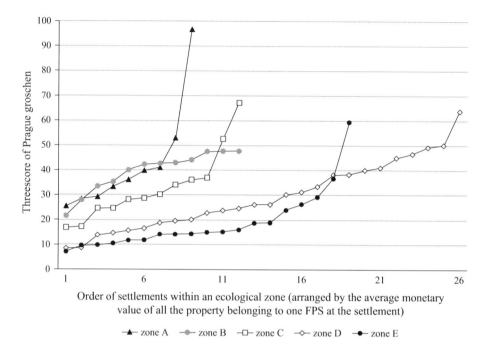

Figure 15.13. Average value of the total property falling to one taxpayer at a settlement in the individual geographic zones of the city-state of Cheb, 1438.

Source: Ar Cheb, book 1067, *Klosteuerbuch 1438*.
Note: Pinpoint depiction of every settlement by ecological zone. For detailed graphs for each property item, cf. *app. 15.5.*

Table 15.9. The most frequent intervals of monetary values of all the property and partial items per taxpayer at a settlement in 1438 and 1456.

	1438	1456	1438					1456				
Monetary value	Average		A	B	C	D	E	A	B	C	D	E
All property	15–30	15–30	30–45		15–30		< 15	30–75	30–45	15–30		
Tenure right to the land-holding	5–10	10–15	10–20		10–15		5–10	10–20		15–20	10–15	5–10
Livestock	9–12	9–12	15–18		9–12		3–9	> 15	> 18	6–12		6–9
Non-land-holding plots	–	–	> 6		< 6		0.0	> 8		< 6		< 2

Source: Cf. *app. 15.7–15.8.*
Note: Values in threescore of Prague groschen.

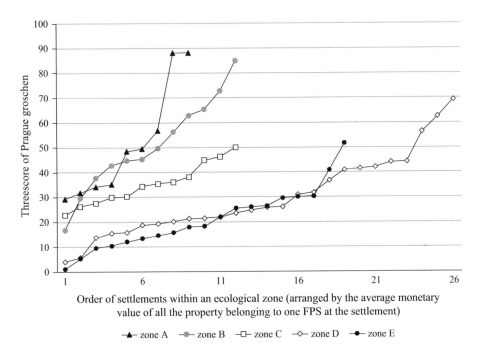

Figure 15.14. **The average value of the total property falling to one taxpayer at a settlement in the individual geographic zones of the city-state of Cheb, 1456.**

Source: Ar Cheb, book 1084, *Klosteuerbuch (Schätzungsbuch) 1456.*
Note: Pinpoint depiction of every settlement by ecological zone. For detailed graphs for each property item, cf. *app. 15.5.*

The question is: how stable were the overall characteristics of settlements between 1438 and 1456? Did the overall wealth accumulated in the settlement and its distribution amongst FPSs remain the same or did it change? Did the settlements change their relative position, or did they stay in roughly the same ranges? Looking at the average values provides at least an approximate answer.

We may gain a rough insight by analyzing the correlation coefficient between the values in 1438 and 1456 (*tab. 15.10*); the graphic representation is more detailed (*figs. 15.17–15.21*).[597] We find the highest degree of stability in the size of the settlements, because in a large amount of them, the number of landholdings remained consistent or changed by one or two. The general tendency was

597   *App. 15.8.*

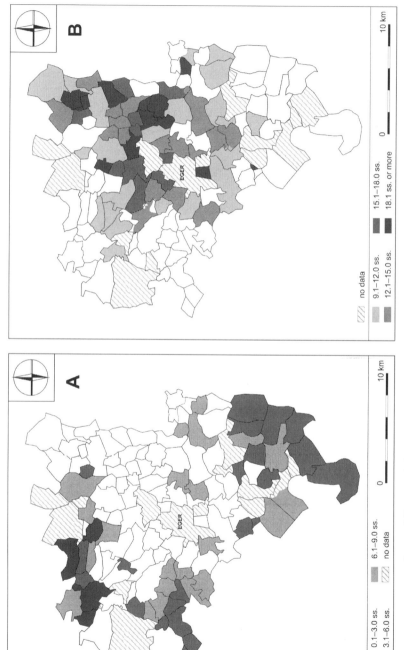

Figure 15.15. Average values of livestock (A–B) in individual settlements in the city-state of Cheb, 1438. Figure (A) shows low values, figure (B) high values. The zonality is striking; the values were generally higher in the heart of the city-state of Cheb and along the Ohře River than in the peripheral submountainous zones.

Source: Ar Cheb, book 1067, Klosteuerbuch 1438. Note: ss. – threescore

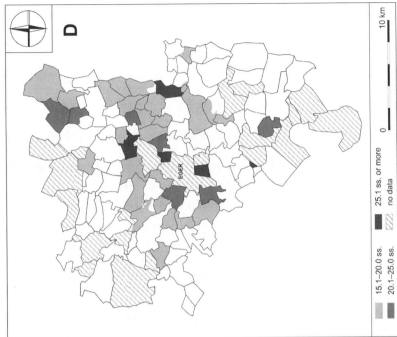

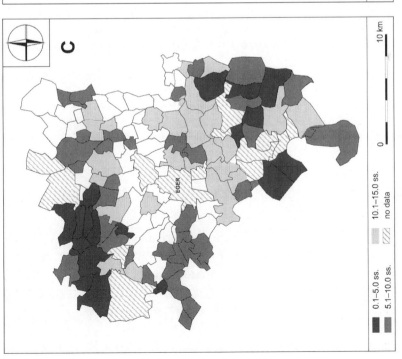

Figure 15.16. Average values of the tenure right to a landholding (C–D) in individual settlements in the city-state of Cheb, 1438. Figure (C) shows low values, figure (D) high values. The zonality is striking; the values were generally higher in the heart of the city-state of Cheb and along the Ohře River than in the peripheral submountainous zones.

Source: Ar Cheb, book 1067, *Klosteuerbuch 1438. Note:* ss. – threescore

a tiny decline. We find the lowest degree of stability in the average values of non-landholding plots. Just a few settlements kept their original average value, while a large proportion changed their status. If we look at *appendix 15.8*, we can gain an impression of the different settlements in the different value ranges in 1438 and 1456. The fluctuation of non-landholding plots between FPSs in various settlements may also explain the changes in the average values of all property.

The average nominal value of the tenure right to the landholdings and of the livestock held by one FPS in a settlement from 1438–1456 increased slightly in most cases, which can be explained by inflation and the devaluation of the Prague groschen. Notable are the more distinct fluctuations, which imply that several settlements had improved or declined economically. The dominant trend in the late medieval city-state of Cheb was stability, but at the same time some settlements may have followed an individual development trajectory.

Table 15.10. **Correlation between characteristics of settlements in the city-state of Cheb, 1438 and 1456.**

	Correlation coefficient (1438–1456)
Number of FPSs with landholdings	0.96
Average value of overall property	0.75
Average value of the tenure right to the landholding	0.76
Average value of livestock	0.82
Average value of other property	0.53

Source: Ar Cheb, book 1067, *Klosteuerbuch 1438*; book 1084, *Klosteuerbuch (Schätzungsbuch) 1456*.
Note: Cf. *app. 15.7a–f; figs. 15.20–15.24*.

15.8 Summary

The evaluation of the property position of all FPSs in the city-state of Cheb for both 1438 and 1456 demonstrated an expected diversity between the main ecological zones. Extremely rich FPSs were more frequent in favorable zones in terms of agriculture and market production than in unfavorable zones. We should perceive more valuable property as being better equipped and having more commercialized landholdings with a larger amount of arable land, horses, and cattle. The situation in the city-state of Cheb indicates that the

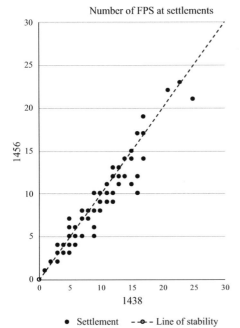

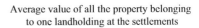

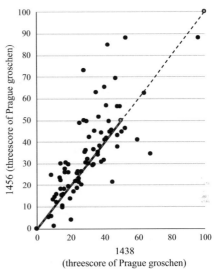

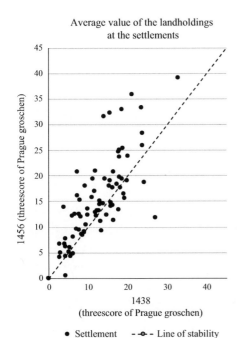

Figures 15.17–15.19. Change in the characteristics of settlements in the city-state of Cheb from 1438-1456.

Source: Ar Cheb, book 1067, *Klosteuerbuch 1438*; book 1084, *Klosteuerbuch (Schätzungsbuch) 1456*.

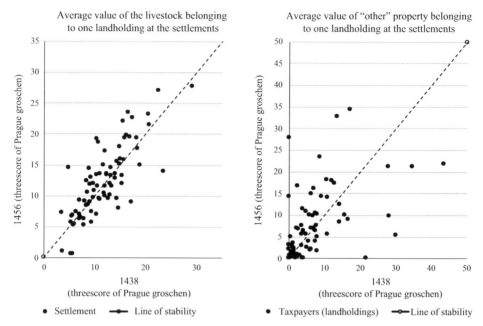

Figures 15.20–15.21. **Change in the characteristics of settlements in the city-state of Cheb from 1438–1456.**

Source: Ar Cheb, book 1067, *Klosteuerbuch 1438*; book 1084, *Klosteuerbuch (Schätzungsbuch) 1456*.

geographically contingent socioeconomic diversity that is well-documented for Early Modern Bohemia had its roots in the Late Middle Ages. Large and market-oriented landholdings predominated in agriculturally favorable zones; medium, mostly subsistence-oriented landholdings were more characteristic of the less favorable hilly areas.

The monetary value helps us reconstruct the number of horses and cattle and thereby also the operational size of a landholding. This is a prerequisite for reconstructing socioeconomic stratification. The equivalent of an ideal, medium-sized, and self-sufficient landholding—the basis of economic models of Czech agrarian history—would have livestock worth around 12 threescore of Prague groschen in the late medieval city-state of Cheb. However, the city-state of Cheb differed from early modern Bohemia in that the majority of the peasantry was not subject to the burden of labor duties.

Model calculations show us that medium-large peasant landholdings with an area of agricultural land ranging from one-quarter to one hide (37%) prevailed in the city-state of Cheb as a whole. Large peasant landholdings (23%) were also considerably represented on one pole and smallholders without a horse-paired team on the other pole (27%).

Settlements in the city-state of Cheb were mostly small, the number of landholdings ranging mostly between 10 and 15. If we compare them based on the average monetary values of all property and main items of property held by one taxpayer, we find that the settlements situated in one ecological zone are usually very similar to each other, although some escape the general trend. The highest average monetary values were in the agriculturally optimal zones A and B, whereas the lowest were in the cold submountainous zone E.

The basic characteristics of a large section of the settlements did not change between 1438 and 1456. The number of landholdings and also the average monetary value of property held by one taxpayer remained stable.

Only the average values of non-landholding plots held by one taxpayer showed noticeable fluctuation between 1438 and 1456. Such properties circulated among settlements due to either migrating taxpayers (FPSs) or landholding transfers between them.

16.
Cheb burghers
and the land market

16.1 Rural land market activity of the Cheb burghers

The peasantry was not the sole actor in the land market in the Cheb country-side; Cheb's burghers also played a role. Without knowing about the activities of Cheb's burghers in connection with rural land, the picture of the peasantry would be incomplete. We aim to determine the degree of the commercial (entrepreneurial) activities of the burghers and their numbers in separate seg-ments of the land market in the Cheb countryside.[598]

Agrarian historians point out the significant role that burghers played in shaping the flexible land market in the Late Middle Ages. However, our current ideas are of a rather qualitative nature, and the quantitative analysis is lacking.[599] In the city-state of Cheb it is possible to observe that the city itself influenced the praxis of land transfer, namely, by (i) the collection of land tax, which caused further homogenization of the legal framework;[600] (ii) the

---

598 On the general problem most recently, see Rezia Krauer, "Die Beteiligung städtischer Akteure am ländlichen Bodenmarkt. Die Region St. Gallen im 13. und 14. Jahrhundert" (PhD diss., Universität Zürich, 2018); Werner Rösener, "Aspekte der Stadt-Land-Bezie-hungen im spätmittelalterlichen Deutschland," *Peasants and townsmen in medieval Europe. Studia in honorem Adriaan Verhulst*, Jean-Marie Duvosquel and Erik Thoen (Gent: Snoeck-Ducaju, 1995), 663–680, on 674; Isenmann, *Die deutsche Stadt*, 679–680; Scott, *Town*, 205.

599 Cerman, "Social Structure," 67–68; Bavel van,and Hoppenbrouwers, "Landholding," 20.

600 For more, see Bavel van and Hoppenbrouwers, "Landholding," 16.

partial registration of purchases and sales; and (iii) the penetration of testamentary practice and city legal customs into the rural area.

Castles and land rent

Like the nobility, burghers also operated in the market with (1) castles and their associated demesne farms and (2) fixed land rents. These activities impeded the flexibility of the land market, and we do not perceive them as progressive in terms of commercialization.

Cheb's burgher families or nobility of burgher origin held 6–7 of the 8 small *castles* in the rural area of Cheb.[601] Nevertheless, the acquisition and possession of prestigious rural property was of no commercial significance; it was rather a channel of vertical socioeconomic mobility and an opportunity for a break from the city. In 1480, none of the seven holders of the castles whose families were of burgher origin had citizenship anymore. On the contrary, all of them identified with the landed nobility and refused (although unsuccessfully) to have their "subject" tenants pay the land tax.[602]

According to the register of the city tax from 1446, at least 42 burghers received **land rent** (a total of 811 grain "kars" [ca. 754 hectoliters], including rye and oats, usually at the rate of 1:1).[603] The standard estimated price of one "kar" of grain rent was then 4 threescore of Prague groschen. We calculate that approximately 8 Cheb "kars" of rye (thus 16 "kars" of the grain rent) were necessary to ensure the subsistence needs of one complete burgher family. Only 17 burghers exceeded this limit, which indicates the notional boundary of commercial activities with grain; the maximum amount of an individual's collected rent was 66.5 "kars."

According to the *1469 Land Tax Register*, land rent was collected by 72 Cheb burghers (913 "kars"),[604] but the boundary of 16 "kars" was only surpassed by one-quarter of the burghers; 54 "kars" was the maximum.[605] Not only was the Cheb burghers' possession of land rent very fragmented, but it also did not generally have much commercial significance. It seems that the grain payments

---

601   Sturm, *Districtus Egranus*, 190–237; Gradl, *Die Chroniken*, 390–422.
602   Heisinger, "Die Egerer Klosteuerbücher," 94–96.
603   Ar Cheb, book 1424, *Losungsbuch 1446*.
604   Burghers that owned castles and strongholds not included.
605   Ar Cheb, book 1096, *Losungsbuch 1469*.

rather served to ensure and supplement the food supply of the burgher families, and thus did not go to the market. Ecclesiastical institutions received land
rent for similar reasons. Land rent was also a suitable financial investment and
a means of providing for one's offspring.

"Free" landholdings and non-landholding plots[606]

The burghers were further involved in the rural land market with (1) "free"
landholdings and (2) non-landholding plots, where they competed with the
peasants. Here, we will use the data from the 1446 *City Tax Register*.

In terms of rural *non-landholding plots*, 46 burghers owned 88.5 "tagwerks"
of meadow and 16.5 unmeasured meadows. A total of 33 burghers then owned
106 measured arable "morgens" and 4 unmeasured fields. Thus, on average one
holder had 3 "tagwerks" of meadow and 3.7 arable "morgens." The maximum
was 8 "tagwerks" of meadow and 10 arable "morgens."

In total comparison, the burghers held a smaller portion of the total amount
of rural non-landholding plots than the peasants, namely 19% of the meadows
and 24% of the fields in terms of size, and 21% of the meadows and 25% of the
fields in terms of price (*tab. 16.1–16.2*). The rest belonged to the peasants. All
this suggests that burghers were actually engaged in the land market for subsistence reasons; evidence of strong entrepreneurial activities is lacking. These
plots enabled the burgher households to only expand the farmland adjacent to
the town.

The average price of the non-landholding plots varied depending on their
location, with those in the city's farmland usually being more expensive than
those in the rural area, which were less expensive. Additionally, rural non-
landholding plots also differed from one another according to whether they
were held by peasants (usually less expensive) or burghers (more expensive).[607]
Hence, burghers either acquired higher-quality plots and/or their activities
increased the prices.

Regarding the direct possession of **demesne farms** by Cheb burghers, it is
useful to add the testimony of the land tax registers (1424, 1438, 1456) and city
tax registers (1446). According to them, the burghers held 12 demesne farms

---

606   See also Klír, "Land transfer," 182–184.
607   *App. 16.1a–b.*

Table 16.1. **The distribution of the rural non-landholding plots and "free" landholdings (demesne farms) between the peasants and burghers in the city-state of Cheb, 1446–1456.**

| 1456/ 1446 | Threescore gr. | | | Number | | | % | | | Holders | |
	Meadows	Fields	"Free" land-holdings/ demesne farms	Meadows	Fields	"Free" land-holdings/ demesne farms	Meadows	Fields	"Free" land-holdings/ demesne farms	Meadows	Fields
Peasants	2,415.7	1,225.1	30	78.6	75.5	71.4	114	75
Burghers	656	398	12	21.4	24.5	28.6	46	33
Total	3,071.7	1,623.1	42	100.0	100.0	100.0	160	108

According to: Klír, "Land transfer," 184, tab. 16.
Source: Ar Cheb, book 1424, *Losungsbuch* 1446; book 1084, *Klosteuerbuch (Schätzungsbuch) 1456*.
Note: city – data from 1446; countryside – data from 1456

(mainly in the immediate vicinity of Cheb), which can be considered as equivalent to the largest "free" landholdings. These demesne farms were, for the most part, retained by burghers over the long-term. Nevertheless, their share was ultimately low, as the number of "free" landholdings in the hands of the peasantry was around 30.

Price structure of the property of Cheb burghers

The register of Cheb city tax from 1446 provides insight into the structure of the properties of almost all of the Cheb burghers (*tab. 16.3; figs. 16.1–16.3*; 1,222 true taxpayers of the city tax). From the overall synopsis, the marginal importance of the rural area properties is clear, among which the most significant item was land rent (6.5%). The very low property percentage of demesne farms and non-landholding plots (4.0% in total) is almost astonishing and testifies to the relatively small commercial importance of direct land possession for late medieval Cheb burghers. Their behavior on the land market did not bear the signs of economic progressivity or a growth initiator, but rather the pursuit of subsistence or—for the richest—a rise among the landed nobility.

The distribution of the monetary values of the burghers' property corresponds to the secular cycle, with very low grain prices. Arable agriculture, which also systematically influenced livestock production, did not open up the possibility of property expansion. Burghers' investment in agricultural land was therefore almost surprisingly low, unlike their investments into trade and urban craft production. The acquisition of castles did have significance, though not of an economic nature but rather a social one.

Table 16.2. **The distribution of the rural non-landholding plots between the peasants and burghers in the city-state of Cheb, 1446–1456.**

1446/1456	Measured plots		%	
	"tagwerks"	"morgens"	Meadows	Fields
Peasants	378.3	336	81.0	76.0
Burghers	88.5	106	19.0	24.0
Total	466.8	442	100.0	100.0

According to: Klír, "Land transfer," 184, tab. 17.
Source: Ar Cheb, book 1424, *Losungsbuch 1446*; book 1084, *Klosteuerbuch (Schätzungsbuch) 1456*.
Note: city – data from 1446; countryside – data from 1456

Table 16.3. **Share of the main property items on the assigned city tax in Cheb, 1446.**

	Asset	%
Town	Houses in Cheb	28.1
	Moveable property – mercantile	18.2
	Meadows and fields in Cheb	11.3
	Other	31.9
Rural area	Land rent and tithes	6.5
	Demesne farms in the hinterland of Cheb and the rural area	2.2
	Meadows and fields outside of Cheb	1.8
Total		100.0

Source: Ar Cheb, book 1424, *Losungsbuch 1446*.

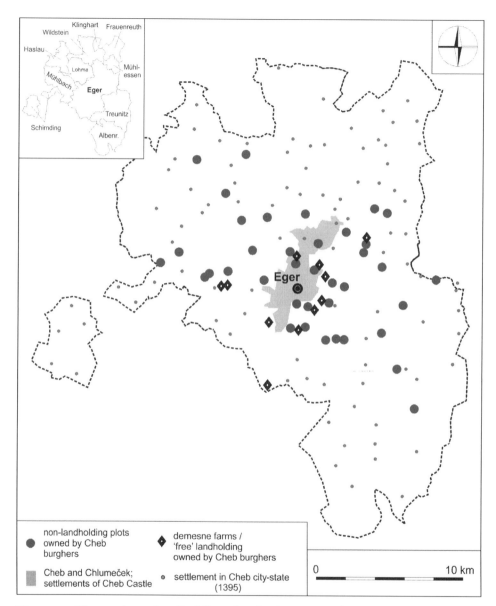

Figure 16.1. **The rural non-landholding plots in the possession of Cheb burghers, 1446.**

Source: Ar Cheb, book 1424, *Losungsbuch 1446.* The demesne farms are partially complemented after the Ar Cheb, book 1060, *Klosteuerbuch 1424.*

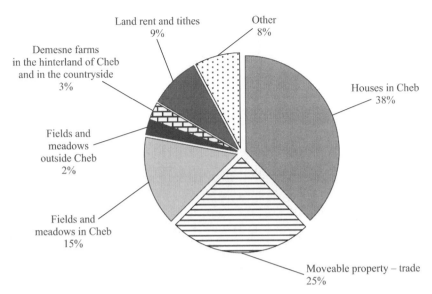

Figure 16.2. The distribution of the taxable property of the Cheb burghers by monetary values, 1446.

Source: Ar Cheb, book 1424, Losungsbuch 1446.

16.2 Agrarian producers in the city of Cheb

The picture of the socioeconomic structure of agrarian producers in the city-state of Cheb would be incomplete without insight into the situation in the city of Cheb. The question is: how many burghers owned agricultural land and did this land have a subsistence or market purpose? Our main source is yet again the 1446 city tax register for its list and characteristics of individual taxpayers' property.[608]

In 1446, the city of Cheb was comprised of 1,222 taxpayers, with a prescribed city tax, where almost one-half owned a house, one-fifth owned a garden, and one-sixth owned other agricultural land such as fields and meadows (*tab. 16.4*). Suburban burghers were three times more likely than inner city burghers to own agricultural land. Thirty-two percent of suburban burghers owned a field or a meadow, whereas for those in the inner city it was only 12%. Tenure of

608   Ar Cheb, book 1424, *Losungsbuch 1446.*

Table 16.4. **Characteristics of taxpayers in the city of Cheb, 1446.**

	Absolute terms			%		
	Inner city	Suburbs	Total	Inner city	Suburbs	Total
Taxpayers according to name	1,072	399	1,477	72.9*	27.1*	100.0*
Taxpayers with prescribed tax	891	331	1,222	72.9*	27.1*	100.0*
Taxpayers with an explicitly listed fireplace	738	275	1,013	72.9*	27.1*	100.0*
Taxpayers with a house, including houses with a garden	363	234	597	40.7**	70.7**	48.9**
Taxpayers with a garden, including houses with a garden	87	158	245	9.8**	47.7**	20.0**
Taxpayers with both a field and a meadow	34	42	76	3.8**	12.7**	6.2**
Taxpayers with only a field	57	54	111	6.4**	16.3**	9.1**
Taxpayers with only a meadow	15	9	24	1.7**	2.7**	2.0**
Total number of taxpayers with agricultural land (field and/or meadow)	106	105	211	11.9**	31.7**	17.3**

Source: Ar Cheb, book Nr. 1424, *Losungsbuch 1446.*
Note:
* proportion of total
** proportion of taxpayers with prescribed tax in the inner city or the suburbs

arable land was more frequent than tenure of meadows. Most of the land lay within the farmland of Cheb or the immediate neighborhood, although tenure of fields in more remote settlements was not exceptional.

In the city's farmland, measured meadows were held by 51 burghers (129.3 "tagwerks"), unmeasured meadows by 26 burghers (26.5 meadows), measured fields by 233 burghers (799.3 "morgens"), and unmeasured fields by 23 burghers (24 fields). Even here, land possession was related to subsistence (*tab. 16.3–16.4*).[609] Comparing burghers with peasants, it is clear that burghers were engaged predominantly in rural land transfer with non-landholding meadows and only to a small extent with arable plots.

Regarding the size of the area, we can only analyze the tenure of measured fields ("morgen") and meadows ("tagwerk"). Eighty-seven percent of tenants in total owned arable land with an area of less than 10 "morgens" (ca. 5.5 ha); an area of 2–4 "morgens" (ca. 1–2 ha) was most frequent for the fields of one tenant (*fig. 16.3*).[610] A small area and fragmentation of land tenure indicate intensive manual labor using a hoe and spade rather than a plough. This meant that burghers could use the labor of women and children, fertilize better, grow a diverse spectrum of produce, flexibly alternate sowing procedures, and reduce the area of fallow land, thus achieving relatively high yields. The fragmented land tenure in Cheb's farmland allowed for the effective usage of the free labor capacity of the burghers and the land.[611]

On average, the number of meadows held by one tenant was half the number of fields. Overall, 84% of tenants owned meadows the size of less than 5 "tagwerks" (ca. 2.9 ha), mostly around 1–2 "tagwerks" (ca. 0.6–1.2 ha; *fig. 16.4*).[612] These figures suggest that burghers were more likely to keep cattle for subsistence purposes.

In conclusion, it is evident that the city of Cheb itself contained the largest number of small and subsistence-oriented agrarian producers in the city-

---

609   *App. 16.1a–b.*

610   *App. 16.2a.*

611   In general terms, cf. Jean-Michel Boehler, "Routine oder Innovation in der Landwirtschaft: ‚Kleinbäuerlich' geprägte Regionen westlich des Rheins im 18. Jahrhundert," in *Ländliche Gesellschaften in Deutschland und Frankreich, 18.–19. Jahrhundert,* ed. Reiner Prass, Jürgen Schlumbohm, Gérard G. Béaur, and Christophe Duhamelle, Veröffentlichungen des Max-Planck-Instituts für Geschichte 187 (Göttingen: Vandenhoeck & Ruprecht, 2003), 101–123, on 107–118.

612   *App. 16.2b.*

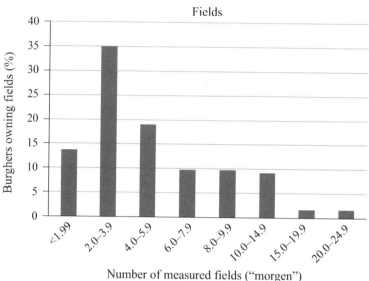

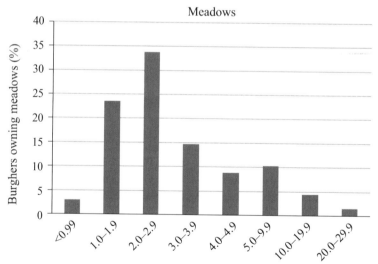

Figures 16.3–16.4. **Area of "morgens" and "tagwerks" in the hands of Cheb burghers in the city's farmland, 1446.**

Source: Ar Cheb, book 1424, *Losungsbuch 1446.*
Note: 1 "morgen" / 1 "tagwerk" = 0.57 ha.

state of Cheb. Even so, such producers (the Cheb burghers) were able to put a portion of their surplus on the market according to the changing situation, and profit from the potential high demand of the city's population, price fluctuations, easy access to their land, and opportunity to balance their work capacity ideally between the agrarian and non-agrarian spheres.[613] The fundamental thing is that the number of smallholders in the city was more or less equal to the total number of smallholders without paired horse teams in the whole Cheb countryside. From our analysis, we can formulate the following hypothesis, which should be the object of further research: a large number of the smallholders living in the town of Cheb could satisfy the city's demand for flexible hired wage labor, which created an impervious barrier around the town that did not advance the expansion of sub-peasant groups in the surrounding countryside.[614]

16.3 Summary

In addition to peasants, burghers also entered the landholding and non-landholding plots market. Peasants were interested in actively using "subject" landholdings, whereas burghers sought land rent. Real competition occurred in the "free" landholding and non-landholding plot market.

In comparison to other European areas, the late medieval city-state of Cheb was among the areas with low landlord restrictions on land transfer, where— to a large extent caused by the city—the institutional and market mechanisms made possible the accumulation of land wealth and the flexible management of economic resources. Nevertheless, the burghers of Cheb did not have a strong or systematic interest in the commercial investment in land and agricultural business; their activities had a subsistence background and were oriented around the non-landholding plots in the vicinity of Cheb. Of the total rural non-landholding plots, one-quarter to one-fifth fell to burghers; the rest was controlled by the peasants. Burghers also had relatively little interest in "free" landholdings, which allowed property to be disposed of flexibly. Only a few of

---

613 Boehler, "Routine," 110.
614 Unfortunately, we know hardly anything about a demand for wage laborers in the Cheb countryside.

them, usually in the closest hinterland of Cheb, were controlled in the long-term by burghers, and these landholdings then functioned as demesne farms and often also as residences. The model by which the Cheb burghers acted thus corresponds to a period with minimum grain prices that did not encourage agricultural business.

Analysis of the city of Cheb revealed that almost as many small agrarian producers with land tenure up to 5.5 ha of arable land lived in the city as in the entire city-state of Cheb. The large number of smallholders with an available labor capacity, primarily living in the Cheb suburbs, did not contribute to the growth of "sub-peasant" groups in the Cheb countryside. Hypothetically, we posit that the socioeconomic structure of agrarian producers in the city was complementary and systemically connected with the socioeconomic structure of the peasantry in the countryside.

◂ Plate 6: **Vackovec (Watzkenreuth). View of the fortified house and the surrounding buildings (1900). In the middle of the 15th century, Hans Ruprecht held the free landholding with the tower-like building and was granted citizenship, but retained the country estate. The photograph shows several layers of the farmstead over time – the late-medieval tower-like structure, followed by the early modern dwelling house, with its ornately timbered upper floor, surrounded by modern brick farm buildings. Small wooden buildings of post and beam construction are in the foreground along the road.**

V.
Socioeconomic Mobility and Migration

The previous portion of this work introduced the reader to the issue of the socioeconomic stratification of the Cheb peasantry, its historical context, and the differentiating and equalizing powers that it generated. Now, we turn our attention to an actual analysis of socioeconomic mobility and migration.

17.
Questions and methods

17.1 Analyzed phenomena

In the following chapters, we test models explaining the socioeconomic stratification and mobility of the European peasantry. We test primarily the *polarization model*, the *cycle model*, and the *model of uneven reproduction*. Each of
these models predicts certain relationships between wealth and (1) the continuity of landholding tenure, i.e., the rate of family replacement on the same
landholding, (2) the trajectory of socioeconomic mobility across a life cycle and
between generations, and (3) migration. These three empirical phenomena are
not independent of each other, but they are different and measured in different
ways.[615] According to the nature of the sources that we have available to us
for addressing the separate issues, we examine a time span in the city-state of
Cheb of either 18 years (1438–1456) or 14 years (1442–1456). We address the
following research sub-areas:

I. Family ties to the land: The relationship between wealth and the continuity of property tenure

1) *Analysis of the connection between the material wealth of family property societies (FPSs) and continuity of property tenure in 1438–1456.*
   We ask: How many FPSs recorded in 1438 endured on the same landholding until 1456? How many FPSs dissolved but had some familial continuity

---

615   This commentary according to Jonas Lindström.

on the same landholding? Was stability of property tenure characteristic of relatively wealthy FPSs, and was the degree of family continuity higher than for poor FPSs? Did poor FPSs more frequently abandon or change their landholdings? *Chap. 18.*

2) *Analysis of the connection between the value of the landholding and the intensity of landholding transfers in 1442–1456.*

The question is: How many transfers occurred in individual landholdings during the focus period? And what type of transfer did this involve? In other words, were these intrafamilial transfers a result of inheritance procedures (transfers between relatives) or market transfer due to the tenant moving from one landholding to another? Again, we are interested in whether the degree of intrafamilial transfers differed for large and valuable landholdings compared to smallholdings. *Chap. 19.*

II. Relationship between wealth and socioeconomic mobility

3) *Analysis of the socioeconomic mobility of FPSs and the intergenerational mobility of GFPSs[616] on the same landholding.*

For the period 1438–1456, we examine whether the rich and poor FPSs that were settled on the same landholding differed in terms of wealth accumulation. We also ask whether the level of the wealth of the FPS influenced the wealth of the family successors on the same landholding. *Chap. 20.* We address the fate of FPSs that moved from one landholding to another in *chapter 22.*

4) *Analysis of tax fluctuations on the same landholding.*

In this chapter, we deal with the potential objection that the socioeconomic position of an FPS from 1438–1456 could fluctuate and that the developments in property that we interpolate were not linear. We therefore focus on the nominal value of tax prescribed for each landholding over a two-year period and establish the extent to which the property trajectory of an FPS was direct or indirect. *Chap. 21.*

---

616   GFP – a genetically connected family property society.

III. Migration analysis

5) *Analysis of the socioeconomic aspects of migration.*
We examine how a tenant's (FPS's) property situation changed upon them moving from one landholding to another. Did tenants of poor landholdings move to even poorer landholdings, or did they then inhabit wealthier landholdings? Where did the tenants of wealthy landholdings move to? Did moving within a settlement and out of a settlement differ in these aspects? ***Chap. 22.***
Further, we examine the extent to which FPSs formed a geographically ramified system and whether a change of the FPS on one landholding could trigger a chain reaction across the region. ***Chap. 22.***
6) *Mobility between city and countryside.*
We follow the property position of persons and families that migrated from the countryside to the city of Cheb. ***Chap. 23.***

17.2 Analytical units

FPSs and GFPSs

On the analytical level, we work with FAMILY PROPERTY SOCIETIES (FPSs). Each FPS was unique; it was created at a certain moment and then ended with the death (or retirement) of the tenant or his widow. The FPS was shaped by familial and kinship ties. We label two FPSs that can be connected by a family tie as a GENETICALLY CONNECTED FPS (GFPS). In the sources, we identify a GFPS based on the same name (usually tenant → his son) or the label of the family tie (tenant → his son-in-law). The disappearance of an FPS from one landholding does not mean its end. There have been cases when one FPS during its existence alternated between one or more landholdings. Members of the same FPS could change, so we judge its continuity according to the tenant—the taxpayer listed in the land tax registers.

Landholdings

The core of property tenure of each FPS was the landholding, which could have various legal and socioeconomic statuses. In the city-state of Cheb, one

FPS usually held one "subject" landholding with livestock. Approximately 5–6% of FPSs held rights of tenure to more than one landholding.

We may describe a landholding in two ways, both of which are equally important: firstly, according to the monetary value of the tenure right, which for "subject" landholdings was the "purchase" right; and secondly, according to livestock values, usually draft horses, cattle, and sheep. Both values express qualitative and quantitative aspects of tenure. The value of the "purchase" right expresses the degree of attainability of the landholding, and the value of draft horses, together with the value of cattle, expresses the size of the economic operation of the landholding, demands on the labor force, and also the area of the cultivated land (cf. *chap. 14*).

17.3 Ecological zonality

We analyze FPSs and their landholdings both for the city-state of Cheb as a whole and also in terms of the ecological zones. The reason for this is that extremely rich FPSs were more frequent in favorable zones in terms of agriculture and market production than in unfavorable zones (cf. esp. *chap. 15*). If we assessed the peasantry of the city-state of Cheb as a whole, the relative distribution of FPSs according to wealth would reflect the distribution of ecological zones. The FPSs at the top of the socioeconomic pyramid in the unfavorable zone E would be just average in terms of wealth in comparison with FPSs in the agriculturally optimal zones A and B. By assessing FPSs and landholdings in each zone separately, we can tell the extent to which certain phenomena are general and to what extent they are geographically specific.

17.4 Catastrophic events

Our results may be distorted by the fact that certain rural settlements were plundered or burnt to the ground during local military conflicts.[617] A down-

---

617   Klír, "Procesy pustnutí," 724–733.

wardly mobile FPS could therefore correlate with the tenants of plundered landholdings, while an upwardly mobile FPS could therefore correlate with the tenants of unplundered landholdings. For this reason, in our analysis of the absolute socioeconomic mobility of FPSs and GFPSs, we included the catastrophe factor and tested its significance (*chap. 20.3*). We have not taken into account all catastrophes reported from 1429–1456,[618] but only those that occurred after 1450.

During the focus period, a local conflict between the city of Cheb and the Burgrave of Meissen, Henry II of Plauen, which occurred in 1452, was the greatest scourge in the region, destroying around one-fifth of the settlements in the city-state of Cheb. Various disasters hit individual landholdings across the entire city-state of Cheb, and the tax registers inform us fairly accurately about these events (cf. *chap. 12.4*).[619]

17.5 Statistical methods

Research into the socioeconomic mobility of past and contemporaneous peasant populations applies a wide range of statistical approaches and methods that can simplify reality. In this study, we apply two of them:[620]

1) The classic and oldest method is to order peasant households/families according to wealth, and then divide them into smaller groups (ranges) and examine whether the same family remained in the same group or if it changed its position. The groups may be compiled in two ways: firstly, in a way that would reflect certain absolute values of wealth,[621] and secondly,

618   Klír et al., *Knihy*, 163–166.
619   Klír, "Procesy pustnutí," 727–728.
620   On other methods cf. esp. Gregory Clark, "Measuring inequality through the strength of inheritance," *Current Anthropology* 51 (2010): 101–102; Shenk et al., "Intergenerational Wealth," 81; Borgerhoff et al., "Intergenerational"; McGuire and McC. Netting, "Leveling Peasants," 275–277, fig. 3.
621   For illustration, see the approach of Russian agrarian economists. Cf. Alexander Tschaja-now, *Die Lehre von der bäuerlichen Wirtschaft. Versuch einer Theorie der Familienwirtschaft im Landbau* (Berlin: Parey, 1923; reprint: Frankfurt, New York: Campus-Verlag, 1987), 23, 97–100, 104, Tab. 10, 67–71, 76; Shanin, "Socio-Economic Mobility"; Shanin, "Measuring," 234–242.

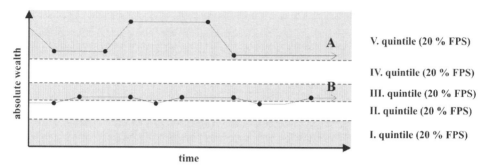

Figure 17.1. **Interpretation of quintiles. FPS (A) appears stable because its position remains in the same quintile, even though the absolute value of its property fluctuates dramatically and falls in the final third. Conversely, FPS (B) runs between quintiles and therefore appears unstable, despite that its position changes just minimally in terms of absolute values. During interpretation, it is therefore essential to follow the absolute definition of quintiles.**

Source: Prepared by the author.
Note: Cf. *app.* C–G.

by evenly dividing the population into equally large quantiles—most often medians, tertiles, quartiles, quintiles, and deciles.[622] Such an approach has the advantage of being simple and illustrative, while it risks distorting the testimony if the groups are compiled incommensurately (*fig. 17.1*). The range of quantiles that we worked with within this study is summarized in *appendices A–C.*

2) One may also proceed graphically and pinpoint the property position of each peasant family in two time segments. The two-dimensional graph may be based on an ordinary linear or even a logarithmic scale. A stability diagonal is usually formed in the graph.[623] The advantage of graphic depiction lies in its completeness; the disadvantage, in reduced clarity.

622   Quartiles were applied, for instance, by Lindström, *Distribution,* esp. 167–168.
623   E.g., Attwood, "Why some," 502–503, fig. 5.

17.6 **Length of the focus period**

The length of the analyzed period, which is 14 or 18 years, is relatively short and does not exceed the average reproduction period of one generation. It is therefore unsurprising that some FPSs remained at the same landholding for the entire period. Nevertheless, the resolution of the set questions is not threatened in any way by the short focus period, because we assume that in the period of the assessment of the peasant property in 1438, the tenants and their families were in various stages of their life cycles. If there were no socio-economic or cultural "filter," then in the following 14 years the FPS would end due to the influence of biological circumstances, evenly across all property, legal, and socioeconomic categories and ecological zones. However, if a socio-economic "filter" existed, we would find differences between the property categories. In this study, we focus on the relative differences.

18.
Continuity and stability of family tenure: 1438–1456

18.1 Introduction

Our objective is to establish whether the degree of wealth influenced the stability and continuity of property tenure, in other words, on family ties to the land. The focus of our interest are cases where an FPS endured on the *same landholding* for the entire focus period of 1438–1456, or, if it did not endure, was still maintained by a community of relatives headed by a widow, son, brother, or other close relative of the original tenant.

We analyze the following phenomena:

a) The proportion of landholdings where the tenant and his FPS did not change between 1438 and 1456—i.e., continuity was maintained on the landholding (= continuous FPS).

b) The proportion of landholdings where, although the tenants changed once or more, the landholding remained in the family—the successor of the FPS became a GFPS (= continuous GFPS).

c) The overall proportion of landholdings that remained in the hands of the same family (= /a/+/b/).

We analyze separately FPSs with tenure of (1) "subject" and "free" landholdings, (2) one or more landholdings or parts thereof, and (3) *Hof* landholdings, *Herberge* landholdings, and *Höfel* landholdings.

18.2 Method[624]

Data processing

Our analysis follows the *1438 Land Tax Register* and the *1456 Taxation Book*.[625] The first step was to transfer the data contained in both books into two separate databases. For each taxpayer (i.e., head of an FPS), we noted the monetary value of his taxed property and separate items—the value of the tenure right to the landholding, livestock values, non-landholding plots, and potentially further items. Other information was also recorded, such as the legal status of the items.

In the second step, we linked up both databases by identifying identical landholdings. Connecting a landholding from 1438 with the identical landholding in 1456 was no easy task, since the order of the landholdings (taxpayers) within one settlement was different not only in the 1438 register and the *1456 Taxation Book*, but also in ordinary annual registers. For this reason, it was necessary to compare the entries in all the tax registers surviving for 1438–1456 and follow ongoing changes in landholding tenants. Even so, it proved impossible to reconstruct a complete chain and to identify all landholdings across the registers.

Throughout 1438–1456, organic changes occurred, such as the disappearance, splitting, and merging of some landholdings.[626] We followed all such phenomena and included them in the database. In the database, we also entered data on concrete changes in tenants, continuity within one family (more precisely, those with the same surname), widows at the head of FPSs, etc. Also examined were all interventions into the economic operation of landholdings, such as fires, looting, and loss of horses and cattle.

As for the size of the analyzed set, the *1438 Land Tax Register* cites 950 taxpayers or FPSs, of which 901 demonstrably held a landholding (*tab. 18.1–18.2*). It proved to be impossible for various reasons to analyze all FPSs, since for some only the tax rate was shown but not the estimated property, or else the landholding was empty, etc. In total, we have data in 1438 for just 833 FPSs

---

624   See also Klír, "Land transfer," 167–170.
625   Klír et al., *Knihy*.
626   Between 1442 and 1456, 14 landholdings were divided into two parts, taking the total number of landholdings that could be assessed to 547. In the same time period, 37 landholdings merged.

Table 18.1. **Statistical overview of the analyzed data in the city-state of Cheb, 1438–1456.**

	1438	1456
FPSs (taxpayers)	950	783
FPSs with landholdings	901	739
Assessable set of FPSs	833	699
Assessable set of FPSs in 96 localities*	799	548
Linked landholdings	504	
Continuous FPSs on the same landholding	226	
Genetically linked FPSs (GFPSs) on the same landholding	55	

Source: Ar Cheb, book 1067, *Klosteuerbuch 1438*; book 1084, *Klosteuerbuch (Schätzungsbuch) 1456.*
Note: FPS – family property society; * – settlements with taxpayers listed by name and characterized in detail in 1438 and 1456.

Table 18.2. **Representation of ecological zones in the focus sample, 1438–1456.**

Ecological zone	A	B	C	D	E	Total
Linked landholdings (1438–1456)	53	58	91	165	137	504
Continuous FPSs on the same landholding (i.e., tenant continuity)	25	34	43	76	48	226
Genetically linked FPSs (GFPSs) on the same landholding (i.e., generational exchange, continuity of family, not tenant)	4	10	9	19	12	55

Source: Ar Cheb, book 1067, *Klosteuerbuch 1438*; book 1084, *Klosteuerbuch (Schätzungsbuch) 1456.*
Note: FPS – family property society.

at our disposal; in 1456 there are 699 of such analyzable FPSs. Data for 504 landholdings have proved to be possible to link together.[627] In addition to such linked landholdings, we could also include those where we lost tenant continuity immediately between the 1438 register and the nearest subsequent 1442

---

627 It was irrelevant for us whether this particular FPS held a landholding that was possible to identify in the 1438 register and in the 1456 *Taxation Book*; in this we differ from the approach of previous studies, so we have been able to establish the results more precisely, but the final interpretation remains unchanged. Klír, "Socioeconomic Mobility"; Klír, "Sociálně-ekonomická mobilita."

register. This is because if it was not possible to find a certain tenant in the 1442 register who had been listed in 1438, it automatically meant that the landholding's tenant had changed.

Analytical method

The method we have chosen is quantile analysis. We ordered all FPSs and their landholdings in ascending order for both 1438 and 1456 and for both the entire city-state of Cheb and each ecological zone separately, according to the monetary value of (1) all taxed property, (2) "purchase" right to the landholding, and (3) livestock. Subsequently, we divided the series of "subject" FPSs into five identically large sections—quintiles—both for the city-state of Cheb as a whole and for the separate ecological zones. The first quintile contained 20% of the poorest FPSs and the fifth quintile contained 20% of the wealthiest FPSs. Due to their low number, we divided the FPSs with "free" landholdings into tertiles and the FPSs with several landholdings in their tenure into medians (*app. A–B*).

Of course, a concrete FPS may have belonged in a different quantile according to the value of livestock, the value of tenure right to the landholding, or the total value of the property (*tab. 18.3*). The majority of the FPS tenants of "subject" landholdings always belonged in the same or neighboring quintile (72%).

Table 18.3. **Overview of the property position of FPSs in quintiles according to the total value of property, landholding, and livestock in the city-state of Cheb, 1438.**

	FPSs always in the identical quintile	FPSs in different quintiles (number expresses the extent of difference)				Incomplete data*	Total
		1	2	3	4		
Number	199	263	107	32	6	35	642
%	31.0	41.0	16.7	5.0	0.9	5.5	100.0

Source: Ar Cheb, book 1067, *Klosteuerbuch 1438*.

Note: Quintile identicalness means that, for instance, one FPS falls into the first quintile according to the total value of property, landholding, and livestock. A quintile differentiation of 2 means that, for instance, an FPS falls into the second quintile according to landholding value and in the fourth quintile according to livestock value.

* – value of property item not listed in tax register

The important thing is that the economic resources of a landholding represented an integral system, and in effect, wealthy FPSs were often linked to landholdings with a tenure right of high monetary value. In other words, a large number of horses, cattle, and sheep usually indicated a landholding with a corresponding size of farmland and buildings, from the point of view of quantity, quality, or social prestige. Nonetheless, this was not a strict rule, but rather a generally applicable tendency (cf. *chap. 14*).

Demographic data – identifying family relations

In reconstructing family ties, we rely in principle on name matches (correspondence). We consider an FPS to be continuous if a person of identical name is cited as heading the FPS every year in the land tax register. We also consider an FPS to be continuous in a situation where the name is made more precise, such as when a baptismal name is added to the surname. Change of tenant could be identified if the tax officials differentiated father and son in the register using the adjectives or *"alt"* and *"jung."*

Evidence of the disintegration of the original FPS and the creation of a GFPS can be found in cases where the name of the original taxpayer in the tax register is replaced by a new name, but kinship can still be assumed. Most often, this involved situations in which the new taxpayer had the same surname as the preceding taxpayer, or where a mention is made in the register that the new taxpayer is a son or son-in-law. Widows were possible to recognize using the genitive suffix *"-in"* (*tab. 18.4*). However, we are unable to identify many types of kinship and succession in the female line. The number of GFPSs will

Table 18.4. **Example of the identification of the intrafamilial landholding transfer (FPS → GFPS).**

Settlement	Number of landholdings	Interval	Name in the tax register
Horní Lažany / Losau, Ober-	3	1438–1453	Hensel Prentel
		1454–1455	Hanns Prentelin
		1456	Hanns Prenttel

According to: Klír, "Land transfer," 169, tab. 7.
Source: The registers of the Cheb land tax from 1438, 1442–1456; book 1084, *Klosteuerbuch (Schätzungsbuch) 1456.*

thus be underestimated in our analysis in favor of continuous FPSs and discontinuous tenure of landholdings (*tab. 18.6*).

From a methodological viewpoint, it is important that surnames (in the sense of family names) were mostly stabilized in the city-state of Cheb by the 15th century. Nevertheless, it is pointless to trace the continuity of names in the case of occupational names that could have been passed on with the landholding, so we have excluded such persons and their landholdings ("Fischer," "Schmid," and "Mülner").[628]

Our records are slightly distorted in situations in which the original tenant died, leaving behind non-adult orphans, with the landholding then subsequently passing to the widow who married again soon after. The name of the second husband would then appear in the register as the new tenant who was responsible for the landholding and taxes only until the orphans came of age. In such cases, family continuity looks like discontinuity. For this reason, we carefully studied the complete sequence of tenants for all landholdings. A surname formula X → Y → X actually occurred for several landholdings (*tab. 18.5*).[629]

Table 18.5. **Case of identification of landholding transfer within one family, probably via a guardian or the widow's new husband (FPS → GFPS).**

Village	Nr.	Range	Name	Sequence
Jesenice / Gaßnitz	18	1438–1447	Maier Fridel	X
		1448–1452	Wolfel Custer	Y
		1453 and onward	Maierfridel	X

Source: Registers of the Cheb land tax from 1438, 1442–1456; book 1084, *Klosteuerbuch (Schätzungsbuch)* 1456.
Note: The transfer was probably mediated by the guardian or husband of the widow.

Systematic error

In our analysis, we may assume a systematic error due to the fact that we judge family relations mainly based on matching names, which means that we see patrilineal succession (following the male line) but not matrilineal (following

---

628   For more on the method of identification of identical peasants according to name in medieval written sources, see, e.g., DeWindt, "Redefining," 169–171.
629   Drahov/Trogau 5; Starý Rybník/Altenteich 8; Jesenice/Gaßnitz 18 and 23.

Table 18.6. **Testimonial value of data found for assessing continuity and stability of landholding tenure.**

Identified in our records as		In reality, may also partially include
Continuous FPS	overestimated	GFPS
GFPS	underestimated	–
Discontinuous tenure	overestimated	GFPS

the female line). We may approximately quantify the extent of this error by comparison with the Early Modern Period.

We assume that we can identify patrilineal succession in tax registers according to matching names, while we can identify matrilineal succession according to widow and in some cases also according to son-in-law. Of all available studies, the results of Josef Grulich from his research on an early modern district of Vřesce (South Bohemia) are best suited for comparison, because they were classified in a manner that we can apply.[630] If we were to identify intrafamilial landholding transfers for the Vřesce district based only on matching names, we would identify around 75% of the cases. If we identified all sons-in-law correctly, around 90% would be correct. According to these analogies, the main body of intrafamilial landholding transfers that we are capable of identifying based on matching surnames are transfers from father to son and from widowed mother to son. The proportion of such transfers represents the lower threshold of our systematic error; according to early modern data, this was around 60%. In this case, for comparison we also use other studies concerning the Early Modern Period.[631]

The data we have found on the total number of continuous FPSs, GFPSs, and discontinuity in the tenure of Cheb landholdings must be assessed with care, since it only approximately approaches past reality. Identified family transfers of FPS → GFPS predominantly include transfers between father or widowed mother and son. We can estimate that there were in fact one-sixth to one-third more family transfers.

From the point of view of interpretation, the main thing is that data for all ecological zones and for rich and poor are burdened with more or less the same

---

630   *App. 18.1a.* Grulich, *Populační vývoj,* 302–309.
631   *App. 18.1b.* Velková, *Krutá vrchnost;* Zeitlhofer, *Besitzwechsel,* 208. Unfortunately, we cannot use Štefanová, *Erbschaftspraxis,* 76, 80.

systematic error. The relative differences should therefore be close to reality. Despite all skepticism, the analysis of land tax registers should fairly reliably demonstrate the differences between the fates of rich and poor and between the lifetime prospects of families in different ecological zones.

18.3 "Subject" landholdings – the city-state of Cheb as a whole

Continuity of the same tenant (FPS)

In the city-state of Cheb as a whole, almost 75% of FPSs recorded in 1438 had disintegrated by 1456 (fig. 18.1).[632] The degree of continuity was not distributed evenly, but to a certain extent depended on the original property position. In all cases, the lowest degree of continuity is found in the poorest quintile

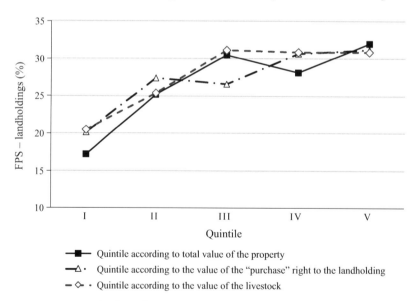

— ■ — Quintile according to total value of the property

— △ · Quintile according to the value of the "purchase" right to the landholding

— ◇ · Quintile according to the value of the livestock

Figure 18.1. **Continuity of tenants on the same "subject" landholdings (FPS) in the city-state of Cheb, 1438–1456.**

Source: Cf. app. 18.2a.

632   *App. 18.2a.*

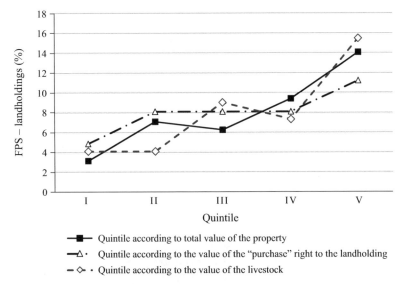

Figure 18.2. The familial continuity on the same "subject" landholdings (GFPS) in the city-state of Cheb, 1438–1456.

Source: Cf. app. 18.2a.

(17–21%) and the highest in the richest quintile (31–32%), regardless of whether we follow quintiles set according to total property values, values of "purchase" right to the landholding, or values of livestock.

Landholding transfer within one family (GFPS)

Also, the degree of family reproduction on the same landholding shows striking dependence on property position (*fig. 18.2*).[633] The proportion of GFPSs created from disintegrated FPSs based on kinship, as far as we can judge according to matching names, was in the region of 3–15%. In the poorest quintiles, the proportion was always noticeably lower (3–4%) than in the richest quintiles (11–15%). In quintiles set according to the total value of property, the difference was almost five-fold, in quintiles according to the value of "purchase" right to a landholding it was two-fold, and for livestock, the difference was almost four-fold.

633   *App. 18.2b.*

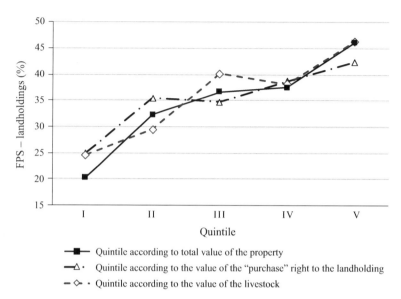

Figure 18.3. **The continuity of family property societies (FPS+GFPS) in the city-state of Cheb, 1438–1456.**

Source: Cf. app. 18.2a.

Continuity of family property tenure (FPS plus GFPS)

If we follow familial continuity on the same landholding in general (i.e., the sum of proportions of continuous FPSs and GFPSs), significant differences between quintiles naturally occur again (*fig. 18.3*).[634] We find familial continuity on the same landholding in 19–25% of FPSs in the poorest quintile and in 42–46% in the richest quintile. The likelihood of a family reproducing on the same landholding for the entire focus period was twice as probable on the richest landholdings compared to the poorest.

Extremely poor and rich FPSs

For orientation, we examined the extent to which this general trend influenced extremely poor and rich FPSs; specifically it applied in 5% of the poorest and 5% of the richest FPSs recorded for the year 1438. The values for 5% of the

634   *App. 18.2c.*

poorest FPSs are similar to the values in quintile I, and the values for 5% of the richest FPSs are similar to the values in quintile V. The average values in quintiles were not distorted significantly by FPSs with property extremes.

18.4 "Subject" landholdings – the city-state of Cheb according to ecological zones

The city-state of Cheb was not geographically or economically uniform, so the question arises as to the degree of disparity in individual zones. For each zone, we have various numbers of taxpayers, but always a sufficiently large sample in statistical terms. We ordered taxpayers in each zone separately and set a special quintile range for each particular zone.[635]

Continuity of the same tenant (FPS)

Although we can see small differences in tenant continuity between zones as a whole, the same tendency applies (fig. 18.4).[636] The total proportion of tenants (FPSs) who remained on landholdings throughout the focus period was more or less identical in zones A–B and D (28–30%), slightly lower in zone C (26–27%), and lowest in zone E (24–25%). The proportion of continuous FPSs rose in the property quintile in zones A and C–E, where a minimum of continuous FPSs lay in a poorer quintile than the maximum number. Specifically, a minimum (8–25%) lay most often in quintiles I and II and the maximum (32–54%) in quintiles IV and V, regardless of whether we assess the total value of property, "purchase" right to the landholding, or livestock values. We have not established a connection between the proportion of FPSs and the property quintile in zone B where a minimum (8–23%) were located in a richer quintile than the maximum (33–42%). This zone did not follow the tendency that applied in most of the city-state of Cheb.

---

635   This means, amongst other things, that, for instance, the value of the taxpayers' overall property in quintile IV in zone E in absolute terms was identical with the wealth of landholdings in quintiles I and II in zone A. In other words, a relatively rich landholding lying in zone E would be relatively poor if it were to lie in zone A.

636   App. 18.3a; fig. 18.4; App. 18.4a.

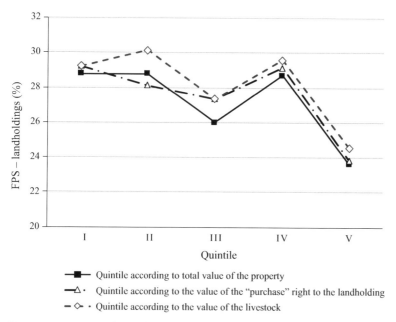

Figure 18.4. Proportion of "subject" landholdings, where the same tenant endured between 1438 and 1456 (continuity of FPS). Synoptic graph for the zones as a whole.

Source: Cf. app. 18.4b.

Landholding transfer within one family (GFPS)

The proportion of GFPSs that ensured the continuity of family tenure in the focus period rose in the quintiles set according to the total values of property and livestock in all zones.[637] In all cases, a minimum (0–4%) lay in poorer quintiles than the maximum (13–31%). Specifically, the minimum lay most often in quintiles I and II, and the maximum in quintile V (with just one exception). If we assess quintiles set according to the value of the "purchase" right to a landholding, we find a similar tendency in zones A and C–E, with the situation being different only in zone B (*fig. 18.5*). The connection between property position and continuity of family tenure is very accentuated and applicable across all zones.

---

637   *App. 18.4b; App. 18.3b.*

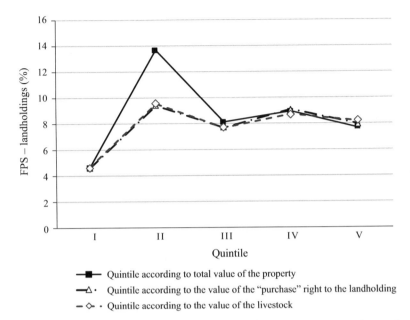

Figure 18.5. **Proportion of "subject" landholdings where, despite a change in tenant between 1438 and 1456, familial continuity of tenure (GFPS) was maintained. Synoptic graph for the zones as a whole.**

Source: Cf. tab. 18.4.
Note: We do not distinguish between variously wealthy FPSs.

Continuity of family property tenure (FPSs and GFPSs)

Family property continuity was highest in zones B and D (38–42%), lower in zones A and C (33–35%), and the lowest in zone E (31–33%).[638] The connection between continuity of family tenure and property position is best shown by quintiles set based on livestock values. In this case, the highest proportion of FPSs and GFPSs (45–69%) appeared in quintile V and in one case in quintile IV. The lowest values occurred most frequently in quintile I (15–28%) and once in quintile III. A similarly positive correlation between the continuity of family property tenure and property position is shown in quintiles set according to the total value of property and "purchase" right to a landholding in zones A and C–E. The connection is less accentuated only in zone B.

Summary

Analysis of continuity and stability according to property quintiles showed that rich FPSs in all zones reproduced on the same landholding considerably more frequently than poor FPSs. The highest degree of familial stability and continuity was demonstrated in FPS reproduction in the agroclimatically favorable zones A and B and the lowest in zone D and submountainous zone E. In light of the results from *chap. 18.3*, this is unsurprising, since the wealth of the FPSs in zones A and B was higher on average than in other zones. At the same time, we can investigate internal differences between zones that in effect are internal differences between generally wealthier FPSs and generally poorer FPSs. Overall, it therefore applies that the greatest stability and continuity in the city-state of Cheb was displayed by rich FPSs in the agroclimatically favorable zones A and B, while the least stability by poor FPSs in zone D and submountainous zone E.

In summary, we can confirm that the general tendency for the city-state of Cheb can be found in zones A and C–E, and less distinctively in zone B.

18.5 Landholding categories

During the Early Modern Period, there was a higher degree of fluctuation of tenants on smallholdings than on peasant fullholdings. The natural question, therefore, is: what differences existed between landholdings of various socioeconomic categories in the late medieval city-state of Cheb? Given that the values of *Herberge* landholdings were on average lower than that of *Hof* landholdings, we would expect also a smaller degree of familial continuity on *Herberge* landholdings and a higher degree on *Hof* landholdings. This expectation was fully confirmed. During the focus period, the degree of familial reproduction was actually twice as high on *Hof* landholdings than on *Herberge* landholdings (*tab. 18.7*).[639]

---

639 *App. 18.5.*

Table 18.7. Level of the continuity of tenure according to the socioeconomic categories of the landholdings in the individual geographic zones of the city-state of Cheb, 1438-1456.

Zone	Herberge landholdings				Hof landholdings				Höfel landholdings			
	Number	FPS	GFPS	FPS+GFPS	Number	FPS	GFPS	FPS+GFPS	Number	FPS	GFPS	FPS+GFPS
		%				%				%		
A	3	0.0	0.0	0.0	63	28.6	4.8	33.3	3	33.3	0.0	33.3
B	5	40.0	20.0	60.0	58	22.4	8.6	31.0	5	60.0	0.0	60.0
C	29	3.4	3.4	6.9	93	32.3	9.7	41.9	3	33.3	0.0	33.3
D	22	18.2	4.5	22.7	173	29.5	9.8	39.3	7	42.9	0.0	42.9
E	22	18.2	0.0	18.2	152	25.0	7.2	32.2	12	8.3	25.0	33.3
Total	81	13.6	3.7	17.3	539	27.8	8.3	36.2	30	30.0	10.0	40.0

Source: Ar Cheb, book 1067, Klosteuerbuch 1438; book 1084, Klosteuerbuch (Schätzungsbuch) 1456.
Note: Cf. figs. 18.16–18.18.

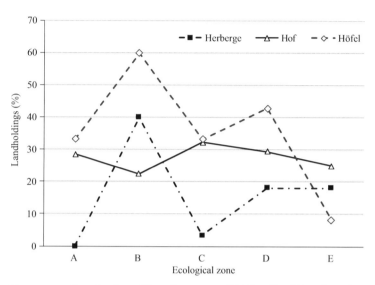

Figure 18.6. Continuity of family tenure (FPS) of "subject" Hof, Herberge, and Höfel landholdings in the city-state of Cheb in various ecological zones, 1438–1456.

Source: Cf. tab. 18.15.

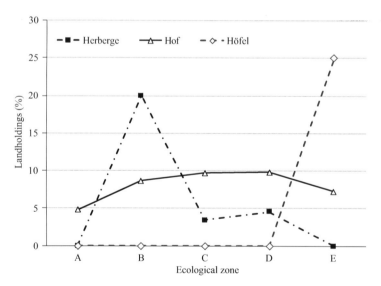

Figure 18.7. The familial continuity assured by transfer of the subject landholdings of the various socioeconomic categories (GFPS) of the landholdings in the individual geographic zones of the city-state of Cheb, 1438–1456.

Source: Cf. tab. 18.15.

Continuity of the same tenant (FPS)

On average, for 1438–1456, there was no change in tenants on 14% of *Herberge*, 28% of *Hof*, and 30% of *Höfel* landholdings (*fig. 18.6; tab. 18.7*). Tenant stability on *Hof* landholdings was twice as high than on *Herberge* landholdings. As for *Hof* landholdings, the individual ecological zones did not differ much in terms of the degree of tenant stability (22–32%). It makes sense only to statistically evaluate *Herberge* landholdings in zones C–E. In zones D–E, tenants remained on 18% of *Herberge* landholdings, in zone C only on 3%. Thus, differences between these zones were considerable.

Landholding transfer within one family (GFPS)

The average proportion of GFPSs that ensured familial continuity of property tenure was only 4% in *Herberge* landholdings, 8% in *Hof* landholdings, and 10% in *Höfel* landholdings (*fig. 18.7; tab. 18.7*). The relative difference was therefore double again. As for *Hof* landholdings, we find the lowest proportion of GFPSs in zone A (5%), while in other zones the proportion was approximately balanced (7–10%).

Continuity of family property tenure (FPSs and GFPSs)

The continuity of property tenure in the city-state of Cheb as a whole in the focus period was maintained on 17% of *Herberge*, 36% of *Hof*, and 40% of *Höfel* landholdings, although the bearers of this continuity for the most part were long-term tenants (continuity of FPSs), not GFPSs (*fig. 18.8; tab. 18.7*). As for *Hof* landholdings, we register a higher degree of continuity in ecological zones C–D (39–42%) and lower in A–B and E (31–33%). In other words, we find a greater fluctuation of tenants in geographically extreme zones. The differences were not particularly distinct, however.

18.6 "Free" landholdings

In 1438 and 1456, a total of 31 FPSs with tenure of "free" landholdings were recorded. As a whole, an FPS with tenure of a "free" landholding had similar

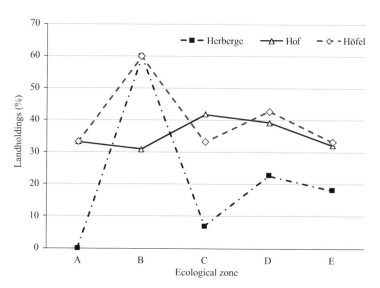

Figure 18.8. Familial continuity on the subject landholdings of the various socioeconomic categories of the landholdings in the individual geographic zones of the city-state of Cheb (FPS + GFPS), 1438–1456.

Source: Cf. tab. 18.15.
Note: Cf. figs. 18.6–18.7.

expectations as "subject" landholdings in the wealthiest, fifth property quintile—the degree of familial continuity exceeded 50%, the proportion of FPSs constituting 39–40%, continuity GFPSs 13%. However, if we divide FPSs into tertiles according to property position, we can see differences (*figs. 18.9–18.11*).[640] In the wealthier FPSs we can see a really extraordinary degree of familial continuity (60–80%; tertiles II and III). This value exceeds the average values recorded for the wealthiest "subject" landholdings by about one-quarter. Conversely, the degree of familial continuity was just 30% on average in tertile I. The degree of stability and continuity of family tenure therefore did not depend primarily on legal status, but again on the value of the taxpayer's property.[641]

640   *App. 18.6a.*
641   For similar results, see Lindström, *Distribution*, 63–67.

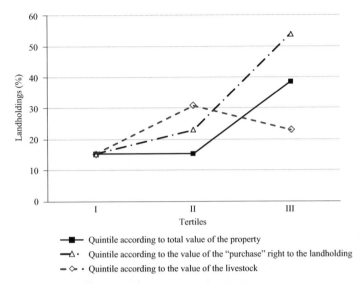

Figure 18.9. **The continuity of the tenant (FPS) on "free" landholdings in the city-state of Cheb, 1438–1456.**

Source: Cf. app. 18.6a.

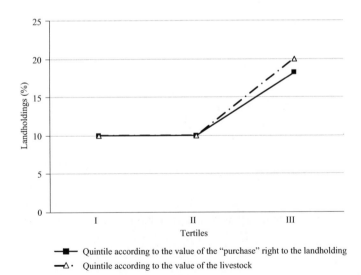

Figure 18.10. **Familial continuity on "free" landholdings assured by transfer (GFPS), 1438–1456.**

Source: Cf. app. 18.6a.

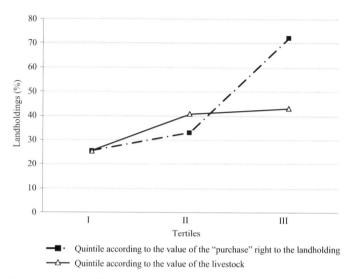

Figure 18.11. **Familial continuity on "free" landholdings (FPS+GFPS) in the city-state of Cheb, 1438–1456.**

Source: Cf. *app. 18.6a.*
Note: Cf. *figs. 18.9–18.10.*

18.7 Complex tenure

We followed the stability and continuity of FPSs with more than one "subject" landholding in their possession in 1438, according to the tenure of the main landholding under which the tenant is listed in the land tax registers. We analyzed a total of 36 such FPSs that usually had tenure of two *Hof* landholdings or a *Hof* landholding with one or two additional *Herberge* landholdings. FPSs with several landholdings followed the trajectory of the wealthiest FPSs in the fifth property quintile.[642] A common characteristic of FPSs in such a position was the degree of familial continuity and reproduction on the same main landholding (47%). The values are almost identical if we divide such FPSs into medians, i.e., into poorer and richer halves.

642　App. 19.6b.

18.8 **Summary and interpretation**

All of our analyses demonstrated a positive relationship between familial stability or continuity of property tenure and monetary value of property.

1. Wealthy FPSs endured on the same landholding for our entire focus period considerably more often than poor FPSs.
2. Where a rich FPS disappeared from a landholding, we find familial continuity in the form of a GFPS in its place more often than was the case for a poor FPS.

This noticeable positive correlation was evident for "subject" landholdings both in the city-state of Cheb assessed as a whole and in the separate ecological zones, although less strikingly. In agroclimatically unfavorable zones, this indicated differences between poor FPSs, while in agriculturally attractive zones, it indicated differences between wealthier FPSs (if we know that there were more wealthy households in attractive zones and more poor ones in unfavorable zones). Therefore, in the favorable zones A and B, the correlation between continuity of family tenure and property position unsurprisingly manifested itself less noticeably—a large proportion of FPSs followed the general trajectory of wealthy FPSs.

The positive connection between the value of property and the continuity of tenure was also demonstrated by a special analysis according to socioeconomic and legal categories:

3. FPSs on *Herberge* landholdings demonstrated characteristics similar to FPSs in the poorest property quintile.
4. Conversely, FPSs with tenure of "free" landholdings and FPSs with tenure of several "subject" landholdings followed the trajectory of FPSs in the richest quintile, except for those whose property value was low.

The question is: what happened when family tenure on landholdings was discontinued? We are unable to establish whether the FPS disintegrated due to the death of the tenant and/or whether they simply moved to another landholding. This is related to the fact that the differing degrees of familial continuity could have depended on the type of landholding transfer. A small degree of familial continuity could have been due to "*inter vivos*" market transfers, while a large degree of continuity could have been due to transfers in inheritance procedure, i.e., "*causa morti*." We shall address this question in the following chapter.

From a demographic point of view, accentuated differences exist between the stability and continuity of family tenure in the richest FPSs that held "free" landholdings and the poorest FPSs in agroclimatically unfavorable zones. We register continuity and stability in 85% of the former and just 15% of the latter. We believe that rich FPSs on "free" landholdings reproduced more or less absolutely and the remaining 15% may in reality have been simply matrilineal intrafamilial transfers. On the other hand, the poorest FPSs left their landholdings in great numbers, and non-family, "*inter vivos*," transfers prevailed, and intrafamilial transfers occurred only in situations when the tenant died on the landholding. Although the difference in the degree of familial continuity of tenure between the richest and poorest taxpayers in the late medieval city-state of Cheb was approximately fourfold, this was not necessarily due to the higher death rate and lower reproductive potential of the poor, but to differing intensities and types of landholding transfer.

The results of the analysis point more to a *model of uneven reproduction* than to a *cyclic model* of socioeconomic mobility. At the same time, they do not confirm the *model of uneven reproduction* since we do not know the fate of the tenants and FPSs leaving poor landholdings.

19.
Landholding transfers: 1442-1456

19.1 Introduction

The preceding chapter showed that average poor tenants and their FPSs maintained tenure of a landholding for a shorter period than rich tenants, and they also passed landholdings down to their male offspring less frequently. We may consider the positive relationship between the wealth and continuity of family tenure of the same landholding as proven.[643] In this chapter, we move our focus from FPSs to the actual landholdings and we will be examining:

1. The ratio between intrafamilial and market transfers.
2. Whether the intensity and nature of transfers were dependent on the legal status, socioeconomic categories, operational size, and monetary value of a landholding.

The relative position of the monetary value of tenure right to a certain landholding and livestock was not stable but changed over time. We therefore assess each landholding according to its position in 1438 and then in 1456. In the first case, this involves establishing a correlation between the characteris-

---

643 From the point of view of interpretation, the *model of uneven reproduction* assumes differing intensities of transfers between variously rich landholdings and differing degrees of family replacement on a landholding. As for change of family on a landholding, historical demography speaks of what is known as the replacement rate, which expresses the number of transfers of a landholding within the family and outside it. The period that we follow is fairly short, and farmers were replaced only in a few of the landholdings, so the replacement rate may be followed only in isolated cases.

tics of a landholding and its prospects (1438/1442→1456; *chap. 19.3*), and in the second, the correlation between the value of the landholding and its past (1456→1442/1438; *chap. 19.4.*).

Our analysis is burdened by simplification, which involves applying the characteristics and monetary value of a 1438 landholding to all transfers that the landholding underwent during the time segment 1438–1456.

The identified issues can alternatively be approached through the targeted monitoring of the annual replacement rate of the tenants of the landholdings and also the migration rate depending on the property status. In this regard, we refer readers to a special study published elsewhere.[644]

19.2 Method[645]

Analyzed set

As with the preceding chapter, we based our analysis on a database of land-holdings in 1438 and 1456, to which we added all changes in tenant occurring between 1442 and 1456.[646] In our analysis, we included only those landholdings we could link up according to entries in 1438 and 1456, and for which we know the monetary value of the "purchase" right and of livestock (*tab. 19.1–19.2*). Landholdings that in the meantime disappeared from land tax registers or alternatively appeared newly (i.e., landholdings that had undergone demise, merging, fission, or conversely had newly come into being) were left aside.

Types of transfer

No clear border may be traced between intrafamilial and market transfers, since intrafamilial transfers can involve market-based transactions, including when inheritance occurs in the form of a sale.[647] Another problem lies in the

---

644   Klír, "Local migration," in print.
645   Summarized in Klír, "Land transfer," 167–172.
646   We had to leave out the period 1439–1441 due to the absence of surviving complete registers.
647   Bavel van and Hoppenbrouwers, "Landholding," 18.

Table 19.1. **Fates of tenants of landholdings recorded in the city-state of Cheb, 1442–1456 (degree of stable tenure and landholding transfers in the city-state of Cheb).**

	Tenants	
	recorded in 1442	newly registered in 1443 or later
Dead or departed from their landholding by 1456 (i.e., tenants named in the 1442 register, or later, who were no longer listed in the *1456 Taxation Book*)	451	492
Remained on the same landholding until 1456 (i.e., tenants named in the 1442 register, or later, who were no longer listed in the *1456 Taxation Book*)	345	406
Total	796	837

Source: Ar Cheb, books 1069–1083, *Klosteuerbücher 1442–1456*; book 1084, *Klosteuerbuch (Schätzungsbuch)* 1456.

definition of the family and the reconstruction of familial relationships.[648] In the city-state of Cheb, our research is limited by the nature of the written sources, so at best we may make an educated guess as to the real ratio between intrafamilial and market transfers. We can differentiate just three specific categories of transfer (*tab. 19.3*).

Family relations

We determined kinship between taxpayers as in the preceding chapter—based on whether the names of two successive tenants matched. Again, we disregarded occupational surnames, since a match of such names did not necessarily mean kinship.

The final database included 1,694 items, i.e., 1,694 individual tenants of individual landholdings. Some persons in the database appeared more than once if they lived on more than one landholding during their lifetime. A total of 345 tenants remained on the same landholding for the whole focus period (43% of everyone from 1442); 899 were new arrivals, and 857 departed.

648 Štefanová, *Erbschaftspraxis*, 73–74.

Table 19.2. **Overview of types of landholding transfer in the city-state of Cheb, 1442-1456.**

		Number of cases	%	
Newly registered tenants on the landholdings (1443–1456)		**899**	**100.0**	
Intrafamilial transfers	Succession of the widow	52	5.8	15.6
	Succession of another family member	88	9.8	
"Commercial" land market transfer	Tenant arrives from a different landholding in the city-state of Cheb	188	20.9	84.4
Not specified	–	571	63.5	
Departures from the landholdings, 1442-1456 (including deaths)		**857**	**100.0**	
Intrafamilial transfers	Departure/death of the widow	52	6.1	16.3
	Departure/death of another family member	88	10.3	
"Commercial" land market transfer	Tenant moves to a different landholding in the city-state of Cheb	167	19.5	83.7
	Tenant moves to the city and becomes a burgher	33	3.9	
Not specified	–	517	60.3	

Source: From Klír, "Land transfer," 171–172, tab. 9. Data according to Ar Cheb, books 1069–1083, *Klosteuer-bücher 1442–1456*; book 1084, *Klosteuerbuch (Schätzungsbuch) 1456*.

Migration

The Cheb land tax registers illuminated some aspects of the geographic mobility of the Cheb peasantry, namely the moving of a tenant from one landholding to another. In the database, we have identified cases when in a certain year there was an alternation of the tenants of a certain landholding, but in the same year or next year the original tenant appeared at another landholding, either in the same settlement or elsewhere in the city-state of Cheb (*tab. 19.4a–b*). We have included in the analysis unique persons identified by their baptismal and family name or by a less common family name. It was crucial that the likelihood of correctly identifying the same person appearing in close temporal connection at various landholdings be as high as possible based on name cor-

Table 19.3. **The types of transfers recognizable in the registers of the Cheb
land tax in 1438, 1442–1456.**

	Indication in the land tax registers	Interpretation
1.	Same family name of two subsequent tenants (name match); or record of kinship relationship	intrafamilial transfers in the male line, partially also the female line – most often *causa morti*, a transfer within the inheritance procedures
2.	The same name (taxpayer) disappears at one landholding and also appears at another	commercial land market transfers *inter vivos* – the original tenant did not die but moved to another landholding in the city-state of Cheb (a transfer connected with migration)
3.	Total change of the name of the tenant of the landholding (taxpayer)	intrafamilial and/or commercial land market transfers – transfer within the wider family or in a female line that we are unable to recognize – the tenant retired, and the handover of the landholding occurred outside of the family – departure of the tenant to a place where they cannot be found (outside of the city-state of Cheb or left for the town) – decline of the tenant among the landless

Source: From Klír, "Land transfer," 168, tab. 6. Data according to Ar Cheb, books 1067, 1069–1083, *Klosteuerbücher 1438, 1442–1456*; book 1084, *Klosteuerbuch (Schätzungsbuch) 1456.*

respondence. In some cases, proof of mobility is indisputable since, in his new abode, the taxpayer was named according to place of origin (*tab. 19.4b*).

Those with occupational surnames were excluded from the analyzed set, unless the surname was specified by a less frequently occurring baptismal name. Conversely, we included in the analyzed set cases where an original tenant did not appear on other landholdings until 2 years later. The analysis of migration from the countryside to Cheb was not negligible, and we deal with it separately in *chapter 23*.

The migrations of certain peasant groups are impossible to find in the land tax registers. This applies firstly to persons who crossed between peasant and sub-peasant strata, secondly to persons who moved between landholdings and were subject and not subject to the Cheb land tax.[649] Nevertheless, some

649 (1) In cases of new persons arriving on a landholding, we are unable to differentiate between persons who originally had not been settled on a landholding and had come from sub-peasant groups; for instance, they had been amongst the landless, a servant or an inmate-lodger,

Table 19.4a. Example of the identification of migration in the city-state of Cheb.

Settlement	Reference number of landholdings	Interval	Name in the tax register
Dolní Pelhřimov / Pilmersreuth (Unter-)	2	1442–1448	Nickel Stark mit sein kind
Horní Hraničná / Kunreuth (Ober-)	10	from 1449	Nickel Stargk

Source: From Klír, "Land transfer," 170, tab. 8. Data according to Ar Cheb, books 1067, 1069–1083, *Klosteuerbücher 1438, 1442–1456*; book 1084, *Klosteuerbuch (Schätzungsbuch) 1456.*

Table 19.4b. Example of the identification of multiple migrations in the city-state of Cheb.

Settlement	Reference number of landholdings	Interval	Name in the tax register
Žírovice / Sirmitz	4	1443–1448	Nikel Per
Vojtanov / Voitersreuth (Vorden-)	4	1447–1452	Nickel Per
Horní Lomany / Lohma (Ober-)	12	from 1453	Perr von Feydersßrewt

Source: Ar Cheb, books 1067, 1069–1083, *Klosteuerbücher 1438, 1442–1456*; book 1084, *Klosteuerbuch (Schätzungsbuch) 1456.*

of the peasants who moved to the city may be identified amongst new citizens (*chap. 24*).

For these reasons, it is difficult to interpret differences in the degree of migration between individual settlements, since in settlements on the edge of the city-state of Cheb or in isolated enclaves, the degree of record-keeping

or had come from one of the suburbs of Cheb. (2) As for departures, we cannot differentiate between persons who had left the peasant or smallholder strata, whether through loss of land property or departure to the city. (3) We are unable to identify the persons migrating from outside of the city-state of Cheb of Cheb or from settlements not subject to the Cheb land tax. Records therefore fail to capture moving from/to the settlements of Cheb Castle and the city hospital. (4) Also unidentifiable are persons arriving from landholdings or leaving for landholdings in settlements where, despite the fact that the land tax was collected, they were not described in detail in the registers—the larger of such localities include Marktredwitz, Libá (Liebenstein), Hazlov (Haslau), and Skalná (Wildstein).

is worse than in settlements lying closer to the center.[650] For this reason, it is difficult to determine whether some parts of the city-state of Cheb were more prone to immigration or emigration.

Migration in the city-state of Cheb played a significant role in landholding transfer. Despite many limitations, we established that a whole one-fifth of property transfers were cases of the tenant moving to another landholding, either within the same village or to a different one. Approximately one-twentieth of tenants moved to Cheb, gaining citizenship. The real extent of the movement between landholdings was certainly higher, since migration outside Cheb land tax territory accounted for an increase that we cannot see in the land tax registers. Some tenants moved from and to several landholdings during the focus period (more in *chap. 22.2*).

Notes on the analysis

+ For our analysis of property transfers involving landholdings, we applied the same procedure and quantiles as in *chapter 18*. However, the number of landholdings in the separate quintiles is not the same, as some of the landholdings have been excluded from the analysis.
+ We did not calculate the average number of property transfers for all landholdings, but just for those where the tenant changed at least once.
+ As for intrafamilial transfers, we differentiated between succession by the widow and a male relative, most frequently probably the son.
+ Given that we could identify migration in the registers only when the same tenant in one year left one landholding and then in the same or subsequent year appeared on a different landholding, moving out and moving in (departures and arrivals) should be balanced overall. If we look at the value quintiles, this is naturally not the case, since the tenant could have moved between landholdings of varying value. In each quintile, we may evaluate not only the proportion of transfers connected with migration, but also whether moving out or moving in was the predominant trend.

---

650   We are best informed about migration within the city-state of Cheb and least informed in settlements in distant and isolated enclaves surrounded by settlements belonging to Waldsassen Monastery and the burgraves of Nuremberg and their vassals.

19.3 Analysis of landholdings according to their characteristics in 1438

This subchapter concentrates on the quantiles set according to the monetary value of tenure right to a landholding and the value of livestock in 1438 (*app. A*). We focus our attention on (1) the degree of continuity of tenure, (2) the intensity of replacement of landholding tenants, (3) the nature of landholding transfers, and (4) migration. In particular we analyze "subject" "free" landholdings and landholdings that were part of a complex tenure.[651]

A. "Subject" landholdings – The city-state of Cheb as a whole

In our analysis, we included a total of 465 landholdings and 485 transfers in terms of "purchase" right, and 432 landholdings and 453 transfers in terms of livestock monetary values.

I. Continuity of the tenure

Tenants of landholdings (FPSs) in the focus period remained unchanged in 43% or 42% of the landholdings, according to whether we are looking at "purchase" right or livestock value (*fig. 19.1*).[652] In the richest quintile, the degree of stability was always higher than in the poorest quintile. In categories set according to "purchase" right, we find more or less the same proportion of identical tenants in quintiles II–IV (37–42% or 42–46%), while they differ more dramatically in quintile V in values according to "purchase" right (54%) and in quintile I according to livestock values (33%).

The relatively higher degree of continuity between 1442–1456 compared to 1438–1442 is evident. The difference is considerably higher than we would have expected proportionally. We may find an explanation for this in the catastrophic failed harvest of 1437 and the severe wave of plague and famine described in Nuremberg sources from 1438–1439.[653]

---

651   Our analyzed set also includes some settlements that, despite not appearing in the 1456 Taxation Book, were described in the *1438 Land Tax Register*, and detailed, extant data exists in the ordinary tax registers, including the 1456 register (Rathsam, Starý Rybník/ Altenteich). We ignore mills because it was difficult to determine intrafamilial property transfers.

652   *App. 19.2a–b.*

653   Cf. *chap. 5.10.* Bauernfeind, *Materielle Grundstrukturen,* 182–187.

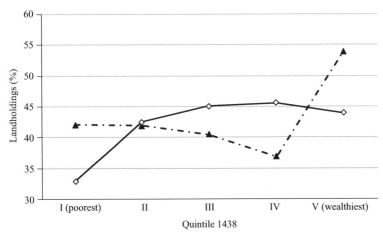

Figure 19.1. **The continuity of tenants (FPS) on "subject" landholdings in the city-state of Cheb, 1442–1456.**

Source: Cf. *app. 19.2a–e.*
Note: The city-state of Cheb as a whole, judged by the property quintiles for 1438.

Unsurprisingly the results are relatively similar to those in the preceding *chap. 18.* The differences arise because we worked with the shorter time interval of 1442–1456 and with a less numerous set of landholdings, since we excluded those that were impossible to identify between 1438 and 1442.

2. Frequency of the transfers

The average number of property transfers per landholding where at least one change in tenant occurred during the time segment of interest was 1.84 or 1.82 (*figs. 19.2–19.4*).[654] In this analysis, the correlation between the number of transfers and the value of the landholding was very clear. The more valuable the landholding, either in terms of the value of the "purchase" right or livestock, the less its tenants changed. Landholdings with the lowest "purchase" right and livestock values changed tenure on average 2.1–2.3 times, while landholdings with the highest values changed 1.3–1.5 times.

654   *App. 19.6c–e.*

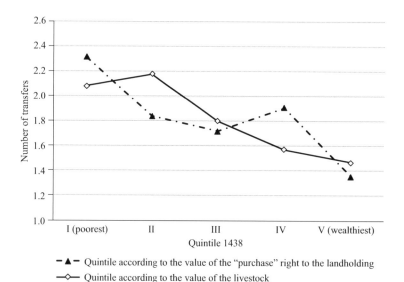

━▲━ Quintile according to the value of the "purchase" right to the landholding
━◇━ Quintile according to the value of the livestock

Figure 19.2. The average number of property transfers per landholding that changed tenants in 1442–1456.

Source: Cf. *app. 19.2a–e.*
Note: The city-state of Cheb as a whole, judged by the property quintiles for 1438.

3. Transfers within a family

The average proportion of landholdings handed down within a family was fairly low, at least according to name match, totaling 21% of all transfers when counting widows or 15% not including widows. The separate quintiles differed widely in this respect, especially in terms of livestock values.[655] The differences between the poorest and the richest quintile were 1.7–1.8 times in terms of "purchase" right value and 2.8–3.6 times in terms of livestock value. In other words, while intrafamilial transfers, including widows, applied to just 13.7% and 21.2% of all transfers in the poorest quintile, the figure was 38% and 39% in the richest quintile. The difference is quite striking.

The total amount of landholdings handed down within a family is probably far too low compared to the real situation. Nevertheless, the relative numbers and the comparison between the quintiles are important.[656]

---

655   *App. 19.1; app. 19.6c–e.*
656   Many thanks to J. Lindström for this comment.

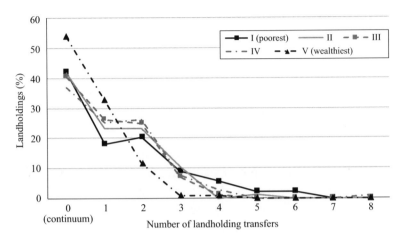

Figure 19.3. The differences between variously wealthy landholdings according to the number of property transfers, 1442–1456. Quintiles according to the value of "purchase" right in 1438.

Source: Cf. *app. 19.2a–e.*
Note: The city-state of Cheb as a whole.

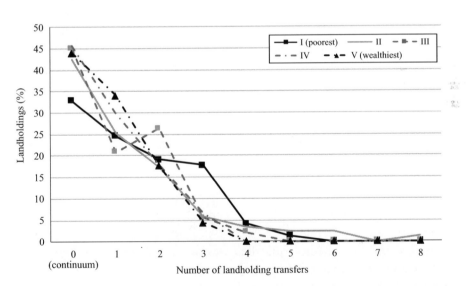

Figure 19.4. The differences between variously wealthy landholdings according to the number of property transfers, 1442–1456. Quintiles according to the value of livestock in 1438.

Source: Cf. *app. 19.2a–e.*
Note: The city-state of Cheb as a whole.

4. Transfers due to migration

On average, tenant migration accounted for 17% ("purchase" right) and 18% (livestock) of all property transfers.[657] Moving in may be identified in 15% and 16% of property transfers. In the poorest quintile, the tenant moving out accounted for 17% and 24% of all property transfers, while moving in accounted for 11% and 15% (*app. 19.1*). In the richest quintile, the tenant moving out accounted for 12% of all property transfers, while moving in occurred in 15% and 16%. Differences between value quintiles may be explained by the fact that tenants moving had socioeconomic aspects—tenants moved from less to more valuable landholdings. In poorer landholdings, it was more likely that the tenant would leave it than the widow or son taking over the tenure, whereas the opposite was true for rich landholdings.

B. "Subject" landholdings – various ecological zones

The question is to what extent the tendencies and correlations found in the city-state of Cheb as a whole may be generalized and to what extent the various ecological zones differed from each other. Our research is limited by the fact that in the most favorable zones (A–B), we analyzed just 42 landholdings and 42–46 transfers, while in other zones, we analyzed 84–143 landholdings and 135–147 transfers (C–E). Therefore, in certain situations in zones A–B we come up against problems arising from the statistically low frequency.

In our analysis, we used the same quintiles as we did for the analysis of eco-logical zones in the preceding *chapter 18*. Therefore, in each ecological zone we worked with quintiles with a different absolute span.

1. Continuity of the tenure

The overall proportion of landholdings whose tenant did not change during the focus period of 1442–1456 was approximately 43% in zones A and C–D, while the proportion was higher (48% and 51%) in zone B, and lower (38%) in zone E. The link to the value quintiles, whether set according to "purchase" right or livestock value, is not entirely clear cut (*fig. 19.5*).[658] Nevertheless, we

---

657   *App. 19.1; app. 19.2.c–e.*
658   *App. 19.3a–b.*

find the lowest degree of continuity mostly in quintiles I and II (min. 10%) and the highest in quintiles III–V (max. 60%).

2. Frequency of the transfers

When a change of tenant occurred on a landholding, landholdings underwent on average 1.8–1.9 transfers in zones A and C–E, while in zone B 1.4 transfers took place per landholding according to "purchase" right value and 1.6 transfers according to livestock value. All zones showed a correlation between the intensity of landholding transfers and value quintiles, whether set based on "purchase" right or livestock values.[659] The greatest intensity occurs usually in quintile I or II, where the average was 2.0–3.2 transfers per landholding. The smallest intensity occurs in quintile IV or V, where the average was 1.0–1.5 transfers per landholding. The differences between the poorest and the richest landholdings were approximately double.

3. Transfers within a family

The highest number of intrafamilial transfers (according to matching names) occurred in the agriculturally favorable zones A and B, amounting to 26–44%.[660] In the less favorable zones C–E, the figure was just 19–25%. If we exclude transfers to the widow, the percentage of intrafamilial transfers falls to 18–26% in zones A and B and to 10–20% in zones C–E. In zones C–E we can see a clear link between the intensity of intrafamilial transfers and value quintiles. The relatively fewest intrafamilial landholding transfers can be found in quintiles I and II, where they represented a maximum of 13% of all transfers. We found the most intrafamilial transfers in quintiles IV and V, where they accounted for 21–32% of all transfers. Differences between quintiles were therefore manifold.[661]

4. Transfers due to migration

We found the most demonstrable incidences of a tenant moving from one landholding to another in zone A, where moving out accounted for 28–29%

---

659   *App. 19.3b; App. 19.4a–b, 4f.*
660   *App. 19.3c–d; App. 19.4a–d, 4g–h.*
661   It is not possible to evaluate differences between separate value quintiles in zones A and B due to the low number of such cases.

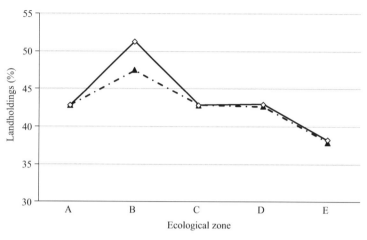

Figure 19.5. **The continuity of tenants (FPS) on subject landholdings, 1442-1456. The city-state of Cheb by ecological zone.**

Source: Cf. app. 19.9a–b, 9e.
Note: Property quintiles for 1438.

of all transfers.[662] Leaving this zone aside, the proportion of transfers due to the tenant moving out rose slightly due to worsening natural conditions for agriculture. In zone B, transfers connected with moving out accounted for 12% and 15% of all cases; in zone C, 15–16%; in zone D, 17%; and in zone E, 20–21%.

The various ecological zones were very similar regarding the proportion of landholding transfers involving moving in, which can be identified in 13–18% of all landholding transfers.

Due to a systematic error, we have traced fewer cases of moving than was the reality. Past reality may be most faithfully demonstrated by the results for zone A, located in the center of the city-state of Cheb. The migration of tenants between landholdings was behind at least one-third of the property transfers here.

662   *App. 19.2c–d, 4g–i; 19.3c–d.*

C. "Free" landholdings

We know the monetary value as of 1438 for 31 "free" landholdings. The monetary values of tenure right to the landholdings were fairly different, so we divide them further into tertiles. We may trace the intensity and nature of property transfers for 23 landholdings where 13 and 14 transfers took place. A total of 13 transactions concerned landholdings for which we know the livestock value, and 14 transfers concerned landholdings for which we know the value of "free" tenure right.

The same tenant remained on half of the "free" landholdings between 1442–1456.[663] The figure in the first tertile was considerably lower (29% and 33%), in the second tertile considerably higher (75%), and in the third tertile higher as well (50% and 44%). The degree of continuity of tenants on "free" landholdings corresponded to the degree of continuity on the richest "subject" landholdings.

D. Socioeconomic category of the landholdings[664]

It is possible to follow the differences between *Hof* and *Herberge* landholdings only according to the data of the *1438 Land Tax Register*. We have judged the frequency and character of the landholding transfers for 46 *Herberge*, 379 *Hof*, and 21 *Höfel* according to the classification for 1438.

Regarding tenure continuity, the same tenant remained significantly more often at *Hof* and *Höfel* landholdings (43%) than at *Herberge* landholdings (26%) (*tab. 19.5*).

If the tenant had already changed, then 2.4–2.5 of the landholding transfers fell to the *Herberge* and *Höfel* landholding, whereas at *Hof* landholdings it was only 1.7 of the transfers (*tab. 19.6*).

Within a family, *Höfel* landholdings were transferred the most often—that is, in 35% of the cases and without widows in 28% of the cases (*tab. 19.6*). With *Hof* landholdings, the share of the intrafamilial transfers was distinctly lower (23% with widows and 16% without widows); we find the lowest share with *Herberge* landholdings (14% and 11%).

663   *App. 19.5a–b.*
664   Summarized in Klír, "Land transfer," 176.

Demonstrably, most transfers due to the tenant moving out to another landholding occurred with *Höfel* landholdings (24%) and the fewest with *Herberge*
landholdings (12%) (*tab. 19.6*). Values for *Hof* landholdings lie somewhere in
between (19%). We do not find such a degree of difference in cases of moving
in, which can be identified at approximately the same rate of 15–17% in all
landholding categories. The question is how to explain the striking difference
between the level of migration connected with *Hof* and *Herberge* landholdings.

Table 19.5. **Distribution of the number of transfers according to the
socioeconomic category of the landholding in the city-state of Cheb as a whole,
1442–1456.**

Landholding	Land-holdings	Share of landholdings with a certain number of transfers %				Total %
		0 (continuity)	1	2	3 or more	
Hof	379	42.7	28.8	19.3	9.3	87.3
Herberge	46	26.1	19.6	21.7	32.7	10.6
Höfel	21	42.9	9.5	33.3	14.3	4.8
Total	434	42.2	27.6	20.7	9.5	100.0

According to: Klír, "Land transfer," 179, tab. 14.
Source: Ar Cheb, books 1067, 1069–1083, *Klosteuerbücher 1438, 1442–1456*; book 1084, *Klosteuerbuch
(Schätzungsbuch) 1456.*
Note: Socioeconomic categories of the landholding according to Ar Cheb, book 1067, *Klosteuerbuch 1438.*

Table 19.6. **Intensity and character of transfers according to the socioeconomic
category of the landholding in the city-state of Cheb as a whole, 1442–1456.**

Land-holding	Total evaluated transfers	Average number of transfers per landholding	%		Migration	
			Undeter-mined	Intra-familial	Moving out	Moving in
Hof	377	0.99	58.60	22.8	18.6	15.1
Herberge	84	1.83	73.80	14.3	11.9	15.5
Höfel	29	1.38	41.40	34.5	24.1	17.2
Total	438	1.01	57.70	22.4	19.9	17.1

According to: Klír, "Land transfer," 179, tab. 15.
Source: Ar Cheb, books 1067, 1069–1083, *Klosteuerbücher 1438, 1442–1456*; book 1084, *Klosteuerbuch
(Schätzungsbuch) 1456.*
Note: Socioeconomic categories of the landholding according to Ar Cheb, book 1067, *Klosteuerbuch 1438.*

Summary

The results of the analysis correspond to the assumptions of the *model of uneven reproduction*. The degree of property continuity, intensity of transfers, and proportion of intrafamilial transfers were not distributed evenly between landholdings and ecological zones but correlated with the monetary value of the landholding. This applies whether we measure according to the value of the tenure right or livestock.

+ The average number of property transfers on the poorest landholdings was twice or three times higher than on rich landholdings. In the agriculturally favorable zone B, the intensity of the transfers of landholdings of all property categories was very low in general, which may be explained by the fact that even locally poor landholdings in favorable zones were relatively rich compared to less favorable zones.
+ The number of *intrafamilial transfers* correlated even more closely with the value of the landholding. While intrafamilial transfers were the exception for the poorest groups of landholdings and fluctuated below 15%, the percentage for the richest landholdings was 40%. Therefore, the differences between ecological zones were even more contrasting. In agriculturally favorable zones the proportion of intrafamilial transfers was around 50%, while in less favorable zones the figure did not exceed 25% even in the richest of landholdings. In other words, the prospects for familial continuity for the richest landholdings in less favorable zones were similar to those for the poorest landholdings in agriculturally favorable zones.
+ The main thing is that we find a higher degree of correlation between intrafamilial transfers and landholding values for quintiles set according to livestock values than according to "purchase" right values. Therefore, fundamental for the fate and intensity of property transfers involving landholdings was their operational size, i.e., their real economic operation.
+ "Free" landholdings had similar prospects to the richest "subject" landholdings in agriculturally favorable zones.
+ Unsurprisingly, the *Herberge* landholdings followed a trajectory characteristic of the poorest landholdings.
+ The proportion of transfers associated with tenant migration from one landholding to another was fairly high. On average, this was 20%. The highest likelihood of tracing a case of moving was in ecological zone A, since it was located in the center of the city-state of Cheb. The hope that the tenant did

not leave the confines of the city-state of Cheb when moving is therefore higher here than in other zones, where peasant mobility was largely directed outside of the city-state of Cheb. It is then no great surprise that almost 28.6% of transfers in zone A involve the departure of a tenant, while in other zones this figure is 12–20%. We may therefore claim that in the richer land-holdings intrafamilial transfers (mostly due to *causa morti*) clearly prevailed over the departure of the tenant, while in poorer landholdings the situation was the opposite.

19.4 Analysis of landholdings according to their characteristics in 1456[665]

In this subchapter, we again concentrate on the same phenomena, but this time we base our analysis on quantiles set according to the value of tenure right to a landholding and the value of livestock as of 1456, rather than 1438 (*app. B*). The analyzed sample is almost one-third more numerous than the previous one, so the results are easier to generalize. While in the previous chapter we examined the correlation between the characteristics of a landholding and its prospects (1438/1442→1456), now, conversely, we examine the correlation between the value of the landholding and its past (1456→1442/1438).

Analysis of the characteristics of 1438 showed that more valuable landhold-ings underwent fewer transfers than less valuable landholdings. If the results from the analysis of 1456 are the same, we may ask whether it was the value of landholdings that influenced the intensity of transfers or conversely if the intensity of transfers determined the value of landholdings. In other words, (1) did valuable landholdings undergo fewer transfers because they were valu-able or (2) were valuable landholdings valuable because they underwent fewer transfers?

---

665   Summarized in Klír, "Land transfer," 172–176.

A. "Subject" landholdings – the city-state of Cheb as a whole

Transfers in the time segment of 1442–1456 were observed for 632 "subject" landholdings for which the value of the "purchase" right was known, and for 565 landholdings for which the livestock value was known in 1456. With the first, there were 569 transfers; with the second, 564 transfers. The set of landholdings for which we know the values of the "purchase" right largely intersects with the set of landholdings for which we know livestock values. A portion of the landholdings, however, appears only in one of the sets and not in the other. For this reason, the number of evaluated transfers is also different.

Continuity of the tenure
The share of the landholdings at which the tenant (FPS) did not change in the focus period rose clearly, and relatively fluidly, with the value of the "purchase" right to the landholding and with the value of the livestock (*fig. 19.6*).[666] The overall average was 45% or 42%, but whereas in the first quintile it was only 32% (value of the "purchase" right) and 26% (value of livestock), in the fifth it was already 54% and 58%. The difference between the extreme quintiles was thus approximately double. The quintiles set according to the value of the livestock show a greater correlation with the degree of the continuity of the tenant than the quintiles set according to the value of the "purchase" right to the landholding.

Frequency of the transfers
The number of transfers per landholding was usually between one and two (31% and 16%); only rarely were there more. For a landholding where the tenant changed, there was on average 1.7 transfers (*figs. 19.7–19.9*).[667] With the landholdings in the lower quintiles, this average was significantly higher than in the higher quintiles, while we always find the extreme values in quintiles I and V. In the case of the quintiles set based on the value of the "purchase" right, there were 1.35–1.85 transfers to a landholding, and according to the value of livestock, as much as 1.4–2.0. The difference thus was 1.5 times.

666   *App. 19.7a–b.*
667   *App. 19.7c–d.*

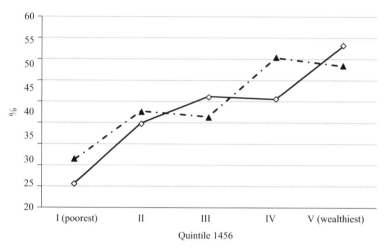

▲ Quintile according to the value of the "purchase" right to the landholding
◇ Quintile according to the value of the livestock

Figure 19.6. The continuity of tenants (FPS) on subject landholdings in the city-state of Cheb, 1442–1456.

Source: From Klír, "Land transfer," 173, fig. 2. Data according to *app. 19.7a–e.*
Note: The city-state of Cheb as a whole, judged according to the total property quintiles for 1456.

Intrafamilial transfers

Of the 569 or 564 landholding transfers, there were on average 20% (without widows 14%) per family according to name matching,[668] but these figures differed significantly in the various quintiles (*fig. 19.7*). For landholdings with a lower value of the "purchase" right and livestock, fewer transfers occurred within the family than on the wealthier landholdings. We again find the extreme values, which differed by 3–4 times, in quintiles I and V. Whereas in quintile I, 12% of the transfers demonstrably took place within the family, in quintile V, it was 32% or 40% of the transfers, depending on whether we are considering the quintiles determined by the values of the "purchase" right or of livestock. We again find that with the poorest and smallest landholdings, intrafamilial transfers were exceptional but were, on the contrary, common on the wealthier and large landholdings.

668   *App. 19.6.–19.7e.*

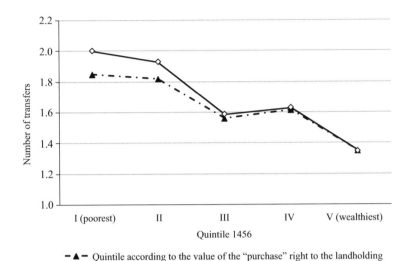

Figure 19.7. **The average number of property transfers of a landholding that changed its tenant in 1442-1456.**

Source: From Klír, "Land transfer," 174, fig. 3. Data according to *app. 19.7a–e.*
Note: The city-state of Cheb as a whole, judged according to the total property quintiles for 1456.

Transfers due to migration

It proved possible to identify relocation from one landholding to another in 22% or 20% of all landholding transfers, based on whether we analyze the data set for "purchase" right values or livestock values.[669] No great differences were found between the various quintiles set according to the value of the "purchase" right; the percentage of departures ranged between 20% and 23%.[670] The percentage of arrivals ranged between 17% and 25%. In the quintiles set according to livestock values, we see a very low proportion of departures in quintiles II and V (13–14%) and arrivals in quintile I (15%). It once again proved that tenants moved out of poorer landholdings more frequently than richerones.[671]

---

669   *App. 19.6; App. 19.7e.*
670   *App. 19.6; App. 19.7e.*
671   It remains to be explained why the numbers of identified departures and arrivals are not balanced. The discrepancy was due to the fact that in the end we excluded one landholding of a pair of landholdings between which we had identified mobility.

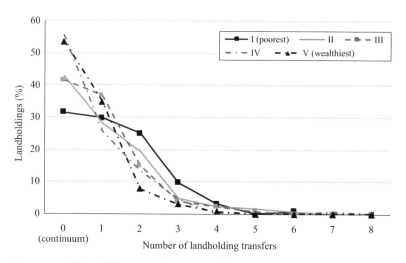

Figure 19.8. The differences between the variously wealthy landholdings according to the number of property transfers, 1442–1456. Quintiles according to the value of the "purchase" right in 1456.

Source: From Klír, "Land transfer," 173, fig. 4. Data according to *app. 19.7a–e.*
Note: The city-state of Cheb as a whole.

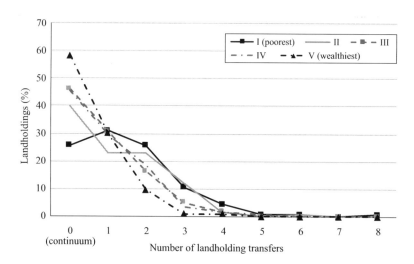

Figure 19.9. The differences between the variously wealthy landholdings according to the number of property transfers, 1442–1456. Quintiles according to the value of the livestock in 1456.

Source: From Klír, "Land transfer," 173, fig. 5. Data according to *app. 19.7a–e.*
Note: The city-state of Cheb as a whole.

B. "Subject" landholdings – individual ecological zones

We have noticed that similar tendencies and correlations apply to the entire city-state of Cheb, even when we set the property quintiles for each ecological zone separately. This also affords a very good illustration of the quantitative differences between them. The picture is a little blurred, due to the fairly low number of landholdings in zones A and B, which in some cases are therefore better evaluated together.

1. Continuity of tenure
The degree of continuity of family tenure rose in all zones with the monetary values of both "purchase" right and livestock on the landholding.[672] In agriculturally favorable zones, continuity of the same tenant was overall greater than in less favorable zones (*fig. 19.10*). While in zones A and B, the same tenants remained on average on 49% ("purchase" right) and 52% (livestock) of landholdings. In zones C and D, the figures were 43–45% and 43–48% respectively, and in zone E, 38% and 39%. The maximum in all zones lay in quintiles IV or V, while it was overall the highest in zone A in quintile IV, as determined by the value of the "purchase" right (75%) and lowest in zone E in quintile V (52%). The minimum lay most often in quintiles I and II (7×) and, more rarely, in quintiles III–IV (3×). The lowest degree of continuity of all was in zones C and E in quintile I (22%). For quintiles set based on "purchase" right, the minimums demonstrated in zones A and B correspond to the maximums in zone E. We find the lowest degree of correlation between value quintiles and continuity of property tenure in zones A and B. Continuity was generally high in these zones, but in the richer quintiles it was sometimes higher than in poorer quintiles. This may be explained by the fact that even the relatively poor landholdings situated in these zones were rich in the context of the city-state of Cheb as a whole.

2. Number of transfers
Ecological zones differed in the average number of property transfers undergone by a landholding where at least one change of tenant occurred.[673] We find

---

672   *App. 19.9a–b, 9d.*
673   *App. 19.8b; app. 19.9c–e.*

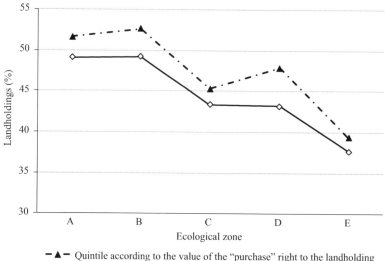

Figure 19.10. **The continuity of tenants (FPS) on "subject" landholdings, 1442-1456. The city-state of Cheb by ecological zone.**

Source: Cf. app. 19.9a–b, 9e.
Note: Property quintiles for 1456.

the lowest average in zone B (1.3–1.4), mainly lower averages in zone A (1.6), and mainly higher averages in zones C–E (1.7–1.8). More striking differences existed between separate quintiles than between ecological zones. Therefore, it is necessary to address separately the quintiles set according to "purchase" right and livestock kept on the landholding.

The average number of property transfers per landholding fell as the value of the "purchase" right grew. The highest intensity of transfers can be seen mainly in quintile I and once in quintile II (1.6–2.6), the lowest in quintile V and once in quintile IV (1.2–1.5). In the case of quintiles set according to livestock values, we see an identical tendency with ranges of 1.8–2.4 for maximums and 1.2–1.3 for minimums, with zone A as the exception. In this zone, the maximum lay in quintile III and the minimum in quintile IV. The greatest contrasts between quintiles are to be found in zones A, C, and E, and smaller contrasts in zones B and D.

3. Intrafamilial transfers

The greatest proportion of intrafamilial transfers were identified in zones A and B, with averages of 31% and 40% in "purchase" right value quintiles and 37% and 25% in livestock value quintiles.[674] In the other zones (C and E), the averages were noticeably lower, at 20–22% and 18–20%. If we did not include widows, the average would be lower.

In the various zones, internal differences are evident between quintiles according to both "purchase" right and livestock. The greatest proportion of intrafamilial transfers occurred in quintile V and, less frequently, in quintile IV, while the gap between maximums ranged from 33–100% in quintiles set according to "purchase" right and 27–60% according to livestock; extreme values lay in all cases in zone B. The minimums ranged from 0–14% and lay mainly in quintile I (6×).

In summary, in zones A and B intrafamilial transfers were common for landholdings more or less in all quintiles and was the rule for landholdings of greater value. In other zones, intrafamilial transfers were very rare for landholdings in poorer quintiles and common only for richer landholdings.

4. Transfers due to migration

Significant differences between zones and quintiles are evident in the proportion of transfers due to the tenant relocating from one landholding to another.[675] The highest proportion of transfers where we have identified migration logically occurred in the central zone A. In this zone, we can identify migration relatively more often and probably more fully. Conversely, other zones were peripheral to a certain extent, and tenant migration was strongly linked to areas outside of the city-state of Cheb, which reduced the chances of tracing such mobility. In other words, the values established for zone A should most faithfully reflect past reality, while in other zones the proportion of transfers attributed to migration are probably considerably underestimated.

The average proportion of transfers involving departure (moving out) was 29% ("purchase" right) and 33% (livestock) in zone A, and for those involving arrival (moving in) it was 42% and 37%. These figures are doubled in com-

674   *App. 19.8c–d; app. 19.9g–h.*
675   *App. 19.8c–d; app. 19.9g–i.*

parison with intrafamilial transfers. In other zones, the average proportion of transfers involving departure was 17–25% and arrival 15–25%.

It is important to follow differences between separate property quintiles and between the proportion of arrivals and departures. In principle, we can differentiate most emigration quintiles and most immigration quintiles. No clear tendency can be seen except for the poorest quintile I (according to livestock), where, except for zones A and B, departure predominated over arrival. Furthermore, the situation is significant in the richest quintile in zones A and B, where we did not observe any departures but did observe a fairly high proportion of arrivals. This indicates that the opportunity for property-related ascension opened up to tenants moving from landholding to landholding.

C. "Free" landholdings

For 1456, data are available for 20 "free" landholdings that were held by peasants and with which it is also possible to follow transfers in 1442–1456. The set of landholdings for which we know the value of tenure right is equally as large as the set of landholdings for which we know the livestock values. However, the landholdings included in both sets are not absolutely identical. Due to the relatively low number of landholdings and high-value differences, we have divided the "free" landholdings into terciles in both cases. Comparing the terciles based on the value of tenure right to the landholding yields different results than comparing them based on the value of livestock.[676] For this reason, we assess them separately.

Value of the tenure right
All of the investigated characteristics closely correlated with the monetary value of the tenure right to the "free" landholdings. The average share of landholdings on which the tenant did not change was 55% and corresponded to the average of the wealthiest "subject" landholdings. Nevertheless, in the first tercile this share was 0%, whereas in the second and third it was 86% and 71% respectively, indicating a staggering degree of continuity. In other words, rich "free" landholdings in 1442–1456 changed tenants only exceptionally.

676 *App. 19.10a–b.*

On a landholding that had already changed its tenant, there was an average of 1.2 transfers. In the first tercile, however, it was 1.3, while in the others 1.0. The share of discovered intrafamilial transfers was on average 36%. The demonstrable departure of a tenant to another landholding was not recorded even once, while arrivals were recorded two times, which represents 18% of all the landholding transfers.

Value of livestock
The investigated characteristics also closely correlated with the value of the livestock bred on a "free" landholding. The share of continual tenants was on average 60%, in the first tercile it was 50%, in the second and third 71% and 57%, respectively. On a landholding where a change of tenant (or tenants) had taken place, there was an average of 1.25 transfers. This figure was higher in the first and second terciles than in the third. The share of intrafamilial transfers reached 40%; it was the lowest in the first tercile (25%) and the highest in the third (67%). The departure of a tenant to another landholding was not demonstrated even once, whereas arrivals were demonstrated twice, representing 20% of all transfers.

D. Complex tenure

Here we investigate the past of "subject" landholdings that were part of complex tenure in 1456. When doing this, in all cases we assess the main landholding under which the tenant was registered in the tax registers. Therefore, in this case we ignore differences in the value of tenure right to a landholding and the value of livestock.

The assessed set consisted of 35 landholdings in total, forming part of complex tenure in 1456, for which we also know the tenant and property transfers during 1442–1456.[677] The proportion of identical tenants was exceptionally large, totaling 66%. Where a landholding underwent any change of tenant at all, an average of 1.3 transfers took place. The proportion of intrafamilial transfers was only average (19%), and the proportion of transfers taking place due to migration was proven only in 13% of cases. Overall, 29% of cases of complex property tenure were a continuation of the complex tenure of 1438, the remain-

677 *App. 19.11a–b.*

der not coming into existence until the interim period that we are studying. In other words, the precondition for the existence of complex tenure in the city-state of Cheb was the continuity of the tenant who, as a rule, did not depart from the landholding that formed the core of such tenure. After their death or departure to a retirement dwelling, the complex tenure usually disintegrated.

Summary

An analysis of the fate of FPSs and landholdings sorted into property quintiles according to the monetary values listed for 1456 showed similar correlations and tendencies to those sorted according to the data of 1438. The degree of property continuity and intensity and types of transfer correlated positively with the monetary value and operational size of the landholding. And a comparative glance at the graphs shows that the general tendencies identified in *chapter 18* became even more evident and regular.

- The degree of *familial continuity* of property tenure in the city-state of Cheb as a whole rose steadily along with the value of the "purchase" right to the landholding and livestock, respectively from 26% and 32% up to 58% and 54%. This tendency is more evident here than in the case of quintiles set according to the values of 1438. Furthermore, the correlation between the position of the landholding in the quintile set according to the values of 1456 and the intensity of landholding transfers was more balanced than according to the values of 1438. This leads us to assume that a high monetary value of the "purchase" right to a landholding encouraged continuity of tenure. At the same time, less valuable landholdings underwent property transfers more frequently than more valuable landholdings.
- For landholdings sorted into quintiles according to the values in 1456, the nature of up to twice as many property transfers could be established than for landholdings sorted according to the values in 1438. The proportion of *intrafamilial transfers* rose along with value quintiles evidently more fluidly and with greater contrast than was the case with the categorization of 1438. The proportion of transfers taking place due to migration no longer correlates so markedly with value quintiles.
- We also find significant differences *between ecological zones* because in the agriculturally favorable zones A–B, landholdings tended to be more valuable and larger, while in zones C–E, landholdings were smaller and poorer (*tab. 19.7*). Therefore, in zones A–B, (1) the stability of landholding tenure

and the proportion of intrafamilial transfers were higher and also (2) the differences between various quintiles were less dramatic than in other zones. The intensity of landholding transfers was generally lower in zones A–B. No cases of departures to different landholdings are described for zones A and B, only arrivals from landholdings located in other zones.

+ *"Free" landholdings* followed the same disposal trajectory as the most valuable and largest "subject" landholdings. Their tenants did not leave them, the degree of familial continuity was almost absolute, and their bonds to the land unusually strong.

+ The fates of landholdings that were part of *complex landholding tenure* in 1456, as well as a comparison with 1438, confirm that the precondition for the accumulation of property and growth in the value of a landholding was the continuity of tenure.

+ The tendencies documented for the city-state of Cheb as a whole are not as evident *within separate ecological zones*. This may be explained by the fact

Table 19.7. **Length of tenure of "subject" landholdings by one tenant (FPS) in the late medieval city-state of Cheb, 1442–1456.**

Ecological zone		14 or 15 years or more* (%)	18 or 20 years or more* (%)
A		49.2–51.7*	28.8–29.2
B		49.3–52.6*	28.1–30.2
C	"subject" landholdings	43.4–45.3*	26.0–27.4
D		43.2–47.9*	28.7–29.6
E		37.7–39.4*	23.6–24.6
The city-state of Cheb as a whole	"free" landholdings	55.0–60.0	28.8–29.2

Source: Ar Cheb, books 1069–1083, *Klosteuerbücher 1442–1456*; book 1084, *Klosteuerbuch (Schätzungsbuch) 1456*.

Note: This is only the minimum proportion of tenants whose tenure covered the analyzed time interval. We cannot see tenants who, although their tenure also covered or even exceeded the time interval, arrived on the landholding before 1438 and ended before 1456 or arrived after 1442 but exceeded the time interval outside of the analyzed period, i.e., after 1456. The data in the table therefore have only relative testimonial value and show significant differences between legal categories and ecological zones. The interval value includes the data set based on the quintiles according to the total value of the property, landholdings, and livestock.

* – data for the set of landholdings evaluated according to monetary values as at 1456.

that property differences within ecological zones were not so contrasting. It is possible that if we were to analyze just certain ecological zones, we might not find any positive correlation between the value of a landholding and familial continuity of tenure.

+ The share of landholding transfers issued by *widows* seems more or less constant; no significant differences were found between the zones or the property categories.

20.
Socioeconomic mobility of FPSs and GFPSs

20.1 Formulation of the issue

In this chapter, we focus on whether rich and poor FPSs or GFPSs that remained on the same landholding between 1438 and 1456 differed from each other (1) in the trajectory of socioeconomic (i.e., property) mobility in the course of the life cycle and (2) in the degree of intergenerational property mobility. In most cases, we assess the socioeconomic mobility of richer FPSs, since these reproduced more frequently on the same landholding and therefore are overrepresented in our analysis set.

Property mobility of FPSs

We examine the property mobility of FPSs between 1438 and 1456 in cases where the FPS did not disintegrate and at the same time reproduced for the entire period on the same landholding (so-called continuous FPS; we look at the trajectory of families moving from landholding to landholding in *chapter 22*). From the point of view of evaluating the sources, this means that a person with the same surname or same baptismal name and surname is listed both in the *1438 Land Tax Register* and in the *1456 Taxation Book*, and at the same time, no mention of any change or discontinuity appears in the registers for 1442–1456. We ignore potential distortion when a landholding was taken over by a son bearing the same name as his father without this fact appearing in a land tax register.

In the database, we identified and linked together 183 such FPSs with one "subject" landholding in their hands, 12 FPSs with a "free" landholding, and 8 FPSs with tenure of more than one landholding. The number of continuous FPSs that we included in our analysis was slightly reduced by the absence of monetary values for certain property items. The numbers of FPSs in our sets for analysis of the total values of property, "purchase" right, and livestock therefore differ slightly.

Intergenerational property mobility

It also proved possible to follow the intergenerational property mobility of families, i.e., the degree of transfer of material wealth most often between parents and children. This involved cases where the original FPSs formally dissolved but the landholding was passed from father or widowed mother to child with the same surname, most often the son. In our set, we also included cases where the landholding was demonstrably passed down to the son-in-law of the original tenant or where the widow became involved in the property chain. In such cases, we may speak of a family reproducing on the same landholding. Of course, the familial continuity of a GFPS could be maintained in various ways, including through kinship on many landholdings, although due to the presence of different surnames and the absence of data concerning kinship ties, this is impossible to discover, and therefore such cases are missing from our records and analysis. In total, we have identified 38 proven cases of GFPSs holding just one "subject" landholding and 2 GFPSs succeeding an FPS with more than one landholding. However, again, the necessary monetary data was available for only a fraction of such cases.

During the analysis, we differentiated between GFPSs according to the number of intrafamilial transfers and we have not included transfers to widows in these numbers.

The "age" of FPSs and GFPSs

Although we do not know the exact age of continuous FPSs as of 1438, they must have already been relatively old by 1456, enduring at least 18 years, with most of them reaching the end of their demographic cycle. The situation was the opposite with GFPSs, most of which were young, created after 1438, and therefore at the beginning, or in the middle, of their cycle.

20.2 Relative socioeconomic mobility of FPSs and GFPSs

We test the models of socioeconomic mobility by analyzing the degree to which the relative property position rose or fell between 1438 and 1456 for (1) FPSs that retained the same tenant and the same landholding for the entire period and (2) GFPSs, i.e., societies usually headed by a male descendant or son-in-law of the original tenant on the same landholding. In the first case, we analyze the property shift of FPSs during one life cycle, and in the second we analyze intergenerational property mobility. With GFPSs, we differentiate whether one or two landholding transfers took place. We also separately evaluate situations in which male succession passed through the widow as a temporary head of the FPS.

At this point, the absolute monetary value of the property of a concrete FPS is not as important as its relative position compared to other FPSs. During our analysis, we used identical positions of FPSs and GFPSs in the quintiles that we worked with in *chapters 18–19 (app. A–B)*. We examined how (1) the position of an FPS changed in quintiles set according to characteristics from 1438 and 1456 respectively, and (2) how the relative position of GFPSs differed in 1456 from that of the original FPS in 1438. We ignored values of non-landholding plots, which are in any case reflected in the total value of property.

In the case of the *stability, differentiating, and leveling model,* the position of all FPSs should remain stable regardless of the quintile in which they lie. Development should be similar, regardless of whether we investigate the value of overall property, "purchase" right to the landholding, or livestock. However, the trajectory of absolute divisions between quintiles and their range should look different—in the *stability* model these would remain more or less stable, in the differentiating model they would move apart, and in the leveling model they would approach each other.

In the *cycle model*, the positions of individual FPSs would change either (1) perfectly, i.e., FPSs in the first quintile would move to the fifth and vice versa, or merely (2) partially, i.e., an FPS from the fifth quintile would fall to the fourth or the third and vice versa. The position in terms of livestock values would be the most dynamic, while the position in terms of the value of the "purchase" right would be the least dynamic. The perfect version of the cycle model assumes the flow of material wealth across the entire peasant community (Russian peasantry of the 19th/20th centuries), the moderate version only within one peasant's stratum or neighboring strata (e.g., small and medium peasants, medium and large peasants alternating). For FPSs that maintained the same tenant between 1438 and 1456, a rise in property is assumed, while for GFPSs, a fall in property is assumed.

The *model of uneven reproduction* assumes a more complicated property trajectory. As with the differentiating model, it emphasizes the growth of property in rich FPSs and a decrease in property in poor FPSs. In line with the cycle model, it also assumes a division of property from extremely rich FPSs and a temporary decline in terms of property. The main tendency in all quintiles would be stability; in quintile IV, this would be accompanied by a significant rise in property, while logically in quintile V a significant decline would occur. The most stable would be the position of FPSs lying in the first quintile. We assume a more frequent rise in quintile IV and a fall in quintile V for GFPSs on the same landholding than with continuous FPSs. The most striking change is a change in position in terms of the value of livestock, the lowest in terms of the value of "purchase" right.

Of course, our research capabilities are limited for many reasons. Firstly, each FPS experienced a unique development that was influenced by several factors that we did not take into account. It is further the case that between 1438 and 1456, individual FPSs were at various phases of their life cycle—some were freshly created, others older—so their demographic characteristics were different. Thirdly, we homogenize the status of FPSs within one quintile.

I. "Subject" landholdings

A. Property mobility of FPSs – tenants of one "subject" landholding

We assessed the change in the relative position of FPSs in 178–183 cases, according to the value of tenure right, livestock, and non-landholding plots (*figs. 20.1; 20.3; 20.5*).[678] It may be stated that:

+ The property position of FPSs most often remained stable, even though we may find different values in individual quintiles.
+ The greatest degree of stability is demonstrated in the poorest and the richest quintiles, i.e., quintile I (42–52%) and quintile V (55–70%).
+ If any change in the relative property position of an FPS occurred, either upwards or downwards, as a rule it was not at all significant. In total, 78–97%

---

678   *App. 20.1a–f.*

of all FPSs remained in the same quintile or moved up or down by one quintile, whatever property item was used to assess the FPS.

+ Generally, the highest degree of stability was demonstrated by FPSs when
assessing the total value of property and, conversely, the lowest when assessing livestock values.

B. Genetically connected FPSs (GFPS) – tenants of one "subject" landholding

We assessed 23 and 25 GFPSs with one landholding transfer and 5 GFPSs
with two landholding transfers. The results differed if we assessed a change
in the position of the GFPS according to the total value of the property or
according to the value of the "purchase" right or the value of livestock. From the
analysis, we determined that:

+ According to the total value of property, the position of GFPSs either
remained the same or declined, usually by one quintile. The same applies
also to GFPSs with two transfers (*fig. 20.2*).[679] Only in one case was an
increase of one quintile observed.

+ The relative position according to the value of the "purchase" right and livestock remained the same, declined, or improved by one or two quintiles,
more or less to approximately the same degree (*figs. 20.4; 20.6*).[680] In GFPSs
with two transfers, we find greater fluctuations; in one case, the GFPS
shifted from quintile I to quintile V.

If we assess the richest GFPSs, their relative position according to total
value of property and "purchase" right remained the most stable (56 and 57%),
while the position was least stable according to the value of livestock (38%);
in this case, most GFPSs declined by one quintile compared to the preceding
FPS (50%). This finding corresponds well to situations in which livestock was
divided up or sold off during the inheritance procedure, while the integrity of
the "subject" farmland remained intact.

The analysis of the total value of property for GFPSs revealed a relatively
impaired position, while the value of the "purchase" right or livestock was more
or less balanced. This may be explained by the disposal of individual non-
landholding plots. The primary heir received the landholding, where they had

679   *App. 20.1a–b.*
680   *App. 21c–f.*

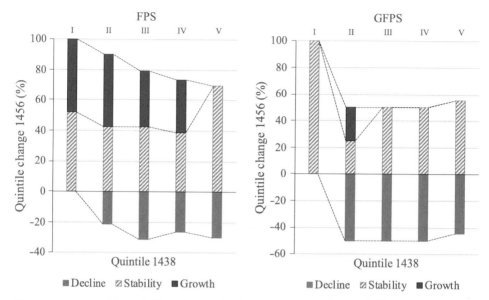

Figures 20.1–20.2. **The relative change in the monetary values of all property held by continuous family property societies (FPSs) and genetically connected family property societies (GFPSs) with one landholding transfer in the city-state of Cheb, 1438 and 1456.**

Source: Cf. *app. 20.1a–b.*

Note: The gray columns represent the proportion of FPSs or GFPSs that rose to a higher property category. The black columns represent the proportion of FPSs or GFPSs that fell into a lower property category. The hatched columns represent the proportion of FPSs or GFPSs whose position did not change.

to keep a certain basic number of horses and cattle, but non-landholding plots could be passed down to other heirs. However, it is possible to imagine a situation where the primary heir had to pay off their other siblings, but they could improve their property position with a good marriage. The number of siblings and the suitability of the marriage greatly predetermined property-related rise or fall.

C. Comparison of FPSs mobility and intergenerational mobility (GFPSs)

The relative property position of FPSs that endured for the entire focus period on the same landholding most often remained stable, regardless of which property item or quintile we assess (*figs. 20.7–20.9*). The position of GFPSs was

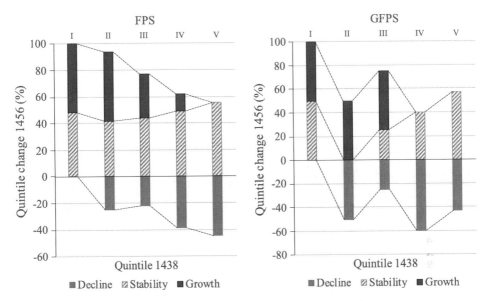

Figures 20.3–20.4. **The relative change in the monetary value of the "purchase" right to landholdings held by continuous family property societies (FPS) and genetically connected family property societies with one property transfer (GFPS) in the city-state of Cheb, 1438–1456.**

Source: Cf. *app. 20.1c–d.*

Note: The gray columns represent the proportion of FPSs or GFPSs that rose to a higher property category. The black columns represent the proportion of FPSs or GFPSs that fell into a lower property category. The hatched columns represent the proportion of FPSs or GFPSs whose position did not change.

much more often downward compared to the preceding FPS, to the greatest extent according to total values of all property and livestock. GFPSs usually maintained the same position as the preceding FPS according to the value of the "purchase" right. This means that intergenerational transfer within one family usually entailed a property-related fall.

II. "Free" landholdings

The analyzed set comprises 30 FPSs that in 1438 had tenure of a "free" landholding and for which we also know the monetary value, and 20 FPSs with the same characteristics for 1456. We ordered these FPSs in ascending order according to the value of property, tenure right to the landholding, and value

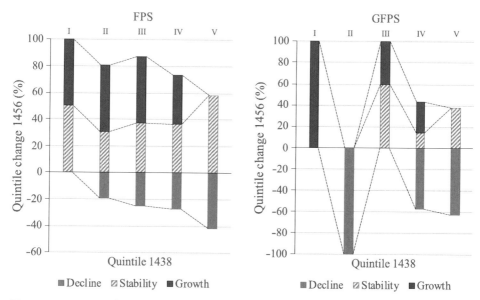

Figures 20.5–20.6. The relative change in the monetary values of livestock held by continuous family property societies (FPSs) and genetically connected family property societies (GFPSs) with one landholding transfer in the city-state of Cheb, 1438–1456.

Source: Cf. *app. 20.1e–f.*

Note: The gray columns represent the proportion of FPSs or GFPSs that rose to a higher property category. The black columns represent the proportion of FPSs or GFPSs that fell into a lower property category. The hatched columns represent the proportion of FPSs or GFPSs whose position did not change.

of livestock, subsequently dividing them into tertiles.[681] We assessed relative property mobility in 9 continuous FPSs and 3 GFPSs with two landholding transfers, one of which always involved a widow. The interpretation was naturally limited by the low frequency of cases.

The property position of FPSs most often remained stable if we evaluate the total value of property and tenure right to the landholding. As for livestock values, a fall in property predominated. For GFPSs, a fall predominated in all areas.

---

681   *App. 20.2.*

III. Complex "subject" landholdings

We evaluated relative property mobility for 8 FPSs that in 1438 had tenure of more than one "subject" landholding and for which we also know the necessary monetary value; in addition, we evaluated one GFPS with one landholding transfer and two GFPSs with two landholding transfers, of which one transfer always involved a widow. To determine the relative property position, we used the absolute values delineating quintiles for tenants of "subject" landholdings.[682]

Despite that a large portion of FPSs and also GFPSs remained only on one landholding until 1456, their relative position measured according to total property value remained the same in all cases. Stability within quintiles was perfect, despite absolute fluctuation. If we evaluate the value of the "purchase" right to the landholding, a relative fall predominated for FPSs, often very extreme. As for relative position measured according to livestock values, we found both stability and upward and downward mobility. There is no reason to evaluate GFPS mobility given the low number of cases.

Summary

The relative property position of continuous FPSs remained more or less stable between 1438 and 1456; therefore, FPSs remained in the same quintile or crossed into a neighboring quintile. This pattern does not correspond to the *cycle reproduction model*. For intergenerational landholding transfers, we found that although the successor GFPS underwent a relative decline in terms of total property value, their relative position most often remained stable in terms of the value of the "purchase" right to the landholding or livestock values. This supports the adequacy of the *model of uneven reproduction*, whereby rich FPSs maintained their position and also had rich successors (GFPS), even when their initial position may have been weakened due to the contemporaneous demographic situation and the need to provide for other heirs. FPSs holding "free" landholdings followed a similar tendency to that of the richest FPSs with tenure of one "subject" landholding. The same applied also to FPSs with tenure of several "subject" landholdings, although even the fission of complex tenure and its fragmentation usually did not mean a fall into lower property quintiles.

682 *App. 20.3a–b.*

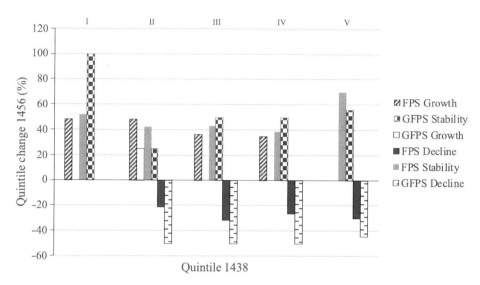

Figure 20.7. Comparison of the relative change in the monetary values of all property held by continuous FPSs and GFPSs in the city-state of Cheb, 1438–1456.

Source: Cf. *figs. 20.1–20.2.*

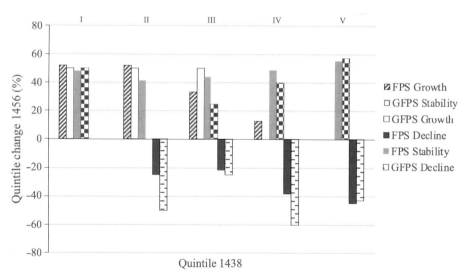

Figure 20.8. Comparison of the relative change in the monetary values of the "purchase" right to "subject" landholdings held by continuous FPSs and GFPSs in the city-state of Cheb, 1438–1456.

Source: Cf. *figs. 20.3–20.4.*

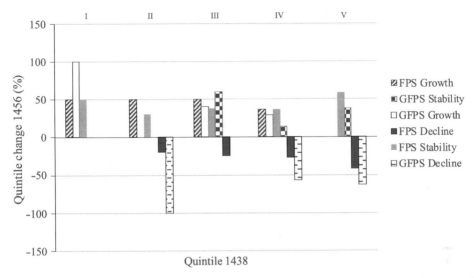

Figure 20.9. **Comparison of the relative change in the monetary values of livestock held by continuous FPSs and GFPSs in the city-state of Cheb, 1438–1456.**

Source: Cf. figs. 20.5–20.6.

20.3 Absolute socioeconomic mobility

In the previous chapter, we tested models of socioeconomic mobility by analyzing the change in the relative property position of individual FPSs and GFPSs. We can also verify these findings by examining in detail the absolute change in property position. Using this procedure, we can eliminate distortion caused by (1) the homogenization of the property position of all FPSs and GFPSs within one quintile and (2) the varyingly wide absolute ranges of the quintiles (cf. *chap. 17.5*).

In XY scatter plot graphs, we demonstrate the socioeconomic mobility of those FPSs that did not disintegrate during the focus period. In addition, we should add:

* Each FPS is indicated by a point whose position is determined by the value of property or main property items in 1438 (x-axis) and in 1456 (y-axis).
* The two diagonals represent the line of nominal value stability, which ignores inflation, and real value stability, which takes into account inflation of 127%. The closer an FPS is to these lines, the more the value of its property was similar in the focus period. A position directly on the line means perfect

stability. A position above the lines means a property rise, and a position below the lines means a property fall. The vertical distance from the diagonals expresses absolute exchange of monetary value.

* The graphs marked with an × indicate FPSs whose landholding was hit by disaster during 1450–1456.
* We do not divide FPSs according to ecological zones.

We summarize and simplify the testimony of the scatter plot graphs in bar charts that express the percentage of FPSs where the monetary value of property rose, fell, or remained stable. We calculate the difference between 1438 and 1456 separately for nominal values and for values for which we take into account the inflation trend—we multiply the monetary value of 1438 by the coefficient 1.27. We consider any difference of up to one threescore of Prague groschen as stability, a positive difference of over one threescore of groschen as a rise, and a negative difference as a fall. The disadvantage of the bar chart summaries is that they do not take into account the absolute size of the differences, but this is expressed in the scatter plot graphs.

Comparison of nominal and non-inflation-related monetary values is suitable for evaluating changes in the value of the "purchase" right, since it may be assumed that the head of the FPSs continued to cite the same monetary values to the tax officials. On the other hand, the inflation trend should be taken into account, especially in comparison with livestock values.[683]

I. "Subject" landholdings

A. Property mobility of FPSs – tenants of one "subject" landholding

We examined property mobility within the life cycle of FPSs in 170–178 cases. To enhance clarity, we have divided the monetary value cited in 1438 (1) into 6 ranges of 10 threescore of Prague groschen for total property value, (2) into 6 ranges of 10 threescore of groschen for "purchase" right value, and (3) into 7 ranges of 3 threescore of groschen for livestock value.

---

683   We leave out of our analysis 8 cases where continuous FPS with tenure of a "subject" land-
      holding endured under the widow, 3 cases of widows with tenure of "free" landholdings,
      8 cases where two genetically connected FPSs followed each other (FPS→GFPS→GFPS),
      and 3 cases of GFPSs with tenure of several "subject" landholdings.

Total property value
Regarding the total property value, most FPSs changed their position to varying degrees, sometimes very radically (*figs. 20.10; 20.11–20.12*).[684] On a nominal level, in all value categories, the predominant change was a rise, most distinct in the poorer FPSs with property of less than 10 threescore of Prague groschen (increase of 80%), least distinct in the rich FPSs with property worth 30–50 threescore (58–59%), and again distinct in the richest FPSs with property worth more that 50 threescore (75%). If we take inflation into account, the proportion of upward mobility was naturally less, and in the value category of 30–39 threescore downward mobility predominated (77%). In principle, it was true that along with the rising value of property, the probability of socioeconomic rise fell, except for the richest FPSs. In the 10 richest landholdings, growth in the value of property was prevalent (70%), sometimes by several dozen threescore, so the resulting values lie somewhere off the scatter graph. The relevant data is contained in *table 20.1.*

A surprising aspect is that mobility among FPSs whose landholdings were hit by catastrophe shortly before 1456 did not differ greatly. It seems that the consequences of these events were quickly overcome and did not leave significant traces behind them.

Table 20.1. **Changes in the total value of extremely rich FPSs (70 threescore or more) in the city-state of Cheb, 1438–1456.**

	Reduction in property value			Increase in property value						
1438	87	94	133	70	73	85	87	91	145	166
1456	77	24	77	97	98	110	160	156	211	258

Source: Ar Cheb, book 1067, *Klosteuerbuch 1438;* book 1084, *Klosteuerbuch (Schätzungsbuch) 1456.*
Note: Monetary values in threescore of Prague groschen.

The value of "purchase" right
A dynamic picture similar to the change in total property values is also illustrated by changes in the values of "purchase" right to landholdings (*figs. 20.13–20.15*).[685] The value of the "purchase" right changed for many FPSs—

684   *App. 20.7a.*
685   *App. 20.7b.*

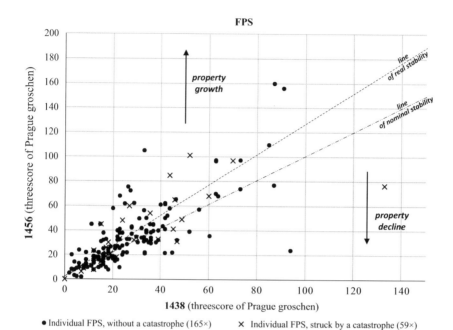

Figure 20.10. **Comparison of the monetary values of all property held by continuous family property societies (FPSs) in the city-state of Cheb, 1438 and 1456.**

Source: Ar Cheb, book 1067, *Klosteuerbuch 1438;* book 1084, *Klosteuerbuch (Schätzungsbuch) 1456.*
Note: Extremely high values omitted.

some were more, some less—while the separate value categories had an overall tendency to differ slightly. On a nominal level, values of up to 15 threescore of Prague groschen in almost all cases increased or remained the same (over 90%); with the smallest values of up to 5 threescore, a rise was predominant (68%), and with values of 10–15 threescore, stability was predominant (54%). With higher values, the upward and downward tendencies were balanced (25–32%), but overall stability predominated (39–40%). The general trend was fairly clear, with the probability of a rise in price falling steadily with the value of the "purchase" right (67% → 25%).

Taking inflation into account, a different picture emerges. An increase in the value of the "purchase" right predominated only for values of up to 5 threescore; otherwise, in all cases a fall dominated, the proportion of which increased steadily along with the rising value. The difference between the nominal and

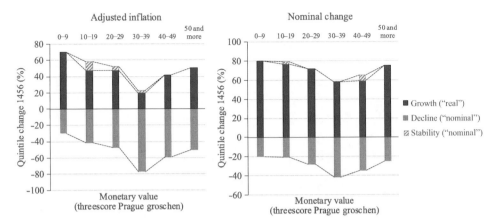

Figures 20.11–20.12. Change in the monetary values of all property held by continuous family property societies (FPSs) in the city-state of Cheb, 1438–1456.

Source: Cf. app. 20.7a. Note: Cf. fig. 20.10.

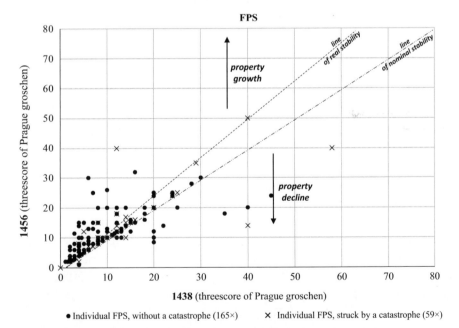

Figure 20.13. Comparison of the monetary values of the "purchase" right to landholdings held by continuous family property societies (FPSs) in the city-state of Cheb, 1438–1456.

Source: Ar Cheb, book 1067, Klosteuerbuch 1438; book 1084, Klosteuerbuch (Schätzungsbuch) 1456. Note: Extremely high values omitted.

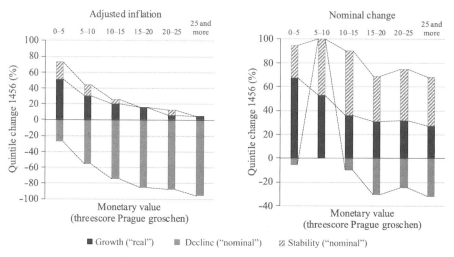

Figures 20.14–20.15. Change in the monetary values of the "purchase" right to landholdings held by continuous family property societies (FPSs) in the city-state of Cheb, 1438–1456.

Source: Cf. app. 20.7b.
Note: Extremely high values omitted. Cf. fig. 20.13.

inflationary values may be explained by the fact that between 1438 and 1456 there was stability or a little growth in the value of the "purchase" right, so when including the fairly high level of inflation in calculations, almost all values fell slightly. But even here it was true that the probability of a fall increased steadily with the value of the "purchase" right (27% → 96%). The values of burned-down or plundered landholdings behaved similarly, lying in the 20–30 three-score range, demonstrating a surprising stability.

The detailed graph depicts FPSs that held a "subject" landholding worth up to 40 threescore (*fig. 20.16*). The vertical and horizontal orientation lines indicate approximate thresholds that differentiated smallholdings and peasant fullholdings. We do not take into account inflation between 1438 and 1456, which would move the horizontal lines slightly higher. We see that even though deviations in absolute monetary values from the diagonals expressing stability were often significant, in most cases a landholding remained in the same operational category. On the other hand, landholdings whose values changed fairly radically are also evident.

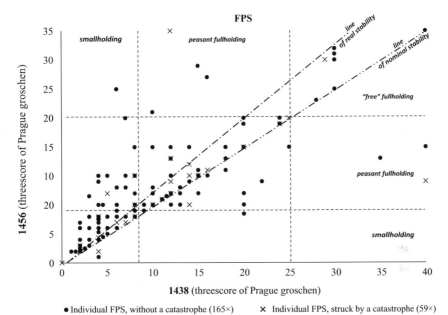

Figure 20.16. Comparison of the monetary values of the "purchase" right to landholdings held by continuous family property societies (FPSs) in the city-state of Cheb, 1438–1456.

Source: Ar Cheb, book 1067, *Klosteuerbuch 1438*; book 1084, *Klosteuerbuch (Schätzungsbuch) 1456*.
Note: Only FPSs holding no more than one landholding selected. Values over 30 threescore of Prague groschen omitted. More on the horizontal and vertical lines, cf. *tab. 14.2–14.3.*

Value of livestock

We see a fairly clear trend in the values of livestock held by FPSs (*figs. 20.17–20.19*).[686] In the lowest values (up to 3 threescore of Prague groschen) the probability of a rise was highest (nominally: 77%; taking inflation into account, 65%), in the highest values (19 threescore or more) the probability of a fall was greatest (nominally: 62%; taking inflation into account, 77%). The tendency between these extremes was not completely steady, but with a rising value the probability of a rise decreased, and the probability of a fall increased. Both tendencies were in approximate balance in values in the 10–12 threescore range, both nominally and taking inflation into account. Regarding the livestock value, we do not register any difference between FPSs whose properties

---

686   *App. 20.7c.*

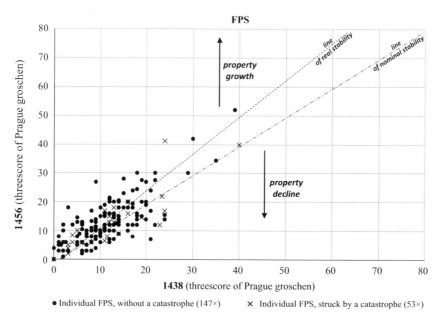

Figure 20.17. Comparison of the monetary values of livestock held by continuous family property societies (FPSs) in the city-state of Cheb, 1438 and 1456.

Source: Ar Cheb, book 1067, Klosteuerbuch 1438; book 1084, Klosteuerbuch (Schätzungsbuch) 1456.

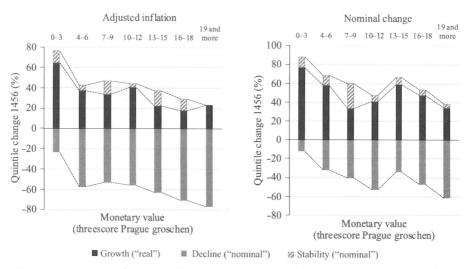

Figures 20.18–20.19. Change in the monetary values of livestock held by continuous family property societies (FPSs) in the city-state of Cheb, 1438–1456.

Source: Cf. app. 20.7c. Note: Cf. fig. 20.17.

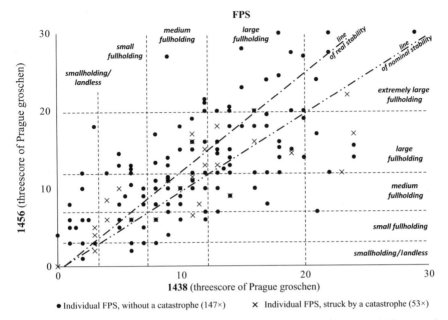

Figure 20.20. **Comparison of the monetary values of livestock held by continuous family property societies (FPSs) in the city-state of Cheb, 1438–1456.**

Source: Ar Cheb, book 1067, *Klosteuerbuch 1438*; book 1084, *Klosteuerbuch (Schätzungsbuch) 1456.*
Note: Only FPSs holding no more than one landholding selected. Values over 30 threescore of Prague groschen omitted. More on the horizontal and vertical lines, cf. *tab. 15.17.*

were plundered between 1450–1456 and FPSs that were spared. The catastrophe factor played no significant role.

The detailed graph contains FPSs that held one landholding and the livestock of which was never valued at more than 30 threescore (*fig. 20.20*). For basic orientation we draw vertical and horizontal lines indicating the operational categories of landholdings; we ignore inflation between 1438 and 1456. It is evident from the graph that along with the rising value of livestock and the extent of absolute fluctuation, in most cases the operational category of a landholding did not change fundamentally or, at most, moved into the neighboring category. Very few FPSs managed to avoid this oscillation. We explain this relative stability as an attempt to achieve a balance between a fairly fixed quantity of arable fields and meadows and horses as draft animals and cattle. On the other hand, even so, the fluctuation in value, and thereby also in the number of horses and cattle, was surprisingly high.

Non-landholding plots[687]

The most dynamic item held by FPSs were non-landholding plots. In 1438, 63 continuous FPSs held such plots, 21 of which had completely disappeared by 1456. Of those FPSs that did not have tenure of non-landholding plots in 1438, 55 of them held at least one in 1456. In 1456, a total of 97 FPSs held non-landholding plots (*figs. 20.21–20.22*).[688] For simplification, we only assess the nominal values of non-landholding plots and ignore inflation trends. Plundering and fires again had no evident effect.

The graphs show a clear tendency. The more valuable the non-landholding plots held by FPSs in 1438, the greater the likelihood that the value in 1456 would be higher, and vice versa. In the lowest value category (up to 3 threescore of Prague groschen) the values for almost one-third of the FPSs (29%) had risen by 1456, although the majority lost tenure of non-landholding plots completely. In the 4–6 threescore category, 36% of the FPSs gained in value, and in categories 7–19, a whole 58–60% of them gained in value. In the over 20 threescore category, 50% of the FPSs gained in value. As for non-landholding plots, wealth really yielded wealth. If we look at the tenants of non-landholding plots, we are looking at the wealthiest section of the Cheb peasantry, which was capable of accumulating further economic resources. It is also true that we see the life cycle of the FPS best in the dynamics of the tenure of the non-landholding plots.

B. Genetically connected FPSs (GFPS) – tenants of one "subject" landholding

We traced 22–25 cases of intergenerational property mobility of FPSs/GFPSs holding "subject" landholdings. This involved the following landholding transfers:

man → man with same surname
man → widow → man with same surname
man → son-in-law

---

687   Klír, "Land transfer," 180–182.
688   *App. 20.7d.*

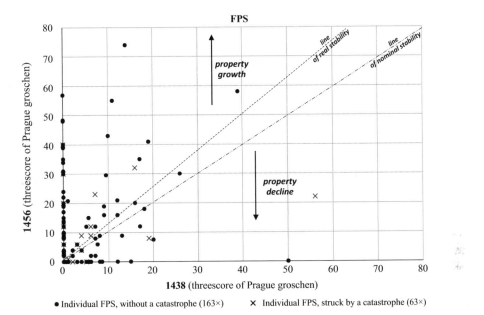

● Individual FPS, without a catastrophe (163×)   × Individual FPS, struck by a catastrophe (63×)

Figure 20.21. Comparison of the monetary values of non-landholding plots held by continuous family property societies (FPSs) in the city-state of Cheb, 1438–1456.

Source: From Klír, "Land transfer," 181, fig. 6. Data according to Ar Cheb, book 1067, *Klosteuerbuch 1438*; book 1084, *Klosteuerbuch (Schätzungsbuch) 1456*. *Note:* Extreme values omitted.

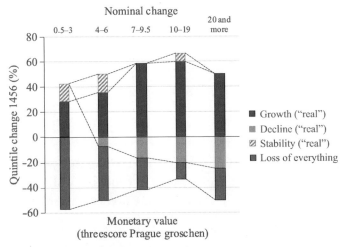

Figure 20.22. Change in the monetary values of non-landholding plots held by continuous family property societies (FPSs) in the city-state of Cheb, 1438–1456.

Source: Cf. app. 20.7d. *Note:* Cf. fig. 20.21.

Given the low number of GFPSs, we divide the monetary values only into 3 ranges. None of the property items were affected by the catastrophic events documented between 1450 and 1456.

Total property value
Intergenerational changes in the total value of all property among geneti-cally connected FPSs (GFPSs) demonstrate more exaggerated dynamics than we saw in the life cycle of the same FPS above (*figs. 20.23–20.25*).[689] On a nominal level, in values up to 20 threescore of Prague groschen, most often an increase occurred (71%), and this tendency prevailed over a reduction in the 20–39 threescore range as well (44%), while in higher values a fall in value prevailed (56%). When taking inflation into account, a fall in property values in all categories prevailed, while in values up to 20 threescore the fall was approx-imately balanced by stability and rise (57%), but in values of 40 threescore or more a fall dominated strongly (89%). In other words, the originally poor FPSs were followed by GFPSs with property that either was of the same worth or was more valuable. Conversely, the successors of rich FPSs could most often expect a drop in property value (for extremes *tab. 20.2*).

Table 20.2. **Changes in the total value of extremely rich FPSs and their successors (120 threescore of Prague groschen or more). Notably, only an extreme reduction of the value of the property is documented.**

Year	Only reduction in property value		
1438	201	220	324
1456	24	62	40

Source: Ar Cheb, book 1067, Klosteuerbuch 1438; book 1084, Klosteuerbuch (Schätzungsbuch) 1456.
Note: Monetary values in threescore of Prague groschen.

"Purchase" right
The change in the value of the "purchase" right to "subject" landholdings in GFPSs shows a trend similar to the change in overall property value (*figs. 20.26–20.28*).[690] On a nominal level, an increase in value predominated in all categories, but for lower values, the proportion of upward cases was higher

689   *App. 20.8a.*
690   *App. 20.8b.*

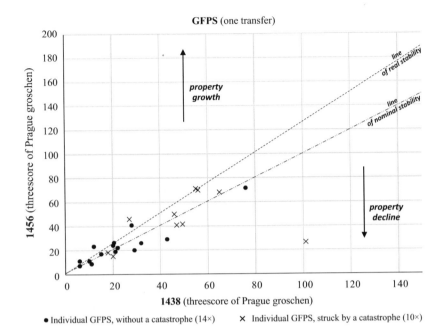

GFPS (one transfer)

• Individual GFPS, without a catastrophe (14×)   × Individual GFPS, struck by a catastrophe (10×)

Figure 20.23. Comparison of the monetary values of all property held by genetically connected family property societies (GFPSs) in the city-state of Cheb, 1438 and 1456.

Source: Ar Cheb, book 1067, *Klosteuerbuch 1438*; book 1084, *Klosteuerbuch (Schätzungsbuch) 1456.*
Note: Extremely high values omitted.

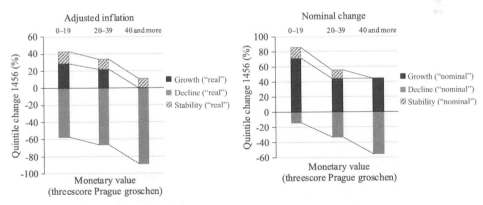

Figures 20.24–20.25. Change in the monetary values of all property held by genetically connected family property societies (GFPSs) in the city-state of Cheb, 1438–1456.

Source: Cf. *app. 20.8a. Note:* Cf. *fig. 20.23.*

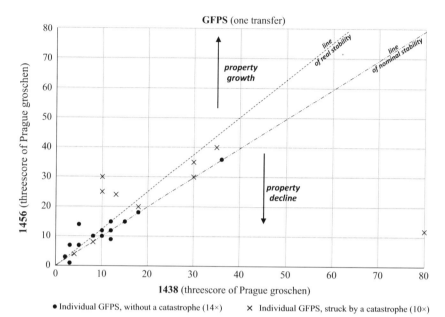

Figure 20.26. Comparison of the monetary values of the "purchase" right to landholdings held by genetically connected family property societies (GFPS) in the city-state of Cheb, 1438–1456.

Source: Ar Cheb, book 1067, *Klosteuerbuch 1438*; book 1084, *Klosteuerbuch (Schätzungsbuch) 1456*.
Note: Extremely high values omitted.

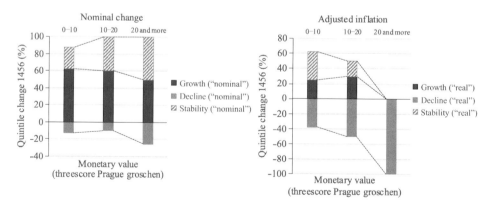

Figures 20.27–20.28. Change in the monetary values of the "purchase" right to landholdings held by genetically connected family property societies (GRMS) in the city-state of Cheb, 1438–1456.

Source: Cf. app. 20.8b. Source: Cf. fig. 20.26.

than for higher values (63% → 50%). For downward cases, the tendency was the opposite; for lower values, the proportion was less than for higher values (13% → 25%). If we take inflation into account, the trend is similar; in the category of highest values of "purchase" right, a reduction in values dominates (100%; for extremes *tab. 20.3*).

Table 20.3. **Changes in GFPSs with extremely high values of the "purchase" right (55 threescore of Prague groschen or more). Notably, only an extreme reduction of the value of the property is documented.**

Year	only reduction in monetary value of the "purchase" right to the landholding		
1438	70	80	240
1456	13	12	40

Source: Ar Cheb, book 1067, *Klosteuerbuch 1438*; book 1084, *Klosteuerbuch (Schätzungsbuch) 1456*.
Note: Monetary values in threescore of Prague groschen.

Livestock

The relationship between the original value of the livestock of an FPS in 1438 and its successor—a GFPS in 1456—shows a clear-cut tendency (*figs. 20.29–31*).[691] The higher the original value of the livestock, the higher the probability of a fall or just a slight rise. In values of up to 9 threescore of Prague groschen, a nominal rise dominated (75%); in the range 10–15 threescore, a fall was more prevalent (40%) than a rise (20%), and in values over 16 threescore, a fall in value dominated (67%). If we take inflation into account, a fall in value dominated already from the over 10 threescore range (90%). The differences are so striking that some GFPSs could end up in a different economic category than the original FPS.

Non-landholding plots[692]

We have 8 cases at our disposal where it is possible to compare the value of non-landholding land held by a "subject" FPS and the successor GFPS (*figs. 20.32–20.33*).[693] In lower values (0.5–6 threescore) two FPSs achieved

---

691   *App. 20.8c.*
692   See *also* Klír, "Land transfer," 180–182.
693   *App. 20.8d.*

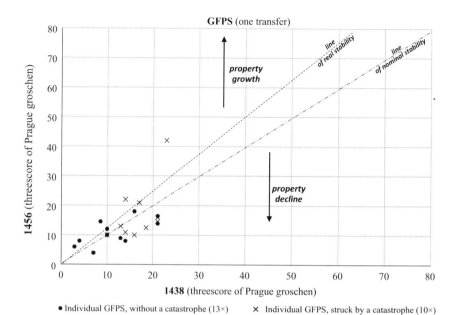

Figure 20.29. **Comparison of the monetary values of livestock held by genetically connected family property societies (GFPSs) in the city-state of Cheb, 1438–1456.**

Source: Ar Cheb, book 1067, Klosteuerbuch 1438; book 1084, Klosteuerbuch (Schätzungsbuch) 1456.

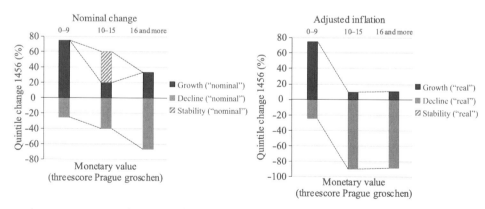

Figures 20.30–20.31. **Change in the monetary values of livestock held by genetically connected family property societies (GFPSs) in the city-state of Cheb, 1438–1456.**

Source: Cf. app. 20.8c. Source: Cf. fig. 20.29.

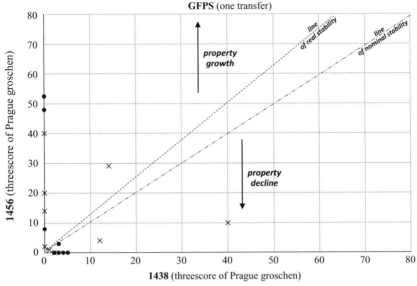

GFPS (one transfer)

• Individual GFPS, without a catastrophe (6×)   ✕ Individual GFPS, struck by a catastrophe (9×)

Figure 20.32. Comparison of the monetary values of non-landholding plots held by genetically connected family property societies (GFPS) in the city-state of Cheb, 1438–1456.

According to: Klír, "Land transfer," 182, fig. 7.
Source: Ar Cheb, book 1067, *Klosteuerbuch 1438*; book 1084, *Klosteuerbuch (Schätzungsbuch) 1456*.
Note: Extreme values omitted.

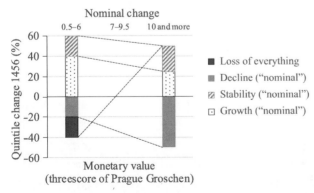

Figure 20.33. Change in the monetary values of non-landholding plots held by genetically connected family property societies (GFPSs) in the city-state of Cheb, 1438 and 1456.

Source: Cf. app. 20.8d. Note: Cf. fig. 20.32.

improvement, while one lost tenure of all of its property; the situation was the opposite in higher values (10 threescore or more).

C. Comparison of FPSs' mobility and intergenerational mobility (GFPSs)

To compare property mobility within the life cycle of one FPS and intergenerational mobility of FPSs/GFPSs, we must adapt the ranges used in the analysis of FPSs to fit the ranges used in the analysis of GFPSs. For simplicity, we compare only the nominal values, and we indicate the inflation trend only graphically.

When looking at the **total value of property**, with both FPSs and GFPSs, it is evident that, together with the monetary value, the proportion of upward cases fell and the proportion of downward cases rose.[694] This tendency was more distinct in GFPSs (nominal rises in extreme intervals: 71% → 44%; falls: 14% → 56%) than in FPSs (nominal rises in extreme intervals: 78% → 68%; falls: 14% → 56%). For intergenerational transfer, a greater probability of a property fall and a lesser probability of a rise existed than for continuous FPSs. In both cases, the probability of a property fall rose as the monetary value of the property rose.

For the **value of the "purchase" right**, the opposite applied.[695] The probability of a nominal increase in value was generally higher in cases of intergenerational transfer of an FPS/GFPS than in a continuous FPS. The explanation is the following. If the tenant of the landholding did not change, the valuation of monetary value in most cases remained the same, while in the event of property transfer, the landholding was newly valued. In both cases, the probability of an increase in the value of the "purchase" right decreased the higher the original value was. In GFPSs, this tendency was more distinct (nominal rises in extreme intervals: 63% → 50%; falls: 13% → 25%) than in FPSs (nominal rises in extreme intervals: 59% → 29%; falls: 2% → 29%).

With rising **livestock values**, again the probability of a rise decreased, and the probability of a fall increased, although this was not as clear-cut as with the values of the "purchase" right.[696] In GFPSs this tendency was more distinct (nominal rises: 75% → 33%; falls: 25% → 67%) than in FPSs (nominal rises: 67% → 47%; falls: 22% → 47%). In intergenerational transfers, a greater prob-

---

694   *App. 20.4a; app. 20.9a.*
695   *App. 20.4b; app. 20.9b.*
696   *App. 20.4c; app. 20.9c.*

ability of a reduction in the amount of livestock and a lesser probability of an increase existed than in continuous FPSs.

A comparison of changes in the value of non-landholding plots between continuous FPSs and FPS/GFPSs comes up against the problem of low numbers.[697] We can assess 63 cases for FPSs, but only 8 cases for FPS/GFPSs. For this reason, we did not perform a more detailed evaluation and interpretation of the changes according to the values of the non-landholding plots.

The results of the comparison of property mobility of FPSs and FPS/GFPSs in 1438–1456 draws a fairly sharp picture. On the level of the predominating trends, it was the case that:

+ In the course of its existence, an FPS accumulated freely disposable property, specifically livestock and non-landholding plots, the values of which rose with the degree of continuity of the FPS.
+ Intergenerational transfer within families usually meant property decline; as a result of paying off siblings, a GFPS could lose its non-landholding plots and some of its livestock.
+ Conversely, the value of the "purchase" right to a landholding was set slightly higher in the new assessment.
+ For continuous FPSs and intergenerational transfer of FPS/GFPSs, the probability of a property rise or fall correlated with the property value.
+ The value of the property of rich FPSs and GFPSs increased less often than that of poor, and vice versa.

II. "Free" landholdings

We assessed 9–11 continuous FPSs that had tenure of a "free" landholding. In the total value of the property, the value of the tenure right, and the value of the livestock, we see a similar tendency as in continuous FPSs holding a "subject" landholding.[698] With the rising monetary value of 1438, by 1456 the chance for an increase in property position fell, and conversely, the risk of its declining rose. Shifts in the value of non-landholding plots are not possible to interpret in clear-cut terms.[699]

---

697   *App. 20.4d; app. 20.9d.*
698   *App. 20.5; app. 20.10a–c.*
699   *App. 20.5.*

As a rule, the property position of GFPSs was much worse compared to the preceding FPS.

III. Complex "subject" landholdings

In the researched set, we assessed 8 continuity FPSs that had tenure of more than one "subject" landholding in 1438.

+ According to the **total value of the property,** they belong in the range of 20 threescore of Prague groschen or more. On a nominal level, between 1438 and 1456, most of them suffered a decline (63%), which is opposite to the trend for FPSs with tenure of just one "subject" landholding, where the majority in the same property range enjoyed a rise (58–77%).[700]
+ According to **"purchase" right** values, such continuous FPSs in 1438 were unsurprisingly among the richest (10 threescore or more). By 1456, most of them had suffered decline on a nominal level (63%), while with FPSs with only one "subject" landholding, stability was predominant (39–40%) and decline was rare (10–32%).[701]
+ According to the value of **livestock,** 5 continuity FPSs were among the richest of all (16 threescore or more); by 1456, 3 of them had declined (60%) and 2 had improved.[702] In this respect, it tallies with the continuity FPSs that held one "subject" landholding.
+ Improvements, i.e., their accumulation, predominated for **non-landholding plots.**[703]

Summary

Every FPS had its own unique reproduction conditions; every tenant and his family behaved differently. Therefore, the data unsurprisingly presented in the summary tables do not correspond completely to any of the socioeconomic mobility models. We may rule out the premise that the position and repro-duction of most FPSs were fixed, as predicted by the *stability model,* or that a considerable number of them would undergo dramatic change in line with

700   *App. 20.6; app. 20.11a.*
701   *App. 20.6; app. 20.11b.*
702   *App. 20.6; app. 20.11c.*
703   *App. 20.6.*

the *cycle model*. As with the peasantry of the Early Modern Period, we also encounter stability, continuity, and change in the late medieval city-state of Cheb.[704] But we are interested in quantitative differences, and these speak in favor of the *model of uneven reproduction*.

A comparison of continuous FPSs in 1438 and 1456 showed that a greater chance existed for rich FPSs that their position would decline than for poor FPSs. Specifically:

+ As for the **total value of property,** in principle it was true that the probability of a socioeconomic rise fell as its value increased, except for a small group containing the richest FPSs.
+ A similar trend may be identified in the **value of the "purchase" right** to a landholding. The probability of a price rise fell steadily with its value.
+ We find a negative correlation between the value of **livestock** in 1438 and the probability of it rising by 1456. The probability of values increasing dominated for the lowest starting values, whereas the probability of values decreasing dominated for the highest starting values. Interestingly, both tendencies were in approximate balance for values in the 10–12 threescore range, which corresponded to the value of a paired team of horses and 4–6 cows and heifers. This finding corresponds to the idea that a certain optimal threshold existed for the operational size of the landholding that poorer FPSs attempted to reach by expanding their property, and richer FPSs tried to remain above it. In this case, the law of equilibrium between the means of production and the labor force applied.
+ In the values of **non-landholding plots,** the basic tendency differed. The more valuable the non-landholding plots held by FPSs in 1438, the greater the likelihood that the value in 1456 would be higher, and vice versa. In this case, it seems that the richest families consciously applied specific strategies, thanks to which their wealth yielded wealth.

The absolute property trajectory of the GFPS was identical in principle to that of the FPS but was also more distinctive. The originally poor FPSs were followed by GFPSs with property that was either of the same worth or more valuable. Conversely, more often than not a decline in property awaited the successor of rich FPSs.

---

704   Lindström, *Distribution*, 167.

Generally speaking, in the course of their existence, FPSs accumulated property, while intergenerational transfer within the family usually meant a drop in the total value of property and livestock, which is an indication of paying off siblings in property. This aligns with the finding that the value of the "purchase" right to a landholding either did not change or rose slightly. For continuous FPSs and intergenerational transfer of FPS/GFPSs it is also true that the probability of a property rise negatively correlated with the property value.

As far as we can tell from the analyzable cases, FPSs and GFPSs with tenure of "free" landholdings or several "subject" landholdings followed the tendency of the richest FPSs that held a "subject" landholding.

It should be added that the property mobility of those FPSs whose landholdings were hit by a catastrophe between 1450 and 1456 did not differ from other landholdings. The consequences of these catastrophic events—including the widespread plundering of the city-state of Cheb in 1452, which devastated one-fifth of the city-state's settlements—were soon overcome and did not leave any significant economic trace.

20.4 Interpretation

The results of the analysis of relative and absolute socioeconomic mobility must be interpreted with care for many reasons, but nevertheless they do correspond to the *model of uneven reproduction (fig. 20.34)*. To sum up:

1. Property stability and change are documented; however, it is the quantitative differences that are important. A large number of the analyzed FPSs during their existence maintained more or less their original property position, but a considerable proportion of them did change it. It can be seen that rich FPSs had a tendency to become poorer, and poor FPSs to become richer. Nevertheless, a narrow segment of the richest FPSs were able to continue accumulating property. The greatest dynamism may be seen in non-landholding plots, with many FPSs losing them completely, and others newly gaining them, although the prevailing tendency was growth. Multidirectional property mobility would testify to the significant influence of demographic factors (life cycles) and the application of the principle of fragmentation. However, the growing value of the property of a narrow stratum of the richest FPSs corresponds to the principle of the accumulation of

disposable property and to the prediction of neoclassical economics and Marxist models.

2. Mobility of GFPSs demonstrated a greater bond to property category than in the case of FPSs. Poor families tended to maintain or expand their property, while rich families tended to divide it. As a rule, the property amassed by the richest stratum of FPS did not withstand generational replacement but rather disintegrated. This pattern again testifies to the fundamental weight of the principle of fragmentation against a backdrop of demographic factors and contemporaneous inheritance practices, as modeled by neopopulationist theories. Small properties could not be further divided, and free labor capacity forced peasants to endeavor to maintain or increase resources. Conversely, large properties, sometimes comprising several landholdings and other items, were potentially divided up among several heirs, or the heir had no motivation to maintain them. Siblings increased the risk of the socioeconomic decline of the main heir of "subject" landholdings and had fewer opportunities for economic rise.

3. Based on threshold property values around 20–30 threescore of Prague groschen where the upward and downward tendency of FPSs were balanced, we can hypothetically expect a balanced size category of a medium-large landholding that fully satisfied the needs of the family and also optimally sourced their labor capacity. Such a landholding with an ideal balance of means of production, labor force, and yields would comprise livestock worth 10–12 threescore (a paired team of horses + 4–6 cows); the rest of the monetary value would include the "purchase" right and/or non-landholding plots. Although further expansion of property was welcomed, subjectively it was much less important than achieving balance, and so the sale or division of property above the threshold value was fairly acceptable for the family. In the event of scarcity, when a landholding had not achieved the point of balance, the opposite applied. The peasant was strongly motivated to acquire property and choose a corresponding demographic (marital) or economic strategy. Property mobility was therefore greatly influenced by the demographic cycle of the family and the individuality of the particular peasant. In this respect, we should recall the similarly formulated models of A. V. Chayanov.[705]

---

705 Tschajanow, *Die Lehre*, esp. 35–41. An innovative theoretical rationale for the result of subjective decision making, even if for a different situation, is offered by Dribe, *Leaving*, 81–105.

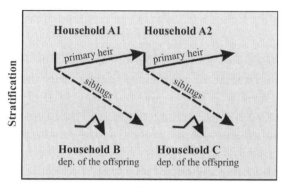

Figure 20.34. Diagram of variations to the model of uneven reproduction. Socioeconomic mobility differs not only between rich and poor families, but also between the offspring of the rich.

Source: Cf. fig. 3.1–F. Note: dep. – departure

4. Non-landholding and fairly freely disposable land plots had a special function. As a rule, they were not enormously large in area and did not significantly increase the labor burden of the FPS, but they did facilitate its focused optimization. It was also a suitable means of accumulating wealth, which played a large role in the endowment of offspring and in inheritance proceedings.

The positive interdependence between property size and (1) continuous family property tenure and (2) the trajectory of the socioeconomic mobility of FPSs and GFPSs fully corresponds with the predictions of the *model of uneven reproduction* and opposes the *cyclic social mobility* model. The model of uneven reproduction, as formulated for Halesowen in pre-plague England and for Björskog in early modern Sweden has yet to be proven in our case. It assumes that tenants on poorer landholdings were pushed out by the offspring of richer FPSs. It is therefore necessary to establish the reason for the higher degree of discontinuity of poorer FPSs. Was it due to moving to even poorer landholdings and descending into landlessness? Or conversely was it due to moving to vacant and richer landholdings? These questions are addressed in *chap. 22.*

21.
Fluctuation of tax
on landholdings, 1442–1456

21.1 Research objectives and method

In the previous chapter, we formulated our theories concerning the analysis of socioeconomic mobility based on the monetary value of the taxed property and its main constituent components for 1438 and 1456. We simplified the exceptionally diverse reality and in principle assumed that the development in 1438–1456 was linear in principle. Conversely, this chapter aims to analyze the degree of oscillation during 1442–1456. We base our study on the amount of the land tax set and paid annually. We address the following questions:

1) To what extent did the level of the tax fluctuate? Did continuity or change prevail?
2) In this respect, to what extent did landholdings that had not undergone any property transfer (continuous FPSs) differ from other landholdings?
3) What tendencies in the level of prescribed tax prevailed at the landholdings with continuous FPSs and the other landholdings?

The level of prescribed land tax was based on the monetary value of property, but their relation was not completely straightforward, because the tax rate was individual and took into account the taxpayer's ability to pay. Therefore, a tax of the same level could be prescribed to properties of differing values and vice versa. Differences in the tax rate from one taxpayer to the next were not dramatically different and were a matter of percentage points or at most 20% or 30% (*chap. 12*).

Method

Annual data on the level of the Cheb land tax are available from 1442. Our analysis of the situation is confined to two-year intervals between 1443–1451, the year-to-year interval between 1442–1443 and 1455–1456, and a four-year interval from 1451–1455. This four-year interval was chosen due to the mass tax land remission in 1453 caused by the plundering of the city-state of Cheb in 1452.

For the sample analyzed, we include only those landholdings that could be identified in all the *1442–1456 Land Tax Registers*. We ignored mills and complex tenure comprising several landholdings. We analyze "subject" and "free" landholdings separately.

In the focus period, the land tax was increased several times for all tax-payers; therefore, it was not stable on an absolute level, even though the relative property position of taxpayers (landholdings) did not change. Therefore, the relative differences, not the absolute ones, are important.

Due to the necessity of analyzing the relative differences between land-holdings and also due to the large quantity of data, we selected the following procedure. In each monitored year we ordered taxpayers ("subject" landhold-ings) according to the level of prescribed tax, further dividing them into quintiles (*app.* C).[706] Then we examined whether landholdings had remained in the same quintiles or, on the contrary, if they had moved between them. Nat-urally, separate quintiles cover differently sized tax ranges (*chap. 17.5; fig. 17.1*), some being relatively large and the landholding remaining within them even after a high absolute change of prescribed tax (quintile V), while some are relatively narrow and even a slight absolute change means a change of quintile (quintiles II and III). But what is most essential here is not the difference in stability and oscillation between quintiles, but primarily it is the differences between the landholdings with a different number and nature of property transfers. For "free" landholdings we used tertiles.

706   If several taxpayers had been prescribed the same tax, we took into account the tax amounts in the following years.

21.2 Analysis

"Subject" landholdings

We investigated the degree of stability and fluctuation of the prescribed land tax both for the whole landholding dataset (i.e., all landholdings) as well as for specific types of landholdings that (1) remained in the tenure of the same FPS / continuous FPS, (2) was transferred within the same family/GFPS, (3) despite being transferred within the same family continuity was later interrupted, and (4) were never transferred within the same family (*figs. 21.1–21.4*).[707]

The most common trend evident from 1442–1456 was a relatively stable landholding position, which generally fluctuated only within the same quintile. Of 528 landholdings, 43% remained in the same quintile during the examined 14 years; both of the extreme quintiles appear to be the most stable—quintile I (56% of stable landholdings) and quintile V (63% of stable landholdings)—whereas with the rest of them, only one-third of the landholdings remained in the same quintile without any interruption (31–33%). For landholdings in the continuous tenure of an FPS or GFPS, a slightly higher degree of stability was evident (46% and 47%) than for the rest of the landholdings (33% and 40%).

Number of transitions of a landholding between quintiles
Most landholdings changed their position once or twice (46%), a few of them three to five times (12%). Naturally, if the level of prescribed tax approached a quintile boundary, even a landholding with a relatively stable amount of tax could appear alternately once in one, then later in the neighboring quintile (*fig. 17.1*). A high number of changes therefore does not necessarily mean a fluctuating nominal value of tax, but just indicates one of the disadvantages of our quintile approach. A revealing, albeit extreme, example of this type is demonstrated in four landholdings whose trajectory from 1438–1456 followed a multidirectional pattern: quintile III→IV→III→IV→III. At least some of the shifts of just one quintile could in reality express something close to relative stability. In 23% of landholdings, the tax amount changed quintile only once and by just one quintile, and although in the other 20% one or two changes occurred, the shift occurred within two neighboring quintiles. In other words,

707   *App. 21.1a–c.*

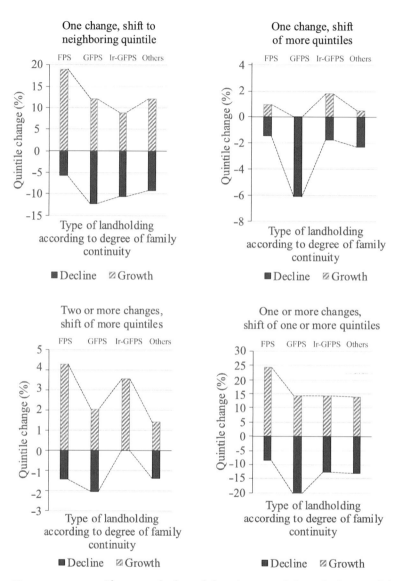

Figures 21.1–21.4. **Characteristics of the change of the relative position of "subject" landholdings according to the tax land burden in 1442–1456. The share of the family property societies (FPSs) that remained in the same category is not displayed.**

Source: Cf. *app. 21.1a–b.*

Note: The hatched columns represent the proportion of property societies that went into a relatively higher tax category. The black columns, on the other hand, represent the proportion of property societies that suffered a decline. Cf. *app. 21.1a–b.*

85% of the landholdings either did not change their relative position at all or only slightly.

Degree of quintile change

What we consider to be substantial:

+ A distinct, specific landholding in the continuous tenure of the same FPS means a rise of one or more quintiles.
+ If a landholding changed its relative tax position just once, then for a continuous FPS this meant an increase in approximately three-quarters of the cases, whereas for other landholdings the upward and downward tendencies were balanced, and for intrafamilial transfer (GFPS) a fall prevailed.
+ If a landholding changed its position more than once, then for a continuous FPS we can see an exclusively upward tendency noticeably more often than for the rest of the landholdings.
+ For continuous FPSs, the change was also fairly smooth; a single leap of two quintiles or more can be documented in only 5% of cases, whereas for the rest of the landholdings it can be documented in 12% of cases, and for interrupted GFPSs in as many as 14% of cases and for GFPSs in 6% of cases.

This is all consistent with the findings of the previous chapters, which indicate that the continuity of FPSs on the same landholding usually enabled a gradual accumulation of property, whereas the disintegration of FPSs and a transfer to the primary heirs (GFPS) was more often connected with property decline.

The position of 13% of landholdings changed in a wider range from two to four quintiles. The continuous rise or fall of the tax amount across several quintiles would not be surprising, since some of the landholdings and FPSs could go through radical changes that would ultimately lead to a great change of the property position (cf. *chap. 21*). The question is: what was the proportion of landholdings whose position did not change linearly but went through ups and downs in a way that could not be established through a mere mechanical comparison of the property position in 1438 and 1456?

Trajectory of the change

When a landholding changed quintile then on a single occasion it shifted most often to the neighboring one (91% of most of the changes). Therefore, the shifts were mostly undramatic. Some landholdings changed their position several times, but they also followed only an upward or downward trajectory (4% of all landholdings). The majority of landholdings that changed their position just once were better off (15% of all landholdings); in fewer cases their position worsened (8% of all landholdings). It is again true that continuous FPSs were more likely to have an upward trajectory, whereas for the remainder of the landholdings, both tendencies were equal.

Altogether, 40 landholdings (8% of all landholdings) changed their position twice or more times and at the same time had (a) a wider range than just two neighboring quintiles and (b) a more complicated trajectory. An important question for continuous FPSs and for GFPSs is: to what extent did they experience this complex property development that cannot be detected by a simple comparison of the property position in 1438 and 1456? Of the 40 total landholdings in which we had identified a rather complex, saltatory, and fluctuating trajectory of the tax amount, 9 were continuous FPSs and two were GFPSs, which is an insignificant proportion of the total.

"Free" landholdings

We have at our disposal an uninterrupted sequence of tax amounts for 21 "free" landholdings. If we compared them together with "subject" landholdings, then more than two-thirds of them would fall into quintile V. This is why we assess them separately and divide them into tertiles.[708]

The prevailing trend was stability (47%) or a change by one tertile or oscillation in the framework of two neighboring tertiles (42%). In one case, the landholding shifted from the first to the third tertile and in another case it was the other way around (11%). So multidirectional and, at the same time, dramatic oscillation cannot be proven for the "free" landholdings.

21.3 Summary and interpretation

The main aim of this chapter was to address the objection that the property position of an FPS at only two randomly selected points in time (1438, 1456) does not have sufficient interpretational potential, because the trajectory of

708   *App. 21.1d.*

socioeconomic mobility did not necessarily have to be linear, but rather oscillating. Therefore, in this chapter, we studied in great detail fluctuations in the nominal value of tax being paid by landholdings at two- or three-year intervals. We found that:

+ Whether or not they remained with the same FPS for the entire focus period, the majority of landholdings did not experience a dramatic change from the point of view of tax burden, and their position stayed the same or changed by just one quintile (85%).
+ If a landholding changed its position more dramatically, it generally followed either an upward or downward trajectory.
+ Under 8% of landholdings escaped this pattern, but we covered only 11 of these landholdings in our analyses of the socioeconomic mobility of FPSs and GFPSs in *chapter 20*.

In summary, the results and interpretations presented in *chapter 20* are not distorted by the fact that the relative property position of an FPS on the same landholding would oscillate dramatically and also multidirectionally from year to year. The analysis of the tax burden also confirmed that the continuity of an FPS on the same landholding usually enabled the gradual accumulation of property, whereas the disintegration of an FPS and a passing to the primary heir (GFPS) usually brought a property split.

22.
Migration

(figs. 22.19–22.22; table ID in appendix)

22.1 Introduction

This chapter aims to find correlations between socioeconomic mobility and the migration of peasants in the city-state of Cheb. This is a fundamental interpretive item that will show what the prospects were for poor FPSs and whether their migration from one landholding to another was connected with a socioeconomic rise or fall. In other words, it can reveal the extent to which migration worked as a channel of socioeconomic mobility. We are also interested in the question of the distances FPSs moved, whether they stayed within their home area or broke their ties and moved a longer distance away.

In our analysis, we cover all landholding transfers recorded between 1442 and 1456. The analyzed set of landholdings is the same set analyzed in *chapter 19*. Of course, we can only evaluate the migration of tenants within the city-state of Cheb and, even then, only partially. We excluded from our analysis 33 cases where tenants moved from a rural landholding to the city where they gained citizenship. These cases are dealt with specifically in *chapter 23*.

From the point of view of testing different models of socioeconomic mobility of the peasantry, it is essential to ask whether, by moving, the tenants acquired richer or poorer landholdings than their original ones. In principle, we can base our thoughts on two types of data: first, on the level of prescribed land tax and, second, on the monetary value of the "purchase" right to the landholdings. We will analyze separately (1) moving within the same settlement and moving between different settlements, (2) "subject" and "free" tenure, and (3) tenure comprising several landholdings.

From the basic overview, it is evident that relocation of peasants between landholdings during the period covered in our study was balanced; in every five-year period, we managed to identify about 40 cases of migration.[709] Therefore, we treat the focus period 1442–1456 as a whole.

22.2 Comparison based on land tax level[710]

The level of prescribed land tax enables us to see whether the total monetary value of a peasant's property rose, fell, or stayed the same upon moving from one landholding to another. The fundamental advantage of using the nominal value of tax as data is the fact that we know the data for every year and every tenant and therefore also for every move from one landholding to another. The fact that we know the previous payment history of the migrating peasant on his original landholding and subsequent development on the target landholding is also important for a detailed perspective and interpretation.

However, the options for interpretation and research are limited. Firstly, the land tax was not always static from year to year, e.g., in 1443, 1447, and 1456 there was a universal increase in tax. Therefore, moving during these years meant a greater likelihood that the taxpayer would pay a nominally higher amount on the target landholding than on the original landholding. The problem caused by annual tax increases can nevertheless be solved by evaluating not the absolute values but rather the relative position within quintiles.

Secondly, the land tax prescribed for the tenant coming to a target landholding could be lower for various reasons, mainly when they moved to an abandoned landholding, and only in the following year could their tax be increased. In these cases, there is a greater probability that moving will seem to be a socioeconomic fall. The solution is to follow developments in tax in the longer term.

709   *App. 22.2a.*
710   Summarized also in Klír, "Local migration," 206–208.

Relative level of land tax

To evaluate the relative position of the taxpayer according to the amount of the land tax prescribed, we use the same categorization into quintiles as in *chapters 18–20*.

Individual property categories differed widely in their share of the overall number of moves, both upon moving between landholdings within the same settlement (28 evaluated situations; *figs. 22.1–22.2*)[711] and between settlements (137 situations; *figs. 22.3–22.4*).[712] Almost one-third of departures and arrivals were of the tenants from the poorest landholdings, then the proportion gradually fell and the wealthiest property category accounts for only 7–10% of the total established mobility.

+ Significant differences can be found in the economic consequences of a tenant moving between landholdings within the same settlement and moving between settlements (*fig. 22.5*). Moving within the same settlement resulted mostly in maintaining the same property position or in its decline. Only 22% of the poorest significantly improved their situation by moving within the settlement; in the other quintiles, except for quintile V, it was more, at 25–40%.

+ Moving between settlements represented a jump to a higher quintile for 47% of the poorest taxpayers. Thanks to migration, the position of 41% of the taxpayers in quintile II rose, whereas for 31% of them, it fell. In the quintiles III and IV, falls prevailed over rises. The taxpayers from the wealthiest quintile V made their situation worse by changing landholdings in 46% of the cases. So, on the level of general tendency, (1) the probability of migration decreased as the property category became wealthier, while simultaneously, (2) the likelihood of experiencing a decline in socioeconomic status increased. Hence, a tenant moving between settlements generally involved socioeconomic mobility: for the poor, it was a chance for an upward rise, while for the rich it was more likely a property fall.

Jumps in property value due to moving were usually not dramatic; overall, a shift of just one quintile prevailed. No case of a tenant passing from quintile I to quintile V is documented; we found just four cases of a fall into quintile IV.

711   App. 22.1a.
712   App. 22.1b.

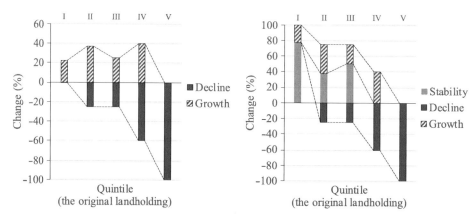

Figures 22.1–22.2. Relative change of the taxpayer's position when moving within the same settlement, 1438-1456.

Source: Cf. app. 22.1a.

Note: Fig. 22.1 – without the taxpayers whose position remained relatively stable. Fig. 22.2 – including the taxpayers whose position remained relatively stable. The gray columns represent the proportion of taxpayers who by moving from one landholding to another reached a higher property category. The black columns represent the opposite. The hatched columns represent the proportion of taxpayers whose property position remained relatively stable, even after moving (only fig. 22.2).

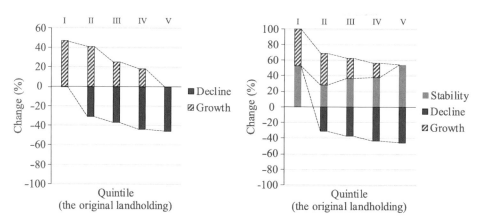

Figures 22.3–22.4. Relative change of the taxpayer's position when moving within the same settlement, 1438-1456.

Source: Cf. App. 22.1b.

Note: Fig. 22.3 – without the taxpayers whose position remained relatively stable. Fig. 22.4 – including the taxpayers whose position remained relatively stable. The gray columns represent the proportion of taxpayers who by moving from one landholding to another reached a higher property category. The black columns represent the opposite. The hatched columns represent the proportion of taxpayers whose property position remained relatively stable, even after moving (only fig. 22.4).

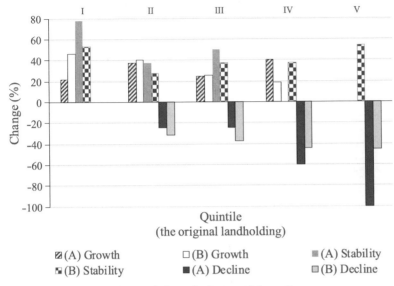

Figure 22.5. **Comparison of the relative position of a taxpayer upon moving within the same settlement and between settlements, 1438–1456.**

Source: Cf. Figs. 22.1–22.4.

Only one fall from quintile II to quintile V is documented. We found a profound decline several times in taxpayers departing from the wealthiest landholdings, but this could have involved moving into a retired tenant's dwelling.

Multiple migrations between landholdings

We identified 11 taxpayers in the analyzed set who moved twice during the period in question, meaning they farmed on three landholdings in a row. From a topographic point of view, we can see cases when a taxpayer (cf. *tab. 22.1*):
a) on his second move returned to their original landholding (1×)
b) on his second move returned to their original settlement, but to a different landholding (1×)
c) moved in all cases to a different settlement (9×)

From the point of view of socioeconomic mobility, we differentiate case(s) of:
i) rise (2×)   iii) fall (3×)
ii) stability (5×)   iv) complex trajectory (1×)

Table 22.1. **List of taxpayers with multiple migrations within the city-state of Cheb, 1438–1456.**

Taxpayer's name	Settlement and reference number of the landholding	Range	Tax according to quintile (simplified)	Type of migration
Maier Fridel	*Gaßnitz 18* Scheibenreuth 16 *Gaßnitz 18*	1438–1447 1449–1452 1456 and onward	2→3→4 3→2 3→2	(a) – (ii)
Wolffel Pögel; Wolffel	*Konradsgrün 16* Scheibenreuth 14 *Konradsgrün 8*	1447–1448 1449–1450 1451–1452	1 1 1	(b) – (ii)
Jurg Haloz	Liebeneck 2 Mühlbach 12 Kunreuth, Unter- 6	1444–1446 1447 1448 and onward	1 2 2→3	(c) – (i)
Hans Kuncz	Lindau, Unter- 4 Stabnitz x7 Gaßnitz 3	1442–1444 1445–1455 1456 and onward	1 1 2	(c) – (i)
Vl[rich] Abesser	Konradsgrün 5 Palitz 4 Taubrath 4	1438–1448 1450–1453 1454 and onward	1 1 1	(c) – (ii)
Hans Krawthan	Trogau 6 Kropitz 6 Sirmitz 6	1442 1443–1444 1445–1449	2 3 3	(c) – (ii)
Elbel	Kunreuth, Ober- 12 Pograt 10 Altenteich x8	1438 1442–1444 1445–1446	3 3 1	(c) – (iii)
Fichtner	Voitersreuth, Vorden- 4 Sirmitz 2 Trogau 6	1438–1446 1447 1448–1449	3 2 1	(c) – (iii)
Helm	Kötschwitz 2 Ensenbruck 6 Pograt 12	1438 1442–1449 1450 and onward	5 3→2 2	(c) – (iii)
Stadelman	Stadel 2 Sirmitz 4 Sorgen 3	1443–1449 1449–1455 1456 and onward	4 1→2 4→2	(c) – (iv)
Nikel Pehr	Sirmitz 4 Voitersreuth, Vorden- 4 Lohma, Ober- 12	1443–1448 1447–1452 1453 and onward	3 3 2→3	(c) – (ii)

Source: Ar Cheb, books 1067, 1069–1083, *Klosteuerbücher 1438, 1442–1456*; book 1084, *Klosteuerbuch (Schätzungsbuch) 1456.*

Note: Only German settlement names listed. A settlement name in italics indicates that the taxpayer moved out and later returned to it.

On a quantitative level, moving between settlements significantly predominated (75%) over returning to the original settlements. Despite multiple migrations, half of taxpayers maintained more or less an identical position; the others were either worse off or better off.

Taxpayers' payment history

In the preceding subchapters, we examined the quantitative proportion of cases where moving was linked to property stability or change. We have yet to consider the taxpayers' payment history on the original and target landholding. In most cases, the relative property position of the taxpayer—measured according to the nominal value of land tax—did not change or oscillated within two neighboring quintiles. Nevertheless, several taxpayers had an interesting history behind them or before them that, while difficult to analyze in quantitative terms, gives us an idea of the unique nature of each life story. We chose 18 situations of more complex socioeconomic mobility, as well as migration that can be divided into four model groups (*tab.* 22.2):

A. On the original landholding, the property position of the taxpayer changed for the worse, but moving represented a rise and renewal of the original position (3×).
B. The property position of the taxpayer had begun to change for the better already on the original landholding; the moving reinforced the rise and/or the rise continued even after moving (8×).
C. The property position of the taxpayer had worsened already before moving; the moving reinforced the fall and/or the fall continued even after moving (3×).
D. Moving represented property decline, but in subsequent years the taxpayer returned to his original level (4×).

Nominal value of tax

One downside of quantile analysis is the homogenization of different situations within one quantile, in our case within a quintile. We can sharpen our focus and investigate not how the relative value changed but how the nominal value of tax changed. Given the annual tax increases, there is no sense in evaluating the proportion of rises and falls alone, rather one should examine the

Table 22.2. **Taxpayers with a more complex payment history in the city-state of Cheb, 1442–1456.**

Taxpayer's name	Settlement and reference number of the landholding	Developments in land tax (simplified)	Type
Hanns Doman	Schlada 7 / Schöba 4	5→4→3 / 5→4	A.
Peter Doman	Höflas (Trebendorf) 4 / Trebendorf 6	4→2→3 / 4	A.
Jorg Solch; Jurg Solich (1444)	Zettendorf 8 / Markhausen 5	4→3→2 / 4	A.
Hans Rupprecht	Hartessenreuth 1 / Harlas 2	2→4→3 / 3	B.
Freÿsleben	Rathsam 13 / Kunreuth (Unter-) 3	2→1→2 / 3→4→5	B.
Hans Kern	Voitersreuth (Vorden-) 1 / Stadel 2	1→2→3→2 / 5→4	B.
Hans Erlpeck; Erlpeck von Ob[er]ndorff (1449)	Rohr 2 / Oberndorf 9	2→3 / 5→4	B.
Hans Heberl	Gaßnitz 14 / Gaßnitz 8	3→4 / 5→4→5	B.
Nickel Kern	Voitersreuth (Vorden-) 2 / Hagengrün 3	1→3 / 3→4	B.
Merckel	Frauenreuth 16 / Haid 3	2→3 / 4→3→4→3→4	B.
Nickel Mülner	Haid 9 / Watzgenreuth 3	2 / 3→4	B.
Stubner	Stabnitz 6 / Konradsgrün 6	3→1→2 / 1	C.
Hans Adler	Seichenreuth 7 / Lohma (Unter-) 3	4→2 / 3→2→3	C.
Peter Furma[n]	Gaßnitz 17 / Scheibenreuth 6	3→2 / 2→1	D.
Sigel Greÿl	Scheibenreuth 7 / Scheibenreuth 8	4 / 2→3→4	D.
Hans Sulch	Markhausen 6 / Zettendorf 7	4 / 3→4→5→4	D.
Hans Fischer	Reichersdorf 4 / Reichersdorf 7	3 / 2→3→4	D.
Nickl Lyebhart	Haid 3 / Haid 6	5 / 4→3	D.

Source: Ar Cheb, books 1069–1083, *Klosteuerbücher 1442–1456*; book 1084, *Klosteuerbuch (Schätzungsbuch) 1456.*
Note: Only the German settlement names are listed.

differences between various property categories that are set based on levels of land tax in ranges of 10 Prague groschen.

We evaluated 34 cases of moving within the same settlement where a property value fall prevailed (50%) over a rise (32%); the rest were able to maintain relatively the same position (18%) (*figs. 22.6; 22.8.*).[713] We evaluated 121 cases of moving between settlements where, on the other hand, a property rise prevailed (51%) over a fall (40%); only 9% of taxpayers were able to maintain more or less the same position (*figs. 22.7; 22.9*).[714] The results of the analysis are as follows:

+ In cases of moving both within the same settlement as well as between settlements, the worse the original property-related position was, the greater the possibility that by moving, the property position of the taxpayer would rise.
+ When moving between settlements, there was almost an 80% likelihood of a property rise in the category of peasants with tax in the range of 1–10 Prague groschen and almost a 60% likelihood in the range of 11–20 Prague groschen. With the higher values, the probability that moving would involve a property decline prevailed.
+ When moving within the same settlement, the taxpayers in the lowest property category with tax in the range of 1–10 groschen had almost a 50% likelihood of improving their property position, and the likelihood that it would remain the same was 33%. For the higher property categories with tax of 11 groschen or more, moving was, on the other hand, more likely to mean a property fall.

Analysis again showed that the socioeconomic impact of a tenant moving from one "subject" landholding to another differed based (1) on the original property position and (2) on whether moving took place within the same settlement or between different settlements.

Our knowledge of the socioeconomic aspects of migration could be enhanced by establishing just how great a jump in property value occurred when a tenant moved (*figs. 22.10–22.11*).[715] If we divide up the peasants based on the nominal value of land tax paid into relatively wide categories of 10 Prague groschen, then in the category of up to 30 groschen, peasants remained in the same category after the majority of moves (67–89%) or shifted up or down by one category (11–44%). For the less wealthy peasants, even this kind of change could mean a relatively significant property rise or fall. Moving within the same settlement

713   *App. 22.2b.*
714   *App. 22.2b.*
715   *App. 22.2c–e.*

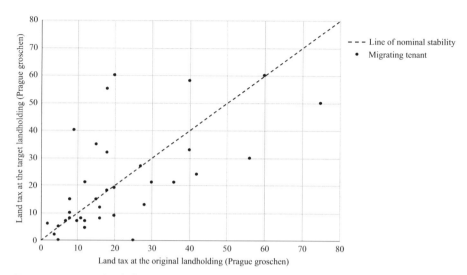

Figure 22.6. **Nominal change in the value of land tax upon a move by a tenant (FPS) between landholdings within the same settlement in the city-state of Cheb, 1442-1456.**

Source: Ar Cheb, books 1067, 1069–1083, *Klosteuerbücher 1438, 1442–1456*; book 1084, *Klosteuerbuch (Schätzungsbuch) 1456.*

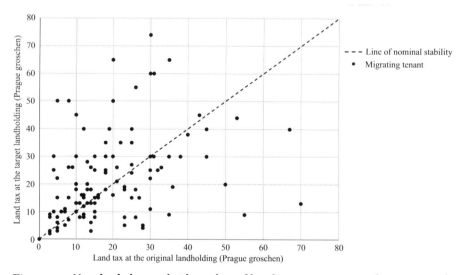

Figure 22.7. **Nominal change in the value of land tax upon a move by a tenant (FPS) between settlements in the city-state of Cheb, 1442-1456.**

Source: Ar Cheb, books 1067, 1069–1083, *Klosteuerbücher 1438, 1442–1456*; book 1084, *Klosteuerbuch (Schätzungsbuch) 1456.*

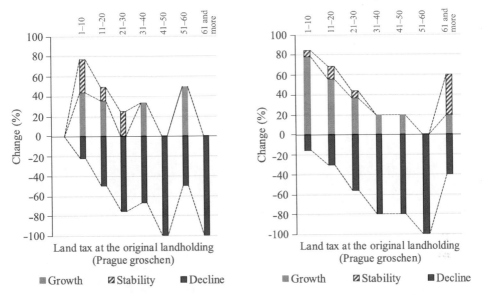

Figures 22.8–22.9. Nominal change in the value of land tax upon a move by a tenant (FPS) between landholdings within the same settlement (fig. 22.8) and between settlements (fig. 22.9) in the city-state of Cheb.

Source: Cf. *app. 22.2c.*

Note: The gray columns represent the proportion of taxpayers who after moving to a target landholding were paying higher tax than that on the original landholding. The black columns represent the opposite. The hatched columns represent the proportion of taxpayers who paid the same amount of tax.

on average brought less significant change than moving between settlements. In the tax category of over 30 groschen, the moving already meant a significant property change, usually downward.

There was not a single case detected where the tenant of a "free" landholding moved to a "subject" landholding. This is in line with the previous finding (*chap. 18.7; 19.3–19.4*) that the ties to "free" landholdings were relatively strong and the landholdings were passed down within the family fairly frequently. Two cases are documented in which a peasant who had tenure of a "subject" landholding moved to a "free" landholding. In both cases, it involved moving between settlements connected with a significant property rise.[716]

716   ID 333 and ID 1823 in an *appendix on the CD.*

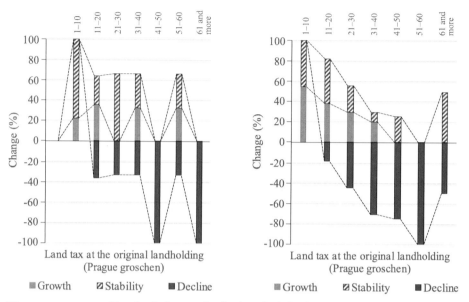

Figures 22.10–22.11. **Nominal change in the level of the land tax upon a move by a tenant (FPS) between landholdings within the same settlement (fig. 22.10) and between settlements (fig. 22.11) in the city-state of Cheb, 1442–1456.**

Source: Cf. app. 22.2d.

Note: The gray columns represent the proportion of taxpayers who after moving to a target landholding were paying higher tax than on the original landholding. The black columns represent the opposite. The hatched columns represent the proportion of taxpayers who paid the same amount of tax.

22.3 Comparison based on the value of tenure right

The level of prescribed land tax reflected the actual total value of a taxpayer's property. Thus, the analysis presented in the previous subchapter does not tell us directly whether the taxpayers moved from a wealthy landholding to a poor one or vice versa. Therefore, here we concentrate on the value of the tenure right to the landholdings, specifically the value of the "purchase" right. The advantage of this approach is that our findings will not be distorted by the continuous rises in tax. The disadvantage is that we do not know the value of the "purchase" right to the landholdings upon the taxpayer moving, only for 1438 and 1456.

In the broadest possible scope, we can use the values of the "purchase" right to the landholdings for (a) 1438, (b) 1456, (c) 1438 and 1456, or (d) 1456 and

1438.[717] Working with the values of the "purchase" right to the landholdings from 1456 seems to be the most effective, because we can find them for two-thirds of all moves.

Relative change

We examine the socioeconomic impacts of migration according to quintiles set up according to the value of the "purchase" right to the landholdings (*app. C–D*). From this point of view, we may evaluate 23 cases of a peasant moving within the same settlement and 80 cases of moving between settlements (*figs. 22.12–22.14*).[718]

+ Moving within the same settlement most often involved a fall of one quintile or more, while moving between settlements involved, conversely, a rise. Given the low frequency, there is no point in interpreting the values according to the separate quintiles.
+ In cases of moving between settlements, the degree of migration clearly rose with the falling value of the "purchase" right. Moving between settlements was twice as likely for a tenant with a landholding in the first, poorest quintile than for a tenant in quintile V. When moving from a landholding in quintile I or II, the tenant was most often better off (56–59%) or his position stayed relatively the same (28–40%); in the case of quintiles III and IV, the likelihood of a fall or rise were more or less balanced, for the tenants in quintile V (i.e., on the wealthiest landholdings), a property fall was most likely (60%). All in all, in all quintiles it was most likely that the property position of a tenant would remain the same or changed by one quintile (63–83%).

Nominal change

We can additionally evaluate the socioeconomic impact of migration according to the property ranges for the monetary values of the "purchase" right to landholdings (*figs. 22.15–22.16*).[719] In most cases, only those tenants who left the poorest landholdings with a value of "purchase" right of up to 4 threescore of Prague groschen improved their position by moving within the same set-

717   *App. 22.4.*
718   *App. 22.3a–b.*
719   *App. 22.5a–d.*

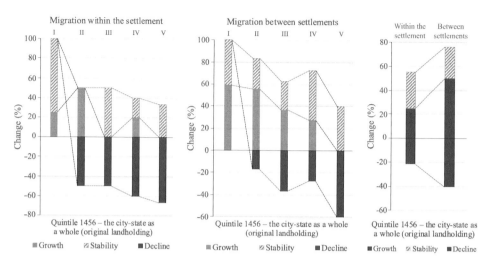

Figures 22.12–22.14. Relative change of the "purchase" right to a landholding when a tenant moved between landholdings within the same settlement (fig. 22.12) and between settlements (fig. 22.13), including comparison of both types of moves (fig. 22.14). The city-state of Cheb as a whole, 1442–1456.

Source: Cf. app. 22.3a–b.

Note: Gray columns represent the proportion of taxpayers who acquired a landholding with a relatively higher value of the "purchase" right than their original landholding. The black columns represent the opposite. Hatched columns describe the proportion of taxpayers who moved to a landholding with relatively the same value of the "purchase" right.

tlement. For moving between settlements, this threshold was higher—around 8 threescore of groschen. In the 9–12 threescore of groschen range, the rise and fall were balanced; from 13 threescore of groschen, a fall in the property values prevailed. The property rises were not in any way dramatic; most tenants with a landholding with a value of 12 threescore of groschen moved to a landholding of the same or similar property range (63–83%). The property falls or rises of tenants on wealthy landholdings were often more significant.

22.4 Comparison based on socioeconomic landholding category, 1438

The data from the *1438 Land Tax Register* allow us to examine whether various types of landholdings can be connected to varying degrees of migra-

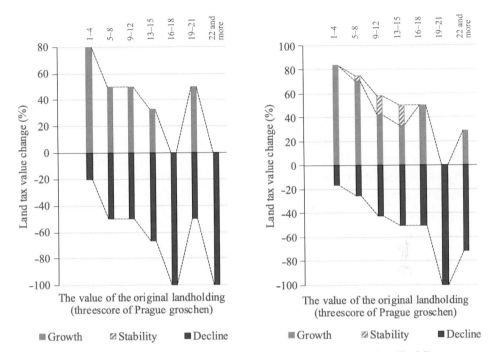

Figures 22.15–22.16. **Nominal change of the "purchase" right to a landholding upon a tenant moving between landholdings within the same settlement (fig. 22.15) and between settlements (fig. 22.16). The city-state of Cheb as a whole, 1442–1456.**

Source: Cf. app. 22.5a–d.

Note: Gray columns represent the proportion of taxpayers who acquired a landholding *with a relatively higher value* of "purchase" right than their original landholding. The red columns represent the opposite. Hatched columns describe the proportion of taxpayers who moved to a landholding with relatively the same value of the "purchase" right.

tion.[720] Cheb's "subject" landholdings comprised 12% *Herberge*, 83% *Hof*, and 5% *Höfel* landholdings. We find similar proportions in moves from landholding to landholding. The types of the original and target landholdings could be identified in 13 cases of moving within the same settlement and in 44 cases of moving between settlements. Among original landholdings, *Herberge* consti-

720 *App. 22.6a–b.*

tuted 11–15%, *Hof* 75–77%, and *Höfel* 8–14%. In summary, we may state that
Herberge and *Hof* landholdings were left at approximately the same rate.

As for landholdings to which peasants arrived, we find differences between
migration within the same settlement and between settlements.

+ Within the same settlement, tenants moved from *Herberge* landholdings to
  other *Herberge* landholdings and from *Hof* landholdings to *Hof* or *Herberge*
  landholdings. Moving to *Herberge* landholdings was fairly frequent (39%).
  We cannot rule out the possibility that some moves were simply the departure of the tenant to a retirement dwelling.

+ In the case of moving between settlements, we find that most often tenants
  moved from *Herberge* landholdings to *Hof* landholdings (80%) and from
  Hof landholdings again mainly to other *Hof* landholdings (76%), or more
  rarely to *Herberge* landholdings or to *Höfel* landholdings (12%). In the case
  of *Höfel* landholdings, moving to a landholding of the same type predominated (83%). Overall, the high proportion of *Höfel* landholdings among
  target landholdings is striking (21%), exceeding their average proportion in
  the whole fourfold.

In summary, the socioeconomic category of landholdings to which peasants
arrived reflects a higher likelihood of property decline when moving within the
same settlement, and stability or improvement when moving between different
settlements.

22.6 Geographical distance

We analyzed the geographical distance between the original and the target
landholding of a migrating tenant (FPS) in ranges of three kilometers (*tab. 22.3;
fig. 22.17*). A large proportion of moves took place within the same settlement
or nearby settlements up to 6 km away (82%). Only a small proportion of
moves took place over longer distances, while the number of moves recorded
in the 12–18 km range is so low that it may have been significantly distorted by
an error stemming from the surname match method (*figs. 22.19–22.22*).

The database that we evaluated included only migration within the part
of the city-state of Cheb that was subject to land tax. Nevertheless, tenants
moving between geographically fairly close landholdings prevailed to such an
extent that it may be considered a typical feature of moving in the Late Middle

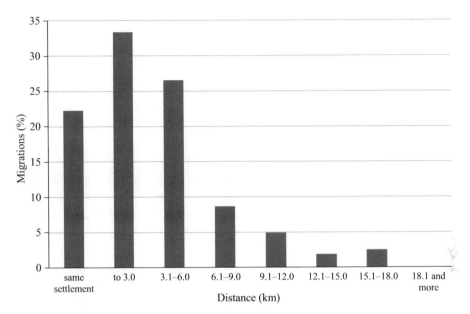

Figure 22.17. **Distance between the original and target landholding of a migrating tenant (FPS) in the city-state of Cheb, 1442–1456.**

Source: Cf. tab. 22.3.

Table 22.3. **Distance between the original and target landholding of a migrating tenant (FPS) in the city-state of Cheb, 1442–1456.**

	Distance (km)								Total
	Identical settlements	up to 3.0	3.1–6.0	6.1–9.0	9.1–12.0	12.1–15.0	15.1–18.0	18.1 or more	
Cases	36	54	43	14	8	3	4	0	162
%	22.2	33.3	26.5	8.6	4.9	1.9	2.5	0.0	100.0
Not including moves within the same settlement (%)	–	42.9	34.1	11.1	6.3	2.4	3.2	0.0	100.0

Source: Ar Cheb, books 1067, 1069–1083, Klosteuerbücher 1438, 1442–1456; book 1084, Klosteuerbuch (Schätzungsbuch) 1456.
Note: Cf. fig. 22.17.

Ages. Although we do not know the real geographical horizon of the late medieval peasant, the active radius of moving from landholding to landholding (i.e., the migration horizon) should indicate the intensively developed social and family bonds and the overall environment that the peasant knew well. The perimeter of this horizon of familiarity was not at all distant, stretching just 6 km, so moving up to that distance probably did not result in the breaking of established ties with peasants and the original home. At the same time, there do not seem to be any significant differences in tax levels between tenants in various property categories. The average nominal value of tax for tenants who moved a distance of up to 6 km was 22 Prague groschen on the original landholding and 25 groschen on the target landholding, while the situation for tenants moving farther away was 26 groschen and 25 groschen, respectively.

22.7 Migration chains and the domino effect[721]

In the analyzed set, we identified a total of 165 migrations of a tenant from one landholding to another in 1442–1456. The vacated landholding may have been taken on by a completely new tenant who until then had not farmed another landholding or a tenant who moved in from another landholding. One can imagine a domino effect where a change on one landholding led to migrations and changes on other landholdings. It is extraordinarily difficult to follow the concrete causality of social and demographic events across a certain region; nevertheless, we have attempted to do so. Amongst the 165 movements, we identified:

+ 113 simple moves (69%), i.e., cases where the vacated landholding was occupied by a person who until then had not appeared in the land tax registers.
+ 52 moves (31%) that were part of a migration chain, i.e., the vacant landholding was occupied by a person who had moved from a different landholding registered in the land tax registers.[722] Of these 52 moves, 40 were part of a chain of three landholdings and 12 were part of a chain of four land-

---

721   Summarized also in Klír, "Local migration," 208–209.
722   *App. 22.7.*

holdings. A migration chain comprising five or more landholdings proved impossible to identify.

Given the restrictions of our research, all of the above numbers are minimums. If the real number of moves is underrepresented for a range of reasons, the moving chains are underrepresented several times more.

A taxpayer's move may have been connected with a reduction of the monetary value of his property, or vice versa, or else his property position may not have changed. Variability was significant. We are interested in the quantitatively prevailing tendencies and ask whether the migration chains had an upward or downward tendency.

In the first case, the most propertied taxpayer occupied the first vacated landholding, while the poorest would be at the end of the chain. In other words, moving was connected with socioeconomic rise, so the later the taxpayer's position in the chain, the lower the value of the property. In the second case, the situation would be the opposite: moving was accompanied by socioeconomic decline. A state of stability may also be imagined. To solve the question, we analyze chains comprising three landholdings that are statistically sufficiently numerous. Essential for the analysis is of course knowledge of the nominal value of tax for all moves and taxpayers.

The analyzed set comprised 19 cases—migration chains. Almost half of them demonstrated upward socioeconomic mobility, a quarter downward, and a quarter stable or fluctuating (*tab. 22.4*). This corresponds also to the tax quintiles occupied by the landholdings in various positions in the chain (*tab. 22.5*; *fig. 22.18*). Compared to the others, the first (i.e., the trigger landholdings) had relatively fewer taxpayers in quintiles I and II and, conversely, more in quintiles IV and V. The proportion of second landholdings to third (i.e., the last landholding) is similar. On the level of weak tendency, migration tended to mean socioeconomic rise, i.e., a taxpayer from a poorer landholding came to occupy a vacated landholding.

Migration chains are one of the most striking examples of the peasantry as a mutually interconnected system that comprised both socioeconomic and geographic aspects. The departure of a tenant from one of the landholdings of Cheb may have attracted a tenant from another landholding whose departure could continue the migration process like a domino effect. The existence of a fairly large number of moving chains documents a sufficient quantity of vacant landholdings and also the geographical permeability of peasant families for whom no serious obstacles stood in the way of moving.

Table 22.4. **Socioeconomic tendencies in migration chains involving three landholdings in the city-state of Cheb, 1442–1456.**

Tendency	Absolute terms	%
Upward – the highest quintile documented for the first (trigger) landholding, lowest quintile for the third landholding.	9	47.4
Downward – the highest quintile documented for the third landholding, lowest quintile for the first (trigger) landholding.	5	26.3
Stable – the same quintile for all landholdings.	3	15.8
Oscillating – both the first and third landholding in the same quintile, the second higher or lower.	2	10.5
Total	19	100.0

Source: Ar Cheb, books 1069–1083, *Klosteuerbücher 1442–1456*; book 1084, *Klosteuerbuch (Schätzungsbuch) 1456*.

Table 22.5. **Representation of quintiles set according to the value of land tax on landholdings that were part of migration chains involving three landholdings in the city-state of Cheb, 1442–1456.**

	Quintile											
	Absolute terms					Total	%					Total
Order	I	II	III	IV	V		I	II	III	IV	V	
1. landholding (trigger)	4	5	6	2	2	19	21.1	26.3	31.6	10.5	10.5	100.0
2. landholding	8	3	5	3	0	19	42.1	15.8	26.3	15.8	0.0	100.0
3. landholding (final)	7	6	6	0	0	19	36.8	31.6	31.6	0.0	0.0	100.0
Total	19	14	17	5	2	57	35.1	28.1	35.1	15.8	12.3	100.0

Source: Ar Cheb, books 1069–1083, *Klosteuerbücher 1442–1456*; book 1084, *Klosteuerbuch (Schätzungsbuch) 1456*.

22.8 Summary and explanation

We have analyzed the mutual connection between socioeconomic mobility and migration from many points of view, the results of which paint a fairly uniform and complete picture.

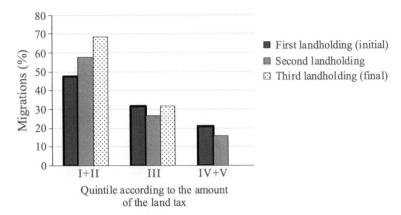

Figure 22.18. Representation of quintiles set according to the value of land tax on landholdings that were part of migration chains involving three landholdings in the city-state of Cheb, 1442–1456.

Source: Cf. tab. 22.5.

- The socioeconomic impact of a tenant moving from one landholding to another depended on the tenant's original property position. The lower the original property position, the greater the likelihood that moving would bring the tenant a property rise. We also identified differences between moving within the same settlement and between different settlements. In the first case, the probability of a socioeconomic rise was significantly lower than in the second case. Moving within the same settlement also usually brought a less pronounced change than moving between settlements.
- As for changes in relative socioeconomic position expressed in value quintiles, stability was most frequent on average. Tenants leaving the poorest landholdings were, nevertheless, better off in most cases, while tenants leaving the richest landholdings, conversely, were worse off. It was also true that the degree of migration rose as the values of the "purchase" right to landholdings fell. It was lowest for landholdings in quintile I and highest in quintile V.
- As for migration between different categories of landholding (*Hof* × *Höfel* landholding), we identify the greatest risk of property decline—in the shape of the exchange of a *Hof* landholding for a *Herberge* landholding—in moving within the same settlement and stability or improvement in moving between settlements.
- When analyzing quintiles set separately for various ecological zones, we find a similar tendency as when assessing quintiles set for the city-state of Cheb

as a whole but even more clearly. The trajectory of socioeconomic rise and also the level of migration itself were always closely related to the value of the "purchase" right of the previous landholding. A move by a tenant with tenure of a landholding in quintile I was three times more likely than by a tenant holding a landholding in quintile V.

* Geographical analysis shows that most cases of tenants moving from one landholding to another took place in the same settlement or a short distance away, not exceeding 6 km (82%). Therefore, even after moving, the tenant generally remained within a familiar social, economic, and ecological environment, and old ties were not broken.[723] The Cheb countryside may therefore be imagined as a continuum of mutually entwined peasant communities, which, from the point of view of individuals, did not extend beyond the horizon of neighboring settlements up to 6 km away, i.e., about a one- or two-hour walk. A parish church usually stood within the boundaries of this perimeter. The actual geographical horizon and activities of peasants were certainly more extensive: a range of settlements lay 12–18 km away from Cheb and the city-state of Cheb was 25–30 km across.

* In conclusion, it is necessary to at least consider what demographic events could happen during the migration of peasants. Did married couples and complete peasant households move, or was migration connected with the marriage of widows and widowers? Unfortunately, we do not know.

* Moving from landholding to landholding was most frequently connected with socioeconomic rise; richer landholdings therefore more easily found new tenants and poorer ones were more liable to be left unoccupied. Ultimately, migration could lead to the abandonment of the landholding at the end of the migration chain.

Naturally, we ask ourselves why smallholdings and poor peasant landholdings were very rarely handed over within the family and why tenants left other landholdings, usually wealthier ones. We also ask why, on the contrary, tenants remained on wealthy landholdings until their death or retirement, and why they were taken over by their descendants. It would be optimal to clarify the observed phenomena in the form of micro-studies, but the Cheb fiscal sources do not allow their elaboration due to their one-sidedness. The necessary

---

723   Cf., e.g., Grulich, *Migration*, esp. 8, 20–21, 45.

data are not available elsewhere in the eastern part of Central Europe either (cf. *chap. 4.1*). Nevertheless, Bruno Lienen's findings for two villages in the Paderborn Uplands (Westphalia) and, in part, those by Konrad Wanner for the city-state of Zurich, provide at least a partial answer.[724]

Thanks to the rich and diverse documents of the Böddeken monastery, Bruno Lienen was able to clarify the causal links between population development, the change in the peasantry's legal framework, land transfer, and local migration; and changes in the economic strategies of peasant farming between the 14th and 16th centuries. The unprecedented mobility of the peasantry, the collapse of the original normative landholdings, and flexible property transfers occurred as a result of the population depression and the fall in grain prices in the second half of the 14th century. Ties to the land were loosened, and as a result, peasants lost interest in hereditary tenure, as they could rent land from different landlords, in different places, and for different times. Peasant families therefore migrated between landholdings according to where the landlords offered them the most favorable conditions. Emotional ties to landholdings were lacking; any relationship to a landholding was based primarily on its economic benefits. Some peasants alternated between several landholdings during their lives, and the size of their land equipment fluctuated greatly. The original normative landholdings remained only as "urbarian" units (i.e., organizational units listed in the estate register), while the real land equipment of peasant households was flexible and usually included multiple original "urbarian" landholdings or parts thereof.[725]

In a situation where it was possible to easily acquire landholdings and flexibly change their land equipment, tenants did not have to go into retirement and hand over their land to their children during their lifetime, because the children left for vacant landholdings during the lifetimes of their parents, and the parents, if their strength was no longer sufficient and it was unnecessary to feed the children, reduced the amount of cultivated land. Alternatively, the size of the leased and cultivated land corresponded to the demographic situation

---

724 Cf. Klír, "Local Migration," 216–218.
725 Bruno Lienen, "Aspekte des Wandels bäuerlicher Betriebe zwischen dem 14. und dem 17. Jahrhundert an Beispielen aus Tudorf (Kreis Paderborn)," *Westfälische Forschungen* (1991): 288–315; Bruno Lienen, "Obern- und Niederntudorf 1300–1600: Beiträge zur Geschichte der ländlichen Gesellschaft Westfalens im Spätmittelalter" (PhD diss., Universität Bielefeld, 1992), http://bieson.ub.uni-bielefeld.de/volltexte/2006/901/. Cf. Klír, "Local Migration," 216–218.

of the family, which corresponds to the cyclical reproduction model. The rate of family transfers was therefore relatively low, reaching 31% before 1480. The described pattern changed in the last quarter of the 15th century due to population growth, the influx of people from overcrowded neighboring areas, and rising grain prices. As in Ottobeuren, for example, in the second half of the 16th century, new normative landholdings stabilized in Padernborn, and strong bonds were formed between families and landholdings. The share of family transfers from the end of the 15th century was a full 80%; at the same time, the practice of leaving for retirement appeared.

Konrad Wanner found similar behavior based on an analysis of the information-rich estate registers of the Benedictine monastery in Rheinau in the canton of Zurich. The Rheinau estate registers also revealed a flexible land market and a surplus of land, from which the peasants chose the unit of land with a rent that was the most advantageous for them. Land, of which the relatively highest land rent was paid, remained uncultivated. In addition to intensive land transfers, local migrations of peasant households were also documented. Twelve of the original seventeen peasants remained in one of the case-study villages for about ten years, but only two of them retained the same land tenure (1399–1400). Even features of cyclical property mobility were identified—large landholdings shrank, small ones grew larger, and some were even newly created. Even in the Zurich district, the late medieval land transfer regime ended with population growth in the last decades of the 15th century.[726]

For the Cheb peasantry, we can quantify the high rate of change in landholdings and the rate of migration, thus shifting the existing mosaic of knowledge gained in the Padernborn and Zurich districts. Another benefit is the identification and quantification of the social conditionality of the rate of change and migration. In the city-state of Cheb, we can see the flexibility of the land market and the size of the landholdings in the living circulation of non-landholding plots and also in the merging and division of some normative landholdings. With the help of the Padernborn and Zurich microstudies, we can explain the Cheb data quite convincingly, although so far only as a hypothesis.

We say that the level of family continuity on large and wealthy landholdings was higher not only because they offered a better standard of living, but also because they enabled livelihoods for adult offspring who could remain on the

---

726   Wanner, *Siedlungen*, 207–211. Cf. Klír, "Local Migration," 216–218.

farms as a part of the labor force and take them over in old age or upon the death of their parents. This is evidenced by Randolph C. Head's demographic analyses of the city-state of Zurich.[727] In Cheb, there was a higher rate of conversion of poor landholdings because their holders left for better landholdings if they became available. In addition, due to limited economic resources, adolescent offspring left the poor homesteads as soon as possible and did not return after their parents' deaths. The high degree of change thus went hand in hand with a minimal degree of family continuity.

727   Head, "Haushalt."

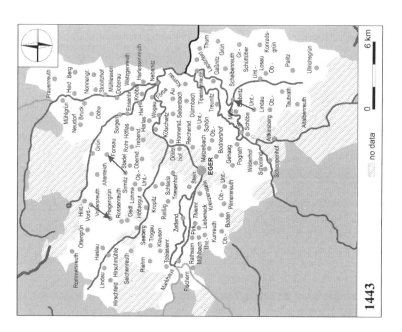

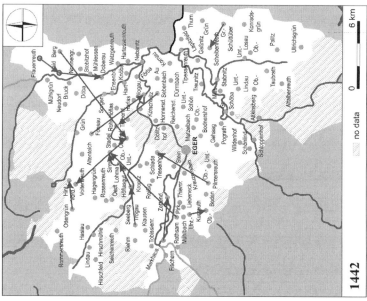

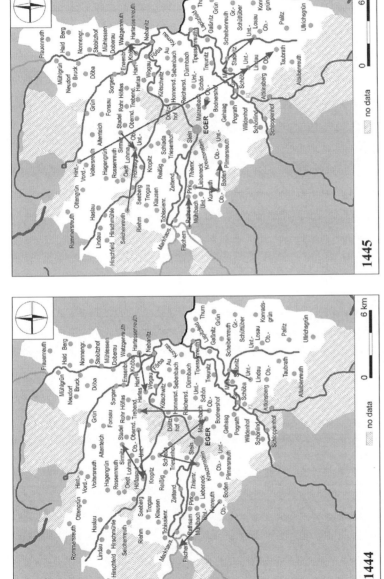

Figure 22.19. Moving by tenants (taxpayers) between settlements, 1442–1445. Categorized according to the year of moving out of the original landholding. The taxpayer most often did not appear on the new landholding until the following year.

Source: Registers of the Cheb land tax. *Note:* Categorized according to the year of the move from the original landholding. The taxpayer most often appeared at the target landholding the next year. Blank map showing only the relevant settlements that were analyzed. For easier orientation, the city of Cheb (Eger), Cheb Castle settlements, and the settlement below Ostroh Castle (Seeberg) have been added.

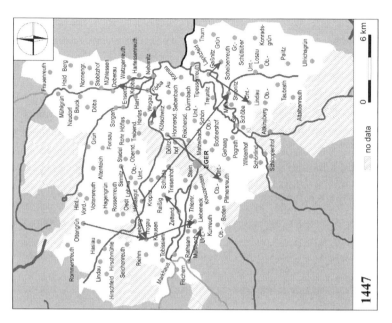

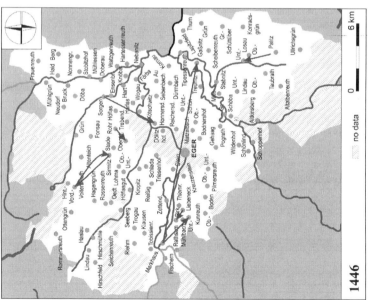

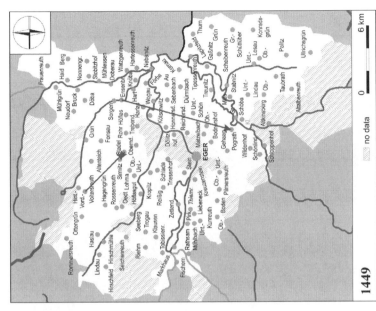

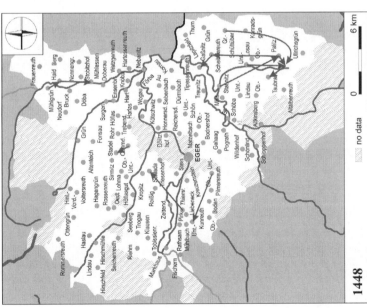

Figure 22.20. **Moving by tenants (taxpayers) between settlements, 1446–1449. Categorized according to the year of moving out of the original landholding. The taxpayer most often did not appear on the new landholding until the following year.**

Source: Registers of the Cheb land tax. *Note:* Categorized according to the year of the move from the original landholding. The taxpayer most often appeared at the target landholding the next year. Blank map showing only the relevant settlements that were analyzed. For easier orientation, the city of Cheb (Eger), Cheb Castle settlements, and the settlement below Ostroh Castle (Seeberg) have been added.

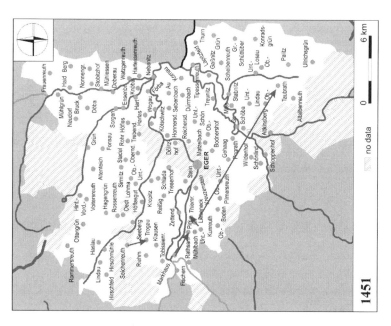

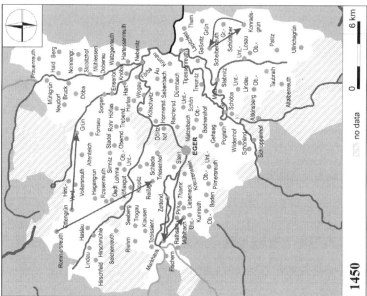

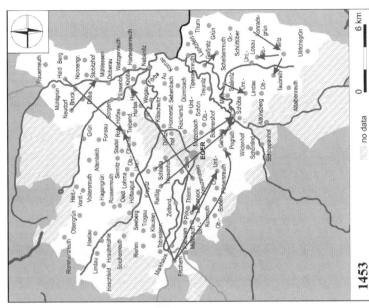

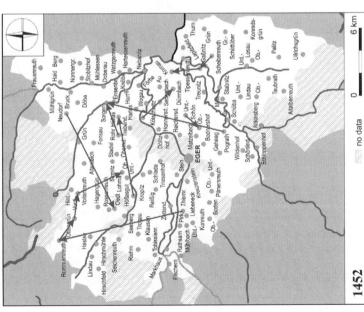

Figure 22.21. Moving by tenants (taxpayers) between settlements, 1450–1453. Categorized according to the year of moving out of the original landholding. The taxpayer most often did not appear on the new landholding until the following year.

Source: Registers of the Cheb land tax. *Note:* Categorized according to the year of the move from the original landholding. The taxpayer most often appeared at the target landholding the next year. Blank map showing only the relevant settlements that were analyzed. For easier orientation, the city of Cheb (Eger), Cheb Castle settlements, and the settlement below Ostroh Castle (Seeberg) have been added.

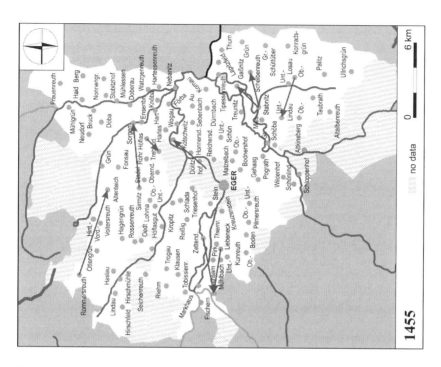

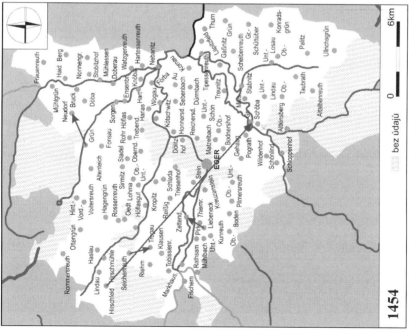

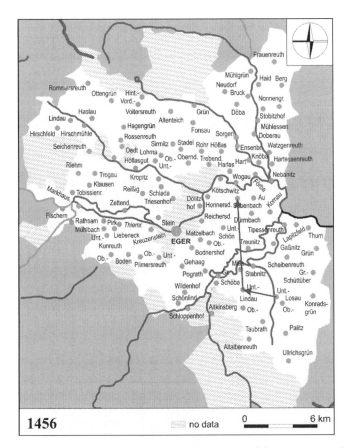

1456   no data   0   6 km

Figure 22.22. **Moving by tenants (taxpayers) between settlements, 1454–1456. Categorized according to the year of moving out of the original landholding. The taxpayer most often did not appear on the new landholding until the following year. Moving in 1456 includes only those cases where the taxpayer appeared at a new landholding already in 1456.**

Source: Registers of the Cheb land tax. *Note:* Categorized according to the year of the move from the original landholding. The taxpayer most often appeared at the target landholding the next year. Blank map showing only the relevant settlements that were analyzed. For easier orientation, the city of Cheb (Eger), Cheb Castle settlements, and the settlement below Ostroh Castle (Seeberg) have been added.

23.
Migration to the city
of Cheb

23.1 Introduction

Migration between the city and the countryside took many forms; written sources for Cheb, however, shed light only on the situations of certain socio-economic groups:[728]

---

728   For the peasantry moving to cities in general, see Volker Stamm, "Gab es eine bäuerliche Landflucht im Hochmittelalter?: Land- Stadt-Bewegungen als Auflösungsfaktor der klassischen Grundherrschaft," *Historische Zeitschrift* 276 (2003): 305–322; Norbert Becker, "Landflucht am unteren Niederrhein als Spiegel des gesellschaftlichen Umbruchs," *Annalen des Historischen Vereins für den Niederrhein* 196 (1994): 7–30. For the definition of moving in the context of medieval cities, cf. Gilomen, "Neue Forschungen," 14–15. More recently, see esp. Rainer Christoph Schwinges, ed., *Neubürger im späten Mittelalter. Migration und Austausch in der Städtelandschaft des Alten Reiches (1250–1550)*, Zeitschrift für historische Forschung. Beiheft 30 (Berlin: Duncker & Humblot, 2002); Hans-Jörg Gilomen, ed., *Migration in die Städte. Ausschluss – Assimilierung – Integration – Multikulturalität – Migrations vers les villes. Exclusion – assimilation – intégration – multiculturalité*, Schweizerische Gesellschaft für Wirtschafts- und Sozialgeschichte 16 (Zürich: Chronos, 2000); Martin Musílek, *Patroni, klienti, příbuzní. Sociální svět Starého Města pražského ve 14. století* [Patrons, clients, and relatives: The social world of Old Town Prague in the 14th Century] (Prague: Casablanca, 2015), 148–165. For cities in Franconia / Upper Palatinate and Swabia in the vicinity of Cheb, cf. Hektor Ammann, "Vom Lebensraum der mittelalterlichen Stadt. Eine Untersuchung an schwäbischen Beispielen," *Berichte zur deutschen Landeskunde* 31 (1963), 284–316; Roland Gerber, "Die Einbürgerungsfrequenzen spätmittelalterlicher Städte im regionalen Vergleich," in *Neubürger im späten Mittelalter. Migration und Austausch in der Städtelandschaft des Alten Reiches (1250–1550)*, ed. Rainer Christoph Schwinges, Zeitschrift für histori-

* Tenants of rural landholdings moving to the city who had retained or, alternatively, sold off their rural properties.
* Heirs and widows of rural tenants who had settled in the city.
* Very occasionally, the opposite situation is documented where a person surrendered their citizenship and moved to the countryside.
* The relationship between the city and the countryside also had a purely property-related aspect—burghers acquired properties in the countryside, and vice versa, peasants acquired agricultural land in the city's farmland. This intermingling of property is reflected fairly well in city and land tax registers.

It is essential for the study of urban immigration that citizenship in late medieval Cheb was not bound to the possession of a house or other real estate. Therefore, we can reconstruct the migration horizon here in greater completeness than, for example, in the case of pre-Hussite Prague.[729]

In the following passages, we divide the question of urban migration into four parts. In the first part, we focus on the main sources concerning Cheb for studying urban migration and methodological problems. In the second part, we examine the main principles and characteristics of migration to the city during the focus period (1442–1456); we reconstruct and simultaneously interpret the "collection" area, including its zonality. In principle, while doing this, we respect approaches that have been developed during the general study of urban migration and interaction between the city and its hinterland.[730] In the third part, we look at the socioeconomic aspects of migration, analyzing the amount and socioeconomic status of migrating peasants, both in their original settlement and in their destination, the city of Cheb. The fourth part addresses the property dispositions that facilitated rural-urban migration.

---

sche Forschung. Beiheft 30 (Berlin: Duncker & Humblot, 2002), 251–288, on esp. 267–270, 277–281.

729   Cf. Musílek, *Patroni*.

730   More recently, see esp. Rainer Christoph Schwinges, ed., *Neubürger im späten Mittelalter. Migration und Austausch in der Städtelandschaft des Alten Reiches (1250–1550)*, Zeitschrift für historische Forschung. Beiheft 30 (Berlin: Duncker & Humblot, 2002); Gerber, "Die Einbürgerungsfrequenzen," 257–264.

23.2 **Sources**

We usually acquire information about urban migration during the Late Middle Ages thanks to various types of city books; in imperial territory, these are most often the registers of new burghers.[731] We identify their place of origin either according to direct data or indirectly according to surname.[732] A new burgher register is lacking for Cheb, the earliest dating to just 1815.[733] Their testimony may be substituted by other types of city books.[734] For the Late Middle Ages, this means:

a) City income books (*Allgemeine Umgeldbücher*)
b) City tax registers (*Losungsbücher*)
c) Land tax registers (*Klosteuerbücher*)

City income books began to be systematically kept after the reform of the city office and financial administration in 1441, with the earliest of such books concerning the accounting year of 1442 (summer 1442 – summer 1443).[735] The income books were kept until 1765 and have survived in an almost uninterrupted series; for the medieval period, books are missing for 8 years (1451, 1466, 1475, 1502–1505, 1513).[736] Late medieval income books were fairly uniform and clearly laid out in structure; entries were categorized into main chapters according to type of income. One of these categories comprised entries of income acquired from fees for the granting of citizenship, entitled "*Von der Burger-*

---

731 On this period, see esp. Rainer Christoph Schwinges, "Neubürger und Bürgerbücher im Reich des späten Mittelalters: Eine Einführung über die Quellen," in *Neubürger im späten Mittelalter. Migration und Austausch in der Städtelandschaft des Alten Reiches (1250–1550)*, ed. Rainer Christoph Schwinges, Zeitschrift für historische Forschung. Beiheft 30 (Berlin: Duncker & Humblot, 2002), 17–50; Rainer Christoph Schwinges, "Bürgermigration im Alten Reich des 14.-16. Jahrhunderts," in *Migration in die Städte. Ausschluss Assimilierung – Integration – Multikulturalität – Migrations vers les villes. Exclusion – assimilation – intégration – multiculturalité*, ed. Hans-Jörg Gilomen, Schweizerische Gesellschaft für Wirtschafts- und Sozialgeschichte 16 (Zürich: Chronos, 2000), 17–37, on 21–28; Gilomen, "Neue Forschungen," 12.

732 On the methodology for searching according to surname, cf. Becker, "Das Land," 104.

733 Heribert Sturm, "Die Egerer Ungeldbücher als bevölkerungsgeschichtliche Quelle," *Zeitschrift für sudetendeutsche Geschichte* 2 (1938): 189–200, on 189.

734 Namely, registers that are otherwise used as control sources during analysis of ledgers of new burghers. Cf. Schwinges, "Neubürger und Bürgerbücher," 371.

735 Klír et al., *Knihy*, 62–63.

736 Sturm, "Die Egerer Ungeldbücher," 190.

rechten" (i.e., income from citizenship admission fees), to which one page was devoted but usually only partially filled. Entries listed the person's name and sometimes also their geographical origin, value of fee, and date of payment (*tab. 23.1*).[737] For instance:

> *"It[em] aber eingenom[m]en von den Nickel Fisch[er] vo[n] Woga II ss gr. zu purg[er]recht am Mitboch vor Oc[u]li"*[738]

Late medieval entries concerning income from citizenship admission fees have been addressed by the Cheb archivist Heribert Sturm (focus period 1442–1490).[739] He believed that the annual entries in these books were more or less full lists of newly accepted burghers, since persons appeared in it who for some reason did not or could not pay a monetary fee. In the first situation, it was stated in the book why the fee was waived; in the second, it was noted in some cases that, for instance, the person in question would work off the monetary fee.

An almost uninterrupted series of **city tax registers** starting in 1390 and finishing in 1758 has survived, missing registers for just eight years in the Middle Ages (1405, 1416–1417, 1421, 1423–1424, 1435, 1503).[740] For some city taxpayers, their place of origin was cited as a part of their name, e.g., *"Ruppel Fischer von Liebneck"* or *"Simo[n] von Tachaw."*[741] Sometimes geographical origin was included in the surname itself (e.g., *"Niclas Voydersrewtt[er]"*), although in such cases this did not usually concern new citizens but rather the offspring of a family that had long since moved to the city.[742] As of 1457, scribes began recording the names of new burghers on the back inside cover, even if just as a simple column below a title such as *"Czu New purg[ern]."*[743] A comparison of entries from the tax registers and income books showed:[744]

---

737   We provide a complete transcription of entries for 1442–1456 in *app. 26.1.*
738   Ar Cheb, book 2148, *Allgemeine Umgeldbücher 1446*, fol. 40r. Cf. *app. 26.1.*
739   Sturm, "Die Egerer Ungeldbücher," 193–200.
740   Sturm, "Die Egerer Ungeldbücher," 189.
741   Klír et al., *Knihy*, 138–144; Ar Cheb, book 1424, *Losungsbuch 1446*, fol. 8r, 16r.
742   Ar Cheb, book 1424, *Losungsbuch 1446*, fol. 66r; for more on names also cf. Musílek, *Patroni*, 149.
743   As seen in, e.g.: Ar Cheb, book 1438, *Losungsbuch 1460.*
744   We investigated the income books and registers of 1457–1470.

a) Entries in the registers related to persons who had gained citizenship in the preceding year. The first list of names of new burghers contained in the 1457 register therefore corresponds with entries in the 1456 *City Income Book*.[745]
b) The names were transferred to the register from the income book, although in simplified form and sometimes not all of them in full.

The testimony of the city tax register is unique in that it at least partially informs us of the geographical origin of burghers living together at one moment in time.

City land tax registers, surviving with gaps from 1392 and more or less complete from 1441, recorded situations in which a taxpayer moved to Cheb and gained citizenship and so began to pay tax on their rural properties to the city tax authorities.[746] If such a person kept his properties in the countryside, records of this continued to be kept in the land tax registers either with a note such as *"purg[er] hynnen"* or simply *"ist hynnen"* or similar (*see app. 23.2a–b*) but without data concerning payment, or these rural properties, and any other related property, could have been completely excluded from the land tax register. The analysis of the land tax registers is significant for research on Cheb rural-urban migration in three ways. Firstly, it permits us to discover the socio-economic status of some new burghers on their original landholding in the countryside. Secondly, it helps identify new burghers whose place of origin does not appear in either income books or city tax registers. Thirdly, it gives us some insight into migration at a time when standardized accounts books were not kept by the city office (1392–1441).

23.3 Migration horizon of Cheb's new burghers

General remarks

In our analysis of the geographical origin of new burghers, we apply the concept of the migration horizon, which refers to the long-term "collection" area of

745   Ar Cheb, book 1435, *Losungsbuch 1457*; book nr. 2157, *Allgemeine Umgeldbücher 1456*, fol. 38r.
746   Klír et al., *Knihy*, 138–144.

a given city's population.[747] The migration horizon is perceived as a reflection of one part of the social space, i.e., of the social networks, relationships, and interactions between selected medieval people. The scope and structure of the migration horizon inform us of the social, economic, demographic, and cultural foundations of the city and its status concerning other settlements.[748]

A model and empirically supported perception of the migration horizon of late medieval cities is offered by the results of the wide-ranging project concerning the city of Bern titled *Neubürger im späten Mittelalter. Migration und Austausch in der Städtelandschaft des alten Reiches, 1250–1550*.[749] On the analytical level, it identifies three geographically and socially differing zones (segments) of the migration horizon of a medieval city—the so-called migration core, a wider economic zone, and a long-distance zone.[750]

I. The *proximate zone* or *migration core* is defined as the city's immediate hinterland and its dominant population resource. No cities, towns, or market villages are located in this area, and almost all of the places of origin of new burghers are rural settlements. On the map indicating the origin of new burghers, the migration core of a certain city appears to be a spatially compact zone.[751]

II. The *wider economic zone* is understood to be the territory where cities, towns, and market villages are all sources of new burghers. The places of origin of new burghers are also rural settlements, but they do not cover a compact territory; rather, they have a diffuse structure (the rural population here is significantly absorbed by other, closer cities).[752] In the wider economic zone, which represents an area crisscrossed by a network of direct commercial contacts with other cities, the migration of craftsmen from cities predominates.

---

747   Schwinges, "Neubürger und Bürgerbücher," 372, 398. Cf. Musílek, *Patroni*, 148–165.
748   Schwinges, "Neubürger und Bürgerbücher," 403.
749   Schwinges, "Neubürger und Bürgerbücher"; Schwinges, "Bürgermigration."
750   Schwinges, "Neubürger und Bürgerbücher," 402–403.
751   In historiography, the migration core is sometimes delineated quite subjectively as a space from which the majority of new burghers come from. Extensive migration cores are then construed that include not just the nearby hinterland of the city (the migration core in a narrower sense), but also part of the economic zone. Cf. Musílek, *Patroni*, 165.
752   For more on the phenomenon of the so-called "nearest city," cf. Becker, "Das Land," 108–111. For more, see Schwinges, "Neubürger und Bürgerbücher," 378–406.

III. In the *distant zone*, the only place of origin of new burghers are cities, but not all cities in this zone. New burghers predominantly include highly specialized craftsmen and professionals with higher levels of education. In the case of university cities, this zone partially overlaps with the university migration zone.

The separate segments of the migration horizon of medieval cities reflected its level of centrality and its citizens' social networks. The migration core constituted the scope of the local market radius and also the city's demands as to population, subsistence, and raw materials. Geographically, its shape should resemble a perfect circle. The wider economic and distant zones were dependent on the extent and intensity of regional and interregional economic contacts, and their geographical shape largely reflected the trade route network. The scope and structure of the migration horizon were unique to each medieval city, since they depended upon (1) the needs of the city and its political strength, (2) the potential of its hinterland, and (3) the migration horizon of neighboring cities. A geographically extensive migration core or economic zone did not necessarily mean a strong city but could indicate a weak hinterland in terms of population and just a slightly urbanized landscape, as was the case, for instance, with the Hanseatic cities on the coasts of the Baltic Sea.[753]

The identification of the scope of the separate migration zones of a medieval city is dependent on the source base, the method of record-keeping of new burghers, and the length of the analyzed time segment. Previous research has shown that the scope and structure of migration zones of late medieval imperial cities were stable in the long-term; therefore, at least approximate information may be provided both by a sample in the form of randomly selected time segments and also through the detailed analysis of shorter time segments.[754]

Migration horizon, 1442–1490

The geographical origin of Cheb's new burghers in the Late Middle Ages (1442–1490) was analyzed by Heribert Sturm according to the city income books.[755] The place of origin was specified in the books for 36% of new burghers, the remaining 64% being most likely persons who came from Cheb

753 Schwinges, "Neubürger und Bürgerbücher," 403–404.
754 Schwinges, "Neubürger und Bürgerbücher," 398–399.
755 Klír, *Rolnictvo*, app. 26.2.

itself, especially the sons and sons-in-law of established burghers.[756] The proportion of persons with place of origin specified is lower in the case of Cheb than in other cities.[757] As far as Heribert Sturm could determine, new burghers with places of origin outside Cheb hailed predominantly from rural settlements rather than from other cities (3:1).[758] Sturm's tables also show that Cheb's migration core did not exceed a perimeter of 15 km. Up to this distance, new burghers predominantly included immigrants from rural settlements as opposed to immigrants from cities (*figs. 23.1–23.2*). Eighty-six percent of new burghers hailed from the migration core. New burghers hailing from another city had moved a distance of 15–30 km (27%), 31–50 km (31%), or most frequently, further (39%).

The amount of the citizenship admission fee was not fixed in the Late Middle Ages but differed individually according to the applicant's property position. This differs from an earlier and isolated surviving item of data from the mid-14th century, when a sum of 20 pounds of hellers (or 4.5 Rheinish guilders) was required for citizenship admission.[759] Nothing suggests that the level of the fee was adjusted according to the geographical origin of the new burgher, as it was, for instance, in Göttingen.[760]

Migration horizon in detail, 1442–1456[761]

Heribert Sturm's findings are too general for the purposes of our study of the socioeconomic mobility and migration of the Cheb peasantry; therefore, in the following passages we analyze the situation in the time segment 1442–1456. While doing so, we are aware that the findings cannot be generalized to apply to the 15th century or the Late Middle Ages as a whole.

756   Schwinges, "Neubürger und Bürgerbücher," 196–200.
757   Cf. Musílek, *Patroni*, 148; Schwinges, "Neubürger und Bürgerbücher."
758   Klír, *Rolnictvo*, app. 26.2b.
759   Sturm, "Die Egerer Ungeldbücher," 193; data published by Karl Siegl, *Alt-Eger in seinen Gesetzen und Verordnungen* (Augsburg, Kassel: Johannes Stauda, 1927), 25. On the situation regarding coins around the mid-14th century, cf. Castelin, "Chebské mincovnictví," 77–78. On the significance of the amount of the citizenship admission fee, cf. Musílek, *Patroni*, 165–166.
760   Schwinges, "Neubürger und Bürgerbücher," 396.
761   Summarized also in Klír, "Local migration," 210–214.

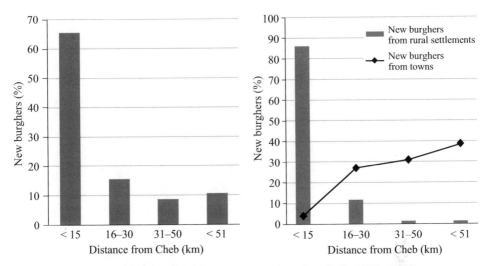

Figures 23.1–23.2. Migration horizon of new burghers in Cheb, 1442–1490. The migration core of the city with a perimeter of up to 15 km is clearly visible (fig. 23.1). Up to this distance, new burghers from the countryside were predominant. Afterwards the ratio turned in favor of new burghers from cities and towns (fig. 23.2).

Source: Data according to Sturm, "Die Egerer Ungeldbücher," 197–198. Adapted.
Note: Cf. Klír, *Rolnictvo,* app. 26.2b.

All city income books for the focus period have survived, except for 1451.[762] In a total of 14 books, 114 names were recorded, with most in 1448 (17 names) and the fewest in 1450 (2 names); therefore, on average 8 names a year. Geographical origin was not entered for 52% of new burghers, but it proved possible to establish this data for one-tenth of them in the land tax registers.[763] So, we have reliable information as to the place of origin of 61 new burghers (*fig. 23.12*). The citizenship admission fee ranged between 8 and 360 Prague groschen (1 to 4 Rhenish guilders); on average, the figure was 76 groschen.[764]

762   *App. 23.1.*
763   *App. 23.2b.*
764   The Rhenish guilder to Prague groschen exchange rate ranged between 1:22 in 1442 to 1:28 in 1456.

Overall, the highest fees were prescribed for new burghers arriving from the Cheb countryside.[765]

We cross-checked the testimony of the city income books using the information-rich Cheb *1446 City Tax Register*, which, of the 1,400 taxpayers' names, listed 56 names in a form like "*Simo[n] von Tachaw*," including 14 widows (*fig. 23.13*).[766] The *1442–1456 City Income Books* and the *1446 City Tax Register* provided almost surprisingly corresponding testimony.

Migration core

The scope of the migration core of Cheb's new burghers may be narrowed to a perimeter of approximately 8–10 km from Cheb (*fig. 23.3*).[767] Seventy-four percent of new burghers, according to the income book, or 72%, according to the city tax register of 1446, hailed from this territory. The geographical border of Cheb's migration core seems remarkably sharp if we look at the number of new burghers per unit of area (*fig. 23.4.*). While the average was one to two new burghers per 10 km², up to a distance of 5–10 km, the figure for a distance of 11–15 km was only 0.2 new burghers and with even fewer further afield. Migration to the city was therefore exceptionally attractive for peasants in its vicinity, while with increasing distance the attractiveness of Cheb fell exponentially (*fig. 23.4*). The perimeter of 8–10 km corresponded to the local market radius of a medieval city, at the same time representing a distance that could be overcome in 2–3 hours on foot, i.e., a return journey could be made during one day.

It was found that the migration core of Cheb did not cover the entire territory of the city-state but was smaller—comprising primarily the parish of Cheb and also the most fertile parts of the Cheb Basin along the banks of the Ohře and Odrava Rivers (*figs. 23.5; 23.12–23.13*). The intensity of migration to the city within the migration core may be expressed more precisely using relative figures—on average 0.6 new burghers came from 100 landholdings in the parish of Cheb every year, while from the parish of Dřenice, which had a similar population, the figure was 4–5x lower (*fig. 23.6*).[768] As for the proportion of immigrants from the countryside and from cities, up to a distance of

---

765   Klír, *Rolnictvo*, app. 26.5a.
766   Ar Cheb, book 1424, *Losungsbuch 1446*. Cf. Klír, *Rolnictvo*, app. 26.5b.
767   Klír, *Rolnictvo*, app. 26.3a.
768   Klír, *Rolnictvo*, app. 26.3b–d.

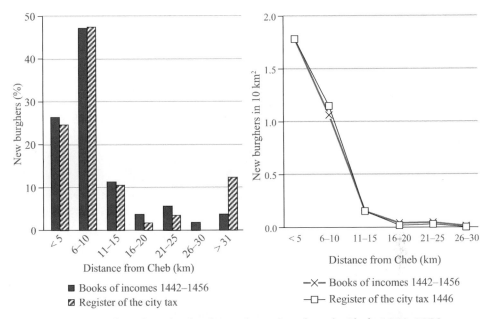

Figures 23.3–23.4. The migration horizon of new burghers in Cheb, 1442–1456. The migration core of the city is clear (perimeter up to 10 km). The attractiveness of the city fell exponentially, along with geographical distance (fig. 23.4).

Source: Ar Cheb, books 2144–2157, *Umgeldbücher 1442–1450, 1452–1456*; book 1424, *Losungsbuch 1446*.
Note: Cf. Klír, *Rolnictvo*, app. 26.3e.

16–20 km a place of origin in a rural settlement prevailed, while thereafter the proportion turned in favor of cities (*figs. 23.7–23.8*).[769]

The wider economic zone
Amongst Cheb's new burghers we find immigrants from almost all cities, towns, and market villages lying up to 25–40 km away. This segment of the migration horizon was geographically asymmetric, extending along trade routes stretching farthest into Upper Franconia and Bohemia, less far into Vogtland and the Upper Palatinate. Cheb's commercial and economic networks fairly evenly covered the entire area between the Fichtel Mountains, the Ore Mountains,

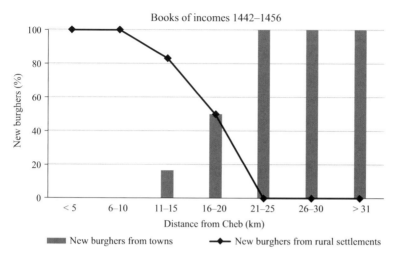

Figure 23.5. Parish pertaining to the place of origin of new burghers arriving in Cheb from the city-state of Cheb, 1442–1456.

Source: Ar Cheb, books 2144–2157, *Umgeldbücher 1442–1450, 1452–1456*; book 1424, *Losungsbuch 1446*.
Parish pertinence according to Ar Cheb, book 974, *Musterungsbuch der Bauernschaft*.
Note: Cf. Klír, *Rolnictvo*, app. 26.3b.

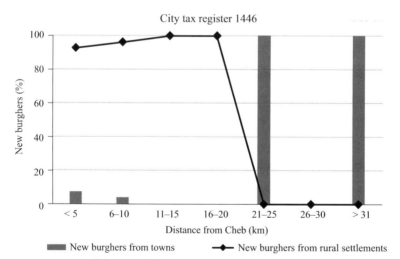

Figure 23.6. Parish pertaining to the place of origin of new burghers arriving in Cheb from the city-state of Cheb, 1442–1456. Average number of immigrants pertaining to 100 landholdings lying in the parish.

Source: Ar Cheb, books 2144–2157, *Umgeldbücher 1442–1450, 1452–1456*; book 1424, *Losungsbuch 1446*.
Parish pertinence according to Ar Cheb, book 974, *Musterungsbuch der Bauernschaft*.
Note: Cf. Klír, *Rolnictvo*, app. 26.3d.

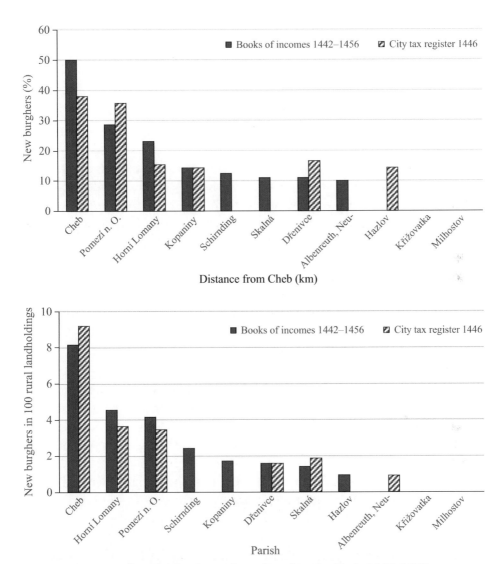

Figures 23.7–23.8. Migration horizon of new burghers in Cheb, 1442–1456.
Up to a distance of 15 km, new burghers from the countryside were predominant.
Afterwards the ratio turned in favor of new burghers from cities.

Source: Ar Cheb, books 2144–2157, *Umgeldbücher 1442–1450, 1452–1456*; book 1424, *Losungsbuch 1446*.
Parish pertinence according to Ar Cheb, book 974, *Musterungsbuch der Bauernschaft*.
Note: Cf. Klír, *Rolnictvo*, app. 26.3e.

and Slavkov Forest, and also the trade routes to Nuremberg, Cheb, Regensburg, and Leipzig.

Long-distance contact zone
The third segment of Cheb's migration horizon may be reconstructed at least
approximately according to the most distant places of origin of new burghers.
In the *1442–1456 City Income Books*, these places included Hof in Upper
Franconia and Kadaň in Bohemia (ca. 50 and 80 km away, respectively); in
the *1446 City Tax Register* they included Zwickau (ca. 85 km) and Olomouc
in Moravia (ca. 400 km), which was an extreme case. The absence of new burghers from Prague and prominent imperial cities suggests the secondary and
rather transit-related significance of Cheb during the focus period.

23.4 Socioeconomic aspects[770]

Property position of Cheb's new burghers in the city

The property position of Cheb's new burghers may be examined using the city
tax registers. As an example, we chose the 1446 register, which contained the
nominal value of tax registered for 1,222 taxpayers, 48 of whom, according to
their names, originated from outside Cheb, including 13 widows. We ordered
all of the taxpayers of Cheb according to the level of prescribed tax and divided
them into five quintiles containing in all cases 244 or 245 persons. Subsequently, we analyzed the quintile position of taxpayers from outside Cheb
and examined whether they belonged more to the poorer or richer section of
Cheb's burghers.

Burghers who had moved into Cheb from the countryside of the city-state
tended to be among the richer taxpayers—three times as many belonged to the
richest quintile than to the poorest (*fig. 23.9*).[771] Burghers who had moved from
the wider Cheb region, or from places even further afield, tended to belong to
the poorer groups in terms of property. However, given the low number of

---

770 Summarized also in Klír, "Local migration," 210–214.
771 Cf. Klír, *Rolnictvo*, app. 26.5a–b.

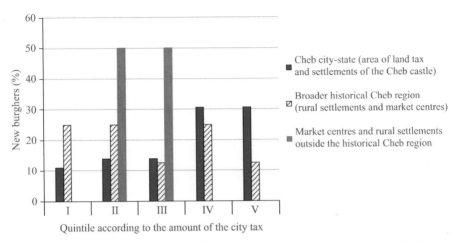

Figure 23.9. Property position of Cheb's burghers bearing a surname of the type "Simo[n] von Tachaw" in the 1446 Tax Register.

Source: Ar Cheb, book 1424, *Losungsbuch* 1446.
Note: Forty-eight of the 56 names of the type *"Simo[n] von Tachaw"* could be analyzed. Socioeconomic position was established for a total of 1,222 Cheb taxpayers. Cf. Klír, *Rolnictvo*, app. 26.5a–b.

cases assessed, the results for burghers from places farther afield cannot be generalized.

Property position of new burghers in their place of origin

A total of 33 new burghers who had moved into the city from the countryside had been previously registered among taxpayers in the Cheb land tax registers (*fig. 23.10; app. 23.2a*). With these persons, it may be determined what tax they were paying before and therefore too their relative property position. We can use the same quintiles as in *chapter 21*. We can also find the amount that they paid for the citizenship admission fee. The analysis showed that:

+ Approximately half of those who gained citizenship and left a rural landholding were among the richest group of land taxpayers (quintile V). The other half were among the medium-rich taxpayers (quintiles II–IV).
+ The poorest taxpayers of Cheb land tax (quintile I) did not figure among new burghers, with one exception. We assume that these individuals were tenants of smallholdings and the landless who without a doubt also left for the city but did not acquire any property or citizenship and were probably among the paupers of the city.

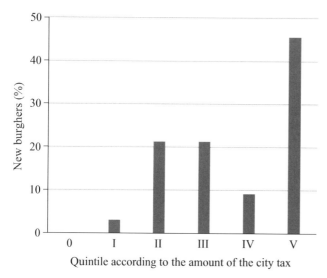

Figure 23.10. The original property position of Cheb's new burghers who had moved to the city from rural landholdings, 1442–1456.

Source: Ar Cheb, books 1069–1083, *Klosteurbücher 1442–1456*; book 1084, *Klosteuerbuch (Schätzungsbuch)* 1456; Ar Cheb, books 2144–2157, *Umgeldbücher 1442–1450, 1452–1456*.
Note: Cf. *app. 23.2a.* * – payment in Rheinish guilders converted according to a ratio of 1:25

+ The original property position was also reflected in the prescribed amount of the citizenship admission fee. The highest fee was collected from the richest rural immigrants; in two cases this represented the highest amount at all—4 threescore of Prague groschen.
+ Among new burghers, we also found tenants of "subject" and "free" landholdings.

Sociotopography: Immigration attractiveness of city districts

The city tax registers recorded taxpayers in a topographic manner, with 16 inner city districts and 12 suburban districts. This enabled us to determine which city districts attracted new burghers. For our sample, we again analyzed the *1446 City Tax Register (fig. 23.11)*. While doing this, we orientated ourselves according to the taxpayer's name, and we differentiated between origin within the city-state of Cheb (the land tax district and the Cheb Castle villages) and outside it. We analyzed a total of 1,400 taxpayers' names, among which 56 persons had names indicating place of origin such as *"Simo[n] von Tachaw."*

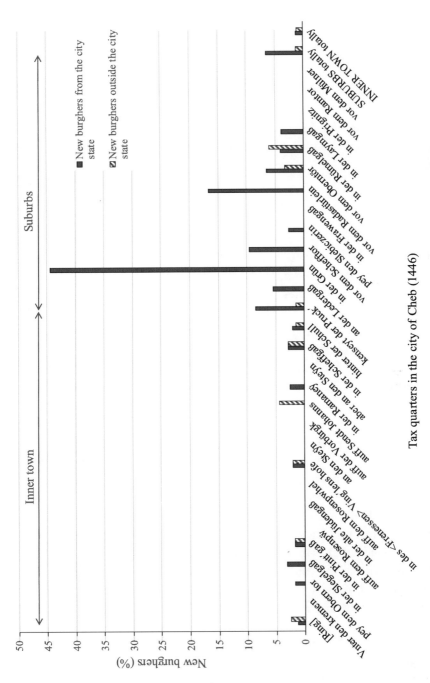

Fig. 23.11. The proportion of Cheb burghers with a known non-city origin in 1446. The difference between the inner city and the suburbs is striking.

Source: Ar Cheb, book 1424, Losungsbuch 1446.

The relative results are important, since the numbers of burghers of non-Cheb origin may have been higher in reality. The analysis showed that:

+ Three times as many persons of non-city origin lived in the suburbs than in the inner city.
+ The number of persons in the inner city who had moved there from the city-state of Cheb and from outside it was balanced, while persons from the city-state of Cheb clearly dominated in the suburbs (80%).
+ The highest proportion of new burghers of non-city origin was in the suburbs *"In der Grün"* (min. 44%) and *"Vor dem Radastürlein"* (min. 17%).

23.5 Property dispositions

The land and city tax registers also provide other data,[772] according to which we may follow, on the one hand, the property dispositions that accompanied migration and, on the other hand, the land transfers between city and country-side (*tab. 23.1*). The data for new burghers who moved to the city from the countryside and whose property situation may be determined according to the *1446 City Tax Register* are especially important. We consider the following to be particularly substantial:

+ Tenants of rural landholdings who acquired citizenship would thereafter also retain their "free" landholding, if they held one, while they would conversely sell a "subject" landholding (A).
+ Records exist of heirs of rural property who gained or had already gained citizenship previously (B–C). In six cases, this involved the offspring of the richest land taxpayers belonging to quintile V; in three cases, these were the offspring of less propertied land taxpayers in quintiles III–IV (quintiles according to total property in 1438; cf. *chap. 19–20*).
+ With propertied families, cases fairly often occurred in which the rural landholding was taken over by one of the descendants, while the others left for the city (C). We find information about such persons in the event that they were paid off with a non-landholding plot that they taxed via the land tax. A similar type of group existed in the form of widows who departed for the city to either live with their sons or daughters or remarry (B).

772   *App. 23.2b.*

Table 23.1. **Change in taxpayers' payment obligations between the city and the countryside 1442–1456.**

Situation			
Type		**Subtype**	**Concrete situation number in appendix 23.2.**
A	A taxpayer holding a landholding gained citizenship.	1. Landholding transferred immediately or after just a few years by a different person.	1, 6, 20
		2. The taxpayer got rid of a landholding but retained non-landholding plots and other properties.	3, 13, 9*, 17, 28*, 35*
		3. A new burgher retained a rural landholding and also other items of property that can no longer be followed in the land tax registers but can be found in the *1446 City Tax Register*.	11*
B	A widow and/or primary heir had citizenship in the city.	– -	4, 12, 15, 24, 29–30, 32
C	Secondary heirs had citizenship in the city.	– -	16, 21, 27, 31, 33
D	A burgher acquired (taxed) properties in the countryside that traditionally had been taxed under the land tax.	1. Entire landholding.	18, 25–26
		2. Non-landholding plots.	5, 8, 22–23, 36
E	A peasant (land tax taxpayer) acquired properties in the countryside that traditionally had been taxed under city tax.	– -	7, 10
F	A person surrendered their citizenship and became subject to the land tax.	– -	34

Source: Ar Cheb, books 1069–1083, *Klosteurbücher 1442–1456*; book 1084, *Klosteuerbuch (Schätzungsbuch)* 1456; book 1424, *Losungsbuch 1446*.
Note: Cf. app. 23.2b.
* – the property situation of a new burgher may be studied in the *1446 City Tax Register*.

23.6 Summary

No new burghers' registers were kept in late medieval Cheb; however, the city income books (1442–1765) and tax registers (1390–1758) provided the same function. The city income books in particular can be a fully-fledged resource for analyzing the geographical origin of Cheb's new burghers, since they recorded the citizenship admission fees, and the name of a new burgher was standardly supplemented with information concerning his place of origin. Origin outside of the city could be proven in a third (1442–1490) and/or half of all recorded new burghers (1442–1456). New burghers were predominantly immigrants from rural settlements (ca. three-quarters), as opposed to people from other cities.

In line with the methodological approach of R. C. Schwinges's team, we divide the migration horizon of late medieval Cheb into three distinct zones: the migration core, the wider economic zone, and the long-distance relations zone. Cheb's migration core stretched to a distance of 8–10 km from the city, and up to three-quarters of new burghers came from it in 1442–1456. Our defined migration core did not cover the entire city-state of Cheb but primarily comprised the parish of Cheb and also the agriculturally favorable belt along the banks of the Ohře River and to some extent the Odrava River. The wider economic zone stretched to a distance of 25–40 km, following the course of trade routes, was asymmetrical in shape, and the immigrants from this zone mainly included a range of craftsmen. Given the short focus segment, we were able to reconstruct the long-distance migration zone only tentatively, although in principle it could have comprised a large section of imperial cities as well as the most prominent Bohemian and Moravian cities.

Against the backdrop of established knowledge about immigration and emigration, we may classify Cheb as a typical transit city to which people from the immediate rural surroundings or from smaller market centers tended to move, while conversely, the richer burghers tended to move out to distant cities of the same or greater economic significance.

Migration from the countryside to the city was significant, and it covered one-twentieth of all the landholding transfers of landholdings in Cheb's territory (*tab. 19.2*). In the group of the wealthiest peasants, however, this share was substantially greater. The poorest section of the peasantry (i.e., smallholders and the landless) did not figure among new burghers. Without a doubt, such people also left the countryside for Cheb, but they most likely simply increased

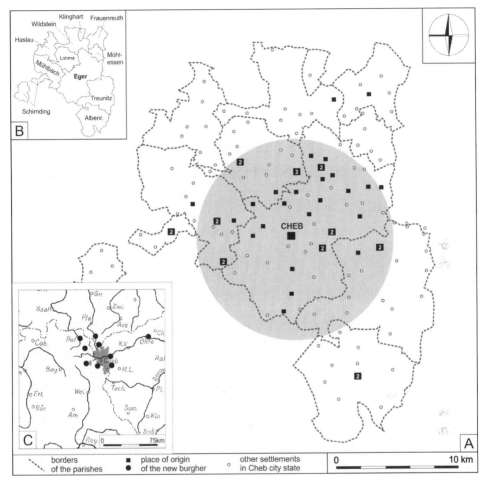

Figure 23.12. The place of origin of the newly accepted burghers in Cheb between 1442 and 1456.

Source: City income books. Cf. *app. 23.1.*
Note: A – immigrants from the city-state of Cheb (migration core with 10-km perimeter in gray);
B – parishes in the city-state of Cheb; C – immigrants from outside of the city-state of Cheb (in gray).

the numbers of urban paupers and therefore do not appear in the records. New burghers paid a citizenship admission fee corresponding to their property position, and sometimes they kept possession of at least some of their rural properties. New burghers moving from the countryside settled most often in the suburbs of Cheb and were among the richer taxpayers of city tax.

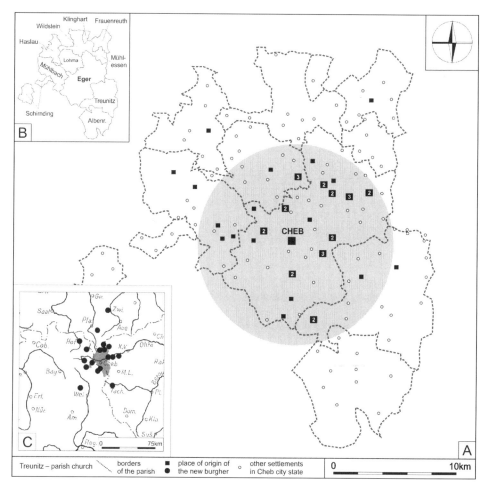

Figure 23.13. The origin of the immigrants to Cheb that can be established according to surnames of the type "Simo[n] von Tachaw" in the 1446 Tax Register.

Source: Ar Cheb, book nr. 1424, *Losungsbuch 1446.*

Note: A – immigrants from the city-state of Cheb (migration core with 10-km perimeter in gray); B – parishes in the city-state of Cheb; C – immigrants from outside of the city-state of Cheb (in gray; Olomouc in Moravia not illustrated).

The extensive urban migration of the wealthiest Cheb peasants can be another explanation of why there was not an accumulation of peasant property in the countryside. The richest peasants could have preferred to purchase in the city over increasing their own agrarian production.

24.
Abandonment as a reflection of social mobility

24.1 Research objectives

In *chapters 20–23* we described the socioeconomic mobility and migration of the peasantry in the late medieval city-state of Cheb. We can talk about a type of uneven reproduction where migration was a route of social ascent. If the poorer landholdings were left in favor of the wealthier ones, this raises a natural question as to whether the process of abandonment can be explained in this way. In the following chapters, we will test the hypothesis that late medieval abandonment was the reverse side of a regime of uneven reproduction where migration was the channel of upward social mobility.

Analysis of the peasants of the city-state of Cheb in 1424/1438–1456/1469 showed a population and landscape where almost no long-term vacant land-holdings and no abandonment of settlements existed even during the periods of mortality crises or military conflicts. However, the city-state of Cheb was not an isolated island, and its inhabitants did not live in a vacuum. But was the extraordinarily stable Cheb city-state, in terms of population and settlements, accompanied by an increased emigration and depopulation of the surrounding submountainous and mountainous areas? Such a question cannot be solved after 1412–1413 based on tax registers, for they only inform us about a part of the original Cheb region. Our attention diverts to the oldest surviving registers, from 1392–1409, which were created when the Cheb land tax included a wider area and a third more locations.[773] The question is whether depopulation and abandonment occurred in this belt specifically (*chap. 24.5*).

24.2 Sources

The Cheb *1392–1409 Land Tax Registers* did not have a fixed form. The oldest tax register, from 1392, recorded for each settlement the overall prescribed amount, the degree to which it was paid, and in many settlements, by name and individually, the actually paying persons and therefore not all potential taxpayers. The overall final sum collected from one location was recorded. The register contains a total of 203 settlements; some did not have a prescribed tax for various reasons, or in some, the peasants may have not paid. In many settlements, the prescribed tax was collected, but only *en masse*; therefore, we do not know the names of individual taxpayers. We know the internal structure of just 102 settlements, with a total of 929 individual taxpayers.[774]

The following *1395 Land Tax Register* was of a similar nature, but it seems that it was not completely finalized.[775]

The following clean copies of land tax registers, covering the period from 1397–1409 with some gaps, were kept in a simpler way. Next to the names of settlements, the overall prescribed sum was listed with a comment stating whether it was paid in full or not, and if not, it listed the reason. The names of the taxpayers are missing completely. In the tax registers from 1397, the clerks quite systematically labeled currently abandoned villages, which they continued to do in the years to come.[776]

---

773   Klír et al., *Knihy*, 124–131.
774   Ar Cheb, book 1009, *Klosteuerbuch 1392* (original); book 1053, *Klosteuerbuch 1392* (copy); Klír et al., *Knihy*, 74–81; Heisinger, "Die Egerer Klosteuerbücher," 8–12, 105–124.
775   Ar Cheb, book 1054, *Klosteuerbuch 1395*.
776   Ar Cheb, book 1055, *Klosteuerbuch 1397* (copy); book 1056, *Klosteuerbuch 1401*; book 1057, *Klosteuerbuch 1404*; book 1058, *Klosteuerbuch 1408*; book 1059, *Klosteuerbuch 1409*. The register of 1409 was compiled from three parts by Heisinger, "Die Egerer Klosteuerbücher," 14. Some loose sheets have most likely been lost from the tax register because villages normally listed together are missing.

24.3 **Methods**

In the surviving tax registers from 1392–1409, we traced for each settlement
how high the tax amount was and to what extent this obligation was satisfied.
Then we noted all additional comments by the clerk, which usually shed light
on why some of the taxpayers did not pay the tax or why it was waived. We
ignored the data from the register of 1395 because it was not always certain why
no tax was prescribed for a large number of settlements and why so many of
the other settlements did not pay it.

The analyzed set included 176 settlements that were under the control of
the Cheb city council in 1392–1409 and where there was at least one taxpayer
who should pay the land tax. Settlements marked as abandoned were retained
in the analyzed set (*fig. 24.1*). For each year, we assigned a specific settlement to
one of the following categories for each year:

1. Taxpayers paid the total amount of prescribed land tax. In this category, we
   included several settlements where individual taxpayers failed to meet their
   tax obligations, but the reason was not their economic weakness but because
   they owed allegiance to a landlord who did not respect the authority of the
   Cheb city council (*fig. 24.1*; black field).
2. Some taxpayers did not pay their taxes at all or only partially. The register said that the tax was partially or totally waived in a given year, or it
   was just noted that they had not paid the tax. The reason was listed only
   rarely—a fire or a failed harvest as the result of weather fluctuation (*fig. 24.1*;
   dark gray field).
3. None of the taxpayers paid the tax, which also may or may not have been
   noted in the register (*fig. 24.1*; light gray field).
4. The settlement was explicitly marked as abandoned (*fig. 24.1*; in the field
   "+").

Several main groups of settlements emerged in the analyzed set according to
their payment ability (*figs. 24.2–24.3*):

A. Non-problematic settlements, where land tax was always paid by all of the
   taxpayers during the whole period.
B. Settlements where taxpayers paid the total tax in the majority of the analyzed years and paid it partially or not at all only once or twice.
C. Problematic settlements where the total tax was paid only in one to three
   years.
D. Settlements that were listed as abandoned during the majority of the following period.

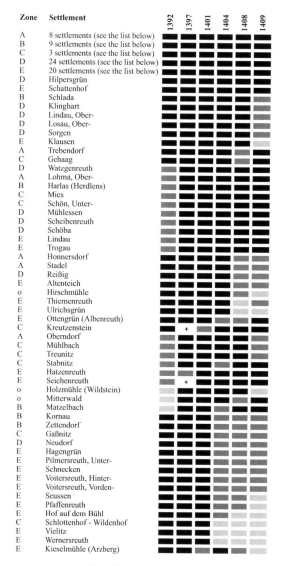

Figure 24.1. Collection of Cheb land tax in 1392–1409, reflecting the process of abandonment.

Black field – required tax amount collected in full. **Dark gray field** – tax amount collected only in part.
Light gray field – tax amount not paid at all. + – settlement listed as abandoned.
Source: Ar Cheb, books 1009, 1054–1059, *Klosteuerbücher 1392, 1397 (copy from 1769), 1401, 1404, 1408, 1409.*
Cf. Klír, *Rolnictvo,* app. 30.1.
Note: Settlements where the prescribed tax amount was collected each year (listed in summary in the table): **Zone A:** Lehenstein; Dölitz(hof); Höflas (Trebendorf); Reichersdorf; Rohr; Sirmitz; Triesenhof;

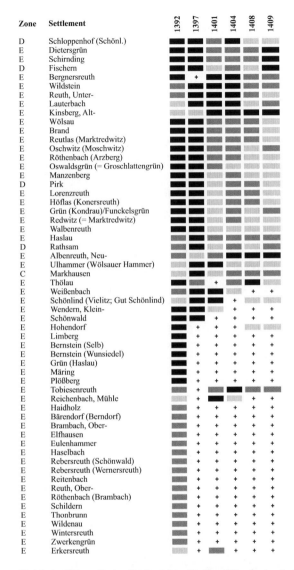

Zone	Settlement	1392	1397	1401	1404	1408	1409
D	Schloppenhof (Schönl.)						
E	Dietersgrün						
E	Schirnding						
D	Fischern						
E	Bergnersreuth						
E	Wildstein						
E	Reuth, Unter-						
E	Lauterbach						
E	Kinsberg, Alt-						
E	Wölsau						
E	Brand						
E	Reutlas (Marktredwitz)						
E	Oschwitz (Moschwitz)						
E	Röthenbach (Arzberg)						
E	Oswaldsgrün (= Groschlattengrün)						
E	Manzenberg						
D	Pirk						
E	Lorenzreuth						
E	Höflas (Konersreuth)						
E	Grün (Kondrau)/Funckelsgrün						
E	Redwitz (= Marktredwitz)						
E	Walbenreuth						
E	Haslau						
D	Rathsam						
E	Albenreuth, Neu-						
E	Ulhammer (Wölsauer Hammer)						
C	Markhausen						
E	Thölau						
E	Weißenbach						
E	Schönlind (Vielitz; Gut Schönlind)						
E	Wendern, Klein-						
E	Schönwald						
E	Hohendorf						
E	Limberg						
E	Bernstein (Selb)						
E	Bernstein (Wunsiedel)						
E	Grün (Haslau)						
E	Märing						
E	Plößberg						
E	Tobiesenreuth						
E	Reichenbach, Mühle						
E	Haidholz						
E	Bärendorf (Berndorf)						
E	Brambach, Ober-						
E	Elfhausen						
E	Eulenhammer						
E	Haselbach						
E	Rebersreuth (Schönwald)						
E	Rebersreuth (Wernersreuth)						
E	Reitenbach						
E	Reuth, Ober-						
E	Röthenbach (Brambach)						
E	Schildern						
E	Thonbrunn						
E	Wildenau						
E	Wintersreuth						
E	Zwerkengrün						
E	Erkersreuth						

Hohlerhof. **Zone B:** Au; Förba; Hart; Knöba; Kötschwitz; Lohma, Unter-; Nebanitz; Stein; Wogau. **Zone C:** Dürrnbach; Sebenbach; Schön, Ober-. **Zone D:** Döba; Thurn; Tipessenreuth; Berg; Bruck; Doberau; Dürr; Ensenbruck; Fonsau; Frauenreuth; Grün (Thurn); Haid; Hartessenreuth; Höflas(gut) (Lohma); Kropitz; Lapitzfeld; Liebeneck; Lindau, Unter-; Losau, Unter-; Mühlgrün; Nonnengrün; Pograt; Schüttüber, Groß-; Stobitzhof. **Zone E:** Taubrat; Albenreuth, Alt-; Boden (St. Anna); Bodnershof (Leubnershof); Grün (Wildstein); Hirschfeld; Konradsgrün; Kunreuth, Ober-; Kunreuth, Unter-; Liebenstein; Oedt; Ottengrün (Haslau); Palitz; Pilmersreuth, Ober-; Riehm; Rommersreuth; Rossenreuth; Schönlind (Schloppenhof); Schönberg; Gosel.

Data from the hard-to-interpret year 1395 were not documented.

24.4 The two faces of the uneven reproduction regime

The results presented in *figure 24.1* show that, on a general trend level, settlements where we investigated social mobility and migration in 1438–1456 were different in nature in 1392–1409 than the settlements that were not included in the analyzed set. This set included mainly prosperous and attractive settlements situated in the Cheb Basin, the counter-pole to which were unstable and periodically depopulated submountainous and mountainous zones.

Expressed in concrete figures, entirely or almost problem-free settlements accounted for a full 86% of the analyzed set, problematic settlements 14%, while almost abandoned settlements were not categorized in the set. Conversely, problematic and abandoned settlements accounted for 81% of the non-analyzed set. We see a similar tendency if we assess the distribution of various types of settlements. A total of 91% of problem-free settlements were assessed, compared to only 35% of problematic settlements (*figs. 24.2–24.3*).

24.5 Correlation with natural conditions

Various types of settlements assessed according to ability to pay the land tax were distributed unevenly in various ecological zones (*tab. 24.1–24.2*). It was discovered that the worse the ecological zone, the greater the likelihood that the settlement would not pay tax in full or would soon be abandoned. None of the settlements located in zone A can be marked as problematic or even abandoned; 62% of them were completely problem-free. Conversely, in zone E most settlements were problematic regarding paying the land tax (66%), and just 22% were problem-free. As natural conditions worsened, the economic threat to settlements grew.

Nevertheless, the correlation between negative payment ability and natural conditions may also be indirect. A settlement in the geographically unfavorable zone usually meant worse access to Cheb as the main marketplace, greater vulnerability to local violent conflicts, and also the stronger influence of the landlord, who could overburden their "subject" tenants and prevent them from paying land tax to Cheb. However, we have eliminated this last factor ("fighting over rent") by excluding settlements belonging to the Burgraves of Nuremberg and others to which this might apply.

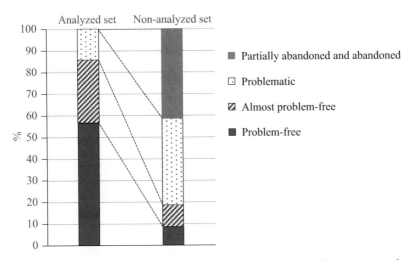

Figure 24.2. Proportion of settlements with varying abilities to pay the land tax (1392-1409) in the set for which we analyzed social mobility in 1438-1456 in chap. 19-23.

Source: Ar Cheb, books 1009, 1054–1059, *Klosteuerbücher 1392, 1397 (copy from 1769), 1401, 1404, 1408, 1409.* Cf. Klír, *Rolnictvo*, app. 30.2.

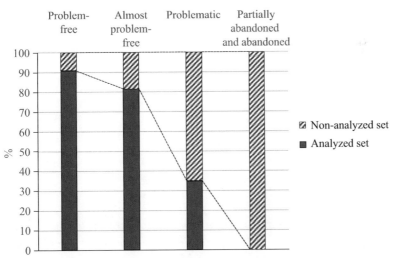

Figure 24.3. Proportion of settlements with varying abilities to pay the land tax (1392-1409) in the set for which we analyzed social mobility in 1438-1456 in chap. 19-23.

Source: Ar Cheb, books 1009, 1054–1059, *Klosteuerbücher 1392, 1397 (copy from 1769), 1401, 1404, 1408, 1409.* Cf. Klír, *Rolnictvo*, app. 30.2.

Table 24.1. **Distribution of settlements with varying payment abilities according to ecological zones in the Cheb region (1392–1409). Absolute values.**

Payment of land tax	Zone					Total
	A	B	C	D	E	
1. Without problems	8	9	3	25	21	66
2. Insignificant problems	5	3	8	9	13	38
3. Problematic	0	2	3	3	35	43
4. Almost abandoned and abandoned villages	0	0	0	0	29	29
Total	13	14	14	37	98	176

Source: Ar Cheb, books 1009, 1054–1059, *Klosteuerbücher 1392, 1397 (copy from 1769), 1401, 1404, 1408, 1409.*

Table 24.2. **Distribution of settlements with varying payment abilities according to geographical zones in the Cheb region (1392–1409). Relative values.**

Payment of land tax	Zone					Total
	A	B	C	D	E	
1. Without problems	12.1	13.6	4.5	37.9	31.8	37.5
2. Insignificant problems	13.2	7.9	21.1	23.7	34.2	21.6
3. Problematic	0.0	4.7	7.0	7.0	81.4	24.4
4. Almost abandoned and abandoned villages	0.0	0.0	0.0	0.0	100.0	16.5
Total	7.4	8.0	8.0	21.0	55.7	100.0

Source: Ar Cheb, books 1009, 1054–1059, *Klosteuerbücher 1392, 1397 (copy from 1769), 1401, 1404, 1408, 1409.*

24.6 Summary

The primary precondition for abandonment was the fact that tenants had the option to move, and in certain situations, moving was the preferred option for adaptation and social rise.[777] A significant role was certainly the fact that

---

777 From the Czech historical literature, see the lucidly written Grulich, *Migrace*, 8–74; for high and late medieval Bohemia and Moravia, see Graus, *Dějiny*, 244–246, 256–257; Míka,

the position of the landlord was weak in the Cheb region, and the moving of "subject" tenants in reality was not controlled. Although records exist in a range of transalpine areas of restrictions limiting departure from a manor or country, either in the form of prescribed norms or an oath, such records are lacking for the Cheb region in the period investigated.[778] Another favorable circumstance could have been that the costs of migration were low; a large proportion of farmsteads were, construction-wise, fairly simple and had relatively cheap furnishings that the peasants mainly acquired and renovated with their own hands.[779] Therefore, the farmer did not lose much in moving, since the target farmstead did not require great costs; the decisive step was to acquire draft animals and beef cattle.[780] Strong ties formed only around wealthy landholdings and great farmsteads. The short distances involved also made moving easier, since, even after the change, the tenant and his household remained in a very familiar environment.

Analysis of settlements paying Cheb land tax in 1392–1409 showed that the system of uneven reproduction on peasant landholdings had two contrasting faces in the Late Middle Ages. One comprised the regions that were stable in terms of population and economy, represented in our case by the Cheb Basin, and the second comprised the adjacent zones hit by depopulation, typically in submountainous and mountainous terrains.

Settlements where Cheb land tax was collected around the year 1400 could be divided into three categories: (1) stable in terms of population and economic stability; (2) unstable; and (3) permanently or temporarily abandoned. While

---

Poddaný lid, 189–203. For the Early Modern Period, see Grulich, *Migrace*; Petráň, *Poddaný lid*, 241–251.

778 Hans-Martin Maurer, "Masseneide gegen Abwanderung im 14. Jahrhundert. Quellen zur territorialen Rechts- und Bevölkerungsgeschichte," *Zeitschrift für Württembergische Landesgeschichte* 39 (1980): 30–99; Gero Kirchner, "Probleme der spätmittelalterlichen Klostergrundherrschaft in Bayern. Landflucht und bäuerliches Erbrecht. Ein Beitrag zur Genesis des Territorialstaates," *Zeitschrift für Bayerische Landesgeschichte* 19 (1956): 1–94, on 45–63; Wilhelm Abel, *Die Wüstungen des ausgehenden Mittelalters*, Quellen und Forschungen zur Agrargeschichte 1 (Stuttgart: Fischer, 1955), 53–57; Cerman, *Villagers*, 23, Table 2.1; Graus, *Dějiny*, 244–248.

779 Cf., e.g., Pavel Vařeka, *Archeologie středověkého domu 1. Proměny vesnického obydlí v Evropě v průběhu staletí. 6.–15. století*, Archaeologica (Plzeň: Dryada, 2004); Jan Klápště, *The archaeology of Prague and the medieval Czech lands, 1100–1600*, Studies in the Archaeology of Medieval Europe (Shefield: Equinox, 2016); Rösener, *Bauern*, 73–95.

780 Achilles, *Überlegungen*, 11.

problem-free settlements remained part of the Cheb territory (the city-state of Cheb) even after 1412, most of the others split off. The dark side to the extraordinarily stable areas of the Cheb region in terms of population and settlements could have been the increased emigration and depopulation of the surrounding submountainous and mountainous areas. We assume that the direction of migrations flows, indirectly documented around 1400, was also of a similar nature around 1450, although in this case abandonment of settlements did not occur.

The generally formulated principles in chapters 20–24 apply, and we shall supplement them with another fundamental finding. The price of population-related and economic stability of some regions was the depopulation and disintegration of peasant communities in other regions. It is therefore clear that living and abandoned villages cannot be addressed separately since all were linked by the same social processes and formed one system. Indeed, the abandonment of settlements in the Late Middle Ages and the type of uneven production system in which migration was a route to achieve social rise were expressions of the same socioeconomic process—or more accurately, *regime*. At the same time, migration of the late medieval peasantry increased the differences between various settlements and regions—remaining stable, flexible, and innovative in one region, while aggravating the crisis in other regions.

◂ Plate 7: **Nebanice (Nebanitz). A cottage at the confluence of the Ohře and Plesná Rivers (so-called Schwalbenhäusel; September 9, 1900). The dwellings of fishermen, shepherds, and other landless people maintained their traditional structural form for a long time. The ground floor was timbered, the gable half-timbered.**

Summary and Conclusion

European historians are able to describe in detail the reproductive system, socioeconomic mobility, and migration of the early modern peasantry operating in conditions of long-term population and economic growth. However, we do not know enough about the form of these social processes in peasant communities, which faced a fundamentally different environment of population stagnation and agrarian depression during the Late Middle Ages. One of the few European regions where the socioeconomic mobility and migration of the peasantry can be traced to the required detail and quantity for this period is the city-state of Cheb, thanks to fascinating fiscal sources, which provide annual insight into the interior of 80–100 rural settlements and 800–900 landholdings, covering approximately 400km².

The structure of the work was based on the notion that the socioeconomic stratification, mobility, and migration of the peasantry were always and everywhere determined by several generally valid and often contradictory forces, but their concrete impact depended on historically variable factors. Thus, the situation of each peasant population was unique. In the case of the late medieval city-state of Cheb, the Cheb peasant communities notably were (i) only weakly monetized and the majority of family property transfers were material or in kind, (ii) subject to weak landlord control, and (iii) able to generate a relatively large agricultural surplus, drawn only in part by rent. The stability of the social system relied on local migration, which, in an environment of population stagnation and abundance of land, dampened the effects of polarizing forces. Peasant communities were divided into a group of (A) dominating peasant families, controlling wealthy "subject" or even "free" landholdings stably and in the long-term and often capable of materially securing all their descendants; and a group of (B) poorer peasants and smallholders families, whose members fluctuated between landholdings and settlements, where migration was usually the channel of upward social mobility.

I. Socioeconomic structure and institutions

Historical context and geographical zonality

In the Late Middle Ages, the city-state of Cheb was among the largest in terms of area and also the most compact of the imperial city-states, such as Nuremberg and Rothenburg ob der Tauber in Franconia or Ulm in Swabia. However, unlike them, the city-state of Cheb did not emerge as a gradual consolidation of territorial, jurisdictional, or even landlords' rights (i.e., formation from below) but by the assumption of sovereign power by the city council (i.e., formation from above). The Cheb territory largely overlaps with the market and consumption area of the late medieval city. It was directly supplied with agricultural products from a circle with a perimeter of about 12 km, from distant places rather indirectly through a network of transit locations (*chap. 5.1; 5.4*).

In this monograph, we have followed the peasantry in the peak period of the city-state of Cheb, in essence defined as the period between the Hussite and Hungarian wars. The analyzed interval of 1438–1456 was relatively calm politically, socially, demographically, and in terms of prices, although at its beginning there was likely a substantial mortality crisis (1438/1439). It was also an exceptionally cold period, which did not, however, bring a dramatic decline in agricultural production. The historical context of the peasant population that we investigated differed substantially from that of the Early Modern Period, which has so far been the focus of most studies of a similar nature because the early modern peasant communities of Central Europe operated in a period of a growing labor-rent manorial estate, demographic growth, price revolution, monetized family relationships, and, in some locations, also mining booms or protoindustrialization (*chap. 5.1; 5.8–5.10*).

The city-state of Cheb was not homogenous but rather divided into several ecologically diverse zones which differed in social, economic, and also demographic structure. One pole consisted of agroclimatically favorable areas with commercially oriented agriculture, large and highly valued landholdings, and a significant land tax burden; the second pole consisted of a relatively harsh submontane climate with subsistence agriculture. The overall lower wealth of peasant households in less favorable agriculture zones was also reflected in the different degrees of socioeconomic stratification, socioeconomic mobility, migration, and the intensity of land transfers. If we were to analyze the individual ecological zones separately, our results would not be statistically as clear as the analysis of the city-state of Cheb as a whole (*chap. 5.2–5.7*).

Sources

Our findings are based on an analysis of the annually recorded lists of the payers of the Cheb land tax, which has been preserved completely and continually since 1442. We have supplemented their testimony with the monetary values of the main property items of each household, which were preserved in the 1438 *Land Tax Register* and in the property 1456 *Taxation Book*. This is why we have framed the center of gravity of the analysis in precisely these years. From other contemporary written sources, we used a particularly informative register of the Cheb city tax (1446), books of municipal incomes, and the estate land register of the Cheb Poor Clares (*chap. 6.1; 6.3*).

The Cheb land tax registers are a rich source, the testimonial potential of which has no precise analogy in late medieval transalpine Europe because the land tax in other regions was either not yet collected annually or a continuous series of registers were not preserved (*chap. 6.2*).

The monetary values of the property items listed in the tax registers reflected the prices used for property transfers within the peasant communities. Their testimony should thus be similar to the data in later land-transfers registers. Nevertheless, there is a fundamental difference because both types of documents were different institutional instruments and shaped social reality in a different way. The advent of land-transfers registers was a manifestation of the bureaucratization of the administration and a tool for regulating and controlling the transfers of "subject" land, whether by the peasant elites or the landlords. The knowledge of peasant communities based on land-transfers registers will thus always be burdened by the fact that the very existence of this source implies a distinct historical context. The Cheb tax registers are unique in this respect, as they allow the information limit of land-transfers registers to be exceeded (*chap. 14.2*).

We consider the monetary value of the property of the peasant households to be a relatively true image of the market capacity and the level of the agrarian commercialization of the landholding, and thus a suitable means for analyzing socioeconomic stratification and mobility. Naturally, market as well as institutional factors influenced the specific amounts of the monetary values. The market component would have been the strongest with the monetary values of freely disposable property (livestock, non-landholding plots), the institutional component with the "purchase" right (emphyteusis) to "subject" landholdings (*chap. 14.1–14.7*).

Institutional framework

The peasant land property circulated in two different economic as well as legal systems. The larger part of the land resources was compact, impartible, and transferred as an integral part of a "subject" landholding, which was held by the "purchase" right. This land was subject to relatively strong institutional control by landlords and also by the peasant communities themselves. The tenants had broad dispositional rights to the purchased landholding, and if they fulfilled certain formal conditions, they could leave, sell, or hand over and will the land-holding to one of their offspring. The division or merger of landholdings was not common, but it did occur (*chap. 7.3–7.4*).

The smaller, although quantitatively large, part of the land resources was outside traditional institutional control and was divisible, available, and cir-culated relatively freely on the market. Flexible *fief right* also applied to it, as is known from the neighboring Bavarian and Franconian regions. Property disposition of land under fief right did not actually differ from disposition of land under town law, so they were often unsurprisingly in the hands of Cheb burghers (*chap. 7.2; 7.4*).

Sometimes, entire landholdings were governed by fief right. These were not burdened by land rent, only land tax. Roughly 5% of the landholdings in the city-state of Cheb were in this category. These landholdings can be labeled as "free," although their legal status could have more specific forms. Because of its progressive nature, the land tax burdened "free" landholdings several times more than "subject" landholdings. This largely diminished the economic exclu-sivity of "free" landholdings, but the exclusivity in property disposition rights remained (*chap. 7.2; 7.4*).

Individual landholdings did not have the same status within the peasant community, and access to a common pool of economic resources. A dis-tinction was made between full-fledged peasant's landholdings (*Hof* land-holdings), smallholders, and cottagers (*Herberge* landholdings), which usually did not own draft animals. The *Herberge* landholdings were generally among the poorest group of landholdings, and tenants quickly alternated on them (*chap. 8.2*).

The analysis showed that the socioeconomic structure of the Cheb country-side complemented the socioeconomic structure of the city. The countryside was characterized by self-sufficient landholdings (*Hof*), with smallholdings making up only one-fifth (*Herberge*). However, these proportions change significantly if we include the small and subsistence-oriented agrarian producers living directly in the city of Cheb, especially in the suburbs. The absolute number of smallholders of agricultural land living in the city was equal to the number of tenants of smallholdings in the Cheb countryside as a whole. This had extremely serious consequences. Small agricultural producers living directly in Cheb could, in the long-term, satisfy the city's demand for a flexible wage labor force, thus preventing the growth of non-peasant classes in the countryside (*chap. 15.2; 15.5; 16.2*).

Surplus extraction

Landlord rights in the late medieval city-state of Cheb were exceptionally fragmented and dispersed. Only a minimum of settlements were compact in terms of property. Over one-third of the landlord rights were controlled by Cheb's ecclesiastical institutions, and tens of Cheb's patrician families shared the other third, of which only a few owned more than ten "subject" landholdings. Manors, in the sense of economically consolidated dominions, were lacking, and the land rent was most often characterized by in-kind payments, with labor rents being minimal. The fragmentation and spatial dispersion of landlord rights, their circulation among the patrician families, and the absence of labor rent indicate relatively weak landlord control over the land transfers of "subject" land (*chap. 9*).

The land tax, land rent, and ecclesiastical tithe formed the rent, which fell with various burdens on all of the tenants or holders of Cheb landholdings. The tenants of the "subject" landholdings paid all of the parts of the rent; the holders of the "free" landholdings paid only the land tax and ecclesiastical tithe. The **land rent** had a fixed nature based on the extent of the "subject" holding and favored some "subject" landholdings while relatively overburdening others. Nevertheless, almost all of the "subject" landholdings created a sufficiently high surplus to be able to bear the additional burden of the land tax (*chap. 10–11*).

The **land tax** was regular, property-based, direct, and progressive in nature. It was also distributed in a different way than the land rent because it came from the amount of money that the peasant households could accumulate during the year. The amount of the land tax, therefore, reflected and respected the level of commercialization of the individual landholdings. Generally, the share of the land tax decreased on the overall burden of the serf landholdings as the amount of the land rent rose (*chap. 12*).

Both forms of rent drew from the seasonal agricultural surplus and were temporally and physically complementary. The land rent, mainly of an in-kind nature, drew on the grain surplus at the beginning of the autumn, after the end of the field work (St. Michael). The land tax, which was monetary in nature, drew indirectly from the livestock surplus after the end of the common grazing (St. Martin). We therefore believe that the implementation of a monetary land tax was related to the shift of the center of gravity of commercial agriculture from grain to livestock production. If the land tax had not been implemented and the land rent had also remained fixed, the Cheb peasantry would likely have differentiated very quickly, and at least some of the peasants would have been able to accumulate an extraordinarily high surplus thanks to livestock production. Paradoxically, the introduction of the land tax had a leveling effect, which stabilized the socioeconomic stratification of the Cheb rural area (*chap. 10–12*).

The total amount of the land rent and land tax was relatively high; a large number of the "subject" landholdings paid so much that the sum could ideally feed several adult individuals. This indicates that peasant landholdings had a high degree of surplus and also a reserve that could be drawn upon in years of crisis. This further explains the great regenerative potential and resilience of Cheb landholdings, which throughout the 15th century to a great extent avoided "social fallow" and abandonment (*chap. 12.4; 13*).

The third part of the rent (*the ecclesiastical tithe*) had an exceptionally variable nature; for some "subject" landholdings it was negligible, for others it was a more noticeable burden. Based on the little specific data that we have, we conclude that it was one-tenth to one-quarter of the land rent (*chap. 13.5*).

The analysis of the land rents, land taxes, and ecclesiastical tithes demonstrated that the rent as a whole was set for the minimal production level of the landholding, under which they did not fall in the analyzed period even in the agriculturally unfavorable years. Naturally, this conclusion is not true across the board; we are only speaking of a general trend, including approximately 95–99% of the landholdings. The majority of the peasants thus certainly still had a disposable surplus in their hands, the specific amount of which fluctuated year-to-year. For the study of socioeconomic mobility and migration, it was a substantial finding that peasants could in principle accumulate considerable wealth. Socioeconomic differentiation of the Cheb peasantry was therefore possible, but it did not occur significantly (*chap. 13*).

Monetization of the Cheb peasantry

Family hereditary right in the city-state of Cheb can be characterized as impartible inheritance (of a landholding). The landholding was acquired by only one of the offspring, who was responsible for providing for the parents and dealing with the other siblings. However, unlike the Early Modern Period, this distinct inheritance system did not lead to the general monetization and commercialization of the Cheb peasantry because it could work without debt and the circulation of higher sums of money. The main reason for this was the period's price relations, namely the low prices of the "purchase" right to "subject" landholdings on the one hand, and relatively high prices of beef cattle and non-landholding plots of land on the other. While the primary heir acquired a landholding, the other siblings could be satisfied by the non-landholding plots, if available, and/or cattle. Freely disposable non-landholding plots, although only a small part of Cheb's land resources, were of extraordinary stabilizing importance in the context of impartible inheritance (of a landholding). The functioning of impartible inheritance with the marginal role of money assumed a sufficient number of "subject" lands and landholdings, which could be taken by the second-born sons, and was therefore bound to a period of population stagnation, mortality crises, and low prices of agricultural products (*chap. 14.8*).

The land rent did not force the peasants to monetize either, as it was typically demanded in kind. The only external monetization factor of the late medieval peasants of Cheb was the land tax, for which the peasants paid cash mainly through the seasonal sale of cattle. The main arguments for the claim of the generally low monetization of the Cheb peasantry are, firstly, model calculations and, secondly, the fact that the peasants, with some exceptions, did not seek financial resources on the well documented urban credit market (*chap. 14.9*).

II. Socioeconomic mobility and migration

Research methods

The theoretical and methodological inspirations for the monograph were the peasantological research and the agrarian historical and demographic studies from the milieu of medieval England and early modern Transalpine Europe (*chap. 3–4*). On the analytical level, we investigated (1) the development of the property position of families that remained on identical landholdings throughout the period under review; (2) the difference in the property position of two consecutive, related families on the same landholding, and thus, to a great extent, the intergenerational property transmission; (3) the rate of family transfers; (4) the rate of transfers that were accompanied by rural-rural or rural-urban migration; (5) the socioeconomic position of the migrating tenant on the original and target landholdings; (6) the number of property transfers that individual landholdings underwent; and (7) the fluctuations of the land taxes prescribed to individual landholdings. We have excluded settlements with a higher degree of centrality from the analysis due to the lack of complete and balanced data (*chap. 17*).

The elementary analyzed units were both the *families* and the *landholdings*. To meet the needs of the research and comply with legal terminology, we have specified the term *family* as a family property society (FPS) and in the case of family ties as a genetically connected family property society (GFPS). However, in this summary, we use only the term *family* for simplicity (*chap. 17.2; 18.2*).

The family and familial relations that we used in our analyses do not correspond to reality but only approximate it. The reconstruction of families and real familial ties was not possible based on the accessible sources; we therefore used the *method of the correspondence of names*, which largely enabled us to identify the family relationships in the male and, to a lesser extent, female lines. We are aware of the systematic errors that burden our results. The comparison with the early modern Czech records allowed us to set the approximate degree of this error at 25% (*chap. 17.2; 18.2*).

We determined migration patterns also based on the correspondence of names and close temporal connection, when in one year the registers stopped listing a taxpayer at one landholding and in the same or next year began to mention him at another. The detected migration values are, of course, only minimal. Only migration to the city of Cheb or migration between landholdings that were subject to land revenue tax and were kept by name in the land tax registers could be monitored (*chap. 18.2*).

We worked with the monetary values of (i) all of the property as a whole, (ii) the tenure right to a landholding, usually the "purchase" right, (iii) the livestock, and (iv) non-landholding plots. We have drawn the relevant data from two points in time—1438 and 1456. We also used data on the amount of the prescribed land tax in two-year time segments between 1438 and 1456 (1442, 1443 /2x/, 1445, 1447, 1449, 1453, 1455). Considering the relatively narrow span of the analyzed time segment, we left aside an interpretation of the absolute values but focused on observing the differences between (a) families with various property positions (rich × poor), (b) various sizes of landholdings measured by the number of livestock, and (c) landholdings of various legal statuses and socioeconomic categories. We assumed that at the time of the taxation of the peasant property in 1438, the tenants and their families were in various phases of the life cycle. If there was no socioeconomic or general institutional filter, then the families should die out at an equal rate in all property categories, ecological zones, and institutional conditions due to the influence of biological factors in the subsequent years, but if there was a socioeconomic filter, we will find differences between the property categories and the ecological zones in any subsequent time segment. This premise allowed us to meet the set aims also based on an analysis of a short time segment, during which a large number of peasant families survived (*chap. 17; 18.2*).

We relied on a quantitative approach to gain insight into the relatively dominating trends. We used quantile analysis of the statistical methods abundantly, dividing the analyzed sample into the same parts in terms of number. We also worked with an interval analysis, dividing the sample into parts that are different in number but firmly fixed in content. We also combined both methods. However, we approached the reconstruction of the institutional framework by the route of qualitative analysis (*chap. 17.5*).

Due to the large geographical scope and diversity, we analyzed the city-state of Cheb not only as a whole, but also analyzed each of its five main ecological zones separately. On a quantitative level, we worked with a set of 80–100 settlements, 600–800 landholdings, and 2,000 taxpayers, with the specific numbers varying for different sub-questions (*chap. 15–16; 18*).

Main results

In accordance with the methodologically inspiring approaches of early modern agrarian history, we conceptualized several main models of socioeconomic stratification, mobility, and the unequal distribution of economic resources. The first is the *differentiation model*, which assumes the gradual concentration of resources and the accumulation of wealth in the hands of a narrow group of the wealthiest peasant households, thus also increasing socioeconomic differentiation. The second, the *cycle model*, emphasizes the biological, institutional, and individually conditioned forces acting against the differentiating tendencies, which led to the constant circulation of resources among individual peasant families. According to this model, the socioeconomic trajectory of peasant families was similar in the entirety of their duration but differed in the time segments according to the specific phase of the life cycle. Third, we tested the *model of uneven reproduction*, highlighting the different reproductive possibilities and the socioeconomic mobility of rich and poor families, as well as the differences between the individual offspring of the wealthy. For families on rich landholdings, stability and continuity were characteristic, but the accumulated surplus was not invested—it was used to support the offspring. In other words, the wealthy had enough resources that they could divide them. The families on poor landholdings reproduced less successfully, and a high migration rate was typical for them.

So far, the situation of the Cheb peasantry in 1438–1456 is best characterized by the *model of uneven reproduction*. All of the analyses showed that:

1) The socioeconomic stratification did not change much; the property inequalities did not deepen (*chap. 15.4*).
2) Wealthy families reproduced relatively continuously on the same landholdings; the poor, on the contrary, left their original landholdings (*chap. 18–19*).
3) The property position of rich families remained relatively stable, and their landed property was sometimes so large that it could be divided among several descendants (*chap. 20*).

Wealthy families had a strong tie to their landholding; the tenants remained on them often until their death. The rich landholdings were therefore often transferred by inheritance (*intrafamilial transfer*). In contrast, poor families were not tied to their landholdings by anything firm, and the tenants often abandoned and transferred them outside of the circle of their relatives throughout their active life (*chap. 18–19*).

If a wealthy tenant had left their rural landholding during their lifetime, they often did so to move to Cheb and join the rich burghers. This finding is well in line with the image we have of late medieval peasant elites. Their wealth was of diverse origins, not only from the tenure of agricultural land and production but also from financial business, services, and non-agrarian market activities. In addition, the richest peasants were often linked to both the city and the non-peasant segment of the rural population. Against the backdrop of the period's economic conditions, peasant elites unsurprisingly preferred to buy citizenship and property in the city and to do business over increasing their own agricultural production. The relatively significant migration of the richest peasants to the city would also explain why there was no long-term accumulation of property and land in the countryside. Neither did the Cheb burghers themselves, who sought above all the land rent arising from "subject" landholdings, attempt to create agricultural commerce (*chap. 16.1; 23*).

What happened to the families of predominantly poor peasants who left their homes? Did a descent among the "sub-peasant" and hired classes await them as in the overpopulated medieval English Halesowen or in early modern Europe? The analysis of the Cheb sources proved that this was not the case, because for poor peasants, local migration was an efficient channel of upward socioeconomic mobility. The direction of the shift depended largely on the initial property position. The poorer the landholding the family (household) left, the greater the chance that it would end up on a richer landholding. The property position of poor families usually improved after migration. For the most part, leaving their original landholding did not mean the loss of their home base, because over 80% of the moves took place within the settlement or in a circle of up to 6 km. A large number of the migrating families thus likely remained for their entire life cycle in a well-known social milieu and natural environment; its geographic horizon and social space did not change more significantly. This might also explain in part the high frequency of the moves of families from landholding to landholding. Of all of the land transfers that we evaluated, about 20% of them were between relatives, 20% were unrelated and connected with migration, and 4% were related to migration to the city. The remaining half were transfers outside of the closer family for which we know nothing more about the fate of the family of the tenants. Some families alternated between even more than two landholdings during their lives (*chap. 22*).

A detailed analysis revealed an important phenomenon that we logically assumed to exist: the "domino" effect of chain migration. The trigger was the release of a relatively rich landholding occupied by a middle-wealthy family who left vacant the landholding, which was then occupied by another, relatively poorer family, behind whom once again was left a vacant landholding. In the sources, we have reconstructed migration chains of three or even four landholdings. It is possible to imagine situations occurring during mortality crises when the poorest landholding at the end of the chain was not occupied and left abandoned. Chain migration is a manifestation of the peasantry as a demographically, socially, and economically interconnected system whose parts interact with one another (*chap. 21.7*).

The link between property position and socioeconomic mobility and migration was demonstrated for the "subject" landholdings, which accounted for approximately 95% of the whole. The "free" landholdings did not avoid the overall trend, as they followed the trajectory of the richest group of "subject" landholdings.

The question, of course, arises as to why the poor landholdings were very rarely transferred within the family and why the tenants left them for other, usually richer landholdings. Further questions arise as to why, on the contrary, tenants often stayed on wealthy landholdings until their deaths and why they were taken over by their offspring. So far, the answer can only be found on a hypothetical level, thanks to micro-studies from some German regions (e.g., the Padernborn region or the city-state of Zurich). We argue that the high degree of familial continuity on large and wealthy landholdings was due not only to better living conditions but also to the fact that the size and wealth of these landholdings made it possible to absorb the entire family labor force and also to provide sustenance for adult offspring. As a result, offspring were able to stay on the landholdings and take them over in the event of their parents' old age or death. The rate of the conversion of poor Cheb landholdings was higher because their tenants left for better landholdings if they became available. In addition, due to limited economic resources, adolescents left the poor landholdings as soon as possible and did not return after their parents' deaths. A high degree of change thus automatically accompanied the minimum degree of familial continuity (*chap. 21.9*).

The strength of the *model of uneven reproduction* lies in the fact that it includes all of the crucial factors influencing the socioeconomic mobility of the peasantry and also respects the specifics of the feudal period. It assumes the principle of imperfect exploitation of the surplus by rent, the action of market relations, and the relevant socioeconomic differentiation, which, however, manifested itself not in a deepening of the inequality between the relatively fixed "subject" landholdings but in the migration of poorer families and the local continuity of the wealthy. Rich families did accumulate surplus, but with different consequences than the Marxist–Leninist approaches had predicted. The *model of uneven reproduction* also takes into account the natural family cycle and the associated changeable labor capacity of the nuclear family, which, against the backdrop of a limited land market, led to a more permanent integration of additional labor forces or sophisticated marriage strategies. The principle of fission was not left aside but was implemented primarily in the cases of extremely wealthy families (*chap. 21*).

Through analyzing the registers of the Cheb land tax, the system of socioeconomic mobility and migration of the peasantry was reconstructed, the principles and basic features of which should be generally true for the period of the late medieval agrarian depression. We concluded this, first of all, because it is the opposite of the model that was found, for instance, for the overpopulated town of Halesowen in England or early modern Europe, such as in the Swedish village and parish of Björskog, and secondly because the same phenomena that have been proven for the Cheb peasantry can be proven also elsewhere in Europe in various forms between ca. 1340 and 1480. If we leave aside the general overviews and emphasize specific case studies, then the hectic mobility of the land, the migration of the peasants, the shrinking of large landholdings, the growth of small landholdings, and the lack of labor forces have been convincingly described, e.g., in the late medieval Paderborn and Zurich regions. The life trajectory of the English peasantry was described similarly. Furthermore, the local peasant communities seem to be partially fictitious, as they were components of a fluid population (*chap. 4.1; 19; 22–23*).

Abandonment processes

In this study, we discovered that during a period of population stagnation, migration served as a significant and widely used channel of socioeconomic mobility, where its direction was related to the economic position of the landholdings and property position of the tenants. Economically weaker landholdings were abandoned in favor of stronger ones, which would partially explain the phenomenon of the late medieval abandonment and desertion of rural settlements in agriculturally unfavorable regions. We therefore tested the hypothesis that late medieval depopulation was the reverse side of the regime of uneven reproduction with migration as a means of socioeconomic ascent.

The chronology, spatial distribution, and intensity of depopulation in the late medieval Cheb region proved that the rural area of the time was filled with massive social and landscape contrasts. Whereas in the center of the historical Cheb region (city-state) abandonment did not happen even at times of mortality crises and war conflicts, in the surrounding mountainous zones a significant number of the settlements, and in some microregions even the majority, were at least temporarily abandoned. We therefore formulated a model concept that the Cheb Basin created a social and demographic system with its surroundings interconnected by peasant migration. In the period of late medieval population stagnation, the prosperity and population density of one region meant the depopulation and the abandonment of another (*chap. 24*).

In general, therefore, it is true that the explanation for the causes of the disappearance of some settlements did not lie in themselves but in the functioning of the broader late medieval social, economic, and demographic system.

Conclusion

The presented study builds on existing knowledge about the status and development of the peasantry in the Late Middle Ages, as summarized for the Czech lands by Jaroslav Čechura, František Šmahel, and Eduard Maur, and in the broader Central European context by Markus Cerman and Shami Ghosh. Its original contribution lies, firstly, in the fact that it expands our knowledge of hitherto unexplored spheres and, at the same time, quantifies key social processes on a larger scale for the first time (*chap. 17–24*).

Of the knowledge we had previously lacked about social processes within the peasantry, we can now mention (i) quantification of the rate of change and migration rate on landholdings, as well as evidence of their socioeconomic conditionality; (ii) quantitative knowledge of local migration as a channel of predominantly upward socioeconomic mobility; and (iii) in the case of rural-urban migration, a comparison of the socioeconomic status of migrant peasants in the starting locality and in the city, (iv) revealing specific cases of chain migration and its connection with the processes of settlement abandonment in the Late Middle Ages.

It was also confirmed that the status and fate of the peasantry did not differ significantly in the late medieval western and eastern parts of Central Europe. The phenomena observed in the city-state of Cheb has analogies at least in a wide strip north of the Alps, from today's western Germany through Switzerland and from Saxony to Silesia and Moravia. At the same time, however, significant differences were found at the regional and micro-regional levels, in the case of the city-state of Cheb between the agriculturally favorable zone in the nearest hinterland of the city on the one hand, and the more distant, climatically harsher foothill and mountainous terrains on the other.

Archival Sources

Ústřední archiv zeměměřictví a katastru
[Central Archive of Geodesy and Cadastre, Czech Republic, Prague]

Fond Stabilní katastr
[Fonds of the Stable cadastre]

Nr. 41 *Culturensquellete, k.k. Mappierungs Inspektorats . . .*, district Eger (Nr. 41)
Nr. 42 *Culturensquellete, k.k. Mappierungs Inspektorats . . .*, Grasslitz (Nr. 42).
(also accessible online: http://archivnimapy.cuzk.cz/uazk/pohledy/archiv.html
/18 July 2018/)

Národní archiv
**Oddělení fondů samosprávy a státní správy do roku 1848 a církevních institucí
(1. oddělení)**
[National Archives, Czech Republic, Prague, Department of Self-Government, State
Administration until 1848, and Ecclesiastical Institutions Fonds (1st Department)]

Fond Hraniční spisy
[Fonds Border files]

NA, HS, Fasc. O, Num. 37, Nr. 19 *Zins und Rent zur der Pfleg zur Eger. Ausgeschrieben
worden am Montag nach Sebastiani L: octavo aus den Zetteln die her Kanczler
Franckeng[rüner] zugeschickt hat.*

Státní oblastní archiv v Plzni, Státní okresní archiv v Chebu
[State Regional Archive Pilsen, State District Archive Cheb]

Fond Město Cheb
Cheb City Fund

Ar Cheb, book 894	*Schuldprotokolle 1387–1416*
Ar Cheb, book 895	*Schuldprotokolle 1416–1429*
Ar Cheb, book 896	*Schuldprotokolle 1429–1439*
Ar Cheb, book 897	*Schuldprotokolle 1439–1452*
Ar Cheb, book 898	*Schuldprotokolle 1452–1470*
	[City court's records / Books of obligations]
Ar Cheb, book 933	*Zins- und Copienbuch, 16. Jh.*
	[Register of St. Nicholas parish church in the city of Cheb]
Ar Cheb, book 974	*Musterungsbuch der Bauernschaft 1395*
	[Inventory of the Cheb Land Militia from 1395]
Ar Cheb, book 975	*Salbuch der Klarissinen vom Jahre 1476*
	[Copy Book of the Cheb Poor Clares from 1476]
Ar Cheb, book 984	*Chronik des Hans Schönstetters 1390–1576*
	[The Chronicle of Hanuš Schönstetter]
	(also accessible at www.portafontium.eu/chronicle
	/soap-ch/00001-mesto-cheb-schoenstetter-1576-sig521
	?language=de /12 August 2018/)
Ar Cheb, book 984	*Urbar der Clarissinnen ab 1464*
	[Urbarium of the Poor Clares from 1464]
Ar Cheb, book 1414	*Losungsbuch 1436*
Ar Cheb, book 1416	*Losungsbuch 1438*
Ar Cheb, book 1424	*Losungsbuch 1446*
Ar Cheb, book 1434	*Losungsbuch 1456*
	[Registers of city tax]
Ar Cheb, book 1009	*Klosteuerbuch 1392*
Ar Cheb, book 1054	*Klosteuerbuch 1395*
Ar Cheb, book 1055	*Klosteuerbuch 1397* (copy from 1769)
Ar Cheb, books 1056–1059	*Klosteuerbücher 1401, 1404, 1408, 1409*
Ar Cheb, book 1060	*Klosteuerbuch 1424*
Ar Cheb, book 1061	*Klosteuerbuch 1429*
Ar Cheb, book 1062	*Klosteuerbuch 1431* (correctly 1429, fragment)
Ar Cheb, books 1063–1065	*Klosteuerbücher 1432, 1433, and 1434* (an animal has chewed upon most of the book from 1434)
Ar Cheb, book 1066	*Klosteuerbuch 1434–1438* (more precisely 1435)
Ar Cheb, book 1067	*Klosteuerbuch 1438* (copy from 1769; edition Klír et al., *Knihy*, 284–423)
Ar Cheb, books 1068–1083	*Klosteuerbücher 1441–1456*
	[Registers of the Cheb land tax]
Ar Cheb, book 1084	*Klosteuerbuch (Schätzungsbuch) 1456* (edition Klír et al., *Knihy*, 437–532)
	[Land taxation book]

Ar Cheb, books 1085–1105   *Klosteuerbücher 1457–1478*
                                [Registers of the Cheb land tax]
Ar Cheb, books 2144–2152   *Umgeldbücher 1442–1450*
Ar Cheb, books 2153–2169   *Umgeldbücher 1452–1469*
                                [Books of city incomes from 1442–1450, 1452–1469]
Ar Cheb, book 2423–2438   *Ausgabenbuch 1441–1456*
Ar Cheb, book 2451   *Ausgabenbuch 1469*
                                [Books of city expenditures from 1441–1456, 1469]

◀ Plate 8: **Cheb (Eger). The city archive (former convent of the Poor Clares), office of Karl Siegel, now room No. 22 (ca. 1920). View from the window to the door and the open safe.**

Bibliography

Abel, Wilhelm. *Agrarkrisen und Agrarkonjunktur. Eine Geschichte der Land- und Ernährungswirtschaft Mitteleuropas seit dem hohen Mittelalter.* Hamburg – Berlin: Parey, 1978.

Abel, Wilhelm. *Massenarmut und Hungerkrisen im vorindustriellen Europa. Versuch einer Synopsis.* Hamburg – Berlin: Parey, 1974.

Abel, Wilhelm. *Strukturen und Krisen der spätmittelalterlichen Wirtschaft,* Quellen und Forschungen zur Agrargeschichte 32. Stuttgart: Fischer, 1980.

Achilles, Walter. *Landwirtschaft in der frühen Neuzeit,* Enzyklopädie deutscher Geschichte 10. Munich: Oldenbourg, 1991.

Achilles, Walter. "Überlegungen zum Einkommen der Bauern im späten Mittelalter." *Zeitschrift für Agrargeschichte und Agrarsoziologie* 31 (1983): 5–26.

Akram-Lodhi, A. Haroon, and Kay Cristóbal, eds. *Peasants and globalization: Political economy, rural transformation and the agrarian question.* London – New York: Routledge, 2009.

Alfani, Guido, and Erik Thoen, eds. *Inequality in rural Europe (Late Middle Ages-18th century).* Corn publication series 18. Turnhout: Brepols, 2020.

Alfani, Guido. "Economic inequality in preindustrial Europe, 1300–1800: Methods and results from the EINITE project." In *Disuguaglianza economica nelle società preindustriali: cause ed effetti / Economic inequality in pre-industrial societies: causes and effect,* ed. Giampiero Nigro, 21–36. Datini Studies in Economic History. Firenze: Firenze University Press, 2020.

Alfonso, Antón María Isabel, ed. *The rural history of medieval European societies: Trends and perspectives,* The medieval countryside 1. Turnhout: Brepols, 2007.

Ammannm, Hektor. "Vom Lebensraum der mittelalterlichen Stadt. Eine Untersuchung an schwäbischen Beispielen." *Berichte zur deutschen Landeskunde* 31 (1963), 284–316.

Ammannm, Hektor. "Wie gross war die mittelalterliche Stadt?" (1956). In *Die Stadt des Mittelalters 1,* ed. Carl Hasse, 408–415. Wege der Forschung 243. Darmstadt: Wissenschaftliche Buchgesellschaft, 1977.

Aparisi, Frederic. "Village entrepreneurs: The economic foundations of Valencian rural elites in the fifteenth century." *Agricultural History* 89 (2015): 336–357.

Aparisi, Frederic Romero, and Royo Pérez, Vicent, eds. *Beyond lords and peasants: Rural elites and economic differentiation in pre-modern Europe*. Valencia: Publicacions de la Universitat de València, 2014.

Aston, Trevor H., and Charles H. E. Philpin, eds. *The Brenner debate. Agrarian class structure and economic development in pre-industrial Europe*, Past and Present Publications. Cambridge: Cambridge University Press, 1985.

Attwood, Donald W. "Why some of the poor get richer: Economic change and mobility in rural western India [and Comments]." *Current Anthropology* 20 (1979): 495–516.

Bader, Matthias. "Lehenswesen in Altbayern." 16. 09. 2013; In *Historisches Lexikon Bayerns*, <www.historisches-lexikon-bayerns.de/Lexikon/Lehenswesen in Altbayern>.

Bauernfeind, Walter. *Materielle Grundstrukturen im Spätmittelalter und der Frühen Neuzeit. Preisentwicklung und Agrarkonjunktur am Nürnberger Getreidemarkt von 1399 bis 1670*, Nürnberger Werkstücke zur Stadt- und Landesgeschichte 50. Neustadt a. d. Aisch: Korn und Berg, 1993.

Baum, Hans-Peter. "Lehenswesen in Franken." 13. 02. 2014; In *Historisches Lexikon Bayerns*, <www.historisches-lexikon-bayerns.de/Lexikon/Lehenswesen_in _Franken>.

Baliazin, Vladimir Nikolaevich. *Professor Aleksandr Chaianov, 1888–1937*. Moscow: Agropromizdat, 1990.

Bavel van, Bas J. P., "Looking for the islands of equality in a sea of inequality. Why did some societies in pre-industrial Europe have relatively low levels of wealth inequality?" In *Disuguaglianza economica nelle società preindustriali: cause ed effetti / Economic inequality in pre-industrial societies: causes and effect*, ed. Giampiero Nigro, 431–456. Datini Studies in Economic History. Firenze: Firenze University Press, 2020.

Bavel van, Bas J. P., ed. *Social relations: Property and power*, Rural economy and society in North-Western Europe, 500–2000, 1. Turnhout: Brepols, 2010.

Bavel van, Bas J. P., and Peter C. M. Hoppenbrouwers, eds. *Landholding and land transfer in the North Sea area (late Middle Ages – 19th century)*, CORN publication series 5. Turnhout: Brepols, 2004.

Bavel van, Bas J. P., and Peter C. P. Hoppenbrouwers. "Landholding and land transfer in the North Sea area (late Middle Ages – 19th century)." In *Landholding and land transfer in the North Sea area (late Middle Ages – 19th century)*, ed. Bas J. P. Van Bavel, and Peter C. M. Hoppenbrouwers, 13–43. CORN publication series 5. Turnhout: Brepols, 2004.

Béaur, Gérard, and Jean-Michel Chevet. "Institutional changes and agricultural growth." In *Property rights, land markets and economic growth in the European countryside (thirteenth–twentieth centuries)*, ed. Gérard Béaur, et al., 19–65. Rural history in Europe 1. Turnhout: Brepols, 2013.

Béaur, Gérard, and Jürgen Schlumbohm. "Einleitung: Probleme einer deutsch-französischen Geschichte ländlicher Gesellschaften." In *Ländliche Gesellschaften in Deutschland und Frankreich, 18.–19. Jahrhundert*, ed. Reiner Prass, Jürgen Schlumbohm, Gérard G. Béaur, and Christophe Duhamelle, 11–29. Veröffentlichungen des Max-Planck-Instituts für Geschichte 187. Göttingen: Vandenhoeck & Ruprecht, 2003.

Beck, Rainer. *Unterfinning. Ländliche Welt vor Anbruch der Moderne*. Munich: Beck, 2004.

Becker, Norbert. *Das Land am unteren Niederrhein. Untersuchungen zur Verfassungs-, Wirtschafts- und Sozialgeschichte des ländlichen Raumes vom Hohen Mittelalter bis zur Frühen Neuzeit (1100–1600)*, Rheinisches Archiv 128. Cologne: Böhlau, 1992.

Becker, Norbert. "Landflucht am unteren Niederrhein als Spiegel des gesellschaftlichen Umbruchs." *Annalen des Historischen Vereins für den Niederrhein* 196 (1994): 7–30.

Bernard, Walter. *Das Waldhufendorf in Schlesien: Ein Beitrag zur Siedlungsgeographie Schlesiens*, Veröffentlichungen der Schlesischen Gesellschaft für Erdkunde E. V. und des Geographischen Instituts der Universität Breslau 12. Wrocław: Marcus, 1931.

Bernstein, Henry. "V. I. Lenin and A. V. Chayanov: Looking back, looking forward." *Journal of Peasant Studies* 36 (2009): 55–81.

Berthe, Maurice, ed. *Endettement paysan et crédit rural dans l'Europe médiévale et moderne: actes des XVIIes Journées Internationales d'Histoire de l'Abbaye de Flaran, Septembre 1995*, Flaran 17. Toulouse: Presses universitaires du Midi, 1998.

Blickle, Peter. *Kommunalismus: Skizzen einer gesellschaftlichen Organisationsform, Band 1: Oberdeutschland; Band 2: Europa*. Munich: R. Oldenbourg Verlag, 2000.

Boehler, Jean-Michel. "Routine oder Innovation in der Landwirtschaft: „Kleinbäuerlich" geprägte Regionen westlich des Rheins im 18. Jahrhundert." In *Ländliche Gesellschaften in Deutschland und Frankreich, 18.–19. Jahrhundert*, ed. Reiner Prass, Jürgen Schlumbohm, Gérard G. Béaur, and Christophe Duhamelle, 101–123. Veröffentlichungen des Max-Planck-Instituts für Geschichte 187. Göttingen: Vandenhoeck & Ruprecht, 2003.

Boháč, Zdeněk. "Postup osídlení a demografický vývoj českých zemí do 15. století" [History of the settlement and the demographic development in the Czech Lands up to the 15th century]. *Historická demografie* 12 (1987): 59–87.

Böhm, Astrid. "Das Iatromathematische Hausbuch des Codex ÖNB, 3085 (fol. 1r–39v). Stoffgeschichtliche Einordnung, dynamisch-mehrstufige Edition und Glossar." M. A. thesis, Karl-Franzens-Universität Graz, Graz, 2014.

Bok, Václav. "Hospodářský vývoj kláštera chotěšovského do roku 1421." Dissertation, Charles University, Prague, 1961.

Boukal, Jan. "Rytíř Kryštof z Týna. Válečník a diplomat pozdního středověku." [Knight Christoph of Týn. Warrior and diplomat of the Late Middle Ages]. B. A. Thesis, Charles University, Prague, 2013.

Bowles, Samuel, et al. "The emergence and persistence of inequality in premodern societies: Introduction to the special section." *Current Anthropology* 51 (2010): 7–17.

Brakensiek, Stefan. "Grund und Boden – eine Ware? ein Markt zwischen familialen Strategien und herrschaftlichen Kontrollen." In *Ländliche Gesellschaften in Deutschland und Frankreich, 18.–19. Jahrhundert*, ed. Reiner Prass, Jürgen Schlumbohm, Gérard G. Béaur, and Christophe Duhamelle, 269–290. Veröffentlichungen des Max-Planck-Instituts für Geschichte 187. Göttingen: Vandenhoeck & Ruprecht, 2003.

Braun, Hermann. "Sitte und Brauchtum im Jahreskreis." In *Eger und das Egerland: Volkskunst und Brauchtum*, ed. Lorenz Schreiner, 371–395. Munich: Lang Müller, 1988.

Braun, Peter. "Die Herren von Sparneck. Stammbaum, Verbreitung, Kurzinventar." *Archiv für die Geschichte von Oberfranken* 82 (2002): 71–106.

Brázdil, Rudolf, Martin Možný, Tomáš Klír, et al. "Climate variability and changes in the agricultural cycle in the Czech Lands from the sixteenth century to the present." *Theoretical and Applied Climatology* 2018: 1–21.

Brázdil, Rudolf, and Oldřich Kotyza. *History of Weather and Climate in the Czech Lands 1. Period 1000–1500*, Zürcher Geographische Schriften 62. Zürich: ETH, 1995.

Brázdil, Rudolf, and Oldřich Kotyza. "Kolísání klimatu v českých zemích v první polovině našeho tisíciletí" [Climate fluctuation in the Czech lands during the first part of the last millenium]. *Archeologické rozhledy* 49 (1997): 663–699.

Brázdil, Rudolf, and Oldřich Kotyza. "Současná historická klimatologie a možnosti jejího využití v historickém výzkumu" [Contemporary historical climatology and possibilities of its utilisation in the historical research]. In *Historie a interdisciplinární výzkum*, 17–59. Časopis Matice moravské, Supplementum 1. Brno: Matice moravská, 2002.

Briggs, Chris Daniel. *Credit and village society in fourteenth-century England*. Oxford: Oxford University Press, 2009.

Briggs, Chris Daniel. "Money and rural credit in the Later Middle Ages revisited." In *Money, prices, and wages: Essays in honour of Professor Nicholas Mayhew*, ed. Marin R. Allen, and D'Maris Coffman, 129–142. Palgrave studies in the history of finance. Basingstoke: Palgrave Macmillan, 2015.

Briggs, Chris Daniel, and C. Jaco Zuijderduijn, eds. *Land and credit: Mortgages in the Medieval and Early Modern European countryside*, Palgrave studies in the history of finance. London: Palgrave Macmillan, 2018.

Brunner, Otto. "Das „ganze Haus" und die alteuropäische „Ökonomik." In *Neue Wege der Verfassungs- und Sozialgeschichte*, Otto Bruner, 103–127. Göttingen: Vandenhoeck & Rupprecht, 1980.

Büntgen, Ulf, and Lena Hellman. "The Little Ice Age in scientific perspective: Cold spells and caveats." *Journal of Interdisciplinary History* 44 (2014): 353–368.

Burdová, Pavla, Dagmar Culková, and Eliška Čáňová, eds. *Tereziánský katastr český, sv. 4, Dominikál.* Prague: Archivní správa ministerstva vnitra ČR, 1970.

Byres, Terry J. "Differentiation of the peasantry under feudalism and the transition to capitalism: In defence of Rodney Hilton." *Journal of Agrarian Change* 6 (2006): 17–68.

Carocci, Sandro. "Social Mobility and the Middle Ages." *Continuity and Change* 26 (2011): 367–404.

Carocci, Sandro, and Isabella Lazzarini. "Introduction." In *Social mobility in medieval Italy (1100–1500)*, ed. Sandro Carocci, and Isabella Lazzarini, 9–20. Viella historical research 8. Roma, 2018.

Carocci, Sandro, and Isabella Lazzarini, ed. *Social mobility in medieval Italy (1100–1500)*, Viella historical research 8. Roma, 2018.

Castelin, Karel. "Chebské mincovnictví v době grošové (1305–1520)." *Numismatický sborník* 3 (1956): 73–113.

Cerman, Markus. "Bodenmärkte und ländliche Wirtschaft in vergleichender Sicht: England und das östliche Mitteleuropa im Spätmittelalter." *Jahrbuch für Wirtschaftsgeschichte* 2 (2004): 125–150.

Cerman, Markus. "Mittelalterliche Ursprünge der unterbäuerlichen Schichten." In *Untertanen, Herrschaft und Staat in Böhmen und im "Alten Reich." Sozialgeschichtliche Strukturen*, ed. Markus Cerman, and Robert Luft, 323–350. Veröffentlichungen des Collegium Carolinum 99. Munich: Oldenbourg, 2005.

Cerman, Markus. "Open fields, tenurial rights and the development of land markets in medieval East-central Europe." In *Property rights, land in market and economic growth*, ed. Gérard Béaur, 405–424. Rural history in Europe 1. Turnhout: Brepols, 2013.

Cerman, Markus. "Social structure and land markets in Late Mediaeval Central and East-central Europe." *Continuity and Change* 23 (2008): 55–100.

Cerman, Markus. *Villagers and lords in Eastern Europe*, 1300–1800, Studies in European history. Basingstoke, 2012.

Cerman, Markus, Eduard Maur, and Hermann Zeitlhofer. "Sozialstruktur und Besitztransfer in frühneuzeitlichen gutsherrschaftlichen Gesellschaften in vergleichender Perspektive: Ergebnisse des Projekts 'Soziale Strukturen in Böhmen.'" In *Soziale Strukturen in Böhmen. Ein regionaler Vergleich von Wirtschaft und Gesellschaft in Gutsherrschaften, 16.–19. Jahrhundert*, ed. Markus Cerman, and Hermann Zeitlhofer, 262–285. Sozial- und Wirtschaftshistorische Studien 28. Vienna – Munich, 2002.

Cerman, Markus, and Eduard Maur. "Die wirtschaftliche und soziale Entwicklung im frühneuzeitlichen Böhmen aus mikro- und makrohistorischer Sicht." In *Soziale Strukturen in Böhmen. Ein regionaler Vergleich von Wirtschaft und Gesellschaft in*

Gutsherrschaften, 16.–19. Jahrhundert, ed. Markus Cerman, and Hermann Zeitlhofer, 101–110. Sozial- und Wirtschaftshistorische Studien 28. Vienna – Munich, 2002.

Cerman, Markus, and Eduard Maur. "*Proměny vesnických sociálních struktur v Čechách 1650–1750,*" [Der Wandel der ländischen Sozialstrukturen in Böhmen, 1650–1750]. *Český časopis historický* 98 (2000): 737–774.

Cerman, Markus, and Hermann Zeitlhofer, eds. *Soziale Strukturen in Böhmen. Ein regionaler Vergleich von Wirtschaft und Gesellschaft in Gutsherrschaften, 16.–19. Jahrhundert*, Sozial- und Wirtschaftshistorische Studien 28. Vienna – Munich, 2002.

Cerman, Markus, and Robert Luft, eds. *Untertanen, Herrschaft und Staat in Böhmen und im "Alten Reich": sozialgeschichtliche Studien zur Frühen Neuzeit*, Veröffentlichungen des Collegium Carolinum 99. Munich: Oldenbourg, 2005.

Chaianov, Aleksandr Vasil'evich. *Izbrannye proizvedenija*, ed. Evgeniija Viktorovna Serova. Moscow: Moskovskii rabochii, 1989.

Chaianov, Aleksandr Vasil'evich. *Krest'janskoe khozijaistvo: izbrannye trudy*, ed. A. A. Nikonov. Moscow: Ekonomika, 1989.

Chaianov, Aleksandr Vasil'evich. *A.V. Chaianov: Chelovek—uchenyi—grazhdanin*. Moscow: Izdatel'stvo mSChA, 1998.

Chaianov, Aleksandr Vasil'evich. *Organizatsiia krest'ianskogo khoziaistva*. Moscow: Kooperativnoe Izdatel'stvo, 1925.

Chaianov, Aleksandr Vasil'evich. *Bjudzhetnye issledovanija: istorija i metody*. Leningrad, 1929.

Chaianov, Aleksandr Vasil'evich. *Ocherki po Ekonomike Trudovogo Selskogo Khazyaistva*. Moscow: Narodnyi komissariat zemledeliya, 1924.

Chaianov, Aleksandr Vasil'evich, and Gennadij Aleksander Studenskii, *Istoriya byudzhetnykh issledovanii*. Moscow: Izd. Tsentral'nogo statisticheskogo upravleniya, 1922.

Chalupa, Aleš. "Venkovské obyvatelstvo v Čechách v tereziánských katastrech (1700–1750)" [La population tchéque de la campagne dans les cadastres thérésiens (1700–1750)]. *Sborník Národního muzea v Praze, řada A – Historie* 23 (1969): 197–378.

Chalupa, Aleš, Marie Lišková, Josef Nuhlíček, and František Rajtoral, eds. *Tereziánský katastr český*, sv. 1, Rustikál, kraje A–CH. Prague: Archivní správa ministerstva vnitra ČR, 1964.

Chevalier, Jacques. "There is nothing simple about simple commodity production." *Studies in Political Economy* 7 (1982): 89–124.

Chevalier, Jacques. "There is nothing simple about simple commodity production." *Journal of Peasant Studies* 10 (1983): 153–186.

Chocholáč, Bronislav. "Grundbücher in Böhmen und Mähren." In *Quellenkunde der Habsburgermonarchie (16.–18. Jahrhundert). Ein exemplarisches Handbuch*, ed. Josef Pauser, Martin Scheutz, and Thomas Winkelbauer, 530–539. Mitteilungen des

Instituts für Österreichische Geschichtsforschung, Ergänzungsband 44. Vienna – Munich: Oldenbourg, 2004.

Chocholáč, Bronislav. "Güterpreise, Verschuldung und Ratensystem: Eine Fallstudie zu den finanziellen Transaktionen der Untertanen bei Besitzübertragungen in Westmähren im späten 16. und im 17. Jahrhundert." In *Untertanen, Herrschaft und Staat in Böhmen und im "Alten Reich." Sozialgeschichtliche Strukturen*, ed. Markus Cerman, and Robert Luft, 89–125. Veröffentlichungen des Collegium Carolinum 99. Munich: Oldenbourg 2005.

Chocholáč, Bronislav. "O studiu pozemkových knih" [Über das Studium der Gründbücher]. *Sborník prací Filozofické fakulty brněnské univerzity, řada historická* (C) 42/40 (1993): 51–61.

Chocholáč, Bronislav. "Poddanský úvěr na Moravě v 16. a 17. století" [Kredit der Unteranenbevölkerung in Mähren im 16. und 17. Jahrhundert]. *Český časopis historický* 99 (2001): 59–84.

Chocholáč, Bronislav. *Selské peníze: Sonda do finančního hospodaření poddaných na západní Moravě koncem 16. a v 17. století* [Das Bauerngeld. Finanzwirtschaft der Bauern in Westmähren am Ende des 16. und im 17. Jahrhundert]. Knižnice Matice moravské 4. Brno: Matice moravská, 1999.

Clark, Gregory. "Measuring inequality through the strength of inheritance." *Current Anthropology* 51 (2010): 101–102.

Cole, John W., and Eric R. Wolf. *The hidden frontier: Ecology and ethnicity in an Alpine valley*. New York: Academic Press, 1974.

Cruyningen, Piet J., and Erik Thoen. "Food supply, demand and trade: Aspects of the economic relationship between town and countryside (Middle Ages – 19th Century)." Book introduction. In *Food supply, demand and trade. Aspects of the economic relationship between town and countryside (Middle Ages – 19th Century)*, ed. Piet J. van Cruyningen, and Erik Thoen, 1–6. CORN 14. Turnhout: Brepols, 2012.

Curtis, Daniel R. *Coping with crisis: The resilience and vulnerability of pre-industrial settlements*, Rural worlds: Economic, social, and cultural histories of agricultures and rural societies. London – New York: Routledge, 2016. 2nd edition.

Čechura, Jaroslav. "Liber antiquus kláštera v Plasech z let 1339–1441" [Der 'Liber antiquus' des Klosters Plass aus den Jahren 1339–1441]. *Časopis Národního muzea v Praze, Řada A – Historie* 153 (1984): 166–179.

Čechura, Jaroslav. *Adelige Grundherrn als Unternehmer: Zur Struktur südböhmischer Dominien vor 1620*, Sozial- und wirtschaftshistorische Studien 25. Munich: Oldenbourg Verlag, 2000.

Čechura, Jaroslav. "Die Bauernschaft in Böhmen während des Spätmittelalters: Perspektiven neuer Orientierungen." *Bohemia* 31 (1990): 283–311.

Čechura, Jaroslav. *Die Struktur der Grundherrschaften im mittelalterlichen Böhmen unter besonderer Berücksichtigung der Klosterherrschaften*. Quellen und Forschungen zur Agrargeschichte 39. Stuttgart: Steiner 1994.

Čechura, Jaroslav. "Dvě studie k sociálně ekonomickému vývoji klášterního velkostatku v předhusitských Čechách" [Zwei Studien zur sozialökonomischen Entwicklung des Klostergrossgrundbesitzes im vorhussitischen Böhmen]. *Sborník Národního Muzea v Praze, řada A – Historie* 42 (1988): 1–72.

Čechura, Jaroslav. "František Graus jako vítěz. (Dějiny venkovského lidu v Čechách v době předhusitské II.)." In *František Graus: Člověk a historik, Sborník z pracovního semináře Výzkumného centra pro dějiny vědy konaného 10. prosince 2002, 69–88. Prague: Výzkumné centrum pro dějiny vědy, 2004.

Čechura, Jaroslav. "Chotěšov v 15. století" [Chotěšov im 15. Jahrhundert]. *Minulostí Západočeského kraje* 27 (1991): 51–78.

Čechura, Jaroslav. "K některým otázkám hospodářského a správního systému cisterciáckých klášterů (Zlatá koruna v předhusitském období.)" [Zu einigen Fragen des Wirtschafts- und Verwaltungssystems des Zisterzienserklostern (Kloster Goldenkron in der vorhussitischen Zeit)]. *Československý časopis historický* 29 (1981): 228–257.

Čechura, Jaroslav. "Krize pozdního středověku – mýtus 20. století?" In *Středověký kaleidoskop pro muže s hůlkou: věnováno Františku Šmahelovi k životnímu jubileu, 34–45. Prague: Nakladatelství Lidové noviny, 2016.

Čechura, Jaroslav. "Mikrohistorie a raněnovověká studia: možnosti a meze jednoho historiografického konceptu" [Mikrogeschichte und Frühneuzeitstudien. Möglichkeiten und Grenzen eines hisoriographischen Konzepts]. *Časopis Matice moravské* 135 (2016): 361–393.

Čechura, Jaroslav. "Mor, krize a husitská revoluce" [Die Pest, die Krise und die hussitische Revolution]. *Český časopis historický* 92 (1994): 286–303.

Čechura, Jaroslav. "Rolnictvo v Čechách v pozdním středověku. Perspektivy dalšího studia." *Český časopis historický* 88 (1990): 465–498.

Čechura, Jaroslav. *Sedláci si dělají, co chtějí: sborník vybraných prací profesora Jaroslava Čechury*. Ed. Veronika Boháčová – Veronika Kucrová. Prague: Nakladatelství Lidové noviny, 2012.

Čechura, Jaroslav. "Sedlák." In *Člověk českého středověku*, ed. František Šmahel, and Martin Nodl, 436–459. Prague: Argo, 2002.

Čechura, Jaroslav. "Teorie agrární krize pozdního středověku: teoretický základ koncepce hospodářského a sociálního vývoje předhusitských Čech: metodologická studie" [Die Theorie von der Agrarkrise des späten Mittelalters: theoretische Grundlagen eines Entwurfs der wirtschaftlichen und sozialen Entwicklung im vorhussitischen Böhmen]. *Archaeologia historica* 12 (1987): 129–141.

Čechura, Jaroslav. "Zákup na statcích vyšehradské kapituly ve 14. a 15. století" [Der Ankauf an den Gütern des Wyschehrader Domkapitels im 14. und 15. Jahrhundert]. *Právněhistorické studie* 34 (1997): 39–62.

Černý, Václav. *Hospodářské instrukce. Přehled zemědělských dějin v době patrimonijního velkostatku v XV. – XVI. století* [Wirtschaftsinstruktionen – Übersicht einer Geschichte der Landwirtschaft zur Zeit der Patrimonialherrschaft im XV.–XIX. Jahrh. Les instructions économiques – Esquisse d'une histoire de l'agriculture pendant le régime seigneurial aux XVe–XIXe siècles]. Prameny a základy vydávané Československou akademií zemědělskou A 2. Prague: Československá akademie zemědělská, 1930.

Černý, Zbyněk. *Příznivé světlo: chebské fotografické ateliéry (1849–1945)* [Gutes Licht: Egerer Fotoateliers (1849–1945)]. Cheb: Muzeum Cheb, 2016.

Čornej, Petr, et al. *Dějiny zemí Koruny české. I., Od příchodu Slovanů do roku 1740.* Prague: Paseka, 1997.

Čornej, Petr. "Epidemie a kalamity v letech 1419–1471 očima českých kronikářů." *Documenta Pragensia* 7 (1987): 193–224.

Demade, Julien. "Grundrente, Jahreszyklus und monetarische Zirkulation: Zur Funktionsweise des spätmittelalterlichen Feudalismus." *Historische Anthropologie* 17 (2009): 222–244.

Demade, Julien. "The Medieval countryside in German-language historiography since the 1930s." In *The rural history of medieval European societies: Trends and perspectives,* ed. Antón María Isabel Alfonso, 173–252. The medieval countryside 1. Turnhout: Brepols, 2007.

Demek, Jaromír, and Petr Mackovičin, eds. *Zeměpisný lexikon ČR. Hory a nížiny.* Brno: AOPK ČR, 2006.

Derndorfer, Jürgen, and Roman Deutinger, eds. *Das Lehnswesen im Hochmittelalter. Forschungskonstrukte – Quellenbefunde – Deutungsrelevanz.* Mittelalter-Forschungen 34. Ostfildern: Thorbecke, 2010.

DeWindt, Anne Reiber. "Redefining the peasant community in medieval England: The regional perspective." *Journal of British Studies* 26 (1987): 163–207.

Döberl, Michael. *Die Landgrafschaft der Leuchtenberger. Eine verfassungsgeschichtliche Studie mit anhängenden Regesten und Urkunden.* Munich: Killinger 1893.

Dribe, Martin. *Leaving home in a peasant society: Economic fluctuations, household dynamics and youth migration in Southern Sweden, 1829–1866.* Lund Studies in Economic History 13. Lund: Lund University, 2000.

Durdík, Jan. "Vojenská hotovost chebského venkova v roce 1395." *Historie a vojenství* 1966: 561–583.

Duvosquel, Jean-Marie, and Erik Thoen, eds. *Peasants and townsmen in medieval Europe. Studia in honorem Adriaan Verhulst.* Gent: Snoeck-Ducaju, 1995.

Dyer, Christopher. "The English mediaeval village community and its Decline." *Journal of British Studies* 33 (1994): 407–429.

Dyer, Christopher. "Social mobility in medieval England." In *Social mobility in medieval Italy (1100–1500)*, ed. Sandro Carocci, and Isabella Lazzarini, 23–43. Viella historical research 8. Roma: Viella, 2018.

Dyer, Christopher. "Trade, urban hinterlands, and market integration, 1300–1600: A summing up." In *Trade, urban hinterlands and market integration c. 1300–1600*, ed. James A. Galloway, 103–109. Centre for Metropolitan History. Working Papers Series 3. London: Centre for Metropolitan History, Institute of Historical Research, 2000.

Dyer, Christopher. "Villages in crisis: Social dislocation and desertion, 1370–1520." In *Deserted Villages Revisited*, ed. Christopher Dyer, and Richard Jones, 28–45. Explorations in Local and Regional History 3. Hatfield: University of Hertfordshire Press, 2010.

Ehmer, Josef, and Michael Mitterauer. "Zur Einführung: Familienstruktur und Arbeitsorganisation in ländlichen Gesellschaften." In *Familienstruktur und Arbeitsorganisation in ländlichen Gesellschaften*, ed. Josef Ehmer, and Michael Mitterauer, 7–30. Vienna: Böhlau, 1986.

Eklof, Ben, and Stephen Frank, eds. *The world of the Russian peasant: Post-emancipation culture and society*. Boston: Unwin Hyman, 1990.

Ellis, Frank. *Peasant economics: Farm households and agrarian development*. Wye Studies in Agricultural and Rural Development. Cambridge: Cambridge University Press, 2003.

Epstein, Stephan R., ed. *Town and country in Europe 1300–1800*. Themes in international urban history 5. Cambridge: Cambridge University Press, 2001.

Ertl, Thomas, Thomas Frank, and Samuel Nussbaum, eds. *Busy tenants. Peasant land markets in Central Europe (15th to 16th century)*. Vierteljahrschrift für Sozial- und Wirtschaftsgeschichte, Beiheft 253. Stuttgart: Franz Steiner Verlag, 2021.

Ettel, Ernst. *Beiträge zur Siedlungsgeschichte des Egerer Kreises unter besonderer Berücksichtigung der Orts- und Flurformen*. Quellen und Erörterungen 4. Pressath: Bodner / Otnant-Gesellschaft für Geschichte und Kultur in der Euregio Egrensis, 2004.

Faussner, Hans Constantin. "Vom salmannischen Eigen zum Beutellehen. Zum bäuerlichen Grundeigentum im bayerisch-österreichischen Rechtsgebiet." *Forschungen zur Rechtsarchäologie und rechtlichen Volkskunde* 12 (1990): 11–37.

Fischer, Gretl. *Die Flurnamen des Gerichtsbezirkes Eger*. Sudetendeutsches Flurnamen-Buch 4. Reichenberg: Kraus / Deutsche Gesellschaft der Wissenschaften und Künste für die Tschechoslowakis, 1941.

Freiburg, Hubert. "Agrarkonjunktur und Agrarstruktur in vorindustrieller Zeit. Die Aussagekraft der säkularen Wellen der Preise und Löhne im Hinblick auf die Entwicklung der bäuerlichen Einkommen." *Vierteljahrschrift für Sozial- und Wirtschaftsgeschichte* 64 (1977): 289–327.

Gałęski, Bogusław. *Basic concepts of rural sociology*. Manchester: Manchester University Press, 1972.

Galloway, James A., ed. *Trade, urban hinterlands and market integration c. 1300–1600*. Centre for Metropolitan History. Working Papers Series 3. London: Centre for Metropolitan History, Institute of Historical Research, 2000.

Gerber, Roland. "Die Einbürgerungsfrequenzen spätmittelalterlicher Städte im regionalen Vergleich." In *Neubürger im späten Mittelalter. Migration und Austausch in der Städtelandschaft des Alten Reiches (1250–1550)*, ed. Rainer Christoph Schwinges, 251–288. Zeitschrift für historische Forschung. Beiheft 30. Berlin: Duncker & Humblot, 2002.

Ghosh, Shami. "Rural Economies and Transitions to Capitalism: Germany and England Compared (c. 1200–c. 1800)." *Journal of Agrarian Change* 16 (2016): 255–290.

Giles, Kate, and Christopher Dyer, ed. *Town and country in the middle ages: Contrasts, contacts and interconnections, 1100–1500*. Monograph series. The Society for Medieval Archaeology 22. Leeds: Taylor & Francis Group, 2005.

Gilomen, Hans-Jörg, ed. *Migration in die Städte. Ausschluss – Assimilierung – Integration – Multikulturalität – Migrations vers les villes. Exclusion – assimilation – intégration – multiculturalité*. Schweizerische Gesellschaft für Wirtschafts- und Sozialgeschichte 16. Zürich: Chronos, 2000.

Gilomen, Hans-Jörg. "Neue Forschungen zur Migration im Spätmittelalter und in der Frühen Neuzeit. Einleitung." In *Migration in die Städte. Ausschluss – Assimilierung – Integration – Multikulturalität – Migrations vers les villes. Exclusion – assimilation – intégration – multiculturalité*, ed. Hans-Jörg Gilomen, 1–16. Schweizerische Gesellschaft für Wirtschafts- und Sozialgeschichte 16. Zürich: Chronos, 2000.

Gindely, Antonín. *Geschichte der böhmischen Finanzen von 1526 bis 1618*. Vienna: Kaiserlich-Königliche Hof- und Staatsdruckere, 1868.

Glaser, Rüdiger, and Dirk Riemann. "A thousand-year record of temperature variations for Germany and Central Europe based on documentary data." *Journal of Quaternary Science* 24 (2009): 437–449.

Glaser, Rüdiger, and Dirk Riemann. "Klimageschichte im späten Mittelalter und in der frühen Neuzeit in Südwestdeutschland im Kontext der mitteleuropäischen Klimaentwicklung." In *Landnutzung und Landschaftsentwicklung im deutschen Südwesten: zur Umweltgeschichte im späten Mittelalter und in der frühen Neuzeit*, ed. Lorenz Sönke, and Peter Rückert, 219–232. Veröffentlichungen der Kommission für geschichtliche Landeskunde in Baden-Württemberg, Reihe B 173. Stuttgart: W. Kohlhammer, 2009.

Górecki, Piotr. "Medieval peasants and their world in Polish historiography." In *The rural history of medieval European societies: Trends and perspectives*, ed. Antón María Isabel Alfonso, 253–296. The medieval countryside 1. Turnhout: Brepols, 2007.

Gradl, Heinrich. *Die Chroniken der Stadt Eger*. Prague: Verlag des Vereines für Geschichte der Deutschen in Böhmen, 1884.

Gradl, Heinrich. *Geschichte des Egerlandes (bis 1437)*. Prague: H. Dominicus (Th. Gruß), 1893.

Gradl, Heinrich, ed. *Monumenta Egrana: Denkmäler des Egerlandes, als Quellen für dessen Geschichte. I. Band (805–1322)*. Eger: A. E. Witz, 1886.

Gräf, Holger Thomas, and Katrin Keller, eds. *Städtelandschaft = Réseau urbain = Urban network: Städte im regionalen Kontext in Spätmittelalter und früher Neuzeit*. Städteforschung A 62. Cologne: Böhlau, 2004.

Graham, Crow, and Allan Graham. *Community life: An introduction to local social relations*. New York – London: Harvester Wheatsheaf, 1994.

Graus, František. *Dějiny venkovského lidu v Čechách v době předhusitské II. Od poloviny 13. stol. do roku 1419*. Studie a prameny 13. Prague: Státní nakladatelství politické literatury, 1957.

Graus, František. "From resistance to revolt: The late medieval peasant wars in the context of social crisis." *Journal of Peasant Studies* 3 (1975): 1–9.

Graus, František. "Krize středověku a husitství" [Die Krise des Mittelalters und das Hussitentum]. *Československý časopis historický* 17 (1969): 507–526.

Graus, František. *Pest – Geissler – Judenmorde. Das 14. Jahrhundert als Krisenzeit*, Veröffentlichungen des Max-Planck-Instituts für Geschichte 86. Göttingen: Vandenhoeck & Ruprecht, 1994.

Graus, František. "Vývoj feudální renty v Čechách v 14. a 15. století." *Československý časopis historický* 7 (1959): 301–303.

Grimm, Jacob, and Wilhelm Grimm. *Das Deutsche Wörterbuch von Jacob Grimm und Wilhelm Grimm*, <http://dwb.uni-trier.de/de/das-woerterbuch/das-dwb/>.

Grove, Jean M. *The Little Ice Age*. London: Routledge, 1988.

Grulich, Josef. *Migrace městského a vesnického obyvatelstva: Farnost České Budějovice 1750–1824*. Monographia historica 13. České Budějovice: University of South Bohemia in České Budějovice, 2013.

Grulich, Josef. *Migrační strategie: město, předměstí a vesnice na panství České Budějovice ve druhé polovině 18. století*. Monographia historica 17. České Budějovice: University of South Bohemia in České Budějovice, 2018.

Grulich, Josef. *Populační vývoj a životní cyklus venkovského obyvatelstva na jihu Čech v 16. až 18. století* [Die demographische Entwicklung und der Lebenszyklus der Dorfbewohner (Südbohmen, 16.–18. Jahrhundert)]. Monographia historica 10. České Budějovice: University of South Bohemia in České Budějovice, 2008.

Gründler, Carl August. *Polemik des germanischen Rechts Land- und Lehnrecht (jus controversum germanicum privatum et feudale)*. Bd. 4. Leipzig: Reimann, 1838.

Grüner, Sebastian, and Alois John. *Über die ältesten Sitten und Gebräuche der Egerländer: 1825 für J. W. von Goethe niedergeschrieben*. Beiträge zur deutsch-böhmischen Volkskunde 4/1. Prague: J. G. Calve, 1901.

Gusinde, Konrad. *Schönwald. Beiträge zur Volkskunde und Geschichte eines deutschen Dorfes im polnischen Oberschlesien.* Wort und Brauch 10. Wrocław: M. & H. Marcus, 1912.

Guzowski, Piotr. "Monetisation and economic inequality among peasants in medieval Poland." In *Monetisation and commercialisation in the Baltic Sea, 1050–1450,* ed. Dariusz Adamczyk, and Beata Mozejko, 98–122. London – New York: Routledge, 2021.

Guzowski, Piotr. "Village court records and peasant credit in fifteenth- and sixteenth-century Poland." *Continuity and change* 29 (2014): 115–142.

Haas, Antonín, ed. *Sbírka pramenů práva městského království českého IV/1, Privilegia nekrálovských měst českých z let 1232–1452.* Prague: Nakladatelství Československé akademie věd, 1954.

Hagen, William W. Review of *The Peasants of Ottobeuren, 1487–1726: A rural society in Early Modern Europe* by Govind P. Sreenivasan. *Journal of Modern History* 78 (2006): 752–754.

Hamblen, Bethany Jane. "Communities of the hinterland: Social networks and geographical mobility beyond the walls of late medieval York." PhD dissertation, University of York, York, 2008.

Hanzal, Josef. "Poznámky ke studiu ceny poddanské nemovitosti v 16.–17. století." In *Příspěvky k dějinám cen nemovitostí v 16.–18. století,* 39–48. Prague: Charles University, 1963.

Harrison, Mark. "Resource allocation and agrarian class formation: The problem of social mobility among Russian peasant households, 1880–1930." *Journal of Peasant Studies* 4 (1977): 127–161.

Hatcher, John, and Mark Bailey . *Modelling the Middle Ages.* Oxford: Oxford University Press, 2001.

Head, Randolph C. "Haushalt und Familie in Landschaft und Stadt Zürich, nach Steuerbüchern des 15. Jahrhunderts." *Zeitschrift für Agrargeschichte und Agrarsoziologie* 40 (1992): 113–132.

Head, Randolph C. The Review of *The Peasants of Ottobeuren, 1487–1726: A rural society in Early Modern Europe* by Govind P. Sreenivasan. *American Historical Review* 110 (2005): 1614–1615.

Heinritz, Herbert. "Bergbau in Oberfranken." 11. 05. 2009. In *Historisches Lexikon Bayerns,* <www.historisches-lexikon-bayerns.de/Lexikon/Bergbau in Oberfranken>.

Heinzle, Birgit. "Transactions Intertwined. Land Transfer Among Tenants in the Aflenz and Veitsch Estate." In *Busy tenants: Peasant land markets in Central Europe (15th to 16th century),* ed. Thomas Ertl, Thomas Frank and Samuel Nussbaum, 75–108. Vierteljahrschrift für Sozial- und Wirtschaftsgeschichte, Beiheft 253. Stuttgart: Franz Steiner Verlag, 2021.

Heisiner, Wilhelm. "Die Egerer Klosteuerbücher als Quellen für die Bevölkerungs- und Wirtschaftsgeschichte des Egerlandes im späten Mittelalter." Dissertation, Deutsche Universität, Prague, 1938.

Hemmerle, Josef. "Kolonisation und Lehenbesitz der Herren von Nothaft im westlichen Böhmen." Stifter-Jahrbuch 4 (1955): 57–78.

Henningsen, Ute. Besitz und Einkünfte der Herren von Rosenberg in Böhmen nach dem Urbar von 1379–1384. Historische und landeskundliche Ostmitteleuropa-Studien 5. Marburg: J.-G.-Herder-Institut, 1989.

Hensch, Mathias. "Montanarchäologie in der Oberpfalz – von der Forschung vergessen?" Bericht der bayerischen Bodendenkmalpflege 43/44 (2002/2003): 273–287.

Hill, Thomas. Die Stadt und ihr Markt. Bremens Umlands- und Außenbeziehungen im Mittelalter (12.–15. Jahrhundert), Vierteljahrschrift für Sozial- und Wirtschaftsgeschichte. Beihefte 172. Stuttgart: Steiner, 2004.

Himl, Pavel. Die ‚armben Leüte‘ und die Macht. Die Untertanen der südböhmischen Herrschaft Český Krumlov / Krumau im Spannungsfeld zwischen Gemeinde, Obrigkeit und Kirche (1680–1781). Quellen und Forschungen zur Agrargeschichte 48. Stuttgart: Steiner, 2003.

Himl, Pavel. "Marginální vrstvy raně novověké společnosti." In Základní problémy studia raného novověku, ed. Marie Šedivá Koldinská and Ivo Cerman, et al., 370–409. České dějiny 6. Prague: Nakladatelství Lidové noviny, 2013.

Hirschmann, Norbert. "Zum bergbaulichen Verbrauchszentrum Oberpfalz im 16. Jahrhundert: Möglichkeiten und Grenzen einer Analyse anhand von Zoll- und Mautakten sowie verwandtem Quellenmaterial." In Bergbaureviere als Verbrauchszentren, ed. Ekkehard Westermann, 59–84. Vierteljahrschrift für Sozial- und Wirtschaftsgeschichte. Beihefte 130. Stuttgart: Steiner, 1997.

Hofman, Gustav. Metrologická příručka pro Čechy, Moravu a Slezsko do zavedení metrické soustavy. Pilsen: Státní oblastní archiv, 1984.

Hoffmann, Richard Charles. Land, liberties, and lordship in a late medieval countryside: Agrarian structures and change in a Duchy of Wroclaw, The Middle Ages series. Philadelphia: University of Pennsylvania Press, 1989.

Hoffmann, Hermann, ed. Das älteste Lehenbuch des Hochstifts Würzburg 1303–1345 (Vol. 1–2), Quellen und Forschungen zur Geschichte des Bistums und Hochstifts Würzburg 25. Würzburg: Schöningh, 1973.

Höllerich, Reinhard. "Der historische Bergbau im Rehauer Gebiet: Zur Rekonstruktion einer Bergbaulandschaft." Archiv für die Geschichte von Oberfranken 96 (2016): 71–97.

Holzfurtner, Ludwig. "Die Grundleihepraxis oberbayerischer Grundherren im späten Mittelalter." Zeitschrift für Bayerische Landesgeschichte 48 (1985): 647–676.

Hopcroft, Rosemary L. Regions, institutions, and agrarian change in European history, Economics, Cognition, and Society. Ann Arbor: University of Michigan Press, 1999.

Hoppe, Göran, and John Langton. *Peasantry to capitalism: Western Östergötland in the nineteenth Century*, Cambridge Studies in Historical Geography 22. Cambridge: Cambridge University Press, 1994.

Hoppenbrouwers, Peter C. M., and Jan Luiten van Zanden, eds. *Peasants into farmers? The transformation of rural economy and society in the low countries (Middle ages – 19th century) in light of the Brenner debate*, CORN publication series 4. Turnhout: Brepols, 2001.

Horský, Jan. "Pojmy, objekty, vztahy a systémy. Poznámky o místě historické demografie ve vývoji dějepisectví" [Concepts, objects, relations and systems. Notes on local historical demographics in the development of history], *Lidé města* 14 (2012): 421–455.

Horský, Jan, Iva Sedláčková, and Markéta Seligová. "Ein einheitliches „altes demographisches Regime" oder die Bindung eines demographischen Verhaltens zu "Ökotypen." *Historická demografie* 20 (1996): 57–91.

Horský, Jan, and Markéta Seligová. *Rodina našich předků*, Knižnice Dějin a současnosti 2. Prague: Nakladatelství Lidové noviny, 1997.

Huppertz, Barthel. *Räume und Schichten bäuerlicher Kulturformen in Deutschland: Ein Beitrag zur Deutschen Bauerngeschichte*. Bonn: Ludv. Röhrscheid, 1939.

Husa, Václav. "K methodice studia dějin lidových hnutí v období pozdního feudalismu." In Václav Husa and Josef Petráň, *Příspěvky k dějinám třídních bojů v Čechách I. Nevolnické povstání r. 1775*, 5–34, Acta Universitatis Carolinae, Historica VI. Prague: Charles University, 1955.

Husa, Václav. "Třídní boje – tabu československého dějepisectví" [Les luttes de classe – un tabou de l'historiographie tchécoslovaque]. *Dějiny a přítomnost* 1 (1937): 39–47.

Irsigler, Franz, and Herbert Eiden. "Environs and hinterland: Cologne and Nuremberg in the Later Middle Ages." In *Trade, urban hinterlands, and market integration c. 1300–1600*, ed. James A. Galloway, 43–57. Centre for Metropolitan History. Working Papers Series 3. London: Centre for Metropolitan History, Institute of Historical Research, 2000.

Isenmann, Eberhard. *Die deutsche Stadt im Mittelalter 1150–1550: Stadtgestalt, Recht, Verfassung, Stadtregiment, Kirche, Gesellschaft, Wirtschaft*. Cologne – Weimar – Vienna: Böhlau, 2014.

Jänichen, Hans. *Beiträge zur Wirtschaftsgeschichte des schwäbischen Dorfes*, Veröffentlichungen der Kommission für geschichtliche Landeskunde in Baden-Württemberg. Reihe B 60. Stuttgart: Kohlhammer, 1970.

Jánský, Jiří. *Kronika česko-bavorské hranice 2 – Chronik der böhmisch-bayerischen Grenze 2. (1427–1437)*. Domažlice: Nakladatelství Český les, 2003.

Jánský, Jiří. *Kronika česko-bavorské hranice 3 – Chronik der böhmisch-bayerischen Grenze 3. (1437–1457)*. Domažlice: Nakladatelství Český les, 2003.

Jánský, Jiří. *Kronika česko-bavorské hranice 4 – Chronik der böhmisch-bayerischen Grenze 4. (1458–1478)*. Domažlice: Nakladatelství Český les, 2004.

John, Alois. "Das egerländer Volkstum und die Ursachen seines Verfalls" (1896). In *Egerländer Heimatsbuch. Gesammelte Aufsätze*, ed. Alois John, 234–242. Eger: Selbstverlag, 1907.

John, Alois. *Oberlohma: Geschichte und Volkskunde eines egerländer Dorfes*, Beiträge zur deutsch-böhmischen Volkskunde IV/2. Prague: J. G. Calve'sche k.u.k. Hof- u. Universitäts- Buchhandlung (Josef Koch), 1903.

John, Alois. "Saat und Ernte im Egerlande (1896)." In *Egerländer Heimatsbuch. Gesammelte Aufsätze*, ed. Alois John, 207–217. Eger: Selbstverlag, 1907.

John, Alois. *Sitte, Brauch und Volksglaube im deutschen Westböhmen*, Beiträge zur deutsch-böhmischen Volkskunde 6. Reichenberg: Kraus, 1924.

Johnson, Robert E. "Family life-cycles and economic stratification: A case-study in rural Russia." *Journal of Social History* 30 (1997): 705–731.

Kadlec, Jaroslav. *Dějiny kláštera Svaté Koruny*. České Budějovice: Knihkupectví ČAT "U zlatého klasu," 1949.

Karel, Tomáš, and Vilém Knoll. "Hrady na Chebsku jako reprezentanti moci" [Die Burgen des Egerlandes als Machtrepräsentanten]. *Castellologica bohemica* 16 (2016): 153–178.

Käubler, Rudolf. *Die ländlichen Siedelungen des Egerlandes*. Leipzig: Verlag der Werksgemeinschaft, 1935.

Kejř, Jiří, and Vladimír Procházka. "Právně historické glosy k dějinám venkovského lidu v Čechách v době předhusitské." *Právněhistorické studie* 5 (1959): 291–321.

Kenzler, Hauke. *Die hoch- und spätmittelalterliche Besiedlung des Erzgebirges: Strategien zur Kolonisation eines landwirtschaftlichen Ungunstraumes*, Bamberger Schriften zur Archäologie des Mittelalters und der Neuzeit 4. Bonn: Habelt, 2012.

Kitsikopoulos, Harry. "Introduction." In *Agrarian change and crisis in Europe, 1200–1500*, ed. Harry Kitsikopoulos, 1–22. Routledge research in medieval studies 1. New York: Routledge, 2011.

Kitsikopoulos, Harry, ed. *Agrarian change and crisis in Europe, 1200–1500*, Routledge research in medieval studies 1. New York: Routledge, 2011.

Kitsikopoulos, Harry. "Social and economic theory in medieval studies." In *Handbook of medieval studies: terms, methods, trends*, ed. Albrecht Classen, 1270–1292. Berlin – New York: De Gruyter, 2010.

Kitsikopoulos, Harry. "Standards of living and capital formation in pre-plague England: A peasant budget model." *Economic History Review* 53 (2000): 237–261.

Klebel, Ernst. "Freies Eigen und Beutellehen in Ober- und Niederbayern." *Zeitschrift für Bayerische Landesgeschichte* 11 (1938): 45–85.

Klein, Herbert. "Ritterlehen und Beutellehen in Salzburg." *Mitteilungen der Gesellschaft für Salzburger Landeskunde* 80 (1940): 87–128.

Klír, Tomáš. "Agrarsysteme des vorindustriellen Dorfes. Zur Interpretation mittelalterlicher Ortswüstungen im Niederungs- und Mittelgebirgsmilieu." In *Stadt – Land – Burg. Festschrift für Sabine Felgenhauer-Schmiedt zum 70. Geburtstag*, ed. Claudia Theune, et al., 139–157. Internationale Archäologie, Studia honoraria 34. Rahden/West.: Leidorf, 2013.

Klír, Tomáš. "Land transfer in a late medieval city state: Cheb Region 1438–1456." In *Busy tenants: Peasant land markets in Central Europe (15th to 16th century)*, ed. Thomas Ertl, Thomas Frank, and Samuel Nussbaum, 151–192. Vierteljahrschrift für Sozial- und Wirtschaftsgeschichte, Beiheft 253. Stuttgart: Franz Steiner Verlag, 2021.

Klír, Tomáš. "Local migration of peasants in the Late Middle Ages: A quantitative analysis of the Cheb city state 1442–1456." *Journal of Migration History* 8 (2022): 191–219.

Klír, Tomáš. *Osídlení zemědělsky marginálních půd v mladším středověku a raném novověku* [Besiedlung und landwirtschaftliche Nutzung marginaler Böden im späten Mittelalter und der frühen Neuzeit – The settlements and agriculture of the margins in the later Middle Age and Early Modern Period], Dissertationes archaeologicae Brunenses/Pragensesque 5. Prague: Charles University, 2008.

Klír, Tomáš. "Procesy pustnutí, válečné škody a tzv. sociální úhory. Chebsko v pozdním středověku" [The processes of village abandonment, war damage, and social fallows: The Cheb region in the Late Middle Ages]. *Archaeologia historica* 42 (2017): 547–577.

Klír, Tomáš. *Rolnictvo na pozdně středověkém Chebsku v pozdním středověku: sociální mobilita, migrace a procesy pustnutí* [Peasantry in the Cheb city-state in the Late Middle Ages: Social mobility, migration, and abandonment of settlements]. Prague: Karolinum, 2020.

Klír, Tomáš. "Rural credit and monetarisation of the peasantry in the late Middle Ages: The Eger city state c. 1450." In *A history of the credit market in Central Europe: The Middle Ages and Early Modern Period*, ed. Pavla Slavíčková, 113–130. London – New York: Routledge, 2020.

Klír, Tomáš. "Sociálně-ekonomická mobilita rolnictva v pozdním středověku. Chebsko v letech 1438–1456" [The socio-economic mobility of peasants in the Late Middle Ages: The Cheb district in the years 1438–1456]. In *Wieś miniona, lecz obecna. Ślady dawnych wsi i ich badania*, ed. Przemysław Nocuń, Agnieszka Przybyła-Dumin, and Krzysztof Fokt, 159–231. Monografie i materiały MGPE 13. Chorzów: Muzeum "Górnośląski Park Etnograficzny w Chorzowie," 2018.

Klír, Tomáš. "Sociální mobilita rolnictva a procesy pustnutí v pozdním středověku. Díl 2. Sociální a geografická mobilita rolnictva v pozdním středověku: Chebsko 1392–1469" [Social mobility of the peasantry and the processes of abandonment in the Late Medieval Period. Volume 2. Social and geographical mobility of the peasantry in the Late Medieval Period: The Cheb Region 1392–1469]. Inaugural dissertation, Charles University, Prague, 2018.

Klír, Tomáš. "Socioeconomic mobility and property transmission among peasants: The Cheb region (Czech Republic) in the Late Middle Ages." In *Settlement change across Medieval Europe: Old paradigms and new vistas*, ed. Brady Niall, and Claudia Theune, 341–355. Ruralia 12. Leiden: Seidestone, 2019.

Klír, Tomáš. *Zánik a pustnutí venkovských sídlišť v pozdním středověku: Chebsko a Slavkovský les* [The abandonment of rural settlements in the Late Middle Ages: The region of Cheb and the Slavkov Forest]. Prague: Karolinum, 2023.

Klír, Tomáš. "Zaniklé středověké vsi ve výzkumném záměru Ústavu pro archeologii Univerzity Karlovy v Praze. Zaniklý Spindelbach (Krušné hory), Kří a Hol (střední Čechy)" [Research of deserted medieval villages conducted by the Institute of Archaeology at Charles University in Prague]. In *Wieś zaginiona. Stan i perspektywy badań*, ed. Przemysław Nocuń, Agnieszka Przybyła-Dumin, and Krzysztof Fokt, 17–59. Monografie i materiały MGPE 5. Chorzów: Muzeum "Górnośląski Park Etnograficzny w Chorzowie," 2016.

Klír, Tomáš, et al. *Knihy chebské zemské berně z let 1438 a 1456* [Die Egerer Landsteuerbücher von 1438 und 1456], Libri Civitatis X. Prague: Faculty of Arts of Charles University, 2016.

Klír, Tomáš, and Dana Vodáková. "Economy and population of an Early Modern village: Milčice – home of the most famous Bohemian peasant F. J. Vavák." *Historie – otázky – problémy* 9 (2017): 106–151.

Klír, Tomáš, and Michal Beránek. "A social-economic interpretation of the layouts of deserted villages: An example of a deserted village at the 'V Žáku' site in Klánovice Forest in Prague." In *Studies in Post-medieval Archaeology 4*, ed. Jaromír Žegklitz, 289–364. Prague: Archaia, 2012.

Konersmann, Frank. "Von Betriebsgrössen zu Wirtschaftspraktiken: Die Betriebsgrössenfrage in der deutschen Agrar- und Sozialgeschichte." In *Ländliche Gesellschaften in Deutschland und Frankreich, 18.–19. Jahrhundert*, ed. Reiner Prass, Jürgen Schlumbohm, Gérard G. Béaur, and Christophe Duhamelle, 125–143. Veröffentlichungen des Max-Planck-Instituts für Geschichte 187. Göttingen: Vandenhoeck & Ruprecht, 2003.

Kopsidis, Michael. *Agrarentwicklung: Historische Agrarrevolutionen und Entwicklungsökonomie*, Grundzüge der modernen Wirtschaftsgeschichte 6. Stuttgart: Steiner, 2006.

Kosminskij, Eugenij Aleksevic. *Studies in the agrarian history of England in the thirteenth century*. Oxford: Basil Blackwell, 1956.

Kostlán, Antonín. "'Cenová revoluce' a její odraz v hospodářském vývoji Čech" ["Die Preisrevolution" und ihr Widerhall in der wirtschaftlichen Entwicklung Böhmens]. *Folia Historica Bohemica* 11 (1987): 161–212.

Kostlán, Antonín. "Feudální zatížení českého venkova po husitské revoluci. K hospodářským a sociálním dějinám jagellonského období českých dějin (1471–1526)." CSc dissertation, Historický ústav ČSAV, Prague, 1988.

Kostlán, Antonín. "K rozsahu poddanských povinností od 15. do první poloviny 17. století ve světle odhadů a cen feudální držby." *Folia Historica Bohemica* 10 (1986): 205–248.

Koumar, Jiří. "'Má doplaceno, žádnému nic nedluží . . .': Finanční aspekty majetkového transferu poddanské nemovitosti na mělnickém panství v 17. století" ["Er hat alles beglichen, er schuldet niemandem etwas . . ." Finanzielle Aspekte des Vermögenstransfers einer Untertanenliegenschaft im Dominium Mělník im 17. Jahrhundert]. *Ústecký sborník historický* 1 (2011): 7–43.

Koutná-Karg, Dana. "Das Register des Klosters Chotieschau." *Verhandlungen des Historischen Vereins für Oberpfalz und Regensburg* 131 (1991): 305–312.

Krauer, Rezia. "Die Beteiligung städtischer Akteure am ländlichen Bodenmarkt. Die Region St. Gallen im 13. und 14. Jahrhundert." PhD dissertation, Universität Zürich, Zürich, 2018.

Krenzlin, Anneliese. *Beiträge zur Kulturlandschaftsgenese in Mitteleuropa. Gesammelte Aufsätze aus vier Jahrzehnten*, Erkundliches Wissen 63, Geographische Zeitschrift – Beihefte. Wiesbaden: Steiner, 1983.

Krofta, Kamil. *Dějiny selského stavu: Přehled dějin selského stavu v Čechách a na Moravě*, Laichterův výbor nejlepších spisů poučných 80, Dílo Kamila Krofty 3, ed. Emil Janoušek. Prague: Jan Laichter, 1949.

Krofta, Kamil. "Začátky české berně." *Český časopis historický* 36 (1930): 1–26, 237–257, 437–490.

Křivka, Josef. *Zadlužení poddanského zemědělství na roudnickém panství v 18. století*, Rozpravy ČSAV. Řada společenských věd 1986/2. Prague: Academia, 1986.

Kubů, František. *Chebský městský stát: Počátky a vrcholné období do počátku 16. století*. Cheb: Veduta, 2006.

Kubů, František. "Ozbrojené síly chebského městského státu." *Sborník Chebského muzea* 2001: 9–23.

Kubů, František. *Die staufische Ministerialität im Egerland. Ein Beitrag zur Siedlungs- und Verwaltungsgeschichte*, Otnant-Gesellschaft für Geschichte und Kultur in der Euregio Egrensis. Quellen und Erörterungen 1. Pressath: Bodner, 1995.

Kula, Witold. *An economic theory of feudal system: Towards a model of the Polish economy 1500–1800*. London: NLB and Humanities Press, 1976.

Kurpelová, Margita, Lubomír Coufal, and Jaroslav Čulík. *Agroklimatické podmienky ČSSR*. Bratislava: Príroda, 1975.

Lambrecht, Thijs, and Wouter Ryckbosch. "Economic inequality in the rural Southern Low Countries during the fifteenth century: Sources, data and reflections." In *Disuguaglianza economica nelle società preindustriali: Cause ed effetti / Economic inequality in pre-industrial societies: Causes and effect*, ed. Giampiero Nigro, 205–229. Datini Studies in Economic History. Firenze: Firenze University Press, 2020.

Langhammer, Rudolf. *Waldsassen. Kloster und Stadt 1. Aus der Geschichte der ehedem reichsunmittelbaren und gefürsteten Zisterzienserabtei bis zur Reformation.* Waldsassen: Albert Angerer, 1936.

Lee, John S. *Cambridge and its economic region, 1450–1560.* Hertfordshire: University of Hertfordshire Press, 2001.

Lehner, Johann Baptist. "Beiträge zur Kirchengeschichte des Egerlandes." *Jahresbericht des Vereins zur Erforschung der Regensburger Diözesangeschichte* 12 (1939): 79–211.

Lehner, Johann Baptist. "Ein Pfarreienverzeichnis des Bistums Regensburg aus dem Jahre 1326." *Jahresbericht des Vereins zur Erforschung der Regensburger Diözesangeschichte* 2 (1927): 24–36.

Leingärtner, Georg. *Die Wüstungsbewegungen im Landgericht Amberg vom ausgehenden Mittelalter bis zur Neuorganisation des Landgerichts im Jahre 1803*, Münchener Historische Studien, Abt. Bayerische Geschichte 3. Kallmünz: M. Lassleben, 1956.

Lenski, Gerhard Emmanuel. *Power and privilege: A theory of social stratification*, McGraw-Hill Series in Sociology. New York: McGraw-Hill, 1966.

Levi, Giovanni. *Das immaterielle Erbe. Eine bäuerliche Welt an der Schwelle zur Moderne.* Berlin: Wagenbach, 1986.

Lienen, Bruno. "Aspekte des Wandels bäuerlicher Betriebe zwischen dem 14. und dem 17. Jahrhundert an Beispielen aus Tudorf (Kreis Paderborn)." *Westfälische Forschungen* 1991: 288–315.

Lienen, Bruno. "Obern- und Niederntudorf 1300–1600: Beiträge zur Geschichte der ländlichen Gesellschaft Westfalens im Spätmittelalter." PhD thesis, Universität Bielefeld, 1992 (available at http://bieson.ub.uni-bielefeld.de/volltexte/2006/901/ [18.1. 2021]).

Lindström, Jonas. *Distribution and differences: Stratification and the system of reproduction in a Swedish peasant community 1620–1820*, Studia Historica Upsalensia 235. Uppsala: Uppsala Universitet, 2009.

Littlejohn, James. *Social stratification: An introduction*, Studies in Sociology 7. New York: Routledge, 2021. (1st edition 1972 by George Allen & Unwin Ltd)

Löwe, Heinz-Dietrich. "Differentiation in Russian peasant society: Causes and trends, 1880–1905." In *Land commune and peasant community in Russia: Communal forms in imperial and early Soviet society*, ed. Robert Bartlett, 165–195. London: Springer, 1990.

Lůžek, Bořivoj. "Špitální dvůr v Dobroměřicích v letech 1517–1542." *Sborník Československé akademie zemědělských věd* 2 (1957): 175–201.

Macek, Josef. *Jagellonský věk v českých zemích (1471–1526) 1. Hospodářská základna a moc.* Prague: Academia, 1992.

Majer, Jiří. "Konjunkturen und Krisen im böhmischen Silberbergbau des Spätmittelalters und der Frühen Neuzeit: Zu ihren Ursachen und Folgen." In *Konjunkturen im europäischen Bergbau in vorindustrieller Zeit. Festschrift für Ekkehard Westermann zum 60. Geburtstag*, ed. Christoph Bartels, 73–83. Vierteljahrschrift für Sozial- und Wirtschaftsgeschichte. Beihefte 155. Stuttgart: Steiner, 2000.

Majer, Jiří. *Těžba cínu ve Slavkovském lese v 16. století*. Prague: Národní technické muzeum, 1970.

Maťa, Petr, and Michal Dragoun. *Lán ve středověkých Čechách*. In *Acta Universitatis Carolinae: Philosophica et Historica. Z pomocných věd historických* 12, 103–110. Prague: Charles University, 1995 [1997].

Matějek, František. *Cesta poddaného lidu na Moravě ke znevolnění*, Knižnice Matice moravské 5. Brno: Matice moravská, 2000.

Matějek, František. *Feudální velkostatek a poddaný na Moravě. S přihlédnutím k přilehlému území Slezska a Polska: Studie o přeměnách na feudálním velkostatku v druhé polovině 15. a v první polovině 16. století*, Studie a prameny 18. Prague: Nakladatelství Československé akademie věd, 1959.

Maur, Eduard. *Český komorní velkostatek v 17. století: Příspěvek k otázce „druhého nevolnictví" v českých zemích*, Acta Universitatis Carolinae. Philosophica et historica. Monographia 59. Prague: Charles University, 1976.

Maur, Eduard. The review of "Český tereziánský katastr." In *Acta Universitatis Carolinae – Philosophica et Historica 3, Studia Historica* 8, 127–131. Prague: Charles University, 1972.

Maur, Eduard. "Das bäuerliche Erbrecht und die Erbschaftspraxis in Böhmen im 16.–18. Jahrhundert." *Historická demografie* 20 (1996): 93–118.

Maur, Eduard. "Dějiny rodiny v české historiografii." In *Rodina a domácnost v 16.–20. století*, 9–22, Acta Universitatis Carolinae. Philosophica et historica 2/2006, Studia historica 60. Prague: Karolinum, 2010.

Maur, Eduard. *Gutsherrschaft und „zweite Leibeigenschaft" in Böhmen: Studien zur Wirtschafts-, Sozial- und Bevölkerungsgeschichte (14.–18. Jahrhundert)*, Sozial- und wirtschaftshistorische Studien 26. Vienna: Verlag für Geschichte und Politik, Munich: Oldenbourg, 2001.

Maur, Eduard. "K způsobu tvoření a splácení cen poddanských nemovitostí v 17. a počátkem 18. století." In *Příspěvky k dějinám cen nemovitostí v 16.–18. století*, 71–154. Prague: Charles University, 1963.

Maur, Eduard. "Nejstarší chotěšovské pozemkové knihy (1497–1566) – významný pramen pro poznání populačního vývoje Čech v 16. století" [The oldest Chotěšov land registry books (1497–1566) – an important source for the research of the population development of Bohemia in the 16th century]. *Historická demografie* 41 (2017): 131–149.

Maur, Eduard. "Obyvatelstvo českých zemí ve středověku." In *Dějiny obyvatelstva českých zemí*, ed. Ludmila Fialová, et al., 35–73. Prague: Mladá fronta, 1996.

Maur, Eduard. "Poddaní točnického panství v druhé polovině 17. století. Příspěvek k využití katastrů, soupisů obyvatelstva a pozemkových knih pro studium hospodářského a sociálního postavení venkovského lidu." *Sborník archivních prací* 14 (1964): 57–87; 15 (1965): 277–297.

Maur, Eduard. "Příspěvek k demografické problematice předhusitských Čech (1346–1419)". In *Acta Universitatis Carolinae – Phil. et Hist., Studia historica* 34, 7–71. Prague: Charles University, 1989.

Maur, Eduard. "Venkov v raném novověku." In *Základní problémy studia raného novověku*, ed. Marie Šedivá Koldinská and Ivo Cerman, et al., 307–334. České dějiny 6. Prague: Nakladatelství Lidové noviny, 2013.

Maur, Eduard. Review of *Besitzwechsel und sozialer Wandel: Lebensläufe und sozioökonomische Entwicklungen im südlichen Böhmerwald, 1640–1840*, by Hermann Zeitlhofer, *Historie – otázky – problémy* 9 (2017): 301–303.

Maur, Eduard, and Šárka Nekvapil Jirásková. *Historik bez hranic: Z díla profesora Eduarda Maura*. Pardubice: University of Pardubice, 2017.

McDonough, Susan. "Being a neighbor: Ideas and ideals of neighborliness in the medieval west." *History Compass* 15/9 (September 2017): 1–11. https://doi.org/10.1111/hic3.12406.

McGuire, Randall, and Robert McC. Netting. "Leveling peasants? The maintenance of equality in a Swiss Alpine community." *American Ethnologist* 9 (1982): 269–290.

McGuire, Randall H. "Breaking down cultural complexity: Inequality and heterogeneity." *Advances in Archaeological Method and Theory* 6 (1983): 91–142.

Medick, Hans. *Weben und Überleben in Laichingen. 1650–1900. Lokalgeschichte als Allgemeine Geschichte*, Veröffentlichungen des Max-Planck-Instituts für Geschichte 126. Göttingen: Vandenhoeck & Ruprecht, 1997.

Mengel, David Ch. "A Plague on Bohemia? Mapping the Black Death." *Past and Present* 211 (2011): 3–34.

Metz, Rainer. *Geld, Währung und Preisentwicklung. Der Niederrheinraum im europäischen Vergleich 1350–1800*, Schriftenreihe des Instituts für Bankhistorische Forschungen 14. Frankfurt a. M.: Knapp, 1990.

Meynen, Emil, and Josef Schmitüsen. *Handbuch der naturräumlichen Gliederung Deutschlands*. Remagen: Bundesanstalt für Landeskunde, Bad Godesberg: Bundesanstalt für Landeskunde und Raumforschung, 1953–1962.

Míka, Alois. "Nástin vývoje cen zemědělského zboží v Čechách v letech 1424–1547." *Československý časopis historický* 7 (1959): 545–571.

Míka, Alois. *Poddaný lid v Čechách v první polovině 16. století*, Studie a prameny 19. Prague: Nakladatelství Československé akademie věd, 1960.

Mikulec, Jiří. "Dějiny venkovského poddaného lidu v 17. a 18. století a česká historiografie posledních dvaceti let." *Český časopis historický* 88 (1990): 119–130.

Mitterauer, Michael. "Formen ländlicher Familienwirtschaft." In *Familienstruktur und Arbeitsorganisation in ländlichen Gesellschaften*, ed. Josef Ehmer, and Michael Mitterauer, 185–323. Vienna: Böhlau, 1986.

Mlynaříková, Barbora. *Geografický horizont prostého člověka v Čechách v letech 1740–1830*, sv. I–2, Národopisná knižnice 39. Prague: Etnologický ústav Akademie věd České republiky, 2001.

Moon, David. *The Russian peasantry 1600–1930. The world the peasants made*. London – New York: Longman, 1999.

Morgan, Kelly. "Debating the Little Ice Age." *Journal of Interdisciplinary History* 45 (2014): 57–68.

Morávková, Naďa. *František Graus a československá poválečná historiografie*. Prague: Academia, 2013.

Mulder, Monique Borgerhoff, et al. "Intergenerational wealth transmission and the dynamics of inequality in small-scale societies." *Science* 326.5953 (2009): 682–688.

Müller, Miriam. "A divided class? Peasants and peasant communities in Later Medieval England." In *Rodney Hilton's Middle Ages: An exploration of historical themes*, ed. Christopher Dyer, 115–131. Past and Present Supplements 195, Suppl. 2. Oxford: Oxford Journals, 2007.

Musílek, Martin. *Patroni, klienti, příbuzní. Sociální svět Starého Města pražského ve 14. století* [Patrons, clients, and relatives: The social world of Old Town Prague in the 14th Century]. Prague: Casablanca, 2015.

Muggenthaler, Hans. *Kolonisatorische und wirtschaftliche Tätigkeit eines deutschen Zisterzienserklosters im 12. und 13. Jahrhundert*, Deutsche Geschichtsbücherei 2. Munich: Hugo Schmidt, 1924.

Myśliwski, Grzegorz. "Central Europe." In *Agrarian change and crisis in Europe, 1200–1500*, ed. Harry Kitsikopoulos, 250–291. Routledge research in medieval studies I. New York: Routledge, 2011.

Nabholz, Hans, and Edwin Hauser, eds. *Die Steuerbücher von Stadt und Landschaft Zürich des XIV. und XV. Jahrhunderts, 2/1: Steuergesetzgebung von 1401–1470, Steuerrödel von 1401–1450*. Zürich: Beer, 1939.

Nabholz, Hans, and Friedrich Hegi, eds. *Die Steuerbücher von Stadt und Landschaft Zürich des XIV. und XV. Jahrhunderts, 1: Die Steuerrödel des XIV. Jahrhunderts, 1357–1379*. Zürich: Beer, 1918.

Netting, Robert McC. *Balancing on an Alp: Ecological change and continuity in a Swiss mountain community*. Cambridge: Cambridge University Press, 1981.

Netting, Robert McC. *Smallholders, householders. Farm families and the ecology of intensive, sustainable agriculture*. Stanford: Stanford University Press, 1993.

Nigro, Giampiero, ed. *Disuguaglianza economica nelle società preindustriali: cause ed effetti / Economic inequality in pre-industrial societies: causes and effect*, Datini Studies in Economic History. Firenze: Firenze University Press, 2020.

Nikonow, Alexander Alexandrowitsch, and Eberhard Schulze. *Drei Jahrhunderte Agrarwissenschaft in Russland. Von 1700 bis zur Gegenwart*, Studies on the Agricultural and Food Sector in Central and Eastern Europe. Halle: IAMO, 2004.

Nikulin, Alexander M. "An Omitted Intellectual Tradition: The Chaianov School on Collective Farming." *Jahrbücher für Geschichte Osteuropas* 65 (2017): 423–444.

Nikulin, Alexander, and Irina Trotsuk. "Pitirim Sorokin's contribution to rural sociology: Russian, European and American milestones of a scientific career." *The Journal of Peasant Studies* 45 (2018): 1203–1220.

Nitz, Hans-Jürgen. "Grenzzonen als Innovationsräume der Siedlungsplanung. Dargestellt am Beispiel der fränkisch-deutschen Nordostgrenze im 8. bis 11. Jahrhundert." *Siedlungsforschung* 9 (1991): 101–134.

Nodl, Martin. "František Graus – Proměny pojetí krize pozdního středověku." In *František Graus: Člověk a historik, Sborník z pracovního semináře Výzkumného centra pro dějiny vědy konaného 10. prosince 2002*, 99–118. Prague: Výzkumné centrum pro dějiny vědy, 2004.

Nodl, Martin. "Sociální aspekty pozdně středověkého městského přistěhovalectví." In *Sociální svět středověkého města*, ed. Martin Nodl, 3–96. Colloquia mediaevalia Pragensia 5. Prague: Filosofia, 2006.

North, Michael, ed. *Geldumlauf, Währungssysteme und Zahlungsverkehr in Nordwesteuropa 1300–1800. Beiträge zur Geldgeschichte der späten Hansezeit*, Quellen und Darstellungen zur hansischen Geschichte 35. Cologne – Vienna: Böhlau, 1989.

Nový, Rostislav. "Hospodářský region Prahy na přelomu 14. a 15. století.") *Československý časopis historický* 19 (1971): 397–418.

Nový, Rostislav. "Hospodářství a sociální poměry doby Karla IV." In *Karolus Quartus. Piae memoriae fundatoris sui Universitas Carolina D.D.D.*, 39–74. Prague: Charles University, 1984.

Nový, Rostislav. "Review of *Issledovanija po agrarnoj istorii Čechii 14 - načalo 15 vv, Moskva 1963*," by Boris Timofeevich Rubtsov, *Československý časopis historický* 12 (1964): 541–544.

Nový, Rostislav. "Struktura feudální renty v předhusitských Čechách." *Československý časopis historický* 9 (1961): 60–74.

Nový, Rostislav. "Studie o předhusitských urbářích I." *Sborník historický* 13 (1965): 5–64.

Ogilvie, Sheilagh. "Vesnická obec a tzv. 'druhé nevolnictví' v raně novověkých Čechách" [Communities and the 'Second Serfdom' in Early Modern Bohemia]. *Český časopis historický* 107 (2009): 46–94.

Ogilvie, Sheilagh, and Alexander Klein. "Occupational structure in the Czech lands under the second serfdom." *Economic History Review* 69 (2015): 493–521.

Ogilvie, Sheilagh, and André W. Carus. "Institutions and economic growth in historical perspective." In *Handbook of Economic Growth* 2A, ed. Steven N. Durlauf, and Philippe Aghion, 405–514. Amsterdam: Elsevier, 2014.

Ogilvie, Sheilagh, and Jeremy Edwards. "Frauen und „zweite Leibeigenschaft" in Böhmen." *Bohemia* 44 (2003): 101–145.

Ogilvie, Sheilagh. *State corporatism and proto-Industry: The Württemberg Black Forest, 1580–1797*. Cambridge: Cambridge University Press, 1997.

Palloth, Judith. *Land reform in Russia: Peasant responses to Stolypin's project of rural transformation*. Oxford: Clarendon Press, 1999.

Patzold, Stefan. *Das Lehnswesen*. Munich: Beck, 2012.

Pauly, Michel, and Martin Uhrmacher. "Das Versorgungsgebiet der Stadt Luxemburg im späten Mittelalter." In *Städtische Wirtschaft im Mittelalter: Festschrift für Franz Irsigler zum 70. Geburtstag*, ed. Rudolf Holbach, 211–254. Cologne: Böhlau, 2011.

Pekař, Josef. *České katastry*. Prague: Historický klub, 1932.

Petráň, Josef. "Doprava a cestování." In *Dějiny hmotné kultury I (2). Kultura každodenního života od 13. do 15. století*, ed. Josef Petráň, 812–826. Prague: Státní pedagogické nakladatelství, 1985.

Petráň, Josef. *Poddaný lid v Čechách na prahu třicetileté války* [Serfs in Bohemia on the verge of the Thirty Years' War]. Prague: Nakladatelství Československé akademie věd, 1964.

Petráň, Josef. *Zemědělská výroba v Čechách v druhé polovině 16. a počátkem 17. století*, Acta Universitatis Carolinae, Philosophica et Historica, Monographiae 5. Prague: Charles University, 1963.

Petráň, Josef, ed. *Problémy cen, mezd a materiálních podmínek života od 16. do poloviny 19. století*, Acta Universitatis Carolinae. Philosophica et Historica 1. Prague: Charles University, 1971.

Petráň, Josef, ed. *Problémy cen, mezd a materiálních podmínek života lidu v Čechách v 17.–19. století II*, Acta Universitatis Carolinae. Philosophica et Historica 3. Prague: Charles University, 1977.

Petráň, Josef, et al. "Současný stav bádání o dějinách cen a mezd." *Československý časopis historický* 21 (1973): 45–72.

Petrusek, Miloslav. "Od víry ve společnost bez trestů ke společnosti altruistické a nezištné lásky (Na okraj Sorokinovy Krise našeho věku)" [From faith in a society without punishments to a society of altruistic love (on the margins of Sorokin's Crisis of our age)]. In *Aktéři, systémy, rizika*, ed. Jiří Šubrt, 9–25. Acta Universitatis Carolinae, Philosophica et Historica 1/2006, Studia Sociologica 15. Prague: Karolinum, 2009.

Petrusek, Miloslav, Hana Maříková, and Alena Vodáková, et al. *Velký sociologický slovník*, sv. 1 a 2. Prague: Karolinum, 1996.

Placht, Otto. *České daně 1517–1652*. Prague: Jednota československých matematiků a fysiků, 1924.

Pospisil, Leopold. *Obernberg: A quantitative analysis of a Tirolean peasant economy*, Memoirs of The Connecticut Academy of Arts and Sciences 24. New Haven: Connecticut Academy of Arts and Sciences, 1995.

Procházka, Vladimír. *Česká poddanská nemovitost v pozemkových knihách 16. a 17. století*, Právněhistorická knižnice 6. Prague: Nakladatelství Československé akademie věd, 1963.

Postan, Michael M. "The charters of the villeins." In *Essays on medieval agriculture and general problems of the medieval economy*, ed. Michael M. Postan, 107–149. Cambridge: Cambridge University Press, 1973.

Postles, David. "Migration and mobility in a less mature economy: English internal migration, c. 1200–1350." *Social History* 25 (2000): 285–299.

Pražáková Seligová, Markéta. *Život poddaných v 18. století: osud, nebo volba?: K demografickým, hospodářským, sociálním a rodinným aspektům života venkovských poddaných na panství Horní Police* [The lives of serfs in the 18th century: Destiny or choice? Towards demographic, economic, social and family aspects of the lives of rural serfs living in the estate of Horní Police]. Prague: Togga, 2015.

Prökl, Vincenz. *Eger und Das Egerland: Historisch, statistisch und topographisch dargestellt*, 2. sv. Prague – Eger: V. Prökl, 1845.

Raftis, James Ambrose. *Tenure and mobility: Studies in the social history of the mediaeval English village*. Toronto: Pontifical Institut of Mediaeval Studies, 1964.

Raiser, Elisabeth. *Städtische Territorialpolitik im Mittelalter. Eine vergleichende Untersuchung ihrer verschiedenen Formen am Beispiel Lübecks und Zürichs*, Historische Studien 406. Lübeck – Hamburg: Matthiesen, 1969.

Razi, Zvi. *Life, marriage, and death in a medieval parish: Economy, society, and demography in Halesowen 1270–1400*, Past and present publications. Cambridge: Cambridge University Press, 1980.

Rebel, Hermann. *Peasant classes: The bureaucratizations of property and family relations under early Habsburg absolutism. 1511–1636*. Princeton: Princeton University Press, 1983.

Ress, Franz Michael. "Geschichte und wirtschaftliche Bedeutung der oberpfälzischen Eisenindustrie von den Anfängen bis zur Zeit des 30jährigen Krieges." *Verhandlungen des Historischen Vereins für Oberpfalz und Regensburg* 91 (1950): 5–186.

Reynolds, Susan. *Fiefs and vassals: The medieval evidence reinterpreted*. Oxford: Oxford University Press, 1994.

Robisheaux, Thomas. *Rural society and the search for order in Early Modern Germany*. Cambridge: Cambridge University Press, 1989.

Rödel, Dietrich. *Das erste Salbuch des Hochstifts Würzburg. Agrargeschichtliche Analyse einer spätmittelalterlichen Quellen*, Studien zur bayerischen Verfassungs- und Sozialgeschichte 13. Munich: Kommission für Bayerische Landesgeschichte, 1987.

Rödel, Dietrich. "Die spätmittelalterliche Dorfbevölkerung in Mainfranken." *Strukturen der Gesellschaft im Mittelalter. Interdisziplinäre Mediävistik in Würzburg*, ed. Dietrich Rödel, and Joachim Schneider, 281–301. Wiesbaden: Reichert, 1996.

Roseberry, William. "Rent, differentiation, and the development of capitalism among peasants." *American Anthropologist* 78 (1977): 45–58.

Rösener, Werner. "Aspekte der Stadt-Land-Beziehungen im spätmittelalterlichen Deutschland." *Peasants and townsmen in medieval Europe. Studia in honorem Adriaan Verhulst*, Jean-Marie Duvosquel, and Erik Thoen, 663–680. Gent: Snoeck-Ducaju, 1995.

Rösener, Werner. *Bauern im Mittelalter*. Munich: Beck, ³1987.

Rozinskaya, Natalia, Alexander Sorokin, and Dmitry Artamonov. "Peasants' inequality and stratification: Evidence from pre-revolutionary Russia." *Scandinavian Economic History Review* 69 (2021): 253–277.

Rubtsov, Boris Timofeevich. "Dopis redakci (doplnění a opravy k článku B.T. Rubcov, K otázce …)." *Československý časopis historický* 9 (1961): 927–928.

Rubtsov, Boris Timofeevich. *Evoljucija feodal'noj renty v Čechii (XIV – načalo XV v.)*, Moscow: s.n., 1958.

Rubtsov, Boris Timofeevich. *Issledovaniia po agrarnoi istorii Chekhii, XIV-nachalo XV v.* Moscow: Izd-vo Akademii nauk SSSR, 1963.

Rubtsov, Boris Timofeevich. "Ještě o některých sporných otázkách agrárního vývoje v předhusitských Čechách." *Československý časopis historický* 18 (1970): 601–608.

Rubtsov, Boris Timofeevich. "K otázce *některých zvláštností vývoje feudální renty v Čechách ve 14. a na počátku 15. století*." *Československý časopis historický* 8 (1960): 856–863.

Sabean, David Warren. *Property, production, and family in Neckarhausen, 1700–1870.* Cambridge: Cambridge University Press, 1990.

Salverda, Wiemer, Brian Nolan, and Timothy M. Smeeding, eds. *The Oxford Handbook of Economic Inequality.* Oxford: Oxford University Press, 2011.

Sapov, V. V., ed. *Pitirim Aleksandrovich Sorokin. Nauchnoe izdanie*, Filosofiiā Rossii pervoĭ poloviny dvadtsatogo veka) Moscow: ROSSPĖN, 2013.

Scott, James C. *The moral economy of the peasant: Rebellion and subsistence in Southeast Asia.* New Haven: Yale University Press, 1976.

Scott, Tom. *The city-state in Europe, 1000–1600: Hinterland, territory, region.* Oxford: Oxford University Press, 2012.

Scott, Tom. "The city-state in the German-speaking lands." In *Politics and reformations: Essays in honor of Thomas A. Brady, Jr.*, ed. Christopher Ocker, et al., 3–66. Studies in medieval and reformation traditions 128. Leiden, 2007.

Scott, Tom. *Town, country, and regions in reformation Germany*, Studies in Medieval and Reformation Traditions. Leiden: Brill, 2005.

Scott, Tom. "Town and country in Germany, 1350–1600." In *Town and country in Europe 1300–1800*, ed. S. R. Epstein, 202–228. Themes in international urban history 5. Cambridge: Cambridge University Press, 2001.

Sedláček, August. *Paměti a doklady o staročeských mírách a váhách*, Rozpravy České akademie věd a umění I/66. Prague: Česká akademie věd a umění, 1923.

Seitz, Reinhard H., and Helmut Wolf. "Zum Erzbergbau im Stiftsland Waldsassen." *Acta Albertina Ratisbonensia* 31 (1971): 15–56.

Seligová, Markéta. "Die Entwicklung der Familie auf der Herrschaft Děčín in der Mitte des 17 Jh. unter Berücksichtigung seines wirtschaftlichen Charakters." *Historická demografie* 20 (1996): 119–175.

Shanin, Theodor. "Defining peasants: Conceptualizations and deconceptualizations." In *Defining peasants. Essays concerning rural societies, expolary economies, and learning from them in the contemporary world*, ed. Theodor Shanin, 49–74. Oxford: Blackwell, 1990.

Shanin, Theodor. "Chayanov's message." In *A. V. Chayanov on the theory of peasant economy*, ed. Daniel Thorner, 15–18. Manchester: Manchester University Press, 1986.

Shanin, Theodor. "Introduction: Peasantry as a concept." In *Peasants and peasant societies: Selected readings*, ed. Theodor Shanin, 1–11. Oxford: Blackwell, 1990.

Shanin, Theodor. *Late Marx and the Russian road: Marx and the "peripheries of capitalism"*. New York: Monthly Review Press, 1983.

Shanin, Theodor. "Measuring peasant capitalism." In *Defining peasants. Essays concerning rural societies, expolary economies, and learning from them in the contemporary world*, ed. Theodor Shanin, 229–247. Oxford: Blackwell, 1990.

Shanin, Theodor. "Peasantry: Delineation of a sociological concept and a field of study." *European Journal of Sociology* 12 (1971): 289–300.

Shanin, Theodor. "Socio-economic mobility and the rural history of Russia 1905–30." In *Defining peasants: Essays concerning rural societies, expolary economies, and learning from them in the contemporary world*, ed. Theodor Shanin, 209–227. Oxford: Blackwell, 1990.

Shanin, Theodor. *The awkward class: Political sociology of peasantry in a developing society: Russia 1910–1925*. Oxford: Clarendon Press, 1972.

Shenk, Mary K., et al. "Intergenerational wealth transmission among agriculturalists: Foundations of agrarian inequality." *Current Anthropology* 51 (2010): 65–83.

Schaïk van, Remigius Wenceslaus Maria. *Belasting, bevolking en bezit in Gelre en Zutphen 1350–1550*, Middeleeuwse studies en bronnen 6. Hilversum: Verloren, 1987.

Schaïk van, Remigius Wenceslaus Maria. "Taxation, public finances, and the state-making process in the Late Middle Ages: The case of the duchy of Guelders." *Journal of Medieval History* 19 (1993): 251–271.

Schaïk van, Remigius Wenceslaus Maria, ed. *Economies, public finances, and the impact of institutional changes in interregional perspective: The Low countries and neighbouring German territories (14th–17th centuries)*, Studies in European urban history 36. Turnhout: Brepols, 2015.

Schirmer, Uwe. *Das Amt Grimma 1485–1548. Demographische, wirtschaftliche und soziale Verhältnisse in einem kursächsischen Amt am Ende des Mittelalters und zu Beginn der Neuzeit*, Schriften der Rudolf-Kötzschke-Gesellschaft 2. Beucha: Sax Verlag, 1996.

Schmidtill, Ernst. *Zur Geschichte des Eisenerzbergbaus im südlichen Fichtelgebirge*, Die Plassenburg 18. Bayreuth: Freunde der Plassenburg EV, 1963.

Schmitz, Hans-Jürgen. *Faktoren der Preisbildung für Getreide und Wein in der Zeit von 800 bis 1350*, Quellen und Forschungen zur Agrargeschichte 20. Stuttgart: Fischer, 1968.

Schofield, Philip R. "Dealing in crisis: External credit and the early fourteenth-century English village." *Medieval merchants and money: Essays in honour of James L. Bolton*, ed. Matthew Davies, and Martin Allen, 253–270. London: University of London Press, 2016.

Schofield, Philip R. *Peasant and community in late medieval England, 1200–1500*, Medieval culture and society. Basingstoke: Springer, 2003.

Schofield, Philip R., and Thijs Lambrecht, ed. *Credit and the rural economy in North-western Europe, c. 1200–c. 1850*, CORN publication series 12. Turnhout: Brepols, 2009.

Schofield, Philip R., and Nicholas J. Mayhew, ed. *Credit and debt in medieval England, c.1180–c.1350*, Oxford: Oxbow Books, 2002.

Schreiber, Rudolf. *Das Elbogener Urbar der Grafen Schlick von 1525*, Sudetendeutsches historisches Archiv 1. Prague: Deutsche Gesellschaft der Wissenschaften und Künste für die Tschechoslowakische Republik, 1934.

Schreiber, Rudolf. *Der Elbogener Kreis und seine Enklaven nach dem dreissigjährigen Kriege*, Sudetendeutsches historisches Archiv 2. Prague: Deutsche Gesellschaft der Wissenschaften und Künste für die Tschechoslowakische Republik, 1935.

Schulze, Eberhard, ed. *Alexander Wasiljewitsch Tschajanow. Die Tragödie eines grossen Agrarökonomen*, Studies on the Agricultural and Food Sector in Central and Eastern Europe 12. Kiel: IAMO, 2001.

Schwabenicky, Wolfgang. *Der mittelalterliche Bergbau im Erzgebirgsvorland und im westlichen Erzgebirge*. Chemnitz: Klaus Gumnior, 2009.

Schwinges, Rainer Christoph, ed. *Neubürger im späten Mittelalter. Migration und Austausch in der Städtelandschaft des Alten Reiches (1250–1550)*, Zeitschrift für historische Forschung. Beiheft 30. Berlin: Duncker & Humblot, 2002.

Schwinges, Rainer Christoph. "Neubürger und Bürgerbücher im Reich des späten Mittelalters: Eine Einführung über die Quellen." In *Neubürger im späten Mittelalter. Migration und Austausch in der Städtelandschaft des Alten Reiches (1250–1550)*, ed. Rainer Christoph Schwinges, 17–50. Zeitschrift für historische Forschung. Beiheft 30. Berlin: Duncker & Humblot, 2002.

Schwinges, Rainer Christoph. "Bürgermigration im Alten Reich des 14.-16. Jahrhunderts." In *Migration in die Städte. Ausschluss - Assimilierung - Integration - Multikulturalität - Migrations vers les villes. Exclusion - assimilation - intégration - multiculturalité*, ed. Hans-Jörg Gilomen, 17–37. Schweizerische Gesellschaft für Wirtschafts- und Sozialgeschichte 16. Zürich: Chronos, 2000.

Siegl, Karl. *Alt-Eger in seinen Gesetzen und Verordnungen.* Augsburg – Kassel: Johannes Stauda, 1927.

Siegl, Karl. "Das älteste Egerer Stadtsteuerbuch vom Jahre 1390." *Kalender für das Egerland* 21 (1931): 83–106; 22 (1932): 55–78.

Siegl, Karl. "Das Salbuch der Egerer Klarissinen vom Jahre 1476 im Egerer Stadtarchiv." *Mittheilungen des Vereines für Geschichte der Deutschen in Böhmen* 43 (1905): 207–252, 293–317, 450–479; 44 (1906): 77–105 (as a monograph: Prague, 1905).

Siegl, Karl. "Geschichte der Egerer Burgpflege." *Mittheilungen des Vereines für Geschichte der Deutschen in Böhmen* 50 (1912): 546–594 (as a monograph: Prague, 1912).

Singer, Friedrich Wilhelm, ed. *Das Landbuch der Sechsämter von 1499.* Landkreis Wunsiedel im Fichtelgebirge: Wunsiedel, 1993. 2nd edition.

Singer, Friedrich Wilhelm, ed. *Das Nothaftische Lehensbuch von 1360. Besitz und Verwaltung der Reichsministerialen Nothaft im Historischen Egerland, Faksimile und Übertragung des Originals im Bayerischen Hauptstaatsarchiv München.* Arzberg – Hohenberg: G. Arzberger, 1996.

Slavík, František Augustin. "O popisu Čech po třicetileté válce." *Zprávy zemského archivu království českého* 3 (1910): 17–114.

Sonderegger, Stefan. "Active Manorial Lords and Peasant Farmers in the Economic Life of the Late Middle Ages: Results from New Swiss and German Research." In *Peasants, Lords, and State: Comparing Peasant Conditions in Scandinavia and the Eastern Alpine Region, 1000–1750,* ed. Tore Iversen, John Ragnar Myking, and Stefan Sonderegger, 292–318. The Northern World 89. Leiden and Boston: Brill, 2020.

Sorokin, Pitirim. *Social Mobility.* New York: Harper & Brothers, 1927.

Sorokin, Pitirim. *Sociologické nauky přítomnosti,* Laichterova filosofická knihovna 13. Translated by transl. Blažena Jirsová. Prague: Jan Laichter, 1936.

Sorokin, Pitirim, and Edward A. Tiryakin, ed. *Sociological theory, values, and socio-cultural change: Essays in honor of Pitirim A. Sorokin.* New York: Free Press of Glencoe, 2017.

Spiess, Karl-Heinz, and Thomas Willich, ed. *Das Lehnswesen in Deutschland im hohen und späten Mittelalter.* Stuttgart: Steiner, 2011.

Spittler, Gert. "Tschajanow und die Theorie der Familienwirtschaft." In *Die Lehre von der bäuerlichen Wirtschaft. Versuch einer Theorie der Familienwirtschaft im Landbau,* Aleksander Tschajanow, vii–xxxvii. Frankfurt – New York: Campus-Verlag, 1987.

Sprandel, Rolf. „Der Würzburger Lehenhof 1345–1372." *Zeitschrift für Bayerische Landesgeschichte* 47 (1984): 791–794.

Sreenivasan, Govind P. *The Peasants of Ottobeuren, 1487–1726: A rural society in Early Modern Europe,* Past and Present Publications. Cambridge: Cambridge University Press, 2004.

Stamm, Volker. "Gab es eine bäuerliche Landflucht im Hochmittelalter?: Land-Stadt-Bewegungen als Auflösungsfaktor der klassischen Grundherrschaft." *Historische Zeitschrift* 276 (2003): 305–322.

Stark, Harald. "Die Stammlehen der Familie Nothaft im Egerland." *Archiv für die Geschichte von Oberfranken* 75 (1995): 39–69.

Stark, Harald, and Herbert Maurer. *Die Familie Notthaft – auf Spurensuche im Egerland, in Bayern und Schwaben.* Weissenstadt: Heinz Späthling, 2006.

Stark, Harald, et al. *Po stopách šlechtického rodu Notthafftů – Notthaffti v Čechách a v Bavorsku / Auf den Spuren eines Adelsgeschlechts – die Notthaffte in Böhmen und Bayern.* Cheb: HB Print, 2007.

Steiner, Johann. "Alte Masse und Gewichte des Egerlandes." *Unser Egerland* 30 (1926): 74–77.

Sturm, Heribert. "Der Egerer Losungsschreiber Hans Schönstetter und seine Chronik." In *Heimat und Volk: Forschungsbeiträge zur sudetendeutschen Geschichte: Festschrift für Universitätsprofessor Dr. Wilhelm Wostry zum 60. Geburtstage,* ed. Anton Ernstberger, 247–285. Brünn: Rudolf M. Rohrer, 1937.

Sturm, Heribert. "Die Egerer Ungeldbücher als bevölkerungsgeschichtliche Quelle." *Zeitschrift für sudetendeutsche Geschichte* 2 (1938): 189–200.

Sturm, Heribert. *Districtus Egranus. Eine ursprünglich bayerische Region,* Historischer Atlas von Bayern – Altbayern II/2. Munich: Kommission for Bayerische Landesgeschrifte, 1981.

Sturm, Heribert. *Eger. Geschichte einer Reichsstadt.* Augsburg: Kraft, 1951.

Sturm, Heribert. "Egerländer Pfarreien in der Diözese Regensburg." *Jahrbuch der Egerländer* 6 (1956), 38–44.

Sturm, Heribert. *Inventar der Amtsbücher, des Stadtarchivs Eger mit mit alphabetischen Verzeichnis, angelegt in den Monaten Oktober 1945 bis Mai 1946,* rkp. SOkA Cheb.

Sturm, Heribert. *Tirschenreuth,* Historischer Atlas von Bayern – Altbayern 21. Munich: Kommission for Bayerische Landesgeschrifte, 1970.

Šach, František. "Potažní zvířata v českých zemích v průběhu šesti století." *Vědecké práce Československého zemědělského muzea* 16 (1977): 5–28.

Šanderová, Jadwiga. *Sociální stratifikace. Problém, vybrané teorie, výzkum.* Prague: Karolinum, 2004.

Šimeček, Zdeněk. "O poddanských poměrech v nejjižnější oblasti Čech v období před-husitském." *Československý časopis historický* 19 (1971): 568–574.

Šmahel, František. "Dvanáct pramenných sond k sociálním poměrům na Táborsku od poloviny 14. do konce 15. století." *Husitský Tábor* 9 (1987): 277–322.

Šmahel, František. *Husitská revoluce I. Doba vymknutá z kloubů.* Prague: Karolinum, 1995.

Šmahel, František. "Táborské vesnice na Podblanicku v letech 1420–1547." *Sborník vlastivědných prací z Podblanicka* 22 (1981): 171–201.

Štefanová, Dana. *Erbschaftspraxis, Besitztransfer und Handlungsspielräume von Untertanen in der Gutsherrschaft. Die Herrschaft Frýdlant in Nordböhmen, 1558–1750*, Sozial- und wirtschaftshistorische Studien 34. Vienna: Verlag für Geschichte und Politik, 2009.

Štefanová, Dana. "Schöppenbücher." In *Quellenkunde der Habsburgermonarchie (16.–18. Jahrhundert). Ein exemplarisches Handbuch*, ed. Josef Pauser, Martin Scheutz, and Thomas Winkelbauer, 511–515. Mitteilungen des Instituts für Österreichische Geschichtsforschung, Ergänzungsband 44. Vienna – Munich: Oldenbourg, 2004.

Šusta, Josef. "Úroční rejstřík kláštera zlatokorunského z počátku 15. věku." *Český časopis historický* 13 (1907): 312–322.

Tchayanov, Aleksander. "The organization and development of agricultural economics in Russia." *Journal of Farm Economics* 12 (1930): 270–277.

Thorner, Daniel, et al., ed. *A. V. Chayanov on the theory of peasant economy*. Manchester: Manchester University Press, 1986.

Tietz-Strödel, Marion. "Ländlich-bäuerliche Architektur im Egerland unter besonderer Berücksichtigung von Fachwerk und Vierseithof." In *Eger und das Egerland. Volkskunst und Brauchtum*, ed. Lorenz Schreiner, 130–193. Munich: Langen Müller, 1988.

Třeštík, Dušan. "Příspěvky k sociální diferenciaci venkovského lidu v šestnáctém století." *Sborník historický* 4 (1956): 189–225.

Tschajanow, Alexander. *Die Lehre von der bäuerlichen Wirtschaft. Versuch einer Theorie der Familienwirtschaft im Landbau*. Berlin: Parey, 1923 (reprint: Frankfurt – New York: Campus-Verlag, 1987).

Úlovec, Jiří. *Hrady, zámky a tvrze na Chebsku*. Cheb: Chebské muzeum, 1998.

Vacek, František. "Emfyteuse v Čechách ve XIII. a XIV. století II." *Agrární archiv* 1919: 130–144.

Válka, Josef. "K problému ceny poddanské usedlosti v 16.–17. století." In *Ceny, mzdy a měna* 2, s.p. Brno: Komise pro dějiny cen, mezd a měny, 1963.

Vanhaute, Eric, Isabelle Devos, and Lambrecht Thijs, eds. *Making a living: Family, income and labour*, Rural economy and society in North-Western Europe, 500–2000. Turnhout: Brepols, 2011.

Ploeg van der, Jan W. *Peasants and the art of farming: A Chayanovian manifesto*, Agrarian Change and Peasant Studies Series. Winnipeg: Fernwood, 2013.

Ploeg van der, Jan W. "The genesis and further unfolding of farming styles research." *Historische Anthropologie* 20 (2013): 427–439.

Vaniš, Jaroslav. "Ceny v Lounech v druhé polovině 15. století" [The prices in Louny in the 2nd Half of the 15th century]. *Hospodářské dějiny* 8 (1981): 5–93.

Vaniš, Jaroslav. "Příspěvek k měnovým poměrům doby Jiřího z Poděbrad." *Numismatické listy* 16 (1961): 65–77.

Velička, Tomáš. "Lantkrabata z Leuchtenberka v politice lucemburských králů a jejich lenní knihy s ohledem na majetky na Chebsku a Loketsku." *Sborník muzea Karlovarského kraje* 22 (2014): 169–212.

Velková, Alice. *Krutá vrchnost, ubozí poddaní? Proměny venkovské rodiny a společnosti v 18. a první polovině 19. století na příkladu západočeského panství Šťáhlavy* [Cruel landlords, poor subjects? Trasformations of the rural family and society in the 18th and the first half of the 19th centuries], Opera Instituti historici Pragae, Řada A, Monographia 27. Prague: Historický ústav, 2009.

Velková, Alice. "Proměny venkovské společnosti v letech 1700–1850" [Transformations of rural society between 1700–1850]. *Český časopis historický* 105 (2007): 809–857.

Viazzo, Pier Paolo. *Upland communities: Environment, population, and social structure in the Alps since the sixteenth century*, Cambridge studies in population, economy, and society in past time 8) Cambridge: Cambridge University Press, 1989.

Vogeler, Georg. "Die böhmischen Berna-Register als „Steuerbücher deutscher Territorien"?." In *Böhmen und das Deutsche Reich: Ideen- und Kulturtransfer im Vergleich (13.–16. Jahrhundert)*, ed. Eva Schlotheuber, and Hubertus Seibert, 203–222. Veröffentlichungen des Collegium Carolinum 116. Munich: R. Oldenbourg, 2009, 203–222.

Vogeler, Georg. "Spätmittelalterliche Steuerbücher deutscher Territorien, Teil 1: Überlieferung und hilfswissenschaftliche Analyse." *Archiv für Diplomatik* 49 (2003): 165–295.

Vogeler, Georg. "Spätmittelalterliche Steuerbücher deutscher Territorien, Teil 2: Funktionale Analyse und Typologie." *Archiv für Diplomatik* 50 (2004): 57–204.

Volf, Miloslav. "Vývoj gruntovní knihy ve světle zákonů a hospodářských instrukcí." *Zprávy českého zemského archivu* 8 (1939): 43–108.

Völkl, Georg, ed. "Das älteste Leuchtenberger Lehenbuch." *Verhandlungen des Historischen Vereins für Oberpfalz und Regensburg* 96 (1955): 277–404.

Wagner, Illuminatus. *Geschichte der Landgrafen von Leuchtenberg I*. Kallmünz: Laßleben, 1940.

Wanner, Konrad. *Siedlungen, Kontinuität und Wüstungen im nördlichen Kanton Zürich (9.-15. Jahrhundert)*, Geist und Werk der Zeiten. Arbeiten aus dem Historischen Seminar der Universität Zürich 64. Bern: P. Lang, 1984.

Warde, Paul. "Subsistence and sales: The peasant economy of Württemberg in the early seventeenth century." *The Economic History Review* 56 (2006): 289–319.

Whittenburg, James P., and Randall G. Pemberton. "Measuring inequality: A Fortran program for the Gini index, Schutz coefficient, and Lorenz curve." *Historical Methods Newsletter* 10 (1977): 77–84.

Whittle, Jane C. *The development of agrarian capitalism: land and labour in Norfolk, 1440–1580*, Oxford historical monographs. Oxford: Oxford University Press, 2000.

Wiendlová, Zdena. "Geografický horizont středočeských vesničanů na konci 14. století." *Český časopis historický* 93 (1995): 65–85.

Wickham, Chris. "Conclusions." In *Le marché de la terre au Moyen Âge*, ed. Laurent Feller, and Chris Wickham, 625–642. Collection de l'École Française de Rome 350. Rome: École Française de Rome, 2005.

Wild, Joachim. "Schriftlichkeit und Verwaltung am Beispiel der Lehenbücher in Bayern." In *Schriftlichkeit und Lebenspraxis im Mittelalter. Erfassen, Bewahren, Verändern*, ed. Hagen Keller, Christel Meier, and Thomas Scharff, 69–77. Münstersche Mittelalterschriften 76. Munich: Fink, 1999.

Wolf, Adam, ed. "Die Selbstbiographie Christophs von Thein. 1453–1516". *Archiv für österreichische Geschichte* 53 (1875): 105–123

Wolf, Eric R. *Peasants*. Englewood Cliffs, US: Prentice-Hall Englewood, 1966.

Wolf, Helmut. *Eisenerzbergbau und Eisenverhüttung in der Oberpfalz von den Anfängen bis zur Gegenwart*, Hefte zur bayerischen Geschichte und Kultur 3. Munich: Haus der Bayerischen Geschichte, 1986.

Wyżga, Mateusz. *Homo movens. Mobilność chłopów w mikroregionie krakowskim w XVI–XVIII wieku*. Kraków: Wydawnictwo Naukowe Uniwersytetu Pedagogicznego, 2019.

Zehentmeier, Sabine. "Sigmund Wann (um 1400–1469). Unternehmer, Handelsherr, Bankier und Stifter." In *Religion Kultur Geschichte: Beiträge zur historischen Kulturforschung vom Mittelalter bis zur Gegenwart; Festschrift für Klaus Guth zum 80. Geburtstag*, ed. Heidrun Alzheimer, Michael Imhof, and Ulrich Wirz, 63–74. Petersberg: Michael Imhof, 2015.

Zeitlhofer, Hermann. *Besitzwechsel und sozialer Wandel: Lebensläufe und sozioökonomische Entwicklungen im südlichen Böhmerwald, 1640–1840*, Sozial- und wirtschaftshistorische Studien 36. Vienna – Cologne: Böhlau, 2014.

Zelenka, Jan. *Beneficium et feudum: Podoba a proměny lenního institutu*, Práce Historického ústavu AV ČR, řada A, Monographia = Opera Instituti Historici Pragae, Series A, Monographia 66. Prague: Historický ústav, 2016.

Zweynert, Joachim, et al. "The Enigma of A.V. Chayanov." In *Economics in Russia: Studies in intellectual history*." ed. Joachim Zweynert, and Vincent Barnett, 91–105. Aldershot: Ashgate, 2008.

List of Plates

Plate 1: Cheb. View from the northwest. Ca 1935.
Ar Cheb, fund no. 1059 – Kreuzinger collection of negatives, signature 96.16.

Plate 2: Okrouhlá (Scheibenreuth). A shepherd boy near Březová Mýť. 1893.
Ar Cheb, fund no. 770 – Haberzettl's collection of photographs, inv. no. 409, signature 23.8 (cf. inv. no. 665, signature 132.16).

Plate 3: Starý Hrozňatov (Kinsberg, Alt-). View from the southeast, with the castle in the background. 1899.
Ar Cheb, fund no. 770 – Haberzettl's collection of photographs, inv. no. 130, signature 7.1.

Plate 4: Horní Lomany (Lohma, Ober-). Two women with sticks in the vicinity of Antonínovy Výšiny. 19.3. 1905.
Ar Cheb, fond. no. 48 – Alois John, sign. 10.13.

Plate 5: Doubrava (Taubrath). A farmstead with a pigeon loft. 1940.
Ar Cheb, fond. no. 742 – Hanika's collection of photographs, signature 114.

Plate 6: Vackovec (Watzkenreuth). View of the fortified house and surrounding buildings. 1900.
Ar Cheb, fund no. 770 – Haberzettl's collection of photographs, inv. no. 191, signature 10.16.

Plate 7: Nebanice (Nebanitz). Timbered house (so-called Schwalbenhäusel). 9 September 1900.
Ar Cheb, fund no. 770 – Haberzettl's collection of photographs, inv. no. 612, signature 129.4 (cf. inv. no. 421, signature 24.5).

Plate 8: Cheb. The city archive (former convent of the Poor Clares), Karel Siegel's office, now room No. 22. Ca 1920.
Ar Cheb, fund no. 763 – Collection of historical photographs, sign. 044.03.

Plate 9: Bříza (Pirk). Cheb peasant couple in costume in front of their living house. A well-known pair of the prototype in Cheb costume. Ca 1900.
Ar Cheb, fund no. 770 – Haberzettl's collection of photographs, inv. no. 422, signature 24.6

German Equivalents of Czech Settlement Names

Czech settlement name	German settlement name
Aš	Asch
Boden I	Boden (Alt-Albenreuth)
Boden II	Boden (St. Anna)
Bor	Haid
Bříza	Pirk
Cetnov	Zettendorf
Děvín	Döba
Dlouhé Mosty	Langenbruck
Dobrošov	Tobiesenreuth
Dolnice	Dölitzhof
Doubek	Aag
Doubrava u Vackovce	Doberau
Doubrava u Lipové	Taubrath
Doubrava u Aše	Grün (Neuberg)
Drahov	Trogau
Dřenice	Treunitz
Dvoreček	Höflasgut (Lohma)
Dvorek	Höflas (Trebendorf)
Dvory Dolní	Schön, Unter-
Dvory Horní	Schön, Ober-
Háje	Gehaag
Hartoušov	Hartessenreuth
Hazlov	Haslau
Hluboká	Nonnengrün
Hněvín	Knöba
Horka	Berg
Horní Ves	Oberndorf
Hradiště	Reichersdorf
Hraničná Dolní	Kunreuth, Unter-
Hraničná Horní	Kunreuth, Ober-
Hůrka	Riehm

Cheb	Eger
Chlumeček	Lehenstein
Chocovice	Kötschwitz
Chvoječná	Sebenbach
Jesenice	Gaßnitz
Jindřichov	Honnersdorf
Klest	Reißig
Kopanina	Frauenreuth
Kopaniny	Krugsreuth
Kozly	Gosel
Krapice	Kropitz
Krásná	Schönbach, Ober-
Krásná	Schönbach, Unter-
Krásná Lípa	Schönlind (Schloppenhof)
Křižovatka	Klinghart
Lažany Dolní	Losau, Unter-
Lažany Horní	Losau, Ober-
Lesina	Hart
Lesinka	Harlas
Lesní Mlýn	Holzmühle (Wildstein)
Libá	Liebenstein
Lipina Dolní	Lindau, Unter-
Lipina Horní	Lindau, Ober-
Lipná	Lindau
Lipoltov	Lapitzfeld
Lomany Dolní	Lohma, Unter-
Lomany Horní	Lohma, Ober-
Loužek	Au
Maškov	Matzelbach
Mechová	Mies
Milhostov	Mühlessen
Mlýnek	Mühlgrün
Mostek	Bruck
Mýtina	Albenreuth, Alt-

Mýtinka	Rossenreuth
Nebanice	Nebanitz
Nová Ves	Neudorf
Nový Drahov	Rohr
Obilná	Kornau
Okrouhlá	Scheibenreuth
Oldřichov	Ulrichsgrün
Ostroh	Seeberg
Otov u Hazlova	Ottengrün (Haslau)
Palič	Palitz
Paseky Dolní	Reuth, Nieder-
Paseky Horní	Reuth, Ober-
Pelhřimov Dolní	Pilmersreuth, Unter-
Pelhřimov Horní	Pilmersreuth, Ober-
Podhoří	Kreutzenstein
Podhrad	Pograt
Polná	Hirschfeld
Pomezí nad Ohří	Mühlbach
Pomezná	Markhausen
Potočiště	Dürrnbach
Poustka	Oedt
Povodí	Ensenbruck
Rybáře	Fischern
Salajna	Konradsgrün
Skalka	Rommersreuth
Skalka	Stein
Skalná	Wildstein
Slapany	Schloppenhof (Wildenhof)
Slatina	Schlada
Smrčí	Klausen(hof)
Starost	Sorgen
Starý Hrozňatov	Kinsberg
Starý Rybník	Altenteich
Stebnice	Stabnitz

Stodola	Stadel
Střížov	Triesenhof
Studánka	Thonbrunn
Stupice	Stobitzhof
Suchá	Dürr
Šitboř Velká	Schüttüber, Groß-
Šneky	Schnecken
Štítary	Schildern
Táborská	Seichenreuth
Trpěš	Tipessenreuth
Tršnice	Tirschnitz
Třebeň	Trebendorf
Tůně	Liebeneck
Tuřany	Thurn
Újezd	Märing
Úval	Grün (Thurn)
Vackovec	Watzgenreuth
Vernéřov	Wernersreuth
Vojtanov	Voitersreuth
Vokov	Wogau
Vonšov	Fonsau
Vrbová	Förba
Všeboř Velká a Malá	Schöba
Výhledy	Grün, Steingrün (Haslau)
Zelená	Grün (Wildstein)
Zelený Háj	Hagengrün
Žírovice	Sirmitz

Czech Equivalents of German Settlement Names

German settlement name	Czech settlement name
Aag	Doubek
Albenreuth, Alt-	Mýtina
Albenreuth, Neu-	–
Altenteich	Starý Rybník
Asch	Aš
Au	Loužek
Bärendorf	–
Berg	Horka
Bergnersreuth	–
Bernstein (Selb)	–
Bernstein (Wunsiedel)	–
Boden (Alt-Albenreuth)	Boden
Boden (St. Anna)	Boden
Bodnershof	–
Brambach, Ober-	–
Brambach, Unter-	–
Brand	–
Bruck	Mostek
Brunn	–
Dietersgrün	–
Döba	Děvín
Doberau	Doubrava
Dölitzhof	Dolnice
Dürr	Suchá
Dürrnbach	Potočiště
Eger	Cheb
Elfhausen	–
Ensenbruck	Povodí
Erkersreuth	–
Eulenhammer	–
Fischern	(Rybáře)

Fonsau	Vonšov
Förba	Vrbová
Frauenreuth	Kopanina
Garmersreuth	-
Gaßnitz	Jesenice
Gehaag	Háje
Gosel	Kozly
Groschlattengrün	-
Grün, Steingrün (Haslau)	Výhledy
Grün (Kondrau)	-
Grün (Neuberg)	Doubrava u Aše
Grün (Thurn)	Úval
Grün (Wildstein)	Zelená
Hagengrün	Zelený Háj
Haid	Bor
Haidholz	-
Hardek	-
Harlas	Lesinka
Hart	Lesina
Hartessenreuth	Hartoušov
Haselbach	-
Haslau	Hazlov
Hatzenreuth	-
Hilpersgrün	-
Hirschfeld	Polná
Hirschmühle	-
Hof auf dem Bühl	-
Höflas (Konnersreuth)	-
Höflas (Trebendorf)	Dvorek
Höflasgut (Lohma)	Dvoreček
Hohendorf	-
Hohlerhof	-
Höchstädt i. Fichtelgebirge	-
Holzmühle (Wildstein)	Lesní Mlýn

Honnersdorf	Jindřichov
Kieselmühle (Arzberg)	–
Kinsberg	Starý Hrozňatov
Klausen(hof)	Smrčí
Klinghart	Křižovatka
Knöba	Hněvín
Konnersreuth, Markt	–
Konradsgrün	Salajna
Korbersdorf	–
Kornau	Obilná
Kötschwitz	Chocovice
Kreutzenstein	Podhoří
Kropitz	Krapice
Krugsreuth	Kopaniny
Kunreuth, Ober-	Hraničná Horní
Kunreuth, Unter-	Hraničná Dolní
Langenbruck	Dlouhé Mosty
Lapitzfeld	Lipoltov
Lauterbach	–
Lehenstein	Chlumeček
Liebeneck	Tůně
Liebenstein	Libá
Limberg	–
Lindau	Lipná
Lindau, Ober-	Lipina Horní
Lindau, Unter-	Lipina Dolní
Lohma, Ober-	Lomany Horní
Lohma, Unter-	Lomany Dolní
Lorenzreuth	–
Losau, Ober-	Lažany Horní
Losau, Unter-	Lažany Dolní
Manzenberg	–
Märing	Újezd
Markhausen	Pomezná

Matzelbach	Maškov
Meußelsdorf	–
Mies	Mechová
Mitterwald	–
Mugel, Alt-	–
Mühlbach	Pomezí nad Ohří
Mühlessen	Milhostov
Mühlgrün	Mlýnek
Nebanitz	Nebanice
Neudorf	Nová Ves
Neuhausen, Ober-	–
Neuhausen, Unter-	–
Nonnengrün	Hluboká
Oberndorf	Horní Ves
Oedt	Poustka
Oschwitz	–
Ottengrün (Albenreuth)	–
Ottengrün (Haslau)	Otov u Hazlova
Palitz	Palič
Pechtnersreuth	–
Pfaffenreuth	–
Pilmersreuth, Ober-	Pelhřimov Horní
Pilmersreuth, Unter-	Pelhřimov Dolní
Pirk	Bříza
Plößberg	–
Pograt	Podhrad
Querenbach	–
Rathsam	–
Rauschenstein, Rauchensteig	–
Rebersreuth (Schönwald)	–
Rebersreuth (Wernersreut)	–
Redwitz (= Marktredwitz)	–
Reichenbach (mlýn)	–
Reichersdorf	Hradiště

Reißig	Klest
Reuth, Ober-	Paseky Horní
Reuth, Nieder-	Paseky Dolní
Reutlas (Marktredwitz)	–
Riehm	Hůrka
Rodenbach	–
Rohr	Nový Drahov
Rommersreuth	Skalka
Rosenhof	–
Rossenreuth	Mýtinka
Röthenbach (Arzberg)	–
Röthenbach (Brambach)	–
Rügersgrün	–
Sebenbach	Chvoječná
Seeberg	Ostroh
Seichenreuth	Táborská
Selb	–
Seußen	–
Schachten	–
Scheibenreuth	Okrouhlá
Schildern	Štítary
Schirnding	–
Schlada	Slatina
Schloppach	–
Schloppenhof (Wildenhof)	Slapany
Schlottenhof	–
Schnecken	Šneky
Schöba	Všeboř Velká a Malá
Schön, Ober-	Dvory Horní
Schön, Unter-	Dvory Dolní
Schönbach, Ober-	Krásná
Schönbach, Unter-	Krásná
Schönberg	–
Schönlind (Eulenhammer)	–

Schönlind (Selb), Gutschönlind	–
Schönlind (Schloppenhof)	Krásná Lípa
Schönwald	–
Schüttüber, Groß-	Šitboř Velká
Sirmitz	Žírovice
Sorgen	Starost
Stabnitz	Stebnice
Stadel	Stodola
Stein	Skalka
Stobitzhof	Stupice
Taubrath	Doubrava
Thiemreuth	–
Thölau	–
Thonbrunn	Studánka
Thurn	Tuřany
Tipessenreuth	Trpěš
Tirschnitz	Tršnice
Tobiesenreuth	Dobrošov
Trebendorf	Třebeň
Treunitz	Dřenice
Triesenhof	Střížov
Trogau	Drahov
Ulrichsgrün	Oldřichov
Vielitz	–
Voitersreuth	Vojtanov
Walbenreuth	–
Watzgenreuth	Vackovec
Weißenbach	–
Wendern, Klein-	–
Wernersreuth	Vernéřov
Wildenau	–
Wildstein	Skalná
Wintersreuth	–
Wogau	Vokov

Wölsau	–
Wölsauer Hammer	–
Woltersgrün, Ober-	–
Woltersgrün, Unter-	–
Zettendorf	Cetnov
Zwerkengrün	–

◀ Plate 9: **Bříza (Pirk). Cheb peasant couple in costume in front of the living house (ca 1900). Cheb peasants spoke the North Bavarian dialect, as did the inhabitants of the adjacent Western Bohemia and a wide swath on the border of historic Bavaria and Franconia.**

Index

The index includes the entries listed in the printed part of the monograph. Digital appendices are not excerpted. Cross-referencing is used when some entries are more general or more widely used (e.g., debt → credit market). If the entries overlap in meaning, we use the "cf." reference. Settlement names are presented in their current official form; for settlements in the Czech part of the Cheb region, the former German name is added in brackets.

A

abandonment 11, 38, 117, 262, 480, 515–24, 534, 541–3

abandonment cf. contraction of agricultural areas

Abel, Wilhelm, German historian and economist 128, 130

accounts books → city accounts books

accumulation of capital 51, 56, 61–2, 69–74, 79, 86, 188, 207, 282, 303, 305–6, 349, 358, 415, 446–8, 455, 457, 514, 538–9

accumulation of capital cf. capital

adaptation 62, 522

administrative division cf. city-state of Cheb

administrative division of the city-state of Cheb 21–2, 106–8, 136

agrarian crisis 128–9, 138, 209, 529, 541

agrarian crisis cf. crisis of the late Middle Ages

agrarian cycles 120–1, 137, 214, 230, 297

agrarian depression → agrarian crisis

agrarian economists, Russia 56–7, 361

agrarian institutions → economic institutions

agrarian reforms 57

agrarian sociology 51–6

agrarian technology → agricultural system

agrarian terms → agrarian cycles

agricultural production 36, 45–6, 62, 69, 85, 124, 128–31, 136–7, 208, 218, 242, 267, 310, 314, 530, 539

agricultural system 120–1, 161, 230, 321

agricultural yields 53, 71, 129–30, 134, 137, 206, 232–233, 302, 347, 412, 449

agricultural yields cf. crop failure

Alagna, village in Italy 61

Albenreuth, Neu- → Neualbenreuth

Albrecht II of Germany, King of the Romans, Hungary, Croatia and Bohemia 103

Albrecht Nothaft of Weißenstein → Nothaft

Alps 33, 61–2, 117, 321, 543

Altmugel, village in the Upper Palatinate 122

anthropological approaches 36, 43, 45, 48, 60–3, 67, 76–7, 91, 208, 361

anthropology → anthropological approaches

arable land → fields

archer 212–3

archive → Cheb archive

armiger 178, 211–3

Arzberg, settlement in Upper Franconia 122–3

Augsburg, city in Swabia 48, 130

Austria 15, 77, 88, 147, 149, 180